IRISH
RECORDS

SOURCES FOR FAMILY
& LOCAL HISTORY

BY JAMES G. RYAN, Ph.D.

Ancestry Publishing

P.O. Box 476
Salt Lake City, UT 84110

FLYLEAF PRESS

4 Spencer Villas
Glenageary
Co. Dublin
Ireland
Phone (01) 806228

*Irish Records:
Sources for Family
& Local History*
is available ex-
clusively in Ire-
land from The
Flyleaf Press.

Ryan, James G., 1950-
    Irish records.

    Bibliography: p.
    Includes index.
        1. Ireland – Genealogy – Bibliography.
    2. Ireland – History, Local-Sources – Bibliography.
    I. Title
    Z5313.I7R83   1988   [CS483]   016.929'3415 87-70107
    ISBN   0-916489-22-1

Robert J. Welsh, Managing Editor
Design and Production by Robb Barr
Cover Design by Newman Passey Design, Inc.

First Printing 1988
10 9 8 7 6 5 4 3 2 1

Printed in the United States of America.

Dedication

To my family —
the best you could find.

This book is essentially a book of reference and thanks are therefore primarily due to the hundreds of researchers and organizations to whose work it refers. Without their contributions this book would have no purpose. Thanks are also due to the following for providing illustrations and information: the National Library of Ireland for the parish maps, barony maps, and many other illustrations; the Public Record Office of Ireland for illustrations and for the use of their list of Church of Ireland parish records; the Representative Church Body Library; the Office of the Registrar General; the Family History Library of the Church of Jesus Christ of Latter-day Saints; the Federation for Ulster Local Studies; and the Northwest Center for Learning and Development. Thanks are also due to the journals from which illustrations have been shown.

Thanks are due to the following for comments on parts of the draft manuscript: Mr. Michael Costello of the Kerry County Library, Mr. Jarlath Glynn of the Wexford County Library, Dr. Chris O'Mahoney of the Mid-west Archives and Ms. Una Palcic of the Sligo Family Research Society.

I would also like to thank Rachel Devoy, Michelle Power, and Mary Cahill for typing the manuscript. Finally, I want to thank my wife, Kathryn, and my parents for their encouragement and their comments on the drafts.

Contents

Preface

Although there are several guides to Irish family history records, most of them are organized according to the type of records they cover (e.g., parish records, wills, etc.) or according to the institution holding the records (e.g., Public Record Office holdings, etc.). Neither of these systems, however, is ideally suited to the needs of the genealogist or historian who is armed only with the information that a certain person came from a certain county on a certain (or uncertain) date.

Unfortunately, Irish family records are sparse. In the time period of greatest interest, the late eighteenth and early/middle nineteenth centuries, most of the Irish population (and particularly those who emigrated) lived as small tenant farmers or laborers. These activities required few written records. Even such events as births and marriages were not generally recorded by the state until 1864 and were not recorded by the Catholic Church, in most cases, until after 1800. Because of this, every source of available information can be valuable. Indeed, many of the very best sources of information are those dealing with only one town or county. A detailed guide to these local sources is therefore very valuable.

This guide lists available records for each county in Ireland. They are listed, within each county, under the following headings: A Brief History; Census and Census Substitutes; Church Records (Church of Ireland, Presbyterian, and Roman Catholic); Commercial and Social Directories; Family History; Gravestone Inscriptions; Newspapers; Wills and Administrations; Miscellaneous Sources; and Research Sources and Services.

It is hoped that the result will be a more usable reference for the genealogist and historian.

James Ryan
Co. Dublin, Ireland
1988

Introduction

How to Use This Guide

There are no definitive ways of ensuring success in family research. In some cases a researcher can start with a large amount of information on a family's vital data, names, and areas of residence and find nothing. In other cases persistent researchers with only the bare essentials of data have, through hard work and creative research, succeeded. Initiative is an important ingredient in finding Irish roots, particularly where family details are sparse. Once the normal sources such as parish registers and land valuation records have been consulted, imaginative use of local historical accounts can produce further information about the family and its circumstances. Alternatively, it can point the way towards other sources of information. In short, the more that is known about life in the area at the relevant period, the more one can try to imagine the ancestor's situation and the aspects of their life which might have been recorded.

Principles for Family Research

This guide is designed to facilitate family research by providing a comprehensive listing of all the record sources in the county from which an ancestor came. The objective of the family researcher is to add to the stock of information about his/her ancestors from the records available. This essentially means adding more "elements of identity" to their ancestors. Elements of identity are names, dates, places, and relationships which distinguish one person from another and thus help to ensure that the researcher is following the right lines. For example, if a researcher knows that his ancestor was a Michael Ryan born in Tipperary in the early 1830s, it would be virtually impossible to establish a definite family line because there were many people of that name born at that time and place. If the exact birthdate or place is known, then the possibilities are greatly improved.

The principles on which family research should be done are simple. First, the researcher must work from what is already known to what is unknown and concentrate on adding to the known elements of identity of their ancestors. The best approach is to work on the ancestor about whom most is known. By adding new elements of identity to this person, more information will inevitably be found about other earlier relatives, siblings, etc. What the researcher should *not* do is to find a family of the same name in the ancestor's area and try to establish a link. Many Irish family names are associated with particular areas and other families of the same name should therefore be expected to be found. An exception to this rule is where the name is very rare and a linkage therefore reasonable. Build from what is already known and, if the apparently "right" family is found, try to prove that it is not, for instance, by looking for evidence of the named person in Ireland after the ancestor left.

Second, the researcher should work from the more recent events in the ancestor's life to the less recent. As records generally improve with time, it may, for example, be easier to find a person's birthdate by looking at death records and gravestone inscriptions. In the case of emigrant ancestors, both of these principles suggest that all possible information on the person in the immigrant country should be collected before attempting to trace ancestry in Ireland.

What the Records Can Tell

The following is a guide to the information about elements of identity which various sources can provide:

Where did they live?

A precise "address" for an ancestor is one of the most valuable elements of identity, particularly in searching for ancestors with names which are locally very common. Records which provide both names and definite addresses are therefore very valuable ways of linking people with places. The two major records used for these purpose are *Griffith's Valuation Survey* in the mid 1800s and the *Tithe Applotment Survey* (see Census and Census Substitutes section p. xxvii) in the early 1800s. Both of these are indexed in the "Surname Index" compiled by the National Library of Ireland, which indicates how many house/land holders with a particular family name were recorded in *Griffith's Valuation Survey*, and also whether (but not how many) landholders of that name are in the *Tithe Applotment Survey*. By examining the original records indicated in the index, the full names of those listed and the townland in which they lived can be established.

For ancestors who lived in larger towns, a further useful source is commercial directories (see p. xxxii). *Griffith's Valuation Survey* also lists the householders in towns and villages. The *Tithe Applotment Survey,* however, only lists holders of certain types of agricultural land.

For the latter part of the nineteenth century, a good source is the civil register of births, deaths, and marriages which started in 1864 (see Civil Register of Birth, Marriage, and Death section p. xvii). If, for instance, it is known when the parent of an emigrant died, the death certificate may give the family home address. Marriage certificates are particularly useful as they give the addresses of both partners. Birth records also give the parents' address.

There are a range of other censuses and census substitutes listed for each county, some of which have names arranged alphabetically and give addresses.

Who were their relatives?

If an address has been found, the most obvious way of identifying other family members is to check local church records of birth and marriage. To do this it will be necessary to identify the church which served the area and consult its records, if they exist. This can be done using the guides in the Church Records section in each chapter. Note that several counties now have indexed parish records either on computer or card index (see Research Sources and Services section in the county of interest).

After 1864, official certificates of death, birth, and marriage are also available (Church of Ireland marriage certificates are available from 1845). Marriage certificates give the names of the bride's and groom's fathers. Death records are less useful since they only list the name of the person present at death, whose relationship to the deceased is often not stated. Birth records give names of parents (including mother's maiden name). The full list of details specified on each of these certificates is listed in the Civil Register of Birth, Marriage, and Death section (p. xvii). Other useful sources include gravestone inscriptions, wills, marriage license bonds, and newspaper birth, marriage, and death notices. A few of the more detailed censuses also list entire households and give relationships of the residents. Finally, there are pedigrees and family histories (see Family Histories sections). These exist mainly for more prominent families. If the family are large landowners or otherwise prominent members of society they are likely to be listed in one of these directories (see p. xxxii). People in either of these categories are also more likely to be mentioned in newspaper birth, death, marriage, or business notices.

What were their occupations?

The range of possible occupations in the eighteenth and nineteenth centuries was far less than it is now, particularly in Ireland where there was little industrialization. If the ancestor was a tradesman or retailer, a commercial directory for the area may be a useful way to determine the exact nature of the business. It was also common for businesses to place notices of change of premises, change of ownership, etc., in local newspapers. These can be a very valuable source of information.

The majority of the population, and particularly of those who emigrated, were either small tenant farmers or laborers. A listing in *Griffith's Valuation Survey* as a landholder (as distinct from just a householder) is a fair indication that the person concerned was a farmer. Listings of laborers are very scarce.

Many of the directories listed in the records of each county also separately list various professionals, e.g., medical doctors, lawyers, clergy, and various categories of public officials such as sheriffs, bailiffs, etc. Local public officials are also often listed in the reports and minute books of county and borough councils.

There are specific directories available for some professions.

For medical doctors, Croly's *Irish Medical Directory* (1846) lists general practitioners and other medical graduates. This information is also available in the *Medical Directory for Ireland,* issued most years from 1852 to 1860 and in the *Irish Medical Directory* which appeared

annually from 1872. Clergymen are also found in some directories: Catholic priests are listed in the *Catholic Directory,* issued annually from 1836. There are many other listings of priests in various diocesan history journals and local history journals. Church of Ireland ministers are listed in various publications: the *Ecclesiastical Registry* by Samuel Lea (1814); *Irish Ecclesiastical Register,* issued in 1817, 1818, 1824, and 1827; the *Ecclesiastical Register* by J. Erick (1830); *Bourn's Churchman's Almanac and Irish Ecclesiastical Directory* (1841); *Irish Ecclesiastical Directory* (1841 and 1842); *Irish Clergy List* (1843); Oldham's *Clerical Directory of Ireland* (1858); and James Charles's *Irish Church Directory,* issued in 1862 and annually since then. Presbyterian church members are not well documented. The only specific directory is McComb's *Presbyterian Almanac* of 1857.

Copies of these directories are available in various Irish or other libraries.

Irish Place-names and Family Names

Place-names

The majority of Irish place-names, and particularly townland names, are derived from the Gaelic, or Irish, language. Some components of these names, e.g., Bally-, -more, or -beg are particularly common. A good description of the origins of Irish place-names is given in *Irish Names of Places* (1893) and *Irish Local Names Explained* (1884. Reprint. Baltimore: Genealogical Publishing Company, 1979), both by P.W. Joyce. Because these names are ancient there are often variations in the way in which they are spelled, particularly in earlier documents. Note, for instance, the variations in spelling between the names of many parishes and those of the corresponding Catholic parishes (e.g., Killadysert versus Kildysert).

It is common for researchers to have names of the places of origin of their ancestors, which are not listed in any guide. This may be because the name was taken down or remembered from the pronunciation used by an ancestor who may have been illiterate, Irish-speaking, or both.

>
> the enchantress Murna. When the wind blows strongly in certain directions, a loud whistling sound comes from some crevices in the rock, which can be heard distinctly half a mile off; and the peasantry who know nothing of such learned explanations, and care less, will tell you, among many other dim legends of the lady Murna, that this sound is the humming of her spinning wheel.
>
> III. The genitive of *ua* or *o* (a grandson) is *ui*, which is pronounced the same as *ee* or *y* in English; and consequently when a local name consists of a noun followed by a family name with *O* (such as O'Brien) in the genitive singular, the *ui* is usually (but not always) represented in anglicised names by *y*. This is very plainly seen in Cloonykelly near Athleague in Roscommon, *Cluain-Ui-Cheallaigh*, O'Kelly's meadow; in Drumyarkin in Fermanagh (near Clones), O'Harkin's *drum* or hillridge. Cloonybrien, near Boyle in Roscommon, where a portion of the Annals of Lough Key was copied, is called in Irish *Cluain-I-Bhraoin*, O'Breen's meadow. Knockycosker, north of Kilbeggan in Westmeath, is written by the Four Masters *Cnoc-Ui-Choscraigh*, O'Cosgry's hill. The barony of Iraghticonor in the north of Kerry, is called in Irish *Oireacht-Ui-Chonchobhair*, O'Conor's *iraght* or inheritance.
>
> In the parish of Moycullen in Galway there is a townland, now called Gortyloughlin; but as we find it written Gurtyloughnane in an old county map, it is obvious that here *n* has been changed to *l*—a very usual phonetic corruption (1st Vol., Pt. I., c. III.), and that the Irish name is *Gort-Ui-Lachtnain*, the field of O'Lachtnan or O'Loughnane —a well-known family name. This townland includes the demesne and house of Danesfield, the name of which is an attempted translation of the

Extract from *The Origin and History of Irish Names of Places* by P.W. Joyce. Gill & Son, Dublin, 1893.

place-name. In compiling censuses during the last century, for instance, indexes of townlands were compiled and have been published.

Alphabetical Index to the Towns and Townlands of Ireland (Dublin: Alexander Thom and Company, 1877) lists townlands alphabetically and gives, for each, the parish, barony, county, and Poor Law Union to which it belongs. The parishes, baronies, and Poor Law Unions are also listed separately.

General Alphabetical Index to the Townlands and Towns, Parishes and Baronies of Ireland...1851 (Reprint. Baltimore: Genealogical Publishing Company Inc., 1984) is based on the 1851 census and gives much the same information as the above index.

Having found where an ancestor lived, some further background information on the area may be gleaned from the following publications:

Topographical Dictionary of Ireland by Samuel Lewis (1837) lists all the parishes, baronies, towns, villages, and counties in Ireland with local administrative details, an account of agriculture and industry, major local houses ("seats") and their owners, and other local information.

Parliamentary Gazetteer of Ireland (Fullerton and Company, 1846) gives much the same information as the above.

Local history journals are also a good source of information on the history and other aspects of particular counties (see Research Sources and Services section p. xlii). The Irish Place-Names Commission in the Ordnance Survey Office can usually assist in finding the accepted variant for difficult place-names where the above sources fail.

Maps are available for various periods and

Thus the spelling will reflect the phonetics used. Examples include Mallah for Mallow, Carsaveen for Cahirciveen, etc. Some imagination is necessary to relate these names to their currently accepted forms. A knowledge of local accents is also very valuable in these situations.

There are several good sources for finding a

CENSUS OF IRELAND

FOR THE YEAR

1851.

GENERAL ALPHABETICAL INDEX

TO THE

TOWNLANDS AND TOWNS OF IRELAND,

With the Number of the Sheet of the Ordnance Survey Maps in which they appear ; the Areas of the Townlands in Statute Acres ; the County, Barony, Parish, and Poor Law Union in which they are situated ; also the Volume and Page of the Townland Census of 1851—which contain the Population and Number of Houses in 1841 and 1851, and the Poor Law Valuation in 1851.

⁎ The names of Towns are printed in SMALL CAPITALS, and those of *Islands* which are not Townlands in *Italics*.

No. of Sheet of the Ordnance Survey Maps.	Townlands and Towns.	Area in Statute Acres.	County.	Barony.	Parish.	Poor Law Union in 1857.	Townland Census of 1851, Part I.	
		A. R. P.					Vol.	Page
34	Abartagh	34 2 32	Waterford	Decies within Drum	Clashmore	Youghal	II.	351
97	Abberanville	24 0 29	Galway	Athenry	Kiltullagh	Loughrea	IV.	4
93	Abbernadoorny	62 3 27	Donegal	Banagh	Killymard	Donegal	III.	111
58	Abbert	178 3 30*a*	Galway	Tiaquin	Monivea	Tuam	IV.	78
58, 59	Abbert Demesne	1,293 2 21*b*	Galway	Tiaquin	Monivea	Tuam	IV.	78
4	Abbeville	943 2 7	Tipperary, N.R.	Lower Ormond	Lorrha	Borrisokane	II.	285
118	Abbey	27 0 22	Cork, W.R.	Bantry	Kilmocomoge	Bantry	II.	119
116,117,125	Abbey	334 3 28	Galway	Leitrim	Ballynakill	Portumna	IV.	50
58	Abbey	875 3 7	Galway	Tiaquin	Abbeyknockmoy	Tuam	IV.	75
56	Abbey	222 3 21	Limerick	Coshlea	Kilflyn	Kilmallock	II.	240
13	Abbeycartron	219 2 20	Longford	Longford	Templemichael	Longford	I.	160
16	Abbeycartron	32 1 3	Roscommon	Roscommon	Elphin	Strokestown	IV.	209
18,19,22,23	Abbeyderg	867 2 21	Longford	Moydow	Taghsheenod	Ballymahon	I.	162
21	ABBEYDORNEY T.	—	Kerry	Clanmaurice	O'Dorney	Tralee	II.	173
4	Abbeydown	454 3 6	Wexford	Scarawalsh	Moyacomb	Shillelagh	I.	325
3	Abbey East	301 0 12	Clare	Burren	Abbey	Ballyvaghan	II.	11
47	Abbeyfarm	55 1 12	Limerick	Kilmallock	St. Peter's & St. Paul's	Kilmallock	II.	250
42, 51	Abbeyfeale East	1,350 3 23	Limerick	Glenquin	Abbeyfeale	Newcastle	II.	244
42	ABBEYFEALE T.	—	Limerick	Glenquin	Abbeyfeale	Newcastle	II.	244
42	Abbeyfeale West	718 2 4*c*	Limerick	Glenquin	Abbeyfeale	Newcastle	II.	244
86	Abbeyfield	18 0 36	Galway	Kilconnell	Kilconnell	Ballinasloe	IV.	40
107	Abbeygormacan	94 1 18	Galway	Longford	Abbeygormacan	Ballinasloe	IV.	56
33	Abbeygrey or Monasternalea	503 1 14	Galway	Killian	Athleague	Mountbellew	IV.	43
33	Abbeygrey or Monasternalea	157 3 37	Galway	Killian	Killeroran	Mountbellew	IV.	44
20	Abbeygrove	59 0 25	Kilkenny	Gowran	Blanchvilleskill	Kilkenny	I.	93
29	Abbeyhalfquarter	247 0 29	Sligo	Tireragh	Kilmoremoy	Ballina	IV.	235
107	Abbey Island	17 1 33	Donegal	Tirhugh	Kilbarron	Ballyshannon	III.	148
106	Abbey Island	83 1 23	Kerry	Dunkerron South	Kilcrohane	Cahersiveen	II.	183
20	Abbey Land	9 0 3	Cavan	Upper Loughtee	Urney	Cavan	III.	86
14	Abbeyland	68 3 19*d*	Kildare	Clane	Clane	Naas	I.	53
40	Abbeyland	144 2 3	Kildare	Kilkea and Moone	Castledermot	Athy	I.	59
15, 20	Abbey Land	9 0 11	Longford	Ardagh	Mostrim	Granard	I.	152
27	Abbeyland	92 2 23	Meath	Lower Duleek	Duleek	Drogheda	I.	195
25	Abbeyland	327 2 33	Meath	Lower Navan	Navan	Navan	I.	215
6, 7	Abbeyland	75 1 25	Westmeath	Corkaree	Multyfarnham	Mullingar	I.	263
11	Abbeyland and Charlestown or Ballynamonaster	230 1 6	Westmeath	Moygoish	Kilbixy	Mullingar	I.	279
100, 108	Abbeyland Great	812 1 6	Galway	Longford	Clonfert	Ballinasloe	IV.	56
101	Abbeyland Little	231 3 5	Galway	Longford	Clonfert	Ballinasloe	IV.	56
17	Abbeyland North	26 0 8	Galway	Dunmore	Dunmore	Tuam	IV.	33
112	Abbey-lands	20 3 14	Cork, E.R.	Kinsale	Kinsale	Kinsale	II.	100

(*a*) Including 3A. 2R. 16P. water.
(*b*) Including 12A. 3R. 24P. water.

(*c*) Including 6A. 3R. 5P. water.
(*d*) Including 5A. 3R. 32P. water.

B

First page of the Townland and Towns index from the *General Alphabetical Index to the Townlands and Towns, Parishes and Baronies of Ireland*. Thom's, Dublin, 1861.

exist : those of an ancient chapel at Rosslare, called St. Breoch's, or St. Bridget's, were taken down some years since.

ROSSLEA, or ROYSLEA, a village, in that part of the parish of CLONES which is in the barony of CLONKELLY, county of FERMANAGH, and province of ULSTER, 4 miles (N. N. E.) from Clones, on the road from Lisnaskea to Monaghan ; containing 355 inhabitants. The place is romantically situated near the celebrated mountain of Carnmore, in a fine meadow district, several townlands of which are rich pasture land, especially those of Lisnabrack and Salloo, where vast numbers of oxen are annually fed for the English market. The village consists of one irregularly built street, containing 71 houses, and is connected with the new line of road on the mountain from Enniskillen to Belfast by a bridge over the river Fin. In the vicinity is Lake View, the residence of the Rev. T. Bogue, P. P., a beautiful villa, overlooking the lake of Island Hill and commanding a fine view of several other small lakes in the neighbourhood ; it is surrounded with grounds tastefully laid out and richly embellished. Here is a flax-mill belonging to Mr. Lynch. Fairs are held on the 8th of every month ; a constabulary police force is stationed here, and petty sessions and manorial courts are held in the court-house, a neat building in the centre of the village. The R. C. chapel is a very handsome edifice of stone, with a tower and campanile turret : the interior is highly embellished ; the windows are enriched with stained glass, and over the altar-piece is a fine painting. Carnmore mountain is of lofty elevation, and abounds with wild and romantic scenery ; from its summit are seen 32 lakes, including Lough Erne ; and its deep glens are inhabited by a numerous class of peasantry of singular habits and of great originality of character.

ROSSLEE, a parish, in the barony of CARRA, county of MAYO, and province of CONNAUGHT, 6 miles (S. S. E.) from Castlebar, on the road to Hollymount ; containing 886 inhabitants. The land is chiefly in pasture and under tillage ; there is but little bog. Thomastown is the seat of T. V. Clendening, Esq. ; Mount Pleasant, of G. Mahon, Esq. ; Castle Lucas, of G. Ormsby, Esq. ; and Lakemount, of J. O'Dowd, Esq. It is a rectory and vicarage, in the diocese of Tuam, forming part of the union of Balla : the tithes amount to £80. In the R. C. divisions it is part of the union or district of Balla. Here is a private school of about 30 boys and 20 girls. At Clogher Lucas are the ruins of an old castle.

ROSSMANOGUE, a parish, partly in the barony of SCARAWALSH, but chiefly in that of GOREY, county of WEXFORD, and province of LEINSTER, 5 miles (N. E.) from Ferns ; containing 1211 inhabitants. This parish, which is situated on the river Bann, and is skirted by the high road from Camolin to Carnew, comprises 4451½ statute acres, as applotted under the tithe act, chiefly in tillage : on its border is a small red bog. It is a rectory, in the diocese of Ferns, forming part of the union and corps of the prebend of Tomb in the cathedral of Ferns : the tithes amount to £165. 4. 7¼ ; and there is a glebe of 14 acres. The church is in ruins. In the R. C. divisions it is part of the union or district of Camolin ; the chapel is at Craneford, adjoining which is a residence for the priest. About 100 children

538

are educated in two private schools. The late Rt. Hon. George Ogle, of Bellevue, in this county, author of "Molly Asthore" and other admired ballads, received the earlier part of his education under the Rev. Mr. Millar, then rector of this parish.

ROSSMERE, ROSSMIRE, or ROSSMORE, a parish, partly in the barony of DECIES-without-DRUM, but chiefly in that of UPPERTHIRD, county of WATERFORD, and province of MUNSTER ; containing, with the post-town of Kilmacthomas (which is separately described), 2484 inhabitants. It forms a narrow slip of land separating the portions of Upperthird barony ; and within its limits, at Newtown, on the confines of the three baronies of Upperthird, Middlethird, and Decies-without-Drum, it was designed to build a new town, of which the streets were marked out and paved, but only a few houses were built, and these have since mostly gone to ruin. It is a vicarage, in the diocese of Lismore, and in the patronage of the Duke of Devonshire, in whom the rectory is impropriate : the tithes amount to £500, of which £300 is payable to the impropriator, and the remainder to the vicar. The church is a modern structure, towards the erection of which the late Board of First Fruits granted a loan of £750, in 1831 ; and there is a R. C. chapel. About 150 children are educated in two private schools ; and there is a Sunday school under the superintendence of the curate.

ROSSNOWLOUGH, an ecclesiastical district, in the barony of TYRHUGH, county of DONEGAL, and province of ULSTER, 3 miles (N. W.) from Ballyshannon, on the west of the road to Donegal and on the sea coast ; containing 1006 inhabitants. In the year 1830, nine townlands, comprising 2403½ statute acres, were separated from the parish of Drumholm and constituted the ecclesiastical district parish of Rossnowlough. It is a perpetual curacy, in the diocese of Raphoe, and in the patronage of the Vicar of Drumholm : the gross value of the benefice is £108. 8. 9., of which £75 is paid by the vicar, and £25 from Primate Boulter's fund ; the remainder is the annual value of the glebe. The church was erected in 1831, by aid of a gift of £800 from the late Board of First Fruits. In the R. C. divisions it is in the district of Drumholm. About 360 children are educated in six public schools, of which one is supported by the trustees of Erasmus Smith's charity, one from Col. Robertson's endowment, and the remainder chiefly by subscription. There are also two private schools, in which are about 130 children ; and two Sunday schools.

ROSSORY, a parish, partly in the barony of GLENAWLEY, but chiefly in that of MAGHERABOY, county of FERMANAGH, and province of ULSTER ; containing, with part of the suburbs of Enniskillen, 4338 inhabitants. This parish, which is situated on the shores of Lough Erne, and on the roads leading respectively from Enniskillen to Sligo and Ballyshannon, comprises, according to the Ordnance survey, 7654 statute acres, of which 2302¼ are in the barony of Glenawley, and 5351¾ in Magheraboy : of these, about 494 acres are water, and by far the greater portion of the remainder is meadow and pasture. The land is of good quality, and that portion of it which is under tillage is in a state of profitable cultivation : there is a moderate proportion of bog, and limestone is quarried for agricul-

Description of various villages and civil parishes from *Topographical Dictionary of Ireland* by Samuel Lewis. London, 1837.

areas. Xerox copies of *Griffith's Valuation Survey* maps are available from the Valuation Office, 6 Ely Place, Dublin 2. These show the boundaries of the holdings of each of those listed in the survey itself. A full set of nineteenth-century maps of a wide range of scales are also available for consultation at the National Library of Ireland (NLI). Current maps of Ireland at the scales of half-inch, one inch, six inches, and twenty-five inches to the mile, as well as other city and specialty maps, are available from the Ordnance Survey Office, Phoenix Park, Dublin 8.

Family Names

Irish family names are mainly derived from Gaelic and Norman names. English and Scottish names are also common, particularly in the northern counties, but also occur elsewhere in the country. Most Scottish names are also derived from Gaelic. Huguenot, Palatine, and Jewish names also occur. To complicate the situation, many English surnames or family names were adopted by Irish families during the seventeenth and eighteenth centuries when Irish names were discouraged. MacGowan, for instance, became Smith, and McDarra became Oakes because these names either were English for, or sounded like, Irish language words with these meanings.

A common feature of Irish names is the "O" or "Mac" prefix. During the eighteenth and early nineteenth centuries, when the Irish language died away in most of the country, there was a gradual dropping of the "O" and to a lesser extent "Mc" from names. During the latter half of the century, when awareness of Gaelic heritage grew, these prefixes were restored. When searching Irish names it is wise to check both forms (e.g., Sullivan and O'Sullivan, Neill and O'Neill).

The spelling of Irish surnames also varies. Although this occurs to some extent in Ireland, (Keogh, Kehoe; O'Mara, O'Meara; O'Loughlin, O'Lochlann, O'Loghlen) it occurs to a much greater extent among Irish emigrants overseas (Ryan, Ryun, Ryne, Rion, etc.; Geraghty, Garritty, Gerritty, etc.). Thus it is often necessary to establish the accepted local spelling of a name before searching. A modern Irish telephone directory is one useful way to find the currently accepted forms of names. In general terms, the spelling form used currently in Ireland is more likely to be the form of spelling used in eighteenth and nineteenth century records. This is not always the case however.

A good source for determining variants of family names is Edward McLysaght's *Surnames of Ireland* (Dublin: Irish Academic Press, 1985); and his other books: *Irish Families,* and *More Irish Families.* Another source is Robert E. Matheson's *Special Report on Surnames in Ireland together with Varieties and Synonyms of Surnames and Christian Names* (1901); reprinted by Genealogical Publishing Co. of Baltimore.

Administrative Divisions

An ancestor's address is a basic element of identity and can be an essential step in obtaining further information. To understand the components of the types of "addresses" commonly cited, it is necessary to know about the administrative areas used.

Many different administrative boundaries were used in Ireland for civil and ecclesiastical purposes. In most cases these divisions observe boundaries set up for other purposes, e.g., county boundaries, but others, such as diocese boundaries, tend to be unique. A short description of the different divisions is given below. A more detailed description is given by Dr. W. Nolan in *Irish Genealogy – A Record Finder* (Dublin: Heraldic Artists, 1981).

Civil Divisions

The civil divisions are described below starting from the smallest unit of land.

Townland. This is the smallest unit of land area used in Ireland. The area varies in size from less than ten acres to several thousand acres. Despite their name these units do not contain towns, indeed some have no occupants at all. There are around 64,000 townlands in Ireland, and they are the most specific "address" usually available for rural dwellers. They are generally organized into civil parishes.

The Counties of Ireland, from *A New Genealogical Atlas of Ireland* by Brian Mitchell. Genealogical Publishing Company, Baltimore, 1986.

Civil parishes. These are important units for record purposes. They generally contain around twenty-five to thirty townlands as well as towns and villages. There are around 2,500 civil parishes in the country. The guides to church records (see Church Records section p. xxix) list the parishes in each county, and they are also shown in the accompanying maps. Parishes are generally listed within each county although they may also be divided by barony. In many cases civil parishes straddle county and barony boundaries.

Barony. A barony is a portion of a county or a group of civil parishes. Historically it was introduced by the Anglo-Normans and is usually based on a tribal territory or "tuatha." Barony boundaries do not always conform to those of the civil parishes within them. There are 273 baronies in Ireland.

County. The county is a major and consistent division of land. The counties were gradually established by the English since the arrival of the Normans. The first counties – Dublin, Kildare, and Louth – were established in the early thirteenth century, whereas the last counties, those of Ulster, were not established until after 1600. There are thirty-two counties, and these are formed into four provinces.

Province. The four provinces of Ireland are Connaught, Leinster, Munster, and Ulster (see map p. xvi). Each comprises a number of counties.

Cities, Towns, and Boroughs. These are separate administrative areas of varying size. Many towns have several civil parishes, whereas some civil parishes have several townships. Other types of classifications of urban areas include the borough, which is a town with a corporation, or, alternatively, a town which sent a representative (i.e., MP) to the Westminister Parliament. A ward is an administrative unit within a city or large town.

Poor Law Unions. These areas were set up under the Poor Law Relief Act (1838). Rates, land-based taxes, were collected within these areas for maintenance of local poor. They were named after a local large town. The same districts later became used as General Registrar's Districts.

General Registrar's Districts. These districts are the areas within which births, deaths, and marriages were collected. The areas do not always conform to county boundaries.

Ecclesiastical Divisions

Church Parish. This is the basic area over which a parish priest or minister presided. Church of Ireland parishes generally conform to the civil parish boundaries. Catholic parish boundaries, which are generally larger, do not. The church records section in each chapter shows the Catholic parish(es) to which each civil parish belonged before 1880.

Diocese. The parishes of both the Catholic church and Church of Ireland are organized into dioceses, each presided over by a bishop. In both churches the dioceses are devised so as to include a certain number of church parishes. Thus the boundaries do not conform to county boundaries. Neither do the dioceses of the two churches conform to each other. Church of Ireland dioceses are important for record purposes such as administration of wills. The Church of Ireland diocese to which each civil parish belonged is shown in the church records section for each county.

Although Roman Catholic dioceses are less useful for record purposes, the Catholic diocese to which each church parish belonged can be determined from the *Catholic Directory* which has been issued annually by the Catholic hierarchy since 1836. This also gives other details about chapels and priests in each Catholic parish.

Civil Register of Birth, Marriage, and Death

An important source of records not dealt with on a county basis is the civil register of births, marriages, and deaths. The central registration of Church of Ireland marriages started in Ireland in 1845. However, the registration of births, marriages, and deaths for the entire population did not begin until 1864. These records are a very valuable source of information, despite their late start.

Civil records are collected within districts called General Registrar's Districts which are generally named from a large town within them. If the townland of residence of an ancestor is

The Church of Ireland Dioceses of Ireland, from *A New Genealogical Atlas of Ireland* by Brian Mitchell. Genealogical Publishing Company, Baltimore, 1986.

18 64. Births Registered in the District of _____ Kilsheelan _____ in the Union of _____ Clonmel _____ in the

Counties of Tipperary & Waterford

No.	Date and Place of Birth	Name (if any)	Sex	Name and Surname and Dwelling Place of Father	Name and Surname and Maiden Surname of Mother	Rank or Profession of Father	Signature, Qualification, and Residence of Informant	When Registered	Signature of Registrar	Baptismal Name, if added after Registration of Birth, and Date.
78	First August 1864 Poor	Anastatia	Female	Richard Madden Poor	Margaret Madden formerly Walsh	Farmer	Margaret Madden mother Madden Poor	Second September 1864	Robert White Registrar	
79	First September 1864 Lismatalud	Daniel	Male	Patrick Casey Lismatahud Villaning	Bridget Casey formerly Villaning	Labourer	Patrick X Casey mark father Lismatalud	Fourth September 1864	Robert White Registrar	
80	Eighth September 1864 Derrinlaun Upper	Bridget	Female	John Hickey Derrinlaun Upper	Margaret Hickey formerly Keily	Small Farmer	John X Hickey mark father Derrinlaun Upper	Ninth September 1864	Robert White Registrar	
81	Eighth September 1864 Kilsheelan	John	Male	John Dohan Kilsheelan	Maryann Dohan formerly Butler	Labourer	John X Dohan mark father Kilsheelan	Eleventh September 1864	Robert White Registrar	

Example of 1864 Civil Registration of Births.

Superintendent Registrar's District of *Edenderry*

Page 397

66. Marriage solemnized at the Roman Catholic Chapel of *Rhode* in the Registrar's District of *Rhode*

in the Union of *Edenderry* in the County of *Kings*

When Married.	Name and Surname.	Age.	Condition.	Rank or Profession.	Residence at the Time of Marriage.	Father's Name and Surname.	Rank or Profession of Father.
23 July 1864	Michael Dunne	26	Bachelor	Baker	Rathangan	Edward Dunne	Farmer
	Elizabeth Taylor	21	Spinster	Farmer	Tyfer Kings Co	Thomas Taylor	Farmer

married in the Roman Catholic Chapel of *Rhode* according to the Rites and Ceremonies of the Roman Catholic Church by me, *Lawrence ____*

| Marriage was solemnized between us, | Michael Dunne Elizabeth Taylor | } | in the Presence of us, | { | George Ennis Bridget Mulready | |

67. Marriage solemnized at the Roman Catholic Chapel of in the Registrar's District of

in the Union of in the County of

When Married.	Name and Surname.	Age.	Condition.	Rank or Profession.	Residence at the Time of Marriage.	Father's Name and Surname.	Rank or Profession of Father.

Example of 1866 Civil Registration of Marriages.

Superintendent Registrar's District _____ Registrar's District _____

18__ DEATHS Registered in the District of _____ in the Union of _____

In the County of _____

No.	Date and Place of Death	Name and Surname	Sex	Condition	Age last Birthday	Rank, Profession, or Occupation	Certified Cause of Death, and Duration of Illness	Signature, Qualification, and Residence of Informant	When Registered	Signature of Registrar

Example of 1865 Civil Registration of Deaths.

known then the registrar's district (which is the same as the Poor Law Union) can be obtained from one of the available indexes to towns and townlands (see Place-names p. xi).

The categories of information which registrars were requested to provide for on the three types of certificates is as follows:

Birth Certificates: provide date and place of birth; name (if any); sex; name, surname, and dwelling place of father; name, surname, and maiden surname of mother; rank or profession of father; signature, qualification, and residence of informant; when registered; signature of registrar; and baptismal name, if added after registration of birth, and date.

Marriage Certificates: state when married; names and surnames of bride and groom; ages; condition (i.e., bachelor, widow, etc.); rank or profession; residence(s) at time of marriage; fathers' names and surnames; and ranks or professions of fathers.

The church in which the marriage was performed and the names of two witnesses and the clergyman are also listed. Witnesses are commonly family members and may provide clues to family linkages. It is common for the age column to state merely "full age" rather than a specific age. For this reason it is useful to note that "spinster" in the condition column refers to an unmarried girl of any age. In many cases it will be noted if a father is deceased.

Death Certificates: state date and place of death; name and surname; sex; condition (i.e., married, etc.); age last birthday; rank, profes-sion, or occupation; certified cause of death and duration of illness; signature, qualification, and residence of informant; and when registered.

These certificates are available from: Registrar General's Office, 8/11 Lombard Street, Dublin 2. Phone (01) 711000.

Register of Land Deeds

Land deeds are the written statements of legal agreements made in relation to land ownership. They generally refer to leases of land but may also concern mortgages, sales, marriage settlements, or other arrangements. Although the collection of registered deeds at the Irish Registry of Deeds is complete, relatively few deeds were ever formally registered. Furthermore, the registry itself is difficult to search, and professional assistance is advisable. The address is Registry of Deeds, King's Inns, Henreietta Street, Dublin 1.

The *Register* is indexed both by the name of the grantor (i.e., the person granting the land) and also by the name of the townland(s) within each county and, in some cases, barony. Many deeds contain valuable genealogical information, particularly leases made for the term of the life of specified persons. The witnesses to deeds were commonly relations of the parties concerned, and this relationship is often stated on the deed.

An excellent description of the registry and its genealogical value is given by Rosemary ffolliott in *Irish Genealogy – A Record Finder*.

Description of Types of Records Listed for Each County

In each county relevant family history sources and research contacts are presented in the following sections: A Brief History; Census and Census Substitutes; Church Records (Church of Ireland, Presbyterian, Roman Catholic); Commercial and Social Directories; Family History; Gravestone Inscriptions; Newspapers; Wills and Administrations; Research Sources and Services; and Miscellaneous Sources. The significance and content of each of the above sections is explained below.

A Brief History

This section is intended to give a general background to the local effects of major national events described in the section of this introduction entitled A Brief History of Ireland. It also describes other local events and factors of relevance to the family researcher. Emphasis is given to events which caused significant changes in population or family structure, e.g., wars and plantations. Plantations occurred in many Irish counties. Settlers from outside Ireland were brought in to occupy land from which the previous occupants had been expelled. In almost all cases these settlers were from England or Scotland. However, there were also smaller immigrations of German and French Huguenots to certain counties. The major family names associated with particular counties are also listed.

Census and Census Substitutes

This section includes censuses and various types of census substitutes, i.e., records which are not official censuses but fulfill the same function by listing local inhabitants. The different types of census substitutes are described below. Official censuses are described first, then each other type in the approximate chronological order of its occurence.

Official Government Censuses

A full census of the entire population of Ireland was first conducted in 1821 and subsequently at ten year intervals. Although the statistical information from each census is available, few individual household returns for the entire country are available for any years other than 1901 and 1911. Almost all of the returns for the other years were destroyed either by government order (1861 to 1891) or in the fire which destroyed the Public Record Office (PRO) in 1922. The returns for 1901 are a very valuable source of information since they provide name, age, and relationship to the head of household of each resident person. Also recorded is the county of birth of each member of the household. This is particularly useful in attempting to trace those who migrated within the country. The remnants are housed in the Public Record Office, The Four Courts, Dublin

7; and in Public Record Office of Northern Ireland, 66 Balmoral Avenue, Belfast BT9 6NY, Northern Ireland.

Civil Survey

Following the defeated rebellion of the Irish Catholics of 1641, there was a massive confiscation of the tribal lands and their redistribution to English adventurers (those who had provided the funds to raise the army which put down the rebellion), soldiers (as payment for services), and other groups. The Civil Survey was conducted in 1654-56 and listed the owners of land in 1640, and the new owners. The parts which survive have been published by the Irish Manuscripts Commission, and the originals are in the PRO.

Books of Survey and Distribution

These are a compilation of information on land ownership, boundaries, etc., drawn from the Civil, Gross, and other surveys. It lists both the 1640 proprietors of lands and the owners following their confiscation and "distribution," the further changes made in the Cromwellian resettlement of 1659, and at the Restoration (when the British monarchy was restored). Four volumes have been published by the Irish Manuscripts Commission and the remaining sets are in the PRO.

Hearth Money Rolls

In the 1660s a tax was levied on Ireland based on the number of hearths in each house. Hearth Money Rolls have not survived for all counties, but those that do give householders' names in each parish. They are held in various archives and many have been published in periodicals.

Subsidy Rolls

This was a form of tax levied in the 1660s on all those whose goods amounted to over £3 value or who had land of over £1 annual valuation. These lists are less comprehensive than Hearth Money Rolls since the poor are excluded but are valuable nonetheless. These are held in various archives, and many have been published in local history periodicals.

CENSUS OF IRELAND, 1901.

(Two Examples of the mode of filling up this Table are given on the other side.)

FORM A.

No. on Form B. 7

RETURN of the MEMBERS of this FAMILY and their VISITORS, BOARDERS, SERVANTS, &c., who slept or abode in this House on the night of SUNDAY, the 31st of MARCH, 1901.

	NAME and SURNAME	RELATION to Head of Family	RELIGIOUS PROFESSION	EDUCATION	AGE (Years)	AGE (Months)	SEX	RANK, PROFESSION, OR OCCUPATION	MARRIAGE	WHERE BORN	IRISH LANGUAGE	If Deaf and Dumb
1	Mathew Shreider	Head of family	Jew	Cannot Read or Write not English	60		M.	Hebrew Teacher	married	Russia		
2	Hannah Shreider	Wife	Jewess	not English	58		F.		married	Russia		
3	Elias Shneider	Son	Jew	read Turkish	24		M.	Dental Mechanic	not married	Russia		
4	Bessie Shreider	Daughter	Jewess	read Turkish	19		F.		not married	Russia		
5	Leah Shreider	Daughter	Jewess	read Turkish	1		F.		not married	Russia		

I hereby certify, as required by the Act 63 Vic, cap. 6, s. 6 (1), that the foregoing Return is correct, according to the best of my knowledge and belief.

Hitmash Solly C.6. 117th (Signature of Enumerator.)

I believe the foregoing to be a true Return.

Mathew Shreider his mark X

(Signature of Head of Family).

Return for the 1901 Census of the Schreider Household, Dublin.

The Parrish of Killincoole

Is bounded on the east with the river of Castle Ring, on the south with the parrish of Derver and Dromiskin, on the west and north with the parrish of Lowth.

The tythes of the said parish both great and small were in the yeare 1640 in the possession of Arlander Usher Clerk as Incumbent there, being presented thereto by Pattrick Gernon of

Killingcoole, patron of the said parrish. The said tythes with tenne acres of glebe land, and one howse and backside with a pidgeon howse in Killincoole, were worth in the yeare 1640. 50li per annum

In this parrish is conteyned the townes of: Allerdstowne, Killincoole and Whiterath

					li
Henry Gernon of Miltowne th' one moytie and Pattrick Barnwall of Allardstowne the other moytye thereof Free lands	Allerdstowne 4 tates	280	Arrable 275 pasture 5		70 00 00

Bounded on the east with the river of Castle-Ring, on the south and southwest with the lands of Derver and Killincoole, on the west with the lands of Cordery and Whiterath, and on the north with Grange and Whiterath, A castle, a farme howse and divers cabbins, the said castle and towne belonging to Pattrick Barnwall.

					li
Pattrick Gernon of Killincoole free lands 120 ac. p(ai)d 10s. per annum	Killincoole 3 tates	180	Arrable 170 pasture 10		40 00 00

Bounded on the east with the lands of Allardstowne, on the south with the lands of Derver, on the west with the lands of Rahessine and on the north with the lands of Allards- towne and Corderrye. The walls of 2 castles the tymber thereof being burnt, a ruinows mill, an old chappell and cabbins.

					li
Stephen Taaffe of Athelare	Whiterath 2 tates	100	Arrable 80 pasture 20		25 00 00

10s. per annum che(ife)

These above named all outlawd for treason

Bounded on the east with the lands of Grange and Allerdstowne, on the south with the lands of Corderye and Allerdstowne, on the west with Mullahosker, on the north with the lands of Grange.
A castle unroofed
Noe commons in this parrish.

Extract from a copy of the Civil Survey giving a description and names of the land-owners of the parish of Killincoole, County Louth, in 1654-56. *Civil Survey.* Vol. 10. R.C. Simington, Irish Manuscripts Commission, Dublin, 1961.

Muster Rolls

These are lists of local militia, yeomen, or other local armed forces. They are generally composed of planters or non-Catholics. Although there are many histories and documents about such military groups, they usually give only the officer's names, whereas muster rolls are generally more detailed.

Census of Ireland (1659)

This gives the names of "tituladoes" (those with title to land) and total number of persons overall. It also lists the numbers of families in each barony with Irish names. Copies are in the RIA, and they have been published by the Irish Manuscripts Commission.

Catholic Qualification Rolls

After 1692 a series of so-called "Penal laws" were enacted which severely restricted the rights of Catholics in land and property ownership and almost all other areas of activity. These restrictions were gradually lifted towards the end of the eighteenth century for those Catholics who took an oath of allegiance and thereby "qualified." In 1778, for example, those taking the oath could take long-term land leases. In 1782 it allowed the buying and selling of land by Catholics. The "Rolls" consist of those taking the oath. In some counties the numbers taking the oath were very small, and the reference is not listed. They are published in the *59th Report of the Deputy Keeper of Public Records of Ireland* (DKPRI), which is held in the NLI, PRO, and elsewhere.

County of Roscommon : Parish of Clontouskert : Ballintobber Bar :

No. of Reference in ye Alphabett	Proprietors Names Anno: 1641	Denominations	Number of Acres unprofitable	Numbr. of Acres profitable	No. of profitable Acres disposed of on ye Acts	To whom soe disposed wth their Title whether by Decree, Certificate or Patent, References to ye Record thereof	No. of ye Book or Roll & of ye Pag or Skin
16	Tirlogh mc Dowell ..	Tulloghusoge 1: Cart. in Cooleshaghteny 1 qr:	—	015..0..00	015..0..00	Wm. Dellamare ⨎	
17	Gillernow mc: Dermot Hanley :: Rory Ballow mc: Teig Hanley ..	Corry 1: Cartron of Cooleshaghteny containing of arrable Land ½ a Cart: / ½ a Cart:	—	028..0..00	028..0..00		
		County of Roscomon Ballintobber Baro: Parish of Clontouskert					
18	Henry Dillon in Keile and Shanballyloske.. Turlogh oge mc Dowell here	Gallagmaghery ½ a qr. Cont. of Arrable Land :: 1: Cart.: / 1: Cart.	—	058..0..00	033..0..00	Wm. Dellamare ⨎	
19	Hugh oge ô Connor in Eden :: In Garryduffe in Gollogh-maghry	Galloghmaghry ye other ½ Quart. containing of Arrable Land .. 1 Cart: / 1 Cart :/In Magalla : 8 qrs.	—	084..0..00	102..0..00 / 7..0..00	Nicholas Mahon / Plus	
20	Xtopher Delahide :: Thomas Dillon	Carrowbane : 1 qr. containing of arrable .. .. ½ gn: / ½ gn:	—	021..0..00	021..0..00		
21	Tumultogh Boy hanly ..	—ibm— / Two gneeves of Carrowbane Cont. of arrable Land .. more of Pasturable Wood	005..0..00	013..0..00 / 016..0..00	013..0..00 / 016..0..00	Wm. Dellamare ⨎	

Extract from a copy of the *Books of Survey and Distribution* showing the 1641 landowners in the Parish of Clontouskert, Co. Roscommon and the persons to whom the properties were subsequently granted. "Books of Survey & Distribution," Vol. 1. R.C. Simington, Irish Manuscripts Commission, Dublin, 1949.

Religious Censuses

In several dioceses and in some parishes, censuses of parishioners were taken, in some cases for ecclesiastical administration purposes and in others for security reasons (since Catholic or "popish" was at many times in Irish history equated to "rebel"). The censuses vary widely in quality and accuracy. Copies are held in various archives and have been published in several sources.

Freeholders Lists

A freeholder was one who held land for life or for several lives, as distinct from short-term leaseholders or annual rent payers. The significance of freeholder status is that freeholders were the major group entitled to vote. The lists for many counties give addresses and other useful details.

Tithe Applotment Survey

Tithes were a form of tax payable by all religious denominations for maintenance of the Church of Ireland, which was the "established" (state recognized) church until 1867. Between 1823 and 1837 a valuation was conducted to determine the tithe payable by each eligible local landholder. Tithes were only payable on certain types of land, and the tithe applotment survey is therefore far from comprehensive. It does not include any urban inhabitants for instance. However, it is a valuable source. The surnames in the survey have been indexed (see *Griffith's Valuation Survey*). The originals are in the PRO.

Griffith's Valuation Survey

Between 1848 and 1864 all of the land of Ireland was surveyed for the purpose of establishing the level of rates (local tax) to be paid by each landholder or leaseholder. *Griffith's Valuation Survey* lists each land- or householder in the country giving the townland and description of the property (e.g., land; house; house and land; or house, outoffices/out buildings, and land). It also lists the landlord and the annual valuation. Because of the shortage of other records this is a very important substitute census, although it obviously does not cover all inhabitants of an area. It is particularly important in emigrant family research as it was carried out during a period when much emigration occurred, and thus it can form a useful link between the information available about the local origins of an emigrant ancestor and the Irish records. The names occurring in both *Griffith's Valuation Survey* and the *Tithe Applotment Survey* books have been indexed for each county in the surname index compiled by the National Library of Ireland. Microfilmed copies of the survey are available in several libraries.

Local Censuses and Map Indices

For some towns and districts there are detailed censuses, the reasons for which are sometimes obscure. Detailed maps, particularly estate maps, of some towns also give the names of holders of land shown.

Lists of Freemen

In medieval cities, members of all trade corporations had to be freemen of the city; a status conferred by the corporation (City Council). In later centuries the status of freeman of specified cities and towns was traditionally given to citizens whom the city wished to honor. They were therefore generally prominent citizens or visitors. However, as this status also conferred voting rights, it was abused in some cities so as to admit voters for certain candidates or parties. Few Catholics were made freemen during the eighteenth century.

Rate Books (or Poor Law Rate Books)

Under the Poor Law Relief Act (1838) landholders were required to contribute towards programs to help the poor in their area. The funds ran the local workhouse or went to "outdoor relief." Districts, called Poor Law Unions, were set up for collection and distribution of these contributions or "rates." These ratepayers would generally be the holders of property of a certain annual valuation. The books list the ratepayers by area, their holding, and valuation.

Appendix (G.)

A RETURN of the several Houses in the Towns in *Ireland*, which Return Members to serve in Parliament; specifying the Streets in which each is situated, its Number, and the Name of the Occupant; together with the Annual Value of each, as estimated and returned by the Valuators appointed to make the Annual Applotment of Rates and Taxes for Municipal Purposes, either under the Provisions of the Act 9 Geo. 4, c. 82, or of any Local or Private Acts passed for the Regulation of these Towns, or of the New Valuation Act, where it has come into operation.

ARMAGH.

Houses of the Yearly Value of £. 10 and upwards.

No.	Inhabitants' Names.	Yearly Value.		No.	Inhabitants' Names.	Yearly Value.	
		£.	s.			£.	s.
	Lower English-street:				Lower English-st.—*cont*[d].		
1	Francis M'Cormick -	10	—	114	John Lyle - - -	12	—
39	Hugh Lynch - - -	10	—	121	Samuel Thompson - -	11	—
40	John Duff - - -	10	10	128	John M'Elroy - -	10	—
41	Henry Mooney - -	10	—				
42	Patrick Cunningham -	10	—		Upper English-street:		
53	Bernard Quin - -	10	—	1	William Caldwell - -	24	10
54	John Garland - -	10	—	2	Edward Parker - -	24	—
57	Edward Murphy - -	10	—	3	Peter M'Kee - . -	20	—
58	Peter Kelly - - -	10	—	4	James Donnelly - -	22	—
59	James M'Elroy - -	12	—	5	Sarah M'Glone - -	19	—
64	John Woods - - -	10	—	6	Edward Hynes - -	30	—
65	James Donoghue - -	13	—	7	Patrick Downey - -	15	—
66	Owen Farley - - -	10	—	8	Edward Corvin - -	18	—
68	James Dunne - -	12	—	9	Thomas Craig - -	45	—
70	Margaret Williamson -	10	—	10	Arthur Branigan - -	19	—
71	Andrew Johnson - -	10	—	11	Bernard Hagan - -	19	—
73	John Allen - - -	10	—	12	George Barnes - -	24	—
74	Peter M'Caghey - -	14	—	13	Miss Atkinson - -	30	—
76	Johnson Nelson - -	22	—	14	James F. Bell - -	50	—
77	John Williams - -	30	—	15	William Blacker - -	100	—
78	James Vogan - -	34	—	16	Mrs. Lyle - - -	70	—
79	John Graham - -	16	—	17	John M'Kinstry - -	90	—
80	Patrick Corvin - -	15	—	18	R. J. Thornton - -	100	—
81	Michael M'Bride - -	19	—	19	Robert C. Hardy - -	70	—
82	Patrick Carberry - -	10	—	20	Leonard Dobbin, jun. -	100	—
83	Patrick Devlin - -	19	—	21	John Stanley - - -	130	—

Extract from Tables showing the Holders of Houses of over £10 annual valuation in the Town of Armagh. This is a sample of the information on ratepayers and voters presented to the Select Committee on Fictitious Votes 1837. Appendix G of the *Parliamentary Papers* 1837, 2 (1).

Estate Rentals

The vast majority of small farmers and town-dwellers rented their properties from large landowners, many of whom lived abroad. The records of these estates can include details of their tenants. The records are scattered and highly variable in value. Only a small number of the available rentals are listed in this book. Estate rentals will often list only the estate's principal tenants, (those from whom the estate directly collected rent). These tenants would, in turn, have rented to subtenants.

To trace estate rentals it is first necessary to find the name of the ancestor's landlord, for instance through *Griffith's Valuation Survey.* A search for the estate records or family papers can then be made. Richard J. Hayes's *Manuscript Sources for the History of Irish Civilisation* (NLI) is one valuable listing of estate papers. Other estate papers and records in private hands are listed in *Analecta Hibernica,* volumes 15, 20, and 25. From 1849 to 1885 the estates of insolvent owners were sold at public auction. Auction notices generally listed properties and tenants names. These records of "Encumbered Estates," indexed by landlord's name, are available in the NLI and PRO.

Voters Lists

Lists of voters, particularly in the large towns and cities, are available for various periods. A large number of lists relating to those entitled to vote was produced as evidence for the "Commission on Fictitious Votes" in 1837 and 1838. These include lists of freemen, marksmen (those entitled to vote by making a mark rather than a signature), and other lists for some of those towns which were entitled to send a member to Parliament.

Church Records

Because of the lack of census information, church records are the most important source of information on family relationships. The value, quality, and accessibility of the records of each denomination are discussed here:

Church of Ireland (Protestant or Episcopalian) Records

These records generally start earlier than Catholic records, the earliest being 1619. Although there was a legal obligation on the Church of Ireland to keep records from 1634, in practice most began after 1750. In 1876 a law was enacted that all Church of Ireland registers be sent for safekeeping to the Public Record Office in Dublin. This was later amended to allow ministers with suitable storage to keep their own registers. Other ministers sent copies, or kept copies, of their books. Almost all of the registers sent to the PRO, approximately half of those in existence, were destroyed in a fire in the PRO in 1922.

Unlike the Catholic parishes, Church of Ireland parishes tend to conform to civil parish boundaries. Details on Church of Ireland parishes for each county are listed under each county. The PRO has done much to obtain copies of available records. Surviving records are therefore kept either in the PRO; in the custody of the local clergyman; or in a few cases, in the RCB Library.

Presbyterian Records

Presbyterian records generally do not begin until after 1819, from which year Presbyterian ministers were required to keep records. However, because marriages in Presbyterian churches or kirks were not recognized until 1845, many Presbyterian marriages took place in the Church of Ireland. Also, the Presbyterian church rarely kept burial records. Note that there are two major Presbyterian churches. The nonsubscribing Presbyterian church is effectively a separate church.

Roman Catholic Church Records

Church records are undoubtedly the most important record source for Catholics. However, because the Catholic church was severely restricted in the eighteenth century under the Penal Laws, there were few well-appointed churches. Local toleration of Catholics did allow churches to function in some areas. However, most records do not begin until after 1820. Urban records tend to be earlier, but even here few begin before 1760.

For doctrinal reasons, Catholic children were baptised as soon as feasible after birth and usually in a church if there was one. On the other hand, except for the very poor, marriages of Catholics were generally conducted in the bride's home. Marriage records are therefore less likely to be accurate than baptismal records. Catholic churches usually did not keep death or burial records although they do occur in some dioceses. An example is the diocese of Ferns where both the date of burial and the age at death are recorded. Catholic record books have been microfilmed and are available in the National Library and at the Family History Library in Salt Lake City. There are also genealogical research services in many counties which have indexed county church records. Indexing of these and other records is in progress in several counties for the purpose of offering research services. These services are listed where available in the Research Sources and Services section for the relevant county.

The records themselves are highly variable in terms of legibility of handwriting, level of detail, and state of preservation. At worst, the handwriting can be virtually illegible, written in Latin using the writer's own abbreviations, giving only the most basic information, e.g., date followed by (birth) "Patrick of James and Honora Murphy." In addition, the ink may be faded, and the register book may be torn at the edges, overwritten, or have pages missing. At best, the records are written in beautiful copperplate handwriting in neat columns giving full details (dates, names, and residences) in well-preserved books. All possible combinations of these variables will be found. Names of witnesses are almost always given and these may sometimes give clues as to other family associations.

One of the major problems is to ascertain the church which an ancestor attended. The Roman Catholic Records section lists all of the civil parishes in each county and indicates the Catholic church which its inhabitants are likely to have attended. This information has been gleaned from a range of sources but principally Lewis's *Topographical Dictionary of Ireland, 1837,* and the "tentative list" provided in the in-

troductory pages of the "Surname Index" to the *Griffith's Valuation Survey* and *Tithe Applotment Survey* compiled by the National Library of Ireland.

A sample entry of information given in Roman Catholic Church Records section and a discussion of the relevance of each of the items of information is given below:

Civil Parish: **Aghagallon**
Map Grid: 80
RC Parish: Aghagallon and Ballinderry
Diocese: CR
Earliest Record: b. 4.1828; m. 5.1828; d. 3.1828
Missing Dates: 7.1848-5.1872
Parish Address: Rev. Joseph Moloney, PP, 5 Aghalee Road, Aghagallon, Craigavon, Co. Armagh

Civil Parish: Lists all of the civil parishes in each county in alphabetical order. The common alternate names for civil parishes are also indicated. Note that there are many different spellings of some of these parishes used.

Map Grid: Lists the reference number of the civil parish on the county map at the end of each county section. The parishes are listed in sequence (left to right and top to bottom) within each of the baronies in the county.

RC Parish: If the church, which the inhabitants of this civil parish would have attended, is within the parish then this column will contain the name of the Catholic parish. This is often not the same as the civil parish name.

If the relevant church is not within the civil parish then this column will refer the reader to the appropriate church and civil parish. Thus "see Rathcormack" means that Rathcormack church serves the inhabitants of this civil parish, and that it is detailed opposite the civil parish of the same name. If the church parish does not have the same name as the civil parish, it will be referred to, for example, as "Ovens, see Athnowen." This means that the name of the church is Ovens, and that it is detailed opposite the civil parish of Athnowen.

In some cases, a civil parish may be served by several surrounding church parishes. In this case the column will state: e.g., "part Skibereen, see Creagh; part Caheragh." This means that part of the parish is served by the church of

Dec	20	MACLATCHY Mary, of Moses, Newry, servant
	21	AICKEN Mary, of Robert
	25	SCOTT Agnus, of Andrew
1780 Jan	1	HARRISON Mary, of James
Feb	7	AICKIN Elizabeth, of John
	20	BRANNEN Elizabeth, of John
1781 Oct	5	TOWNLEY Esther, of James, Newry, Grocer and Merchant
	5	COMBS Mary, of William, Newry, Glazier
	5	MITCHELL Mary, of John, Newry, sadler
	5	NELSON Anne, of . . . , Sugar Island, Smith
Nov	11	TOWNLEY Samuel, of Samuel, junr, Newry, merchant
	22	ROBISON Thomas, of Andrew, Rockhamilton, linen draper
	23	McGUFFIN Letty, of Richard, Newry, shoemaker
	23	GLENN Mary, of George, Newry, Flaxdresser
	26	ANDERSON John, of John, Newry, woollen draper
	28	CALBREATH Matthew, of James, Newry, Hardware merchant
Dec	4	McKINSTRY Robert, of William, Canal Street, Carpenter
	11	PETTY Samuel, of Samuel, High Street, Shoemaker
	12	CUNINGHAM Isabella, of Edward*, Derrylecka, farmer
		*This person's father was a Roman Catholic, his mother a Dissenter, he alone of all the children embraced the Protestant Faith
	13	WHARTON . . . . , of George, Derrylecka, Weaver
	16	MOORE John, of Joseph, Benagh, Weaver
		BELL Mary, of Robert, Newry, Apothecary
1782 Jan	9	McMINN Archibald, of James, Desart, farmer
	11	GREER Deborah, of William, Newry (Liberty), Gent
	13	McCULLOCH John, of William, Scott's Park, Labourer
	20	HARLAND Mary, of Samuel, Pollock's Green, Bleacher
	20	BETTERTON Juliana, of Thos Wm, Newry, Dancing Master and Player
	24	DAVIDSON Jane, of Arthur, Newry, Chandler
	30	LITTLE John, of William, Altnaveagh, Farmer
	30	RIGGS Mary, of Alexr, Cloghoran, Farmer
	30	THOMPSON George, of Ross, Liberty, Merchant
	31	HALL John, of . . . . , High Street, Breeches-maker
Feb	2	BROWN Peter, of Samuel, Pound Street, Slater
	9	PATTY Samuel, of George, High Street, Gardener
	10	GRAHAM Margaret, of Gerard, Derrylackah, Weaver
	11	AIKINS James, of John, Sugar Island, Cabinet maker
	18	DODDS Catherine, of John, Crobane, weaver
	21	. . . . William, of . . . . High Street, servant
Mch	4	EAGER George, of David, Canal Street
	5	TATE . . . , of David, Creeve, Bailif
	8	McMURRAY John, of . . . . , Canal Street, Guager
	10	POLLOCK Elizabeth, of Alexander, High Street, Shoemaker

Extract of Baptisms from a transcript of the "Registers of the First Presbyterian Church of Newry, Co. Down 1779-1796." *Irish Ancestor* 11 (1) (1979).

Skibereen which is described opposite the civil parish of Creagh, and that another part is served by Caheragh church which is described opposite the civil parish of the same name.

Diocese: Lists the Church of Ireland (not Catholic) diocese to which the civil parish belonged prior to 1880. (Inevitably there have been some changes in boundaries which cannot be adequately accounted for here. If the civil parish of interest is on the boundary of two dioceses it may be useful to check records for both dioceses.)

Earliest Record: Lists the earliest record of each of the three types of record in the order of baptism, marriage, and death/burial. The records are listed by the month and year of the starting record. Records which start after 1880 are generally not listed. If the records of the church which serves the area of interest start too late to be of value, it may be useful to check the other surrounding churches. A late start to the records may suggest that the church did not exist before the records started and that a different church was attended at the time.

Missing Dates: Lists the dates for which the records are missing. As can be seen there are very often extensive gaps in the records for various reasons. This item gives the dates (up to 1880) of the gaps in records. Like the starting dates, these are taken from the NLI index to their microfilm collection of Catholic church records. In some cases these have been supplemented with other information regarding additional records. The dates listed show the month and year (all nineteenth-century unless otherwise indicated) in which the records stopped and then resumed, e.g., 2.1865-8.1878 means that the records stop at some date in February 1865 and resume at some date in August 1878.

Parish Address: Lists the current parish priest of the parish and the address. Note that parish clergy generally do not have the time to conduct searches of their records. Most churches have made their records available for microfilming and, in some cases, have also allowed local heritage groups to index the records. Most parish clergy would therefore prefer not to be asked to conduct searches. The circumstances in which it may be necessary to correspond with the parish are (a) if the records are not available otherwise and (b) where the

date of a baptism or marriage has been established by a researcher. Then the parish may provide a certificate verifying the event. There will usually be a charge for either a search or a certificate, and there may also be a long delay.

Commercial and Social Directories

Ireland has a good selection of commercial directories. These list the various tradesmen, professionals, gentry, and, in some cases, inhabitants of Irish towns and cities.

The most comprehensive directories were Pigot's *Commercial Directory of Ireland* of 1820 and 1824 and Slater's *Royal National Commercial Directory of Ireland* of 1846, 1856, 1870 and 1881. These cover most large towns in the country. There are also many local directories, some of which are excellent with detailed lists of occupants by street. Others will only list the more prominent citizens. Most directories include lists of local public officials, magistrates, and gentry, and most have a list of tradesmen. Some of the better directories also include a house-by-house list of occupants on each street and are therefore very valuable in locating urban dwellers. In some cases the directories also list the major farmers in the immediate vicinity of the town.

Directories are particularly good for Dublin. There are annual directories from 1755 to the present day. From 1755 to 1815 *The Treble Almanack* included only merchants and traders; from 1815 to 1834 it contained nobility and gentry as well. In that year Pettigrew and Oulton's *Dublin Almanac* began with a house-to-house listing of the main streets, and from 1835 it also contained an alphabetical list of individuals. This directory ceased publication in 1849, but in the meantime Thom's *Directory* had begun. This contained all of the lists in Pettigrew and Oulton's and other additional information. It has been published every year up to the present.

Copies of the national directories and the Dublin directories are available in several Dublin libraries. Elsewhere, other directories

NOBILITY AND GENTRY.

Note.—The private Residents of the Professional and Trading Classes
will be found under their respective heads.

Achmuty (Mrs. S.) 23, *Rutland-str.*
Acton (Miss M.) 77, *Stephen's-gr. S.*
Adáir (Mrs.) 64, *Mount-street*, and
  Belgrove, Monasterevan.
Adams (Mrs. Isabella) 2, *Russell-st.*
Adams (Sam. esq.) 45, *Eccles-street.*
Adamson (J. esq.) 55, *Aungier-str.*
Adamson (Rev. A.S.) 14, *Blackhall-st.*
Agar (Wm. esq.) 4, *Molesworth-str.*
Airey (Maj. Gen.) 14, *Merr.-sq. N.*
Alexander (Robert, sen. esq.) 12,
  Merrion-square, and *Seapoint.*
Alexander (Sir Wm.) *Booterstown.*
Alexander (W.J.esq.)16,*Fitz-sq.W.*
Alexander (W. esq.) 4, *up. Baggot-s.*
Alexander (W. esq.) 1, *Richmond-pl.*
Allen (Captain) 3, *Richmond-street.*
Allen (Edm. esq.) 3, *low. Fitzw.-str.*
Allen (Lieu.Col.) 36, *l. Gardiner's-s.*
Allen (Lord Viscount) 10, *Merrion-*
  square, S.
Allen (Rich. esq.) 24, *Eccles-street.*
Anderson (E.esq.) 33,*up.Gloucester-s.*
Anderson (Mrs.) 15, *Charlemont-st.*
Anderson (Mrs.) 18, *Mount-street.*
Anderson (Mrs. M.) 12, *Cuffe-str.*
Anderson (Mrs.) 148, *Mecklb.-str.*
Anderson (Rob. esq.) 22, *Brunsw.-s.*
Annesley (Hon.Fra.) 29, *Molesw.-st.*
Annesley (Rev. Mr.) 2, *S. Cumb.-st.*
Anson (Hon. G.) 3d Guards, *Dublin*
  Castle.
Arabin (Henry, esq.) 12, *Clare-str.*
  and *Corka, Clondalkin.*
Archbold (Miss E.) 39, *Gloucester-st.*
Archdall (John, esq.) *Merrion-str.*
Archdall (Hon.Mrs.M)1,*Kildare-p.*
  Castle Archdall, Co. Fermanagh
Archer (Ald.) 9, *Gardiner's-place.*
Archer (Mrs.) 65, *Stephen's-gr. S.*
Archer (John esq.) *North-wall.*
Ardagh (Dean of) 26, *Harcourt-st.*

Armagh (Archd. of) 7, *Mer.-sq. E.*
  and *Aughnacloy.*
Armit (John,esq.) 1, *Kildare-street,*
  and *Newtown-park.*
Armitage (Mrs.) 45, *Bishop-street.*
Armstrong (Capt.) 17, *Prussia-str.*
Armstrong (Col.) 73, *Mount-street.*
Armstrong (Colonel) *Merrion-str.*
Armstrong (E. esq.)51, *Dominick-st*
Armstrong (Mrs. D.) 12, *l. Dorset-st*
Armstrong (Mrs.) 43, *up. Rutl.-str.*
Armstrong (Rev. Mr.)32,*Hardw.-st.*
Armstrong (R. esq.) *up. Baggot-str.*
Armstrong (Tho. esq.) 41, *Bless.-st.*
Arnold (Jas. esq.) 45, *up. Rutland-st.*
  and *Banbridge, Co. Down.*
Arran (Dowager Countess of) 21,
  Kildare-street.
Arthure (B. esq.) 42, *Dominick-str.*
Arthure (Mrs.) 8, *Charlemont-str.*
Arthure (Mrs. J.) 9, *Gloucester-str.*
Ashe (Major) 4, *up. Rutland-street.*
Ashe (Mrs.) 24, *Mount-street.*
Ashe (Mrs. W.) 45, *Leeson-street.*
Ashworth (J. esq.) 5, *S. Cumb.-str.*
Ashworth (R. esq.) 16, *Mer.-sq. N.*
Atkinson (John, esq.) 1, *Ely-place.*
Atkinson(John,esq.)3,*Blessington-st.*
Atkinson (Jos. esq.) 34, *gt. Ship-st.*
Attorney-General (Rt. Hon. the)
  27, *Steph.-gr. N.* & *Carysfort-park.*
Austin (Colonel) *Dublin Castle.*
Aylmer (Lord) *Royal Hospital.*
Aylmer (Mrs. Cath.) 1, *Eccles-str.*
Aylmer (Mrs. E.) 24, *Queen-street,*
Aylward (Nich. esq.) 9, *Temple-str.*
  and *Shankhill Castle, Co. Kilkenny.*
B.
Babington(Mrs.T.)14,*Blessington-s.*
Bacon (James C.esq.) 27,*Temple-str.*
Bacon (Miss S.) 8, *gt. Ship-street.*
Bagot (Mrs. D.) 36, *Leeson-street.*

List of Nobility and Gentry from *Wilson's Dublin Directory* for the year 1820.

are very rare and only available in NLI or TCD Library.

Family History

An ideal for many is to find that their ancestors have been described in detail by some previous researcher. Although this is rarely the case, the possibility always exists. Published histories usually deal with the more prominent families, or "gentry" of Ireland. The publications listed in the Family History section are those which either (a) refer to a family from one specific county or part of a county, or (b) refer to families which are particularly linked with one county. As is usual for listing of Irish family names, the "O" and "Mac" prefixes are ignored. Thus O'Brien and MacCarthy, for instance, will be listed as Brien and Carthy. There are many other references to specific families in local history publications and other sources. Many of these publications are author published and can be difficult to trace. NLI, SLC, and TCD have good collections.

Gravestone Inscriptions

These can be a very useful source of information as, in many cases, they indicate relationships or give the ages or birthdates of those interred. They are extensively researched in some counties (e.g., Wicklow, Wexford, Cork, and Down) and virtually unresearched in others. The records have been published in a wide variety of sources. The records list the name of the graveyard and the place of publication or availability of the transcriptions. Unfortunately, the name of the graveyard is not always the name of the town or even of a local townland. Graveyards are often on ancient monastic sites which predate other boundary names. The location of most is determinable with the "Index to Townlands etc..." (see Placenames section p. xi). In each section the available records are listed by townland (or graveyard) name. Where possible the general location is indicated.

Newspapers

The earliest known Irish newspaper was published in 1649. During the eighteenth century the numbers increased greatly, and by the nineteenth century most large towns had at least one newspaper, and some towns had several. By 1900 Dublin had seen the publication of some seventy different newspaper titles, and Belfast had seen forty.

The availability of newspapers is often difficult to trace. Many newspaper issues do not exist at all, particularly those from the eighteenth century. Newspapers occasionally changed their names or their base of publication or even stopped publishing for long periods.

In this guide the main newspapers for each county are listed. Also listed are the holdings of each paper in the National Library of Ireland; which has one of the best collections of Irish newspapers; in the British Library, London; and in some county libraries. In many cases the local county library will have good runs of the local newspapers.

Announcements of marriages, deaths, and births are the most obvious items of interest in these newspapers. However, these occur primarily only after the mid eighteenth century. Individual papers differed in their policy on advertisements; some contained many, others less. The policy also changed over the lives of some newspapers. Birth, marriage, and death notices, as might be expected, usually refer to the middle and upper classes. The birth notices tend to be less valuable since the name of the child and even the mother is usually not given. Birth notices often take the form "At Bandon, County Cork, the wife of John Barry Esq., of a daughter." On the other hand, marriage announcements are very valuable. There was a widespread practice of city newspapers repeating the notices appearing in provincial newspapers, often in an abridged form. If a notice of a rural "event" is found in a city newspaper, it is usually wise to check some of the local papers as more details may be found. Many papers did not place these small advertisments in one regular column but inserted them throughout the paper where space allowed.

THE INSCRIPTIONS OF MAGHEROSS CEMETERY

by

Rev. Pádraig Ó Mearáin

In the southern end of the town of Carrickmacross stand the remains of a church destroyed in the rebellion of 1641 and rebuilt in 1682. Surrounding this church is the ancient grave-yard of Magheross. Although P. S. Ó Dalaigh in "Sketches of Farney" mentions a headstone dated 1651, the oldest one that we discovered was dated 1664. The last burial in the grave-yard was in 1955.

The references at the end are to the numbers of the tomb-stones.

1. Elizabeth Connolly of Killough, who died at Carrickma-cross October 5th 1855, aged 70 Yrs.

    This stone is erected by the surviving members of the family whom she served devotedly and faithfully for 46 years. Close beside whose burial ground at her own request her remains are now interred.

2. John Clarke of Carrickmacross, aged 85 years. Also his Father. His mother Mary died 28th Dec. 1895, aged 85 years. R.I.P.

    (on the other side)

    And his brothers John, died 7th Nov. 1882. Aged 35 years. Patrick, died 20th April 1890. Aged 55 years. R.I.P.

3. Here lies the body of Patrick Mc. Cabe. He died in January 7th 1775 aged 68 years.
    Erected by Peter Mc Cabe.

4. This stone was erected by Francis Merron, Box, in memory of his father Patrick Merron who departed this life.

5. Erected by Phillip Duffy in memory of his mother who de-parted this life 26th Jany 1827 aged 56 years.
    Requiescat in Pace.

6. I. H. S. John Mc Adden died in ye year of Our Lord 1794.

7. Here lyeth the body of Thomas Marron who departed this life November ye 8th 1774 aged 48 years. This stone was erected by Nean Marron wife to the said Thomas Marron who departed this life. Feb.ry in the 56th year of her age. Also the body of Alexdr. Howes who departed this life July 3rd 1772 in the 7th year of his age.

8. This stone was erected by Henry Carrol in memory of his

Examples of transcripts of "Gravestone Inscriptions from the Cemetery of Magheross near Carrickmacross, Co. Monaghan." *Clogher Record* 5 (1) (1963).

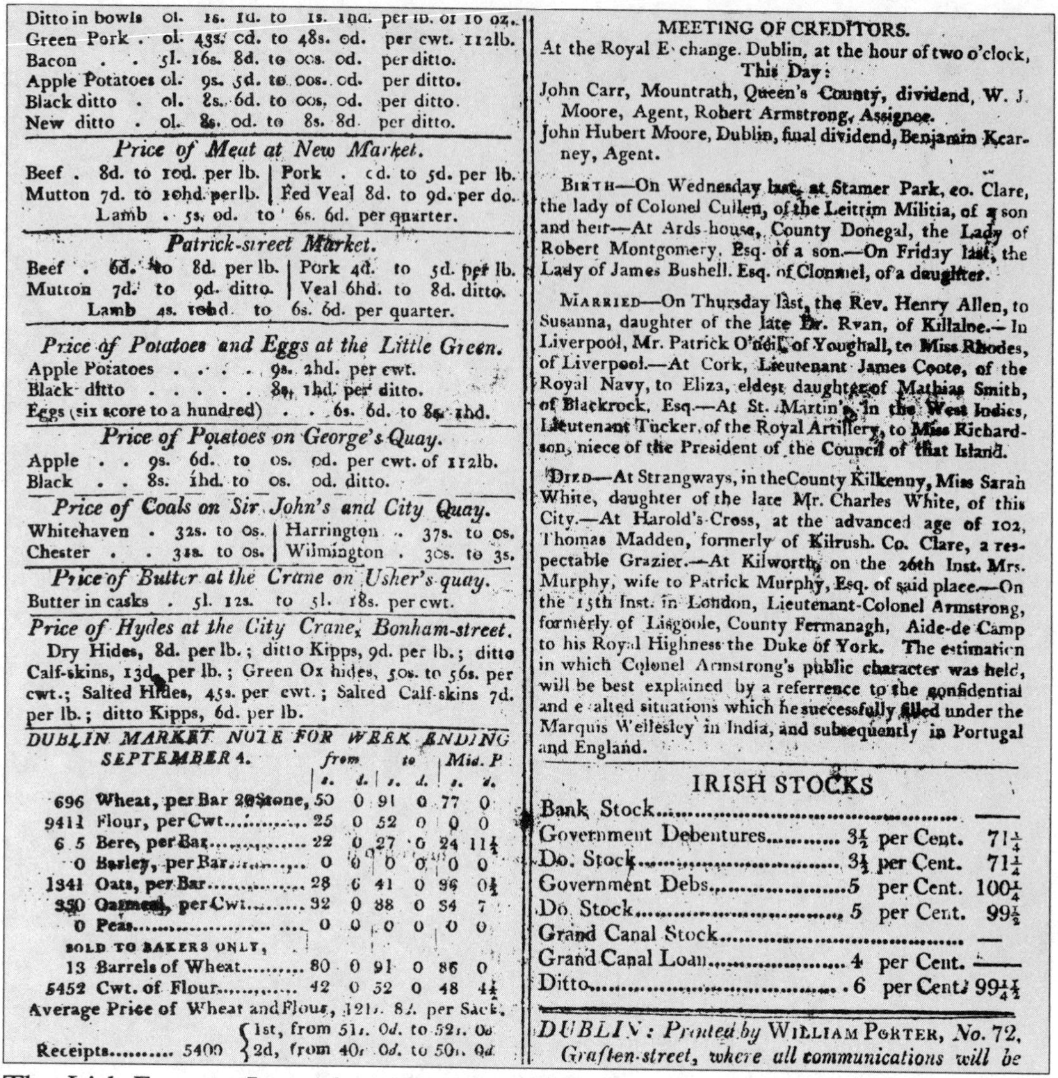

Ditto in bowls 0l. 1s. 1d. to 1s. 1hd. per lb. of 16 oz.
Green Pork . 0l. 43s. 0d. to 48s. 0d. per cwt. 112lb.
Bacon . . 5l. 16s. 8d. to 00s. 0d. per ditto.
Apple Potatoes 0l. 9s. 5d. to 00s. 0d. per ditto.
Black ditto . 0l. 8s. 6d. to 00s. 0d. per ditto.
New ditto . 0l. 8s. 0d. to 8s. 8d. per ditto.

Price of Meat at New Market.

Beef . 8d. to 10d. per lb. | Pork . 0d. to 5d. per lb.
Mutton 7d. to 10hd. per lb. | Fed Veal 8d. to 9d. per do.
Lamb . 5s. 0d. to 6s. 6d. per quarter.

Patrick-street Market.

Beef . 6d. to 8d. per lb. | Pork 4d. to 5d. per lb.
Mutton 7d. to 9d. ditto. | Veal 6hd. to 8d. ditto.
Lamb 4s. 10hd. to 6s. 6d. per quarter.

Price of Potatoes and Eggs at the Little Green.

Apple Potatoes . . . . 9s. 2hd. per cwt.
Black ditto . . . . . 8s. 1hd. per ditto.
Eggs (six score to a hundred) . . 6s. 6d. to 8s. 1hd.

Price of Potatoes on George's Quay.

Apple . . 9s. 6d. to 0s. 0d. per cwt. of 112lb.
Black . . 8s. 1hd. to 0s. 0d. ditto.

Price of Coals on Sir John's and City Quay.

Whitehaven . 32s. to 0s. | Harrington . . 37s. to 0s.
Chester . . 31s. to 0s. | Wilmington . 30s. to 3s.

Price of Butter at the Crane on Usher's-quay.

Butter in casks . 5l. 12s. to 5l. 18s. per cwt.

Price of Hydes at the City Crane, Bonham-street.

Dry Hides, 8d. per lb.; ditto Kipps, 9d. per lb.; ditto Calf-skins, 13d. per lb.; Green Ox hides, 50s. to 56s. per cwt.; Salted Hides, 45s. per cwt.; Salted Calf-skins 7d. per lb.; ditto Kipps, 6d. per lb.

DUBLIN MARKET NOTE FOR WEEK ENDING SEPTEMBER 4.

		from s.	from d.	to s.	to d.	Mid. P. s.	Mid. P. d.
696	Wheat, per Bar 20 Stone,	50	0	91	0	77	0
9411	Flour, per Cwt.	25	0	52	0	0	0
6 5	Bere, per Bar	22	0	27	6	24	11½
0	Barley, per Bar	0	0	0	0	0	0
1341	Oats, per Bar	28	6	41	0	36	0½
350	Oatmeal, per Cwt.	32	0	38	0	34	7
0	Peas	0	0	0	0	0	0
	SOLD TO BAKERS ONLY,						
13	Barrels of Wheat	80	0	91	0	86	0
5452	Cwt. of Flour	42	0	52	0	48	4½

Average Price of Wheat and Flour, 121s. 8d. per Sack.
Receipts.......... 5400 { 1st, from 51s. 0d. to 52s. 0d. / 2d, from 40s. 0d. to 50s. 0d.

MEETING OF CREDITORS.

At the Royal Exchange, Dublin, at the hour of two o'clock, This Day:
John Carr, Mountrath, Queen's County, dividend, W. J. Moore, Agent, Robert Armstrong, Assignee.
John Hubert Moore, Dublin, final dividend, Benjamin Kearney, Agent.

BIRTH—On Wednesday last, at Stamer Park, co. Clare, the lady of Colonel Cullen, of the Leitrim Militia, of a son and heir—At Ards-house, County Donegal, the Lady of Robert Montgomery, Esq. of a son.—On Friday last, the Lady of James Bushell, Esq. of Clonmel, of a daughter.

MARRIED—On Thursday last, the Rev. Henry Allen, to Susanna, daughter of the late Dr. Ryan, of Killaloe.—In Liverpool, Mr. Patrick O'Neil, of Youghall, to Miss Rhodes, of Liverpool.—At Cork, Lieutenant James Coote, of the Royal Navy, to Eliza, eldest daughter of Mathias Smith, of Blackrock, Esq.—At St. Martin's, in the West Indies, Lieutenant Tucker, of the Royal Artillery, to Miss Richardson, niece of the President of the Council of that Island.

DIED—At Strangways, in the County Kilkenny, Miss Sarah White, daughter of the late Mr. Charles White, of this City.—At Harold's-Cross, at the advanced age of 102, Thomas Madden, formerly of Kilrush, Co. Clare, a respectable Grazier.—At Kilworth, on the 26th Inst. Mrs. Murphy, wife to Patrick Murphy, Esq. of said place.—On the 15th Inst. in London, Lieutenant-Colonel Armstrong, formerly of Lisgoole, County Fermanagh, Aide-de-Camp to his Royal Highness the Duke of York. The estimation in which Colonel Armstrong's public character was held, will be best explained by a referrence to the confidential and exalted situations which he successfully filled under the Marquis Wellesley in India, and subsequently in Portugal and England.

IRISH STOCKS

Bank Stock			—
Government Debentures	3½	per Cent.	71¼
Do. Stock	3½	per Cent.	71¼
Government Debs.	5	per Cent.	100¼
Do. Stock	5	per Cent.	99½
Grand Canal Stock			—
Grand Canal Loan	4	per Cent.	—
Ditto	6	per Cent.	99¼½

DUBLIN: Printed by WILLIAM PORTER, *No.* 72, *Graften-street, where all communications will be*

The *Irish Farmers Journal and Weekly Intelligencer,* 5 September 1812.

If the area from which an ancestor came is known, then it is obviously useful to choose a newspaper published close to that area. For this reason the town of publication of each paper is shown. If no success is obtained with the most local paper, check papers from surrounding counties. A look through items such as court notices and other general advertisments in issues of these papers will usually quickly tell whether they contain entries from the area of interest to the researcher.

Basic news items are rarely of interest since names are not frequently given, other than in court cases, etc. Advertisements are an important source of information for tradesmen and other businessmen. These are common in most newspapers.

Wills and Administrations

Wills are legal documents detailing the wishes of deceased persons as to the division of their property. Administrations are legal documents setting out the decisions of a court as to division of the property of those who died without making a will.

Wills

These are a particularly valuable source of genealogical information. They can contain detailed information on relationships between many members of a family group, together with other information on the residences, occupations, history, and circumstances of the family. They are therefore well worth finding if they exist. Until 1858 the church was responsible for proving (i.e., establishing the validity) of wills. From the Reformation until 1858 this meant that the Church of Ireland, as the "established" church, was responsible. Within each Church of Ireland diocese there was a *Consistorial Court* which proved wills of those who had been residents within the diocese, and whose property was also within the diocese. If, however, the testators property in another diocese was of more than £5 value, the will was proven by a *Prerogative Court* which was the responsibility of the Archbishop of Armagh. Furthermore, if the testator had property in England, the will was also proved in the English court at Canterbury and a copy proved in Armagh. These records may also be checked. Recent immigrants to Ireland, in particular, may have retained property in England.

One of the circumstances in which a will might have been proved in the prerogative court is if the testator had land which straddled the border of two dioceses. In the guide to Church of Ireland records in each county, the diocese in which each civil parish is located is shown. From this, and the accompanying map, it can be seen if the land is on the border of another diocese. The other major circumstance in which a testator's will might be in the prerogative court is if he/she was wealthy and therefore had property or goods elsewhere in the country.

Most of the actual will documents (of all types) were destroyed in the fire at the Public Record Office in 1922. The records which are now available are of three types:

Wills. These are the wills which survived the PRO fire, copies, further wills which have been

obtained since 1922, and wills deposited in other archives (see p. xli).

Will Abstracts. Many local or family historians have examined the wills concerned with certain families or areas over the centuries. The notes on the contents of these wills, called abstracts, are available in the PRO and/or in other libraries.

Depending on the purpose for which they were made the abstracts will vary in their detail. They will usually contain the testator's name and address, date of will and probate, executor's name, and the names of the major beneficiaries. The relationship of beneficiaries to the testator is also often indicated. Major abstract collections include Betham's abstracts of Prerogative wills and Eustace's collection of abstracts of wills deposited at the Registry of Deeds.

Will Indexes. The major set of indexes to Irish wills are the books used in the PRO as a guide to finding the wills among their collection. The indexes to Consistorial wills survived the fire although some were damaged. These are in the PRO and are arranged alphabetically by family and Christian name and give the address (in some cases occupation) and year of probate. The indexes to Consistorial wills have been published in various places. The major source is the series of volumes edited by Gertrude Thrift (London: W.P.W. Phillimore, 1909-20. Reprint. Genealogical Publishing Company, 1970). Other sources include the 26th and 30th reports of the DKPRI and local history journals. The sources for indexes are indicated in the relevant section in each county.

Prerogative will indexes are arranged alphabetically by testator's name and also give the address, occupation, and year of probate. They are in two series, the first, up to 1810, and the second from 1811 to 1857. The first series has been published as *Index to the Prerogative Wills of Ireland 1538-1810* edited by Sir Arthur Vicars (1897. Reprint. Baltimore: Genealogical Publishing Company, 1967). The indexes are also available in the PRO.

Administrations

If a person died without making a will, the above two courts also had responsibility for deciding on the distribution of the deceased's

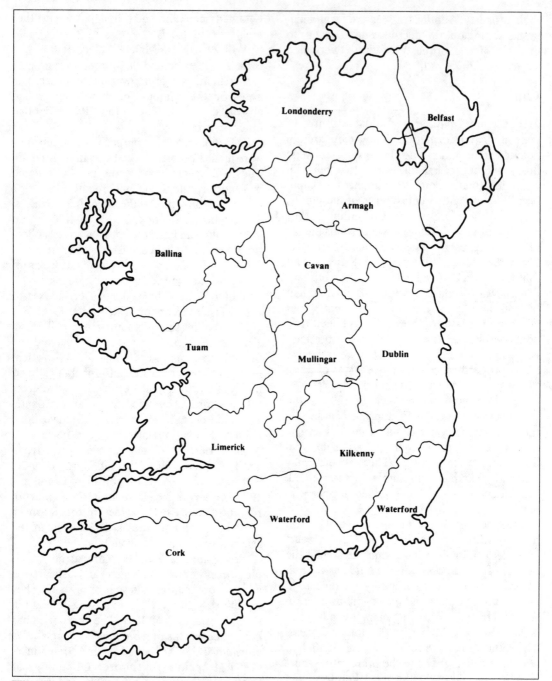

The Probate Districts of Ireland, from *A New Genealogical Atlas of Ireland* by Brian Mitchell. Genealogical Publishing Company, Baltimore, 1986.

147 BROWNE, THOMAS, Cork, gent.

28 Dec. 1713. Narrate, 1 p., 8 March 1717.

Daughter Mary, wife of Hugh Millerd the younger.   Grandson Thomas, son of said Hugh Millerd. Sister Sarah Humpston. Grandson William Kingsmill. Grandson Thomas, son of Edward Browne.

Evan Davis, clerk, tenant in Browne Street. A rent charge formerly granted to St. Peter's Parish, Cork. Brown Street, North East Marsh of Cork.

Witnesses: William Olliffe, Theodore Rheda, merchant, and William Lane, gent., all of Cork city.

Memorial witnessed by: William Olliffe, Ed. Barns.

21, 30, 10695   Hugh Millerd (seal)

148 DILLON, EDMOND, Billogh, parish of Ragharoe, B. Athlone, Co. Roscommon, gent. 18 July 1708. Full, 1 p., 13 March 1717.

My daughters Winifred, Mary and Bridget (heir).

My beloved friend Mr. Joseph Sproule, Gortmacassaughy, Co. Roscommon, gent., and Garrett Dillon, Athleag, said county, merchant, exors. Lands in Co. Roscommon.

Witnesses: Henry Magawly, Ballynahome, Co. Westmeath, gent., Peter Chamberlain, Maynooth, Co. Kildare, gent., Simon Smith, same, gent.

Memorial witnessed by: John Gregson, clerk to Bruen Worthington, notary public, Dublin, Hen. Buckley.

21, 38, 10714   Bridget Dillon als. Kavanagh
                her mark (seal)

149 SAUNDERS, ANDERSON, Newtownsaunders, Co. Wicklow, Esq., 24 Jan. 1717. Narrate, part in full, 1 p., 13 March 1717.

Only son Anderson Saunders. Nephews Richard Saunders, Isaac Dobson, Esq., Morley Saunders, Esq., Robert Saunders Esq., Jeffry Paul, Rathmore, Esq., and Francis Hardy (who is to take name of Saunders if he inherits). Exors. Isaac Dobson, Esq., and Mr. Rowland Bradstock.

Newtownsaunders, and lands in Co. Wicklow. Lands of inheritance in Kingdom of Ireland. Lands in Tipperary.

Page from P.B. Eustace's *Abstracts of Wills from the Registry of Deeds*. The Stationery Office, Dublin, 1956.

1678 **O'Donnoghue**, Geffry, Glanfleckle, co. Kerry, gent.

1804 **O'Donoghue**, Daniel, Killarney, co. Kerry, esq.

1790 ,, Jeffrey, Cork, esq.

1808 ,, Patrick, Killarney, co. Kerry

1808 ,, Robert, Cork city

1630 **O'Donovane**, Daniel, Rahine, or Castle Donovane, co. Cork, gent.   [gent.

1806 **O'Dougherty**, Michael, Cork city, [See O'DOHERTY.]

1797 **O'Dowd**, James, prisoner in the Four Courts Marshalsea

1798 **O'Dowda**, Letitia, Dublin, widow

1628 **O'Doweley**, William M'Donoghe, Biallaragged, co. Kildare, farmer

1781 **O'Driscoll**, Teresa, Annakessy, co. Cork

1627 **O'Duloghry**, John, Dunmoylane, co. Limerick, gent.

1619 **O'Dwyer**, Morogh M'Conagher, Ballyolaghan, co. Tipperary, farmer

1629 **O'Dwyere**, Darby, Milltown, co. Tipperary, esq.

1610 **O'Dwyre**, Gillane neaff, Kilboy, co. Tipperary, gent. (Copy)

1776 **O'Fallon**, Redmond, Athlone

1629 **O'Farrall**, Cornelius, Dublin, gent.

1708 **O'Farrell**, Francis Fergus, Dublin, esq., major-general

1811 ,, Gerald, Dublin city, esq.

1776 ,, Jane, Kilkenny, widow

1798 ,, Michael, Limerick, R. C. priest

1757 ,, Richard, major-genl. of His Majesty's Forces (Copy)

1808 ,, Roger, Lissard, co. Longford

1765 ,, Theobold

1803 **O'Ferrall**, Anne

1803 ,, John, the elder, Sligo, esq.

1593 **O'Fferreshe**, Dowagh M'Edmond M'Donell Duffe, Grange, co. Carlow

1725 **Offey**, John, Bloomsbury-square, Middlesex, esq. (Copy)

1786 ,, John, par. St. James, Westminster, esq. (Copy)

1801 **Offlaherty**, Catherine, Galway town, spinster

1594 **O'Flaerty**, sir Morough ne doe, Aghnemedle, co. Galway, knt.

1763 **O'Flaherty**, Edmond, Aglish, co. Waterford, gent.

1808 ,, Edmond, Lettermore, co. Galway, gent.

1792 ,, John, Gananina, co. Galway, gent.

1778 **O'Flaherty**, Thomas, Clare-street, Dublin, esq.

1804 **O'Flangan**, Jos., Tullamore, King's co., distiller

1803 **O'Flinn**, or **Flinn**, John, Ormondquay, Dublin, grocer

1805 ,, John, Carrick-on-Suir, co. Tipperary

1788 **O'Flyn**, Dorothy, Galway town, widow

1746 **O'Flynn**, Edmond, Forlogh, co. Galway, esq.

1601 **O'Fullny**, Edmond, Athlone, parochianus

1777 **O'Gara**, Farrell, Carrowmacteer, co. Mayo, gent.

1778 ,, Farrell, Carrow Macker, co. Mayo, gent.

1742 **O'Garra**, Mary, widow of Oliver O'G., esq.

1609 **O'Gary**, Manus, Ballycheever, dio. Dublin

1715 **Ogden**, Isaac, Black Pitts, Dublin, brewer

1652 ,, John, Dublin, gent.

1772 **Ogilby**, Alexander, Newtown Limavady, co. Derry

1807 ,, Mary, Newtown Limavady, co. Derry

1740 **Ogle**, Ann, wife to James Ogle, Lurgan, linendraper

1699 ,, Elizabeth, *alias* Smith, London, widow (Copy)

1765 ,, Frances, Dublin, widow

1781 ,, George, Newry, merchant

1712 ,, Henry, Drogheda, alderman

1803 ,, Henry, Newry, co. Armagh, merchant

1748 ,, James, Lurgan, co. Armagh, linendraper

1797 ,, James, Newry, co. Down, linendraper

1728 ,, John, Dublin, innkeeper

1773 ,, John, Drogheda, esq.

1778 ,, John, Waringstown, co. Down

1799 ,, John, Newry, merchant

1735 ,, Luke, Newcastle, Northumberland, gent.

1802 ,, Mary, Dublin, widow

1791 ,, Robert, Dysart Lodge, esq.

1719 ,, Samuel, Dublin, esq.

1743 ,, Susanna, Killaloe, co. Clare, widow

1729 ,, Thomas, Christchurch Yard, Dublin, merchant

1740 ,, Thomas, of lord George Sackville's troop at Thurles

1780 ,, William, Drogheda, alderman

1794 ,, rev. William, Spencerhill, co. Louth, clk.

Page from Sir A. Vicar's *Index to the Prerogative Wills of Ireland 1536-1810*. Dublin, 1897.

property to family and creditors. Having made its decision, the court acted by appointing an administrator (usually a next of kin or major creditor) to look after and distribute the estate of the deceased in the manner set down. The administrator entered a bond for a sum of money as surety that he would do so (hence Administration Bonds). Most of the records of these courts perished in the 1922 fire, but the following are available:

Administrations. Those available are the Prerogative Administrations of 1684-88, 1748-51, and 1839, and the consistorial grant books (see Administration Bonds below).

Abstracts of Administrations. In many of the collections listed in the Major Repositories of Wills and Administration Records section, both wills and administrations have been abstracted. Abstracts of approximately 5,000 pre-1802 administrations were made by Betham. The originals are at the PRO while an indexed copy is at the Genealogical Office. These abstracts contain deceased's name, address, and occupation, date of grant, and to whom made. The Prerogative Court of Canterbury also granted administrations and these are included with the wills in the records for 1828-39 available at the PRO.

Administration Bonds. (See Administrations above.) No original bonds survived the fire. However, the grant books, into which the grants were copied, survived for Cashel (1840-45), Ossory (1848-58), and a damaged copy for Derry and Raphoe (1812-21).

Marriage Licenses

Civil registration of Irish marriages began in 1845 for Church of Ireland marriages and in 1864 for other denominations. Until their disestablishment in 1857, the Church of Ireland was responsible for granting permission to marry. The church used two methods to ensure that neither party had already been married; (1) publishing of "Banns," which gave three weeks public notice of intention to marry so that objections could be made, or (2) marriage license bonds in which the groom (usually) would lodge a sum of money as surety that there was no reason not to marry. This sum was theoretically to insure the church against any damages which might be sought at a later date if it turned out there was an existing impediment to the marriage. Because publishing of banns was cheapest, it was also the most common method.

There are few records of banns. Likewise the original marriage license bonds have not survived. However, indexes and some abstracts of marriage license bonds and grants (the official permission to marry) survive. The indexes give the names of bride and groom and the year of the marriage. The existing records are shown in the Wills and Administrations section under each county.

Major Repositories of Wills and Administration Records

Public Record Office. This is the largest collection of Irish wills anywhere. It includes wills which survived the 1922 fire, copies and originals which have been deposited since, and various collections of will abstracts. The following are the surviving will books held in the PRO:

1. Prerogative Wills for the years 1664-84; 1706-08 (A-W); 1726-28 (A-W); 1728-29 (A-W); 1777 (A-L); 1813 (K-Z); 1834 (A-E).

2. Consistorial Wills. The individual consistorial courts varied as to the care which they took of wills deposited with them. In 1857 the PRO was entrusted with keeping the will documents. When the staff began to assemble the wills, the number of wills actually received from each court varied greatly. None produced all the wills they should have had, few provided many wills before 1780, and some produced very few from any period. Only one consistorial will survived the 1922 fire. The surviving will books are for Connor (1818-20 and 1853-58) and Down (1850-58). All of the indexes survive (see Wills and Administrations section p. xxxvii) and are available at the PRO.

Of particular note among the PRO's collections of abstracts are the Betham Prerogative Will Abstracts. In 1860 Sir William Betham organized the indexing of prerogative wills according to testator's names. He also wrote out brief genealogical abstracts of almost all the pre-1800 wills – amounting to some 37,500 abstracts. The general card index in the PRO covers the wills and will copies and most abstract collections. Abstract collections which are independently indexed in the PRO include the Crossle Collection (mainly seventeenth- and eighteenth-century, with an emphasis on the northwestern counties); and the Jennings Collection of Waterford wills and administrations.

3. The *Irish Will Registers* compiled by the Inland Revenue Commissioners, London, are available from 1828-39 (except part of 1834). They give the names and addresses of testator and executors; dates of will, decease, and probate; main legacies; and names of beneficiaries. This is a very valuable reference for the period 1828-39. The *Indexes to Irish Will Registers* compiled by the Inland Revenue Commissioners in London for the years 1828-79 are also available in the PRO. These give the name and address of testator and executor (often a family member).

Genealogical Office. The GO collection is mainly pre-1800, and many are arranged in series dealing with particular families. These are referenced in the Hayes index. The GO collection is not indexed and thus it is somewhat difficult to determine its exact contents. A general index of their holdings is in *Analecta Hibernica,* Vol. 17.

Registry of Deeds. The Registry of Deeds has a collection of almost 1,500 wills deposited with them in connection with land transfer particularly regarding disputed legacies of land. These wills have been abstracted and published by the Irish Manuscripts Commission as *Registry of Deeds, Dublin, Abstracts of Wills.* Vol. 1, 1708-45 and Vol. 2, 1746-88. Edited by P.B. Eustace (1954-56). Vol. 3, 1785-1832. Edited by E. Ellis and P.B. Eustace (1984).

National Library of Ireland. There are many collections of wills relating to specific families and areas held here. They are not separately indexed. However, Hayes's *Manuscript Sources for the History of Irish Civilization* indexes all NLI holdings by name, area, etc.

Research Sources and Services

This section lists various sources of information which the family researcher can access in Dublin, Belfast, or in the county of interest:

Journals

For many counties in Ireland there is a wealth of detailed local history available to the family researcher. The articles in these journals include detailed histories of specific parishes or townlands, information on local families and institutions, and accounts of the local effects of various events (contemporary accounts of the 1798 rebellion and of the Great Famine being particularly common). For some counties, such as Louth, Cork, and Galway, journals have been published for over 100 years. In some, the volumes are indexed by the places and persons mentioned. Copies are available in NLI and Trinity College, Dublin, Library and elsewhere. Many will accept queries from researchers. In short, all sorts of local historical detail is available in most counties, which may either explain certain events in an ancestor's history or point towards other avenues for research.

Apart from the local journals there are also the following journals which cover local, or family, history in all of Ireland. Non-local publications of interest:

Analecta Hibernica

Gaelic Gleanings

Journal of the Royal Society of Antiquarians of Ireland

Irish Genealogist, c/o Irish Genealogical Research Society, Glenholme, High Oakham Road, Mansfield, Notts, England.

Irish Ancestor, (publication now ceased) c/o Ms. Rosemary ffolliott, Glebe House, Fethard, Co. Tipperary.

Irish Family History, William Street, Tullamore, Co. Offaly.

Libraries and Information Sources

In most counties the major repository of information is the county library. Virtually all of these have local history or local studies sections, generally in the main branch library. Some have very extensive collections of local interest including copies of *Griffith's Valuation Survey, Tithe Applotment Survey,* 1901 and/or 1911 census returns, newspapers, and estate papers.

The major repositories of Irish family history records are in Dublin and Belfast. The records in Dublin relate to all of Ireland but more particularly to the twenty-six counties of the

Republic of Ireland. Those in Belfast relate to the six counties of Northern Ireland and, in some cases, to those Ulster counties which are not within "Northern Ireland" (Cavan, Donegal, and Monaghan). *The archives located in Dublin are the following:*

National Library of Ireland (NLI)
Kildare St.
Dublin 2
Ph: 765521
Holdings include: *Griffith's Valuation Survey,* including: list of householders in each county; Catholic parish registers (microfilm copies of most Catholic registers for all parts of Ireland); local and commercial directories; newspapers (microfilm and original copies of Irish newspapers); estate papers and records; maps; old photographs; and many other sources.

Public Record Office of Ireland (PRO)
Four Courts
Dublin 7
Ph: (01)733833
The PRO holds the original *Tithe Applotment Survey* books for twenty-six counties and copies of the books for northern Irish counties; census returns for 1901 and 1911 and the surviving parts of other censuses; and copies and originals of some surviving Church of Ireland parish registers (see also Representative Church Body Library). The PRO also has many manuscripts of relevance to family and local history, such as estate records, court records, and other government papers.

Genealogical Office (GO)
42 Kildare St.
Dublin 2
Ph: (01) 608670
This office incorporates the State Heraldic Museum and the Office of the Chief Herald. The institution has been in existence continuously since 1552, assigning and ratifying coats of arms for individuals and institutions. The office has a large range of material on family pedigrees, wills, funeral entries (biographies of noblemen who died from 1552 to 1700), and operates a genealogical research service.

Registrar-General's Office
8-11 Lombard St.
Dublin 2
Ph: (01) 711000
This office contains all of the official records of births, marriages, and deaths for all counties since records began in 1864. It also has Church of Ireland (Protestant or Episcopalian) marriage records from April 1845 to 1864. A public research room is available where the indexes to these records can be consulted.

The Registry of Deeds
Henrietta Street
Dublin 1
Records of property transactions since 1708.

State Paper Office
Dublin Castle
Dublin 2
Records of the British administration of Ireland, e.g., records of convicts who were transported, records of the 1798 Rebellion, Fenian Rising, and many others.

Representative Church Body Library (RCB)
Braemor Park
Rathgar, Dublin 14
Ph: (01) 979979
Holds some surviving Church of Ireland parish records, records of the Church of Ireland clergy, and other records and books relevant to the Church of Ireland.

Society of Friends Library (i.e., Quakers)
6 Eustace Street
Dublin
Has records of Quaker meeting houses in Munster, Leinster, and Connaught. Research is conducted for a fee.

Trinity College Library (TCD)
Dublin 2
Ph: (01) 772941
This large library has a fine collection of manuscripts, newspapers, and many examples of illuminated manuscripts and other treasures.

Royal Irish Academy (RIA)
19 Dawson St.
Dublin
Ph: (01) 762570
Has a large collection of manuscript and printed sources.

Dept. of Folklore
University College Dublin
Belfield, Dublin 4
Ph: (01) 693244
Has interesting collections of documents and tapes relating to folklore and customs in various parts of the country.

In Belfast the archives available are the following:

Public Record Office of Northern Ireland (PRONI)
66 Balmoral Avenue
Belfast BT9 6NY
Holds the official records from government departments relating to Northern Ireland from c.1830. It also has large collections of private papers, including estate papers, copies of all surviving Church of Ireland (Episcopalian) parish registers for Northern Ireland, and also registers for some Presbyterian and Roman Catholic churches.

Northern Ireland Registrar-General's Office
Oxford House
Chichester Street
Belfast BT1 4HL
Has records of births, marriages, and deaths from 1864 (and of Protestant marriages from 1845) for the northern counties.

Presbyterian Historical Society
Church House
Fisherwick Place
Belfast BT1 6DW
Has many of the oldest Presbyterian church registers in the province. These may be consulted by arrangement at the Library, Assembly College, Botanic Avenue, Belfast BT7 1JT.

Linen Hall Library
17 Donegall Square North
Belfast BT1

Society of Friends Library
Friends Meeting House, Lisburn
Co. Antrim
Holds records of Quaker meeting houses in Ulster.

Research Services

Because of the accessibility of the archives and records described above, some of the major research services are located in Dublin and Belfast. These perform research for all parts of the country. Those seeking research services can also employ local researchers. In some counties there are local Heritage Centers which have indexed the local parish records and other local records. Possibly the best example is the Clare Heritage Centre (see Research Services section, Co. Clare) which has indexed parish records for forty-seven parishes and twenty-five graveyards in that county, as well as indexed emigrant lists. Where such centers exist they are detailed in the Research Sources and Services section in the relevant county.

Research Services in Dublin include:

Genealogical and Historical Research
Farnham House
4 Henrietta Street
Dublin 1
P.O. Box No. 1501

Hibernian Research Company Ltd.
Windsor House
22 Windsor Road
Rathmines, Dublin 6
Ph: (01) 966522

Irish Research Services
60 Pinewood Avenue
Dublin 11

Dr. J. Ryan
4 Spencer Villas
Glenageary, Co. Dublin
Ph: (01) 806228

Mr. Ian Cantwell
5 Seafield Ave
Monkstown, Co. Dublin

INDEX TO CLERGY OF ROMAN CATHOLIC CHURCH.

NAME, DIOCESE, AND POST TOWN.

Ahern, Michael, Cloyne, Macroom
Ahern, M., Cloyne, Youghal
Ahern, Richard, Cloyne, Mallow
Allen, James, Ard. and Clon., enamore, Longford
Allman, J., Kerry, Castle Island
Ambrose, James, Cork, Monkstown
Ambrose, Robert, Limerick, Newcastle
Anderson, Terence, Dublin, Presb., Seville-place
Ansbro, Laurence, Tuam, Dromgriffin
Ashlin, Stephen, Cloyne, Doneraile
Atkinson, Joseph, Ard. and Clon., Longford
Aylward, Edward, Ferns, Wexford
Aylward, James, Ferns, Enniscorthy
Aylward, Patrick, Ossory, Kilkenny
Bambuck, P., Elphin, Roscommon
Barrett, John, Tuam, Headford
Barrett, P., Killaloe, Dunkerrin
Barrett, E., Cork, Cork
Barrett, T., Cork, Kinsale
Barron, Michael, Waterford, Waterford
Barry, D., Cloyne, Mallow
Barry, Edward, Cloyne, Rathcormack
Barry, James, Cloyne, Middleton
Barry, John, Cloyne, Inniscarra
Barry, John, Cloyne, Carrigtoohill
Barry, John, Cork, Glounthaune R. S. O.
Barry, Michael, Emly, Kilcooly, Thurles
Barry, Patrick, Killaloe, Roscrea
Barry, Robert, Meath, Dunsany
Barton, Luke, Meath, Castle Geoghegan
Barton, P., Kerry, Castletown-Bere
Baxter, James, Dublin, Lucan
Beatson, H., Down and Connor, Belfast
Beauchamp, John, Kildare and Leighlin, Borris
Beasley, J., Kerry, Castletown-Bere
Blaney, J. P., Derry, Draperstown
Beechinor, J., Cloyne, Charleville
Begley, John, Limerick, Shanagolden
Begley, John, Tuam, Tuam
Behan, Hugh, Meath, Trim
Benson, Francis, Achonry, Ballaghadereen
Bergin, James, Kildare, Philipstown
Bermingham, Peter, Clogher, Carrickmacross
Bernard, D., Cork, Bandon
Biggins, R., Tuam, Clifden
Birch, J., Ossory, Knocktopher
Blake, Patrick, Raphoe, Dunfanaghy
Blake, Richard, Meath, Navan
Bodkin, Joseph, Clonfert, Kilrickill
Boggan, J. Ferns, Skreen, Gorey
Boggan, L, Ferns, Duncormick, Wexford
Bolger, David, Ferns, Wexford
Bolger, M., Kildare and Leighlin, Hacketstown
Bolger, P., Kildare, cancroft
Bollasty, Patrick, Meath, Drumconrath, Ardee
Booth, W. J., Armagh, Drogheda
Bourke, John, Cashel, Bruff
Bourke, Joseph, Dublin, Presb., Aughrim-st.
Bourke, Ed., Kildare & Leighlin, Bagenalstown
Bourke, Sylvester, Dublin, Donnybrook
Bourke, Thomas, Dublin, Presb., Harrington-st.
Bourke, William, Killaloe, Kildysart
Bowden, J., Ossory, Kilkenny
Bowes, John, Ossory, Gowran
Bowes, Thomas, Ossory, Kilkenny
Bowes, John, Clonfert, Ballinasloe
Bowes, T. Clonfert, Killimore
Bowes, Bernard, Clonfert, Kilrickill
Bowler, Thomas, Cloyne, Youghal
Boylan, John, Kilmore, Kilnaleck
Boylan, Pk., Clogher, Silverstream, Monaghan
Boylan, T., Ardagh, Drumshambo
Boyle, Hugh, Derry, Victoria Place, Derry
Boyle, John, Raphoe, Falcarragh, Letterkenny
Boyle, John, Killala, Ballina
Boyle, Joseph, Raphoe, Dunfanaghy
Boyle, Patrick, Down, Crossgar
Boyle, Thomas, Derry, Garvagh
Boyle, T., Armagh, Drogheda
Bracken, Michael, Meath, Tullamore
Bracken, W., Meath, Tullamore
Bradley, William, Derry, Castledawson
Brady, Joseph, Derry, Strabane
Bradley, Bernard, Meath, Dunboyne
Bradley, Bernard, Kilmore, Swanlinbar
Brady, E., Kilmore, Kinlough
Brady, Eugene, Kilmore, Bawnboy
Brady, F., Kilmore, Carriganlea
Brady, J., Dublin, Blackrock
Brady, James, Dublin, 47, Westland-row
Brady, Jas., Ardagh, Keadue, Car.-on-Shan.
Brady, John, Kilmore, Belturbet
Brady, Michael, Dublin, Presb., Seville-place
Brady, P. Kilmore, Ballinamore
Brady, Patrick, Armagh, Dundalk
Brady, Patrick, Kilmore, Kilnaleck
Brady, Peter, Kilmore, Cootehill
Brady, Terence, Kilmore, Bailieborough
Brady, Thomas, Kilmore, Cootehill
Brady, William, Ardagh and Clonmacnoise, street, Rathowen
Brannan, F., Kilmore, Garrison
Brannan, J., Dublin, 7, Eblana-av., Kingstown
Brannan, M., Castlerea
Breagry, J., Armagh, Dundalk
Breen, J., Kildare, Ballickmoyler, Carlow
Breen, James, Dublin, Dundrum
Breen, John, Limerick, Athea
Breen, M., Cloyne, Newmarket

Breen, M., Killaloe, Shinrone
Breen, P., Clogher, Irvinestown
Breen, William, Dublin, St. Margarets
Brennan, Denis, Armagh, Drogheda
Brennan, Edward, Ossory, Piltown
Brennan, Edward, Ossory, Rathdowney
Brennan, Edwd., Kildare & Leighlin, Mountrath
Brennan, Geoffrey, Down & Connor, Killough
Brennan, Henry, Ossory, Waterford
Brennan, Hugh, Ardagh, Drumcong, Car.-on-Sh.
Brennan, J., Elphin, Riverstown, Ballymote
Brennan, James, Ossory, Waterford
Brennan, James, Dublin, 47, Westland-row
Brennan, M., Kildare, Stradbally
Brennan, Patrick, Killaloe, Carrigaholt
Brennan, P., Dublin, Glasnevin
Brennan, P. J., Dublin, Skerries
Brennan, Thomas, Ossory, Castlecomer
Breslan, James, Armagh, Coal Island
Bresnahan, Daniel, Limerick, Limerick
Bric, J., Kerry, Killarney
Briody, John, Ard. and Clon., Killoe, Longford
Briody, P., Ardagh, Carrick Fines, Granard
Briody, Patrick, Meath, Athboy
Brisbane, P., Killala, Inniscrone, Ballina
Brock, William, Dublin, Arran-quay
Brogan, John, Meath, Oldcastle
Brophy, Thomas, Ossory, Waterford
Brosnahan, Timothy, Killaloe, Kilkee
Brosnan, P., Kerry, Castlemaine
Brosnan, Very Rev. Thade, Kerry, Cahirciveen
Brosnan, Thomas, Kerry, Tralee
Brosnan, T., Kerry, Tralee
Brown, D., Cloyne, Killinardrisk
Brown, D., Cloyne, Mallow
Brown, Patrick, Kerry, Tralee
Browne, D., Cloyne, Macroom
BROWNE, Most Rev. JAMES, D.D., *Bishop* of Ferns, St. Peter's College, Wexford
Browne, James, Cloyne, Macroom
Browne, John, Ferns, Duncannon, Gorey
Browne, Lawrence, Killaloe, Doonbeg
Browne, Thomas, Limerick, Limerick
Browne, William, Waterford, Waterford
BROWNRIGG, Most Rev. ABRAHAM, D D. *Bishop,* Ossory, Kilkenny
Buchanan, George, Meath, Summerhill
Buckley, C., Cloyne, Buttevant
Buckley, Timothy, Cloyne, Mallow
Buckley, W., Killaloe, Feakle
Buglar, Michael, v.o., Killaloe, Birr
Burdon, D., Cloyne, Buttevant
Burke, David, Down, Loughgiel, Clough
Burke, E. W., Kildare, B.-genalstown
Burke, Edward, Dublin, 33, Stephen's-green
Burke, Edmond, Emly, Kilcooly, Thurles
Burke, J., Tuam, Dunmore
Burke, J., Kerry, Tralee
Burke, James, Waterford, Newcastle, Clonmel
Burke, John, Ross, Timoleague
Burke, J., Kilfenora, Lisdoonvarna
Burke, Mat., Achonry, Swinford
Burke, Michael, Tuam, Ballyhaunis
Burke, Michael, Ardagh, Killoe, Longford
Burke, Thomas, Kilmacduagh, Kilcolgan
Burke, Timothy, Emly, Killenaule
Burke, Thaddeus, Waterford, Car.-on-Suir
Burke, Tobias, Wat. & Lis., Passage, Waterford
Burke, Wm., Watf. & Lis., Kilmacthomas
Burns, J. V., Down, Belfast
Burton, John, Cloyne, Doneraile
Busher, John, Ferns, Tinahely, Enniscorthy
Busher, Thomas, Ferns, Newtownbarry
Butler, M. J., Dublin, Balbriggan
Butterfield, M., Dublin, Presb., Haddington-rd.
Butterly, P., Dublin, Inchicore
Byrne, Charles, Meath, Moate
Byrne, Daniel, Kildare and Leighlin, Carlow
Byrne, Eugene, Dub., 7, Eblana-av., Kingstown
Byrne, F., Armagh, Forkhill
Byrne, George, Kildare and Leighlin, Newbridge
Byrne, J., Kildare and Leighlin, Carlow
Byrne, James, Dromore, Lurgan
Byrne, J. Dublin, Glendalough, Rathdrum
Byrne, John, Armagh, Ardee
Byrne, John, Dublin, 59, Eccles-street
Byrne, John, Kildare & Leighlin, Clonegal
Byrne, Laurence, Armagh, Portadown
Byrne, M., Dublin, Baldoyle
Byrne, Michael, Clonfert, Taghmaconnell
Byrne, Michael, Limerick, Newcastle West
Byrne, Patrick, Waterford & Lismore, Lismore
Byrne, Patrick, Kildare, Ratnangan
Byrne, Patrick, Waterford, Clonmel
Byrne, Peter J., Armagh, Dungannon
Byrne, Richard, Kildare and Leigh, Rathvilly
Byrne, Thomas, Dublin, Arklow
Byrne, Wm., Kildare, Coolkenno, Tullow
Byrnes, James, Emly, Galbally, Tipperary
Byrne, W., Dublin, Cuttlestown
Caffrey, Joseph, Dublin, Fairview
Cahalan, Joseph, Clonfert, Kiltulla, Athenry
Cahill, Cornelius, Cloyne, Glanworth
Cahill, F. Ardagh, Cloone, Mohill
Cahill, Henry, Tuam, Ballyglunin
Cahill, John, Ossory, Knocktopher
Cahill, P., Ardagh, Abbeylara, Granard
Cahill, Richard, Emly, Tipperary
Cahill, T., Ard. & Clonmac., Dromahair
Cahill, Thomas, Ferns, Ballymore, Killinick
Cahill, William, Ossory, Piltown

Cahir, James, Killaloe, Miltownmalbay
Callaghan, A., Achonry, Foxford
Callan, Patrick, Clogher, Annyalla, Monaghan
Callanan, Jonas, Ross, Rosscarbery
Callanan, Jonas, Ross, Timoleague
Callanan, Michael, Waterford, Kilmacthomas
Callary, Michael, Meath, Skryne, Tara
Callary, Philip, Meath, Drogheda
Calligan, M. Killaloe, Killaloe
Campbell, A., Derry, Killeter, Castlederg
Campbell, J., Down, Belfast
Campbell, Joseph, Clogher, Iniskeen
Campbell, P., Dromore, Loughbrickland
Campbell, Patrick, Kilfenora, Liscannor
Campion, Peter, Kildare & Leighlin, Whitehall
Canning, John, Tuam, Westport
Cannon, J. C., Raphoe, Termon
Canton, Joseph, Tuam, Athenry
Cantwell, James, Emly, Killenaule
Cantwell, John, Wat. & Lismore, Clashmore
Cantwell, Patrick, Meath, Enfield
Cantwell, Walter, Emly, Tipperary
Canty, Michael, Limerick, Kilmallock
Canty, Thomas, Emly, Tipperary
Carberry, J., Meath, Collinstown
Carberry, Philip, Dublin, Rathdrum
Carberry, Thomas, Dublin, Ballytore
Carey, James, Killaloe, Corofin
Carey, Jeremiah, Cork, Carrigaline
Carey, John, Meath, Ballymahon
Carey, Joseph, Meath, Garristown
Carey, Michael, Killaloe, Ennis
Carey, Michael, Killaloe, Scariff
Carlin, James, Dromore, Newry
Carlos, Luke, Elphin, Frenchpark
Carmody, James, Kerry, Castleisland
Carmody, Thomas, Kerry, Castletown-Bere
Carolan, F., Armagh, Forkhill
Carolan, P., Dublin, Ballymore-Eustace
Carraher, B., Armagh, Forkhill
Carrick, John, Limerick, Loughill
Carrick, Robert, Dublin, Fingla
Carrigan, Patrick, Ossory, Callan
Carrigan, W., Ossory, Jenkinstown
Carroll, F., Dublin, Presb. Francis-street
Carroll, James, Limerick, Newcastle West
Carroll, John, Ossory, Waterford
Carroll, John, Down and Connor, Coleraine
Carroll, John, Ossory, Kilkenny
Carroll, Luke, Kilmore, Mullagh
Carroll, M., Limerick, Newcastle
Carroll, P., Limerick, Croom
Carver, John, Cloyne, Castletownroche
Casey, John, Waterford, Lismore
Casey, Christopher, Meath, Churchtown, Naas
Casey, Francis L., Cork, Passage West
Casey, James, Elphin, Athleague, Roscommon
Casey, John, Kerry, Cahirciveen
Casey, Michael, Waterf. and Lism. Cappoquin
Casey, P., Waterford and Lismore, Dungarvan
Casey, Thomas, Meath, Kells
Casey, William, Limerick, Abbeyfeale
Cashel, John, Ardagh, Moate
Casserly, James, Ard. & Clon., Clondra, Longford
Cassidy, Edward, Raphoe, Donegal
Cassidy, Francis, Kilmacduagh, Loughrea
Cassidy, F., Rossmuch, Oughterard
Cassidy, J., Cork, Cork
Cassidy, John, Meath, Slane
Cassidy, Thomas, Meath, Longwood
Cassidy, William, Derry, Muff, Donegal
Cassin, W., Ossory, Kilkenny
Caulfield, Patrick, Tuam, Hollymount
Cavanagh, Bartholomew, Tuam, Ballyhaunis
Cavanagh, D. Ferns, Adamstown, Enniscorthy
Cavanagh, M., Ferns, Blackwater, Gorey
Cavanagh, M. Ferns, Ballywilliam, New Ross
Clancy, James, Killaloe, Lerrha
Clancy, John, Emly, Cashel
Clarke, John, Armagh, Dunleer
Clarke, M., Killala, Easky
Clarke, Michael, Dublin, Wicklow
Clarke, Michael, Killala, Killala
Clarke, Owen, Armagh, Donaghmore, Dgannon
Clarke, Patrick, Armagh, Dundalk
Clarke, Patrick, Kilmore, Bailieborough
Clarke, Patrick, Meath, Kingscourt
Clarke, Thomas, Kilmore, Ballinagh
Clavin, James, Meath, Moynalty
Cleary, Denis, Killaloe, O'Callaghan's Mills
Cleary, John, Ferns, Clonroche
Cleary, Michael, Emly, Templemore
Clifford, Edmond, Limerick, Newcastle West
Clifford, Patrick, Clogher, Fintona
Cloney, Silvester, Ferns, Skreen, Gorey
Cloney, Thomas, Ferns, Tagoat
Cloney, Thomas, Ferns, Bridgetown, Wexford
Clune, James, Killaloe, Mountshannon
Cody, Michael, Ossory, Castlecomer
Coen, M., Tuam, Athenry
Coffey, Fras., Dublin, Presb., Arran Quay
COFFEY, Most Rev J., *Bishop of Kerry,* Killarney
Coghlan, J., Cork, Blackrock, Cork
Coghlan, Jas., Clonfert, Loughrea
Coghlan, J., Cork, Bandon
Coghlan, W, Cloyne, Charleville
Coghlan, William, Cloyne, Mallow
Coghlan, W., Cloyne, Charleville
Coglan, J., Waterford, Lismore
Coglan, D., Clonfert, Aughrim
Cole, Dermot, Meath, Navan

Extract from the Index to Clergy of Roman Catholic Churches in *Thom's Official-Directory of the United Kingdom of Great Britain and Ireland* for 1893.

Genealogical Office
Kildare Street
Dublin 2

Dr. Christine Kinealy
10 Grosvenor Road
Rathmines, Dublin 6

Research services in Belfast include the following:

The Ulster Historical Foundation
66 Balmoral Avenue
Belfast BT9 6NY
Ph: (Belfast) (084)681365

Historical Research Associates
7 Lancasterian St.
Carrickfergus, Co. Antrim

Irish Genealogical Services
121 Saintfield Rd.
Belfast, BT8 4HN

Ulster Pedigrees
5 Heathermount Court
Comber, Co. Down, BT23 5NT

Irish World Citizen Organization
124 Donegall St.
Belfast

Societies

There is great interest in local history in Ireland as is shown by the numbers of local history societies listed. Researchers may be interested to correspond with such societies in order to place queries in their newsletters or journals, or indeed to offer information. Although a few societies have permanent headquarters and libraries, most do not and are dependent on voluntary local secretaries. Note that as well as these local societies, there are also publications of a non-local nature which are very relevant to family research.

Miscellaneous Sources

In this section other records of genealogical interest are presented. These include articles dealing with emigration patterns from the county, lists of public officials, and other useful background information. Lists of published wills, administrations, etc., are also included here.

A Brief History of Ireland

Some general background information about Irish history will be useful in understanding the nature and value of the record sources listed in this book. This section, therefore, outlines some of the major events which affected Irish family history.

Current evidence suggests that the earliest arrival of people in Ireland was about 6500 B.C. A number of independent waves of further migrants followed this early invasion. The exact origins of the earlier arrivals are not known, but the bulk of the later arrivals were Celtic, part of the same racial stock as now also inhabit Scotland, Wales, Cornwall in the U.K., and Brittany

in France. These people developed a rich culture in Ireland.

In the old Gaelic cultural system, families and their territories were very closely linked. Indeed, the Gaelic name of a territory and of its people were the same, "tuath." It is therefore possible to identify precisely the territories of the ruling families (O'Neills, O'Briens, O'Connors, etc.). Other families were associated with these ruling families as doctors, lawyers, scribes, historians, etc., and can also be linked with particular territories. For example, the Maguires, ruling family of the area which is now Fermanagh, were associated with the

O'Husseys (bards), the O'Keenans (historians), O'Cassidys (physicians), O'Breslins (lawyers), etc. These territories gradually broke down as the families were dispossessed and new land divisions were imposed by English rule. However, families are generally still well represented in their ancient territories.

The native language of the country is Gaelic, or Irish. Although the Irish language is still spoken in some parts of Ireland and is one of the official languages of the Irish Republic, English is the primary language of the country. Most Gaelic family and place-names are based on Gaelic language forms. The first significant new arrivals to Ireland within recorded history were the Norse and Danish Vikings who arrived in the eighth and ninth centuries, first to raid and later to settle and trade. Many coastal ports, including Waterford, Wexford, and Dublin, were largely developed by these Vikings. Up to and following the defeat of the Vikings by the native Irish in 1014, there was widespread integration of these peoples into the native population. These Scandinavian settlers did not use family names which are passed from father to son as in most of Europe, and as a result, there is little evidence of Viking influence in current family names. Exceptions include the names Sweetman, Harold, and Doyle.

In the twelfth century Ireland was invaded and largely conquered by the Normans, descendants of a mixed Scandinavian-Frankish people who had earlier conquered England and Wales. In time, however, the Normans also became totally integrated with the Irish people, adopting the native dress, customs, and language. Norman names such as Burke, Roche, Fitzgerald, Fitzpatrick, etc., are now among the most common in Ireland.

England nominally controlled all of Ireland from the time of the Norman invasion. In practice however, for several centuries English law only applied in an area around Dublin called the "Pale." The extent of the Pale varied during this time but generally included the current counties of Dublin and parts of Kildare, Meath, Wicklow, and Louth.

In the mid-sixteenth century, Henry VIII began the Tudor "reconquest" of Ireland, gaining the submission of many of the Gaelic chieftains in return for assurances that they would retain lordship of their ancestral territories. He also began the process of destroying Gaelic culture by outlawing Irish language, dress, and even hairstyle!

Gaelic Ireland did not give up easily however, and English rule was only tentatively maintained over many areas from within fortified garrisons. In Ulster, particularly, the O'Neills and O'Donnells fought the "nine years war" with England. This ended with O'Neill's defeat in 1603. The subsequent departure of O'Neill and most of the leading chieftains of Ulster opened the way for the era of "plantation" of Irish territories. In a plantation the native people were removed from their lands and replaced by colonists from England, Scotland, or Wales. This policy was pursued in Ulster with good success. Success was not total, however, because there were not enough planters to occupy all of the areas to be planted and not enough labor to work them. Thus, significant numbers of the native populations stayed in their traditional territories as tenants and laborers. The plantations elsewhere in Ireland had moderate or little success. These plantation schemes are more fully dealt with in the histories of the affected counties.

In 1641 there was a further rebellion by the Catholic population of Ireland which included the Gaelic and "Old English" or Norman people. The Catholics set up a rival parliament in Kilkenny which ruled Ireland for some years. This rebellion was finally defeated by Oliver Cromwell in 1649 and was followed by massive confiscation of land and the forced transplantation of many Catholics to the province of Connaught. Many of the defeated soldiers and others made homeless by the war were transported to the West Indies. The Irish confiscated lands were redistributed to various "adventurers" (those who had financed Cromwell's army), to officers in Cromwells army, and to others favored by the English establishment. The bulk of the population, however, continued to live where they had previously, albeit under new landlords.

From the family history viewpoint this period is significant because the process of confiscation and redistribution required extensive surveys of the land and its owners. Many of these surveys survive.

In order to increase the numbers of Protestant settlers in Ireland, various encouragements were offered to immigrants of that faith. The earliest of these was "an act to encourage Protestant settlers to settle in Ireland," passed in 1662. This helped the influx of French Huguenots into Ireland, particularly after the Revocation of the Edict of Nantes gave them cause to leave France. Many Huguenots were tradesmen, such as goldsmiths, weavers, etc. and many became very successful merchants.

In 1690 James II and William of Orange, contenders for the throne of England, fought a war in Ireland with Catholic support going to James. The war resulted in a defeat for King James, and had a number of devastating consequences for Irish Catholics. The first was that huge numbers of the soldiers who had fought in King James's army were forced to flee overseas. By one estimate, half a million soldiers joined the armies of France and other continental European countries in the fifty years following the end of this war.

Although the Catholic army had negotiated honorable surrender terms (the "Treaty of Limerick") which guaranteed that there would be no general repression of Catholics, this treaty was not honored. Instead, a series of "Penal Laws" were enacted by the English parliament which severely restricted Catholic entry to certain trades, their right to land ownership and inheritance, and many other rights. By the beginning of the eighteenth century it is estimated that only about 5 percent of Ireland was owned by Catholics.

The Penal Laws are very significant from a family history viewpoint as they had the effect of reducing the number and variety of records relating to Catholic families. By limiting the activities of the Roman Catholic Church, and by limiting the numbers and rights of its priests, the Penal Laws in effect hindered the keeping of comprehensive records. By reducing Catholic rights to own land, they also removed Catholic families from inclusion in land records, such as deeds and leases. The Penal Laws also restricted Catholic entry into public office, removed their voting rights, and in general impoverished them, thus cutting down the range of records which they might be expected to have left. For this reason the eighteenth century is known as the "silent century" in Irish family research.

The Penal Laws also applied in some respects to Presbyterians. This was a major cause of the migration of Presbyterians from Ireland to North America and Canada in the eighteenth century. These Presbyterians were the so-called Scots-Irish, the Scottish settlers who came to Ireland in the 1609 plantation of Ulster.

Inspired by the French Revolution of 1789, a new nationalist movement, the United Irishmen, arose in Ireland toward the end of the eighteenth century. This movement culminated in a rebellion in 1798. The rebellion was sporadic, however, and was quickly put down.

The major period of emigration from Ireland started about 1780, but the event which forced the major emigration from Ireland was the Great Famine of 1845 to 1847. The conditions which produced this famine are complex. Briefly, however, Ireland underwent great social change during the eighteenth century. Agriculture developed rapidly in response to the demand from Britain for food. The increase in tillage required an increased workforce, and thus there was a period of relative prosperity for smallholders and laboring classes. Another significant development was that the Irish peasantry became increasingly reliant on the potato as their staple food from the beginning of the century. Since an entire family could support itself on a small area of land, a social revolution occurred. The average age at marriage dropped as it became possible for younger men to support a family by renting a small amount of land on which to grow potatoes (to eat) and cereals (to sell for rent money).

During the nineteenth century there was a consequent large increase in population. In 1687 it is estimated that the population was around 2.2 million. By 1725 it had exceeded 3 million, and by 1772 it was almost 3.6 million. In 1781 it was just over 4 million, and from then until 1820 the rate of increase was approximately 17 percent per decade. The population reached over 8 million in 1841, the highest it had ever been before that time (or has been since). The two major factors which were to change significantly this situation were (a) a decline in the value of agricultural produce and (b) the increasingly common destruction of the potato crop by Potato Blight.

During most of the period of this rapid population increase, the Irish agricultural economy was heavily dependent on export of cereals to England. When the Napoleonic wars ended in 1814, food prices dropped. This meant that small-holdings became increasingly less viable as the small areas planted in cereals were unable to produce enough return to pay the rent. This resulted in large-scale unemployment of the laboring classes, and evictions of many small-holders.

The final blow to these small-holders, however, was the increasing incidence of Potato Blight, a fungal disease which attacks potatoes. The crop partially failed many times between 1800 and 1845. However, in the four years between 1845 and 1848 the crop failed three times, causing what became known as the Great Famine. The result was the death of a million people by starvation or disease and a flood of emigration.

It is estimated that in 1847 alone, around 230,000 people left Ireland for North America and Australia and further thousands for Britain. Some 2 million left between 1845 and 1855, and the process of emigration continued for the remainder of the century and beyond. Between 1845 and 1925 approximately 4.75 million Irish people went to the United States, 70,000 to Canada, and 370,000 to Australia. From its peak of over 8 million in 1841, the population by 1926 had fallen to 4 million and is currently around 5 million.

For those Catholic Irish who remained in Ireland, rights to land, voting, etc., were restored. Toward the end of the nineteenth century the movement for self-government for Ireland, either as a separate parliament within the United Kingdom ("Home Rule") or as an independent state, grew. In 1916 a rebellion began which finally resulted in the establishment of an independent Irish state in 1921.

Until 1921 all of Ireland was within the "United Kingdom of Great Britain and Ireland." In that year twenty-six of the thirty-two counties became independent and later became the Republic of Ireland. Six counties, Antrim, Armagh, Down, Fermanagh, Derry (or Londonderry), and Tyrone, remain part of the United Kingdom. As the records of interest to researchers are generally pre-1921, most of the public records which are dealt with derive from the British administration of Ireland. There are many detailed histories of Ireland available. For the period from 1800 onward a useful general history is *Ireland Since the Famine* by F.S.L Lyons, 1971.

Emigration to the United States and Britain has continued at varying levels ever since the early eighteenth century. In some parts of the country, where the initial level of emigration was high, it became a tradition. Even when the economic situation in Ireland had improved, the attraction of America, in particular, remained. Indeed, in some parts of the country going to America meant reunion with as many family members and friends as were left behind. In his book *20 Years a-Growing*, Maurice O'Sullivan, a native of one such high emigration area, considers his options of going to Dublin or America to work. He imagines his sister's advice from America to "come out here where your own people are, for if you go to Dublin you will never see any of your kinsfolk again!"

Almost none of these events in Irish history affected all counties equally. The local effects in each county are discussed in the county history given at the beginning of each chapter.

Abbreviations Used in the Text and Tables

A and A	Ardfert and Aghadoe (Diocese)		MP	Member of Parliament (i.e., Westminster)
AC	Achonry (Diocese)		ms/s.	manuscript/s
AD	Ardagh (Diocese)		N and M	Newry and Morne (Diocese)
Add.	Additional		n.d.	not dated/no date
AM	Armagh		NLI	National Library of Ireland
b.	birth/born		no/s.	number/s
BL	British Library		N.S.	New Series
CA	Cashel (Diocese)		OS	Ossory (Diocese)
CF	Clonfert (Diocese)		p/p.	page/s
CG	Clogher (Diocese)		Parl.	Parliament/parliamentary
CK	Cork (Diocese)		Ph	phone
CI	Church of Ireland (Protestant or Episcopalian)		PHSA	Presbyterian Historical Society Archives
Co.	County		PRO	Public Record Office
CR	Connor (Diocese)		PRONI	Public Record Office of Northern Ireland
CY	Cloyne (Diocese)		Pub.	published/publisher
d.	death/died		QUB	Queens University, Belfast
DE	Derry (Diocese)		RA	Raphoe (Diocese)
DKPRI	Deputy Keeper of Public Records of Ireland (Report of . . .)		RC	Roman Catholic
DR	Dromore (Diocese)		RCB	Representative Church Body
DU	Dublin (Diocese)		RIA	Royal Irish Academy
DW	Down (Diocese)		RO	Ross (Diocese)
Ed.	Edited		SLC	Family History Library of the Church of Jesus Christ of Latter-day Saints, Salt Lake City, Utah
EL	Elphin (Diocese)			
EM	Emly (Diocese)		SPO	State Paper Office
FE	Ferns (Diocese)		TCD	Trinity College Dublin
Gen.	Genealogy/genealogical		TU	Tuam (Diocese)
GO	Genealogical Office		Vol/s.	Volume/s
Hist.	Historical		WA	Waterford (Diocese)
J.	Journal			
K and K	Killaloe and Kilfenora (Diocese			
KA	Killala (Diocese)			
KD	Kildare (Diocese)			
KF	Kilfenora (Diocese)			
KL	Killaloe (Diocese)			
KM	Kilmore (Diocese)			
KMC	Kilmacduagh (Diocese)			
LC	local custody (records are held by local church)			
LE	Leighlin (Diocese)			
LK	Limerick (Diocese)			
LS	Lismore (Diocese)			
m.	marriage/married			
ME	Meath (Diocese)			
misc.	miscellaneous			

Abbreviations of Periodicals

Anal. Hib.
    Analecta Hibernica

Derry Hist. Soc. J.
    Derry Historical Society Journal

Donegal Ann.
    Donegal Annual

Dublin Hist. Rec.
    Dublin Historical Record

Gen.
  The Genealogist

Hist. Mss. Comm. Rep.
  Historical Manuscripts Commission Report

Ir. Anc.
  Irish Ancestor

Ir. Gen.
  Irish Genealogist

J. Ass. Pres. Mem. Dead
  Journal of the Association for the Preservation of Memorials of the Dead

J. Cork Hist. & Arch. Soc.
  Cork Historical and Archaeological Society Journal

J. Galway Arch. & Hist. Soc.
  Journal of Galway Archaeological and Historical Society

J. Kildare Arch. & Hist. Soc.
  Journal of Kildare Archaeological and Historical Society

J. Louth Arch. & Hist. Soc. (see also *Louth Arch. J.*)
  Journal of Louth Archaeological and Historical Society

J. N. Munster Arch. & Hist. Soc
  Journal of North Munster Archaelogical and Historical Society

J. Waterford & S.E. Ire. Arch. Soc.
  Journal of the Waterford and South-East Ireland Archaeological Society

Kerry Arch. Mag.
  Kerry Archaeological Magazine

L. Gur Hist. Soc. J.
  Lough Gur Historical Society Journal

Louth Arch. J. (see also *J. Louth Arch. & Hist. Soc.*)
  Louth Archaeological Journal

N. Munster Antiq. J.
  North Munster Antiquarian Journal

Reportorium
  Reportorium Novum

R. Ir. Acad. Proc.
  Proceedings of the Royal Irish Acadamy

R.S.A.I.
  Journal of the Royal Society of Antiquarians of Ireland

Ulster Gen. & Hist. Guild Newsletter
  Ulster Genealogical and Historical Guild Newsletter

Ulster J. Arch.
  Ulster Journal of Archaeology

County Antrim

A Brief History

Antrim is on the northwestern coast of Ireland. The major towns are Carrickfergus, Ballymena, Lisburn, and the city of Belfast which is in both Antrim and Down. For practical purposes many Belfast records, particularly church records, are listed together in the appendix.

Under the old Gaelic system this area was part of the territory of the O'Neills and was called Dalriada. The other major Gaelic families were the McQuillans and O'Quinns. Some "Gallowglass" or mercenary families from Scotland settled in Antrim in the thirteenth and fourteenth centuries. These included the Mc-Donnells, Bissels (who became McKeowns), MacNeills, and McAllisters. Two Connaught families, the O'Haras and MacClearys, also migrated to Antrim at this period. The county was little affected by the Norman invasion and the ruling families of the county maintained their independence for several centuries.

In 1594 the major tribes of Ulster, led by Hugh O'Neill, rebelled against English rule. This rebellion lasted until 1603 when the Ulster tribes were finally defeated. Following the defeat and departure of O'Neill and the heads of the major clans, Antrim, like the rest of Ulster, was "planted" with settlers from Britain. Antrim was one of the first counties planted, in advance of the main Ulster plantation which began in 1609. In about 1605 the Lord Deputy, Arthur Chichester, acquired the castle and lands of Belfast. Subsequently, he ruthlessly exterminated the inhabitants of these estates and planted them with English settlers. These came mainly from Devon, Lancashire, and Cheshire and included families named Bradshaw, Bradford, Watson, Taylor, Walker, Jackson, Wilson, Johnson, and Young.

Also in the early 1600s English and Scottish adventurers, such as Clotworthy and Upton, were given confiscated lands in Antrim on the understanding that they would bring over settlers to their new estates. The now common occurrence of names such as Boyd, Fraser, Lindsay, Johnson, Morrison, Patterson, and Maxwell is due to the Scottish settlers brought to the county by these adventurers.

The objectives of plantation, the clearance of the native population and their replacement by British subjects, were most successfully achieved in this county. Many of the native people were removed from the county altogether. As the native Irish population was predominantly Catholic, the Scottish usually Presbyterian, and the English generally Protestant, the proportions of these religions among the population can, in very general terms, be used to estimate the origins of the inhabitants of the county. When religious affiliation was first determined in the census of 1861, the respective proportions of Catholic, Presbyterian, and Protestant in Antrim were 28, 20, and 48 percent.

Antrim, like the other northeastern counties, became a center of the linen industry. The industry was particularly developed by the arrival in the county of many French Huguenot weavers from 1685 onwards. These Huguenots settled in particular in Lisburn and Belfast, and their introduction of French looms and other innovations began a period of prosperity for the industry. By 1700 Belfast had a population of 2,000.

As in the other northern counties, many northern Presbyterians or so-called Scots-Irish left Antrim during the eighteenth and early nineteenth centuries because of the repression of Presbyterians under the Penal Laws (see p. xlviii) which were primarily intended to repress Catholicism. In the eighteenth century Belfast was the center of the Society of the United Irishmen, which was a movement of Catholics and Presbyterians against this repression.

Belfast City is arguably the only city in Ireland to have felt the full effects of the industrial revolution. The city developed rapidly in the nineteenth century largely based on the linen industry and on heavy industry such as shipbuilding. Its rapid growth resulted in further immigration of people from Scotland, northern England, and rural Ireland. By the end of the nineteenth century its population had grown to 300,000.

The county is one of the few whose population has increased since the Great Famine. This is largely due to the growth of Belfast City and surrounding towns. Apart from Dublin, the population of County Antrim is the most urbanized in Ireland. Because of this, commercial directories are particularly valuable sources of information. Some of the 1857 Census returns have also survived. The northern, and non-urbanized, parts of the county are largely agricultural and also have important fishing ports.

Census and Census Substitutes

1635-1796
"The Roll of Freemen – Belfast." In *The Townbook of the Corporation of Belfast 1613-1816.* pp.215-17.

1642
Muster Roll. PRONI T563; SLC film 897012.

1643
"Tax List for Belfast." In *The Townbook of the Corporation of Belfast 1613-1816.* pp.25-27.

1659
"Census" of Ireland. Edited by S. Pender. Dublin: Stationery Office, 1939.

1663-69
Subsidy Roll. PRONI T307.

1666
Hearth Money Roll. PRO film 2745; NLI ms. 9584.

1669
Hearth Money Roll. PRONI T307; NLI ms. 9584 (index on 9585).

"Extracts from Hearth Money Roll for Parishes of Ramoan, Culfreightrin & Rathlin." *The Glynns* 1 (1973): 10-15.

"Extracts from Glenarm Barony." *The Glynns* 5 (1977): 15-16.

1719
"Map of Glenarm" (including names and holdings of the Earl of Antrim's Tenants in the Town and Adjoining Lands). *The Glynns* 9 (1981): 52-61.

1720
List of Landed Gentry in Down and Antrim. RIA ms. 24 K 19.

1734
Map Showing Residents of Ballymoney. SLC film 990232.

1740
Protestant Householders in Parishes of Aghoghill, Armoy, Ballintoy, Ballymena, Ballymoney, Bellewillen, Billy, Clogh,

Drumaul, Dunean, Dunkegan, Dunluce, Finvoy, Kilraghts, Loghall, Manybrooke, Rasharkin, Rathlin, and Ramoan. GO 539; SLC film 100249; RCB Library.

1744
"List of Voters in Belfast." In *The Townbook of the Corporation of Belfast, 1613-1816*. pp. 246-300.

1766
Parish of Aghoghill. RCB Library.

Parishes of Ballentoy and Ballymoney. GO 436; SLC film 258517.

All above parishes on NLI ms. 4173.

1796
See Co. Mayo 1796 (List of Catholics . . .)

1798
List of Persons who Suffered Losses During '98 Rebellion. NLI JLB 94107 (approximately 140 names, addresses, and occupations).

1813
Census of Ballyeaston Congregation (Presbyterian) covering Ballycor, Donagore, Glenwhirry, Grange of Doagh, Kilbride, and Rashee. SLC film 100173.

1824-34
Tithe Applotment Survey (see p. xxvii).

1832-36
"List of Excise License Holders and Applicants in Belfast, Lisburn, and Carrickfergus" (names, occupations, and address). *Parl. Papers* 1837/38, 13 (2): Appendix 10, 13.

1834
Registered Freeholders, Leaseholders, and Householders of Carrickfergus. SLC film 990408.

1837
"Lists of Freemen (since 1831) of Carrickfergus." *Parl. Papers* 1837, 2 (1): Appendix B1; 1837/38, 13 (2): Appendix 3.

"List of Applicants for the Vote in Borough of Belfast." *Parl. Papers* 1837, 2 (2): Appendix 7, 235-45 (gives 772 names, residences, occupations).

"Occupants of Lisburn, Arranged by Street, Giving Property Values." *Parl. Papers* 1837, 2 (1): Appendix G, 211-15.

1838
"Lists of Marksmen (illiterate voters) in Belfast" (over 250 names, occupations, and residences). *Parl. Papers* 1837, 2 (1): Appendix A3; 1837/38, 13 (2): Appendix 4.

1841
Extracts from the Government Census Relating to the Families Johnston, McShane, and Thompson. SLC film 824260.

1851
Government Census Extracts: Parishes of Aghagallon, (townlands from Montiaghs to Tiscallen only), Aghalee, Aghohill (townland of Craigs only), Ballinderry, Ballymoney (townland of Garryduff only), Carncastle, Clough, Craigs, Dunaghy, Grange of Killyglen, Killead (townlands from Ardmore to Carnagliss only), Kilwaughter, Larne, Rasharkin (townlands from Killydonnelly to Tehorny only), Tickmacrevan. PRO; SLC films 597143-53, 597108-13.

1854
List of Applications to be Leaseholders and Householders of Belfast. SLC film 993156.

1856/57
Register of Persons Entitled to Vote (arranged alphabetically by barony; gives over 9,000 names, addresses, nature of qualification to vote, location of freehold, etc.). NLI ILB 324.

1861-62
Griffith's Valuation (see p. xxvii).

1901
Census. PRO.

1911
Census. PRO.

Church Records

Church of Ireland
(For Belfast, see appendix)
(Shows starting date of record)

Parish: **Aghalee**
Existing Records: b. 1782; m. 1782; d. 1782
Status: LC

Parish: **Ahogill**
Existing Records: b. 1811; m. 1811; d. 1811
Status: LC

Parish: **Ardclinis**
Status: Lost

Parish: **Ballinderry**
Existing Records: b. 1805; m. 1840; d. 1805
Status: LC

Parish: **Ballintoy**
Status: Lost

Parish: **Ballyclug**
Existing Records: b. 1841
Status: LC

Parish: **Ballyeaston**
Status: Lost

Parish: **Ballymena** (Kirkinriola)
Existing Records: b. 1815; m. 1807; d. 1780
Status: LC

Parish: **Ballymoney**
Existing Records: b. 1807
Status: LC

Parish: **Ballymire**
Existing Records: b. 1812; m. 1825; d. 1840
Missing dates: m. 1830-45; d. 1841-51
Status: LC

Parish: **Ballyrashane**
Status: Lost

Parish: **Ballyscullion** (Grange)
Status: Lost

Parish: **Ballysillan**
Existing Records: b. 1826; m. 1825; d. 1827
Status: LC

Parish: **Billy**
Status: Lost

Parish: **Carnmoney**
Existing Records: b. 1789; m. 1789; d. 1845
Status: LC

Parish: **Carrickfergus**
Existing Records: b. 1740; m. 1740; d. 1837
Status: LC

Parish: **Christchurch**
Existing Records: b. 1837; m. 1837; d. 1837
Status: LC

Parish: **Christchurch** (Belfast)
Status: LC

Parish: **Christchurch** (Lisburn)
Existing Records: b. 1849
Status: LC

Parish: **Craigs**
Existing Records: b. 1839; m. 1841; d. 1841
Status: LC

Parish: **Culfeightrin**
Status: Lost

Parish: **Cushendun**
Status: Lost

Parish: **Derryaghey** (Lisburn)
Existing Records: b. 1696; m. 1696; d. 1696
Missing Dates: b. 1739-70; m. 1739-1826; d. 1739-1826
Status: LC

Parish: **Derrykeighan**
Status: Lost

Parish: **Donegore**
Status: Lost

Parish: **Drummaul** (Randalstown)
Existing Records: b. 1823; m. 1823; d. 1823
Status: LC

Parish: **Drumtullagh**
Status: Lost

Parish: **Dunaghy**
Status: Lost

Parish: **Duneane**
Status: Lost

Parish: **Dunluce** (Bushmills)
Existing Records: b. 1809; m. 1826; d. 1826
Status: LC

Parish: **Dunseverick**
Existing Records: b. 1832; m. 1833; d. 1833
Status: LC

Parish: **Falls, Lower** (or **St. Luke Belfast**)
Status: Lost

Parish: **Falls, Upper Belfast**
Existing Records: b. 1855
Status: LC

Parish: **Finvoy**
Existing Records: b. 1811; m. 1812; d. 1811
Status: LC

Parish: **Gartree**
Status: Lost

Parish: **Glenavy**
Existing Records: b. 1707; m. 1813; d. 1707
Status: LC

Parish: **Glynn**
Existing Records: b. 1838; m. 1842; d. 1838
Status: LC

Parish: **Inver** and **Larne**
Existing Records: b. 1806; m. 1817; d. 1826
Status: LC

Parish: **Islandmagee**
Status: Lost

Parish: **Jordanstown**
Status: Lost

Parish: **Kilbride** and **Donegore**
Status: Lost

Parish: **Kilbride**
Status: Lost

Parish: **Kildolla**
Status: Lost

Parish: **Killagan**
Status: Lost

Parish: **Killead**
Status: Lost

Parish: **Killwaughter** and **Carncastle**
Status: Lost

Parish: **Lambeg**
Existing Records: b. 1810; m. 1810; d. 1810
Status: LC

Parish: **Layde**
Existing Records: b. 1826; m. 1826; d. 1826
Status: LC

Parish: **Lisburn** or **Blaris**
Existing Records: b. 1639; m. 1661; d. 1661
Missing dates: b. 1647-60
Status: LC

Parish: **Magdalen Asylum** (Belfast)
Existing Records: b. 1855
Status: LC

Parish: **Magheragall**
Existing Records: b. 1771; m. 1772; d. 1772
Status: LC

Parish: **Mariner's Chapel** (Belfast)
Existing Records: b. 1868
Status: LC

Parish: **Muckamore**
Existing Records: b. 1847; d. 1847
Status: LC

Parish: **Newtown Crommelin**
Status: Lost

Parish: **Portglenone**
Status: Lost

Parish: **Raloo**
Status: Lost

Parish: **Ramoan**
Status: Lost

Parish: **Rasharkin**
Status: Lost

Parish: **Rathlin**
Status: Lost

Parish: **St. Andrews** (Belfast)
Status: Lost

Parish: **St. Anne's** (Belfast)
Existing Records: b. 1745; m. 1745; d. 1745
Status: LC

Parish: **St. George** (Belfast)
Existing Records: b. 1819; m. 1824
Status: LC

Parish: **St. John** (Belfast)
Existing Records: b. 1853
Status: LC

Parish: **St. John Malone** (Belfast)
Existing Records: b. 1839; m. 1842
Status: LC

Parish: **St. Mark** (Belfast)
Existing Records: b. 1856
Status: LC

Parish: **St. Mary** (Belfast)
Existing Records: b. 1867; d. 1860
Status: LC

Parish: **St. Mathew** (Belfast)
Status: Lost

Parish: **St. Mathew** (Lisburn)
Status: Lost

Parish: **St. Paul** (Belfast)
Status: Lost

Parish: **St. Philip Drew Memorial** (Belfast)
Existing Records: no records pre-1872
Status: LC

Parish: **Skerry**
Existing Records: b. 1805; m. 1805; d. 1805
Status: LC

Parish: **Stoneyford** (Derryagney)
Existing Records: b. 1845
Status: LC

Parish: **Templecorran**
Existing Records: b. 1848; d. 1856
Status: LC

Parish: **Templepatrick**
Existing Records: b. 1827; m. 1827; d. 1827
Status: LC

Parish: **Tickmacrevan** (Glenarm)
Existing Records: b. 1788; m. 1788; d. 1846
Status: LC

Parish: **Trinity** (Belfast)
Existing Records: b. 1844
Status: LC

Parish: **Whitehouse**
Existing Records: b. 1840
Status: LC

Presbyterian
(For Belfast, see also appendix)

Parish: **Antrim**
Starting Date: 1674

Parish: **Armoy**
Starting Date: 1842

Parish: **Ballycarney**
Starting Date: 1832

Parish: **Ballycastle**
Starting Date: 1829

Parish: **Ballyeaston** (Ballyclare)
Starting Date: 1821

Parish: **Ballylinney** (Ballyclare)
Starting Date: 1837

Parish: **Ballymena**
Starting Date: 1825

Parish: **Ballymoney**
Starting Date: 1817

Parish: **Ballynure**
Starting Date: 1819

Parish: **Ballywillan** (Portrush)
Starting Date: 1816

Parish: **Ballymacarrett** (Belfast)
Starting Date: 1837

Parish: **Ballysillan**
Starting Date: 1839

Parish: **Belfast** (Fisherwick Place)
Starting Date: 1810

Parish: **Belfast** (Rosemary St.)
Starting Date: 1722

Parish: **Broadmills** (Lisburn)
Starting Date: 1824

Parish: **Broughshane**
Starting Date: 1830

Parish: **Buckal**
Starting Date: 1841

Parish: **Carnmoney**
Starting Date: 1798

Parish: **Carrickfergus**
Starting Date: 1823

Parish: **Castlereagh**
Starting Date: 1807

Parish: **Cliftonville**
Starting Date: 1825

Parish: **Cloughwater**
Starting Date: 1852

Parish: **Connor** (Ballymena)
Starting Date: 1819

Parish: **Crumlin**
Starting Date: 1839

Parish: **Cullybackey**
Starting Date: 1812

Parish: **Dongora** (Templepatrick)
Starting Date: 1806

Parish: **Drumbo** (Lisburn)
Starting Date: 1764

Parish: **Dundonald** (Belfast)
Starting Date: 1678

Parish: **Dundron** (Belfast)
Starting Date: 1829

Parish: **Finvoy** (Ballymoney)
Starting Date: 1843

Parish: **Gilnahurk** (Belfast)
Starting Date: 1797

Parish: **Glenarm**
Starting Date: 1850

Parish: **Glenwherry** (Ballymena)
Starting Date: 1845

Parish: **Grange** (Toomebridge)
Starting Date: 1824

Parish: **Kilruaght** (Ballymoney)
Starting Date: 1836

Parish: **Larne**
Starting Date: 1824

Parish: **Loughmourne**
Starting Date: 1848

Parish: **Lylehill** (Templepatrick)
Starting Date: 1832

Parish: **Masside**
Starting Date: 1843

Parish: **Portrush**
Starting Date: 1843

Parish: **Raloo** (Larne)
Starting Date: 1840

Parish: **Randalstown**
Starting Date: 1837

Parish: **Rasharkin**
Starting Date: 1834

Parish: **Templepatrick**
Starting Date: 1831

Parish: **Tobberleigh**
Starting Date: 1831

Roman Catholic

Civil Parish: **Aghagallon**
Map Grid: 80
RC Parish: Aghagallon and Ballinderry
Diocese: CR
Earliest Record: b. 4.1828; m. 5.1828; d. 3.1828
Missing Dates: 7.1848-5.1872
Parish Address: Rev. Joseph Moloney, PP, 5 Aghalee Road, Aghagallon, Craigavon, Co. Armagh

Civil Parish: **Aghalee**
Map Grid: 81
RC Parish: see Aghagallon
Diocese: DR

Civil Parish: **Ahoghill**
Map Grid: 29 and 30
RC Parish: Ahoghill
Diocese: CR
Earliest Record: b. 1833; m. 1833; d. 1833
Missing Dates: d. few, ends 1863

Parish Address: Rev. Gerard McConville, PP, Parochial House, Portglenone Road, Ahoghill, Belfast

Civil Parish: **Antrim**
Map Grid: 48
RC Parish: Antrim
Diocese: CR
Earliest Record: b. 1.1874
Parish Address: Rev. Eamon McEnaney, PP, Parochial House, Antrim, BT41 4HP

Civil Parish: **Ardclinis**
Map Grid: 18
RC Parish: part Layde; part Carnlough, see Tickmacrevan
Diocese: CR

Civil Parish: **Armoy**
Map Grid: 6
RC Parish: Armoy
Diocese: CR
Earliest Record: b. 4.1848; m. 5.1848
Missing Dates: 3.1842-10.1873; 1.1872-11.1873
Parish Address: Rev. Malachy Hurl, PP, Parochial House, Armoy, Ballymoney, Co. Antrim

Civil Parish: **Ballinderry**
Map Grid: 79
RC Parish: see Aghagallon
Diocese: CR

Civil Parish: **Ballintoy**
Map Grid: 2
RC Parish: Ballintoy
Diocese: CR
Earliest Record: b. 4.1872; m. 5.1872
Parish Address: Rev. Patrick McCrea, PP, 53 Ballinlea Road, Ballycastle, Co. Antrim

Civil Parish: **Ballyclug**
Map Grid: 33
RC Parish: Ballymena, see Kirkinriola
Diocese: CR

Civil Parish: **Ballycor**
Map Grid: 47
RC Parish: Ballyclare, see Belfast
Diocese: CR

Civil Parish: **Ballylinny**
Map Grid: 59 and 61
RC Parish: part Ballyclare, see Belfast; part
    Carrickfergus
Diocese: CR

Civil Parish: **Ballymartin**
Map Grid: 70
RC Parish: part Ballyclare, see Belfast; part
    Antrim
Diocese: CR

Civil Parish: **Ballymoney** (see also Co. Derry)
Map Grid: 12
RC Parish: Ballymoney and Derrykeighan
Diocese: CR
Earliest Record: b. 3.1853; m. 4.1853
Parish Address: Rev. Christopher Dallat, PP, 81
    Castle St., Ballymoney, Co. Antrim

Civil Parish: **Ballynure**
Map Grid: 57
RC Parish: part Larne; part Carrickfergus
Diocese: CR

Civil Parish: **Ballyrashane**
Map Grid: 10
RC Parish: Portrush, see Ballywillin
Diocese: CR

Civil Parish: **Ballyscullion** (see Co. Derry)
Map Grid: 40
RC Parish: see Duneane
Diocese: DE

Civil Parish: **Ballywillin**
Map Grid: 7
RC Parish: Portrush and Bushmills
Diocese: CR
Earliest Record: b. 7.1844; m. 5.1848
Parish Address: Rev. Felix McLaughlin, PP,
    Parochial House, Portrush, Co. Antrim

Civil Parish: **Belfast (1)**
RC Parish: Ballyclare
Diocese: CR
Earliest Record: b. 71869; m. 2.1870
Parish Address: Rev. Michael Coppinger, PP,
    Doagh Road, Ballyclare, Co. Antrim

Civil Parish: **Belfast (2)**
RC Parish: Whitehouse, see Templepatrick
Diocese: CR

Civil Parish: **Billy**
Map Grid: 9
RC Parish: see Ballintoy
Diocese: CR

Civil Parish: **Blaris** (see also Co. Down)
Map Grid: 84
RC Parish: Lisburn
Diocese: CR
Earliest Record: not on microfilm
Parish Address: Rev. Joseph Cunningham, PP,
    St. Patrick's Presbytery, 29 Chapel Hill, Lis-
    burn, Co. Antrim

Civil Parish: **Camlin**
Map Grid: 75
RC Parish: see Glenavy
Diocese: CR

Civil Parish: **Carncastle**
Map Grid: 36
RC Parish: part Glenarm, see Tickmacrevan;
    part Larne
Diocese: CR

Civil Parish: **Carnmoney**
Map Grid: 65
RC Parish: part Greencastle; part Whitehouse,
    see Belfast
Diocese: CR

Civil Parish: **Carrickfergus** (St. Nicholas)
Map Grid: 66
RC Parish: Carrickfergus, see Larne for pre-
    1828 Records
Diocese: CR
Earliest Record: b. 12.1828; m. 9.1828
Missing Dates: b. 2.1841-3.1852; m. 10.1840-
    4.1852
Parish Address: Rev. Brendan McGarry, PP,
    Parochial House, Carrickfergus, Co. Antrim

Civil Parish: **Connor**
Map Grid: 35
RC Parish: part Braid or Glenravel, see Skerry;
    part Randalstown, see Drummaul

Diocese: CR
Earliest Record: b. 9.1878; m. 11.1878
Parish Address: Rev. John Moley, Adm., 189 Carnlough Road, Broughshane, Co. Antrim

Civil Parish: **Craigs**
Map Grid: 27
RC Parish: see Rasharkin
Diocese: CR

Civil Parish: **Cranfield**
Map Grid: 45
RC Parish: see Duneane
Diocese: CR

Civil Parish: **Culfeightrin**
Map Grid: 4
RC Parish: Culfreightrin
Diocese: CR
Earliest Record: b. 7.1825; m. 1.1839
Missing Dates: b. 5.1867-1.1868; m. 6.1844-8.1845
Parish Address: Rev. Matthew Dillon, PP, 87 Cushendall Road, Barnish, Ballycastle, Co. Antrim

Civil Parish: **Derryaghy**
Map Grid: 78
RC Parish: Hannastown, Rock, and Derryaghy
Diocese: CR
Earliest Record: b. 10.1855; m. 10.1855
Parish Address: Rev. Thomas Bartley, PP, Kingsway, Finaghy, Belfast BT10 ONE

Civil Parish: **Derrykeighan**
Map Grid: 11
RC Parish: see Ballymoney
Diocese: CR

Civil Parish: **Donegore**
Map Grid: 49
RC Parish: see Antrim
Diocese: CR

Civil Parish: **Drumbeg**
Map Grid: 73A
RC Parish: see Derryaghy
Diocese: DW

Civil Parish: **Drummaul**
Map Grid: 42
RC Parish: Randalstown
Diocese: CR
Earliest Record: b. 10.1825; m. 10.1825
Missing Dates: b. 9.1854-8.1855, 1.1868-9.1871; m. 5.1854-5.1858, 11.1867-?.1871
Parish Address: Rev. Patrick McGarry, PP, Parochial House, Station Road, Randalstown, Co. Antrim

Civil Parish: **Dunaghy**
Map Grid: 25
RC Parish: Glenravel, see Skerry
Diocese: CR

Civil Parish: **Duneane**
Map Grid: 44
RC Parish: Duneane (Toomebridge)
Diocese: CR
Earliest Record: b. 5.1834; m. 5.1835
Missing Dates: m. 2.1847-10.1847
Parish Address: Rev. John Murray, PP, Moneyglass, Toomebridge, Co. Antrim

Civil Parish: **Dunluce**
Map Grid: 8
RC Parish: part Portrush, see Ballywillin
Diocese: CR

Civil Parish: **Finvoy**
Map Grid: 20
RC Parish: Dunloy and Cloughmills
Diocese: CR
Earliest Record: b. 6.1860; m. 6.1877; d. 4.1877
Missing Dates: b. 6.1860, 12.1876-4.1877; m. 12.1876; d. 4.1877
Parish Address: Rev. Hugo Lynch, PP, Parochial House, Dunloy, Ballymena, Co. Antrim

Civil Parish: **Glenavy**
Map Grid: 77
RC Parish: Glenavy and Killead
Diocese: CR
Earliest Record: b. 5.1849; m. 3.1848
Parish Address: Rev. John O'Sullivan, PP, Parochial House, Glenavy, Crumlin, Co. Antrim

Civil Parish: **Glenwhirry**
Map Grid: 34
RC Parish: Braid, see Skerry
Diocese: CR

Civil Parish: **Glynn**
Map Grid: 56
RC Parish: see Larne
Diocese: CR

Civil Parish: **Grange of Ballyscullion**
Map Grid: 41
RC Parish: see Duneane
Diocese: CR

Civil Parish: **Grange of Doagh**
Map Grid: 51
RC Parish: Ballyclare, see Belfast
Diocese: CR

Civil Parish: **Grange of Drumtullagh**
Map Grid: 5
RC Parish: see Ballintoy
Diocese: CR

Civil Parish: **Grange of Dundermot**
Map Grid: 24
RC Parish: Dunloy and Cloughmills, see Finvoy
Diocese: CR

Civil Parish: **Grange of Inispollen**
Map Grid: 16
RC Parish: Craiga and Cushleak (Cushendon),
    see also Culfeightrin
Diocese: CR
Earliest Record: b. 6.1862; m. 6.1862
Parish Address: Rev. Fred MacSorley, PP,
    Cushendun, Co. Antrim

Civil Parish: **Grange of Killyglen**
Map Grid: 38
RC Parish: see Larne
Diocese: CR

Civil Parish: **Grange of Layd**
Map Grid: 15
RC Parish: Cushendun, see Grange of Innispol-
    len
Diocese: CR

Civil Parish: **Grange of Muckamore**
Map Grid: 67
RC Parish: see Antrim
Diocese: CR

Civil Parish: **Grange of Nilteen**
Map Grid: 52
RC Parish: see Antrim
Diocese: CR

Civil Parish: **Grange of Shilvodan**
Map Grid: 43
RC Parish: Braid, see Skerry
Diocese: CR

Civil Parish: **Inver**
Map Grid: 54
RC Parish: see Larne
Diocese: CR

Civil Parish: **Island Magee**
Map Grid: 53
RC Parish: see Larne
Diocese: CR

Civil Parish: **Kilbride**
Map Grid: 50
RC Parish: see Antrim
Diocese: CR

Civil Parish: **Killagan**
Map Grid: 21
RC Parish: part Dunloy, see Finvoy; part Glen-
    ravel, see Skerry
Diocese: CR

Civil Parish: **Killead**
Map Grid: 68 and 69
RC Parish: see Glenavy
Diocese: CR

Civil Parish: **Kilraghts**
Map Grid: 13
RC Parish: see Ballymoney
Diocese: CR

Civil Parish: **Kilroot**
Map Grid: 40
RC Parish: see Duneane
Diocese: CR

Civil Parish: **Kilwaughter**
Map Grid: 37
RC Parish: see Larne
Diocese: CR

Civil Parish: **Kirkinriola**
Map Grid: 28 and 30
RC Parish: Ballymena (Kirkinriola); part Ahogill
Diocese: CR
Earliest Record: b. 1.1848; m. 1.1840
Missing Dates: m. 7.1842-1.1847
Parish Address: Rev. William B. Tumelty, PP, 2 Broughshane Road, Ballymena, Co. Antrim

Civil Parish: **Lambeg**
Map Grid: 73
RC Parish: see Derryaghy
Diocese: CR

Civil Parish: **Larne**
Map Grid: 39
RC Parish: Larne, see Carrickfergus for post-1828
Diocese: CR
Earliest Record: b. 8.1821; m. 9.1821
Parish Address: Rev. Patrick McVeigh, PP, Parochial House, Larne, Co. Antrim

Civil Parish: **Layd**
Map Grid: 17
RC Parish: Cushendall (Layde and Ardclinis); part Cushedun, see Grange of Innispollen
Diocese: CR
Earliest Record: b. 4.1838; m. 7.1837
Missing Dates: b. 3.1844-1.1858; m. 5.1844-3.1860
Parish Address: Rev. F. Park, Parochial House, Cushendall, Ballymena, Co. Antrim

Civil Parish: **Loughguile**
Map Grid: 14
RC Parish: Loughguile
Diocese: CR
Earliest Record: b. 5.1845; m. 5.1845
Parish Address: Rev. Kevin Donnelly, PP, Parochial House, Loughguile, Ballymena, Co. Antrim

Civil Parish: **Magheragall**
Map Grid: 82
RC Parish: see Derryaghy
Diocese: CR

Civil Parish: **Magheramesk**
Map Grid: 83
RC Parish: see Aghagallon
Diocese: CR

Civil Parish: **Newton Crommelin**
Map Grid: 22
RC Parish: see Rasharkin
Diocese: CR

Civil Parish: **Portglenone**
Map Grid: 26
RC Parish: Portglenone (Ahogill before 1864)
Diocese: CR
Earliest Record: b. 1.1864; m. 2.1864
Parish Address: Rev. J. M. Sloane, PP, St. Mary's Presbytery, Portglenone, Co. Antrim

Civil Parish: **Racavan**
Map Grid: 32
RC Parish: Braid, see Skerry
Diocese: CR

Civil Parish: **Raloo**
Map Grid: 55
RC Parish: see Larne
Diocese: CR

Civil Parish: **Ramoan**
Map Grid: 3
RC Parish: Ramoan (Ballycastle)
Diocese: CR
Earliest Record: b. 10.1838; m.10.1838
Parish Address: Rev. Patrick J. O'Hare, PP, Parochial House, Ballycastle, Co. Antrim

Civil Parish: **Rasharkin**
Map Grid: 23
RC Parish: Rasharkin
Diocese: CR
Earliest Record: b. 8.1848; m. 7.1848
Parish Address: Rev. Vincent McKinely, PP, Parochial House, Rasharkin, Ballymena, Co. Antrim

Civil Parish: **Rashee**
Map Grid: 46
RC Parish: Ballyclare, see Belfast
Diocese: CR

Civil Parish: **Rathlin**
Map Grid: 1
RC Parish: see Ramoan
Diocese: CR

Civil Parish: **Shankill**
Map Grid: 72
RC Parish: Greencastle, see Templepatrick
Diocese: CR

Civil Parish: **Skerry**
Map Grid: 31
RC Parish: Braid or Glenravel
Diocese: CR
Earliest Record: b. 7.1825; m. 6.1825
Missing Dates: b. 9.1856-2.1864; m. 9.1832-10.1878
Parish Address: Rev. Francis Teggart, PP, Martinstown, Ballymena, Co. Antrim

Civil Parish: **Templecorran**
Map Grid: 58
RC Parish: see Larne
Diocese: CR

Civil Parish: **Templepatrick**
Map Grid: 56, 62, 63, 64, and 71
RC Parish: part Greencastle (Whitehouse); part Ballyclare
Diocese: CR
Earliest Record: b. 3.1854; m. 4.1854
Parish Address: Greencastle: Rev. Cyril Reilly, PP, 824 Shore Road, Newtownabbey, Co. Antrim

Civil Parish: **Tickmacrevan (1)**
Map Grid: 19
RC Parish: part Carnlough; part Glenarm (see below)
Diocese: CR
Earliest Record: b. 12.1825
Missing Dates: b. 3.1854-6.1857, 12.1862-6.1865
Parish Address: Rev. John Laverty, PP, 51 Bay Road, Carnlough, Ballymena, Co. Antrim

Civil Parish: **Tickmacrevan (2)**
Map Grid: 19
RC Parish: Glenarm (Tickmacrevan)
Diocese: CR
Earliest Record: 5.1859
Parish Address: Rev. William McKeever, PP, Parochial House, Glenarm, Co. Antrim

Civil Parish: **Tullyrusk**
Map Grid: 76
RC Parish: see Glenavy
Diocese: CR

Commercial and Social Directories

1819
Thomas Bradshaw's *General Directory of Newry . . . etc.,* gives alphabetical lists of traders in Belfast and Lisburn.

1820
Belfast Almanac contains lists of streets and thoroughfares and an alphabetic list of traders and their addresses.

Joseph Smyth's *Directory of Belfast and its Vicinity* covers parts of Antrim.

1824
J. Pigot's *City of Dublin & Hibernian Provincial Directory* includes traders, nobility, gentry, and clergy lists of Antrim, Ballycastle, Ballymena, Ballymoney, Belfast, Carrickfergus, Larne, Lisburn, Portglenone, and Randalstown.

1835
William T. Matier's *Belfast Directory* contains lists of traders, merchants, and gentry alphabetically arranged and also a list of prominent people in the surrounding areas.

1839
Matthew Martin's *Belfast Directory* contains alphabetical list of gentry, merchants, and traders; a list of persons classified by professions and trades; residents of each house on the principal streets; and a list of noblemen and gentry residing in the county.

1841

A further edition of the above *Belfast Directory* covers Antrim, Ballymena, Belfast, Carrickfergus, Crumlin, and Lisburn.

1842

Third edition of the *Belfast Directory* covers Antrim, Ballymena, Belfast, Carrickfergus, Crumlin, Larne, and Lisburn.

1850

James Alexander Henderson's *Belfast Directory* contains an alphabetical list of nobility and gentry in and about Belfast; a list of the principal houses on the principal streets; an alphabetical list of gentry, merchants, and traders; a list of persons classified by trades; and covers Belfast and the suburbs of Ballymacarrett, Holywood, Whiteabbey, and Whitehouse.

1852

Henderson's *Belfast and Province of Ulster Directory* has lists of inhabitants, traders, etc., in and around the towns of Antrim, Ballycastle, Ballymoney, Carrickfergus, Larne, Lisburn, and Randalstown.

1854

Further edition of above covering Antrim, Ballyclare, Ballycastle, Ballymena, Ballymoney, Bushmills, Carrickfergus, Crumlin, Dromara, Glenarm, Larne, Lisburn, and Randalstown. Further editions in 1856, 1858, 1861, 1863, 1868, and 1870.

1856

Slater's *Royal National Commercial Directory of Ireland* lists nobility, gentry, clergy, traders, etc., in Antrim, Ballycastle, Ballyclare, Ballymena, Ballymoney, Belfast, Carrickfergus, Crumlin and Glenavy, Cushendall, Glenarm, Larne, Lisburn, Portglenone, and Randalstown.

1860

Hugh Adair's *Belfast Directory* lists the residents of main Belfast streets and of the suburbs of Ardoyne, Ligoniel, Ballynafeigh, Ballymacarrett, Dundonald, the Knock, Newtownbreda, Sydenham, Whiteabbey, and Whitehouse.

1865

R. Wynne's *Business Directory of Belfast* covers Antrim, Ballymena, Ballymoney, Carrickfergus, Larne, Lisburn, and Portrush.

1870

Slater's *Directory of Ireland* contains trade, nobility, and clergy lists for Antrim, Ballycastle, Ballyclare, Ballymena, Ballymoney, Belfast, Carrickfergus, Crumlin and Glenavy, Cushendall, Glenarm, Larne, Lisburn, Portglenone, Portrush, Randalstown, and Whiteabbey.

1877

Revised edition of the *Belfast & Province of Ulster Directory* covers Antrim, Ballyclare, Ballycastle, Ballymena, Ballymoney, Bushmills, Carnlough, Carrickfergus, Crumlin, Dromara, Glenarm, Larne, Lisburn, and Randalstown. Further editions in 1880, 1884, 1887, 1890, 1894, and 1900.

1881

Slater's *Royal National Commercial Directory of Ireland* contains lists of traders, clergy, nobility, and farmers in adjoining parishes of the towns of Antrim, Ballycastle, Ballyclare, Ballymena, Ballymoney, Belfast, Carrickfergus, Glenarm, Larne, Lisburn, Portrush, Randalstown, and Whiteabbey.

1887

The *Derry Almanac* covers Portrush.

1888

Bassett's *Book of Antrim* (does not cover Belfast).

1894

Slater's *Royal National Directory of Ireland* lists traders, police, teachers, farmers, and private residents in each of the towns, villages, and parishes of the county.

Family History

"The Agnews in Co. Antrim." *Ulster J. Arch.* 7, 2nd ser. (1901): 166-71.

Bigger, F. *The Magees of Belfast and Dublin.* Belfast, 1916.

"Caters of Irish Quarter, Carrickfergus." *Ir. Anc.* 10 (1) (1978): 31-33.

"Chiefs of the Antrim MacDonnells Prior to Sorley Boy." *Ulster J. Arch.* 7, 1st ser. (1859): 247-59.

"The Clan of the MacQuillins of Antrim." *Ulster J. Arch.* 8, 1st ser. 8 (1860): 251-68.

Copies of Census Returns for the Following Families and Years: McNeil, 1821–PRO film 5446(4); Hamilton, 1821, 31, 41, 51–PRO film 5246 (9, 12); Moat, 1821, 31, 41, 51–PRO film 5246(6), 5247(1), 5248(14, 35, 37), 5249 (5); Melance, 1831–PRO film 5247(3); Martin, 1841–PRO film 5248(13); Jamison, 1851–PRO film 5249/32.

"Gleanings in Family History from the Antrim Coast, The MacNaghtens and MacNeills." *Ulster J. Arch.* 8, 1st ser. (1860): 127-44.

"Gleanings in Family History from the Antrim Coast, The McAuleys and MacArtneys." *Ulster J. Arch.* 8, 1st ser. (1860): 196-210.

Hamilton–see McNeil.

Hill, George. *Historical Account of the Macdonnells of Antrim.* Belfast, 1873.

Hope, Sir T. *Memoirs of the Fultons of Lisburn.* 1903.

"The McKinleys of Conagher, Co. Antrim, and their Descendants, with Notes about the President of the United States." *Ulster J. Arch.* 3, 2nd ser. (1897): 167-70.

Melance–see McNeil.

Martin–see McNeil.

Moat–see McNeil.

"Notes on the Stewart Family of Co. Antrim." *J. Ass. Pres. Mem. Dead.* 7 (1907-09): 701.

"Notices of the Clan Iar Vor, Clan-Donnell Scots, Especially of the Branch Settled in Ireland." *Ulster J. Arch.* 9, 1st ser. (1861-62): 301-17.

"The Sitlington Family of Dunagorr, Co. Antrim." *Ulster J. Arch.* 15, 2nd ser. (1909): 161-72.

Walsh, Micheline. *The MacDonnells of Antrim and on the Continent* (text of O'Donnell lecture). Dublin, 1960.

Wray–see Co. Donegal.

Gravestone Inscriptions

A series of volumes in the series *Gravestone Inscriptions* has been prepared for this county by George Rutherford and published by the Ulster-Scot Historical Foundation:

Ardclinis: *The Glynns* 4 (1976): 11-16.

Ballykeel: Gravestone Inscription Series, Co. Antrim, No. 1.

Culfeightrin: *Ir. Anc.* 2 (2) (1970).

Glynn: Gravestone Inscription Series, Co. Antrim, No. 2.

Killycrappin: *The Glynns* 5 (1977): 11-14.

Kilmore: *The Glynns* 4 (1976): 11-16.

Kilroot: Gravestone Inscription Series, Co. Antrim, No. 2.

Lambeg: Cassidy, William. *Inscriptions on Old Tombstones in Lambeg Churchyard, Lisburn (1626-1837).*

Lisburn Cathedral: Carmody, W. P. *Lisburn Cathedral and its Past Rectors.* 1926.

Magheragall: *Family Links* 1 (2) (1981): 31-32; and 1 (3) (1982): 26-32.

Shankill: Gravestone Inscription Series (Belfast); Ulster-Scot Hist. Foundation, 1966.

Templecorran: Gravestone Inscription Series, Co. Antrim, No. 2.

Newspapers

One of the best early papers for this county is the *Belfast Newsletter*, which began publication in 1737. The availability of this and all other Belfast newspapers is listed in the appendix.

Title: *Ballymena Advertiser*
Published in: Ballymena, c.1867-92
BL Holdings: 6.1873-7.1892

Title: *Carrickfergus Advertiser*
Published in: Carrickfergus, 1883-current
BL Holdings: 4.1884-1.1931; 10.1946-current

Title: *Larne Times and Weekly Telegraph* (continued as *Larne Times* in 1936, and *East Antrim Times* in 1962)
Published in: Larne, 1891-current
NLI Holdings: 4.1910-12.1915; 6.1921-current
BL Holdings: 1.1893-12.1929; 1.1931-current

Title: *Larne Weekly Reporter*
Published in: Larne, 1881-1904
BL Holdings: 3.1865-3.1861; 4-11.1881; 4.1884-3.1904

Title: *Lisburn Herald*
Published in: Lisburn, 1891-1969
NLI Holdings: 7 Jan. 1905-3 Aug. 1940
BL Holdings: 9.1891-9.1969

Title: *Lisburn Standard*
Published in: Lisburn, 1876-1959
BL Holdings: odd numbers 1878, 1884; 5.1885-12.1924; 1-10.1925; 1.1927-5.1959

Title: *North Antrim Standard*
Published in: Ballymoney, 1887-1922
NLI Holdings: 8.1890-10.1922
BL Holdings: 8.1890-12.1920; 3.1921-10.1922

Title: *Northern Herald* (continued as *Ballymoney Northern Herald* in 1862)
Published in: Ballymoney, 1860-63
NLI Holdings: 10.1860-1.1863
BL Holdings: 7.1862-1.1863

Wills and Administrations

A discussion of the types of records, where they are held, and of their availability and value is given in the Wills and Administrations section of the Introduction. The availability of prerogative wills, administrations, and marriage license records is also described in the relevant parts of the same section. Where available, published sources of these records are given in the Miscellaneous Sources section.

Pre-1858 Wills and Administrations

Prerogative Wills. see p. xli.

Consistorial Wills. County Antrim is mainly in the diocese of Connor, with one parish in each of the dioceses of Derry, Down, and Dromore. The guide to Catholic parish records in this chapter shows the diocese to which each civil parish belonged. The wills of residents of each diocese were usually proven within that diocese (see Wills section, p. xxxvii, for exceptions). The following records survive:

Wills. Connor (1818-20 and 1853-58) and Down (1850-58). PRO; Derry (1612-1858) see Co. Derry; Down (1646-1858) see Co. Down; Dromore (1678-1858) see Co. Down.

Abstracts. Stewart-Kennedy notebooks contain about 500 seventeenth- to nineteenth-century abstracts particularly from Down and Connor dioceses and mainly for testators named Stewart, Clarke, Cunningham, Kennedy, and Wade. TCD Library.

Indexes. Connor 1680-1856 (A-L) and 1636-1857 (M-Y). Also (1810-58) in a volume of combined wills and administrations.

Post-1858 Wills and Administrations

County Antrim was served by the District Registry of Belfast. The surviving records are kept in the PRONI.

Marriage Licenses

Indexes. Down, Connor, and Dromore (1721-1845). PRO; SLC film 100867.

Miscellaneous Sources

"Demographic Study of ... Rathlin Island, 1841-1964." *Ulster Folk* 117 (1971): 70-80.

Dubourdieu, Rev. J. *Statistical Survey of the County of Antrim.* 1812.

"Maps of Carrickfergus." *Ulster J. Arch.* 2 (1895): 2-3.

"The Will Book of the Ballyhagan Meeting of the Society of Friends." *Ir. Gen.* 2 (8) (1950): 225-39.

Research Sources and Services

Journals

Carrickfergus Historical Society Journal (1985-present)

The Corran (published by Larne & District Historical Society, 1975-present)

The Glynns (published by Glens of Antrim Historical Society, 1975-present)

Lisburn Historical Society Journal (1978-present)

North Belfast Historical Magazine (1984-present)

Outline Annual (published by West Belfast Historical Society, 1977-present)

Libraries and Information Sources

Irish and Local Studies Department, Central Library, Royal Avenue, Belfast BT1 1EA, Ph: (084) 43223; Telex 747359

Lisburn Museum, Assembly Buildings, Market Square, Lisburn, Co. Antrim

North Eastern Education & Library Board, Area Library, Demesne Avenue, Ballymena, Co. Antrim, Ph: (080 266) 41531/2/3

Research Services

See research services in Belfast, p. xlvi.

Societies

Antrim Historical Society, Wm. Canning, Dunsilly Lodge, Dunsilly

Ballyclare Historical Society, Mrs. L. Weatherup, 689 Doagh Road, Newtownabbey

Carrickfergus and District Historical Society, Mrs. D. Corcoran, 64 Knocksallagh Park, Greenisland

Glens of Antrim Historical Society (publishes *The Glynns*), Mrs. B. McKay, Gruig, Cushendall

Islandmagee Conservation Society, J.G. Rutherford, 9 Causeway Villas, Ballycarry

Killultagh Historical Society, Mr. T. Lamb, 16 Camlin Park, Crumlin

Larne and District Historical Society (publishes *The Corran*), Mrs. A. Barron, 14 Browndod Road, Millbrook, Larne

Lisburn Historical Society, Miss S. Adams, 11 Halftown Road, Lower Maze, Lisburn

North Belfast Historical Society, Mrs. K. Jenkins, 123 Henderson Ave, Belfast 15, Belfast BT15

CIVIL PARISHES OF COUNTY ANTRIM

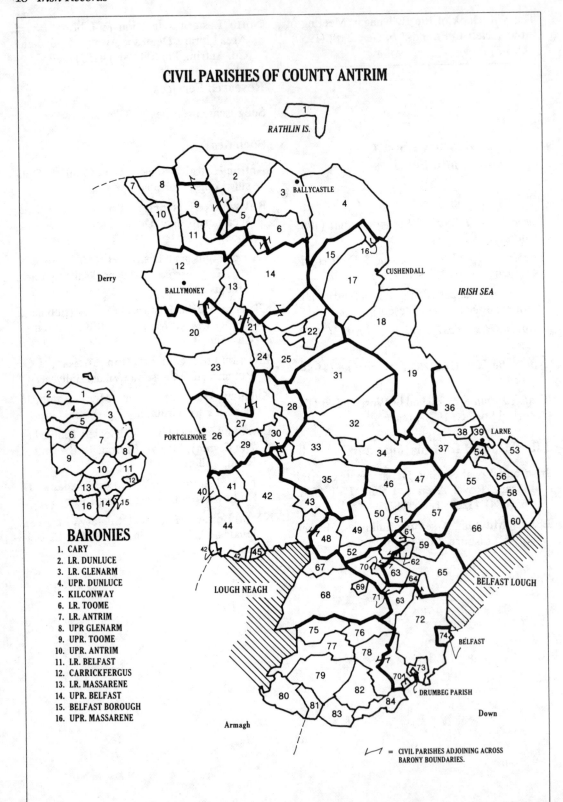

RATHLIN IS.

BALLYCASTLE

CUSHENDALL

Derry

BALLYMONEY

IRISH SEA

PORTGLENONE

LARNE

BELFAST LOUGH

LOUGH NEAGH

BELFAST

DRUMBEG PARISH

Down

Armagh

BARONIES

1. CARY
2. LR. DUNLUCE
3. LR. GLENARM
4. UPR. DUNLUCE
5. KILCONWAY
6. LR. TOOME
7. LR. ANTRIM
8. UPR GLENARM
9. UPR. TOOME
10. UPR. ANTRIM
11. LR. BELFAST
12. CARRICKFERGUS
13. LR. MASSARENE
14. UPR. BELFAST
15. BELFAST BOROUGH
16. UPR. MASSARENE

⌐ = CIVIL PARISHES ADJOINING ACROSS
    BARONY BOUNDARIES.

County Armagh

A Brief History

County Armagh was part of the old Gaelic territory of Uriel or Oriel. The town of Armagh was the ancient seat of the High Kings of Ulster and has also been the ecclesiastical capital of Ireland for some 1500 years.

The main Gaelic families in the area are O'Neill, O'Hanlon, MacCann, MacMahon, O'Keelaghan, McPartlan, MacVeagh, O'Heany, MacSherry, MacAlinden, O'Mulcreevy, O'Heron, O'Garvey, O'Loughran, O'Rogan, O'Hoey, and McEntee or McGinty. Most of these are still much in evidence in the county. Although the Normans invaded this county following their invasion of Ireland in the twelfth century, they did not exercise effective control because of the power of the Gaelic families. This situation of independence from English rule continued for several centuries.

The O'Neill rebellion in 1594 (see Co. Antrim) led to the emigration of Hugh O'Neill and the major families of Ulster, the confiscation of their territories, and in 1609, the English plantation of Ulster by "adventurers."

Among the English adventurers given land in Armagh at this time were the families of Acheson, Brownlow, St. John, McHenry, and Blacker. The plantation of Ulster, which also took place in Cavan, Donegal, Derry, Fermanagh, and Tyrone, was largely successful.

Thousands of settlers, of all social classes, came to Armagh from Scotland and England during the early seventeenth century. The names of the Scottish settlers who came to the county include Boyd, Fraser, Lindsay, Johnston, Morrison, Patterson, and Maxwell. The English settler names include Bradshaw, Bradford, Watson, Taylor, Walker, Jackson, Wilson, Johnson, and Young.

The native population was predominantly Catholic, the Scottish were usually Presbyterian, and English were of the of the Protestant faith. The proportions of these religions among the population can, in very general terms, be used to estimate the origins of the inhabitants of the county. When religious affiliation was first determined in the census of 1861, the respective proportions of Catholic, Presbyterian, and Protestant were 49, 31, and 16 percent.

The Penal Laws, enacted in the 1690s following the accession of the Protestant King William to the English throne, were mainly aimed at restriction of the rights of Catholics. However, they also included various measures which disadvantaged Presbyterians. As a result many Ulster Presbyterians, the so-called Scots-Irish, emigrated to North America during the eighteenth century.

During the seventeenth and eighteenth centuries Armagh became a major center of Ulster's linen industry, particularly around the

town of Lurgan. This industry and other farming activities made the county relatively
prosperous during the seventeenth and
eighteenth centuries. By the nineteenth century
the population had grown to over 200,000
making it one of the most densely populated in
the country. The population density was 511
people to the square mile at the peak population (232,000) in 1841.

The county was relatively less affected than
others by the Great Famine of 1845-47, although it still reduced the population by around
15 percent between 1841 and 1851.

In 1921 the county was one of those which
remained in the United Kingdom when the Irish
Free State was formed. The main towns are Armagh, Portadown, Lurgan, Tanderagee, and
Keady.

Census and Census Substitutes

1602
"First Census of the Fews." *Louth Arch. J.* 8
(2) (1934): 136-38.

1612-13
"Survey of Undertakers Planted in Armagh"
(names, acreages allotted, and account of the
progress of each), *Hist. Mss. Comm. Rep.*
(Hastings mss.) 4 (1947): 159-82.

1630
"Census of Men and Arms on Settlers' Estates" (names and arms, arranged under
name of "undertakers"). *Seanchas
Ardmhacha* 5 (2) (1970): 401-17.

1631
Muster Roll. PRONI T934; BL add. ms.
4770.

1634
Copy of Subsidy Roll, PRO films 2471, 2745.

1641
Book of Survey & Distribution (extract for
Creggan parish). *Louth Arch. J.* 8 (2) (1934):
142-46.

1659
"Census" of Ireland. Edited by S. Pender.
Dublin: Stationery Office, 1939.

"Extract for Fews Baronies." *Louth Arch J.* 8
(2) (1934): 149-52.

1664-65
Hearth Money Roll. GO ms. 538; NLI ms.
9586; PRONI T604; PRO films 2741, 2745;
Also printed in *Anal. Hib.* 8 (1936): 121-202;
SLC film 100181.

"Extract for Barony of Fewes." *Louth Arch.
J.* 8 (2) (1934): 152-56.

1669
"Hearth Money Roll for Parish of Lisburn
and Adjoining Parts of Parishes of
Magheragall and Magheramesk." *Down &
Connor Hist. Soc.* 7 (1936): 85-92.

"Extracts for parish of Aghagallon and adjoining parts of parishes of Magheragall and
Magheramesk." *Down & Connor Hist. Soc.* 6
(1934): 52-54.

"Early Census of Glenravel" (parishes of
Dunaghy & Skerry). *Down & Connor Hist.
Soc.* 5 (1933): 59.

1737
Tythe Payers of Drumcree (from records of
rector). NLI I920041 P1.

1738
A List of the Freeholders of Co. Armagh
c.1738. NLI: P206.

1740
Protestant Householders in Parishes of
Creggan, Derrynoose, Loughgall, Lurgan,
Mullaghbrack, Shankill, and Tynan. GO 539;
PRO 1A 46 100; RCB Library; SLC film
258517.

1755
Poll Book for Co. Armagh. GO ms. 443; SLC
film 100181, 258500.

1766
"Religious Census of Parish of Creggan." GO
ms. 537; SLC film 100173; *Louth Arch. J.* 8
(2) (1934): 156-62.

BARONY OF O'NEILLAND-EAST.

No.	Freeholder's Name.	Place of Abode.	Name of Landlord and Residence.	Value of Freehold	Description.	Situation	Names of Lives or other Tenure.	Date of Registry.
601	Kirk, Robert	Tullygally	Wm. Brownlow, Esq. Lurgan		same	Tullygally	Myself, David and William Kirk	August 25, 1813
602	Kirk, Samuel	Lurgan	same		Lands	same	David, William and Jonathan Kirk	fame
603	Kelly, Richard	Aughacommon	same		Houses & Land	Aughacommon	Anne Cartless	fame
604	Kirk, David	Tullygally	same		Land	Tullygally	Myself, William and Jonathan Kirk	fame
605	Kennedy, Hugh	Lurgan	same		A House	Lurgan	Hugh and John Kennedy	fame
606	Kirk, Samuel	same	same		same	same	Myself, James and William Carroll	fame
607	Kennedy, George	Knocknashane	same		Houses & Land	Knocknashane	George and Anne Kennedy, and Richard Eustice	same
608	Kane, Roger	Turmoyra	same		House & Land	Turmoyra	Prince Augustus, Adol. Frederick, & Henry M'Avoy	same
609	Kelly, Arthur	Cornikinigan	same		same	Cornikinigan	fame fame fame Michael Kelly	same
610	Kane, Owen	Turmoyra	same		Houses & Land	Turmoyra	fame fame fame Thomas Kane	same
611	Kennedy, John	Lurgan	Charles Brownlow, Esq.	FORTY SHILLINGS.	House & Land	Lurgan	John, Jane and Lucy Kennedy	March 2, 1816
612	Kean, Richard	Crossmeatehly	Mr. Sparrow, Tandragee		Houses & Land	Crossmacehly	Richard Kane	August 11, 1817
613	Kelly, John	Lisnisky	same		same	Lisnisky	Samuel Kelly	Sep. 1, 1817
614	Kirk, David	Monbrief	Charles Brownlow, Esq.		House & Land	Monbrief	Prince Augustus, Adol. Frederick, Thomas Brown	Nov. 3, 1817
615	Kerr, James	Legacorry	same		Houses & Land	Legacorry	William, Mary and Margaret Hare	fame
616	Kelly, John	Kinigo	same		same	Kinigo	Henry Pollow	fame
617	Kerr, Owen	Lissaconan	Joseph Greer, Moy		same	Lissaconan	Anne Castles	fame
618	Kelly, Richard	Aughacommon	Charles Brownlow, Esq		House & Land	Aughacommon	Prince Augustus, Adol. Frederick, Henry M'Avoy	August 26, 1818
619	Kane, Patrick	Turmoyra	same		same	Turmoyra	same same Thomas Buron	fame
620	Kirk, David	Monbrief	same		same	Monbrief	Myself, James and John Kennedy (my sons)	fame
621	Kennedy, George	Knocknashane	same		Houses & Land	Knocknashane	Prince Augustus, Adol. Frederick, Thos. Kane	fame
622	Kane, Owen	Turmoyra	same		House & Land	Turmoyra	Prince Augustus, Adol. Frederick, same Michael Kelly	fame
623	Kelly, Arthur	Cornikinigan	same		same	Cornikinigan	same same	fame
624	Kirk, Barrack	Tegnevin	same		Land	Tegnevin	James Taylor	fame
625	Kelly, John	Kinigo	same		Houses	Kinigo	Prince Augustus, Adol. Frederick, David Graham	fame
626	Kennedy, John	Lurgan	fame		same	Lurgan	Arthur, Catherine and Henry Kelly	fame
627	Kerr, Owen	Lissaconan	same		Houses & Land	Lissaconan	Henry Pollow, sen.	fame
628	Kirk, David	Tullygally	same		same	Tullygally	Charles Brownlow, Barrack Kirk, and Brownlow Kirk	fame
629	Kirk, Robert	same	same		House & Land	Tullygally	Myself, David and William Kirk	August 31, 1818
630	Kean, Charles	Tuisin	Miss Sparrow, Tandragee		Houses & Land	Tuisin	Anne Kean	Nov. 19, 1819
631	Kirk, Samuel	Lurgan	C. Brownlow, Esq. Lurgan		Houses	Lurgan	Renewable for ever	August 25, 1813
632	Levingstone, Wm.	Legacorry	Wm. Brownlow, Esq. Lur- gan		House & Land	Legacorry	William Livingstone, John and John M'Collom	same
633	Lownsdale, Fins. son	Drumnakairn	same		Houses & Land	Drumnakairn	Prince Augustus, Adol. Frederick, Geo. Lownsdale	same
634	Lowe, Patrick	Anghavillur	same		House & Land	Anghavillur	Myself	same
635	Lynass, William	Taberlurney	same		same	Taberlurney	Prince Augustus, Adol. Frederick, Thomas Lynnes	fame
636	Latherdale, John	Ballyblough	same		Lands	Ballyblough	Richard Chapman, and Shottle Jackson	fame
637	Lavery, James	Donnygrough	same		House & Land	Ballyblough	The Rev. Brownlow Ford	same
638	Lawson, Alexander	Ballyblough	same		Houses & Land.	Donnygrough	Prince Augustus, Augustus, and Adolphus Frederick	same
639	Lynass, Joseph	Tullygally	same		fame	Ballyblough	William and Jonathan Kirk	same
640	Larkin, Terence	Kinigo	James Ford, Esq.		House & Land	Tullygally	Donald Cobb, and John Corr	same
641	Lownsdale, Thomas	Drumnakairn	Wm. Brownlow, Esq. Lur- gan		fame	Kinigo	Prince Augustus, Adol. Frederick, and Patrick Furfy	same
642	Larkin, John	Killaughey	same		fame	Drumnakairn	Myself	same
643	Levingstone, John	Legacorry	same		same	Killaughey	Wm. (my son) Jane (my daughter) & James M'Murry	same
644	Lynch, William	Bucomell	same		House & Land	Legacorry	William Lynch	same
645	Lownsdale, John	Drumnakane	same		House & Land	Bucomell	Prince Augustus, Adol. Frederick, John Lownsdale	same
646	Lownsdale, James	Ballymagin	same		Land	Drumnakane	Charles Lownsdale	same

Extract from the Barony of O'Neilland East, Co. Armagh of the "Return of Registered Freeholders of £20 and 40 shillings from First January 1813 to First January 1820." NLI IR 94116 al.

Appendix (G.)

A RETURN of the several HOUSES in the Towns in *Ireland*, which Return MEMBERS
to serve in PARLIAMENT; specifying the Streets in which each is situated, its
Number, and the Name of the Occupant; together with the Annual Value of each, as
estimated and returned by the Valuators appointed to make the Annual Applotment
of Rates and Taxes for Municipal Purposes, either under the Provisions of the Act
9 Geo. 4, c. 82, or of any Local or Private Acts passed for the Regulation of these
Towns, or of the New Valuation Act, where it has come into operation.

ARMAGH.

Houses of the Yearly Value of £. 10 and upwards.

No.	Inhabitants' Names.	Yearly Value. £. s.	No.	Inhabitants' Names.	Yearly Value. £. s.
	Lower English-street:			Lower English-st.—*contd.*	
1	Francis M'Cormick -	10 –	114	John Lyle - - -	12 –
39	Hugh Lynch - - -	10 –	121	Samuel Thompson - -	11 –
40	John Duff - - -	10 10	128	John M'Elroy - -	10 –
41	Henry Mooney - -	10 –			
42	Patrick Cunningham -	10 –		Upper English-street:	
53	Bernard Quin - -	10 –	1	William Caldwell - -	24 10
54	John Garland - -	10 –	2	Edward Parker - -	24 –
57	Edward Murphy - -	10 –	3	Peter M'Kee - - -	20 –
58	Peter Kelly - - -	10 –	4	James Donnelly - -	22 –
59	James M'Elroy - -	12 –	5	Sarah M'Glone - -	19 –
64	John Woods - - -	10 –	6	Edward Hynes - -	30 –
65	James Donoghue - -	13 –	7	Patrick Downey - -	15 –
66	Owen Farley - - -	10 –	8	Edward Corvin - -	18 –
68	James Dunne - -	12 –	9	Thomas Craig - -	45 –
70	Margaret Williamson -	10 –	10	Arthur Branigan - -	19 –
71	Andrew Johnson - -	10 –	11	Bernard Hagan - -	19 –
73	John Allen - - -	10 –	12	George Barnes - -	24 –
74	Peter M'Caghey - -	14 –	13	Miss Atkinson - -	30 –
76	Johnson Nelson - -	22 –	14	James F. Bell - -	50 –
77	John Williams - -	30 –	15	William Blacker - -	100 –
78	James Vogan - -	34 –	16	Mrs. Lyle - - -	70 –
79	John Graham - -	16 –	17	John M'Kinstry - -	90 –
80	Patrick Corvin - -	15 –	18	R. J. Thornton - -	100 –
81	Michael M'Bride - -	19 –	19	Robert C. Hardy - -	70 –
82	Patrick Carberry - -	10 –	20	Leonard Dobbin, jun. -	100 –
83	Patrick Devlin - -	19 –	21	John Stanley - - -	130 –
–	Patrick Stores - -	10 –	22	James Moore - - -	40 –

Extract from tables showing the holders of houses of over £10 annual valuation
in the town of Armagh. This is a sample of the information on ratepayers and
voters presented to the Select Committee on Fictitious Votes, 1837. Appendix G
of the *Parliamentary Papers* 1837, 2 (1).

1770

List of inhabitants of Armagh City. SLC film 258621.

1796

"List of Flax Growers of Armagh" (with background to the industry). *Ulster Gen. & Hist. Guild Newsletter* 1 (7) (1981): 204-16. (Gives names in each parish.)

See Co. Mayo 1796 (List of Catholics).

1802

"Game-license Holders." *Ir. Anc.* 8 (1) (1976): p. 35-39.

1813-20

Registered Freeholders of £20 and 40s 1813-1820, Baronies of O'Neilland E. and Upper Orier (1,372 and 1,471 names respectively, arranged alphabetically with residence, location of freehold, etc.). NLI IR 352, p. 2.

Barony of Tureny (395 names), Lower Fews (1,250 names), Upper Fews (365 names). NLI IR 94116 A1.

Lists of Freeholders. SLC film 993156, 258595.

1821

Government Census Remnants for Parish of Kilmore (townlands of Balleney, Corcreevy, Crewcat, Derryhale, Drumnahushin, Listeyborough, and Maynooth). PRONI T450; SLC film 258511, 258621.

1821-31

A List of the Registered Freeholders of Co. Armagh (also listing by Barony for 1813-20). PRONI T862.

1825-35

Tithe Applotment Survey (see p. xxvii).

1833

Extracts of Kilmore Parish Tithe Applotments. NLI I920041 P1.

1834

Mullabrack Parish List (from Tythepayers lists of 1834). NLI I920041 P1.

1837

"Occupants of Armagh, Arranged by Street within 2 Sections" (over and under £10 value). *Parl. Papers* 1837, 11 (1): Appendix G, 176-91.

1839

"Freeholders and Leaseholders in Armagh, Tiranny, O'Neiland West, and O'Neiland East." *Commercial Telegraph* 27 (960) (3 Oct. 1839).

1847

"Castleblayney Poor Law Rate Book." *Clogher Record* 5 (1) (1963): 131-48 (ratepayers in each townland in Castleblayney poor law union).

1852

Registry of Voters in Armagh, Lower Fews, Tiranny, O'Neiland E. and W., Upper Fews, Lower and Upper Orior. SLC film 258499.

1864

Griffith's Valuation (see p. xxvii).

1901

Census. PRO.

1911

Census. PRO.

Church Records

Church of Ireland
(Shows starting date of records)

Parish: **Aghavilly**
Existing Records: b. 1844-76; d. 1846-76
Status: LC

Parish: **Annaghmore**
Existing Records: b. 1856-75; d. 1862-75
Status: LC

Parish: **Armagh**
Existing Records: b. 1750-1875; m. 1750-1845; d. 1750-1845
Status: LC

Parish: **Armaghbreague**
Status: Lost

Parish: **Baleek**
Status: Lost

Parish: **Ballymore**
Existing Records: b. 1783-1871; m. 1783-1845;
d. 1783-1871
Status: LC

Parish: **Ballymoyer**
Existing Records: b. 1820-75; m. 1820-45; d.
1836-75
Status: LC

Parish: **Camlough**
Existing Records: b. 1832-76; m. 1835-45; d.
1833-77
Status: LC

Parish: **Charlemont**
Status: Lost

Parish: **Clare**
Status: Lost

Parish: **Creggan**
Existing Records: b. 1808-75; m. 1808-39; d.
1808-75
Status: LC

Parish: **Derrynose**
Existing Records: b. 1822-75; m. 1822-45; d.
1835-75
Status: LC

Parish: **The Diamond**
Existing Records: b. 1848-77
Status: LC

Parish: **Drumbanagher**
Existing Records: b. 1838-79; m. 1838-45; d.
1838-79
Status: LC

Parish: **Drumcree**
Existing Records: b. 1780-1875; m. 1780-1845;
d. 1780-1875
Status: LC

Parish: **Eglish**
Existing Records: b. 1803-75; m. 1804-75;
d. 1803-75
Status: LC

Parish: **Forkhill**
Status: Lost

Parish: **Grange**
Existing Records: b. 1780-1876; m. 1780-1845;
d. 1780-1875
Status: LC

Parish: **Keady**
Existing Records: b. 1780-1871; m. 1780-1845;
d. 1813-1881
Status: LC

Parish: **Kildooney**
Existing Records: b. 1832-75; m. 1835-45; d.
1837-75
Status: LC

Parish: **Kildarton**
Status: Lost

Parish: **Killeavy** or **Mullaghglass**
Status: Lost

Parish: **Killylea**
Existing Records: b. 1845-75; d. 1845-75
Status: LC

Parish: **Kilmore**
Existing Records: b. 1789-1879; m. 1798-1845;
d. 1824-79
Status: LC

Parish: **Lisnadill**
Status: Lost

Parish: **Loughgall**
Existing Records: b. 1706-1875; m. 1706-1845;
d. 1706-1875
Missing Dates: b. 1730-1778; m. 1730-78; d.
1730-78
Status: LC

Parish: **Loughgilly**
Existing Records: b. 1804-75; m. 1804-45; d.
1804-75
Status: LC

Parish: **Meigh**
Status: Lost

Parish: **Milltown**
Existing Records: b. 1840-75; m. 1840-45; d.
1815-75
Status: LC

Parish: **Moyntaghs** or **Ardmore**
Existing Records: b. 1822-75; m. 1822-45; d.
1822-75
Status: LC

Parish: **Mullaghbrack**
Status: Lost

Parish: **Mullavilly**
Existing Records: b. 1821-74; m. 1821-45; d.
1821-75
Status: LC

Parish: **Newtown Hamilton**
Status: Lost

Parish: **Portadown**
Existing Records: b. 1826-76; m. 1827-45
Status: LC

Parish: **Rich-Hill**
Status: Lost

Parish: **St. Saviour Portadown**
Existing Records: b. 1858-72; d. 1862-76
Status: LC

Parish: **Seagoe**
Existing Records: b. 1683-1865; m. 1683-1845;
d. 1683-1875
Missing Dates: b. 1713-53; m. 1713-53; d. 1713-
53
Status: LC

Parish: **Tynan**
Existing Records: b. 1686-1875; m. 1683-1845;
d. 1683-1875

Missing Dates: b. 1725-1805; m. 1724-1807; d.
1724-1807
Status: LC

Presbyterian

Parish: **Ahorey** (Loughgall)
Starting Date: 1838

Parish: **Armagh**
Starting Date: 1707

Parish: **Bessbrook**
Starting Date: 1854

Parish: **Cladymore**
Starting Date: 1848

Parish: **Clare** (Tandragee)
Starting Date: 1838

Parish: **Cremore**
Starting Date: 1831

Parish: **Donacloney** (Lurgan)
Starting Date: 1798

Parish: **Gilford**
Starting Date: 1843

Parish: **Keady**
Starting Date: 1819

Parish: **Kingmills** (Whitecross)
Starting Date: 1842

Parish: **Knappagh**
Starting Date: 1842

Parish: **Lislooney**
Starting Date: 1836

Parish: **Loughgall**
Starting Date: 1842

Parish: **Lurgan**
Starting Date: 1746

Parish: **Markethill**
Starting Date: 1821

Parish: **Mountnorris**
Starting Date: 1804

Parish: **Newmills** (Portadown)
Starting Date: 1838

Parish: **Newtownhamilton**
Starting Date: 1823

Parish: **Portadown**
Starting Date: 1822

Parish: **Poyntzpass**
Starting Date: 1850

Parish: **Richhill**
Starting Date: 1856

Parish: **Tandragee**
Starting Date: 1835

Parish: **Tullyallen**
Starting Date: 1795

Parish: **Vinecash** (Portadown)
Starting Date: 1838

Roman Catholic

Civil Parish: **Armagh**
Map Grid: 14
RC Parish: Armagh
Diocese: AM
Earliest Record: b. 7.1796; m. 1.1802
Missing Dates: m. 5.1803-1.1817
Parish Address: Rev. Raymond Murray, Parochial House, Abbey St., Armagh

Civil Parish: **Ballymore**
Map Grid: 21
RC Parish: Ballymore and Mullaghbrack (Tandragee)
Diocese: AM
Earliest Record: b. 10.1843; m. 10.1843
Missing Dates: 11.1856-6.1859; 11.1856-7.1859

Parish Address: Rev. Patrick McNulty, PP, Market Street, Tandragee, Craigavon BT62 2BW

Civil Parish: **Ballymyre**
Map Grid: 23
RC Parish: see Loughgilly
Diocese: AM

Civil Parish: **Clonfeacle**
Map Grid: 3
RC Parish: Clonfeacle, see Co. Tyrone
Diocese: AM

Civil Parish: **Creggan** (see also Co. Louth)
Map Grid: 25
RC Parish: Creggan Upper (Crossmaglen)
Diocese: AM
Earliest Record: b. 8.1796; m. 8.1796
Missing Dates: b. 1.1803-9.1812, 5.1829-5.1845; m. 2.1803-12.1812, 7.1829-5.1845, 3.1870-5.1871
Parish Address: Rev. Hugh O'Neill, PP, Parochial House, Crossmaglen, Newry, Co. Down

Civil Parish: **Derrynoose**
Map Grid: 15
RC Parish: Derrynoose
Diocese: AM
Earliest Record: b. 1.1835; m. 7.1846; d. 7.1846
Missing Dates: b. 1.1837-12.1846; d. ends 4.1851
Parish Address: Rev. P. McDonnell, PP, Parochial House, Keady, Co. Armagh

Civil Parish: **Drumcree**
Map Grid: 5
RC Parish: Portadown (Drumcree)
Diocese: AM
Earliest Record: b. 1.1844; m. 2.1844; d. 5.1863
Missing Dates: m. 11.1863-7.1864; d. 12.1863-6.1864
Parish Address: Rev. Patrick Early, PP, Corcrain Villa, Charles St. Portadown, Craigavon, Co. Armagh

Civil Parish: **Eglish**
Map Grid: 11
RC Parish: Eglish
Diocese: AM
Earliest Record: b. 1.1862; m. 1.1862

Parish Address: Rev. John Murphy, PP, Parochial House, 124 Eglish Road, Dungannon, Co. Tyrone

Civil Parish: **Forkhill**
Map Grid: 28
RC Parish: Forkhill (Mullaghbawn)
Diocese: AM
Earliest Record: b. 1.1845; m. 1.1844
Parish Address: Rev. John McGrane, PP, Mullaghbawn, Newry, Co. Down

Civil Parish: **Grange**
Map Grid: 13
RC Parish: see Armagh
Diocese: AM

Civil Parish: **Jonesborough**
Map Grid: 29
RC Parish: see Co. Louth
Diocese: AM

Civil Parish: **Keady**
Map Grid: 16
RC Parish: see Derrynoose
Diocese: AM

Civil Parish: **Kilclooney**
Map Grid: 20
RC Parish: Ballymacnab, see Lisnadill
Diocese: AM

Civil Parish: **Kildarton**
Map Grid: 17
RC Parish: see Armagh
Diocese: AM

Civil Parish: **Killevy (1)**
Map Grid: 26
RC Parish: part Killeavy, Lower (Bessbrook); part Killeavy, Upper, see below
Diocese: AM
Earliest Record: b. 1.1835; m. 1.1835; d. 8.1858
Missing Dates: m. 12.1862-5.1874
Parish Address: Rev. John Bradley, PP, Parochial House, 9 Chapel Road, Bessbrook, Newry, Co. Down

Civil Parish: **Killevy (2)**
Map Grid: 26

RC Parish: Killeavy, Upper (Cloghogue)
Diocese: AM
Earliest Record: b. 10.1832; m. 11.1832
Parish Address: Rev. Henry Devlin, Mountain Lodge, Dublin Road, Newry, Co. Down BT35 8QT

Civil Parish: **Killevy (3)**
Map Grid: 26
RC Parish: Dromintee
Diocese: AM
Earliest Record: b. 6.1853; m. 11.1853
Parish Address: Rev. Charles Vallely, PP, Jonesborough, Newry, Co. Down

Civil Parish: **Killyman**
Map Grid: 2
RC Parish: Dungannon, see Drumglass, Co. Tyrone
Diocese: AM

Civil Parish: **Kilmore**
Map Grid: 6
RC Parish: Kilmore (Mullavilly or Richill)
Diocese: AM
Earliest Record: b. 1.1845; m. 1.1845
Parish Address: Rev. K. Mac Oscar, PP, Mullavilly, Tandragee, Craigavon, Co. Armagh

Civil Parish: **Lisnadill**
Map Grid: 19
RC Parish: Ballymacnab (Kilcluney)
Diocese: AM
Earliest Record: b. 1.1844; m. 1.1844
Parish Address: Rev. Pol Mac Seain, PP, Ballymacnab, Tassagh, Armagh BT60 2QS

Civil Parish: **Loughgall**
Map Grid: 14
RC Parish: Loughgall and Tartaraghan
Diocese: AM
Earliest Record: b. 1.1835; m. 8.1833
Missing Dates: b. 8.1852-10.1854, 5.1858-9.1859; m. 1.1854-2.1860
Parish Address: Rev. Charles Devlin, PP, Parochial House, Loughgall, Co. Armagh

Civil Parish: **Loughgilly**
Map Grid: 22
RC Parish: Loughgilly (Whitecross)
Diocese: AM

Earliest Record: b. 5.1825; m. 2.1825
Missing Dates: b. 12.1844-2.1849; m. 11.1844-2.1849
Parish Address: Rev. Brendan McDonald, PP, Whitecross, Co. Armagh

Civil Parish: **Magheralin**
Map Grid: 10
RC Parish: see Co. Down
Diocese: DR

Civil Parish: **Montiaghs**
Map Grid: 7
RC Parish: Seagoe, see Seagoe
Diocese: DR

Civil Parish: **Mullaghbrack**
Map Grid: 18
RC Parish: see Ballymore
Diocese: AM

Civil Parish: **Newtownhamilton**
Map Grid: 24
RC Parish: Creggan, Lower (Cullyhanna)
Diocese: AM
Earliest Record: b. 2.1845; m. 2.1845
Parish Address: Rev. Kevin Moran, PP, Parochial House, Cullyhanna, Newry, Co. Down

Civil Parish: **Newry**
Map Grid: 27
RC Parish: see Co. Down
Diocese: N and M

Civil Parish: **Seagoe**
Map Grid: 8
RC Parish: part Seagoe or Derrymacash, see also Dromore, Co. Down; part Portadown, see also Drumcree
Diocese: DR
Earliest Record: b. 9.1836; m. 10.1836; d. 4.1837
Parish Address: Rev. Joseph Pettit, PP, 6 Derrymacash Road, Lurgan, Co. Armagh

Civil Parish: **Shankill**
Map Grid: 9
RC Parish: Lurgan, see also Dromore, Co. Down
Diocese: DR
Earliest Record: b. 9.1822; m. 1.1866; d. 1.1866

Parish Address: Rev. Christopher Murray, PP, 70 North St. Lurgan, Co. Armagh

Civil Parish: **Tartaraghan**
Map Grid: 1
RC Parish: see Loughgall
Diocese: AM

Civil Parish: **Tynan**
Map Grid: 12
RC Parish: Tynan (Middletown)
Diocese: AM
Earliest Record: b. 6.1822; m. 6.1822
Missing Dates: b. 8.1834-8.1838, 7.1842-7.1845; m. 10.1834-6.1845
Parish Address: Rev. Michael Toal, PP, Parochial House, Middleton, Armagh

Commercial and Social Directories

1819
Thomas Bradshaw's *General Directory of Newry, Armagh* . . . gives an alphabetic list of the traders in Armagh, Lurgan, Markethill, Portadown, and Tandragee.

1820
J. Pigot's *Commercial Directory of Ireland* contains information on the gentry, nobility, and traders in and around the town of Armagh.

1824
J. Pigot's *City of Dublin & Hibernian Provincial Directory* includes traders, nobility, gentry, and clergy lists for Armagh, Blackwatertown, Lurgan, Portadown, and Tanderagee.

1841
Mathew Martin's *Belfast Directory* contains an alphabetical list of traders, merchants and gentry, residents of the principal streets, and the noblemen and gentry in and around the towns of Armagh, Lurgan, Portadown, and Waringstown.

1842
A further edition of the above covering the same towns.

1846

Slater's *National Commercial Directory of Ireland* lists nobility, clergy, traders, etc., in Armagh, Blackwatertown, Loughgall, Lurgan and Moira, Portadown, and Tanderagee.

1852

Henderson's *Belfast & Province of Ulster Directory* has lists of inhabitants, traders, etc., in and around the towns of Armagh, Blackwatertown, Lurgan, and Portadown.

1856

Slater's *Royal National Commercial Directory of Ireland* lists nobility, gentry, clergy, traders, etc., in Armagh, Keady, Middletown, Richill, Tynan and Markethill, Blackwatertown and Loughgall, Lurgan, Moira and Waringstown, Portadown, and Tanderagee.

1865

R. Wynne's *Business Directory of Belfast* covers Armagh, Lurgan, and Portadown.

1870

Slater's *Directory of Ireland* contains trade, nobility, and clergy lists for Armagh, Crossmaglen, Lurgan, Moy, Newtown Hamilton, Portadown and Tanderagee.

1877

A further edition of Henderson's *Belfast & Province of Ulster Directory* covers Armagh, Blackwatertown, Keady, Lurgan, Moira, Portadown, Richill, Tanderagee, Waringstown, and Donaghcloney. Further editions in 1880, 1884, 1890, 1894, and 1900.

1881

Slater's *Royal National Commercial Directory of Ireland* contains lists of traders, clergy, nobility, and farmers in adjoining parishes of the towns of Armagh, Crossmaglen, Lurgan, Moy, Newtown Hamilton, Portadown, and Tanderagee.

1883

Farrell's *County Armagh Directory & Almanac* contains street directories for Armagh and alphabetical lists for the towns of Lurgan, Portadown, Richill, and Tanderagee.

1888

G.H. Bassett's *Book of Antrim* contains a variety of local information and history as well as a directory of Armagh town and of all the postal districts in the county.

1894

Slater's *Royal National Directory of Ireland* lists traders, police, teachers, farmers, and private residents in each of the towns, villages, and parishes of the county.

Family History

"Blaney of Lurgan, Co. Armagh." *Ir. Anc.* 3 (1) (1971): 32-39.

"The Descendants of Robert McCann of Cloghoge, Co. Armagh." *Ir. Anc.* 5 (1): 1-6.

"Obins of Castleobins." Pedigree in *Swanzy Notebooks.* RCB Library, Dublin.

Phillips, Sir T. *Pedigree of Molyneux of Castle Dillon, Co. Armagh.*

Gravestone Inscriptions

Creggan: *Seanchas Ardmhacha* 6 (2) (1972): 309-32.

Sandy Hill (Armagh City): *Seanchas Ardmhacha* 11 (2) (1985): 395-434.

Newspapers

Title: *Armagh Guardian*
Published in: Armagh, 1844-1982
BL Holdings: 12.1844-in progress

Title: *Armagh Standard* (incorporated with *Ulster Gazette*)
Published in: Armagh, 1879-1909
BL Holdings: 4.1844-6.1909

Title: *Lurgan Gazette*
Published in: Lurgan, 1861-74

Title: *Lurgan Mail* (continued as *Lurgan & Craigavon Mail* in 1977, and as *Lurgan Mail* in 1983)
Published in: Lurgan, 1890-current
NLI Holdings: 12.1904-10.1977
BL Holdings: 12.1897-in progress (except 1926)

Title: *Lurgan Times & Portadown Recorder*
Published in: Lurgan, 1877-1915
BL Holdings: 5.1879-5.1915

Title: *Portadown (Weekly) News* (continued as *Portadown & Lurgan News* from 1872-90)
Published in: Portadown, 1859-current
NLI Holdings: 1.1899-10.1956
BL Holdings: 4-10.1859; 11.1859-5.1822; 6.1872-12.1925; 1927; 1.1929-10.1956

Title: *Ulster Gazette* (continued as *Armagh Gazette* in 1850)
Published in: Armagh, 1844-current
NLI Holdings: 11.1879-12.1913; 6.1921-9.1940; 1.1950-in progress
BL Holdings: 10.1844-1924

Wills and Administrations

A discussion of the types of records, where they are held, their availability and value is given in the Wills section of the Introduction. The availability of prerogative wills, administrations, and marriage license records is also described in the relevant parts of the same section.

Pre-1858 Wills and Administrations

Prerogative Wills. see p. xli.
Consistorial Wills. County Armagh is mainly in the diocese of Armagh; four parishes are in Dromore and one in Newry and Mourne. The guide to Catholic parish records in this chapter shows the diocese to which each civil parish belonged. The wills of residents of each diocese were usually proven within that diocese (see Wills section p. xxxvii for exceptions). The following records survive:

Wills. See p. xxxvii.

Abstracts. "Quaker Wills from the Lisburn Meeting." *Ir. Gen.* (1950). Johnson collection of Will abstracts – Armagh library.

Indexes. Dromore 1678-1858 with the Peculiar of Newry and Mourne 1727-1858; Armagh 1666-1837 (A-L) and 1677-1858 (M-Y), also the District of Drogheda 1691-1846.

Post-1858 Wills and Administrations

This county was served by the District Registry of Armagh. The surviving records are kept in the PRONI.

Marriage Licenses

Indexes. Armagh (1727-1845). PRO; SLC films 100859-860; Dromore – see Co. Antrim

Miscellaneous Sources

"Ballentaken-Beragh in the 17th Century." *Seanchas Ardmhaca* 10 (2) (1982): 455-501.

Coote, Sir Charles. *Statistical Survey of the County of Armagh* (1804).

"Some Lists of Mid-18th Century Linen-drapers in S.E. Ulster." *Ir. Anc.* 11 (1) (1979): 9-14.

Stuart, James. *Historical Memoirs of the City of Armagh (1819).* Edited by the Rev. A. Coleman. 1900.

"The Survey of Armagh and Tyrone, 1622." *Ulster J. Arch.* 23 (1960): 126-37; 27 (1964): 140-54.

Research Sources and Services

Journals

Breifne (see Co. Cavan)
Craigavon Hist. Soc. Review (1972-present)
Down & Connor Hist. Soc. Journal

Seanchas Ardmhacha (published by Armagh Diocesan Historical Society, 1954-present)

Libraries and Information Sources

Armagh County Museum, Charlemont Place, The Mall, Armagh

Irish and Local Studies Dept., Central Library, Royal Avenue, Belfast BT1 1EA

Southern Library Board Headquarters, Brownlow Road, Craigavon, Co. Armagh

Research Services

See research services in Belfast, p. xlvi

Irish World Citizen Organization, 1 Church Place, Lurgan, Co. Armagh

Societies

Armagh Diocesan Historical Society/Cumann Seanchais Ardmhacha, Dr. J.B. Walsh, 14 Ashley Park, Armagh

Armagh Natural History and Philosophical Society, Mr. Whitcroft, c/o Armagh County Museum, The Mall, Armagh

Craigavon Historical Society, D.B. Cassells, 2 Cherryville Park, Upper Toberhewney, Lurgan, Co. Armagh

Creggan Historical Society, Mrs. G. Hanratty, Teer, Crossmaglen, Co. Armagh

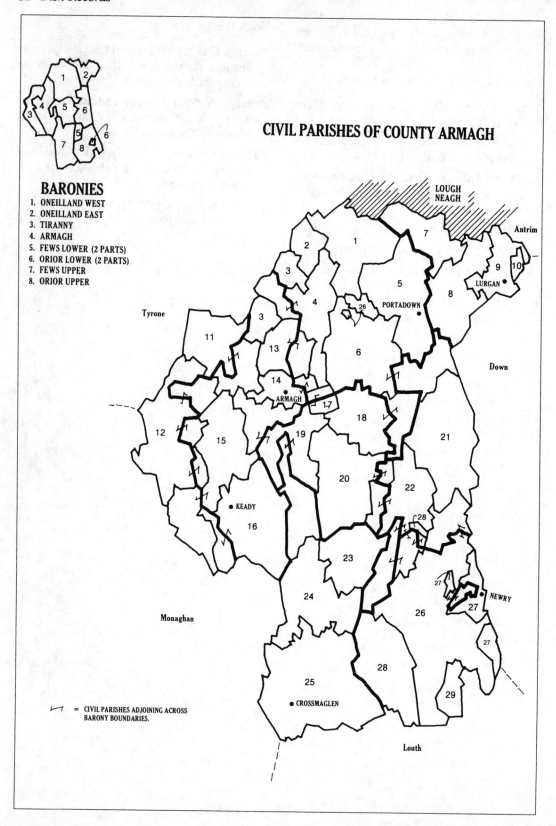

CIVIL PARISHES OF COUNTY ARMAGH

BARONIES
1. ONEILLAND WEST
2. ONEILLAND EAST
3. TIRANNY
4. ARMAGH
5. FEWS LOWER (2 PARTS)
6. ORIOR LOWER (2 PARTS)
7. FEWS UPPER
8. ORIOR UPPER

LOUGH NEAGH

Antrim

Tyrone

Down

Monaghan

Louth

PORTADOWN

LURGAN •

ARMAGH

• KEADY

• CROSSMAGLEN

NEWRY

= CIVIL PARISHES ADJOINING ACROSS
  BARONY BOUNDARIES.

County Carlow

A Brief History

This inland Leinster county contains the towns of Carlow, Muinebeag (or Bagenalstown), Tullow, Leighlinbridge, and Rathvilly.

County Carlow was formerly part of the territory of Ui Kinsellaigh. The major families of the county were Kavanagh, O'Ryan of Idrone, O'Nolan of Forth, O'Neill, and O'Hayden. Following the Norman invasion the county was taken by their leader, Strongbow, and castles were built at Carlow town, Leighlin, and Tullow. The English administration gradually lost their power elsewhere in the county to the powerful McMurrough Kavanaghs who allied themselves with the O'Byrnes and O'Tooles in Wicklow. These native chieftains continued to hold varying degrees of control over the county for several centuries.

The town of Carlow was an important Norman stronghold during the Middle Ages. In 1361 it was walled to protect it from the neighbouring Gaelic chieftains. It was repeatedly attacked and was captured in 1405 by the McMurrough Kavanaghs (see Wexford) and in 1567 by the O'Moores (see Laois). Although a plan for a plantation of the county was put forward during the reign of James I, it was not acted on.

In 1641 the county joined the rebellion of the Catholic Confederacy (see p. xlvii) but the Carlow rebels were finally defeated by Ireton, one of Cromwell's generals, in 1650. Of the English and Norman families who settled in Carlow at various times, the most prominent were Bruen, Butler, Bagenal, Best, Brown, Bunbury, Burton, and Tallon.

During the Great Famine of 1845-47 the county was relatively badly affected. The population in 1841 was 86,000 and by 1851 had fallen by 21 percent to 68,000. Of these people, over 10,000 died of starvation or other causes between 1845 and 1850, and further thousands emigrated.

County Carlow is now an important agricultural center with an extensive sugarbeet and cereal industry. The current population is around 40,000.

Census and Census Substitutes

1659
"Census" of Ireland. Edited by S. Pender. Dublin: Stationery Office, 1939.

1669
"Householders of the Parish of Carlow." *J. Kildare Arch. Soc.* 10 (1918-21): 255-57 (gives names on four streets).

1739

"Tenants of the Lordship of Carlow." *J. Kildare Arch. Soc.* 12 (2) (1937): 99-101.

1767

"Co. Carlow Freeholders." *Ir. Gen.* 12 (1) and (2) (1980): 46-47.

1775

Catholic Qualification Roll Extracts (ninety-three names, addresses, and occupations). 59th Report. DKPRI: 50-84.

1798

List of Persons who Suffered Losses During '98 Rebellion. NLI 94107 (approximately 300 names, addresses, and occupations).

1821

Extracts from the Government Census for Fennagh Parish Relating Only to the Surnames Clowry, Foley, White, Lennon, Rigney, and Gregor. SLC film 100158.

1821-37

Tithe Applotment Survey. (see p. xxvii)

1832-37

"List of Voters Registered in the Borough of Carlow." *Parl. Papers* 1837, 2 (2): 193-96 (over 400 names and street addresses).

1846

Ratepayers in Barragh Electoral Division (names in each townland, description of property, and rate due). NLI film P4547.

1852-53

Griffith's Valuation. (see p. xxvii)

1858-59

Census of the RC Parish of Bagenalstown. Included in Parish register (see Civil Parish of Dunleckney).

1901

Census. PRO.

1911

Census. PRO.

Church Records

Church of Ireland
(Shows starting date of record)

Parish: **Ardoyne**
Status: Lost

Parish: **Barragh**
Status: Lost

Parish: **Bilbo**
Status: Lost

Parish: **Carlow**
Existing Records: b. 1744-1875; m. 1744-1845; d. 1744-1875
Status: PRO and LC

Parish: **Clonagoose** or **Borris**
Status: Lost

Parish: **Clonmulsk**
Status: Lost

Parish: **Clonmore**
Existing Records: b. 1826-82; m. 1826-77; d. 1827-81
Status: LC (copy)

Parish: **Cloydagh**
Status: Lost

Parish: **Dunleckny**
Existing Records: b. 1791-1876; m. 1791-1845; d. 1791-1876
Status: LC

Parish: **Fenagh** (Carlow)
Existing Records: b. 1809-1975; m. 1809-45; d. 1809-75
Status: LC

Parish: **Hackettstown**
Existing Records: b. 1799; m. 1799; d. 1799
Status: LC (copy)

Parish: **Kellitstown**
Status: Lost

Parish: **Killeshin** (Carlow)
Existing Records: b. 1824-76; m. 1824-45; d. 1824-75
Status: LC

Parish: **Kiltennell** (New Ross)
Existing Records: b. 1837-75; m. 1837-75; d. 1837-75
Status: LC

Parish: **Kunneagh**
Status: Lost

Parish: **Lorum**
Status: Lost

Parish: **Myshall**
Existing Records: b. 1814-76; m. 1815-55; d. 1816-77
Status: LC

Parish: **Nurney**
Status: Lost

Parish: **Old Leighlin**
Status: Lost

Parish: **Painestown** (Carlow)
Existing Records: b. 1833-74; m. 1833-45; d. 1833-71
Status: LC

Parish: **Rathvilly**
Existing Records: b. 1826-75; m. 1826-45; d. 1826-75
Status: LC

Parish: **St. Annes**
Existing Records: b. 1859-75
Status: LC

Parish: **St. Mullins**
Status: Lost

Parish: **Staplestown**
Status: Lost

Parish: **Straboe** (see Rathvilly)

Parish: **Tullow**
Existing Records: b. 1696-1875; m. 1696-1845; d. 1696-1875
Status: LC

Parish: **Tullowmagimma**
Status: Lost

Parish: **Urglin-Rutland Church** (Carlow)
Existing Records: b. 1710-1853; m. 1715-1877; d. 1715-1877
Status: LC

Parish: **Wells**
Status: Lost

Roman Catholic

Civil Parish: **Agha**
Map Grid: 32
RC Parish: Leiglinbridge
Diocese: LE
Earliest Record: b. 1.1783; m. 2.1783
Missing Dates: b. 10.1786-12.1819; m. 1.1788-1.1820, 2.1827-7.1827
Parish Address: Rev. John Aughney, PP, Leiglinbridge, Co. Carlow

Civil Parish: **Aghade**
Map Grid: 43
RC Parish: see Ballon
Diocese: LE

Civil Parish: **Ardoyne**
Map Grid: 23
RC Parish: see Ardoyne, Co. Wicklow
Diocese: LE

Civil Parish: **Ardristan**
Map Grid: 25
RC Parish: Tullow, see Tullowphelim
Diocese: LE

Civil Parish: **Ballinacarrig** or **Staplestown**
Map Grid: 6
RC Parish: Tinryland, see Tullowmagimma
Diocese: LE

Civil Parish: **Ballon**
Map Grid: 42
RC Parish: Ballon
Diocese: LE
Earliest Record: b. 1.1785; m. 8.1782; d. 8.1825
Missing Dates: b. 9.1795-7.1816; m. 12.1795-8.1816; d. 12.1834-1.1861
Parish Address: Rev. John Flood, PP, Rathoe, Tullow, Co. Carlow

Civil Parish: **Ballycrogue**
Map Grid: 7
RC Parish: Tinryland, see Tullowmagimma
Diocese: LE

Civil Parish: **Ballyellin**
Map Grid: 36
RC Parish: Bagenalstown, see Dunleckney
Diocese: LE

Civil Parish: **Baltinglass**
Map Grid: 13
RC Parish: see Balinglass, Co. Wicklow
Diocese: LE

Civil Parish: **Barragh**
Map Grid: 45
RC Parish: Clonegal, see Moyacomb
Diocese: LE

Civil Parish: **Carlow**
Map Grid: 4
RC Parish: Carlow
Diocese: LE
Earliest Record: b. 6.1774; m. 11.1769
Missing Dates: b. many gaps to 1820; m. 8.1786-1.1820
Parish Address: Rev. John Fingleton, The Presbytery, Carlow,

Civil Parish: **Clonmelsh**
Map Grid: 5
RC Parish: Leighlinbridge, see Agha
Diocese: LE

Civil Parish: **Clonmore**
Map Grid: 22
RC Parish: Clonmore
Diocese: LE
Earliest Record: b. 11.1819; m. 2.1813
Missing Dates: m. 2.1833-5.1833

Parish Address: Rev. Michael Kaye, PP, Killinure, Tullow, Co. Carlow

Civil Parish: **Clonygoose**
Map Grid: 37
RC Parish: part Borris; part Bagenalstown, see Dunleckney
Diocese: LE
Earliest Record: b. 5.1782; m. 1.1782
Missing Dates: b. 12.1813-2.1825; m. 12.1813-2.1825, 11.1868-2.1869
Parish Address: Rev. Nicholas Moore, PP, Borris, Co. Carlow

Civil Parish: **Cloydagh**
Map Grid: 26
RC Parish: Leighlinbridge, see Agha
Diocese: LE

Civil Parish: **Crecrin** (see also Co. Wicklow)
Map Grid: 21
RC Parish: see Clonmore
Diocese: LE

Civil Parish: **Dunleckney**
Map Grid: 33
RC Parish: Bagenalstown
Diocese: LE
Earliest Record: b. 1.1820; m. 1.1820
Parish Address: Rev. E. Dowling, PP, Muinebheag, Co. Carlow

Civil Parish: **Fennagh**
Map Grid: 24
RC Parish: part Myshall; part Ballon
Diocese: LE

Civil Parish: **Gilbertstown**
Map Grid: 40
RC Parish: see Ballon
Diocese: LE

Civil Parish: **Grangeford**
Map Grid: 9
RC Parish: Tullow, see Tullowphelim
Diocese: LE

Civil Parish: **Hacketstown** (see also Co. Wicklow)
Map Grid: 19
RC Parish: Hacketstown

Diocese: LE
Earliest Record: b. 8.1820; m. 8.1820
Missing Dates: b. 4.1823-7.1826, 9.1826-
10.1827; m. 12.1827-3.1829, 9.1870-2.1877
Parish Address: Rev. W. Hughes, PP, Hack-
etstown, Co. Carlow

Civil Parish: **Haroldstown**
Map Grid: 18
RC Parish: see Hacketstown
Diocese: LE

Civil Parish: **Kellistown**
Map Grid: 8
RC Parish: see Ballon
Diocese: LE

Civil Parish: **Killerrig**
Map Grid: 3
RC Parish: part Tullowphelim; part Leigh-
linbridge, see Agha
Diocese: LE

Civil Parish: **Killinane**
Map Grid: 30
RC Parish: Leighlinbridge, see Agha
Diocese: LE

Civil Parish: **Kiltegan**
Map Grid: 15
RC Parish: see Hacketstown
Diocese: LE

Civil Parish: **Kiltennell**
Map Grid: 38
RC Parish: Borris, see Clonygoose
Diocese: LE

Civil Parish: **Kineagh**
Map Grid: 12
RC Parish: part Castledermot, see Co. Kildare;
part Rathvilly
Diocese: DU

Civil Parish: **Lorum**
Map Grid: 36
RC Parish: Bagenalstown, see Dunleckney

Civil Parish: **Moyacomb** (see also Cos. Wicklow
and Wexford)
Map Grid: 46

RC Parish: Clonegal
Diocese: FE
Earliest Record: b. 1.1833; m. 2.1833
Parish Address: Rev. P. Lawlor, PP, Clonegal,
Enniscorthy, Co. Wexford

Civil Parish: **Myshall**
Map Grid: 44
RC Parish: Myshall
Diocese: LE
Earliest Record: b. 2.1822; m. 9.1822
Missing Dates: b. 5.1846-10.1846; m. 1.1845-
2.1846
Parish Address: Rev. John Hayden, PP,
Myshall, Co. Carlow

Civil Parish: **Nurney**
Map Grid: 31
RC Parish: Bagenalstown, see Dunleckney
Diocese: LE

Civil Parish: **Old Leighlin**
Map Grid: 28
RC Parish: Leighlinbridge, see Agha
Diocese: LE

Civil Parish: **Painestown** (see also Co. Kildare)
Map Grid: 1
RC Parish: see Carlow
Diocese: LE

Civil Parish: **Rahill**
Map Grid: 11
RC Parish: see Rathvilly
Diocese: LE

Civil Parish: **Rathmore**
Map Grid: 17
RC Parish: see Rathvilly
Diocese: LE

Civil Parish: **Rathvilly**
Map Grid: 14
RC Parish: Rathvilly
Diocese: LE
Earliest Record: b. 10.1797; m. 10.1800
Missing Dates: b. 1.1813-6.1813; m. 2.1812-
6.1813
Parish Address: Rev. B. Ryan, PP, Rathvilly,
Co. Carlow

Civil Parish: **St. Mullins (1)** (see also Co. Wexford)
Map Grid: 47

RC Parish: **St. Mullins (2)**
Diocese: LE
Earliest Record: b. 5.1796; m. 6.1796
Missing Dates: b. 3.1810-1.1812, 3.1814-1.1820; m. 2.1807-10.1807, 3.1813-1.1820, 11.1871-2.1872
Parish Address: Rev. Patrick Breen, PP, Glynn, St. Mullins, Co. Carlow

Civil Parish: **Slyguff**
Map Grid: 34
RC Parish: part Borris, see Clonygoose; part Bagenalstown, see Dunleckny
Diocese: LE

Civil Parish: **Straboe**
Map Grid: 16
RC Parish: see Rathvilly
Diocese: LE

Civil Parish: **Templepeter**
Map Grid: 41
RC Parish: see Ballon
Diocese: LE

Civil Parish: **Tullowcreen**
Map Grid: 27
RC Parish: Leighlinbridge, see Agha
Diocese: LE

Civil Parish: **Tullowmagimma**
Map Grid: 10
RC Parish: Tinryland
Diocese: LE
Earliest Record: b. 3.1813; m. 6.1813
Parish Address: Rev. D. Doyle, PP, Tinryland, Co. Carlow

Civil Parish: **Tullowphelim**
Map Grid: 20
RC Parish: Tullow
Diocese: LE
Earliest Record: b. 8.1763; m. 5.1775
Missing Dates: b. 1.1781-1.1798, 1.1802-6.1807; m. 2.1776-1.1799, 2.1800-6.1807, 5.1830-11.1830

Parish Address: Rev. Peter Dunne, Adm. Tullow, Co. Carlow

Civil Parish: **Ullard**
Map Grid: 39
RC Parish: Graignamanagh, see Co. Kilkenny
Diocese: LE

Civil Parish: **Urglin**
Map Grid: 2
RC Parish: part Tullow; part Tinryland, see Tullowmagimma
Diocese: LE

Civil Parish: **Wells**
Map Grid: 29
RC Parish: Leighlinbridge, see Agha
Diocese: LE

Commercial and Social Directories

1788
Richard Lucas' *General Directory of the Kingdom of Ireland* contains lists of traders in Carlow, Old Leighlin, and Leighlinbridge. Also reprinted in *Ir. Gen.* 3 (10) (1965): 392-416.

1820
J. Pigot's *Commercial Directory of Ireland* contains information on the gentry, nobility, and traders in and around the town of Carlow.

1824
J. Pigot's *City of Dublin & Hibernian Provincial Directory* includes traders, nobility, gentry, and clergy lists for the towns of Carlow, Hacketstown, Leighlinbridge, and Tullow.

1839
T. Shearman's *New Commercial Directory for the Cities of Waterford and Kilkenny, Towns of Clonmel, Carrick-on-suir, New Ross, and Carlow*. Lists traders, gentry, etc.

1840
F. Kinder's *New Triennial & Commercial Directory for 1840, '41 & '42*. Contains lists of

traders, nobility, and others for Carlow town (rare volume).

1846

Slater's *National Commercial Directory of Ireland* lists nobility, clergy, traders, etc., in Carlow, Hacketstown, Leighlinbridge, Bagenalstown and Royal Oak, and Tullow.

1856

Slater's *Royal National Commercial Directory of Ireland* lists nobility, gentry, clergy, traders, etc., in Carlow, Hacketstown, Leighlinbridge, Bagenalstown, Borris and Royal Oak, and Tullow.

1870

Slater's *Directory of Ireland* contains trade, nobility, clergy lists for Bagenalstown and Leighlinbridge, Carlow, Hacketstown, and Tullow.

1881

Slater's *Royal National Commercial Directory of Ireland* contains lists of traders, clergy, nobility, and farmers in adjoining parishes of the towns of Bagenalstown and Leighlinbridge, Borris and Old Leighlin, Carlow and Graigue, Hacketstown, and Tullow.

1886

Francis Guy's *Postal Directory* of Munster lists gentry, clergy, traders, principal farmers, teachers, police, etc., in each postal district, and magistrates, clergy, and the professions for the whole county.

1894

Slater's *Royal National Commercial Directory of Ireland* lists traders, police, teachers, farmers, and private residents in each of the towns, villages, and parishes of the county.

Family History

Bewley, Sir Edward. *The Rudkins of the Co. Carlow.* Exeter, 1905; also *Gen.* N.S. 11 (1905): 145-62.

"The Blackneys of Ballyellen" (Co. Carlow). *Ir. Gen.* 3 (1957-58): 44-45, 116.

Copies of 1841 Census Returns for McCall Family. PRO film 5248 (10).

Cullen – Biographical Material. *Reportorium* 1 (1) (1955): 213-27.

"The Dillons of Carlow." *Ir. Gen.* 3 (7) (1962): 245-48.

"The Early Cullen Family." *Reportorium* 1 (1): 185-202.

"The Family of the MacMurrough Kavanaghs." *Carloviana* 1 (3) (1954): 13-16.

"The Vigors of Leighlinbridge." *Carloviana* 2 (8) (1980).

"Vigors Papers" (Burgage, Co. Carlow). *Anal. Hib.* 20 (302): 10.

Gravestone Inscriptions

A series of "Carlow Tombstone Inscriptions" has been published by Muintir Na Tire, Borris, Co. Carlow, 3 vols. to date.

Ballicopagan: Carlow Tombstone Inscriptions, Vol. 2.

Ballymurphy: Carlow Tombstone Inscriptions, Vol. 3.

Borris: Carlow Tombstone Inscriptions, Vol. 2.

Clonagoose: Carlow Tombstone Inscriptions, Vol. 2.

Kilcullen: Carlow Tombstone Inscriptions, Vol. 3.

Killedmond: Carlow Tombstone Inscriptions, Vol. 3.

Kiltennel: Carlow Tombstone Inscriptions, Vol. 3.

New Cemetery: Carlow Tombstone Inscriptions, Vol. 2.

Rathanna: Carlow Tombstone Inscriptions, Vol. 3.

St. Michaels: Carlow Tombstone Inscriptions, Vol. 1.

St. Mullins: Carlow Tombstone Inscriptions, Vol. 1.

Newspapers

The earliest paper published in Carlow is the *Carlow Morning Post* published from 1817. Newspapers from surrounding counties should be consulted for periods before its publication.

Title: *Carlow Independent*
Published in: Carlow, 1875-82
BL Holdings: 6.1879-1.1882

Title: *Carlow Morning Post*
Published in: Carlow, 1817-35
NLI Holdings: 12.1817-5.1820; 1.1828-1.1835
BL Holdings: 1-5 and 11-12.1833; 1.1834-1.1835

Title: *Carlow Nationalist and Leinster Times*
(continued as *Nationalist and Leinster Times* in 1885)
Published in: Carlow, 1883-current
NLI Holdings: 9.1833-in progress
BL Holdings : 9.1833-in progress

Title: *Carlow Post*
Published in: Carlow, 1853-78
NLI Holdings: odd numbers 1858-77
BL Holdings: 10.1853-5.1878

Title: *Carlow Sentinel*
Published in: Carlow, 1832-1920
NLI Holdings: 12.1847-11.1853; 11.1847-2.1881; 8.1883-8.1888; 1.1885-12.1913
BL Holdings: 1.1832-10.1820

Title: *Carlow Standard*
Published in: Carlow, 1832-32
NLI Holdings: 2 Jan.-19 Apr. 1832
BL Holdings: 2 Jan.-19 Apr. 1832

Title: *Carlow Vindicator*
Published in: Carlow, 1892-ca. 1898
BL Holdings: 1-2.1892

Title: *Carlow Weekly News*
Published in: Carlow, 1858-63
BL Holdings: 3.1858-10.1863

Title: *Leinster Reformer*
Published in: Carlow, 1839-41
NLI Holdings: 10.1839-7.1841
BL Holdings: 10.1839-7.1841

Wills and Administrations

A discussion of the types of records, where they are held, their availability, and value is given in the Wills section of the Introduction (p. xxxvii) The availability of prerogative wills, administrations, and marriage license records is also described in the relevant parts of the same section. Where available, published sources of these records are given in the Miscellaneous Sources section.

Pre-1858 Wills and Administrations

Prerogative Wills. see p. xli.
Consistorial Wills. County Carlow is mainly in the diocese of Leighlin with one parish in each of Ferns and Dublin diocese. The guide to Church of Ireland Parish records in this chapter shows the diocese to which each civil parish belonged. The wills of residents of each diocese were usually proven within that diocese (see Wills section for exceptions and those which might have survived).

Indexes. Leighlin (1642-1858). Those to 1800 have been published by Phillimore; Ferns – see Co. Wexford; Dublin – see Co. Dublin

Post-1858 Wills and Administrations

County Carlow was served by the District Registry of Kilkenny. The surviving records are kept in the PRO.

Marriage Licenses

Indexes. Leighlin and Ferns (1691-1845). PRO; GO ms. 612-17 (more complete); SLC film 100169-172. Dublin – see Co. Dublin

A

TOPOGRAPHICAL DICTIONARY

OF

IRELAND.

HAC

HAG

HACKETSTOWN, a market-town and parish, partly in the barony of BALLYNACOR, county of WICKLOW, but chiefly in that of RATHVILLY, county of CARLOW, and province of LEINSTER, 6¼ miles (S. E.) from Baltinglass, on the road from Wicklow to Carlow; containing 4434 inhabitants. In 1798 it sustained two attacks from the insurgent forces, one on the 25th of May, which was successfully repulsed by the yeomanry and a detachment of the Antrim militia; the other on the 25th of June, when a body of insurgents, amounting to several thousands, advanced against it at five in the morning. The garrison, consisting of 170, mostly yeomen, marched out to meet them, but, after a few volleys, were obliged to retreat, the cavalry by the road to Clonmore, and the infantry, 120 in number, into the barrack, where they maintained their position throughout the day behind a breastwork in the rear of it. The town was fired in several places by the rebels, who, after various ineffectual attempts to force an entrance to the barrack and a garrisoned house by which it was flanked, retreated, and in the night the garrison retired on Tullow. The town, which consists of 131 houses, is situated on a rising ground, below which flows a branch of the Slaney, and commands fine views. It is a constabulary police station, and has a penny post to Baltinglass, and a dispensary. A patent was granted in 1635, by Chas. I., to the Earl of Ormonde for a market on Wednesday and fairs on the Tuesday after Nov. 1st, and the Thursday after Trinity Sunday. The market is now held on Thursday, but only during the summer months from March to August, for the sale of meal and potatoes; and the fairs are on Jan. 13th, the first Thursday in Feb., March 12th, April 13th, May 4th, June 2nd, July 13th, Aug. 21st, Sept. 18th, Oct. 17th, the third Thursday in November, and Dec. 21st.

The parish comprises 31,570 statute acres, of which 11,954 are applotted under the tithe act: about one-sixth of the land is arable, nearly one-half pasture, and the remainder bog and waste; the latter is chiefly situated in the eastern part of the parish, and large blocks of granite are dispersed throughout. The principal seats are Woodside, the residence of S. Jones, Esq.; Ballyhelane, of J. Brownrigg, Esq.; and Ballasallagh House, of

VOL. II.—1

J. Hogier, Esq. The living is a rectory, in the diocese of Leighlin, episcopally united in 1693 to the vicarage of Haroldstown, and in the patronage of the Bishop: the tithes amount to £553. 16. 11., and of the benefice to £619. 15. 11. The glebe-house was erected in 1819, by a gift of £300 and a loan of £500 from the late Board of First Fruits; the glebe comprises 8½ acres. The church is a neat building, with a square embattled tower surmounted with pinnacles, which was erected and the church roofed anew, in 1820, by a gift of £600 and a loan of £500 from the late Board of First Fruits; it has recently been repaired by a grant of £559 from the Ecclesiastical Commissioners. In the churchyard is a monument to the memory of Capt. Hardy, who was killed in 1798 while defending the town. In the R. C. divisions it is the head of a union or district, comprising the parishes of Hacketstown and Moyne, and parts of Haroldstown, Clonmore, and Kiltegan; and containing chapels at Hacketstown, Killamote, and Knockanana. Near the church is a very neat place of worship for Wesleyan Methodists, recently erected. The parochial school is supported by the rector and a small payment from the scholars; and there is a national school in the R. C. chapel-yard.

HAGGARDSTOWN, a parish, in the barony of UPPER DUNDALK, county of LOUTH, and province of LEINSTER, 2 miles (S.) from Dundalk, on the road from Dublin to Belfast; containing, with the village of Blackrock, 1011 inhabitants. This parish comprises 1400¼ statute acres, according to the Ordnance survey, nearly the whole of which is very excellent land and under tillage. It is a rectory, in the diocese of Armagh, entirely impropriate in T. Fortescue, Esq.: the tithes amount to £178. 16. 3½. There is neither church, glebe-house, nor glebe. In the R. C. divisions it is the head of a union or district, also called Kilcurley, which comprises the parishes of Haggardstown, Heynstown, Ballybarrack, Philipstown, Dunbin, and part of Baronstown: a handsome chapel was erected here in 1833, and there is another at Baronstown. Here is a school of about 150 children; and there are some remains of the old church and also of an ancient castle.

B

Description of Hacketstown, County Carlow, from *A Topographical Dictionary of Ireland* by Samuel Lewis. London, 1837.

Miscellaneous Sources

Brophy, M. *Carlow Past & Present.* Carlow, 1888.

MacSuibhne, P. *'98 in Carlow.* Carlow, 1974.

MacSuibhne, P. *Clonegal Parish (Carlow).* Carlow, 1975.

Ryan, J. *History of Co. Carlow.* Dublin, 1834.

Research Sources and Services

Journals

Carlow Past & Present

Carloviana

Libraries and Information Sources

Carlow County Library (local history section has good selection of local interest publications), Dublin Street, Carlow Ph: (0503) 31126

Research Services

Carlow County Heritage Society (large collection of relevant reference sources, estate papers, etc.), 4 Sraid Ui Chinneide, Carlow Ph. (0503) 42399

St. Mullins Muintir Na Tire Historical Research, Mr. Pat Doyle, Newtown Borris, Co. Carlow

See also research services in Dublin, p. xliv

Societies

Old Carlow Society (publishes *Carloviana*), Mr. Sean O'Leary, Arus Na Greine, Montgomery Street, Carlow

County Carlow Heritage Society (publishes *Carlow Past & Present*), Mr. Michael Parcell, 4 Kennedy St., Carlow

West Wicklow Historical Society, Mrs. Maeve Baker, Ladystown, Rathvilly, Co. Carlow

BARONIES

1. CARLOW
2. RATHVILLY
3. IDRONE WEST
4. IDRONE EAST
5. FORTH
6. ST. MULLINS UPR.
7. ST. MULLINS LR.

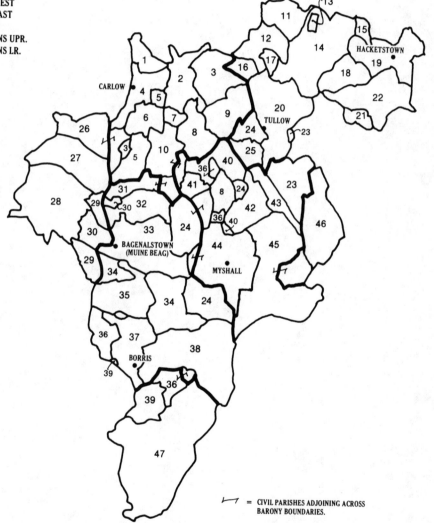

CIVIL PARISHES OF COUNTY CARLOW

⌐ = CIVIL PARISHES ADJOINING ACROSS
BARONY BOUNDARIES.

County Cavan

A Brief History

Originally part of the ancient Kingdom of Breifne, this inland Ulster county contains the towns of Cavan, Bailieborough, Virginia, Belturbet, and Ballyjamesduff.

This part of Breifne was ruled by the O'Reillys whose base was the town of Cavan. Other families associated with the county are (Mc)Brady, O'Mulleady, McGowan (often anglicized as Smith), O'Farrelly, McKiernan, O'Curry, O'Clery, and McIlduff. The O'Reillys retained control over the county for several centuries after the arrival of the Normans in Ireland in 1169. This was due both to the skill of their cavalry and also to the difficulty of the Cavan terrain with its forests, bogs, and lakes.

The boundaries of the county of Cavan were established by the English in 1584, and the county divided into baronies. Most of these were given to different branches of the O'Reillys, with two baronies controlled by the McKernons and McGowans. During the late sixteenth century the O'Reillys and their Cavan allies joined the rebellion of O'Neill against the English (see Co. Tyrone).

Following the defeat of the rebels the land in the county was confiscated and "planted" with English and Scottish settlers in 1609. This was done by granting portions of the county to adventurers (such as Auchmuty) who, in return, undertook to settle an agreed number of English or Scottish families. Pynnar's Survey of the progress of the Ulster plantation during its early stages shows that 286 families were planted in Cavan. The native population retained large parts of the county, however, as there were not enough settlers willing to come to the county.

In 1641 the Catholics in the county, again led by an O'Reilly, joined the Catholic Confederacy (see Co. Kilkenny) in rebellion against England. This rebellion was finally defeated by Cromwell in 1649 and was followed by further confiscations and granting of land in Cavan to English soldiers and others.

The relative proportions of people of Irish, Scottish, and English extraction can, in very general terms, be estimated from the relative proportions of Catholics, Presbyterians, and Episcopalians (Protestants) in the county. In 1861 when the census first collected this information, the respective proportions were 81, 4, and 15 percent respectively.

The county was badly affected by the Great Famine of 1845-47. In 1841 the population was 243,000, and by 1851 it had fallen by almost 30 percent to 174,000. Around 25,000 people died of starvation or disease between 1845 and 1850.

A typical cabin of a smallholder in the area of Ballinaught, County Cavan, in 1835. From *The Miseries and Beauties of Ireland* by Jonathan Binns. London, 1837.

Further thousands migrated to the cities or emigrated. The population of the county is now around 55,000.

Census and Census Substitutes

1612-13
"Survey of Undertakers Planted in Cavan." (names, acreages allotted, and account of the progress of each) *Hist. Mss. Comm. Rep.* (Hastings Mss.) 4 (1947): 159-82.

1630
Muster Roll, c. 1630. PRONI T934; BL add. ms. 4770; printed in *Breifne* 5 (18) (1977-78).

1664
Hearth Money Roll for Parishes of Killeshandra, Kildallan, Killenagh, Templeport, Tomregan. PRONI 184.

1703-04
"Robert Craigies Co. Cavan Tenants." *Ir. Anc.* 8 (2) (1976): 86-87 (parishes of Kildallan and Killeshandra).

1761
Poll-Book for Co. Cavan (lists 1,137 freeholders). PRONI T1522; Cavan Co. Library, Local Studies Dept.

1766
Protestants in Parishes of Kinawley, Lavey, Lurgan, Munterconnaught. RCB Library; SLC film 258517.

1796
See Co. Mayo 1796 (List of Catholics).

1802
"Protestants in Enniskeen Parish." *Ir. Anc.* 5 (2) (1973).

1813-21
List of Freeholders of Co. Cavan (over 5,000 names, addresses, situation of freeholds, etc., alphabetically listed within baronies). NLI IR94119 c2.

1814
"A Census of Protestant Children in Parishes of Drung and Larah, in CI Parish Register." *Ir. Anc.* 10 (1) (1978): 33-37.

AVERAGE SIZE OF FARMS.

The average size of farms in this barony is from eight to twelve acres. The junction of farms has not been very considerable, though every anxiety exists on the part of the landlords to effect it. "The truth is," said one of the witnesses, "the landlords allowed forty-shilling freeholders to become very numerous, and now they would wish to convert them into £10 freeholders."

Here, as elsewhere, the majority of those present concurred in thinking that small holdings produce more in proportion than large ones, and that a small farmer can afford to till his farm better than a large one. The tenants, however, pursue no judicious system of farming, nor is any encouragement given to improvement either by landlords or agents. The only method adopted to recruit exhausted land is to let it rest or lie idle, and leave it to the unassisted care of nature. The usual rotation of crops is as follows:—1st, potatoes; 2nd, oats; 3rd, flax with clover; 4th, clover; 5th and 6th, oats. Some take four or five crops of oats in succession.

About four years before we visited Omagh,

emigration had taken place on a considerable scale; latterly however, it had declined. The occupiers of farms will not give up their holdings on the condition of having their passage money to America paid for them; "they have found it so hard to obtain a living," said one of the witnesses, "that if they have any means of subsistence at all they will not give it up. They know what they have here, but don't know what they may meet with there." The principal emigration had taken place among the industrious classes—those who had acquired a little money. Though carried on to a considerable extent, it has been by no means sufficient to reduce the competition for labour. To produce this effect, it must be not only great but constant. The witnesses were unanimous in considering that if a free passage to America were offered to those who were not in possession of land, great numbers, including many young women, would gladly avail themselves of the opportunity of emigrating. One of the witnesses shrewdly but superficially observed, that emigration made little difference, adding that

A description of the economic condition of smallholders in the Barony of Omagh, Co. Tyrone, in 1835. From *The Miseries and Beauties of Ireland* by Jonathan Binns. London, 1837.

BARONY OF CASTLERAHAN.

No.	Name of Freeholder.	Place of Abode.	Situation of Freehold.	Name of Landlord.	Value of freehold	Name of Lives or other Tenure.	Place and Date of Registry.
1	Bell, Mathias	Derrylaghen.	Derrylaghen.	H. B. Wilson, Esq.		John Magill, Sen.	Cavan, 22d February, 1813.
2	Boylan, John	same.	same.	same.		Connor Maguire.	same. ....
3	Byers, Robert	same.	same.	same.		John Magill, Sen.	same. ....
4	Brady, Nicholas	Drummulard.	Drummulard	Colonel Sankey.		His Royal Highness the Duke of York.	Mt. Nugent, 22d Dec. 1813.
5	Brady, Patrick	Drummolats.	Drummolats.	same.		same.	same. ....
6	Brady, Patrick	same.	same.	same.		same.	same. ....
7	Brady, Michael	same.	same.	same.		same.	same. ....
8	Byers, James	same.	same.	same.		same.	same. ....
9	Brau, John	Carrickashall.	Carrickashall.	Colonel Sankey.		Duke of Clarence.	Cavan, 30th July, 1814.
10	Brey, Thomas	Cormeen.	Cormeen.	Lord Farnham.		James Clearkin, and James O'Neil.	Do. 5th August, 1814.
11	Brady, Charles	Killeilly.	Killeilly.	his own.	£7		same. ....
12	Brady, Andrew	Dromony.	Dromony.	Lord Farnham.		Chas. Coote, Jas. & Robt. Saunderson.	same. ....
13	Byrne, Charles	same.	same.	same.		Chas. Coote, Jas. Saunderson, & Lessee.	same. ....
14	Byers, Robert	Gallonbragh.	Gallonbragh.	same.		Hugh Porter.	same. ....
15	Blackstock, John	Cladangh.	Cladangh.	same.		George, John, and William Blackstock.	same. ....
16	Blackstock, Geo.	same.	same.	same.		same.	same. ....
17	Byers, Robt. Jun.	same.	same.	same.		William, David, and John Byers.	same. ....
18	Byers, William	same.	same.	same.		William, Esther, and William Byers.	same. ....
19	Byers, John	Galnabragher.	Galnabragher.	same.		Hugh Porter.	same. ....
20	Byers, Hugh	same.	same.	same.		same.	same. ....
21	Brady, Patrick	Cormeen.	Cormeen.	same.		James Clearkin.	same. ....
22	Byers, Robert	Tevenanan.	Tevenanan.	same.		Robert and John Byers.	same. ....
23	Brady, Owen	Lisnagerrill.	Lisnagerrill.	same.		Owen Brady, and Hugh and Phillip Tully.	same. ....
24	Burrowes, Hugh	Pottle.	Pottle.	same.		Thomas Hawthorn.	Do. 16th August, 1814.
25	Boylan, Michael	same.	same.	same.		same.	same. ....
26	Boylan, James	same.	same.	same.		same.	same. ....
27	Boylan, Matthew	same.	same.	same.		same.	same. ....
28	Boylan, James	same.	same.	same.		same.	same. ....
29	Boylan, Owen	same.	same.	same.		same.	same. ....
30	Boylan, Patrick	Pollareagh.	Pollareagh.	same.		Park. & Hugh Cosgrove, & Patt. Boylan.	same. ....
31	Blackstock, John	Cladangh.	Cladangh.	same.		George, William, and John Blackstock.	same. ....
32	Briady, Jeremiah	Drumiushillen.	Druminishillen.	Mr. Norton.		Abraham Strong.	Mt. Nugent, 21st Oct 1814.
33	Briady, James	same.	same.	same.		same.	same. ....
34	Briady, Thomas	same.	same.	same.		same.	same. ....
35	Briady, John	same.	same.	same.		same.	same. ....
36	Brady, John	Ballintemple.	Ballintemple.	same.		Charles Brady.	Do. 30th November, 1814.
37	Boylan, Matthew	Mullacaslin.	Mullacaslin.	same.		Duke of Clarence.	same. ....
38	Boylan, William	Tonylion.	Tonylion.	same.		same.	same c ....
39	Boylan, Bryan	same.	same.	same.		same.	same c ....
40	Boylan, Luke, Jun.	same.	same.	same.		same.	same c ....
41	Boylan, Luke	same.	same.	same.		same.	same c ....
42	Boylan, Phillip	same.	same.	same.		same.	same c ....
43	Boylan, Bryan	same.	same.	same.		same.	same c ....
44	Boylan, James	same.	same.	same.		same.	same c ....
45	Boylan, Bryan	same.	same.	same.		same.	same c ....

Extract from "A list of the Freeholders registered in County Cavan since First of January 1813 with those of £50 and £20 previously registered." NLI IR94119 c2

1821

Government Census Remnants: Parishes of Annageliffe, Ballymacue, Castlerahan, Castleterra, Crosserlough, Denn, Drumloman, Drung, Kilbride, Kilmore, Kinawley, Larah, Lavey, Lurgan, Mullagh, Munterconnaught. PRO; SLC films 597154-158.

1824-34

Tithe Applotment Survey (see p. xxvii).

1825

Registry of Freeholders. Jas. O'Brien: Cavan, 1826 (name, residence, and landlord on barony basis). Cavan Co. Library, Local Studies Dept.

1825-32

List of those Registered to Keep Arms (covers 1799-1833, but mainly 1825-32; gives over 1,500 names, alphabetically within baronies, residence, type of arms, etc.). NLI ILB 04 P12.

1841

Government Census Remnants: Killeshandra parish, except townlands of Corranea, Glebe, and Drumberry. PRO; SLC films 100831-838.

Pre-1861

An undated list of the inhabitants of the Barony of Castlerahan is contained in the church records of Kilinkere (list was probably compiled between 1842 and 1861).

1856-57

Griffith's Valuation (see p. xxvii)

1901

Census. PRO.

1911

Census. PRO.

Church Records

Church of Ireland
(Shows starting date of record)

Parish: **Annagelliffe**
Existing Records: b. 1804-75; m. 1804-75; d. 1804-75
Status: LC

Parish: **Arvagh**
Status: Lost

Parish: **Ashfield**
Existing Records: b. 1821-76; m. 1820-37; d. 1818-76
Missing Records: d. 1828-55
Status: PRO

Parish: **Bailieborough** or **Moybologue**
Existing Records: b. 1824-73; m. 1809-51; d. 1809-60
Status: LC

Parish: **Ballinanagh** (see Ballintemple and Kilmore)

Parish: **Ballintemple**
Status: Lost

Parish: **Ballyjamesduff**
Status: Lost

Parish: **Ballymachugh**
Existing Records: b. 1816-76; m. 1815-47; d. 1816-75
Status: LC

Parish: **Belturbet**
Existing Records: b. 1801-70; m. 1801-45; d. 1801-70
Status: LC

Parish: **Billis** (Virginia)
Existing Records: b. 1840-75
Status: LC

Parish: **Castleterra** (Ballyhaise)
Existing Records: b. 1800-77; m. 1785-1845; d. 1820-77
Status: LC

Parish: **Crosserlough** (see Kildrum Ferron)

Parish: **Denn**
Status: Lost

Parish: **Dernakesh**
Existing Records: b. 1837-75; m. 1837-45; d. 1837-75
Status: LC

Parish: **Derryheen**
Status: Lost

Parish: **Derrylane**
Status: Lost

Parish: **Dowra**
Status: Lost

Parish: **Drumgoon** (Cootehill)
Existing Records: b. 1802-75; m. 1802-45; d. 1858-75
Missing Records: b. 1815-24; m. 1815-24
Status: LC

Parish: **Drumlane**
Status: Lost

Parish: **Drumlummin**
Status: Lost

Parish: **Drung**
Existing Records: b. 1785-1875; m. 1785-1845; d. 1785-1875
Status: LC

Parish: **Enniskeen**
Status: Lost

Parish: **Kildallon** (Ballyconnell)
Existing Records: b. 1810-74; m. 1812-63; d. 1785-1875
Status: LC

Parish: **Kildrumferton**
Existing Records: b. 1801-75; m. 1801-52; d. 1803-75
Status: LC

Parish: **Killeshandra**
Existing Records: b. 1735-1866; m. 1735-1840; d. 1735-1875
Status: LC

Parish: **Killinagh**
Status: Lost

Parish: **Killinkere**
Status: Lost

Parish: **Killoughter** (Redhills)
Existing Records: b. 1827-75; m. 1827-45; d. 1827-75
Status: LC

Parish: **Kilmore** (Cavan)
Existing Records: b. 1702-1872; m. 1702-1845; d. 1702-1875
Status: LC

Parish: **Knockbride** (Ballieborough)
Exisiting Records: b. 1825-75; m. 1825-45; d. 1825-75
Status: LC

Parish: **Larah** (see Drung for early entries)
Status: Lost

Parish: **Lavey**
Status: Lost

Parish: **Mullagh**
Status: Lost

Parish: **Munterconnaught**
Status: Lost

Parish: **Quivy** (Beltmobet)
Existing Records: b. 1854-75
Status: LC

Parish: **St. Andrew** (Belturbet)
Status: Lost

Parish: **St. John** (Cloverhill)
Existing Records: b. 1860-76; m. 1861-76
Status: LC (copy)

Parish: **Scrabby**
Status: Lost

Parish: **Shercock**
Status: Lost

Parish: **Stradone** (see Larah)

Parish: **Swanlinbar**
Existing Records: b. 1798-1875; m. 1798-1875;
d. 1798-1875
Status: LC

Parish: **Templeport**
Existing Records: b. 1796-1874; m. 1796-1877;
d. 1797-1877
Status: LC (copy)

Parish: **Tomregan** (Ballyconnell)
Existing Records: b. 1797-1875; m. 1797-1845;
d. 1875-75
Status: LC

Parish: **Trinity, Holy**
Existing Records: 1842-77
Status: LC

Presbyterian

Parish: **Bailieborough**
Starting Date: 1852

Parish: **Ballyjamesduff**
Starting Date: 1845

Parish: **Bellasis**
Starting Date: 1845

Parish: **Cavan**
Starting Date: 1851

Parish: **Cootehill**
Starting Date: 1828

Parish: **Killeshandra**
Starting Date: 1743 (PHSA)

Roman Catholic

Civil Parish: **Annagelliff**
Map Grid: 13
RC Parish: Cavan
Diocese: KM
Earliest Record: b. 7.1812; m. 7.1812
Missing Dates: b. 7.1859-1.1860
Parish Address: Rev. Felim Kelly, Adm., Pres-
bytery, Farnham Street, Cavan

Civil Parish: **Annagh (1)**
Map Grid: 16
RC Parish: Anna West; also Anna East, see
below
Diocese: KM
Earliest Record: b. 1.1849; m. 1.1849; d. 1.1849
Parish Address: Rev. Edward P. Tully, PP, Bel-
turbet, Co. Cavan

Civil Parish: **Annagh (2)**
Map Grid: 16
RC Parish: Anna East
Diocese: KM
Earliest Record: b. 11.1845; m. 7.1847
Parish Address: Rev. Edward P. Tully, PP, Bel-
turbet, Co. Cavan

Civil Parish: **Bailieborough**
Map Grid: 23
RC Parish: Killann
Diocese: KM
Earliest Record: b. 1.1835; m. 1.1835
Missing Dates: b. 11.1849-1.1868; m. 2.1850-
1.1868
Parish Address: Rev. Michael Costello, PP,
Bailieboro, Co. Cavan

Civil Parish: **Ballintemple**
Map Grid: 26
RC Parish: Ballintemple
Diocese: KM
Earliest Record: b. 10.1862; m. 10.1862
Parish Address: Rev. Peter Smith, PP, Ballin-
temple, Ballinagh, Co. Cavan

Civil Parish: **Ballymachugh**
Map Grid: 28
RC Parish: Drumlumman South and Bal-
lymachugh
Diocese: AD
Earliest Record: b. 11.1837; m. 12.1837; d.
12.1837
Missing Dates: b. 8.1873-5.1857; m. 6.1873-
2.1876; d. 9.1869-2.1876
Parish Address: Rev. Patrick Claffey, PP, Car-
rick, Finea, Mullingar, Co. Westmeath

Civil Parish: **Castlerahan**
Map Grid: 32
RC Parish: Castlerahan
Diocese: KM
Earliest Record: b. 2.1752; m. 9.1751
Missing Dates: b. 7.1771-2.1773, 11.1776-
11.1814, 8.1820-10.1828, 5.1841-8.1854;
m. 6.1771-2.1773, 2.1775-11.1814, 6.1820-
5.1832, 11.1841-8.1855
Parish Address: Rev. Michael J. Kelly, PP,
Knocktemple, Virginia, Co. Cavan

Civil Parish: **Castleterra**
Map Grid: 11
RC Parish: Castleterra (Castletara)
Diocese: KM
Earliest Record: b. 6.1763; m. 7.1763
Missing Dates: b. 6.1809-4.1862; m. 4.1793-
10.1808; ends 6.1809
Parish Address: Rev. A. McGrath, PP, Bal-
lyhaise, Cavan, Co. Cavan

Civil Parish: **Crosserlough**
Map Grid: 30
RC Parish: Crosser Lough
Diocese: KM
Earliest Record: b. 10.1843; m. 10.1843;
d. 10.1843
Parish Address: Rev. Patrick McManus, PP,
Kilnaleck, Co. Cavan

Civil Parish: **Denn**
Map Grid: 14
RC Parish: Denn
Diocese: KM
Earliest Record: b. 10.1856; m. 10.1856
Missing Dates: b. many gaps; m. ends 10.1858
Parish Address: Rev. Patrick E. Brady, PP,
Crosskeys, Co. Cavan

Civil Parish: **Drumgoon**
Map Grid: 19
RC Parish: Drumgoon
Diocese: KM
Earliest Record: b. 2.1829; m. 3.1829
Parish Address: Rev. Thomas O'Dowd, PP,
Cootehill, Co. Cavan

Civil Parish: **Drumlane**
Map Grid: 6
RC Parish: Drumlane
Diocese: KM
Earliest Record: b. 1.1836; m. 9.1870
Parish Address: Rev. Joseph Young, PP,
Milltown, Belturbet, Co. Cavan

Civil Parish: **Drumlumman**
Map Grid: 27
RC Parish: Mullahoran (Loughduff and Drum-
lumman North)
Diocese: AD
Earliest Record: b. 1.1859; m. 1.1859; d. 2.1859
Parish Address: Rev. Mark Mimnagh, PP,
Loughduff, Co. Cavan

Civil Parish: **Drumreilly** (see Co. Leitrim)
Map Grid: 4
RC Parish: Drumreilly, see Co. Leitrim
Diocese: AD

Civil Parish: **Drung**
Map Grid: 17
RC Parish: Killesherdany and Drung
Diocese: KM
Earliest Record: b. 6.1803; m. 7.1803
Missing Dates: b. 11.1814-11.1826, 4.1849-
10.1855, 2.1860-1.1867; m. 1.1814-1.1835,
5.1835-1843, 4.1849-10.1855
Parish Address: Rev. Torlach O'Reilly, PP,
Drung, Co. Cavan

Civil Parish: **Enniskeen** (see also Co. Meath)
Map Grid: 24
RC Parish: Kingscourt and Enniskeen
Diocese: ME
Earliest Record: b. 10.1838; m. 8.1838; d. 9.1846
Missing Dates: 8.1854-1.1864
Parish Address: Rev. Richard Teehan, PP,
Parochial House, Kingscourt, Co. Cavan

Civil Parish: **Kilbride**
Map Grid: 29
RC Parish: Kilbride, see Co. Meath
Diocese: ME

Civil Parish: **Kildallan**
Map Grid: 7
RC Parish: Kildallan and Tomregan
Diocese: KM
Earliest Record: b. 4.1867; m. 1.1867
Parish Address: Rev. Thomas A. Tiernan, PP, Kildallan, Belturbet, Co. Cavan

Civil Parish: **Kildrumsherdan**
Map Grid: 18
RC Parish: Killesherdiney, see Drung
Diocese: KM

Civil Parish: **Killashandra**
Map Grid: 8
RC Parish: Killeshandra
Diocese: KM
Earliest Record: b. 1.1835; m.1.1835; d. 1. 1835
Missing Dates: b. 8.1844-3.1845; m. 9.1840-8.1849; d. 5.1852-9.1868
Parish Address: Rev. James Carroll, PP, Killeshandra, Co. Cavan

Civil Parish: **Killinagh**
Map Grid: 1
RC Parish: Killinagh and Blacklion
Diocese: KM
Earliest Record: b. 3.1867; m. 1.1867
Parish Address: Rev. Eugene Dowd, PP, Blacklion, Co. Cavan

Civil Parish: **Killinkere**
Map Grid: 31
RC Parish: Killinkere (Mullagh to 1842)
Diocese: KM
Earliest Record: b. 5.1766; m. 12.1766
Missing Dates: b. 10.1790-1.1842, 4.1862-3.1864; m. 8.1789-1.1842, 11.1861-6.1864
Parish Address: Rev. Patrick McCabe, PP, Killinkere, Virginia, Co. Cavan

Civil Parish: **Kilmore**
Map Grid: 12
RC Parish: Kilmore
Diocese: KM
Earliest Record: b. 5.1859; m. 5.1859; d. 5.1859

Parish Address: Rev. Anthony Smith, PP, Drumcor, Crossdoney, Co. Cavan

Civil Parish: **Kinawley**
Map Grid: 3
RC Parish: Kinawley, see Co. Fermanagh
Diocese: KM

Civil Parish: **Knockbride**
Map Grid: 21
RC Parish: Knockbride
Diocese: KM
Earliest Record: b. 5.1835; m. 1.1835; d. 1.1835
Parish Address: Rev. Vincent Duffy, Tunnyduff, Bailieboro, Co. Cavan

Civil Parish: **Larah**
Map Grid: 20
RC Parish: Larah, Upper and Lower
Diocese: KM
Earliest Record: b. 5.1876
Parish Address: Rev. Michael O'Reilly, PP, Laragh, Stradone, Co. Cavan

Civil Parish: **Lavey**
Map Grid: 15
RC Parish: Lavey
Diocese: KM
Earliest Record: 1.1867
Parish Address: Rev. Sean E.T. O'Reilly, PP, Lavey, Stradone, Co. Cavan

Civil Parish: **Loughan** or **Castlekeeran** (see Co. Meath)
Map Grid: 36
RC Parish: Loughan or Castlekeeran, see Co. Meath
Diocese: ME

Civil Parish: **Lurgan**
Map Grid: 33
RC Parish: Lurgan
Diocese: KM
Earliest Record: b. 1.1755; m. 2.1755
Missing Dates: b. with gaps, 8.1795-11.1821; m. 8.1770-1.1773, 9.1780-11.1821
Parish Address: Rev. Augustine H. Leaden, PP, Virginia, Co. Cavan

Civil Parish: **Moybolgue**
Map Grid: 25

RC Parish: Moybolgue, see Co. Meath
Diocese: KM

Civil Parish: **Mullagh**
Map Grid: 34
RC Parish: Mullagh (see Killinkere for earlier
　　Records)
Diocese: KM
Earliest Record: b. 6.1842; m. 7.1842; d. 9.1842
Missing Dates: d. ends 2.1857
Parish Address: Rev. Patrick Morris, PP, Mul-
　　lagh, Kells, Co. Meath

Civil Parish: **Munterconnaught**
Map Grid: 35
RC Parish: see Castlerahan
Diocese: KM

Civil Parish: **Scrabby**
Map Grid: 9
RC Parish: Granard, see Co. Longford
Diocese: AD

Civil Parish: **Shercock**
Map Grid: 22
RC Parish: Killann, see Bailieborough
Diocese: KM

Civil Parish: **Templeport**
Map Grid: 2
RC Parish: Templeport; part Glengenlin, see
　　Killinagh
Diocese: KM
Earliest Record: b. 9.1836; m. 11.1836; d. 2.1827
Missing Dates: d. ends 12.1845
Parish Address: Rev. Thomas Murray, PP, St.
　　Mogue's, Ballyconnell, Co. Cavan

Civil Parish: **Tomregan** (see also Co. Fer-
　　managh)
Map Grid: 5
RC Parish: Tomregan, see Kildallan
Diocese: KM

Civil Parish: **Urney**
Map Grid: 10
RC Parish: Cavan; see Annagelliff
Diocese: KM

Commercial and Social Directories

1824
J. Pigot's *City of Dublin & Hibernian Provin-
cial Directory* includes lists of traders,
nobility, gentry, and clergy in Bailieboro,
Ballyconnell, Belturbet, Cavan, Cootehill,
Killeshandra, and Kingscourt.

1846
Slater's *National Commercial Directory of
Ireland* lists nobility, clergy, traders, etc., in
Bailieborough, Ballyconnell, Belturbet,
Cavan, Cootehill, Killeshandra, and
Kingscourt.

1852
Henderson's *Belfast and Province of Ulster
Directory* has lists of inhabitants, traders, etc.,
in and around Cavan town.

1854
Further edition of above covers the towns of
Bailieboro, Belturbet, Cavan, and Cootehill.
Further issues in 1856, 1858, 1861, 1863,
1865, 1868, 1870, 1877, 1880, 1884, 1890,
1894, 1900.

1856
Slater's *Royal National Commercial Directory of Ireland* lists nobility, gentry, clergy,
traders, etc., in Bailieboro, Ballyconnell, Belturbet, Cavan, Cootehill, Killeshandra, and
King's Court.

1870
Slater's *Directory of Ireland* contains trade,
nobility, and clergy lists for Bailieborough,
Ballyconnell, Bawnboy, Swanlinbar, Bal-
lyjamesduff, Belturbet, Cavan, Cootehill,
Killeshandra, and Kingscourt.

1881
Slater's *Royal National Commercial Directory of Ireland* contains lists of traders, clergy, nobility, and farmers in adjoining
parishes of the towns of Bailieborough,
Kingscourt, Ballyconnell, Bawnboy, Swanlinbar, Ballyjamesduff, Belturbet, Cavan,
Cootehill, and Killeshandra.

1894

Slater's *Royal National Directory of Ireland* lists traders, police, teachers, farmers, and private residents in each of the towns, villages, and parishes of the county.

Family History

Adams, W. *A Genealogical History of Adams of Cavan.* London, 1903.

Historical and Genealogical Records of the Coote Family. Lausanne, 1900.

"The Babingtons of Cavan." *Breifne* 5 (21) (1982-83).

"Baker of Co. Cavan." Pedigree in *Swanzy Notebooks.* RCB Library, Dublin.

"Burrows of Stradone." Pedigree in *Swanzy Notebooks.* RCB Library, Dublin.

"Colkin of Cavan." Pedigree in *Swanzy Notebooks.* RCB Library, Dublin.

"Some Account of the Family of French of Belturbet." *Ulster J. Arch.* 2nd ser. 8 (1902): 155-60.

Swanzy, H.B. *The Families of French of Belturbet and Nixon of Fermanagh.* Dublin, 1908.

"Humphreys of Knockfad, Co. Cavan." *Ir. Anc.* 13 (2) (1981): 88-89.

Copies of 1841 Census returns of Keaney family. PRO film 5248(6).

"Kernan of Ned, Co. Cavan." *Ir. Gen.* 4 (4) (1971): 323-30.

Kernan, J.D. *Notes on the Descendants of John Kernan of Ned, Co. Cavan.* 3rd ed. Englewood, N.J., 1969.

"Moore of Moyne Hall." Pedigree in *Swanzy Notebooks.* RCB Library, Dublin.

"Moore of Tullyvin." Pedigree in *Swanzy Notebooks.* RCB Library, Dublin.

Lyons, J. *Historical Sketch of the Nugent Family.* Ladestown, 1853.

"Nugent Papers" (Mount Nugent, Co. Cavan). *Anal. Hib.* 20: 125-215.

"Parr of Co. Cavan." Pedigree in *Swanzy Notebooks.* RCB Library, Dublin.

"Perrott of Co. Cavan." Pedigree in *Swanzy Notebooks.* RCB Library, Dublin.

"Wilton of Co. Cavan." Pedigree in *Swanzy Notebooks.* RCB Library, Dublin.

Gravestone Inscriptions

Callowhill: *Breifne* 5 (21) (1982-83).

Castlerahan: *Breifne* 2 (3) (1925-26).

Clonoe (St. Michaels): *Seanchas Ardmhacha* 10 (1) (1980/81): 63-84.

Crosserlough: *Breifne* 5 (17) (1976).

Denn: *Breifne* 2 (2) (1924).

Darver: *Breifne* 1 (3) (1922).

Drumlane: *Breifne* 5 (19) (1979).

Kildrumfertan: *Breifne* 2 (8) (1965).

Lurgan: *Breifne* 1 (4) (1961).

Magherintemple: *Breifne* 2 (6) (1963).

Munterconnacht: *Breifne* 3 (1) (1927-28).

Templeport: *Breifne* 4 (14) (1971).

Newspapers

Title: *Anglo-Celt*
Published in: Cavan, 1846-current
Note: Breaks in publication between 1847 and 1864
NLI Holdings: 2.1846-4.1858; 12.1864-11.1873; 1.1885-12.1886; 1.1887-in progress
BL Holdings: 2.1846-4.1858; 12.1864-11.1869; 7.1870-11.1873; 5.1889-12.1919; 1.1921-in progress

Title: *Cavan Observer*
Published in: Cavan, 1857-64
BL Holdings: 7.1857-10.1864 (except 1-6.1858)

Title: *Cavan Weekly News*
Published in: Cavan, 1864-1907
NLI Holdings: 2.1871-12.1895; odd nos. 1898; 12.1904-7.1907; 7-12.1909
BL Holdings: 12.1864-7.1907

Wills and Administrations

A discussion of the types of records, where they are held, their availability and value is given in the Wills section of the Introduction. The availability of prerogative wills, administrations, and marriage license records is also described in the relevant parts of the same section. Where available, published sources of these records are given in the Miscellaneous Sources section.

Pre-1858 Wills and Administrations

Prerogative Wills. see p. xli.

Consistorial Wills. County Cavan is mainly in the Diocese of Kilmore, with three parishes in each of the dioceses of Meath and Ardagh. The guide to Catholic parish records in this chapter shows the diocese to which each civil parish belonged. The wills of residents of each diocese were usually proven within that diocese (see the Wills section for exceptions). The following records survive:

Wills. See p. xxxvii.

Abstracts. The Upton papers contain abstracts of Cavan family wills, RIA Library; The Swanzy Will Abstracts – cover mainly Clogher and Kilmore, RCB Library.

Indexes. Kilmore Fragments (1682-1858) published by Smyth-Wood.

Post-1858 Wills and Administrations

County Cavan was served by the District Registry of Cavan. The surviving records are kept in the PRO.

Marriage Licenses

Indexes. Kilmore, Ardagh, and Meath (1691-1845). PRO; SLC films 100869

Miscellaneous Sources

"The Management of the Farnham Estates (Co. Cavan) During the Nineteenth Century." *Breifne* 4 (16) (1973-75): 531-60.

O'Connell, P. *The Diocese of Kilmore, its History and Antiquities.* 1937.

Smyth, T.S. *The Civil History of the Town of Cavan.* Cavan, 1934.

"Sources for Cavan Local History." *Breifne* 5 (18) (1977-78): 1.

"The Volunteer Companies of Ulster 1778-1793, III Cavan." *Irish Sword* 7 (1906): 308-09 (officers' names only).

Research Sources and Services

Journals

Breifne (published by Breifne Historical Society, 1958-present)
Heart of Breifne (published by Mrs. Anna Sexton, Grousehall Post Office, Bailieboro, Co. Cavan)

Libraries and Information Sources

Cavan County Library, Farnham Street, Cavan Ph: (049) 31799

Research Services

See Research Services in Dublin, p. xliv

Societies

Breifne Historical Society (publishers of *Breifne*), Mrs. B. Foy, Swellan Lr., Cavan

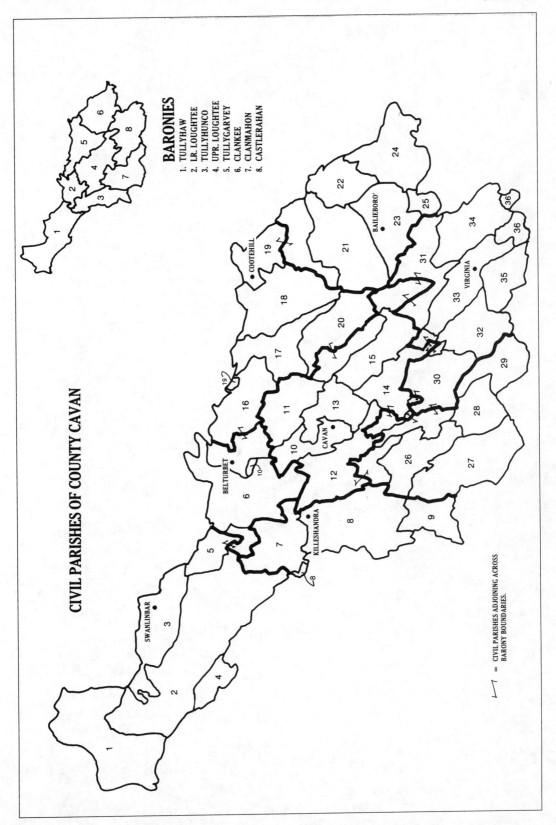

CIVIL PARISHES OF COUNTY CAVAN

BARONIES

1. TULLYHAW
2. LR. LOUGHTEE
3. TULLYHUNCO
4. UPR. LOUGHTEE
5. TULLYGARVEY
6. CLANKEE
7. CLANMAHON
8. CASTLERAHAN

⌐⌐ = CIVIL PARISHES ADJOINING ACROSS
BARONY BOUNDARIES.

County Clare

A Brief History

This Munster county occupies the area between the lower parts of the Shannon River and the west coast. It contains the towns of Ennis, Kilkee, Killaloe, and Kilrush.

In the old Gaelic system the county was part of the Kingdom of Thomond. The major families were those of O'Loughlin, McNamara, and McMahon, and the chief family was the O'Briens. Together, these families are generally referred to as the Dalcassian families.

The O'Briens were a major force in Thomond from earliest times. The Danish vikings raided this county on many occasions during the ninth to eleventh centuries and established settlements in Limerick and on Inniscattery Island. They were finally defeated early in the eleventh century by one of the most famous of the O'Briens, Brian Boru, who also led the Irish army which defeated the powerful Danes of Dublin at the Battle of Clontarf in 1014 (see p. xlvii).

Following the Norman invasion the area was granted to Norman knights, but the Clare chieftains kept them from holding any substantial power in the county. In 1275 it was granted to Thomas de Clare who attempted to take control of the county but was totally defeated by the O'Briens. The O'Briens were later made Earls of Thomond and thereby remained the major force in the county for centuries. Despite the failure of Thomas de Clare or his successor to take control of the territories granted to them in Thomond, the county was nevertheless named after the family when its boundaries were established by the English administration in 1565. Initially it was made part of Connaught, but in 1602 the county was joined with the province of Munster.

The major Norman settlements in the county were at Clare town and at Bunratty. The Norman inhabitants of these towns were either gradually expelled from the county by the Gaelic families, or else adopted the Irish way of life. The Norman castle at Bunratty, for instance, was captured by the O'Briens in 1355 and held by them until the seventeenth century. In the fifteenth century the O'Briens rebuilt the castle on the same site and this castle, restored and refurbished, is now open to the public.

Following the defeat of the 1641 rebellion of the Catholic Confederacy (see p. xlvii and Co. Kilkenny), this county was one of the counties which were set aside to accomodate the "delinquent proprietors," i.e., those proprietors whose land was confiscated because they did not actively oppose the rebellion. Parts of the holdings of the existing Clare landholders were confiscated to accommodate these newcomers.

The county was badly affected by the Great

Famine of 1845-47. The population was 286,000 in 1841 and by 1851 had been reduced to 212,000. Over 50,000 people died between 1845 and 1850 and thousands emigrated, many to Australia. Between 1851 and 1855, for instance, over 37,000 people emigrated from the county. The decline in population continued for the remainder of the century so that by 1891 the population was 124,000. It is currently around 88,000.

County Clare has one of the best local sources of family history research in the form of the Clare Heritage Centre located in Corofin. This center has indexed all of the church records in the county and provides a research service (see Research Sources and Services section).

Census and Census Substitutes

1641

Proprietors of Co. Clare (Book of Survey & Distribution). PRO; NLI ms. 963; also published by Irish Manuscripts Commission, 1967.

1659

"Census" of Ireland. Edited by S. Pender. Dublin: Stationery Office, 1939.

1666-8

Grantees of Co. Clare (same source as 1641 proprietors).

1745

List of Voters at the Parliamentary Election. TCD ms. 2059.

1778

"Extracts from Minute Book of Ennis Volunteers" (with index of those named). *N. Munster Antiq. J.* 6 (4) (1952): 143-151.

1799

"Gentlemen of the Counties of Clare and Limerick Who Were in Favour of the Union in 1799." *Ir. Anc.* 14 (1) (1982): 30-32.

1814-43

Tithe Applotment Survey (see p. xxvii).

1829

List of Freeholders. GO ms. 443; NLI P5556.

1834

Rental of the Roxton Estate, Inchiquin Barony. PRO film 5764.

1866

Census of Kilfenora Catholic Parish (included in parish record see Church Records section).

1901

Census. PRO.

1911

Census. PRO.

Church Records

Church of Ireland
(Shows starting date of records)

Parish: **Ballyvaughan** (see Rathbourney)

Parish: **Clare Abbey**
Status: Lost

Parish: **Clare** (see Clare Abbey)

Parish: **Clondegad**
Status: Lost

Parish: **Clonlea**
Status: Lost

Parish: **Drumcliff**
Existing Records: b. 1744; m. 1744; d. 1744
Missing Dates: b. 1749-84; m. 1749-84; d. 1749-84
Status: LC and PRO

Parish: **Feakle**
Status: Lost

Parish: **Kildysart**
Status: Lost

Parish: **Kilfarboy**
Status: Lost

Parish: **Kilfenora**
Status: Lost

Parish: **Kilfiddane** (see Kilmurry)

Parish: **Kilfieragh** (also see Kilrush)
Existing Dates: b. 1842; m. 1843; d. 1843
Status: PRO

Parish: **Kilfinaghty**
Status: Lost

Parish: **Kilfintinan** (no records)

Parish: **Kilkeedy**
Status: Lost

Parish: **Killaloe**
Existing Records: b. 1679; m. 1672; d. 1783
Status: LC and PRO

Parish: **Killard**
Status: Lost

Parish: **Killinaboy**
Status: Lost

Parish: **Killonaghan** (see Rathbourney)

Parish: **Kilmaley**
Status: Lost

Parish: **Kilmanaheen**
Status: Lost

Parish: **Kilmurry**
Status: Lost

Parish: **Kilnasoolagh** (Newmarket)
Existing Records: b. 1731; m. 1731; d. 1731
Status: LC and PRO

Parish: **Kilrush**
Existing Records: Volume 1 contains some
    loose leaves of entries back to 1741; b. 1773;
    m. 1773; d. 1776
Status: LC and PRO

Parish: **Kilseily**
Status: Lost

Parish: **Kiltinanlea**
Status: Lost

Parish: **Newquay**
Status: Lost

Parish: **O'Briensbridge**
Status: Lost

Parish: **Ogonneloe**
Existing Records: b. 1807; m. 1807; d. 1836
Status: LC and PRO

Parish: **Quin**
Status: Lost

Parish: **Rathbourney**
Status: Lost

Parish: **Scarriff** (see Tomgraney)

Parish: **Sixmilebridge** (see Kilfinaghty)

Parish: **Tomgraney**
Status: Lost

Parish: **Tulloh**
Status: Lost

Roman Catholic

Civil Parish: **Abbey**
Map Grid: 3
RC Parish: see Oughtmanna
Diocese: KF

Civil Parish: **Bunratty**
Map Grid: 76
RC Parish: Newmarket, see Kilnasoolagh
Diocese: KL

Civil Parish: **Carron**
Map Grid: 10
RC Parish: Carron
Diocese: KF

Earliest Record: b. 10.1853; m. 11.1856
Parish Address: Rev. J. Keogh, PP, Carron, Co.
   Clare

Civil Parish: **Clareabbey**
Map Grid: 45
RC Parish: Clareabbey
Diocese: KL
Earliest Record: b. 12.1853; m. 1.1854
Parish Address: Rev. M. McInerney, PP,
   Clarecastle, Co. Clare

Civil Parish: **Clondagad**
Map Grid: 46
RC Parish: Clondagad
Diocese: KL
Earliest Record: b. 10.1846; m. 11.1846
Parish Address: Rev. J. O'Leary, PP, Ballyna-
   cally, Co. Clare

Civil Parish: **Clonlea**
Map Grid: 49
RC Parish: see Killuran
Diocese: KL

Civil Parish: **Clonloghan**
Map Grid: 71
RC Parish: Newmarket, see Kilnasoolagh
Diocese: KL

Civil Parish: **Clonrush**
Map Grid: 38
RC Parish: Clonrush
Diocese: KL
Earliest Record: b. 7.1846; m. 1.1846
Parish Address: Rev. T. McNamara, PP,
   Mountshannon, Co. Clare

Civil Parish: **Clooney (1)** (near Rath)
Map Grid: 18
RC Parish: Ennistymon, see Kilmanaheen
Diocese: KF

Civil Parish: **Clooney (2)** (near Tulla)
Map Grid: 30
RC Parish: see Quin

Civil Parish: **Doora**
Map Grid: 31
RC Parish: Doora
Diocese: KL

Earliest Record: b. 3.1821; m. 1.1823
Parish Address: Rev. P. Meehan, PP, Barefield,
   Ennis, Co. Clare

Civil Parish: **Drumcliff**
Map Grid: 43
RC Parish: Ennis
Diocese: KL
Earliest Record: b. 3.1841; m. 4.1837
Parish Address: Rev. B. O'Donoghue, Adm.,
   Cathedral Presbytery, Ennis, Co. Clare

Civil Parish: **Drumcreehy**
Map Grid: 2
RC Parish: Glanaragh
Diocese: KF
Earliest Record: b. 9.1854
Parish Address: Rev. W. Rooney, PP, Bal-
   lyvaughan, Co. Clare

Civil Parish: **Drumline**
Map Grid: 72
RC Parish: Newmarket, see Kilnasoolagh
Diocese: KL

Civil Parish: **Dysert**
Map Grid: 25
RC Parish: Dysert and Ruan
Diocese: KL
Earliest Record: b. 8.1845; m. 7.1846
Parish Address: Rev. John Donnelly, PP,
   Dysart, Corofin, Co. Clare

Civil Parish: **Feakle (1)**
Map Grid: 33
RC Parish: Feakle Lower; also Killanena, see
   below
Diocese: KL
Earliest Record: b. 4.1860; m. 9.1860
Parish Address: Rev. M. O'Donoghue, PP,
   Feakle, Co. Clare

Civil Parish: **Feakle (2)**
Map Grid: 33
RC Parish: Killanena (Caher Feakle)
Diocese: KL
Earliest Record: b. 2.1842; m. 1.1842
Missing Dates: m. 2.1861-11.1862
Parish Address: Rev. William Teehan, Kil-
   lanena, Co. Clare

Civil Parish: **Feenagh**
Map Grid: 73
RC Parish: Six-Mile-Bridge, see Kilfinaghta
Diocese: KL

Civil Parish: **Gleninagh**
Map Grid: 1
RC Parish: Glanaragh, see Drumcreehy
Diocese: KF

Civil Parish: **Inagh**
Map Grid: 24
RC Parish: Inagh
Diocese: KL
Earliest Record: b. 2.1850; m. 4.1850
Missing Records: m. 7.1865-9.1865
Parish Address: Rev. Patrick Ryan, PP, Inagh, Co. Clare

Civil Parish: **Inishcronan**
Map Grid: 27
RC Parish: Crusheen
Diocese: KL
Earliest Record: b. 2.1860
Parish Address: Rev. E. Vaughan, PP, Crusheen, Ennis, Co. Clare

Civil Parish: **Inishcaltra**
Map Grid: 38
RC Parish: see Clonrush
Diocese: KL

Civil Parish: **Kilballyowen**
Map Grid: 57
RC Parish: Cross or Kilballyowen
Diocese: KL
Earliest Record: b. 2.1878; m. 3.1878
Parish Address: Rev. J. Neylon, PP, Cross, Co. Clare

Civil Parish: **Kilchreest**
Map Grid: 63
RC Parish: Clondegad, see Clondagad
Diocese: KL

Civil Parish: **Kilconry**
Map Grid: 75
RC Parish: Newmarket, see Kilnasoolagh
Diocese: KL

Civil Parish: **Kilcorney**
Map Grid: 9
RC Parish: see Carron
Diocese: KF

Civil Parish: **Kilfarboy**
Map Grid: 39
RC Parish: Milltown Malbay
Diocese: KL
Earliest Record: b. 11.1831; m. 11.1856
Missing Dates: m. 12.1858-2.1859
Parish Address: Rev. Jerome Holohan, PP, Milltown Malbay, Co. Clare

Civil Parish: **Kilfearagh**
Map Grid: 56
RC Parish: Kilkee
Diocese: KL
Earliest Record: b. 3.1869
Parish Address: Rev. Canon H. Kenny, PP, Kilkee, Co. Clare

Civil Parish: **Kilfenora**
Map Grid: 16
RC Parish: Kilfenora
Diocese: KL
Earliest Record: b. 6.1836; m. 12.1865
Missing Dates: b. 5.1847-9.1854
Parish Address: Rev. P. Vaughan, PP, Kilfenora, Co. Clare

Civil Parish: **Kilfiddane**
Map Grid: 62
RC Parish: Kilfidane
Diocese: KL
Earliest Record: b. 8.1868; m. 1.1869
Parish Address: Rev. Kevin Hogan, PP, Cranny, Kilrush, Co. Clare

Civil Parish: **Kilfinaghta**
Map Grid: 74
RC Parish: Six-Mile-Bridge
Diocese: KL
Earliest Record: b. 12.1828; m. 1.1829
Missing Dates: b. 8.1839-12.1839; m. 8.1839-5.1904, 12.1864-2.1865
Parish Address: Rev. R. Carey, PP, Six-Mile-Bridge, Co. Clare

Civil Parish: **Kilfintinan**
Map Grid: 77
RC Parish: Cratloe
Diocese: LK
Earliest Record: b. 11.1802; m. 1.1822
Parish Address: Rev. D. Costello, PP, Cratloe, Co. Clare

Civil Parish: **Kilkeedy**
Map Grid: 20
RC Parish: Kilkeedy
Diocese: KL
Earliest Record: b. 2.1833; m. 2.1871
Missing Dates: b. 1866-1870
Parish Address: Rev. Charles Navin, PP, Tubber, Gort, Co. Galway

Civil Parish: **Killadysert**
Map Grid: 64
RC Parish: Kildysert
Diocese: KL
Earliest Record: b. 7.1829; m. 1.1867
Parish Address: Rev. Flannan Twomey, PP, Kildysart, Co. Clare

Civil Parish: **Killaloe**
Map Grid: 53
RC Parish: Killaloe
Diocese: KL
Earliest Record: b. 5.1828; m. 2.1829
Parish Address: Rev. Canon P. Clune, PP, Killaloe, Co. Clare

Civil Parish: **Killard**
Map Grid: 41
RC Parish: Kilkee, see Kilfearagh
Diocese: KL

Civil Parish: **Killaspuglonane**
Map Grid: 14
RC Parish: Liscannor, see Kilmacrehy
Diocese: KF

Civil Parish: **Killeany**
Map Grid: 8
RC Parish: Killeany, Killymoon, and Killileagh
Diocese: KF
Earliest Record: b. 6.1854; m. 1.1860
Parish Address: Rev. E. Kelly, PP, Lisdoonvarna, Co. Clare

Civil Parish: **Killeely** (see also Co. Limerick)
Map Grid: 78
RC Parish: Parteen and Meelick
Diocese: LK
Earliest Record: b. 9.1831; m. 7.1814
Missing Dates: m. 12.1819-2.1821; 1.1836-2.1847
Parish Address: Rev. Gerard M. Griffin, PP, Parteen, Co. Limerick

Civil Parish: **Killilagh**
Map Grid: 12
RC Parish: see Killeany
Diocese: KF

Civil Parish: **Killimer**
Map Grid: 65
RC Parish: Killimer
Diocese: KL
Earliest Record: b. 1.1859; m. 2.1859
Parish Address: Rev. G. Fitzpatrick, PP, Knockerra, Kilrush, Co. Clare

Civil Parish: **Killinaboy**
Map Grid: 21
RC Parish: Corofin
Diocese: KL
Earliest Record: b. 4.1819; m. 1.1818
Missing Dates: b. 1.1837; m. 2.1844-1.1859
Parish Address: Rev. P. Walsh, PP, Corofin, Co. Clare

Civil Parish: **Killofin**
Map Grid: 66
RC Parish: Kilmurry, see Kilmurryclonderlaw
Diocese: KL

Civil Parish: **Killokennedy**
Map Grid: 51
RC Parish: part Broadford, see Kilseily; part Doonass, see Kiltenanlea
Diocese: KL

Civil Parish: **Killonaghan**
Map Grid: 5
RC Parish: Glanaragh, see Drumcreehy
Diocese: KF

Civil Parish: **Killone**
Map Grid: 44

RC Parish: Killone, see Clareabbey for earlier
   Records
Diocese: KL
Earliest Record: b. 1.1863; m. 2.1863

Civil Parish: **Killuran**
Map Grid: 48
RC Parish: O'Callaghan's Mills
Diocese: KL
Earliest Record: b. 1.1835; m. 1.1835
Parish Address: Rev. E. Fitzgerald, PP,
   O'Callaghan's Mills, Co. Clare

Civil Parish: **Kilmacduane**
Map Grid: 55
RC Parish: Kilmacduane
Diocese: KL
Earliest Record: b. 1.1854; m. 5.1853
Parish Address: Rev. James Keane, PP,
   Cooraclare, Co. Clare

Civil Parish: **Kilmacrehy**
Map Grid: 13
RC Parish: Liscannor
Diocese: KF
Earliest Record: b. 6.1843; m. 2.1866
Parish Address: Rev. T. Kelly, PP, Liscannor,
   Co. Clare

Civil Parish: **Kilmaleery**
Map Grid: 70
RC Parish: Newmarket, see Kilnasoolagh
Diocese: KL

Civil Parish: **Kilmaley**
Map Grid: 42
RC Parish: Inch and Kilmaley
Diocese: KL
Earliest Record: b. 9.1828
Missing Dates: b. ends 2.1873
Parish Address: Rev. A. Madden, PP, Airfield,
   Inch, Ennis, Co. Clare

Civil Parish: **Kilmanaheen**
Map Grid: 17
RC Parish: Ennistymon
Diocese: KF
Earliest Record: b. 1.1870
Parish Address: Rev. Canon P. Lee, PP, Ennis-
   tymon, Co. Clare

Civil Parish: **Kilmihil**
Map Grid: 60
RC Parish: Kilmihil
Diocese: KL
Earliest Record: b. 3.1849; m. 1.1849
Parish Address: Rev. T. Murphy, PP, Kilmihil,
   Co. Clare

Civil Parish: **Kilmoon**
Map Grid: 6
RC Parish: see Killeany
Diocese: KF

Civil Parish: **Kilmurryclonderlaw**
Map Grid: 40
RC Parish: Kilmurry (or Kilmurry McMahon)
Diocese: KL
Earliest Record: b. 11.1845; m. 9.1837; d.
   11.1844
Missing Dates: d. ends 4.1848
Parish Address: Rev. Denis Moloney, PP, Kil-
   murray, Co. Clare

Civil Parish: **Kilmurryibrickane**
Map Grid: 61
RC Parish: Kilmurryibrickane
Diocese: KL
Earliest Record: b. 4.1839; m. 9.1855
Parish Address: Rev. M. Greene, PP, Mullagh,
   Co. Clare

Civil Parish: **Kilmurrynegaul**
Map Grid: 69
RC Parish: Six-Mile-Bridge, see Kilfinaghta
Diocese: KL

Civil Parish: **Kilnamona**
Map Grid: 26
RC Parish: see Inagh
Diocese: KL

Civil Parish: **Kilnasoolagh**
Map Grid: 67
RC Parish: Newmarket
Diocese: KL
Earliest Record: b. 4.1828; m. 1.1828
Parish Address: Rev. Canon J. Carroll, PP,
   Newmarket-on-Fergus, Co. Clare

Civil Parish: **Kilnoe**
Map Grid: 37

RC Parish: Kilnoe
Diocese: KL
Earliest Record: b. 11.1832; m. 11.1832
Parish Address: Rev. W. O'Donoghue, PP, Bodyke, Co. Clare

Civil Parish: **Kilraghtis**
Map Grid: 29
RC Parish: Kilraghtis, see Doora
Diocese: KL

Civil Parish: **Kilrush**
Map Grid: 59
RC Parish: Kilrush
Diocese: KL
Earliest Record: b. 8.1827; m. 1.1829
Missing Dates: b. 12.1831-1.1833
Parish Address: Rev. Peter Ryan, PP, Kilrush, Co. Clare

Civil Parish: **Kilseily**
Map Grid: 50
RC Parish: Broadford
Diocese: KL
Earliest Record: b. 1.1844; m. 2.1844
Parish Address: Rev. M. Clancy, PP, Broadford, Co. Clare

Civil Parish: **Kilshanny**
Map Grid: 15
RC Parish: Kilshanny
Diocese: KF
Earliest Record: b. 6.1854; m. 1.1860
Parish Address: Rev. P. Healy, CC, Kilshanny, Co. Clare

Civil Parish: **Kiltenanlea**
Map Grid: 54
RC Parish: Doonass and Trugh
Diocese: KL
Earliest Record: b. 7.1851; m. 9.1851
Parish Address: Rev. J. Hannon, PP, Clonlara, Co. Clare

Civil Parish: **Kiltoraght**
Map Grid: 19
RC Parish: see Kilfenora
Diocese: KF

Civil Parish: **Moyarta**
Map Grid: 58

RC Parish: Carrigaholt (Moyarta)
Diocese: KL
Earliest Record: b. 2.1853; m. 1.1852
Parish Address: Rev. C. Duffy, PP, Carrigaholt, Co. Clare

Civil Parish: **Moynoe**
Map Grid: 35
RC Parish: Scariff and Moynoe
Diocese: KL
Earliest Record: b. 5.1852; m. 11.1852
Parish Address: Rev. H. J. Nelson, PP, Scariff, Co. Clare

Civil Parish: **Noughaval**
Map Grid: 11
RC Parish: see Carron
Diocese: KF

Civil Parish: **O'Briens-Bridge**
Map Grid: 52
RC Parish: see Kiltenanlea
Diocese: KL

Civil Parish: **Ogonnelloe**
Map Grid: 47
RC Parish: Ogonnelloe
Diocese: KL
Earliest Record: b. 3.1832; m. 2.1857
Missing Dates: b. ends 2.1869; m. ends 2.1869
Parish Address: Rev. S. O'Dea, PP, Ballyheafey, Killaloe, Co. Clare

Civil Parish: **Oughtmanna**
Map Grid: 4
RC Parish: New Quay, see Carron
Diocese: KF

Civil Parish: **Quin**
Map Grid: 32
RC Parish: Quin
Diocese: KL
Earliest Record: b. 1.1816; m. 1.1833
Parish Address: Rev. James O'Dwyer, PP, Quin, Co. Clare

Civil Parish: **Rath**
Map Grid: 22
RC Parish: part Glanaragh, see Drumcreehy; part Corofin, see Killinaboy
Diocese: KL

Civil Parish: **Rathborney**
Map Grid: 7
RC Parish: Glanaragh, see Drumcreehy
Diocese: KF

Civil Parish: **Ruan**
Map Grid: 23
RC Parish: see Dysert
Diocese: KL

Civil Parish: **St. Munchin's**
Map Grid: 79
RC Parish: see Co. Limerick
Diocese: KL

Civil Parish: **St. Patrick's** (see also Co. Limerick)
Map Grid: 80
RC Parish: Parteen, see Killeely
Diocese: LK

Civil Parish: **Templemaley**
Map Grid: 28
RC Parish: see Doora
Diocese: KL

Civil Parish: **Tomfinlough**
Map Grid: 68
RC Parish: Newmarket, see Kilnasoolagh
Diocese: KL

Civil Parish: **Tomgraney**
Map Grid: 34
RC Parish: Tomgraney, see Kilnoe
Diocese: KL

Civil Parish: **Tulla**
Map Grid: 36
RC Parish: Tulla
Diocese: KL
Earliest Record: b. 1.1819; m. 1.1819
Parish Address: Rev. T. Gleeson, PP, Tulla, Co. Clare

Commercial and Social Directories

1788
Richard Lucas's *General Directory of the Kingdom of Ireland* contains lists of traders in Ennis. Reprinted *Ir. Gen.* 4 (1) (1968): 37-46.

1824
J. Pigot's *City of Dublin & Hibernian Provincial Directory* includes traders, nobility, gentry, and clergy lists of Ennis, Killaloe, and Kilrush.

1842
Directory of Kilkee (street directory with householders and number and types of rooms per house). Kilkee: H. Hogan. NLI I61312 hI.

1846
Slater's *National Commercial Directory of Ireland* lists nobility, clergy, traders, etc., in Ennis, Kilkee, Killaloe, Kilrush, and Tulla.

1856
Slater's *Royal National Commercial Directory of Ireland* lists nobility, gentry, clergy, traders, etc., in Ennis, Ennistymon, Kilkee, Killaloe, Kilrush, Milltown Malbay, and Tulla.

1866
G.H. Bassett's *Directory of the City and County of Limerick and of the Principal Towns in the Cos. of Tipperary and Clare* has trader lists for Killaloe, Ennis, and Kilrush and an alphabetical list of the gentry in County Clare.

1870
Slater's *Directory of Ireland* contains trader, nobility, clergy lists for Ennis, Ennistymon, Kilkee, Killaloe, Kilrush, Miltown Malbay, Newmarket-on-Fergus, Sixmilebridge and Cratloe, and Tulla.

1881
Slater's *Royal National Commercial Directory of Ireland* contains lists of traders, clergy, nobility, and farmers in adjoining parishes of the towns of Ennis, Ennistymon, Kilkee, Killaloe, Kilrush, Milltown Malbay, Newmarket-on-Fergus, and Tulla.

1886
Francis Guy's *Postal Directory* of Munster lists gentry, clergy, traders, principal farmers, teachers, and police sergeants in each postal district of the county and has a listing of magistrates, clergy, and the professions for the whole county.

1893

Francis Guy's *Directory of Munster* contains lists of traders and farmers in each of the postal districts of the county and a general alphabetical index to persons in the whole county.

1894

Slater's *Royal National Directory of Ireland* contains lists of traders, police, teachers, farmers, and private residents in each of the towns, villages, and parishes of the county.

Family History

"The Butlers of Co. Clare." *N. Munster Antiq. Soc. J.* 6 (1952): 108-29; 7 (1953): 153-67; 7 (2) (1955): 19-45.

Census Returns Relating to Following Families and Years: Brooks (1841) PRO film 5248(1); Ryan (1851) PRO film 5249 (66, 67).

Collection on History of Kenny, Lysaght, O'Loghlen, and related Clare families. NLI ms. 2109-2110.

"Colpoys of Ballycarr" (Co. Clare). *R.S.A.I.* 27 (1898): 71-72.

"The Cratloe O'Briens." *Ir. Gen.* 6 (1) (1980): 48-53.

"The Families of Corcomroe." *N. Munster Antiq. Soc. J.* 17 (1975): 21-30.

"Finucane of Co. Clare." *Ir. Anc.* 1(1) (1969): 1-11; 1 (2): 144.

"The McNamara Name." *The Other Clare* 5 (1981).

"Nihell of Co. Clare and Co. Limerick." *Ir. Anc.* 4 (1972): 496-506.

"The O'Davorens of Cahermacnaughten, Burren, Co. Clare." *N. Munster Antiq. Soc. J.* 2 (1912-13): 63-93, 149-64.

"O'Halloran of Ballyainveen." *N. Munster Antiq. Soc. J.* 5 (4) (1948): 102-06; 7 (3) (1956): 12-17 (gives diary of births/marriages, etc. from 1758-1912).

"The Sarsfields of Co. Clare." *N. Munster Antiq. Soc. J.*, III (1914-15): 92-107, 170-90, 328-43.

"Some Observations on Thomond Surnames." *N. Munster Antiq. Soc. J.* 5 (1) (1946): 11-14.

"The Studderts of Kilkishen." *The Other Clare* 4 (1980).

Twigge, R.W. *The Pedigrees of MacConmara of...Co. Clare with Some Family Reminiscences.* 1908.

Gravestone Inscriptions

Clare Heritage Centre has indexed several Clare graveyards (see Research Sources and Services section).

Killaloe Cathedral: Year Book of St. Flannan's Cathedral.

Newspapers

The town of Ennis was the centre of newspaper publishing in this county. However, because of its proximity to Limerick city, many of the Limerick city newspapers also contain material of relevance to the south of County Clare. An index to biographical notices in Limerick, Ennis, Clonmel, and Waterford newspapers up to 1821 (50,000 items) is available on microfiche from Ms. R. ffolliott, Glebe House., Fethard, Co. Tipperary. A copy of this is held by the Library of University College, Dublin.

Title: *Clare Advertiser*
Published in: Kilrush, 1868-88
NLI Holdings: 1.1870-5.1873 (odd nos.); 3.1881-12.1885

Title: *Clare Freeman & Ennis Gazette*
Published in: Ennis, 1853-1884
NLI Holdings: 1878-84 (odd nos.)
BL Holdings: 2.1853-1.1884

Title: *Clare Independent & Tipperary Catholic Times* (continued as *Independent and Munster Advertiser* in 1881)
Published in: Ennis, 1876-85

NLI Holdings: 8.1876-12.1885
BL Holdings: 1.1877-12.1885

Title: *Clare Journal & Ennis Advertiser*
Published in: Ennis, 1807-1917
NLI Holdings: 1.1807-9.1809 (incomplete); 1.1854-12.1876; 1-7.1886 (odd nos.); 8.1886-4.1917
BL Holdings: 1.1828-4.1917

Title: *Ennis Chronicle* (continued as *Ennis Chronicle and Clare Advertiser* in 1802)
Published in: Ennis, 1789-1831
NLI Holdings: 1789-92; 1794-97; 1800-11; 1814; 1816; 1818; 1820; 1825-27; 1831
BL Holdings: 1.1828-11.1831

Title: *Kilrush Herald & Kilkee Gazette*
Published in: Kilrush, 1874-1922
BL Holdings: 6.1874-3.1880; 5.1889-6.1922

Wills and Administration

A discussion of the types of records, where they are held, their availability and value is given in the Wills and Administrations section of the Introduction. The availability of prerogative wills, administrations, and marriage license records is also described in the relevant parts of the same section. Where available, published sources of these records are given in the Miscellaneous Sources section.

Pre-1858 Wills and Administrations

Prerogative Wills. see p. xli.
Consistorial Wills. County Clare is mainly in the diocese of Killaloe with two baronies in Kilfenora and four parishes in Limerick. The guide to Catholic parish records for this county shows the diocese to which each civil parish belonged. The wills of residents of each diocese were usually proven within that diocese (see the Wills section for exceptions). The following records survive:

Wills. O'Loughlen Wills (Co. Clare). NLI P2543

Abstracts. Westropp's "Notes on Clare" manuscripts contain abstracts from Clare and Limerick. RIA Library

Indexes. Killaloe and Kilfenora fragments survive from 1653-1858. Those to 1800 have been published by Phillimore. Limerick – see Co. Limerick

Post-1858 Wills and Administrations

County Clare was served by the District Registry of Limerick. The surviving records are kept in the PRO.

Marriage Licenses

Indexes. Killaloe (1691-1845) PRO; SLC film 100869.
Bonds. Killaloe (1680-1720) and (1760-62) *Ir. Gen.* 5(5) 1978: 580-590.
Grants. Killaloe. *Ir. Gen.* 5 (6) (1979): 710-19.

Miscellaneous Sources

"Businessmen of Ennis, Co. Clare Early in the Napoleonic Wars." *Ir. Anc.* 16 (1) (1984): 6-8.

Dunboyne Newscuttings (NLI ms. 3321-79) cover trials, town commission, and church affairs from 1824-28 and 1842-79.

Dutton, Hely. *A Statistical Survey of County Clare.* Royal Dublin society, 1808.

"Emigration from County Clare." *N. Munster Antiq. J.* 17 (1975): 69-76.

"Emigration from the Workhouse at Ennistymon, Co. Clare." *Ir. Anc.* 13 (2) (1981): 79-82.

Frost, J. *History and Topography of Co. Clare to the Beginning of the 18th Century.* 1893; reprinted 1978.

"Funeral Entries from Co. Clare in the 17th Century." *N. Munster Antiq. J.* 17 (1975): 63-67 (records of twelve prominent deaths).

"Game Licenses in Co. Clare 1803-1821." *Ir. Anc.* 14 (2) (1982): 95-98.

Gwynn, A. and O. F. Gleeson, *A History of the Diocese of Killaloe.* Dublin, 1962.

"Magistrates of Co. Clare 1819." *Ir. Anc.* 8 (1): 16-17.

"Magistrates of Co. Clare 1837." *Ir. Anc.* 7 (2): 99-100.

"The Moravian Brethren and Their Church at Corofin." *The Other Clare* 3 (1979): 27-28.

"Schoolmasters in Killaloe Diocese (1808)." *N. Munster Antiq. J.* 11 (1968): 57-63.

White, Rev. P. *History of Co. Clare and of the Dalcassian Clans of Tipperary, Limerick and Galway.* Limerick, 1893.

Research Sources and Services

Journals

Dolgcais

The Other Clare

The North Munster Antiquarian Journal

Libraries and Information Sources

Clare County Library, Mill Road, Ennis, Co. Clare Ph: (065) 21616

Research Services

Clare Heritage Centre (Ignatius Cleary), Corofin, Co. Clare Ph: (065) 27955 (research service on Clare families, with indexes to all Clare parishes, land records, tombstone inscriptions, and ship's passenger lists).

See also research services in Dublin, p. xliv.

Societies

Clare Archaeological & Historical Society, Sister Francis O'Dwyer, Colaiste Muire, College Road, Ennis, Co. Clare

Shannon Archaeological & Historical Society (Publishers of *The Other Clare*), Mrs. Monica O'Brien, Mount Arley, Drumline, Newmarket-on-Fergus, Co. Clare

Tullowphelim Historic Society, Mr. John Keogh, 12 St. Patrick's Park, Tullow, Co. Clare

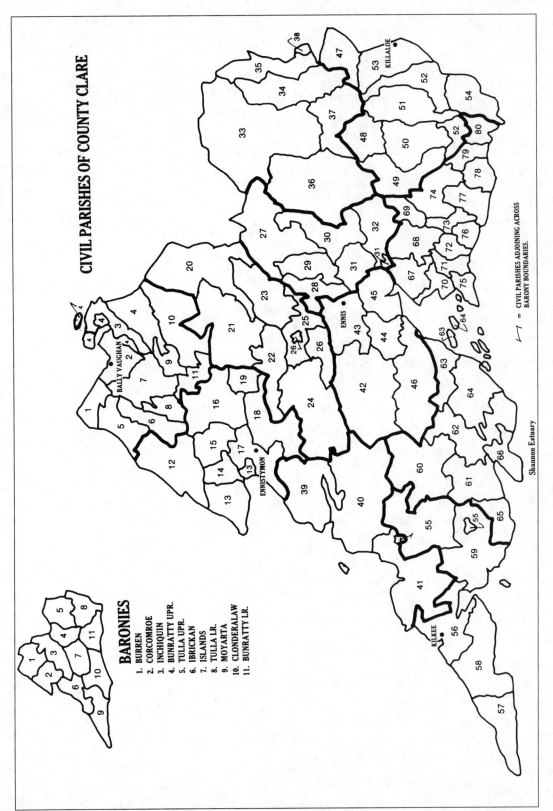

CIVIL PARISHES OF COUNTY CLARE

BARONIES

1. BURREN
2. CORCOMROE
3. INCHIQUIN
4. BUNRATTY UPR.
5. TULLA UPR.
6. IBRICKAN
7. ISLANDS
8. TULLA LR.
9. MOYARTA
10. CLONDERALAW
11. BUNRATTY LR.

BALLYVAUGHAN

ENNISTYMON

ENNIS

KILLALOE

KILKEE

Shannon Estuary

↗ = CIVIL PARISHES ADJOINING ACROSS BARONY BOUNDARIES.

County Cork

A Brief History

This Munster county is the largest in Ireland. The major towns in the county are Cork city, Mallow, Mitchelstown, Youghal, Kanturk, Cobh, Fermoy, Kinsale, Clonakilty, Skibbereen, Bantry, and Bandon.

Before the establishment of the county system, the area of the present County Cork was divided between the territories of Desmond, Muskerry, and Corca Laoidhe. The major Gaelic families in the county were McCarthy, O'Keefe, Murphy, O'Mahony, O'Callaghan, O'Donovan, O'Driscoll, and O'Riordan.

The city of Cork itself was founded in the sixth century by the establishment of a monastery and school on the site by St. Finbarr. This grew into a considerable town. In the early ninth century the Norse Vikings raided and later settled in the town, establishing it as a trading post, and merged with the local inhabitants.

Following the Norman invasion in the twelfth century, the county was granted to the Norman knights, Fitzstephen and De Cogan. These brought over further Anglo-Norman settlers, but the colony never extended much beyond the area around the present Cork city. Like the Norsemen, the Normans in the county gradually merged with the native Irish and adopted the Irish way of life. Gradually over the succeeding centuries the power and holdings of the individual Norman families increased by war and intermarriage. The main names of Norman extraction now found in the county are Barry, Roche, Cogan, and Nagle. The Anglo-Saxon names of Gould and Verling are also found in Cork since Norman times.

The power of many of these Norman and Gaelic families was broken after they supported the unsuccessful revolt of the Earl of Desmond in the late sixteenth century. This resulted in the confiscation of the bulk of the holdings of these families and their distribution, in 1583, to English adventurers. During what is known as the Plantation of Munster, around 15,000 people were brought over and settled in Cork and neighbouring counties. Most of these settlers left again during Hugh O'Neill's war with the English (see Co. Tyrone) and particularly on the approach of his army into Munster in 1598. Although some returned again after his defeat, the plantation was largely a failure. Further English settlers came to the county in the 1650s following the defeat of the 1641 rebellion (see p. xlvii).

In the Great Famine of 1845-47, County Cork was one of the worst affected areas. The population, which peaked at 854,000 in 1841, had fallen to 650,000 in 1851. Almost 150,000

The following is a list of debtors in the Cork City Marshalsea and the County Gaol in 1730–31.

Baily, George	Cork	Ropemaker
Barber, Peter	City	Cooper
Beneson, Robert	Gourtey Cross (Croom) ?	Yeoman
Bonn, Henry	Currivolly, Co. Cork	Gent
Bryan, William	Cork City	Merchant
Butler, William	Cork City	Nailor
Callaghan, Morgan	Killeen, North Liberties	Dairyman
Callan, Teig	Baulan, Co. Cork	Yeoman
Cantlan, Nicholas	Cork City	Taylor
Carthy, James	Cork City	Clothier
Clancy, Thomas	Gloun, Rousk, Cork	Yeoman
Coleman, Thomas	Limerick City	Weaver
Collins, Denis	Cork City	Sawyer
Conan, David	Ballyhouly	Malster
Connell, Bart.	Rathmacully, South Liberties	Farmer
Connell, *Eleanor*	Cork City	Widow
Coppinger, Thomas	Cork	Merchant
Crowley, Florence	Cork City	Porter
Doyle, Edward	Cork (Youghal)	Mariner
Evans, *Catherine*	Cork City	Mealwoman
Field, Stephen	Fairlain (now Wolfe Tone St.)	Mariner

A list of the debtors imprisoned in Cork Jails in 1730-31. Such lists were prepared for presentation at the Quarter Sessions of the Courts and were also posted in the jail. From *Journal of the Cork Hist. & Arch. Soc.* (1942).

people died between 1845 and 1850, and further thousands emigrated. The population is currently around 404,000.

Currently the twenty most common names in Cork are O'Sullivan, Murphy, McCarthy, Mahoney, O'Donovan, Walsh, O'Brien, O'Callaghan, O'Leary, Crowley, Collins, O'Driscoll, O'Connell, Barry, Cronin, Buckley, Daly, Sheehy, O'Riordan, and Kelliher.

Census and Census Substitutes

1641

"Extracts from Civil Survey of Cork" (name, religion, and townland of proprietors in each parish). *J. Cork Hist. & Arch. Soc.* 37 (146) (1932): 83-89; 38 (147) (1933): 39-45; 38 (148) (1933): 72-79; 39 (149) (1934): 33-36; 39 (150) (1934): 79-84; 40 (151) (1935): 43-48; 40 (152) (1935): 91-94; 51 (153) (1936): 37-41; 51 (154) (1936): 97-104.

1654

Parishes of Aghabullog, Aghina, Aglish, Ballinaboy, Ballyvorney, Carnaway, Carrigrohanbeg, Clondrohid, Currykippane, Desertmore, Donoughmore, Drishane, Garrycloyne, Granagh, Inchigeelagh, Inniscarra, Kilbonane, Kilcolman, Kilcorny, Kilmihil, Kilmurry, Kilnamartyr, Knockavilly, Macloneigh, Macroom, Matehy, Moviddy, Templemichael, Whitechurch. *Civil Survey,* Vol. VI; SLC film 973123.

Cork city, with North and South suburbs and liberties. *Civil Survey,* Vol. VI; SLC film 973123.

1659

"Census" of Ireland. edited by S. Pender, Dublin: Stationery Office 1939.

1662-68

Subsidy Rolls Extracts. PRO films 2636, 2643.

1663-64

Extracts from *Civil Survey*: Proprietors of lands confiscated from 1641 owners listed above (see same references).

1730-31

"Debtors in Cork Gaol" (over fifty names, addresses, occupations). *J. Cork Hist. & Arch. Soc.* 47 (165) (1942): 9-23.

1757

Jephson, M.D. "Male, Able-bodied Protestants in Parishes of Brigown, Castletown Roche, Clonmeen, Farrihy, Glanworth, Kilshannig, Marshallstown, Roskeen." Appendix (4) in *An Anglo-Irish Miscellany* (1964).

1766

Religious Census of All Householders (see p. xxvii) in Parishes of Aghabullog, Aghada, Ardagh, and Clonpriest (names of householder's wife and children) Ballyhea, Ballyhooly and Killathy, Brigown, Britway, Carrigdownane, Castlelyons, Castlemartyr, Castletown Roche, Churchtown, Clenor, Clonfert, Clondrohid, Clondullane, Clonmeen, Ruskeen and Kilcummy, Clonmult and Kilmahon, Cloyne and Ballintemple, Coole, Farrihy, Templemologga, Kildorrery, Nathlash Garrycloyne, Whitechurch and Grenagh, Glanworth, Ightermurragh, Imphrick, Inniscarra and Matehy, Killogrohanbeg, Kilnamartyr, Kilshannig, Kilworth and Macrony, Knockmourne and Ballynoe, Lisgoold and Ballykeary, Litter, Macroom, Magourney and Kilcolman, Mallow, Marshalstown, Midleton, Mourne Abbey, Shandrum, Youghal. PRO film 2476.

Parishes of Rathbarry, Ringrone. PRO 1A 46 49.

"Parish of Dunbulloge (Carrignavar)." *J. Cork. Hist. Arch. Soc.* 51 (173): 69-77.

"Religious Census for Kilmichael" (with note on the names and their current status in the area). *J. Cork Hist. & Arch. Soc.* 26 (124) (1920): 69-79.

1768

Tenant Farmers on the Barrymore Estate, (Barrymore Barony). *J. Cork Hist. & Arch.* *Soc.* 51 (173) (1946): 31-40 (name, townland, and holding).

1770

Rental of Bennett Estate [notes on sixty-eight properties, mainly in Cork city and surroundings with details of each and mentioning previous tenants (to 1690s) and neighbors, etc.] NLI film P288.

1771-72

"Debtors in Cork Gaol" (over 150 names). *J. Cork Hist. & Arch. Soc.* 47(165) (1942): 9-23.

1775

Catholic Qualification Roll Extracts (139 names, addresses, and occupations). 59th Report DKPRI: 50-84.

1783

List of Freemen and Freeholders Who Voted in 1783 City of Cork Election (gives names and occupations). NLI P2054.

1793 et seq.

Householders in St. Anne's (Shandon) Parish (list for valuation purposes) in Year 1793 and of Additional Houses Built in Years 1804, 1809, 1821, 1832, 1837, 1844, 1853. *J. Cork. Hist. Arch. Soc.* 47 (165): 87-111 (names and addresses with value of holding).

1817

A List of the Freemen at Large of the City of Cork (arranged alphabetically, gives occupations only). NLI P722.

1823-37

Tithe Applotment Survey (see p. xxvii).

1830

The Census of the Parish of St. Mary Shandon, Cork (circa 1830). *J. Cork Hist. & Arch. Soc.* 49 (169) (1944): 10-18. SLC 941. 5/ A1/59) (gives names of house-owners, other details not related to names).

1830-37

Names, in Alphabetical Order, of Some Householders in the City of Cork (120 names, addresses and occupations). Reports from Committees. *Parl. Papers* 1837-38, 13 (2): 554-57.

BOROUGH OF YOUGHAL.

Number.	NAME.	RESIDENCE.	OCCUPATION.
1	William Ahern	North Main-street	labourer.
2	John Barry	Knockavirry	farmer.
3	Daniel Buckly	North Main-street	shopkeeper.
4	Edmond Bowler	Friar's-street	labourer.
5	William Conway	North Main-street	skinner.
6	John Connor	South Main-street	shopkeeper.
7	Michael Coleman	North Main-street	tailor.
8	Cornelius Hurley	ditto	victualler.
9	Michael Hallahan	ditto	baker.
10	James Hallahan	Meat Shamble-lane	shopkeeper.
11	James Kinneary	Copper-alley	farmer.
12	Denis Kenealy	Cross-lane	gardener.
13	Richard Moore	South Main-street	shoemaker.
14	James M'Guire	North Main-street	wheelwright.
15	John M'Guire	Knockavirry	farmer.
16	Darby M'Grath	Windmill-lane	carman.
17	Garrett Meade	North Main-street	victualler.
18	John Murphy	Fish Shamble-lane	dealer.
19	Maurice Nagle	North Main-street	baker.
20	Robert Power	Cock-lane	weaver.
21	John Prendergast, sen.	North Main-street	publican.
22	Daniel Quinlan	Nile-street	shoemaker.
23	John Ronayne	ditto	tailor.
24	Edmond Seward	South Main-street	fisherman.
25	John Sullivan	Mall-lane	tailor.
26	John Frihey	Shambles-lane	publican.

28 February 1837.   *James Chatterton*, Clerk of the Peace.

Registered Voters in the Borough of Youghal, Co. Cork who were registered as "Marksmen" (i.e., who could vote by making their mark rather than a signature.) This information was prepared as evidence for the Select Committee on Fictitious Votes 1837. *Parliamentary Papers* 1837, 2 (1): Appendix G.

1832-37

Several Lists of Householders in Cork Classified by Valuation and Voting Status (giving residence and occupation for Appendixes 1 and 7). *Parl. Papers* 1837/38, 13 (1): Appendixes 1-5, 301-14; 7-9, 318-23.

1834

List of Protestant Parishioners (including children's names) in Ballymoden, Town of Bandon, Arranged by street. NLI ms. 675.

Casey, Albert. *O'Kief, Coshe Mang, and Slieve Luachra* Vol. 14: 493; SLC film 832809. (Protestant families in Magourney.)

1835

Occupants of Houses of Over £5 Valuation in Youghal (arranged alphabetically with description and value of premises). *Parl. Papers* 1837, 2 (1): Appendix G, 239-49.

The Youghal Poll-Books of 1835 and 1837. 1835 list in *J. Cork Hist. & Arch. Soc.* 83 (238)

(1978): 106-46; 1837 list in *J. Cork Hist. & Arch. Soc.* 84 (239) (1979): 15-43 (voters in local elections; gives names, addresses).

1836/49/52
Census of Kingwilliamstown Estate, Co. Cork (Nohavaldaly Parish) (see also 1849-51). SLC film 101767.

1837
Occupants of Bandon (Bridge) Arranged by Street, Giving Property Values. *Parl. Papers* 1837, 11 (1): Appendix G, 191-98.

List of Nonresident Freemen, City of Cork (mainly Cork Co.). *Parl. Papers* 1837-38, 13 (1): 315-17.

Several Lists of Waste and Poor in Various Parishes in the City of Cork. *Parl. Papers* 1837-38, 13 (1): Appendix 9(2), 10, 11: 323-34.

1838
List of Marksmen (illiterate voters) in Cork City, Mallow, Youghal, Kinsale (gives names, residences, and occupations). *Parl. Papers* 1837/38, 13 (1): Supplemental Appendixes, 5-15; 1837, 13 (2) Appendix 4.

1845-46
Members of Ballineen Agricultural Society 1845/46. *J. Cork. Hist. Arch. Soc.* 51 (173) (1946): 52-60.

1849-51
Emigrants from Kingwilliamstown (part of Nohaval Daly, gives names, ages, and relationships of 191 people with dates of departure, arrival, etc.). In E. Ellis, *Emigrants from Ireland 1847-52* (Baltimore: Genealogical Publishing Company, 1977), 42-53.

1851
Government Census Remnants: Parish of Kilcrumper, (except the townlands of Glenwood, Lisnallagh, and Loughnakilly); Parish of Kilworth, Parish of Leitrim, (except the townlands of Ballymamudthogh, Cronahil, and Propogue); The townlands of Castle Cooke, Kilclogh, Macrony, and Shanaclure in the parish of Macrony. PRO.

1851-53
Griffith's Valuation (see p. xxvii).

1901
Census. PRO.

1911
Census. PRO.

Church Records

Church of Ireland
(Shows starting date of record)

Parish: **Aghadown**
Status: Lost

Parish: **Aglish**
Status: Lost

Parish: **Ahern** or **Aghern**
Status: Lost

Parish: **Ahihagh**
Status: Lost

Parish: **Ardagh**
Status: Lost

Parish: **Ardfield**
Existing Records: b. 1832; m. 1843; d. 1834-36
Status: LC (copy)

Parish: **Athnowen** and **Kilnagleary**
Status: Lost

Parish: **Ballinaboy**
Status: Lost

Parish: **Ballinadee**
Status: Lost

Parish: **Ballintemple** or **Churchtown**
Status: Lost

Parish: **Ballyclough**
Existing Records: b. 1795-1900; m. 1798-1848;
   d. 1796-1900
Status: PRO

Parish: **Ballycotton**
Status: Lost

Parish: **Ballydehob** (chapel of ease to Skull)
Existing Records: b. 1826-75
Status: LC

Parish: **Ballyhooly**
Status: Lost

Parish: **Ballymartle**
Existing Records: b. 1785; m. 1761; d. 1785
Status: LC and PRO

Parish: **Ballymodan**
Exisitng Records: b. 1695; m. 1695; d. 1695
Status: LC and PRO

Parish: **Ballymoney**
Existing Records: b. 1782; m. 1786; d. 1800
Status: LC (copy)

Parish: **Ballyvoe**
Status: Lost

Parish: **Ballyvourney**
Status: Lost

Parish: **Berehaven**
Existing Records: b. 1787; m. 1786; d. 1800
Status: LC and PRO

Parish: **Buffevant**
Status: Lost

Parish: **Caherconlish**
Status: Lost

Parish: **Cannaway**
Status: Lost

Parish: **Carrigaline**
Existing Records: b. 1723; m. 1723; d. 1723
Missing Records: b. 1756-1808; m. 1756-1808;
   d. 1756-1808
Status: LC and PRO

Parish: **Carrigrohanbeg**
Existing Records: b. 1791; m. 1787; d. 1789
Status: LC

Parish: **Carrigtohill**
Existing Records: b. 1776; m. 1779; d. 1776
Status: PRO

Parish: **Castlewaven** or **Castletownsend**
Status: Lost

Parish: **Castlelyons**
Status: Lost

Parish: **Castlemagner**
Status: Lost

Parish: **Castletownroche**
Existing Records: b. 1728; m. 1728; d. 1733
Status: LC and PRO

Parish: **Castleventry**
Existing Records: b. 1825; m. 1825; d. 1825
Status: LC (copy)

Parish: **Christ Church** (Rushbrook)
Existing Records: b. 1866
Status: LC and PRO

Parish: **Churchtown** or **Bruhenny**
Status: Lost

Parish: **Clenore**
Status: Lost

Parish: **Clondrohid**
Existing Records: b. 1770; m. 1770; d. 1778
Status: LC (copy)

Parish: **Clondulane**
Status: Lost

Parish: **Clonfert** (Newmarket)
Status: Lost

Parish: **Clonmeen**
Status: Lost

Parish: **Clonmel** (Queenstown)
Existing Records: b. 1761; m. 1761; d. 1761
Status: PRO

Parish: **Clonmult**
Status: Lost

Parish: **Clonpriest**
Status: Lost

Parish: **Cloyne**
Existing Records: b. 1708; m. 1708; d. 1708
Status: PRO

Parish: **Cobh** (see Clonmel)

Parish: **Corkbeg**
Existing Records: b. 1836; m. 1838; d. 1826
Status: LC and PRO

Parish: **Creagh**
Status: Lost

Parish: **Cullen**
Status: Lost

Parish: **Desertserges**
Existing Records: b. 1837; m. 1837; d. 1837
Status: LC and PRO

Parish: **Doneraile** and **Tenyleroan**
Existing Records: b. 1730; m. 1730; d. 1730
Status: LC

Parish: **Donoughmore**
Status: Lost

Parish: **Douglas**
Existing Records: b. 1792; m. 1730; d. 1730
Status: LC and PRO

Parish: **Drinagh**
Status: Lost

Parish: **Drishane**
Status: Lost

Parish: **Dromdaleague**
Existing Records: b. 1812; m. 1730; d. 1730
Status: LC

Parish: **Dromtarriff**
Status: Lost

Parish: **Dunderrow**
Existing Records: b. 1805; m. 1799; d. 1823
Status: LC (copy)

Parish: **Dungoverney**
Existing Records: b. 1825; m. 1826; d. 1826
Status: LC (copy)

Parish: **Durrus** and **Kilcrohane**
Status: Lost

Parish: **Fanlobbus**
Status: Lost

Parish: **Farihy**
Status: Lost

Parish: **Fermoy**
Existing Records: b. 1801; m. 1826; d. 1826
Status: PRO

Parish: **Frankfield**
Status: Lost

Parish: **Garran-Kinnefeake**
Existing Records: b.1850; d. 1875
Status: PRO

Parish: **Garrycloyne**
Status: Lost

Parish: **Glanworth**
Status: Lost

Parish: **Glengarriff**
Status: LC and PRO

Parish: **Gortroe**
Status: Lost

Parish: **Holy Trinity**
Existing Records: b. 1643; m. 1644; d. 1644
Missing Records: b. 1667-1708; m. 1666-1720;
  d. 1669-1731
Status: LC and PRO

Parish: **Ightermurragh**
Status: Lost

Parish: **Inch**
Existing Records: b. 1815; m. 1644; d. 1644
Status: LC

Parish: **Inchigeelagh**
Status: Lost

Parish: **Inchinabackey**
Status: Lost

Parish: **Innisearra**
Existing Records: b. 1820; m. 1644; d. 1644
Missing Records: b. 1667-1708; m. 1666-1720;
  d. 1669-1731
Status: LC and PRO

Parish: **Innishannon**
Existing Records: b. 1693; m. 1644; d. 1693
Missing Records: b. 1765-87
Status: LC and PRO

Parish: **Inniskenny**
Status: Lost

Parish: **Kanturk**
Status: Lost

Parish: **Kilbanane**
Status: Lost

Parish: **Kulbrin** and **Liscarroll**
Status: Lost

Parish: **Kilbrittoin**
Status: Lost

Parish: **Kilbrogan**
Existing Records: b. 1752; m. 1753; d. 1707
Status: LC and PRO

Parish: **Kilcaskin**
Status: Lost

Parish: **Kilcoe**
Status: Lost

Parish: **Kilcredan**
Status: Lost

Parish: **Kilcully**
Existing Records: b. 1844
Status: LC

Parish: **Kilgariffe**
Status: Lost

Parish: **Killanully**
Existing Records: b. 1831; m. 1838; d. 1836
Status: LC and PRO

Parish: **Killaspugmullane**
Status: Lost

Parish: **Killeagh**
Existing Records: b. 1782; m. 1776; d. 1782
Status: LC (copy)

Parish: **Kilmacabea**
Status: Lost

Parish: **Kilmahon**
Existing Records: b. 1773; m. 1806; d. 1773
Status: PRO

Parish: **Kilmaloda**
Status: Lost

Parish: **Kilmeen**
Existing Records: b. 1806; m. 1806; d. 1844
Status: LC

Parish: **Kilmichael**
Status: Lost

Parish: **Kilmocomoge**
Status: Lost

Parish: **Kilmoe**
Status: Lost

Parish: **Kilnemartyr**
Status: Lost

Parish: **Kilroan** or **Ballydelougher**
Status: Lost

Parish: **Kilshannick**
Existing Records: b. 1731; m. 1806; d. 1844
Status: PRO

Parish: **Kilworth**
Status: Lost

Parish: **Kunneigh**
Existing Records: b. 1794; m. 1795; d. 1796
Status: PRO

Parish: **Kinsale**
Existing Records: b. 1684; m. 1688; d. 1685
Status: PRO

Parish: **Knockavilly**
Existing Records: b. 1837; m. 1844
Status: PRO

Parish: **Knockmourne**
Status: Lost

Parish: **Knocktemple** and **Kilbolane**
Status: Lost

Parish: **Leighmoney**
Status: Lost

Parish: **Lisgood**
Status: Lost

Parish: **Lislee**
Existing Records: b. 1809; m. 1809; d. 1823
Status: PRO

Parish: **Litter**
Status: Lost

Parish: **Macroom**
Existing Records: b. 1727; m. 1736; d. 1727
Status: PRO

Parish: **Magourney**
Existing Records: b. 1757; m. 1756; d. 1758
Status: PRO

Parish: **Mallow**
Existing Records: b. 1780; m. 1756; d. 1758
Status: PRO

Parish: **Marmullane**
Existing Records: b. 1801; m. 1802; d. 1803
Status: PRO

Parish: **Midleton**
Existing Records: b. 1696; m. 1698; d. 1696
Status: LC and PRO

Parish: **Mageely**
Status: Lost

Parish: **Mogeesha**
Existing Records: b. 1852
Status: LC and PRO

Parish: **Monanimy**
Status: Lost

Parish: **Monkstown**
Existing Records: b. 1842; m. 1841; d. 1842
Status: PRO

Parish: **Moviddy**
Status: Lost

Parish: **Nathlash**
Existing Records: b. 1812; m. 1813; d. 1813
Status: LC

Parish: **Nohaval**
Existing Records: b. 1785; m. 1813; d. 1784
Status: PRO

Parish: **Queenstown** (see Clonmel)

Parish: **Rathbarry**
Status: Lost

Parish: **Rathclarin**
Status: Lost

Parish: **Rathcooney**
Existing Records: b. 1749; m. 1813; d. 1784
Status: PRO

Parish: **Rathcormack**
Status: Lost

Parish: **Rincurran**
Existing Records: b. 1793; m. 1793; d. 1827
Status: PRO

Parish: **Ringrone** and **Kilroan**
Status: Lost

Parish: **Ross Cathedral**
Existing Records: b. 1690; m. 1690; d. 1690
Status: PRO

Parish: **Rostellan**
Status: Lost

Parish: **St. Anne, Shandon**
Existing Records: b. 1772; m. 1772; d. 1779
Status: LC

Parish: **St. Brendans**
Status: Lost

Parish: **St. Edmunds**
Status: Lost

Parish: **St. Finnbarr**
Status: Lost

Parish: **St. Lappan**
Status: Lost

Parish: **St. Luke**
Existing Records: b. 1837; m. 1837
Status: LC

Parish: **St. Mary, Shandon**
Existing Records: b. 1802; m. 1803
Status: LC (copy)

Parish: **St. Michael, Blackrock**
Existing Records: b. 1828; m. 1837; d. 1803
Status: PRO

Parish: **St. Nicholas**
Existing Records: b. 1721; m. 1837; d. 1803
Status: LC

Parish: **St. Paul**
Status: Lost

Parish: **St. Peter**
Status: Lost

Parish: **Shandrum**
Status: Lost

Parish: **Skull** (see also Ballydehob)
Status: Lost

Parish: **Teampal-na-bocht**
Existing Records: b.1857
Status: LC

Parish: **Templebredy**
Status: Lost

Parish: **Templemartin**
Existing Records: b. 1806; m. 1808; d. 1810
Status: PRO

Parish: **Templemichael-de-duaghe**
Status: Lost

Parish: **Templecarriga**
Status: Lost

Parish: **Templeomalus**
Status: Lost

Parish: **Templetrines**
Status: Lost

Parish: **Tracton**
Status: Lost

Parish: **Tullagh**
Status: Lost

Parish: **Tullylease**
Status: Lost

Parish: **Wallstown**
Status: Lost

Parish: **Whitechurch**
Status: Lost

Parish: **Youghal**
Existing Records: b. 1665; m. 1665; d. 1665
Missing Records: b. 1720-27; m. 1720-27;
   d. 1720-27
Status: PRO

Presbyterian

Parish: **Bandon**
Starting Date: 1842

Parish: **Cork**
Starting Date: 1832

Parish: **Cobh** (Queenstown)
Starting Date: 1847

Roman Catholic

Civil Parish: **Abbeymahon**
Map Grid: S66
RC Parish: see Donoughmore (2)
Diocese: RO

Civil Parish: **Abbeystowry**
Map Grid: S52
RC Parish: part Skibereen, see Creagh; part Caheragh
Diocese: RO

Civil Parish: **Aghabulloge**
Map Grid: N48
RC Parish: Aghabullogue
Diocese: CY
Earliest Record: b. 1.1820; m. 1.1820
Parish Address: Rev. John Cronin, CC, Aghabullogue, Co. Cork

Civil Parish: **Aghacross**
Map Grid: E32a
RC Parish: see Kildorrery
Diocese: CY

Civil Parish: **Aghada**
Map Grid: E105
RC Parish: Aghada
Diocese: CY
Earliest Record: b. 1.1815; m. 5.1838
Missing Dates: b. 3.1837-3.1838
Parish Address: Rev. John Aherne, PP, Rostellan, Midleton, Co. Cork

Civil Parish: **Aghadown**
Map Grid: S55
RC Parish: Aghadown or Aughadown
Diocese: RO
Earliest Record: b. 6.1822; m. 10.1822

Missing Dates: m. 2.1865-1880
Parish Address: Rev. Jerome Kiely, PP, Lisheen, Skibbereen, Co. Cork

Civil Parish: **Aghern**
Map Grid: 369
RC Parish: see Knockmourne
Diocese: CY

Civil Parish: **Aghinagh**
Map Grid: N50
RC Parish: Aghinagh
Diocese: CK
Earliest Record: b. 4.1848
Parish Address: Rev. P. Carroll, PP, Aghinagh, Co. Cork

Civil Parish: **Aglish**
Map Grid: N56
RC Parish: Ovens, see Athowen
Diocese: CK

Civil Parish: **Aglishdrinagh**
Map Grid: N24
RC Parish: Ballyhea, see Ballyhea
Diocese: CY

Civil Parish: **Ardagh**
Map Grid: E87
RC Parish: see Killeagh

Civil Parish: **Ardfield**
Map Grid: S61
RC Parish: Ardfield and Rathbarry
Diocese: RO
Earliest Record: b. 1.1801; m. 5.1800
Missing Dates: b. 1.1802-1.1803; m. 1812-16
Parish Address: Rev. Denis O'Donoghue, PP, Ardfield, Clonakilty, Co. Cork

Civil Parish: **Ardnageehy**
Map Grid: E42
RC Parish: Watergrasshill
Diocese: CK
Earliest Record: b. 1.1836
Parish Address: Rev. Canon Stephen Harte, PP, Watergrasshill, Co. Cork

Civil Parish: **Ardskeagh**
Map Grid: E2

RC Parish: part Ballyhay, see Ballyhea; part Charleville, see Rathgoggan
Diocese: CY

Civil Parish: **Athowen**
Map Grid: N57
RC Parish: Ovens
Diocese: CK
Earliest Record: b. 9.1816; m. 9.1816
Missing Dates: b. 9.1833-10.1834; m. 8.1833-10.1834, 2.1837-1.1839
Parish Address: Rev. Declan Crowley, PP, Ovens, Co. Cork

Civil Parish: **Ballinaboy**
Map Grid: N70, S25, and E85
RC Parish: Ballinhassig
Diocese: CK
Earliest Record: b. 3.1821; m. 7.1821
Parish Address: Rev. Sean Burke, CC, Ballinhassig, Co. Cork

Civil Parish: **Ballinadee**
Map Grid: N46 and S74
RC Parish: Courcey's Country (Ballinspittal)
Diocese: CK
Earliest Record: b. 9.1819; m. 9.1819
Missing Dates: b. 11.1854-1.1858
Parish Address: Rev. Thomas Kelleher, PP, Ballinspittal, Co. Cork

Civil Parish: **Ballintemple**
Map Grid: E108
RC Parish: see Churchtown
Diocese: CY

Civil Parish: **Ballycaraney**
Map Grid: E53
RC Parish: see Lisgoold
Diocese: CY

Civil Parish: **Ballyclough**
Map Grid: N34
RC Parish: Kilbrin and Ballyclough
Diocese: CY
Earliest Record: b. 8.1807; m. 1.1805
Missing Dates: m. 1.1828
Parish Address: Rev. John Walshe, PP, Ballyclough, Mallow, Co. Cork

Civil Parish: **Ballydeloher**
Map Grid: E59
RC Parish: Glounthaune, see Caherlag
Diocese: CK

Civil Parish: **Ballydeloughy**
Map Grid: E12
RC Parish: Ballindangan, see Glanworth
Diocese: CY

Civil Parish: **Ballyfeard**
Map Grid: S29
RC Parish: see Clontead
Diocese: CK

Civil Parish: **Ballyfoyle**
Map Grid: S35
RC Parish: see Tracton
Diocese: CK

Civil Parish: **Ballyhea**
Map Grid: N20 and E1
RC Parish: Ballyhea; also part Charlville, see Rathgoggan
Diocese: CY
Earliest Record: b. 1.1809; m. 6.1811
Parish Address: Rev. P. Cotter, PP, Ballyhea, Charleville, Co. Cork

Civil Parish: **Ballyhooly**
Map Grid: E27
RC Parish: see Castletownroche
Diocese: CY

Civil Parish: **Ballymartle**
Map Grid: S26
RC Parish: see Clontead
Diocese: CK

Civil Parish: **Ballymodan**
Map Grid: S20
RC Parish: Bandon; also part Kilbritain
Diocese: CK
Earliest Record: b. 1.1836; m. 1.1848
Parish Address: Rev. Canon Patrick Cahalane, PP, VF, Bandon, Co. Cork

Civil Parish: **Ballymoney**
Map Grid: S70

RC Parish: part Dunmanway, see Fanlobbus;
part Enniskean, see Killowen
Diocese: CK

Civil Parish: **Ballynoe**
Map Grid: E70
RC Parish: Ballynoe or Conna, see Knock-
mourne
Diocese: CY

Civil Parish: **Ballyoughtera**
Map Grid: E94
RC Parish: part Imogeela, see Mogeely; part
Midleton
Diocese: CY

Civil Parish: **Ballyspillane**
Map Grid: E62
RC Parish: see Midleton
Diocese: CY

Civil Parish: **Ballyvourney**
Map Grid: N38
RC Parish: Ballyvourney
Diocese: CY
Earliest Record: b. 4.1825
Missing Dates: m. 12.1829 onwards destroyed
by fire
Parish Address: Rev. Patrick O'Hanlon, Bal-
lymakeera, Co. Cork

Civil Parish: **Barnahely**
Map Grid: S41
RC Parish: Passage, see Marmullane
Diocese: CK

Civil Parish: **Bohillane**
Map Grid: E99
RC Parish: Ballymacoda, see Kilmaloda
Diocese: CY

Civil Parish: **Bregoge**
Map Grid: N31
RC Parish: see Buttevant
Diocese: CY

Civil Parish: **Bridgetown**
Map Grid: E25
RC Parish: see Castletownroche
Diocese: CY

Civil Parish: **Brigown**
Map Grid: E33
RC Parish: Mitchelstown
Diocese: CY
Earliest Record: b. 1.1792; m. 1.1822
Missing Dates: b. 7.1801-9.1814
Parish Address: Rev. Canon Patrick Sheehan,
PP, Michelstown, Co. Cork

Civil Parish: **Brinny**
Map Grid: S17
RC Parish: see Inishannon
Diocese: CK

Civil Parish: **Britway**
Map Grid: E50
RC Parish: see Castlelyons
Diocese: CY

Civil Parish: **Buttevant**
Map Grid: N32
RC Parish: Buttevant
Diocese: CY
Earliest Record: b. 7.1814; m. 7.1814
Parish Address: Rev. Canon Michael Cogan,
PP, Buttevant, Co. Cork

Civil Parish: **Caheragh**
Map Grid: S46
RC Parish: Caheragh
Diocese: CK
Earliest Record: b. 6.1818; m. 6.1818
Missing Dates: m. 8.1858-11.1858
Parish Address: Rev. John Tarbett, PP,
Caheragh, Co. Cork

Civil Parish: **Caherduggan**
Map Grid: E8
RC Parish: see Doneraile
Diocese: CY

Civil Parish: **Caherlag**
Map Grid: E60
RC Parish: Glounthaune
Diocese: CK
Earliest Record: b. 8.1864; m. 10.186
Parish Address: Rev. Edward T. Fitzgerald, PP,
Glounthane, Co. Cork

Civil Parish: **Cannaway**
Map Grid: N55

RC Parish: see Kilmurry
Diocese: CK

Civil Parish: **Carrigaline (1)**
Map Grid: E84 and S38
RC Parish: Douglas; also part Passage, see
  Marmullane; see also below
Diocese: CK
Earliest Record: b. 11.1812; m. 11.1812
Parish Address: Rev. Canon T. Crowley, PP,
  Parochial House, Douglas, Co. Cork

Civil Parish: **Carrigaline (2)**
Map Grid: E84 and S38
RC Parish: Carrigaline and Templebrigid
Diocese: CK
Earliest Record: b. 1.1826; m. 1.1826
Parish Address: Rev. Daniel O'Flynn, PP, Car-
  rigaline, Co. Cork

Civil Parish: **Carrigdownane**
Map Grid: E13
RC Parish: see Kildorrery
Diocese: CY

Civil Parish: **Carrigleamleary**
Map Grid: E15
RC Parish: Annakissy, see Clenor
Diocese: CY

Civil Parish: **Carrigrohane**
Map Grid: N64 and E78
RC Parish: Ballincollig and Ballinora
Diocese: CK
Earliest Record: b. 1.1820; m. 1.1825
Missing Dates: b. 3.1828-8.1828; m. 2.1828-
  8.1828, 11.1857-10.1873
Parish Address: Rev. C. McCarthy, PP, Ballin-
  collig, Co. Cork

Civil Parish: **Carrigrohanebeg**
Map Grid: N58
RC Parish: see Innishcarra
Diocese: CY

Civil Parish: **Carrigtohill**
Map Grid: E61
RC Parish: Carrigtwohill
Diocese: CY
Earliest Record: b. 12.1817; m. 11.1817

Parish Address: Rev. Dean John Ahern, PP,
  Carrigtwohill, Co. Cork

Civil Parish: **Castlehaven (1)**
Map Grid: S53
RC Parish: Barryroe East; also Castlehaven, see
  below.
Diocese: RO
Earliest Record: b. 8.1804; m. 11.1771
Parish Address: Rev. Michael O'Cleary, PP,
  Lislevane, Bandon, Co. Cork

Civil Parish: **Castlehaven (2)**
Map Grid: S53
RC Parish: Castlehaven
Diocese: RO
Earliest Record: b. 10.1842; m. 10.1842;
  d. 10.1842
Parish Address: Rev. John Walsh, PP, Union
  Hall, Co. Cork

Civil Parish: **Castlelyons**
Map Grid: E44
RC Parish: Castlelyons
Diocese: CY
Earliest Record: b. 8.1791; m. 1.1830
Missing Dates: 1829
Parish Address: Rev. T. Fitzgerald, PP,
  Castlelyons, Fermoy, Co. Cork

Civil Parish: **Castlemagner**
Map Grid: N10
RC Parish: Castlemagner
Diocese: CY
Earliest Record: b. 5.1832; m. 5.1832
Parish Address: Rev. Philip Foley, PP,
  Castlemagner, Mallow, Co. Cork

Civil Parish: **Castletownroche**
Map Grid: E17
RC Parish: Castletownroche
Diocese: CY
Earliest Record: b. 8.1811; m. 9.1811
Parish Address: Rev. P. O'Keane, PP,
  Castletownroche, Co. Cork

Civil Parish: **Castleventry**
Map Grid: S13
RC Parish: see Kilmeen (1)
Diocese: RO

Civil Parish: **Churchtown**
Map Grid: N27
RC Parish: see Liscarroll
Diocese: CY

Civil Parish: **(Cape) Clear Island**
Map Grid: S58
RC Parish: Rath and the Islands, see Tullagh
Diocese: RO

Civil Parish: **Clenor**
Map Grid: E16
RC Parish: Annakissy (Killavullen)
Diocese: CY
Earliest Record: b. 6.1806; m. 7.1805
Parish Address: Rev. C. O'Flynn, PP, Ballygriffin, Mallow, Co. Cork

Civil Parish: **Clondrohid**
Map Grid: N39
RC Parish: Clondrohid
Diocese: CY
Earliest Record: b. 1807; m. 4.1822
Missing Dates: b. 10.1843-6.1844; m. 6.1847-1.1848
Parish Address: Rev. M. O'Brien, PP, Clondrohid, Macroom, Co. Cork

Civil Parish: **Clondulane**
Map Grid: E38a
RC Parish: see Fermoy
Diocese: CY

Civil Parish: **Clonfert (1)**
Map Grid: N1
RC Parish: Newmarket; also Kanturk, see below
Diocese: CY
Earliest Record: b. 11.1821; m. 1.1822
Missing Dates: b. 10.1865-3.1866; m. 9.1865-3.1866
Parish Address: Rev. Canon E. J. O'Riordan, PP, Newmarket, Co. Cork

Civil Parish: **Clonfert (2)**
Map Grid: N1
RC Parish: Kanturk
Diocese: CY
Earliest Record: b. 7.1822; m. 2.1824; (also Kanturk Workhouse baptisms from 9.1844)

Parish Address: Rev. Canon M. O'Dwyer, PP, Kanturk, Co. Cork

Civil Parish: **Clonmeen**
Map Grid: N13
RC Parish: Clonmeen (Banteer), see also Castlemagner
Diocese: CY
Earliest Record: b. 1.1847; m. 2.1847
Parish Address: Rev. D. C. O'Connell, PP, Banteer, Co. Cork

Civil Parish: **Clonmel**
Map Grid: E66
RC Parish: St. Colman's Cathedral, Cobh (Queenstown)
Diocese: CK
Earliest Record: b. 1812; m. 9.1812
Missing Dates: b. 6.1842-7.1842
Parish Address: Rev. S. Thornhill, Cathedral Terrace, Cobh, Co. Cork

Civil Parish: **Clonmult**
Map Grid: E58
RC Parish: Castlemartyr; see Mogeely (2)
Diocese: CY

Civil Parish: **Clonpriest**
Map Grid: E91
RC Parish: see Youghal
Diocese: CY

Civil Parish: **Clontead**
Map Grid: S84
RC Parish: Clontead and Ballymartle (Belgooly)
Diocese: CK
Earliest Record: b. 4.1836; m.4.1836
Parish Address: Rev. D. Burns, PP, Belgooly, Kinsale, Co. Cork

Civil Parish: **Cloyne**
Map Grid: E98
RC Parish: Cloyne
Diocese: CY
Earliest Record: b. 9.1791; m. 2.1786
Missing Dates: b. 11.1793-10.1803
Parish Address: Rev. D. O'Driscoll, PP, Cloyne, Midleton, Co. Cork

Civil Parish: **Coole**
Map Grid: E45
RC Parish: see Castlelyons
Diocese: CY

Civil Parish: **Cooline**
Map Grid: N23
RC Parish: see Ballyhea
Diocese: CY

Civil Parish: **Corbally**
Map Grid: N66
RC Parish: Ballincollig, see Carrigrohane
Diocese: CK

Civil Parish: **Corcomohide**
Map Grid: N18
RC Parish: see Co. Limerick

Civil Parish: **Corkbeg**
Map Grid: E107
RC Parish: see Aghada
Diocese: CY

Civil Parish: **Cork (city) (1)**
Map Grid: E80
RC Parish: Cathedral (North Parish)
Diocese: CK
Earliest Record: b. 7.1748; m. 7.1748
Missing Dates: m. 5.1764-4.1765
Parish Address: (St. Mary's Cathedral) Rev. Canon D. Forde, Cathedral Presbytery, Cork

Civil Parish: **Cork (city) (2)**
Map Grid: E80
RC Parish: South Parish, see St. Finbar
Diocese: CK

Civil Parish: **Cork (city) (3)**
Map Grid: E80
RC Parish: St. Patrick's
Diocese: CK
Earliest Record: b. 10.1831; m. 7.1832
Parish Address: (St. Patrick's) Rev. J. J. Sullivan, PP, The Acres, Tivoli, Co. Cork

Civil Parish: **Cork St. Nicholas**
Map Grid: E80
RC Parish: Blackrock
Diocese: CK
Earliest Record: b. 7.1810; m. 9.1810

Missing Dates: b. and m. 5.1811-2.1832, 8.1837-2.1839, 6.1839-1.1848
Parish Address: (Blackrock) Rev. Cornelius White, PP, Parochial House, Blackrock, Co. Cork

Civil Parish: **Cork St. Pauls**
Map Grid: E80
RC Parish: see Cork, St. Peters
Diocese: CK

Civil Parish: **Cork St. Peters**
Map Grid: E80
RC Parish: St. Peters and St. Pauls
Diocese: CK
Earliest Record: b. 4.1766; m. 4.1766
Missing Dates: b. 10.1766-11.1780, 9.1803-1.1809; m. 9.1766-10.1780, 10.1803-1.1809, 8.1810-7.1814, 8.1817-5.1834
Parish Address: Rev. Gerald Keohane, PP, The Presbytery, SS. Peter and Paul, Co. Cork

Civil Parish: **Creagh**
Map Grid: S56
RC Parish: Skibbereen
Diocese: RO
Earliest Record: b. 3.1814; m. 11.1837
Parish Address: Rev. James Coombes, The Presbytery, Skibbereen, Co. Cork

Civil Parish: **Cullen (1) (Duhallow)**
Map Grid: N11
RC Parish: part Dromtariff; part Millstreet, see Drishane
Diocese: A and A

Civil Parish: **Cullen (2) (Kinalea)**
Map Grid: S27
RC Parish: see Ballymartle
Diocese: CK

Civil Parish: **Currykippane**
Map Grid: E75
RC Parish: Cathedral, see Cork (city) (1)
Diocese: CK

Civil Parish: **Dangandonovan**
Map Grid: E88
RC Parish: see Killeagh
Diocese: CY

Civil Parish: **Derryvillane**
Map Grid: E11
RC Parish: see Glanworth
Diocese: CY

Civil Parish: **Desert**
Map Grid: S79
RC Parish: Clonakilty, see Kilgarriff
Diocese: RO

Civil Parish: **Desertmore**
Map Grid: N61
RC Parish: Ovens, see Athowen
Diocese: CK

Civil Parish: **Desertserges**
Map Grid: S71
RC Parish: part Enniskeane and Desertserges;
    part Bandon, see Ballymodan
Diocese: CK
Earliest Record: b. 11.1813 (separate registers
    for Enniskeane and Desertserges); m. 9.1813
Parish Address: Enniskeane and Desertserges,
    Rev. Shaw McCarthy, PP, Ahiohill, Co. Cork

Civil Parish: **Donoughmore (1)** (Ibane and Bar-
    ryroe Barony)
Map Grid: S68
RC Parish: Donoughmore; also Barryroe, see
    Castlehaven
Diocese: CY
Earliest Record: b. 4.1803; m. 1.1790
Parish Address: Ver. Rev. John O'Connor, PP,
    Donoughmore, Co. Cork.

Civil Parish: **Donoughmore (2)** (East Muskerry
    Barony)
Map Grid: N49
RC Parish: part Aghabulloge; part Glountane,
    see Kilshannig

Civil Parish: **Doneraile**
Map Grid: E5
RC Parish: Doneraile
Diocese: CY
Earliest Record: b. 4.1815; m. 1.1815
Parish Address: Rev. Canon J. Cotter, PP,
    Doneraile, Co. Cork

Civil Parish: **Drimoleague** (Dromdaleague)
Map Grid: S50
RC Parish: Drimoleague
Diocese: CK
Earliest Record: b. 7.1817; m. 7.1817
Missing Dates: m. 11.1863-12.1876, 1878
Parish Address: Rev. M. Murphy, PP,
    Drimsleague, Co. Cork

Civil Parish: **Drinagh**
Map Grid: S51
RC Parish: see Drimoleague
Diocese: CK

Civil Parish: **Drishane**
Map Grid: N36
RC Parish: Millstreet (Cullen)
Diocese: A and A
Earliest Record: b. 12.1853; m. 1.1855
Parish Address: Rev. Canon P. Browne, PP,
    Millstreet, Co. Cork

Civil Parish: **Dromdowney**
Map Grid: N35
RC Parish: see Ballyclough
Diocese: CY

Civil Parish: **Dromtariff**
Map Grid: N12
RC Parish: Dromtariffe
Diocese: A and A
Earliest Record: b. 2.1832; m. 1.1832
Parish Address: Rev. D. Walsh, PP, Dromagh,
    Mallow, Co. Cork

Civil Parish: **Dunbulloge**
Map Grid: E41
RC Parish: Glanmire, see Rathcooney
Diocese: CK

Civil Parish: **Dunderrow**
Map Grid: N68 and S24
RC Parish: see Kinsale
Diocese: CK

Civil Parish: **Dungourney**
Map Grid: E57
RC Parish: Castlemartyr, see Mogeely (2)
Diocese: CY

Civil Parish: **Dunisky**
Map Grid: N44
RC Parish: see Kilmichael
Diocese: CK

Civil Parish: **Dunmahon**
Map Grid: E20
RC Parish: see Glanworth
Diocese: CY

Civil Parish: **Durrus**
Map Grid: S45
RC Parish: see Kilcrohane
Diocese: CK

Civil Parish: **Fanlobbus**
Map Grid: S9
RC Parish: Dunmanway
Diocese: CK
Earliest Record: b. 6.1818 m. 6.1818
Parish Address: Rev. Canon D. McCarthy, PP,
  Presbytery, Dunmanway, Co. Cork

Civil Parish: **Farahy**
Map Grid: 37
RC Parish: see Kildorrery
Diocese: CY

Civil Parish: **Fermoy**
Map Grid: E38
RC Parish: Fermoy
Diocese: CY
Earliest Record: b. 1.1828; m. 5.1828; (also Fer-
  moy Workhouse baptisms from 4.1854)
Missing Dates: 8.1848-1.1849
Parish Address: Rev. M. O'Connell, Presbytery,
  Fermoy, Co. Cork

Civil Parish: **Garrankinnefeake**
Map Grid: E97
RC Parish: see Aghada
Diocese: CY

Civil Parish: **Garrycloyne**
Map Grid: N54
RC Parish: Blarney
Diocese: CY
Earliest Record: b. 8.1791; m. 9.1778
Missing Dates: b. 6.1792-2.1821, 1.1826-
  10.1826; m. 3.1813-2.1821, 11.1825-12.1826

Parish Address: Rev. Canon Martin Cusack,
  PP, Blarney, Co. Cork

Civil Parish: **Garryvoe**
Map Grid: E100
RC Parish: Ballymacoda, see Kilmacdonagh

Civil Parish: **Glanworth**
Map Grid: E18
RC Parish: Glanworth
Diocese: CY
Earliest Record: b. 1.1836; m. 1.1836
Parish Address: Rev. E. Kenefick, PP, Glan-
  worth, Co. Cork

Civil Parish: **Gortroe**
Map Grid: E49
RC Parish: see Rathcormack
Diocese: CY

Civil Parish: **Grenagh**
Map Grid: N72
RC Parish: Grenagh, see Mourneabbey for pre-
  1840 records
Diocese: CY
Earliest Record: b. 4.1840; m. 4.1840
Parish Address: Rev. Daniel O'Mahony, PP,
  Grenagh, Co. Cork

Civil Parish: **Hackmys**
Map Grid: N22
RC Parish: Charleville, see Rathgoggan
Diocese: CY

Civil Parish: **Holy Trinity** (Christchurch)
Map Grid: E80
RC Parish: part St. Peters and St. Paul; part
  Blackrock, see St. Finbar
Diocese: CK

Civil Parish: **Ightermurragh**
Map Grid: E95
RC Parish: Ballymacoda, see Kilmacdonagh
Diocese: CY

Civil Parish: **Imphrick**
Map Grid: N29 and E4
RC Parish: see Ballyhea
Diocese: CY

Civil Parish: **Inch**
Map Grid: E103
RC Parish: see Aghada
Diocese: CY

Civil Parish: **Inchigeelagh**
Map Grid: N42 and S6
RC Parish: Iveleary
Diocese: CK
Earliest Record: b. 1816; m. 1816
Parish Address: Rev. John Murphy, PP, Inchigeela, Co. Cork

Civil Parish: **Inchinabacky**
Map Grid: E65
RC Parish: see Midleton
Diocese: CY

Civil Parish: **Inishcarra**
Map Grid: N52
RC Parish: Inishcarra
Diocese: CY
Earliest Record: b. 7.1814; m. 8.1814
Missing Dates: b. 9.1844-1.1845
Parish Address: Rev. Canon John Warren, PP, Inniscarra, Co. Cork

Civil Parish: **Inishannon**
Map Grid: S22
RC Parish: Inishannon
Diocese: CK
Earliest Record: b. 8.1825; m. 8.1825
Parish Address: Rev. M. O'Mahony, CC, The Presbytery, Knockavilla, Innishannon, Co. Cork

Civil Parish: **Inishkenny**
Map Grid: N69 and E83
RC Parish: Ballincollig, see Carrigrohane
Diocese: CK

Civil Parish: **Island**
Map Grid: S62
RC Parish: part Clonakilty, see Kilgarriff; part Rathbarry, see Ardfield
Diocese: RO

Civil Parish: **Kilbolane** (see also Co. Limerick)
Map Grid: N17
RC Parish: Freemount, see Knocktemple
Diocese: CY

Civil Parish: **Kilbonane**
Map Grid: N60
RC Parish: see Kilmurry
Diocese: CK

Civil Parish: **Kilbrin**
Map Grid: N7
RC Parish: see Ballyclough
Diocese: CK

Civil Parish: **Kilbrittain**
Map Grid: S73
RC Parish: Kilbrittain
Diocese: CK
Earliest Record: b. 8.1810
Parish Address: Rev. John McCarthy, PP, Kilbrittain, Co. Cork

Civil Parish: **Kilbrogan**
Map Grid: S19
RC Parish: Bandon, see Ballymodan
Diocese: CK

Civil Parish: **Kilbroney**
Map Grid: N30
RC Parish: see Buttevant
Diocese: CY

Civil Parish: **Kilcaskan** (see also Co. Kerry)
Map Grid: S2
RC Parish: Glengarriffe, see Kilmacomoge
Diocese: RO

Civil Parish: **Kilcatherine**
Map Grid: S1
RC Parish: Eyeries
Diocese: RO
Earliest Record: b. 4.1843; m. 2.1824
Parish Address: Rev. Thomas Pierse, PP, Eyries, Co. Cork

Civil Parish: **Kilcoe**
Map Grid: S48
RC Parish: see Aghadown
Diocese: RO

Civil Parish: **Kilcorcoran**
Map Grid: N6
RC Parish: Kanturk, see Clonfert
Diocese: CY

Civil Parish: **Kilcorney**
Map Grid: N37
RC Parish: see Clonmeen
Diocese: CY

Civil Parish: **Kilcredan**
Map Grid: E101
RC Parish: Lady's Bridge, see Kilmacdonagh
Diocese: CY

Civil Parish: **Kilcrohane**
Map Grid: S44
RC Parish: Muintervara or Durrus
Diocese: CK
Earliest Record: b. 5.1820; m. 2.1819
Parish Address: Rev. J. Duggan, CC, Kilcrohane, Bantry, Co. Cork

Civil Parish: **Kilcrumper**
Map Grid: E21
RC Parish: part Fermoy; part Kilworth
Diocese: CY

Civil Parish: **Kilcully**
Map Grid: E74
RC Parish: Glanmire, see Rathcooney
Diocese: CK

Civil Parish: **Kilcummer**
Map Grid: E26
RC Parish: see Castletownroche
Diocese: CY

Civil Parish: **Kildorrery**
Map Grid: E30
RC Parish: Kildorrery
Diocese: CY
Earliest Record: b. 5.1824; m. 1.1803
Missing Dates: b. 9.1853 onwards
Parish Address: Rev. Canon W. Linehan, PP, Kildorrery, Co. Cork

Civil Parish: **Kilfaughnabeg**
Map Grid: S14
RC Parish: see Kilmacabea
Diocese: RO

Civil Parish: **Kilgarriff**
Map Grid: S75
RC Parish: Clonakilty
Diocese: RO

Earliest Record: b. 8.1809; m. 1.1811
Parish Address: Rev. Mgr. M. Daly, PP, Clonakilty, Co. Cork

Civil Parish: **Kilgrogan**
Map Grid: N28
RC Parish: see Liscarroll
Diocese: CY

Civil Parish: **Kilgullane**
Map Grid: E34
RC Parish: see Glanworth
Diocese: CY

Civil Parish: **Kilkerranmore**
Map Grid: S59
RC Parish: part Rosscarbery, see Ross; part Kilmeen; part Rathbarry, see Ardfield

Civil Parish: **Killaconenagh**
Map Grid: S4
RC Parish: Castletownbere, see Kilnamanagh
Diocese: RO

Civil Parish: **Killanully**
Map Grid: E86 and S39
RC Parish: Douglas, see Carrigaline
Diocese: CK

Civil Parish: **Killaspugmullane**
Map Grid: E51
RC Parish: Watergrasshill, see Ardnageehy
Diocese: CK

Civil Parish: **Killathy**
Map Grid: E28
RC Parish: see Castletownroche
Diocese: CY

Civil Parish: **Killeagh**
Map Grid: E90
RC Parish: Killeagh
Diocese: CY
Earliest Record: b. 3.1829; m. 11.1822
Parish Address: Rev. T. Glavin, PP, Killeagh, Co. Cork

Civil Parish: **Killeenemer**
Map Grid: E19
RC Parish: see Glanworth
Diocese: CY

Civil Parish: **Killowen**
Map Grid: S18
RC Parish: see Desertserges
Diocese: CK

Civil Parish: **Kilmacabea**
Map Grid: S11
RC Parish: Kilmacabea
Diocese: RO
Earliest Record: b. 6.1832; m. 7.1832
Missing Dates: m. 2.1865-5.1865
Parish Address: Rev. J. Hurley, PP, Leap, Co. Cork

Civil Parish: **Kilmacdonagh**
Map Grid: E96
RC Parish: Ballymacoda
Diocese: CY
Earliest Record: b. 11.1835; m. 9.1835
Parish Address: Rev. Michael Campbell, Ballymacoda, Co. Cork

Civil Parish: **Kilmaclenan**
Map Grid: N33
RC Parish: see Ballyclough
Diocese: CY

Civil Parish: **Kilmahon**
Map Grid: E104
RC Parish: see Cloyne
Diocese: CY

Civil Parish: **Kilmaloda**
Map Grid: S72
RC Parish: see Timoleague
Diocese: RO

Civil Parish: **Kilmeen (1)**
Map Grid: S10
RC Parish: Kilmeen
Diocese: RO
Earliest Record: b. 8.1821
Parish Address: Rev. J. Casey, PP, Rossmore, Clonakilty, Co. Cork

Civil Parish: **Kilmeen (2)**
Map Grid: N5
RC Parish: Boherbue
Diocese: A and A
Earliest Record: b. 7.1833; m. 3.1863
Missing Dates: b. 12.1860-2.1863

Parish Address: Rev. Donagh O'Donovan, Boherbue, Mallow, Co. Cork

Civil Parish: **Kilmichael**
Map Grid: N45 and S7
RC Parish: Kilmichael
Diocese: CK
Earliest Record: b. 10.1819; m. 1.1819
Missing Dates: m. 2.1850-1.1851
Parish Address: Rev. J. Cremin, CC, Kilmichael, Macroom, Co. Cork

Civil Parish: **Kilmacomogue (1)**
Map Grid: S5
RC Parish: Glengarriffe
Diocese: CK
Earliest Record: 7.1822
Parish Address: Ver. Rev. J. Shine, PP, Glengarriffe, Co. Cork

Civil Parish: **Kilmacomogue (2)**
Map Grid: S5
RC Parish: Bantry
Diocese: CK
Earliest Record: 7.1822 (parts of 1788, 1791-92, 1794-99, 1808-09, 1812-14 and 1822-24 also exist); 5.1788
Missing Dates: 12.1857-1.1872
Parish Address: Rev. Canon D. O'Callaghan, PP, Bantry, Co. Cork

Civil Parish: **Kilmoe**
Map Grid: S49
RC Parish: Goleen (West Schull)
Diocese: CK
Earliest Record: b. 1.1827; m. 1.1827
Parish Address: Rev. William F. Murphy, PP, Goleen, Co. Cork

Civil Parish: **Kilmoney**
Map Grid: S42
RC Parish: see Carrigaline

Civil Parish: **Kilmonogue**
Map Grid: S32
RC Parish: see Clontead
Diocese: CK

Civil Parish: **Kilmurry**
Map Grid: N47
RC Parish: Kilmurry

Diocese: CK
Earliest Record: b. 6.1786; m. 1.1812
Missing Dates: b. 1803-05 mutilated
Parish Address: Rev. D. Kehily, PP, Cloughduv,
   Farnanes, Co. Cork

Civil Parish: **Kilnaglory**
Map Grid: N63 and E82
RC Parish: Ballincollig, see Carrigrohane
Diocese: CK

Civil Parish: **Kilnagross**
Map Grid: S77
RC Parish: Clonakilty, see Kilgarriff
Diocese: RO

Civil Parish: **Kilnamanagh**
Map Grid: S3
RC Parish: Castletownbere
Diocese: RO
Earliest Record: b. 9.1819; m. 7.1819
Parish Address: Rev. Canon John McKenna,
   PP, Castletownbere, Co. Cork

Civil Parish: **Kilnamartry**
Map Grid: N40
RC Parish: Kilnamartyra
Diocese: CY
Earliest Record: b. 1.1803; m. 1.1803
Missing Dates: m. 6.1833-9.1939
Parish Address: Rev. N. O'Connor, PP, Kil-
   namartyra, Macroom, Co. Cork

Civil Parish: **Kilpatrick**
Map Grid: S31
RC Parish: see Tracton
Diocese: CK

Civil Parish: **Kilphelan**
Map Grid: E35
RC Parish: Mitchelstown, see Brigown
Diocese: CY

Civil Parish: **Kilquane (1)**
Map Grid: E3
RC Parish: see Co. Limerick

Civil Parish: **Kilquane (2)**
Map Grid: E50
RC Parish: Glounthaune, see Caherlag
Diocese: CK

Civil Parish: **Kilroan**
Map Grid: S82
RC Parish: Courcey's, see Ballinadee
Diocese: CK

Civil Parish: **Kilroe**
Map Grid: N8
RC Parish: Kanturk, see Clonfert
Diocese: CY

Civil Parish: **Kilshanahan**
Map Grid: E48
RC Parish: Watergrasshill, see Ardnageehy
Diocese: CK

Civil Parish: **Kilshannig**
Map Grid: N16
RC Parish: Glountane, also Kilpadder
Diocese: CY
Earliest Record: b. 5.1829
Missing Dates: b. 8.1844-5.1847
Parish Address: Rev. Mortimer Downing, CC,
   Glountane, Mallow, Co. Cork

Civil Parish: **Kilsillagh**
Map Grid: S69
RC Parish: Barryroe, see Castlehaven
Diocese: RO

Civil Parish: **Kilworth**
Map Grid: E36
RC Parish: Kilworth
Diocese: CY
Earliest Record: b. 9.1829; m. 10.1829
Parish Address: Rev. Canon P. Condon, PP,
   Kilworth, Co. Cork

Civil Parish: **Kinneigh**
Map Grid: S8
RC Parish: part Enniskean, see Killowen; part
   Murragh
Diocese: CK

Civil Parish: **Kinnure**
Map Grid: S33
RC Parish: see Tracton
Diocese: CK

Civil Parish: **Kinsale**
Map Grid: S85
RC Parish: Kinsale

Diocese: CK
Earliest Record: b. 1.1805; m. 8.1828
Missing Dates: b. 7.1806-1.1815
Parish Address: Rev. J. Hyde, PP, The Presbytery, Kinsale, Co. Cork

Civil Parish: **Knockavilly**
Map Grid: N67 and S21
RC Parish: see Inishannon
Diocese: CK

Civil Parish: **Knockmourne**
Map Grid: E68
RC Parish: Conna
Diocese: CY
Earliest Record: b. 9.1834; m. 10.1845
Missing Dates: b. 9.1844-12.1845
Parish Address: Rev. J. Ryan, PP, Conna, Mallow, Co. Cork

Civil Parish: **Knocktemple**
Map Grid: N3
RC Parish: Freemount (Milford)
Diocese: CY
Earliest Record: b. 9.1827; m. 10.1827
Missing Dates: b. 3.1840-1.1858 (except 7.1843-12.1843)
Parish Address: Rev. Gerard Coleman, CC, Freemount, Charleville, Co. Cork

Civil Parish: **Lackeen**
Map Grid: N26
RC Parish: see Liscarroll
Diocese: CY

Civil Parish: **Leighmoney**
Map Grid: S28
RC Parish: see Inishannon
Diocese: CK

Civil Parish: **Leitrim**
Map Grid: E39
RC Parish: see Kilworth
Diocese: CY

Civil Parish: **Liscarroll**
Map Grid: N25
RC Parish: Liscarroll and Churchtown
Diocese: CY
Earliest Record: b. 3.1812; m. 2.1813

Parish Address: Rev. P. J. Twohig, PP, Churchtown, Mallow, Co. Cork

Civil Parish: **Liscleary**
Map Grid: S40
RC Parish: Douglas, see Carrigaline
Diocese: CK

Civil Parish: **Lisgoold**
Map Grid: E54
RC Parish: Lisgoold
Diocese: CY
Earliest Record: b. 7.1807; m. 10.1821
Parish Address: Rev. P. Halliden, PP, Lisgoold, Leamlara, Co. Cork

Civil Parish: **Lislee**
Map Grid: S67
RC Parish: Barryroe, see Castlehaven
Diocese: RO

Civil Parish: **Lismore and Mocollop**
Map Grid: E40
RC Parish: see Co. Waterford
Diocese: LS

Civil Parish: **Litter**
Map Grid: E29
RC Parish: part Fermoy (Templenoe village is in Ballyhooly, see Castletownroche)
Diocese: CY

Civil Parish: **Little Island**
Map Grid: E63
RC Parish: Glounthaune, see Caherlag
Diocese: CK

Civil Parish: **Macloneigh**
Map Grid: N43
RC Parish: see Kilmichael
Diocese: CK

Civil Parish: **Macroney**
Map Grid: E37
RC Parish: see Kilworth
Diocese: CY

Civil Parish: **Macroom**
Map Grid: N41
RC Parish: Macroom
Diocese: CY

Earliest Record: b. 9.1805; m. 1.1780
Missing Dates: b. 11.1843-12.1843
Parish Address: Rev. Mgr. D. O'Connell, PP,
Macroom, Co. Cork

Civil Parish: **Magourney**
Map Grid: N51
RC Parish: see Aghabulloge
Diocese: CY

Civil Parish: **Mallow**
Map Grid: N15 and E14
RC Parish: Mallow
Diocese: CY
Earliest Record: b. 1.1809; m. 4.1757
Missing Dates: b. 7.1809-6.1817, 2.1818-8.1820,
12.1828-4.1832; m. 11.1823-8.1825, 7.1828-
4.1832
Parish Address: Rev. Canon D. O'Callaghan,
PP, Mallow, Co. Cork

Civil Parish: **Marmullane**
Map Grid: S36
RC Parish: Passage
Diocese: CK
Earliest Record: b. 4.1795; m. 4.1795
Missing Dates: m. 5.1831-5.1832
Parish Address: Rev. P. G. Collins, PP, Passage
West, Co. Cork

Civil Parish: **Marshalstown**
Map Grid: E32
RC Parish: Mitchelstown, see Brigown
Diocese: CY

Civil Parish: **Matehy**
Map Grid: N53
RC Parish: see Inishcarra
Diocese: CY

Civil Parish: **Midleton**
Map Grid: E93
RC Parish: Midleton
Diocese: CY
Earliest Record: b. 9.1819; m. 10.1819
Parish Address: Rev. Canon Wm. C. Twohig,
PP, Midleton, Co. Cork

Civil Parish: **Mogeely (1)** (Kinnatalloon)
Map Grid: E71
RC Parish: Conna, see Knockmourne

Civil Parish: **Mogeely (2)**
Map Grid: E89
RC Parish: Imogeela
Diocese: CY
Earliest Record: b. 2.1835; m. 9.1833
Parish Address: (Castlemartyr) Rev. D. Hallis-
sey, PP, Castlemartyr, Co. Cork

Civil Parish: **Mogeesha** (Imokilly)
Map Grid: E64
RC Parish: see Carrigtohill
Diocese: CY

Civil Parish: **Monanimy**
Map Grid: E24
RC Parish: Killavullen, see Clenor
Diocese: CY

Civil Parish: **Monkstown**
Map Grid: S37
RC Parish: Passage, see Marmullane
Diocese: CY

Civil Parish: **Mourneabbey**
Map Grid: N71 and E22
RC Parish: part Mourne Abbey (Ballinamona),
see also Mallow
Diocese: CY
Earliest Record: b. 1.1829; m. 10.1829
Parish Address: Rev. D. McCarthy, PP, Mourne
Abbey, Mallow, Co. Cork

Civil Parish: **Moviddy**
Map Grid: N59
RC Parish: see Kilmurry
Diocese: CK

Civil Parish: **Murragh**
Map Grid: S15
RC Parish: Murragh
Diocese: CK
Earliest Record: b. 1.1834; m. 1.1834
Parish Address: Rev. L. O'Mahony, PP, Baile
Nuis, Bandon, Co. Cork

Civil Parish: **Myross**
Map Grid: S54
RC Parish: see Castlehaven (church)
Diocese: RO

Civil Parish: **Nohaval**
Map Grid: S34
RC Parish: see Tracton
Diocese: CK

Civil Parish: **Nohavaldy**
Map Grid: N4
RC Parish: part Boherbue, see Kilmeen (2)
Diocese: A and A
Earliest Record: b. 11.1835; m. 9.1835
Parish Address: Rev. Michael Campbell, Ballymacoda, Co. Cork

Civil Parish: **Rahan**
Map Grid: E23
RC Parish: part Mallow; part Ballinamona
Diocese: CY

Civil Parish: **Rathbarry**
Map Grid: S60
RC Parish: see Ardfield
Diocese: RO

Civil Parish: **Rathclarin**
Map Grid: S78
RC Parish: see Kilbritain

Civil Parish: **Rathcooney**
Map Grid: E73
RC Parish: Glanmire
Diocese: CK
Earliest Record: b. 11.1806; m. 1.1803
Missing Dates: b. 9.1816-5.1818; m. 5.1817-5.1818
Parish Address: Rev. S. Burke, PP, Glanmire, Co. Cork

Civil Parish: **Rathcormack**
Map Grid: E43
RC Parish: Rathcormack
Diocese: CY
Earliest Record: b. 1.1792; m. 1.1829
Parish Address: Rev. C. Casey, PP, Rathcormac, Fermoy, Co. Cork

Civil Parish: **Rathgoggan**
Map Grid: N21
RC Parish: Charleville
Diocese: CY
Earliest Record: b. 5.1827; m. 8.1774

Missing Dates: m. 11.1792-11.1794, 7.1822-6.1827
Parish Address: Rev. Canon S. Corkery, PP, Charleville, Co. Cork

Civil Parish: **Rincurran**
Map Grid: S86
RC Parish: see Kinsale
Diocese: CK

Civil Parish: **Ringrone**
Map Grid: S81
RC Parish: Courcey's, see Ballinadee
Diocese: CK

Civil Parish: **Rosscarbery** (Ross)
Map Grid: S12
RC Parish: Rosscarbery
Diocese: RO
Earliest Record: b. 11.1814; m. 1.1820
Parish Address: Rev. T. McGrath, PP, Roscarbery, Co. Cork

Civil Parish: **Rosskeen**
Map Grid: N14
RC Parish: see Castlemagner
Diocese: CY

Civil Parish: **Rostellan**
Map Grid: E102
RC Parish: see Aghada
Diocese: CY

Civil Parish: **St. Anne, Shandon**
Map Grid: E77
RC Parish: part Cathedral, see Cork (city) (1); part SS Peter and Paul, see Cork St. Peter

Civil Parish: **St. Finbar**
Map Grid: N62 and E79
RC Parish: part SS Peter and Paul, see Cork St. Peter; part St. Finbars South
Diocese: CK
Earliest Record: b. 8.1756; m. 3.1775
Missing Dates: b. 1.1757-7.1760; 9.1763-3.1774; 7.1777-1.1789
Parish Address: Rev. B. O'Ceallaigh, South Presbytery, Dunbar St. Cork

Civil Parish: **St. Mary, Shandon**
Map Grid: E76
RC Parish: Cathedral, see Cork (city) (1)

Civil Parish: **St. Michael**
Map Grid: E46
RC Parish: see Templemichael
Diocese: CK

Civil Parish: **St. Natlash**
Map Grid: E10
RC Parish: see Kildorrery
Diocese: CY

Civil Parish: **St. Nicholas**
Map Grid: N65 and E81
RC Parish: see Cork
Diocese: CK

Civil Parish: **St. Pauls**
Map Grid: E80
RC Parish: see Cork
Diocese: CK

Civil Parish: **St. Peters**
Map Grid: E80
RC Parish: see Cork

Civil Parish: **Shandrum**
Map Grid: N19
RC Parish: part Shandrum; see also Ballyhea
Diocese: CY
Earliest Record: b. 3.1829
Parish Address: Rev. J. Barry, PP, Shandrum,
   Charleville, Co. Cork

Civil Parish: **Skull**
Map Grid: S47
RC Parish: Skull
Diocese: CK
Earliest Record: b. 10.1807; m. 2.1809
Missing Dates: b. 9.1815-1.1816; m. 11.1815-
   1.1816, 11.1832-2.1833, 9.1870-1.1871
Parish Address: Rev. T. O'Sullivan, PP, Schull,
   Co. Cork

Civil Parish: **Subulter**
Map Grid: N9
Old name: see Ballyclough
Diocese: CY

Civil Parish: **Templebodan**
Map Grid: E55
RC Parish: see Lisgoold
Diocese: CY

Civil Parish: **Templebreedy**
Map Grid: S43
RC Parish: see Carrigaline (church)
Diocese: CK

Civil Parish: **Templebryan**
Map Grid: S76
RC Parish: see Clonakilty, see Kilgarriff
Diocese: RO

Civil Parish: **Templemartin**
Map Grid: S16
RC Parish: part Bandon, see Ballymodan
Diocese: CK

Civil Parish: **Templemichael**
Map Grid: S23
RC Parish: Glanmire, see Rathcooney
Diocese: CK

Civil Parish: **Templemolaga**
Map Grid: E31
RC Parish: see Kildorrery
Diocese: CY

Civil Parish: **Templenacarriga**
Map Grid: E56
RC Parish: see Lisgoold
Diocese: CY

Civil Parish: **Templeomalus**
Map Grid: S63
RC Parish: Clonakilty, see Kilgarriff
Diocese: RO

Civil Parish: **Templequinlan**
Map Grid: S64
RC Parish: see Clonakilty, see Kilgarriff
Diocese: RO

Civil Parish: **Templeroan**
Map Grid: E6
RC Parish: see Doneraile
Diocese: CY

Civil Parish: **Temple Robin** (Great Island)
Map Grid: E67
RC Parish: Cobh, see Clonmel
Diocese: CY

Civil Parish: **Templetrine**
Map Grid: S80
RC Parish: Courcey's, see Ballinadee
Diocese: CK

Civil Parish: **Templeusque**
Map Grid: E47
RC Parish: Glanmire, see Rathcooney
Diocese: CK

Civil Parish: **Timoleague**
Map Grid: S65
RC Parish: Timoleague; also Barryroe, see Castlehaven
Diocese: RO
Earliest Record: b. 11.1842; m. 4.1843
Parish Address: Rev. D. Casey, PP, Timoleague, Co. Cork

Civil Parish: **Tisaxon** or **Teighsasson**
Map Grid: S83
RC Parish: see Kinsale
Diocese: CK

Civil Parish: **Titeskin** (Kilteskin)
Map Grid: E106
RC Parish: see Cloyne
Diocese: CY

Civil Parish: **Trabolgan**
Map Grid: E109
RC Parish: see Aghada
Diocese: CY

Civil Parish: **Tracton**
Map Grid: S30
RC Parish: Tracton Abbey
Diocese: CK
Earliest Record: b. 12.1802; m. 6.1840
Parish Address: Rev. R. Ormond, PP, Minane Bridge, Co. Cork

Civil Parish: **Tullagh**
Map Grid: S57
RC Parish: Inisherkin is part of Rath; remainder is in Skibbereen Parish

Diocese: RO
Earliest Record: b. 7.1818; m. 1.1819
Missing Dates: b. 9.1851-2.1852; m. 8.1851-10.1851
Parish Address: Rev. Brendan Whooley, CC, Rath, Baltimore, Co. Cork

Civil Parish: **Tullilease**
Map Grid: N2
RC Parish: Freemount, see Knocktemple
Diocese: CY

Civil Parish: **Wallstown**
Map Grid: E9
RC Parish: Killavullen, see Clenor
Diocese: CY

Civil Parish: **Whitechurch**
Map Grid: N73 and E72
RC Parish: Blarney, see Garrycloyne
Diocese: CY

Civil Parish: **Youghal**
Map Grid: E92
RC Parish: Youghal
Diocese: CY
Earliest Record: b. 9.1803; m. 12.1801
Missing Dates: 6.1862-6.1866
Parish Address: Rev. Canon D. Dwyer, PP, Youghal, Co. Cork

Commercial and Social Directories

1788

Richard Lucas's *General Directory of the Kingdom of Ireland* contains lists of traders in Bandon, Cork, Cobh, Innishannon, Kinsale, Passage, and Youghal. Also reprinted in *The Irish Genealogist* 4 (1): 37-46.

1797

J. Nixon's *Cork Almanac* contains lists of merchants and traders in the city.

1809

Holden's *Triennial Directory* covers the city of Cork and has alphabetical lists of traders.

1810

West's *Directory of Cork* contains lists of gentry, traders, and professionals.

1812

Connor's *Cork Directory* contains alphabetical lists of merchants and traders. Also issued in 1817, 1821, 1826, and 1828.

1817

Gentlemens and Citizens Cork Almanac published by Geary, gives lists of physicians, bankers, clergy, and public officials.

1820

J. Pigot's *Commercial Directory of Ireland* contains information on the gentry, nobility, and traders in and around the towns of Bandon, Cork, Kinsale, and Youghal.

1824

J. Pigot's *City of Dublin & Hibernian Provincial Directory* includes traders, nobility, gentry, and clergy lists of Bandon, Bantry, Castlelyons, Castlemartyr, Charleville, Clonakilty, Cloyne, Cork, Cobh, Doneraile, Fermoy, Kanturk, Kilworth, Kinsale, Macroom, Mallow, Midleton, Millstreet, Mitchelstown, Newmarket, Rathcormac, Skibbereen, and Youghal.

1842

General Directory of the City and County of Cork with a separate alphabetical listing for city and county of nobility, gentry, and clergy. NLI.

1844

General P.O. Directory of Cork contains general alphabetical directory and trades directory of Cork and list of gentry and traders for each of the following: Ballincollig, Ballinhassig, Ballydehob and Skibbereen, Bandon, Bantry, Blackrock, Buttevant, Carrigaline, Castlelyons, Castlemartyr, Castletown, Castletownroche, Castletownsend, Charleville, Clonakilty, Cloyne, Coachford, Cove, Crookstown, Doneraile, Douglas, Dunmanway, Ennis-

keane, Fermoy, Glanmire, Glounthaun, Inniscarra, Innoshannon, Kildorrery, Killeagh, Killinardish, Kanturk, Kinsale, Kilworth, Macroom, Mallow, Rathcormac, Rosscarbery, Shanagarry, Skibbereen, Tallow, Timoleague, Unionhall, Watergrasshill, Whitegate, and Youghal.

1846

Slater's *National Commercial Directory of Ireland* lists nobility, clergy, traders, etc., in Ballincollig, Bandon and Innishannon, Bantry, Charleville, Clonakilty, Cloyne and Castlemartyr, Cork, Cove, Doneraile, Fermoy, Kanturk, Kilworth, Kinsale, Macroom, Mallow, Midleton, Millstreet, Mitchelstown, Newmarket, Rathcormac, Skibbereen and Castletownsend, and Youghal.

1856

Slater's *Royal National Commercial Directory of Ireland* lists nobility, gentry, clergy, traders, etc., in Ballincollig, Bandon and Innishannon, Bantry and Glengariff, Charleville, Clonakilty, Cloyne and Castlemartyr, Cork, Doneraile, Dunmanway, Fermoy, Kanturk, Kilworth, Kinsale, Macroom, Mallow, Midleton, Millstreet, Mitchelstown, Newmarket, Passage and Monkstown, Queenstown (Cove), Rathcormac and Castlelyons, Ross, Skibbereen, Castletownsend and Baltimore, Skull and Ballydehob, and Youghal.

1870

Slater's *Directory of Ireland* contains trade, nobility, and clergy lists for Ballincollig, Bandon, Bantry, Charleville, Clonakilty, Cloyne and Castlemartyr, Cork, Doneraile, Dunmanway, Fermoy, Kanturk, Kilworth, Kinsale, Macroom, Mallow, Midleton, Millstreet, Mitchelstown, Newmarket, Passage, Queenstown (Cobh), Rathcormac and Castlelyons, Rosscarbery, Skibbereen and Ballydehob, and Youghal.

1875

Guy's *Directory of the City and County of Cork* gives residents, traders, and large farmers in each postal district. Issued annually to 1913.

1881

Slater's *Royal National Commercial Directory of Ireland* contains lists of traders, clergy, nobility, and farmers in adjoining parishes of the towns of Bandon, Bantry and Glengariff, Charleville, Clonakilty, Cloyne and Castlemartyr, Cork, Dunmanway, Fermoy, Kanturk, Kinsale, Macroom, Mallow, Midleton, Millstreet, Mitchelstown, Newmarket, Passage and Monkstown, Queenstown (Cove), Rathcormac and Castlelyons, Rosscarbery, Skibbereen, Castletownsend and Leap, Skull and Ballydehob, and Youghal.

1886

Francis Guy's *Postal Directory* of Munster lists gentry, clergy, traders, principal farmers, teachers, and police sergeants in each postal district of the county and has a listing of magistrates, clergy, and the professions for the whole county. Issued annually from 1889.

1893

Francis Guy's *Directory of Munster* lists traders and farmers in each of the postal districts of the county and a general alphabetical index to persons in the whole county.

1894

Slater's *Royal Directory of Ireland* lists traders, police, teachers, farmers, and private residents in each of the towns, villages, and parishes of the county.

Family History

"Admiral Penn, William Penn, and Their Descendants in Co. Cork." *J. Cork Hist. & Arch. Soc.* N.S. 14 (1908): 105-14, 177-89.

"Barrymore." *J. Cork Hist. & Arch. Soc.* N.S. 5 (1899): 1-17, 77-92, 153-68, 209-24; 6 (1900): 1-11, 65-87, 129-46, 193-209; 7 (1901): 1-16, 65-80, 129-38; 8 (1902): 1-17, 129-50.

Berry, Henry F. "The Old Youghal Family of Stout." *J. Cork Hist. & Arch. Soc.* N.S. 23 (1917): 19-29.

Burke, J. "The O'Driscolls and Other Septs of Corca Laidh." *J. Cork Hist. & Arch. Soc.* N.S. 16 (1910): 24-31.

Caulfield. "Records of the Sarsfield Family of the County Cork." *J. Cork Hist. & Arch. Soc.* N.S., 21 (1915): 82-91, 131-36.

"Chinnery of Co. Cork." *Ir. Anc.* 7 (2) (1975): 67-69.

"The Clann Carthaigh (McCarthy)." *Kerry Arch. Mag..* 1 (1908-12): 160-79, 195-208, 233-51, 320-38, 385-402, 447-66; 2 (1912-14): 3-24, 53-74, 105-22, 181-202; 3 (1914-16): 55-72, 123-39, 206-26, 271-92; 4 (1917): 207-14.

"The Co. Cork Ancestry of the Maddens of Australia." *Ir. Anc.* 16 (1): 14-20.

"Co. Cork Families 1630-5." *J. Cork Hist. & Arch. Soc.* 204 (1961): 126-29, 635-38; 205 (1962): 36-40; 1638-57: 206 (1962): 139-43; (1951): 126-29.

"Cole of Co. Cork." *Gen.* 3 (1879): 289-91.

Cole, R.L. *The Cole Family of West Carbery.* Belfast, 1943.

"Conner Papers." (Manch, Co. Cork). *Anal. Hib.* 15: 153-59.

"The Conran Family of Co. Cork." *Ir. Gen.* 3 (9): 341-50.

Copinger, W.A. *A History of the Copingers or Coppingers of Co. Cork.* Manchester, 1882.

"A Cork Branch of the Rochford Family." *J. Cork Hist. & Arch. Soc.* N.S. 21 (1915): 112-20.

"The Cotter Family of Rockforest, Co. Cork." *J. Cork Hist. & Arch. Soc.* N.S. 43 (1938): 21-31.

"Crone of Co. Cork." *Ir. Anc.* 1 (2) (1969): 77-88.

Day, Robert. "Loftus Family Record." *J. Cork Hist. & Arch. Soc.* N.S. 2 (1896): 491-92.

de Barry. *Etude sur l'histoire des Bary-Barry.* Vieux-Dieu-Les Anvers, 1927.

de Bary, Alfred. *De l'origine des Barry d'Irlande.* Guebwiller, 1900.

"A Defeated Clan, (The O'Crowleys)." *J. Cork Hist. & Arch. Soc.* N.S. 36 (1931): 24-28.

"The Denny Family." In *History of Co. Kerry,.* 242-60 . Dublin, 1910.

"Dennys of Cork." *J. Cork Hist. and Arch. Soc.* N.S. 28 (1922): 45-46.

Donnelly, Eithne. "The Roches, Lords of Fermoy." *J. Cork Hist. & Arch. Soc.* N.S. 38 (1933): 86-91; 39 (1934): 38-40, 57-68; 40 (1935): 37-42, 63-73; 41 (1936): 2-28, 78-84; 42 (1937): 40-52.

"The Descent of the Somervilles of Drishane." *Ir. Gen.* 5 (6) (1979): 704-09.

"The Drews of Mocollop Castle." *J. Cork Hist. & Arch. Soc.* 24 (1918): 4-6.

"The Family of Jackson of Wooldale in the Co. of Cork." *Gen.* N.S. 37 (1920): 29-33.

The Family of Limerick of Schull, Co. Cork. 1909. Also printed in *J. Cork Hist. & Arch. Soc.* N.S. 13: 120-27.

"The Family of Sarsfield." *Herald & Genealogist* 2 (1865): 205-15.

"The Family Register of John Dennehy of Fermoy." *Ir. Gen.* 1(1) (1937): 23-25.

ffolliott, Rosemary. *The Pooles of Mayfield and Other Irish Families.* Dublin, 1958.

Fitzgerald-Uniacke, R.G. "The Uniackes of Youghal." *J. Cork Hist. & Arch. Soc.* N.S. 3 (1894): 113-16, 146-52, 183-91, 210-21, 232-41, 245-55.

"The Fleetwoods of the Co. Cork." *R.S.A.I.* 38 (1908): 103-25.

"A Genealogical Note on the Family of Cramer or Coghill." *J. Cork Hist. & Arch. Soc.* N.S. 16 (1910): 66-81, 143.

"George Chinnery, 1774-1852, With Some Account of his Family and Genealogy." *J. Cork Hist. & Arch. Soc.* N.S. 37 (1932): 11-21; 38 (1933): 1-15.

Gillman, Herbert Webb. "The Chieftains of Pobal-I-Callaghan, Co. Cork." *J. Cork Hist. & Arch. Soc.* N.S. 3 (1897): 201-20.

"Gray of Cork City and Lehana." *Ir. Anc.* 7 (1) (1975): 11.

"Gray of Co. Cork." Pedigree in *Swanzy Notebooks.* RCB Library, Dublin.

"The Harmons of Cork." *Ir. Gen.* 3 (12): 524-28.

"The Herricks of Co. Cork." *Ir. Gen.* 3 (8): 291-98.

"A History of the O'Mahony Septs of Kinelmeky and Ivagha." *J. Cork Hist. & Arch. Soc.* N.S. 12 (1906): 183-95; 13 (1907): 27-36, 73-80, 105-15, 182-92; 14 (1908): 12-21, 74-81, 127-41, 189-99; 15 (1909): 7-18, 63-75, 118-26, 184-96; 16 (1910): 9-24, 97-113.

"History of the O'Sullivans." *J. Cork Hist. & Arch. Soc.* 4 (1898): 120-31, 207-12, 255-78.

Leabhar Chlainn Suibhne: an Account of the MacSweeney Families in Ireland, with Pedigree. Edited by Rev. Paul Walsh. Dublin, 1920.

"Longfield Papers." (Longueville, Co. Cork). *Anal. Hib.* 115: 135-42.

"The Longs of Muskerry and Kinalea." *J. Cork Hist. & Arch. Soc.* N.S. 51 (1946): 1-9.

"The Lords of Ella: the Macdonoghs of Duhallow." *J. Cork Hist. & Arch. Soc.* 3 (1894): 157-62.

MacCarthy, D. *A Historical Pedigree of the MacCarthys.* Exeter, 1880.

McCarthy, Samuel T. *The MacCarthys of Munster.* Dundalk, 1922.

"The MacCarthys of Drishane." *J. Cork Hist. & Arch. Soc.* 23 (1917): 114-15.

"The MacFinnin MacCarthys of Ardtully." *J. Cork Hist. & Arch. Soc.* N.S. 2 (1896): 210-14.

MacLir, Mananaan. *The Synans of Doneraile.* Cork, 1909.

"The Nagles of Mount Nagle (Co. Cork)." *Ir. Gen.* 2 (1954): 337-48.

"Notes on the Cotter Family of Rockforest, Co. Cork." *J. Cork Hist. & Arch. Soc.* N.S. 14 (1908): 1-12.

"Notes on the Family of Ronayne, or Ronan, of Counties Cork and Waterford." *J. Cork Hist. & Arch. Soc.* N.S. 22 (1916): 56-63, 109-14, 178-85; 23 (1917): 93-104, 142-52.

"Notes on the Pedigree of Sherlock of Mitchelstown, Co. Cork." *J. Cork Hist. & Arch. Soc.* N.S. 12 (1906): 50-51.

"Notes on the Stamers Family." *J. Cork Hist. & Arch. Soc.* N.S. 3 (1897): 152-53, 193-94, 232, 304.

O'Connell, Basil. "The Nagles of Mount Nagle (Co. Cork) and Later of Jamestown and Dunower, Barts." *Ir. Gen.* 3 (1955): 377-89.

"O'Crowley Pedigree from the Carew Mss. and Other Sources." *J. Cork Hist. & Arch. Soc.* N.S. 35 (1930): 89.

"The O'Crowleys of Coill t-Sealbhaigh." *J. Cork Hist. & Arch. Soc.* N.S. 56 (1951): 91-94; 57 (1952): 1-6, 105-09; 58 (1953): 7-11.

"The O'Heas of South-west Cork." *J. Cork Hist. & Arch. Soc.* N.S. 51 (1951): 97-107.

"The O'Mullanes." *J. Cork Hist. & Arch. Soc.* N.S. 48 (1953): 97.

"The O'Mullanes and Whitechurch." *J. Cork Hist. & Arch. Soc.* N.S. 48 (1953): 20-21.

"The O'Regans of Carbery." *J. Cork Hist. & Arch. Soc.* N.S. 63 (1958): 18-22.

"The Origins of Co. Cork Kingstons." *J. Cork Hist. & Arch. Soc.* 76 (1981): 75-99.

"The Pedigree and Succession of the House of MacCarthy Mor." *R.S.A.I.* 51 (1921): 32-48.

"The Penroses of Woodhill." *J. Cork Hist. & Arch. Soc.* 241, 242 (1980).

Pratt, John. *The Family of Pratt of Gawsworth and Carrigrohane, Co. Cork.* 1925.

"Roche Papers (Co. Cork)." *Anal. Hib.* 15: 143-52.

"The Rumley Family of Cork." *J. Cork Hist. & Arch. Soc.* N.S. 7 (1901): 127.

Rylands, J.P. *Some Account of the Clayton Family of Thelwall, Co. Chester, Afterwards of St. Dominick's Abbey, Doneraile, and Mallow, Co. Cork.* Liverpool, 1880.

"Some Account of the Roberts Family of Kilmoney." *J. Cork Hist. & Arch. Soc.* N.S. 24 (1929): 107-10.

"Some McCarthys of Blarney and Ballea." *J. Cork Hist. & Arch. Soc.* N.S. 59 (1954): 1-10, 82-88; 60 (1955): 1-5, 75-79.

Somerville, E.E., and Boyle Townshend Somerville, comps. *Records of the Somerville Family of Castlehaven and Drishane, from 1174 to 1904.* Cork, 1940.

"The Somervilles and Their Connections in Cork." *J. Cork Hist. & Arch. Soc.* N.S. 47 (1942): 30-33.

"The Southwells." *J. Cork Hist. & Arch. Soc.* 18 (1912): 141-49.

"Spread of Co. Cork." *Ir. Anc.* 2 (2) (1970): 102-11.

Sullivan, T.D. *Bantry, Berehaven and the O'Sullivan Sept.* Dublin, 1908.

Sweeney, R. Mingo. *Sween, Clan of the Battle-axe, a Brief History of the MacSweeney (Mac Suibhne) Galloglass.* Prince Edward Island: Bonshaw, 1968.

Townshend, R., and D. Townshend. *An Officer of the Long Parliament and His Descendants. An Account of the Life and Times of Colonel Richard Townshend of Castletown (Castle Townshend) and a Chronicle of His Family.* London, 1892.

"The Trants." *J. Cork Hist. & Arch. Soc.* 243, 244 (1981).

"The Trants: an Enterprising Catholic Family in 18th Century Co. Cork." *J. Cork Hist. & Arch. Soc.* 86 (1981): 21-29.

Trimble, D. *The Kingston Family in Co. Cork.* 1929.

"The Wallis Family of Drishane." *J. Cork Hist. & Arch. Soc.* N.S. 67 (1962): 48-51.

"The Waters or Walter Family of Cork." *J. Cork Hist. & Arch. Soc.* N.S. 31 (1926): 7-78; 32 (1927): 17-23, 104-13; 33 (1928): 35-41; 34 (1929): 36-42, 97-105; 35 (1930): 36-43, 102-13; 36 (1931): 26-38, 76-86; 37 (1932): 35-41.

"Wrixon of Co. Cork." Pedigree in *Swanzy Notebooks.* RCB Library, Dublin.

Gravestone Inscriptions

Those records in the *Journal of the Cork Historical & Archaeological Society* (here indicated as *J. Cork Hist. & Arch. Soc.*) are in the series "The Gravestone Inscriptions of Co. Cork" Nos. I to XI. All are indexed by name and place.

The series of volumes entitled *O'Kief, Coshe Mang, and Slieve Luachra* by Albert Casey also contain many records.

Aghinagh: *J. Cork Hist. & Arch. Soc.* 216 (1967): 93-100.

Ballyclough: *O'Kief, Coshe Mang, etc.* 8 (1965).

Ballycurrany: *J. Cork Hist. & Arch. Soc.* 237 (1978): 78-82.

Ballymodan, RC: Genealogical Survey of Bandon, 1985 (see West Cork Heritage Centre).

Ballymadan (St. Peters, CI): Genealogical Survey of Bandon, 1985 (see West Cork Heritage Centre).

Ballyvourney: *O'Kief, Coshe Mang, etc.* 6 (1963).

Bandon (St. Patrick's, RC): Genealogical Survey of Bandon, 1986 (see Ballymodan).

Brinny (Bandon, CI): Genealogical Survey of Bandon, 1986 (see Ballymodan).

Carrigohanebeg: *J. Cork Hist. & Arch. Soc.* 218 (1968): 175-81.

Carrigtwohill: Few records in *J. Cork Hist. & Arch. Soc.* 211 (1965): 26-32.

Castlemagner: *O'Kief, Coshe Mang, etc.* 6 (1963).

Clondrohid: *O'Kief, Coshe Mang, etc.* 6 (1963).

Clonfert: *O'Kief, Coshe Mang, etc.* 6 (1963).

Clonmeen: *O'Kief, Coshe Mang, etc.* 7 (1964); 233, 234 (1976): (95-117; 235 (1977): 11-29 (Lyre and Banteer).

Clonmult: *J. Cork Hist. & Arch. Soc.* 219 (1969): 34-39.

Cobh (Old Churchyard): Published by Great Island Hist. Soc. c/o L. Cassidy, 1 Park View, Cobh, Co. Cork.

Cullen: *O'Kief, Coshe Mang, etc.* 6 (1963).

Dangandonovan: *J. Cork Hist. & Arch. Soc.* 229 (1974): 26-58.

Desertmore: *J. Cork Hist. & Arch. Soc.* 219 (1969): 34-39.

Drishane: *O'Kief, Coshe Mang, etc.* 5 (1963).

Dromagh: *O'Kief, Coshe Mang, etc.* 8 (1965).

Dromtariffe: *O'Kief, Coshe Mang, etc.* 6 (1963).

Dunderrow: *J. Cork Hist. & Arch. Soc.* 224 (1971): 110-27.

Fermoy: *Irish Sword* 51 (1977); 53 (1979) (military stones only).

Inchigeela: *O'Kief, Coshe Mang, etc.* 6 (1963) (see Ballymodan).

Kilbeg (Bandon, CI): Genealogical Survey of Bandon, 1985.

Kilbrin: *O'Kief, Coshe Mang, etc.* 8 (1965).

Kilbrogan (RC): Genealogical Survey of Bandon, 1985 (see Ballymodan).

Kilbrogan: Genealogical Survey of Bandon, 1985 (see Ballymodan, CI).

Kilcorney: *O'Kief, Coshe Mang, etc.* 7 (1964).

Kilcrea Friary: *J. Cork Hist. & Arch. Soc.* 217 (1968): 1-30.

Kilcummin: *O'Kief, Coshe Mang, etc.* 6 (1963).

Killeagh: *J. Cork Hist. & Arch. Soc.* 226 (1972): 76-104; 227 (1973): 40-65.

Kilnaglory: *J. Cork Hist. & Arch. Soc.* 220 (1969): 184-87.

Kilnamartyra: *O'Kief, Coshe Mang, etc.* 6 (1963).

Kilmeen (Barony of Dunhallow): *O'Kief, Coshe Mang, etc.* 6 (1963).

Kinsale (CI): Available from M. McCarthy, 2 Lr. O'Connell Street, Kinsale, Co. Cork.

Lisgoold: *J. Cork Hist. & Arch. Soc.* 237 (1978): 59-65.

Macloneigh: *O'Kief, Coshe Mang, etc.* 8 (1965).

Macroom: *O'Kief, Coshe Mang, etc.* 8 (1965).

Mallow: *O'Kief, Coshe Mang, etc.* 8 (1965).

Mologga: *Ir. Gen.* 2 (12) (1955): 390-92.

Nohovaldaly: *O'Kief, Coshe Mang, etc.* 8 (1965).

St. Finbarr's: Robinson, Rev. Andrew C. *St. Finbarr's Cathedral.* 1897.

Tisaxon: *J. Cork Hist. & Arch. Soc.* 222 (1970): 143-57.

Titeskin: *J. Cork Hist. & Arch. Soc.* 221 (1970): 56-57.

Tullylease: *O'Kief, Coshe Mang, etc.* 8 (1965).

Youghal: Field, W.G. *The Handbook of Youghal.* (1896; reprinted 1973) Contains inscriptions from the Collegiate Church.

Newspapers

A card index to biographical notices in Cork and Kerry newspapers from 1754 to 1827 is available in the Library of University College, Cork. Microfiche copies of this are available in the NLI, the Library of University College, Dublin, and the New York Public Library. Microfiche copies are also available from the compiler, Ms. R. ffolliott, Glebe House, Fethard, Co. Tipperary.

Title: *Constitution* or *Cork Morning Post* (continued as *Cork Constitution* in 1873)
Published in: Cork, 1823-1924
NLI Holdings: 6.1823-12.1827; 1829; 1831-34; 10.1873-7.1922; 1924
BL Holdings: odd numbers 1823; 1.1826-10.1873; 10.1873-12.1924

Title: *Cork Advertiser* (continued as *Constitution* in 1823.)
Published in: Cork, 1799-1824
NLI Holdings: 1-8.1799; 1800; 1-10.1801; 3-12.1803; 2-12.1804; 4-12.1806; 1-8.1807; 11.1811-12.1816; 9.1818-5.1819; 12.1822-6.1823
BL Holdings: odd numbers 1810, 1813, 1823, 1824

Title: *Cork Examiner*
Published in: Cork, 1841-current
NLI Holdings: 8.1841-12.1896; 3.1897-5.1910; 7.1910-in progress
BL Holdings: 8.1841-in progress

Title: *Cork Herald* (continued as *Cork Daily Herald* from 1860)
Published in: Cork, 1856-1901
NLI Holdings: 1870-84; 1896-7.1901
BL Holdings: 4.1858-7.1901

Title: *Munster Advertiser*
Published in: Cork, 1839-41

NLI Holdings: 4.1839-5.1841
BL Holdings: 4.1839-5.1841

Title: *Peoples Press & Cork Weekly Register*
Published in: Cork, 1834-36
BL Holdings: 9.1834-2.1836

Title: *Skibbereen and West Carbery Eagle*
Published in: Skibbereen, 1857-1929
NLI Holdings: 5.1881-12.1884; 4.1899-7.1922; 8.1927-12.1928
BL Holdings: 9.1861-10.1870; 1.1871-7.1922

Title: *Southern Reporter* (continued as *Irish Daily & Southern Reporter* in 1871)
Published in: Cork, 1807-73
NLI Holdings: 6.1807-8.1808; 5.1811-12.1813; 1.1817-4.1819; 1824; 1826; 1827; 1829-7.1832; 1834; 1848; 4.1856-12.1873
BL Holdings: 1.1823-12.1871; odd numbers 1872 and 1873

Title: *Southern Star*
Published in: Skibbereen, 1864-current
NLI Holdings: 6.1921-11.1962
BL Holdings: 2-7.1864; odd numbers 1892; 12.1892-3.1918; 4.1919

Wills and Administrations

A discussion of the types of records, where they are held, their availability, and value is given in the Wills section of the Introduction. The availability of prerogative wills, administrations, and marriage license records is also described in the relevant parts of the same section. Where available, published sources of these records are given in the Miscellaneous Sources section.

Pre-1858 Wills and Administrations

Prerogative Wills. see p. xli.
Consistorial Wills. County Cork is in the dioceses of Cork, Cloyne, Ross, Lismore, Ardfert and Aghadoe, and Limerick. The guide to Catholic parish records in this chapter shows the diocese to which each civil parish belonged. The wills of residents of

	Date of Probate.
Hemington, Thomas, Newmarket	1779
Hendley (*or* Headly), Catherine (widow), Mount Rivers	1791
„ Roger, Ballyvoluck	1736
Henesy, James, Killshaney	1741
„ Laurence, Ballymaloobeg	1781
Hennebry, Maurice, Blarny	1740
Hennessy, George, BallymcMoy (Monition) ...	1779
„ (*or* Henessy), Honor (widow), Richardstown...	1777
„ John, Park	1726
„ (*or* Henessy), Peter, Richardstown ...	1777
Hennesy, John, Killmahan	1740
Herbert, William, ship " Speke "	1780
Herlihy, William, Shanacloune	*1726
„ *See also* Hearlihy and Hierlihy.	
Hewitt, Anne (widow), Castlelyons	*1727
Hickey, William, Mallow	1766
Hicky, Andrew, Castle Redmond	1791
„ Dennis, Ballyganhedagh	1757
„ John oge	1654
Hierlihy (*or* Herlihy), Daniel, Cove	1791
Higgins, Richard, Cork	1780
Hilgrove, Francis, Burgess	1795
Hill, Thomas, Coolegilly	1680
Hindes, John, Kineagh	1629
Hobbs, John, Curroghanyearla	1775
Hodder, John, Bridgetown	1673
„ Margery (widow), Coolemore	1677
„ William, Coolemore	1665
Hodge, John, Middleton	1679
„ William, H.M.S. "Bridgewater"	1749
Hogan, Daniel, Kilcronatt	1775
„ Denis, Newmarket	1682
Hogben, Robert, Barriscourt	1654
Holland, Francis, Dromclogh	1680
„ Susanna (widow), Castleblah	1772
Holmes, Thomas, Ardrabegg	*1753
„ „ Longstown	1774
„ William, Fedane	1687
Homan, Robert, Gortbofinny	1787
Honner, John, Maddam (Copy) (Original in Prerogative)	1670
Honohane, Lyonell, Broghill	1712
Hood, Daniel, Mallow	*1729

Page of Will indexes from the Dioceses of Cloyne, from Phillimore's *Indexes to Irish Wills.* London, 1910.

each diocese were usually proven within that diocese (see the Wills section for exceptions). The following records survive:

Wills. See p. xxxvii.

Abstracts. see p. xxxvii; also McSwiney papers: Abstracts mainly from Cork and Kerry (RIA library); Pre-1800 abstracts from Cork and Cloyne, GO, see *Anal. Hib.* 17 (1949).

Indexes. Cloyne (exist for 1621-1858), PRO. The following have been published: (1621-1800) by Phillimore (see p. xxxvii); (1621-1858) in *O'Kief, Coshe Mang, etc.* by Albert Casey, 8 (1965); (1547-1628) in *J. Cork Hist. & Arch. Soc.* (1895); Cork and Ross (1548-1858) published to 1800 by Phillimore, also in *O'Kief, Coshe Mang, etc.* by A. Casey, 8 (1965). Also, wills from 1548-1833 from the Cork Registry published in *J. Cork Hist. & Arch. Soc.* 1895-98; Lismore – see Co. Waterford; Limerick – see Co. Limerick; Ardfert – see Co. Kerry.

Post-1858 Wills and Administrations

County Cork was served by the District Registry of Cork. The surviving records are kept in the PRO.

Marriage Licenses

Indexes. Cloyne (1630-1845) PRO; SLC film 100863. Cork and Ross (1623-1845) PRO; SLC films 100864-866. Lismore – see Co. Waterford.

Miscellaneous Sources

"Agnes Townsend's Notebook." *Ir. Anc.* 8 (2) (1976): 96-113 (general birth and death information from West Cork area).

"A Brief Directory of the City of Cork 1758 and 1769-1770." *Ir. Gen.* 1 (8) (1940): 254-59.

Cusack, M.F. *A History of the City & County of Cork.* Dublin, 1875.

Donnelly, J.S. *Land and People of 19th Century Cork.* London, 1975.

Gibson, Rev. C.B. *History of the County and City of Cork.* 2 vols. 1861.

"Honorary Freemen of Cork 1690-1946." *J. Cork Hist. & Arch. Soc.* 52 (175): 74-86.

"Mallow Testamentary Records." *Ir. Anc.* 1 (1) (1969): 52-59.

"Maps and Plans of Cork Interest." *J. Cork Hist. & Arch. Soc.* 73 (1968): 72-73.

"The Memorandum Book of David Rochfort. 1750s to 1794." *J. Cork Hist. & Arch. Soc.* 203 (1961): 55-64 (death and marriage records in Garrettstown, Co. Cork). Addendum. 205 (1962): 54-56.

"Register of Boys at St. Stephens Hospital (School) 1773-1802." *J. Cork Hist. & Arch. Soc.* 195 (1957): 46-55 (gives name, age of entry, departure, and to whom apprenticed or other fate of each boy).

Smith, Charles. *The Ancient and Present State of the County and City of Cork (1750).*

"Some Marriage Announcements from *The Cork Mercantile Chronicle* for 1806." *Ir. Gen.* 1 (12) (1942): 356-61.

"Some Notices of Early French Refugees in Cork." *J. Cork Hist. & Arch. Soc.* 24 (117) (1918): 8-15.

Townsend, Rev. H. *A General and Statistical Survey of the County of Cork.* 2 vols. 1815.

White, James Grove. "Historical and Topographical Notes on Buttevant, Mallow, etc." Supplement to *Cork Historical and Archaeological Society's Journal.* 1905-10.

Research Sources and Services

Journals

Journal of Cork Historical & Archaeological Society

Libraries and Information Sources

Cork City Library, Grand Parade, Cork. Ph:
(021) 507110 (has local history section with
extensive local-interest collection)

Cork County Library, Farranlea Road, Cork.
Ph: (021) 46499/46591/46539

Research Services

Cork Archives Institution, Christchurch, Cork

West Cork Heritage Centre, Bandon, Co. Cork
(indexes to many local parishes, gravestones,
etc.)

See also research services in Dublin, p. xliv

Societies

Canovee Historical & Archaeological Society,
Mrs. Sheila Cronin, Caum, Carrigadrohid,
Co. Cork

Charleville & District Historical & Archaeological Society, Mr. J. Binchy, Knights
Lodge, Charleville, Co. Cork

Cobh Historical Society, c/o Cobh Museum
Committee, West End, Cobh, Co. Cork

Cork Historical & Archaeological Society, Mr.
Patrick Holohan, Ballysheehy Lodge,
Clogheen, Co. Cork

Cumann Seanchais Na Banndan (Bandon Local
History Society), Mr. Patrick Caniffe,
Bawnishal, Hare Hill, Bandon, Co. Cork

Mallow Field Club, Mrs. Ita Power, Cork Road,
Mallow, Co. Cork

Timoleague Historical Society, Mr. Robert
Travers, Timoleague House, Bandon, Co.
Cork

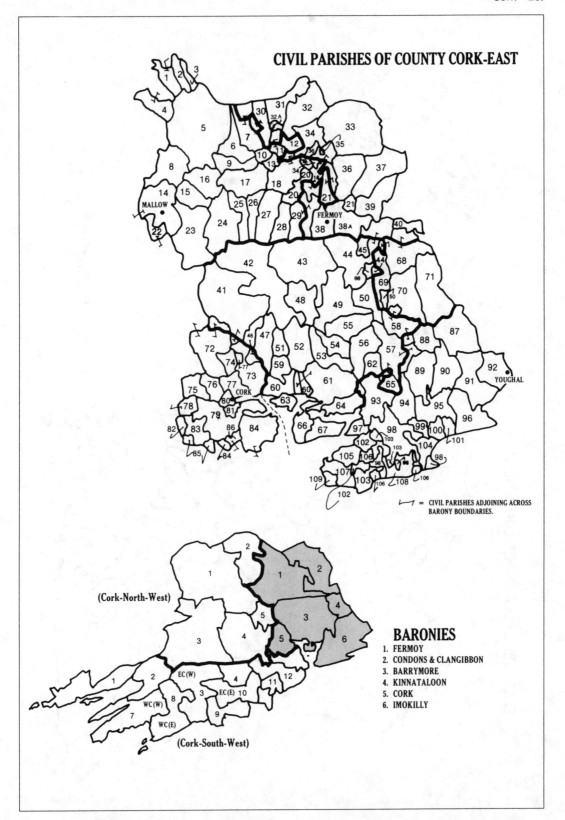

CIVIL PARISHES OF COUNTY CORK-EAST

= CIVIL PARISHES ADJOINING ACROSS BARONY BOUNDARIES.

(Cork-North-West)

(Cork-South-West)

BARONIES

1. FERMOY
2. CONDONS & CLANGIBBON
3. BARRYMORE
4. KINNATALOON
5. CORK
6. IMOKILLY

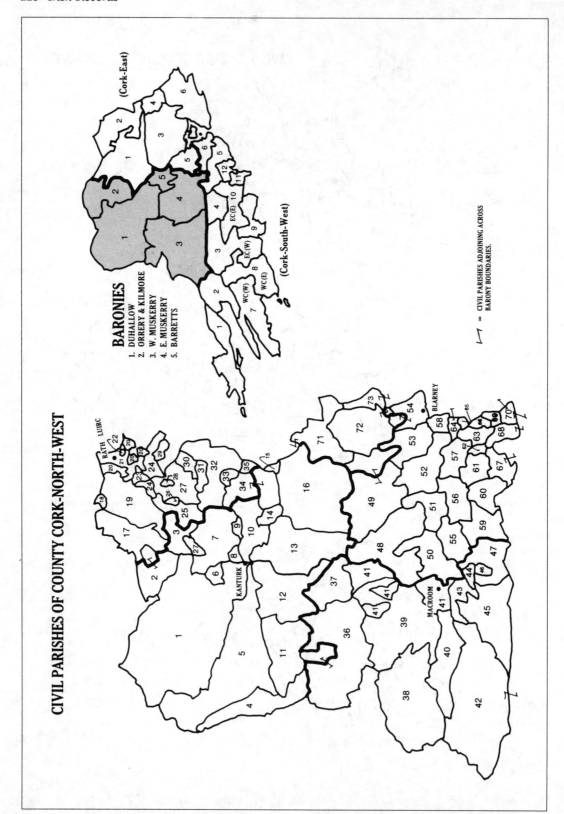

CIVIL PARISHES OF COUNTY CORK-NORTH-WEST

BARONIES
1. DUHALLOW
2. ORRERY & KILMORE
3. W. MUSKERRY
4. E. MUSKERRY
5. BARRETTS

⌐ = CIVIL PARISHES ADJOINING ACROSS BARONY BOUNDARIES.

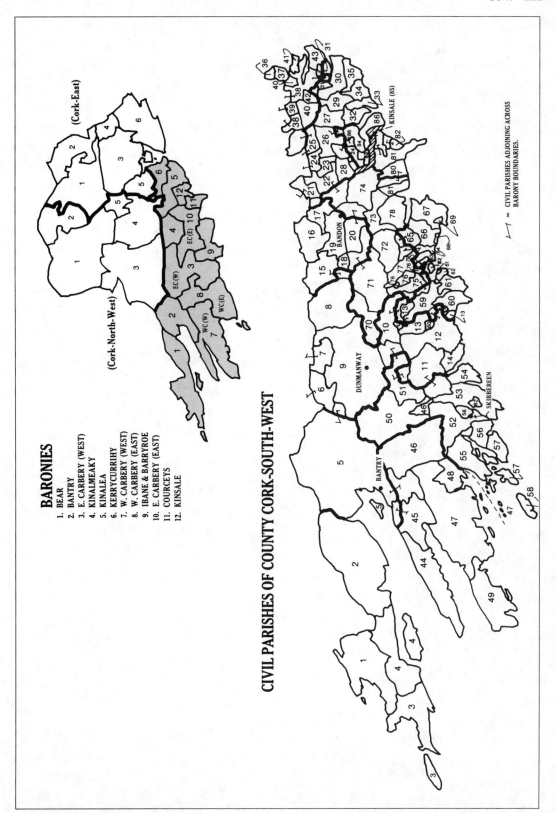

BARONIES

1. BEAR
2. BANTRY
3. E. CARBERY (WEST)
4. KINALMEAKY
5. KINALEA
6. KERRYCURRIHY
7. W. CARBERY (WEST)
8. W. CARBERY (EAST)
9. IBANE & BARRYROE
10. E. CARBERY (EAST)
11. COURCEYS
12. KINSALE

(Cork-East)

(Cork-North-West)

CIVIL PARISHES OF COUNTY CORK-SOUTH-WEST

⌐─┐ = CIVIL PARISHES ADJOINING ACROSS BARONY BOUNDARIES.

KINSALE (85)

BANDON

DUNMANWAY

BANTRY

SKIBBEREEN

County Derry

A Brief History

This Ulster county contains the city of Derry (or Londonderry) and the towns of Coleraine, Limavady, Magherafelt, and Portstewart.

In the old Gaelic system much of Derry was in the old territory of Tirowen. The area was mainly the territory of the O'Cahans or O'Kanes. Other families associated with the area include the O'Connors, O'Donnells, O'Mullan, McCloskey, O'Hegarty, O'Corr, McGurk, McRory, (O')Diamond, McCrilly, McGilligan, O'Deery, and McColgan.

The city of Derry dates back to the foundation of a monastery on the site in A.D. 546. The growth of the monastery and the surrounding settlement made Derry an important town. The town was repeatedly raided by the Danish vikings during the ninth to eleventh centuries.

Neither Derry city nor the old kingdom of Tirowen were affected by the Norman invasion and, like most of the rest of Ulster, it retained its independence from English rule until the beginning of the seventeenth century.

In 1600, during the rebellion of O'Neill and O'Donnell (see p. xlvii and Co. Tyrone) and their allies, the city of Derry was taken by English forces. Following the final defeat of the rebellion most of the county was confiscated from its owners and given to "adventurers" and others for the purpose of planting it with English and Scottish settlers. The O'Cahans were one of the few native families who retained property in the county. Ulster was also divided into counties and was, for a time, known as the county of Coleraine.

In 1609 the plantation of Ulster began and huge areas of Ulster were set aside for the use of settlers from Britain. In an effort to ensure the effective settlement of the new county of Coleraine, it was offered as a business venture to the city of London. Accordingly, in 1613 the county was renamed Londonderry and formally handed over to the city of London by King James. The city decided to administer the county through some of its trade guilds. The county was divided among twelve trade guilds of London, each of which was responsible for the development of its own area.

The London guilds were, by most accounts, less than enthusiastic about the scheme, and there were consequently not as many English settlers as the plantation organizers had expected. By some accounts there were more Irish tenants in the county than in any other. In consequence of this, the London company was heavily fined in 1635 for failing to honor their commitment to plant the county. Nevertheless, a large colony of Protestants was brought into Derry, and the fortification of the city was completed by 1618.

Among the common settler names in the county are those of Elliott, Campbell, Anderson, Baird, Thompson, McClintock, Hamilton, Browne, Barr, Stewart, Smith, Johnston, Irwin, Morrison, Young, and White.

In 1641 the native Irish joined the general rebellion of Irish Catholics. The rebellion was defeated and those involved were severely dealt with.

During the Williamite wars of the early 1690s the city of Derry became a stronghold for the Protestants of the North and withstood a seven-month siege by Jacobite forces.

A general indication of the relative proportions of those of English, Scottish, or native Irish extraction in the county can be gauged from their religious persuasions. In 1861, when the census first ascertained religion, the relative proportions of Catholics (Irish), Protestants (English), and Presbyterians (Scottish) were 45, 17, and 35 percent respectively.

The Penal Laws were specifically enacted at the beginning of the eighteenth century to supress Catholics, but they also affected Presbyterians. For this reason there was considerable emigration of the so-called Scots-Irish from Derry and other Ulster counties during the eighteenth century.

During the Great Famine, County Derry was not as badly affected as others. The population was 222,000 in 1841, and by 1851 it had fallen to 192,000. Derry was an important port of emigration at this time, and there was extensive migration to the city as a result of the famine.

Following the foundation of an independent Irish State in 1921, Derry was one of the six Ulster counties which was kept within the United Kingdom. The name Derry continues to be used in reference to the city and county by most of the population of Ireland. The name Londonderry should also be referred to by researchers.

Census and Census Substitutes

1618

Survey of Derry, City and County, and Coleraine, etc. with Names of Undertakers, Servitors, and Principal Natives. TCD ms. 864 (F.I.9).

1628

Houses and Families in Londonderry, 15 May, 1628. Edited by Rev. R.G.S. King, 1936. SLC film 1363860; NLI IR 94112 L1.

1642/43

Muster Roll. SLC 941.5/ M23m.

1654-56

Civil survey. Vol. 3.

1659

"Census" of Ireland. Edited by S. Pender. Dublin: Stationery Office, 1939.

1662

Extracts from Subsidy Rolls. PRONI T716 (1-17).

1663

Hearth Money Roll. PRONI T307; NLI ms. 9584 (index on 9585).

1740

Protestant Householders in the Parishes of Aghadowy, Anlow, Artrea, Arigall, Ballinderry, Ballynascreen, Ballyscullion, Balten, Banagher, Beleaghron, Belerashane, Belewillin, Boveva, Coleraine, Comber, Desart, Desartlin, Desartmartin, Drummacose, Dunboe, Dungiven, Faughanvale, Glendermot, Killcranoghen, Killowen, Killylagh, Kilrea, Lissan, Macosquin, Maghera, Magherafelt, Tamlaghtfinlaggan, Tamlagh O' Creely, Tamlatard, Tamloght, Templemore, and Termoneny. GO 539; SLC film 100182.

1766

Religious Census of Parishes of Artrea, Desertlin, and Magherafelt. PRO (1A 46 49) and SLC film 258517 (except Desertlin).

Parishes of Bovevagh, Comber, Drumacoose, and Inch. PRO (1A 41 100) and SLC film 258517 (except Comber)

Parish of Desertmartin. RCB Library and SLC film 258517; Protestants in Parishes of Ballymascreen. SLC film 258517

Gubbin Patrick	Middle Rd	Hay Rev G	Shipquay St
Guiggan Patrick	Fergusons Lane	Hays	Richmond St
Haffin John	Foyle St	Hayshaw Mrs	Widows Row
Hagan	Nailors Row	Hazlett Samuel	Ship-Quay
Hagan Bernard	Creevagh Lower	Hazlett William	Kilkea
Hagan James	Bishop St Without	Hazlett William	Shipquay St
Hagan John	Bennetts Lane	Heaney Nicholas	Bennetts Lane
Hagan Patrick	Kilkea	Heany Edward	Bogside St
Hagan Patrick	Nailors Row	Heffernan Robert	Priests Lane
Hall John (2)	Waterloo Place	Hegarty	Fahan St
Hall Mrs	Cunningham Row	Hegarty	Long Tower
Halliday James	Bishop St Without	Hegarty	New Gate off Wapping
Halliday Patrick	Bishop St Without	Hegarty	Wapping
Halliday Tristam	Shantallow	Hegarty Christopher	Fahan St
Hamilton (2)	Ship-Quay	Hegarty Daniel	Foyle St
Hamilton	Thomas St	Hegarty Hugh	Cow Bog
Hamilton David	Bishop St	Hegarty James	Barrack Row
Hamilton Dr	Ferryquay St	Hegarty John	Bishop St Without
Hamilton Dr	Richmond St	Hegarty John	Horse Barrack
Hamilton James	Fahan St	Heggarty	Rossville St
Hamilton John	Bennetts Lane	Henderson Dr	Ballymagrorty
Hamilton John	Fahan St	Henderson Rev W	St Columbs Court
Hamilton John	Foyle St	Henderson William	Ferryquay St
Hamilton John	William St	Henry Barney	William St
Hamilton Mrs	Bogside St	Heslip Edward	William St
Hampton Moss	Ferryquay St	Higgans	St Columbs Wells
Hanigan Neil	Bennetts Lane	Hill John	Diamond
Hanley James	Bogside St	Hill Marcus S	East Wall
Hannigan	Rossville St	Hindman John	Diamond
Harkan Denis	Bridge St	Hindman John S	Foyle St
Harkan Patrick	William St	Hinds Patrick	Foyle Alley
Harkin Bernard	Creggan St	Hinds William	Society St
Harkin Robert	Henrietta St	Hoghey James	Barrack Row
Harkin William	Abbey St	Holland John	Sugar House Lane
Harkin William (2)	William St	Hooton Charles	Fahan St
Harl Robert	Abbey St	Horner Frances	Magazine St
Harlin	Wapping	Horner Francis	Abbey St
Harrigan	Thomas St	Horner Francis	Rossville St
Harrigan Bryan	Abbey St	Horner Leonard	Shipquay St
Harrigan Edward	Horse Barrack	Huffington John	Diamond
Harrigan James	Strand Rd	Huffington William	Cunningham Lane
Harris William	Ballingard	Huffington William	St Columbs Court
Hart General	Culmore	Hughs Miss	Cunningham Row
Hart William	Bishop St Without	Hunter James	Cow Bog
Hart William	Shantallow	Hunter William	Abbey St
Hartford John	Bishop St Without	Hunter William	Ship-Quay
Harvey Henry	Sugar House Lane	Hurlin Daniel	Rossville St
Harvey Richard	Mullennan	Hush Samuel	Orchard Lane
Harvey Thomas	Magazine St	Hutrick Mathew	Nailors Row
Haslett Mrs	Nailors Row	Hutton James	Bogside St
Haslitt	Richmond St	Hyde James (2)	Society St
Hassan James	Weavers Court	Inigly Michael	Bogside St
Hassan John	Long Tower	Irwine Robert	Bishop St Without
Hassan Thomas	Thomas St	Jameson	Long Tower
Hasson	Wapping	Johnston	Rossville St
Hastings Mrs	Wapping	Johnston William	Rossville St
Hattrick J	Cow Bog	Jones Daniel	Fahan St
Hattrick James	Ballingard	Kean James	Cow Bog
Hattrick Joshua	Creggan	Kearney Daniel	Bogside St
Hattrick Robert	Bogside St	Kearney Hugh	East Wall
Haverty James	St Columbs Wells	Kearney James (2)	Fergusons Lane
Havlin Thomas	Wapping Lane	Kearney John	Cow Bog

Sample page of householders in the 1832 Valuation of Derry. From "The First and Second Valuations of the City of Derry." Derry Youth and Community Workshop, 1984.

Banagher, Dungiven, and Leck. RCB Library and SLC film 258517.

1796
See Mayo 1796 (List of Catholics)

1797-1800
Muster Rolls of Co. Derry. SLC film 993910.

1808-13
Freeholders List (alphabetical list A-L only). PRO film 6199.

1821
Extracts from the Government Census Relating Mainly to the Surnames Johnston, McShane, and Thompson. PRO; SLC film 824240.

1823-38
Tithe Applotment Survey (see p. xxvii).

1829
Census of Protestants in Chapel of the Woods Parish. PRONI T308.

1830
Register of Freeholders of City and County. PRONI D834.

1831
Parishes of Aghadowey, Aghanloo, Agivey, Arboe, Artrea, Ballinderry, Balteagh, Banagher, Ballyaughran, Ballymoney, Ballynascreen, Ballyrashane, Ballyscullion, Ballywillin, Bovevagh, Clondermot, Coleraine, Cumber, Desertlyn, Derryloran, Desertmartin, Desertoghill, Drumachose, Dunboe, Dungiven, Errigal, Faughanvale, Kilcrea, Kilcunaghan, Killeagh, Killowen, Lissane, Maghera, Magherafelt, Macosquin, Tamlagh, Tamlagh Finlagan, Tamlaght O'Crilly, Tamlaghtard, Templemore, and Termoneeny. PRO; SLC films 597160-63.

1831-32
The First Valuation of the City of Derry, Parish of Templemore (gives 1,656 householders names with street address). Derry Youth and Community Workshop, 1984.

1832
Petition of Co. Derry Flax-growers, with Signatures. PRO ms. roll.

1832-36
Names of Holders of Applications for Licenses to Sell Liquor in Londonderry and Coleraine (names and addresses). *Parl. Papers* 1837/38, 13 (2) Appendix 10.

1837
List of Those Made Freemen of Londonderry and Coleraine since 1831 (seventy-five names, occupations, and residences). *Parl. Papers* 1837, 11 (1): Appendix B1; 1837/38, 13 (2) Appendix 3.

Name and Residence of Aldermen, Burgesses and Freemen of Coleraine 1831-37 (fifty-one names). *Parl. Papers* 1837, 11 (2): 279-80.

Occupants of Coleraine, Arranged by Street, Giving Property Values. *Parl. Papers* 1837, 11 (1) Appendix G, 198-202.

Occupants of Londonderry, Arranged by Street (giving valuation of property). Also List of Names and Residences (arranged by street) of Those Exempted from Local Tax (with reasons). *Parl. Papers* 1837, 11 (1) Appendix G, 216-25.

1838
Lists of Marksmen, (illiterate voters) in Londonderry and Coleraine (ninety-seven names, occupations, and residences). *Parl. Papers* 1837, 11 (1) Appendix A3; 1837/38, 13 (2) Appendix 4.

1841 and 1851
Extracts from Government Censuses Pertaining to Old Age Pension Claims. PRO; SLC films 258538-41.

1858
The Second Valuation (*Griffith's Valuation*) of the City of Derry (gives 2,923 names with street of residence in parishes of Glendermott and Templemore). Derry Youth and Community Workshop, 1984.

1858-59
Griffith's Valuation (see p. xxvii).

1864-71
Company List of Passengers to Sail from Londonderry (1864-71) (gives name, address, occupation, and age). PRONI

D2892/1/4; *Ulster Gen. & Hist. Guild.* 1 (3) (1979): 80-90.

1868

List of Voters in Londonderry. Arranged alphabetically under (a) how they voted and (b) religion (gives name, address, occupation). NLI JP733.

1901

Census. PRO.

1911

Census. PRO.

Church Records

Church of Ireland
(Shows starting date)

Parish: **Aghadoey**
Status: Lost

Parish: **Aghanloo**
Status: Lost

Parish: **Agherton**
Status: Lost

Parish: **Ballinderry**
Existing Records: b. 1802; m. 1802; d. 1802
Status: LC

Parish: **Ballyeglish**
Existing Records: b.1868; d. 1868
Status: LC

Parish: **Ballynascreen**
Existing Records: b. 1808; m. 1825; d. 1821

Parish: **Ballyscullion**
Existing Records: b. 1776; m. 1776; d. 1776
Status: LC

Parish: **Balteagh**
Status:Lost

Parish: **Banagher** (Derry)
Existing Records: b. 1839; m. 1839; d. 1839
Status: LC

Parish: **Camus** (Bann)
Status: Lost

Parish: **Carrick**
Status: Lost

Parish: **Castledawson**
Existing Records: b. 1844; d. 1844
Status: LC

Parish: **Clonmany**
Status: Lost

Parish: **Clooney**
Existing Records: b. 1867; d. 1867
Status: LC

Parish: **Coleraine**
Existing Records: b. 1769; m. 1769; d. 1769
Status: LC

Parish: **Culmore**
Status: Lost

Parish: **Cumber, Upper**
Existing Records: b. 1811; m. 1826; d. 1826
Status: LC

Parish: **Derry Cathedral**
Existing Records: b. 1642; m. 1642; d. 1642
Missing Records: d. 1776-1829
Status: LC

Parish: **Derry Free Church** (Christ Church)
Existing Records: b. 1855
Status: LC

Parish: **Desertlyn** (Moneymore)
Existing Records: b. 1797; m. 1797; d. 1797
Status: LC

Parish: **Desertmartin**
Existing Records: b.1797; m. 1797; d. 1797
Status: LC

Parish: **Desertoghill**
Status: Lost

Parish: **Drumachose** (Limavady)
Existing Records: b. 1728; m. 1728; d. 1728
Status: LC

Parish: **Dunboe**
Status: Lost

Parish: **Dungiven**
Existing Records: b. 1778; m. 1778; d. 1823
Status: LC

Parish: **Errigal**
Existing Records: b. 1827; m. 1829; d. 1828
Status: LC

Parish: **Formoyle**
Status: Lost

Parish: **Glendermot**
Existing Records: b. 1810; m. 1810; d. 1828
Status: LC

Parish: **Glenely**
Status: Lost

Parish: **Killelagh**
Status: Lost

Parish: **Killowen**
Existing Records: b. 1824; m. 1824; d. 1824
Status: LC

Parish: **Kilrea**
Existing Records: b. 1801; m. 1801; d. 1801
Status: LC

Parish: **Learmount**
Existing Records: b. 1832; m. 1833; d. 1832
Status: LC

Parish: **Lissan**
Existing Records: b. 1753; m. 1752; d. 1753
Missing Records: b. 1796-1803; m. 1794-1816;
    d. 1796-1802
Status: LC

Parish: **Maghera**
Existing Records: b. 1785; m. 1798; d. 1813
Status: LC

Parish: **Magherafelt**
Existing Records: b. 1718; m. 1718; d. 1718
Status: LC

Parish: **Moville, Upper**
Existing Records: b. 1814; m. 1814; d. 1815
Status: LC

Parish: **St. Anne, Ballynascreen**
Status: Lost

Parish: **St. Augustines** (Derry)
Status: Lost

Parish: **Tamlaght**
Existing Records: b. 1801; m. 1801; d. 1801
Status: LC

Parish: **Tamlaghtard**
Existing Records: b. 1747; m. 1747; d. 1747
Missing Records: b. 1776-1819; m. 1776-1819;
    d. 1776-1819
Status: LC

Parish: **Tamlaghtfinlagan**
Existing Records: b. 1796; m. 1796; d. 1796
Status: LC

Parish: **Tamlaght O'Crilly** (Lower)
Status: Lost

Parish: **Tamlaght O'Crilly** (Upper)
Status: Lost

Parish: **Templemore**
Existing Records: b. 1642; m. 1642; d. 1642
Missing Records: d. 1777-1828
Status: LC (1642-1703 is published)

Parish: **Termoneeny**
Existing Records: b. 1821; m. 1821; d. 1846
Status: LC

Presbyterian

Parish: **Ballykelly**
Starting Date: 1699 (PHSA)

Parish: **Banagher** (Derry)
Starting Date: 1834

Parish: **Boveedy** (Kilrea)
Starting Date: 1841

Parish: **Castledawson**
Starting Date: 1835

Parish: **Coleraine**
Starting Date: 1842 (PHSA)

Parish: **Crossgar** (Coleraine)
Starting Date: 1839

Parish: **Cumber** (Claudy)
Starting Date: 1827 (PHSA)

Parish: **Derrymore** (Limavady)
Starting Date: 1825

Parish: **Derry**
Starting Date: 1815

Parish: **Draperstown**
Starting Date: 1837

Parish: **Drumachose** (Limavady)
Starting Date: 1838

Parish: **Dunboe** (Coleraine)
Starting Date: 1843

Parish: **Dungiven**
Starting Date: 1835

Parish: **Faughanvale** (Eglinton)
Starting Date: 1819 (PHSA)

Parish: **Garvagh**
Starting Date: 1795

Parish: **Gortnassy** (Derry)
Starting Date: 1839

Parish: **Killaigh** (Coleraine)
Starting Date: 1805 (PHSA)

Parish: **Kilrea**
Starting Date: 1825

Parish: **Lecompher** (Moneymore)
Starting Date: 1825

Parish: **Limavady**
Starting Date: 1832

Parish: **Maghera**
Starting Date: 1843

Parish: **Magherafelt**
Starting Date: 1703 (PHSA)

Parish: **Magilligan**
Starting Date: 1814

Parish: **Moneymore**
Starting Date: 1827

Parish: **Portstewart**
Starting Date: 1829

Roman Catholic

Civil Parish: **Aghadowey**
Map Grid: 20
RC Parish: see Coleraine
Diocese: DE

Civil Parish: **Aghanloo**
Map Grid: 8
RC Parish: Newtown Limavady (Drumachose, Tamlaght Finlagin, and Aghanloo)
Diocese: DE
Earliest Record: b. 12.1855; m. 4.1856; d. 5.1859
Missing Dates: d. ends 12.1869
Parish Address: Rev. Philip Donnelly, PP, St. Mary's Parochial House, 115 Irish Green Street, Limavady BT49 9AN

Civil Parish: **Agivey**
Map Grid: 21
RC Parish: see Coleraine
Diocese: DE

Civil Parish: **Ardboe**
Map Grid: 46
RC Parish: see Ardboe, Co. Tyrone
Diocese: DE

Civil Parish: **Artrea**
Map Grid: 42
RC Parish: Artrea and Desertlin (Moneymore)
Diocese: AM
Earliest Record: b. 1.1832; m. 4.1830
Missing Dates: b. 3.1834-1.1838, 2.1843-11.1854; m. 7.1843-11.1854, ends 2.1869
Parish Address: Rev. Christopher O'Byrne, PP, Parochial House, Loup, Moneymore, Magherafelt, Co. Derry BT45 7ST

Civil Parish: **Ballinderry**
Map Grid: 48
RC Parish: Ballinderry
Diocese: AM
Earliest Record: b. 12.1826; m. 1.1827
Missing Dates: b. 10.1838-9.1841
Parish Address: Rev. Patrick Fox, PP, Parochial House, Ballinderry, Cookstown, Co. Tyrone

Civil Parish: **Ballyaghran**
Map Grid: 2
RC Parish: see Coleraine
Diocese: CR

Civil Parish: **Ballymoney**
Map Grid: 6
RC Parish: see Co. Antrim
Diocese: CR

Civil Parish: **Ballynascreen**
Map Grid: 36
RC Parish: Ballynascreen or Draperstown (see Dungiven for pre-1834 records)
Diocese: DE
Earliest Record: b. 11.1825; m. 11.1825; d. 11.1825
Missing Dates: b. 2.1834-6.1836; d. ends 4.1832
Parish Address: Rev. Leo Deery, PP, 55 St. Patrick's Street, Draperstown, Magherafelt

Civil Parish: **Ballyrashane**
Map Grid: 4
RC Parish: see Co. Antrim
Diocese: CR

Civil Parish: **Ballyscullion**
Map Grid: 39
RC Parish: Ballyscullion (Bellaghy), see also Magherafelt
Diocese: DE

Earliest Record: b. 9.1844; m. 9.1844
Parish Address: Rev. Michael Flanagan, PP, Ballynease Road, Bellaghy, Magherafelt, Co. Derry

Civil Parish: **Ballywillin**
Map Grid: 1
RC Parish: see Co. Antrim
Diocese: CR

Civil Parish: **Balteagh**
Map Grid: 12
RC Parish: see Errigal
Diocese: DE

Civil Parish: **Banagher**
Map Grid: 15
RC Parish: Banagher (Feeny)
Diocese: DE
Earliest Record: b. 1.1848; m. 12.1851
Parish Address: Rev. John McCullagh, PP, Parochial House, 58 Glenedra Road, Feeny, Co. Derry

Civil Parish: **Bovevagh**
Map Grid: 13
RC Parish: part Banagher; part Newtownlimavady, see Aghanloo
Diocese: DE

Civil Parish: **Carrick**
Map Grid: 11
RC Parish: Newtown Limavady, see Aghanloo
Diocese: DE

Civil Parish: **Clondermot**
Map Grid: 27
RC Parish: Glendermot (Waterside)
Diocese: DE
Earliest Record: b. 1.1864; m. 1.1864
Parish Address: Rev. James Clerkin, PP, 32 Chapel Road, Waterside, Derry BT47 2BB

Civil Parish: **Coleraine**
Map Grid: 3
RC Parish: Coleraine
Diocese: CR
Earliest Record: b. 5.1848; m. 5.1848
Parish Address: Rev. Archibald Molloy, PP, 72 Nursery Ave., Coleraine, Co. Derry BT52 1LR

Civil Parish: **Cumber Lower**
Map Grid: 28
RC Parish: part Glendermot, see Clondermot;
  part Cumber, see below

Civil Parish: **Cumber Upper**
Map Grid: 30
RC Parish: Cumber Upper and Learmount
  (Clandy)
Diocese: DE
Earliest Record: b. 5.1863; m. 9.186
Parish Address: Rev. W. Carolan, PP, Parochial
  House, 9 Church Street, Claudy, Co. Derry

Civil Parish: **Derry City**
Map Grid: 25
RC Parish: see Templemore
Diocese: DE

Civil Parish: **Derryloran**
Map Grid: 45
RC Parish: see Desertcreat, Co. Tyrone
Diocese: AM

Civil Parish: **Desertlyn**
Map Grid: 44
RC Parish: part Artrea; part Magherafelt
Diocese: AM

Civil Parish: **Desertmartin**
Map Grid: 40
RC Parish: Desertmartin and Kilcronaghan
Diocese: DE
Earliest Record: b. 11.1848; m. 11.1848;
  d. 11.1848
Parish Address: Rev. Desmond Kelly, PP, 50
  Tobermore Road, Desertmartin, Co. Derry
  BT45 5LE

Civil Parish: **Desertoghill**
Map Grid: 23
RC Parish: see Kilrea
Diocese: DE

Civil Parish: **Drumachose**
Map Grid: 10
RC Parish: Newtown Limavady, see Aghanloo
Diocese: DE

Civil Parish: **Dunboe**
Map Grid: 16

RC Parish: Dunboe, Macosquin and
  Aghadowey (Coleraine)
Diocese: DE
Earliest Record: b. 8.1843
Parish Address: Rev. Desmond Mullan, PP,
  Laurel Hill, Coleraine, Co. Derry BT51 3AY

Civil Parish: **Dungiven**
Map Grid: 14
RC Parish: Dungiven, see also Ballynascreen
Diocese: DE
Earliest Record: b. 7.1847; m. 9.1864; d. 3.1870
Missing Dates: d. ends 12.1871
Parish Address: Rev. A. Duffy, PP, 19 Chapel
  Road, Dungiven, Co. Derry

Civil Parish: **Errigal**
Map Grid: 22
RC Parish: Errigal (Garvagh)
Diocese: DE
Earliest Record: b. 4.1846; m. 2.1873
Parish Address: Rev. Henry J. O'Kane, PP, 78
  Ballerin Road, Garvagh, Co. Derry BT51
  4EQ

Civil Parish: **Faughanvale**
Map Grid: 26
RC Parish: Faughanvale and Lower Cumber
  (Creggan)
Diocese: DE
Earliest Record: b. 9.1863; m. 11.1860
Parish Address: Rev. Gerard O'Neill, PP, Stel-
  la Maris, Creggan, Eglinton, Co. Derry BT47
  3EA

Civil Parish: **Formoyle**
Map Grid: 18
RC Parish: Magilligan, see Tamlaghtard
Diocese: DE

Civil Parish: **Kilcronaghan**
Map Grid: 37
RC Parish: see Desertmartin
Diocese: DE

Civil Parish: **Kildollagh**
Map Grid: 5
RC Parish: see Coleraine
Diocese: CR

Civil Parish: **Killelagh**
Map Grid: 23
RC Parish: part Errigal; part Kilrea
Diocese: DE

Civil Parish: **Killowen**
Map Grid: 17
RC Parish: Killowen
Diocese: DE

Civil Parish: **Kilrea**
Map Grid: 32
RC Parish: Kilrea and Desertohill
Diocese: DE
Earliest Record: b. 8.1846; m. 8.1846; d. 8.1846
Missing Dates: m. ends 8.1865
Parish Address: Rev. John McGaughey, PP, 4 Garvagh Road, Kilrea, Co. Derry BT51 5QP

Civil Parish: **Learmont**
Map Grid: 31
RC Parish: see Cumber Upper
Diocese: DE

Civil Parish: **Lissan**
Map Grid: 43
RC Parish: Lissan, see Co. Tyrone
Diocese: AM

Civil Parish: **Londonderry City**
Map Grid: 25
RC Parish: see Templemore
Diocese: DE

Civil Parish: **Loughermore**
Map Grid: 29
RC Parish: see Cumber Upper
Diocese: DE

Civil Parish: **Macosquin**
Map Grid: 19
RC Parish: part Coleraine; part Dunboe
Diocese: DE

Civil Parish: **Maghera**
Map Grid: 34
RC Parish: Maghera and Killylough; part Termoneeny
Diocese: DE
Earliest Record: b. 3.1841; m. 5.1841; d. 5.1848
Missing Dates: 5.1853-10.1857

Parish Address: Rev. Bernard McMenamin, PP, 111 Main Street, Maghera BT46 5AB

Civil Parish: **Magherafelt**
Map Grid: 41
RC Parish: Magherafelt and Ardtrea
Diocese: AM
Earliest Record: b. 1.1834; m. 1.1834
Missing Dates: b. 7.1857-1.1858; m. 4.1857-2.1858
Parish Address: Rev. C. L. McKeone, PP, Parochial House, 30 King St., Magherafelt, Co. Derry

Civil Parish: **Tamlaght**
Map Grid: 47
RC Parish: see Co. Tyrone
Diocese: AM

Civil Parish: **Tamlaghtard**
Map Grid: 7
RC Parish: Tamlaghtard or Magilligan
Diocese: DE
Earliest Record: b. 9.1863; m. 10.1863; d. 9.1863
Parish Address: Rev. J. McGlinchey, PP, 71 Duncrun Road, Bellarena, Limavady, Co. Derry

Civil Parish: **Tamlaght Finlagan**
Map Grid: 9
RC Parish: Newtown Limavady, see Aghanloo
Diocese: DE

Civil Parish: **Tamlaght O'Crilly**
Map Grid: 35
RC Parish: see Kilrea
Diocese: DE

Civil Parish: **Templemore**
Map Grid: 24
RC Parish: Templemore (St. Columb's, Long Tower, Derry)
Diocese: DE
Earliest Record: b. 10.1823; m. 11.1823
Missing Dates: b. 9.1826-9.1836, 4.1863-1.1864; m. 9.1826-3.1835, 7.1836-1.1841, 11.1851-1.1854
Parish Address: Rev. Neil McGoldrick, Adm, Parochial House, St. Eugene's Cathedral, Derry

Page 20.

Births and Baptismes in August, 1655.

Ann, the daughter of Hugh Powell, borne July 19th, bap. Aug. 2th.
Ralph, the son of Richard Ball of the bogs side, bap. 3th.
Moses, the son of William Hamilton, baptized the 3th.
Jane, the daughter of John Hunter, baptized the 9th.
Robert, the son of George Holcraft, labourer, bap. the 10th.
James, the son of Hugh McGrañaghan of Taghboine, bap. 16th.
Margarett, the daughter of Andrew Miller, bap. the 16th.
Elizabeth, the daughter of Theophilus Davis, borne August the eleventh, baptized the 16th.
John, the son of William Colewell of Clendermott pish, bap. 19th.
Isabell, the daughter of Robert Lion, baptized the 30th.
James, the son of George Heggerty baptized the 30th.
Thomas, son of Thomas Colwell born Aug. 11th, bap. 30th.
Jennett, daughter of John King born Aug 22th, bap. the 30th.

Birthes and Baptismes in September 1655.

James, son of James Hill, borne and baptized Sep. ye 1st.
Bryan, the son of Turlagh O Devin, baptized the 1st.
Ellinor, the daughter of Donnogh Tooll, baptized the 1st.
Barbara, the daughter of John Graham, borne the 1st, bap. 6th.
Wentworth, son of Wentworth Boucher, souldier, bap. the 11th.
Anne, daughter of Richard Hancie, souldier, baptized Sep. 20th.
Joseph, the son of William Richards, borne and bap. the 23th.
John, the son of Neale McNicholls, borne and bap. 24th.
Mary, the daughter of John Robbinson, bor. 16, bap. 25th.
Margarett, the daughter of Thomas Grier, bor. and bap. 26th.

Birthes and baptismes in October 1655.

James, the son of Andrew Cunningham, bor. Sep. 23th, bap. Octo. 4th.
Manus, son of Henry McKauthery, porter, bap. Octob. ye 7th.
Daniell, son of Thomas Radley, baptized October the 15th.
Elizabeth, the daughter of Alphord Ripley, bor. 12th, bap. 18th.
William, the son of Mr William Tuckey, bor. October 17th, bap. 21th.
John, son of John Heard of Clendermott parish, bap. 22th.
George, son of James Neeper of Cumber parish, bap. 26th.
Jennett, the daughter of William Davis of Doñoghedy, bap. 26th.
Sara, the daughter of Thomas Zanchy, souldier, bap. the 28th.
Henry, the son of Humphrey Godfrey, bor. October the 21th, bap. 30th.
James, the son of James Davis, souldier, baptized the 30th.

Page 28.

Birthes and Baptismes, November 1655.

James, the son of Thomas Hickes, souldier, baptized Nov. ye 10th.
Mul Mureȳ, the son of Hugh McSwyne of Killegh, bap. November 10th.
Thomas, the son of John Stoyle of this parish, baptized the 11th.
Jennett, the daughter of John Mitchell of Birt, baptized the 12th.
Thomas, the son John Reinalds of Clendermott parish, bap. the 15th.
James, son of Edward Erwyne of Clendermott parish, bap. the 15th.

Extract from a published copy of the Baptismal Register of the Parish of Templemore, Co. Derry, in 1655. From the "Register of Derry Cathedral..." Parish Register Society, Dublin 1910.

Civil Parish: **Termoneeny**
Map Grid: 38
RC Parish: Termoneeny (Lavey)
Diocese: DE
Earliest Record: b. 11.1871; m. 12.1873
Parish Address: Rev. Patrick Regan, PP, 65 Moyagall Road, Knockloughrim, Magherafelt, Co. Derry BT45 8PG

Commercial and Social Directories

1820

J. Pigot's *Commercial Directory of Ireland* contains information on the gentry, nobility, and traders in and around the towns of Coleraine and Londonderry.

1824

J. Pigot's *City of Dublin & Hibernian Provincial Directory* includes traders, nobility, gentry, and clergy lists of Castledawson, Coleraine, Dungiven, Kilrea, Londonderry, Maghera, Magherafelt, Moneymore, and Newtown-Limavady.

1842

Matthew Martin's *Belfast Directory* contains an alphabetical list of traders, merchants, and gentry, residents of the principal streets, and the nobility and gentry in and around the towns of Castledawson, Coleraine, Magherafelt, and Moneymore.

1846

Slater's *National Commercial Directory of Ireland* lists nobility, clergy, traders, etc., in Castledawson and Bellaghy, Coleraine, Portstewart, Bushmills and Port Ballintrae, Dungiven, Garvagh and Ballinameen, Kilrea, Londonderry, Maghera, Magherafelt, Moneymore and Coagh, and Newtown-Limavady.

1852

Henderson's *Belfast and Province of Ulster Directory* has lists of inhabitants, traders, etc., in and around the towns of Castledawson, Coleraine, Londonderry, and Maghera.

1854

Further edition of above extended to cover Castledawson, Coleraine, Londonderry, Maghera, Magherafelt, Moneymore. Further editions were issued in 1856, 1858, 1861 (with the addition of Newtown-Limavady) 1865, 1868, 1870, 1877, 1880, 1884, 1894, and 1900.

1856

Slater's *Royal National Commercial Directory of Ireland* lists nobility, gentry, clergy, traders, etc., in Castledawson and Bellaghy, Coleraine, Portstewart, Bushmills and Port Ballintrae, Dungiven, Garvagh and Ballinameen, Kilrea, Londonderry, Maghera, Magherafelt, Moneymore and Coagh, and Newtown-Limavady.

1865

R. Wynne's *Business Directory of Belfast* also covers Coleraine, Londonderry, Newtown-Limavady, Maghera, and Moneymore.

1870

Slater's *Directory of Ireland* contains trade, nobility, and clergy lists for Castledawson, Coleraine, Dungiven, Garvagh, Kilrea, Londonderry, Maghera, Magherafelt, Moneymore, and Newtown-Limavady.

1881

Slater's *Royal National Commercial Directory of Ireland* contains lists of traders, clergy, nobility, and farmers in adjoining parishes of the towns of Coleraine, Dungiven, Kilrea, Limavady, Londonderry, Maghera, Magherafelt, Moneymore, and Coagh.

1887

Derry Almanac of Coleraine, Dungiven, Kilrea, Londonderry, Limavady, and Portstewart.

1894

Slater's *Royal National Directory of Ireland* lists traders, police, teachers, farmers, and private residents in each of the towns, villages, and parishes of the county.

Family History

Bewley, Sir Edmund. *The Folliotts of Londonderry and Chester.* 1902.

Boyle. *Genealogical Memoranda Relating to the Family of Boyle of Limavady.* Londonderry, 1903.

The O'Doherty Information Pack: History and Genealogy. Derry Youth and Community Workshop, 1985.

"Entries from the Family Bible of Alexander and Esther Crookshank. *Ir. Anc.* 9 (2) (1977): 1-2.

Kennedy, F.E. *A Family of Kennedy of Clogher and Londonderry c.1600-1938.* Taunton, 1938.

MacRory, R.A. *The Past – MacRorys of Duneane, Castle-Dawson, Limavady, and Belfast.* Belfast, n.d.

"Richardson of Somerset." Pedigree in *Swanzy Notebooks.* RCB Library, Dublin.

"Some Account of the Sept of the O'Cathains of Ciannachta Glinne-Geimhin. Now the O'Kanes of the Co. of Londonderry." *Ulster J. Arch.* 3 (1855): 1-8, 265-72; 4 (1856): 139-48.

Wray – see Co. Donegal, Family Histories section

Gravestone Inscriptions

Draperstown: (Presbyterian Congregation Church) Published by Ballynascreen Historical Society, 1982.

Maghera and Magherafelt area: Published in *South Derry Historical Society Journal.*

Newspapers

Title: *Coleraine Chronicle* (continued as *Chronicle* in 1967)
Published in: Coleraine, 1844-current
NLI Holdings: 1.1905-11.1967

BL Holdings: 4.1844-in progress
Title: *Coleraine Constitution* (continued as *Northern Constitution* in 1908)
Published in: Coleraine, 1875-current
NLI Holdings: 1.1905-6.1908; 10.1908-in progress
BL Holdings: 4.1877-10.1908; 10.1908-in progress

Title: *Londonderry Chronicle*
Published in: Derry, 1829-72
NLI Holdings: 2-10.1829
BL Holdings: 2-10.1829

Title: *Londonderry Guardian*
Published in: Derry, 1857-71
BL Holdings: 9.1857-9.1871

Title: *Londonderry Journal* (continued as *Derry Journal* in 1880)
Published in: Derry, 1772-current
NLI Holdings: 1.1772-4.1796; 1.1798-12.1809; 1810-1818; 1820-1.1827; 9.1829-1836; 9.1837-12.1847; 1.1848-10.1851; 1852-1855; 9.1860-12.1861; 1858; 1859; 7.1862-12.1863; 1864; 1865; 1866; 9.1933-in progress
BL Holdings: 1.1835-7.1869; 1.1870-in progress

Title: *Londonderry Sentinel* (continued as *Sentinel* in 1974)
Published in: Derry, 1829-current
NLI Holdings: 1.1885-12.1911; 1913; 6.1921-7.1945; 1.1954-5.1974; 7.1924-in progress
BL Holdings: 9.1829-10.1854; 1.1856-7.1869; 1.1870-12.1925; 7.1926-in progress

Title: *Londonderry Standard* (continued as *Derry Standard* in 1888)
Published in: Derry, 1836-1964
NLI Holdings: 1.1853-12.1924; 1.1950-12.1963
BL Holdings: 11.1836-7.1869; 1.1870-1.1964

Wills and Administrations

A discussion of the types of records, where they are held, their availability, and value is given in the Wills section of the Introduction. The availability of prerogative wills, administrations, and marriage license records is also described in the relevant parts of the same section. Where available, published sources of these records are given in the Miscellaneous Sources section.

Pre-1858 Wills and Administrations

Consistorial Wills. County Derry is mainly in the diocese of Derry, with some parishes in Connor and Armagh dioceses. The guide to Catholic parish records in this chapter shows the diocese to which each civil parish belonged. The wills of residents of each diocese were usually proven within that diocese (see Wills section for exceptions). The following records survive:

Wills. Only for Connor Diocese – see Co. Antrim.

Abstracts. see p. xxxvii.

Indexes. Derry (1612-1858) published by Phillimore; Connor – see Co. Antrim; Armagh – see Co. Armagh.

Post-1858 Wills and Administrations

County Derry was served by the District Registry of Londonderry. The surviving records are kept in the PRONI.

Marriage Records

Indexes. Armagh (1727-1845) PRO; SLC films 100859-60. Connor (1721-1845) PRO; SLC film 100867.

Miscellaneous Sources

"Derry Clergy List 1631." *Derriana* (1980): 9-13.

Desertmartin Estate Rental 1877-1886. PRONI D3262 (tenants, holdings, and rent with some comments).

"Mortality in Magherafelt, County Derry in the Early Eighteenth Century." *Ir. Hist. Stud.* 19 (1974): 125-35.

"Popish Clergy in Derry 1704." *Derriana* (1980): 14-25.

"Priests of Derry 1820-1905." *Derriana* (1980): 26-34.

Simpson, R. *The Annals of Derry.* 1847.

Research Sources and Services

Journals

Derriana (published by the Derry Diocesan Historical Society, 1978-present)

South Derry Historical Society Journal (1980-present)

Benbradagh (Dungiven parish magazine)

Libraries and Information Sources

Derry Divisional Library, Bishop Street, Derry

Research Services

North West Centre for Learning and Development, Ltd. (Derry Youth and Community Workshop), 10 Bishop St., Derry, Northern Ireland T748 6PW. Telex: (0504) 268891. (research services, local family history publications, etc.)

Societies

Derry Diocesan Historical Society, Mrs. C. Donnelly, Labby, Draperstown, Co. Derry

Roe Valley Historical Society, Mrs. M. Lueg, Trust Cottage, Limavady, Co. Derry

Londonderry Naturalists Field Club, Mr. T.H. Roulston, Principal's Residence, Belmont House School, Racecourse Road, Derry

Ballinascreen Historical Society, Miss J. Johnston, 73 High Street, Draperstown, Co. Derry

South Derry Historical Society, Mrs. N. O'Connor, 7 Highfield Crescent, Magherafelt, Co. Derry

North West Archaeological and Historical Society, Mr. R. Hamilton, 1 Summerhill, Prehen, Co. Derry

Kilrea Historical Society, Mrs. M. Lennox, Drumane, Kilrea, Co. Londonderry

Coleraine Historical Society, Mrs. J. Cunningham, 43 Knockaduff Road, Aghadowey, Co. Derry

See also research services in Belfast, p. xlvi

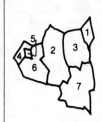

CIVIL PARISHES OF COUNTY DERRY

BARONIES

1. LIBERTIES OF COLERAINE
2. KEENAGHT
3. COLERAINE
4. LIBERTIES OF DERRY
5. CITY OF DERRY
6. TIRKEERAN
7. LOUGHINSHOLIN

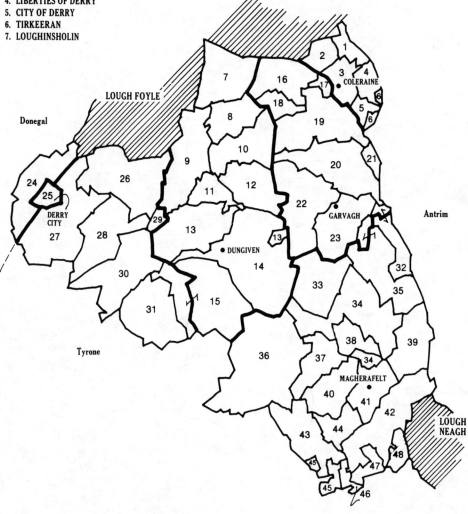

LOUGH FOYLE

Donegal

COLERAINE

Antrim

DERRY CITY

DUNGIVEN

GARVAGH

Tyrone

MAGHERAFELT

LOUGH NEAGH

⌐ = CIVIL PARISHES ADJOINING ACROSS
    BARONY BOUNDARIES.

County Donegal

A Brief History

This Ulster coastal county, which is largely bog and mountain land, contains the towns of Letterkenny, Donegal, Ballyshannon, Lifford, Stranorlar, Killybegs, and Bundoran.

County Donegal was known as the Kingdom of Tirconnell in the old Irish administrative system. It was the territory of the powerful O'Donnell family. The other major families in the county were O'Boyle, O'Doherty, O'Friel, O'Sheil, MacWard, McLoughlin, McDunlevy, McGillespie, MacRearty, McGrath, McGonagle, O'Mulholland, O'Harkin, O'Derry, and O'Strahan. The McSweeneys, also a relatively common name in the county, were a Gallowglass or mercenary family who arrived in the county in the thirteenth century.

This county was little affected by the Norman invasion in the twelfth century and it was not until the late sixteenth century that the English gained any foothold. This was lost again in 1592 when the O'Donnells, under their chief Red Hugh O'Donnell, joined with the O'Neills in a rebellion against the English. This rebellion ended in the defeat of the Ulster Chieftains in 1602, and the county was subsequently included in the plantation of Ulster. Under this scheme the lands were confiscated from the native Irish owners and given to undertakers, i.e., to persons who were granted land on the agreement that they would bring over settlers from England or Scotland.

Among the common settler names in the county are those of Elliott, Campbell, Anderson, Baird, Thompson, McClintock, Hamilton, Browne, Barr, Stewart, Smith, Johnston, Irwin, Morrison, Young, and White.

A general indication of the proportion of native Irish, Scottish, and English can be estimated from the religious persuasions of the inhabitants as the native Irish were generally Catholic, the Scottish Presbyterian, and the English Protestant or Episcopalian. In 1861, when the census first ascertained religion, the proportions of each religion were 75, 11, and 13 percent respectively.

In the eighteenth century the county remained relatively remote. Contemporary maps show few roads in the county, and the accounts of various travellers tell of the unique customs of some of its people. The Penal Laws were specifically enacted at the beginning of the eighteenth century to supress Catholics. However, they also disadvantaged Presbyterians. For this reason there was considerable emigration of the so-called Scots-Irish from Donegal and other Ulster counties during the eighteenth century.

The density of population on the arable land in County Donegal was one of the highest in the country in the early nineteenth century. The county was not as badly affected as many others in the Great Famine of 1845-47. The population was 296,000 in 1841, and by 1851 it had fallen to 255,000. Almost 28,000 people died in the county between 1845 and 1850, and further thousands emigrated.

Census and Census Substitutes

1612-13
Survey of Undertakers Planted in Donegal (names, acreages allotted and account of the progress of each). *Hist. Mss. Comm. Rep.* (Hastings Mss.) 4 (1947): 159-82.

1630
Muster Roll. BL add. ms. 4770; printed in *Donegal Annual* 10 (2) (1972): 124-49.

1642
Muster Roll. SLC film 897012.

1654
Civil Survey, Vol. 3.

1659
"Census" of Ireland. Edited by S. Pender. Dublin: Stationery Office, 1939.

1663-65
Hearth Money Roll Extracts. PRO film 2473.

1665
Hearth Money Roll. GO 538; NLI ms. 9583/4; SLC film 100181, 258502. Lists have been printed for the following parishes in *The Laggan and its Presbyterianism* by A.G. Leahy (1905); Taughboyne (p.89); Clonleigh (p.91); Raphoe (Convoy) (p.92); Donoughmore (p.93); Stranorlar (p.94); Leck (p.94).

1669
Subsidy Roll (Kilmacrenan, Raphoe, Taghboyne, Tirhugh). SLC film 258502; PRONI T307.

1718
"William Connolly's Ballyshannon Estate." *Donegal Ann.* 33 (1981): 27-44 (gives tenants and holdings in 1718 and in 1726 with comments).

1726
See William Connolly, 1718.

1730
"The Murray of Broughton Estate (Southwest Donegal)." *Donegal Ann.* 12 (1) (1977): 22-39 (lists holdings and tenants with comments).

1740
Protestant Householders in Parishes of Cloncaha, Clonmeny, Culdaff, Desertegney, Donagh, Fawne, Movill, and Templemore. GO 539; SLC film 100182.

1761-75
List of Freeholders. SLC film 100181; GO ms. 442.

1761-88
List of Freeholders. NLI ms. 787/8.

1766
Census of Parish of Donoghmore. PRO film 207-08.

Protestants in Parishes of Inch and Leck. PRO 1A 41 100; SLC film 258517.

1767
Register of Freeholders in Co. Donegal. NLI P975.

1770
Names of Owners of Freeholds Entitled to Vote c. 1770 NLI. mss. 987-88.

1782
"Inhabitants of Culdaff Parish." In A.I. Young, *300 Years in Inishowen* 159-60. 1929.

1794
"Protestant Householders in Leck Parish." In *The Laggan and its Presbyterianism* 1: 95.

"Householders in St. Johnston (Parish of Taughboy)." In *The Laggan and its Presbyterianism* 1: 89.

1799
"Protestant Householders in the Parish of Templecrone, Co. Donegal" (list of church wardens of the parish for 1775-90). *Ir. Anc.* 16 (2) (1984): 78-79.

No Armes

[f182ᵛ] Barony de Rapho

The Lady Conningham Widdow of Sir James Conningham,
undertaker of 2,000 acres, her men and armes.

William Conningham
James Calquahan
Andrew mcCorkill
John mcCorkill
Tobias Hood
James Davye
Peter Starret
John mcquchowne
James Knox
Adam Garvance

Swords and Pikes

James mcAdowe
ffyndlay Ewing
Dunkan mcffarlan
Ninian ffoulton
James Scot
William Rankin
Daniell Ramsay
Martin Galbreath
Patrick Porter

Swords and Snaphances

William mcIltherne
David Walker
John Barbor

Swords and Calleuers

James Makee

Sword and halbert

f183   Andrew George
James mcIlman
Michaell Rot(h?)es
Patrick Miller
Robert Muntgomery
Alexander Conningham

Richard Leaky
Robert Staret
John mcIihome
Sallomon Giffin
David Reed
Donnell mcDonnell
Alexander Carlell
William Gafeth

Swords onely

Gilbert Highgate
Patrick Porter
Robert Hasta
William Gambell
John Hunter
John Crawfford
Robert Johnston
Henry Smyth
William Boyes
David Ramsay
William Steward
Robert Crafford
[f183ᵛ] James Conningham
Andrew Conningham
John Crafford
John Hunter
John Wilson
James Bredyne
Mungo Davy
William Richey
John mcIlhome
Henry Hunter
John mcHutchon
James Rankin
William Killy
Robert Pots
William Gambell
John Lyone
James Knox   66

Extract from a County Donegal Muster Roll of 1630 showing the fighting men
available to Lady Conningham, an undertaker in the Barony of Raphoe, and their
arms. From *Donegal Annual* 10(2) (1972).

1802-03
"Protestants in Part of Culdaff Parish." In A.I. Young, *300 Years in Inishowen* 186-87. 1929.

1825-36
Tithe Applotment Survey (see p. xxvii).

1857
Griffith's Valuation (see p. xxvii).

1858-69
Rental of Earl of Leitrim Estate, Barony of Kilmacrenan. NLI ms. 5175-5178.

1901
Census. PRO.

1911
Census. PRO.

Church Records

Church of Ireland
(shows starting date of record)

Parish: **Aghanunshin**
Status: Lost

Parish: **All Saints, Taughboyne**
Status: Lost

Parish: **Ardara**
Existing Records: b. 1829; m. 1829; d. 1830
Status: LC

Parish: **Ballintra** (see Drumholm)

Parish: **Ballyshannon** (see Kilbarron and Finner)

Parish: **Burt**
Existing Records: b. 1802; m. 1802; d. 1802
Status: LC

Parish: **Carndonagh** (see Donagh)

Parish: **Castlefin** (see Donaghmore)

Parish: **Cloncha**
Status: Lost

Parish: **Clondehorky**
Status: Lost

Parish: **Clondevaddock**
Existing Records: b. 1794; m. 1794; d. 1794
Status: LC

Parish: **Convoy**
Status: Lost

Parish: **Conwal**
Status: Lost

Parish: **Culdaff**
Status: Lost

Parish: **Desertegny**
Existing Records: b. 1790; m. 1813; d. 1803
Missing Records: m. 1831-43; d. 1804-32
Status: LC

Parish: **Donagh**
Status: Lost

Parish: **Donaghmore**
Status: Lost

Parish: **Donegal**
Existing Records: b. 1803; m. 1803; d. 1803
Status: LC

Parish: **Drumholm** (Ballintra)
Existing Records: b. 1691; m. 1691; d. 1691
Status: LC

Parish: **Dunboe**
Status: Lost

Parish: **Dunlewey** (Bunerana)
Existing Records: b. 1853
Missing Records: b. 1856
Status: LC

Parish: **Fahan, Upper**
Existing Records: b. 1765; m. 1765; d. 1765
Status: LC

VALUATION OF TENEMENTS.

PARISH OF KILLYBEGS, LOWER.

67

No. and Letters of Reference to Map.		Names.		Description of Tenement.	Area.			Rateable Annual Valuation.						Total Annual Valuation of Rateable Property.		
		Townlands and Occupiers.	Immediate Lessors.					Land.			Buildings.					
					A.	R.	P.	£	s.	d.	£	s.	d.	£	s.	d.
		DRUMBARRAN. *(Ord. S. 75 & 82.)*														
1	{ a	James Evans,	Rev. G. N. Tredennick {	House, offices, and land,	21	0	20	13	10	0	4	10	0	} 30	0	0
	b }			Corn-mill and kiln,	—			—			12	0	0	}		
2		Thomas Mullowney,	Same,	Land,	1	0	10	1	0	0	—			1	0	0
3		Francis M'Clinchy,	Same,	Land,	1	2	30	1	10	0	—			1	10	0
4		Charles Gallagher,	Same,	Land,	0	3	15	1	0	0	—			1	0	0
5	{	Thomas Dever, } Charles Morough, }	Same,	Land,	7	1	30	{ 1	15	0	—			1	15	0
								1	15	0	—			1	15	0
6		James M'Hugh,	Same,	Land,	2	1	20	1	2	0	—			1	2	0
7 A	{	John Maginly (*Shane*),	Same,	Land,	1	2	5	0	13	0	—			} 2	10	0
– B					3	2	35	1	17	0	—			}		
8	{	James Dorian, } Charles Morough, }	Same,	Land,	2	3	15	{ 0	15	0	—			{ 0	15	0
								0	15	0	—			0	15	0
9		Sidney Bresland,	Same,	Land,	1	2	0	0	15	0	—			0	15	0
10		Bernard Magrorty,	Same,	Land,	6	0	22	3	10	0	—			3	10	0
–	a	Patrick Shevlin,	Same,	House and garden,	0	0	24	0	3	0	0	5	0	0	8	0
–	b	James M'Hugh,	Same,	House and garden,	0	0	24	0	3	0	0	12	0	0	15	0
11		William Walker,	Same,	Land,	3	0	35	1	15	0	—			1	15	0
12		Thomas Maloney,	Same,	Land,	4	0	0	2	5	0	—			2	5	0
13		John Boyle,	Same,	Land,	2	2	0	1	10	0	—			1	10	0
14		John O'Donnell,	Same,	Land,	2	3	20	1	10	0	—			1	10	0
15		Dudley O'Donnell,	Same,	Land,	5	0	30	2	10	0	—			2	10	0
–	a	James M'Afee,	Same,	Garden,	0	1	0	0	5	0	—			0	5	0
–	b	National school-house and play ground,	(*See Exemptions.*)													
–	c	Unoccupied,	Rev. Geo. N. Tredennick	House,	—			—			0	10	0	0	10	0
16		Patrick Shevlin,	Same,	Land,	2	1	10	1	5	0	—			1	5	0
17		Michael Fisher,	Same,	Land,	3	1	5	2	0	0	—			2	0	0
18		Charles Gallagher,	Same,	Land,	3	0	15	2	0	0	—			2	0	0
19		Blakeney Gubbins,	Same,	Land,	1	2	30	1	0	0	—			1	0	0
–	a	William Tredennick,	Same,	Ice-house,	—			—			0	5	0	0	5	0
20		John Crimley,	Same,	Land,	2	1	0	1	5	0	—			1	5	0
–	a	John Sheeran,	Same,	Land,	0	3	15	0	15	0	—			0	15	0
		TOWN OF ARDARA. MAIN-STREET.														
21	1	R. C. Chapel, yard, and grave-yard,	(*See Exemptions*).													
–	2	Teague Bresland,	Rev. Geo. N. Tredennick	House, offices, & sm. gar.	—			—			3	0	0	3	0	0
–	3	James Dorian,	Same,	House, office, & sm. gar.	—			—			3	5	0	3	5	0
–	4	Unoccupied,	James Dorian,	House (*in progress*),	—			—			—					
–	5	Patrick Gillespie,	Charles Gallagher,	House & small garden,	—			—			1	5	0	1	5	0
–	6	Charles Gallagher,	Same,	House & small garden,	—			—			1	5	0	1	5	0
–	7	John Boyle,	Rev. Geo. N. Tredennick	House & small garden,	—			—			2	15	0	2	15	0
–	8		John Boyle,	Ruins,	—			—			—					
–	9	Myles Sweeney,	Rev. Geo. N. Tredennick	House, office, & sm. gar.	—			—			1	10	0	1	10	0
–	10	James Heraghty,	Same,	House & small garden,	—			—			1	5	0	1	5	0
–	11	Patrick Kennedy,	Same,	House and garden,	0	0	8	0	2	0	2	13	0	2	15	0
–	12	Francis M'Hugh,	Francis M'Glenchy,	House, office, & garden,	0	0	7	0	2	0	3	13	0	3	15	0
–	13	Manus M'Glenchy,	Rev. Geo. N. Tredennick	House,	—			—			1	10	0	1	10	0
–	14	John Dever,	Same,	House, office, & garden,	0	0	8	0	2	0	3	13	0	3	15	0
–	15	Henry Morrisson,	Same,	House, office, & garden,	0	0	8	0	2	0	2	18	0	3	0	0
–	16	Andrew Mackey,	Same,	House & small garden,	—			—			2	5	0	2	5	0
–	17	John Coen,	Same,	House & small garden,	—			—			1	0	0	1	0	0
–	18	William Given,	Archibald Richey,	House & small garden,	—			—			0	15	0	0	15	0
–	19	Patrick Bresland,	Charles Gallagher,	House, yard, & sm. gar.	—			—			1	0	0	1	0	0
–	20	Dudly O'Donnell,	Owen Craig,	House and office,	—			—			1	0	0	1	0	0
–	21	Patrick Kelly,	Denis Bresland,	House,	—			—			0	15	0	0	15	0
–	22	John Sweeney,	Same,	House & small garden,	—			—			0	15	0	0	15	0
–	23	Unoccupied,	Patrick Boyle,	Ho. (*in progress*) & gar.	0	0	7	0	2	0	—			0	2	0
–	24	Mary Manelis,	Rev. Geo. N. Tredennick	House, offices, & garden,	0	0	8	0	2	0	1	8	0	1	10	0
–	25	John Gallagher,	Patrick Boyle,	House,	—			—			1	0	0	1	0	0
–	26	Charles Gallagher,	Rev. Geo. N. Tredennick	Ho., off., yd., & sm. gar.	—			—			10	10	0	10	10	0
–	27	James Dwyer,	John Evans,	House,	—			—			1	10	0	1	10	0
–	28	Neal Sharp,	Same,	House,	—			—			1	0	0	1	0	0
–	29	John Campbell,	Rev. Geo. N. Tredennick	House,	—			—			0	10	0	0	10	0
–	30	Thomas Manelis,	Same,	House,	—			—			0	10	0	0	10	0
–	31	John Shevlin,	Same,	House,	—			—			0	10	0	0	10	0
–	32	Peter Carolan,	Same,	House,	—			—			0	10	0	0	10	0

Page from the *Griffith's* or *Primary Valuation of Ireland* showing some of the land and lease-holders in the parish of Killybegs Lower, Co. Donegal.

Parish: **Finner**
Existing Records: b. 1815; m. 1815; d. 1815
Status: LC

Parish: **Gartan**
Status: Lost

Parish: **Glencolumbkille**
Existing Records: b. 1827
Status: LC

Parish: **Glenties**
Existing Records: b. 1852; d. 1853
Status: LC

Parish: **Gweedore**
Status: Lost

Parish: **Inch**
Status: Lost

Parish: **Inniskeel**
Existing Records: b. 1826; m. 1827; d. 1852
Status: LC

Parish: **Inver**
Existing Records: b. 1805; m. 1805; d. 1827
Status: LC

Parish: **Kilbarron** (Ballyshannon)
Existing Records: b. 1785; m. 1785; d. 1785
Status: LC

Parish: **Kilcar** (Killybegs)
Existing Records: b. 1819; m. 1819; d. 1818
Status: LC

Parish: **Killaghtee** (Glenties)
Existing Records: b. 1775; m. 1758; d. 1762
Status: LC

Parish: **Killea**
Status: Lost

Parish: **Killybegs**
Existing Records: b. 1787; m. 1809; d. 1809
Missing Records: b. 1797-1808
Status: LC

Parish: **Killygarvan**
Status: Lost

Parish: **Killymard**
Status: Lost

Parish: **Kilmacrenan**
Status: Lost

Parish: **Kilteevogue** (Stranorlar)
Existing Records: b. 1818; d. 1825
Status: LC

Parish: **Laghey**
Status: Lost

Parish: **Leck**
Status: Lost

Parish: **Lettermacward**
Status: Lost

Parish: **Meenglass**
Status: Lost

Parish: **Mevagh**
Status: Lost

Parish: **Milford**
Status: Lost

Parish: **Mount Charles**
Status: Lost

Parish: **Moville Lower**
Status: Lost

Parish: **Muff**
Existing Records: b. 1803; m. 1804; d. 1847
Status: LC

Parish: **Raphoe**
Existing Records: b. 1831; m. 1831; d. 1831
Status: LC

Parish: **Rathmullen** (see Killygarvan)

Parish: **Raymochy**
Status: Lost

Parish: **Raymunterdoney**
Status: Lost

Parish: **Rossnowlagh**
Status: Lost

Parish: **Stranorlar**
Existing Records: b. 1821; m. 1821; d. 1821
Status: LC

Parish: **Taughboyne** (Derry)
Existing Records: b. 1819; m. 1836; d. 1819
Status: LC

Parish: **Templecarn**
Existing Records: b. 1825; m. 1825; d. 1825
Status: LC

Parish: **Templecrone**
Status: Lost

Parish: **Tullaghobegley**
Existing Records: b. 1821; m. 1821; d. 1850
Status: LC

Parish: **Tullyaughnish** (Ramelton)
Existing Records: b. 1798; m. 1788; d. 1788
Status: LC

Presbyterian

Parish: **Ballindrait**
Starting Date: 1819

Parish: **Ballyshannon**
Starting Date: 1836

Parish: **Buncrana**
Starting Date: 1836

Parish: **Burt**
Starting Date: 1834

Parish: **Carnone** (Raphoe)
Starting Date: 1834

Parish: **Carrigart**
Starting Date: 1844

Parish: **Convoy**
Starting Date: 1822

Parish: **Donegal**
Starting Date: 1825

Parish: **Donoughmore** (Castlefin)
Starting Date: 1844

Parish: **Knowhead** (Muff)
Starting Date: 1826

Parish: **Letterkenny**
Starting Date: 1841

Parish: **Monreagh** (Derry)
Starting Date: 1845

Parish: **Moville**
Starting Date: 1834

Parish: **Newtowncunningham**
Starting Date: 1808

Parish: **Ramelton**
Starting Date: 1808

Parish: **Raphoe**
Starting Date: 1829

Parish: **St. Johnston**
Starting Date: 1838

Parish: **Trentagh** (Kilmacrennan)
Starting Date: 1836

Roman Catholic

Civil Parish: **Aghanunshin**
Map Grid: 18
RC Parish: Aghanunshin, see Aughnish
Diocese: RA

Civil Parish: **Allsaints**
Map Grid: 29
RC Parish: see Taughboyne
Diocese: RA

Civil Parish: **Aughnish** (see also Killygarvan)
Map Grid: 16
RC Parish: part Aughnish; part Killygarvan

Diocese: RA
Earliest Record: b. 11.1873; m. 12.1873
Parish Address: Rev. D. Sweeney, PP, Augh-
nish, Ramelton, Co. Donegal

Civil Parish: **Barr of Inch**
Map Grid: 19
RC Parish: see Mintiaghs
Diocese: RA

Civil Parish: **Burt**
Map Grid: 25
RC Parish: Burt, Inch, and Fahan
Diocese: DE
Earliest Record: b. 11.1859; m. 1.1856; d. 4.1860
Missing Dates: d. ends 7.1866
Parish Address: Rev. L. O'Brien, PP, Parochial
House, Fahan, Lifford, Co. Donegal

Civil Parish: **Clonca**
Map Grid: 1
RC Parish: Clonca (Malin)
Diocese: DE
Earliest Record: b. 11.1856; m. 4.1870
Parish Address: Rev. Charles Campbell, PP,
Malin, Lifford, Co. Donegal

Civil Parish: **Clondahorky**
Map Grid: 10
RC Parish: Clondahorky (Dunfanaghy)
Diocese: RA
Earliest Record: b. 10.1877; m. 1.1879
Parish Address: Rev. Thomas Doherty, PP,
Dunfanaghy, Co. Donegal

Civil Parish: **Clondavaddog**
Map Grid: 7
RC Parish: Clondavaddog (Tamney)
Diocese: RA
Earliest Record: b. 2.1847; m. 2.1847; d. 2.1847
Missing Dates: b. 3.1871-5.1873; m. ends 7.1869;
d. ends 2.1869
Parish Address: Rev. Peader Arnold, PP, Tam-
ney, Letterkenny, Co. Donegal

Civil Parish: **Clonleigh**
Map Grid: 35
RC Parish: Clonleigh (Lifford)
Diocese: DE
Earliest Record: b. 4.1773; m. 8.1788

Missing Dates: b. 2.1795-1.1836, 5.1837-3.1853;
m. 9.1781-1843
Parish Address: Rev. William McGaughey, PP,
Murlog, Lifford, Co. Donegal

Civil Parish: **Clonmany**
Map Grid: 2
RC Parish: Clonmany
Diocese: DE
Earliest Record: b. 1.1852
Parish Address: Rev. Hugh Gallagher, PP,
Clonmany, Lifford, Co. Donegal

Civil Parish: **Convoy**
Map Grid: 36
RC Parish: see Raphoe
Diocese: RA

Civil Parish: **Conwal**
Map Grid: 17
RC Parish: Conwal and Leck (Letterkenny)
Diocese: RA
Earliest Record: b. 5.1853; m. 5.1853
Missing Dates: b. 12.1862-3.1868; m. 11.1863-
2.1877
Parish Address: Rev. Kieran McAteer, PP, The
Presbytery, Letterkenny, Co. Donegal

Civil Parish: **Culdaff**
Map Grid: 4
RC Parish: Culdaff
Diocese: DE
Earliest Record: b. 1.1838; m. 1.1849
Missing Dates: b. 11.1841-6.1847
Parish Address: Rev. Bernard Duffy, PP, Cul-
daff, Lifford, Co. Donegal

Civil Parish: **Desertegny**
Map Grid: 20
RC Parish: Desertegny and Lower Fahan
Diocese: DE
Earliest Record: b. 12.1864; m. 11.1871
Parish Address: Rev. Hugh McGurk, PP, St.
Oran's Road, Buncrana, Co. Donegal

Civil Parish: **Donagh**
Map Grid: 3
RC Parish: Donagh
Diocese: DE
Earliest Record: 1.1847

Parish Address: Rev. Hugh O'Neill, PP, Church Road, Carndonagh, Lifrord, Co. Donegal

Civil Parish: **Donaghamore**
Map Grid: 39
RC Parish: Donaghmore (Killygordon)
Diocese: DE
Earliest Record: b. 11.1840; m. 4.1846
Parish Address: Rev. M. Keaveny, PP, Crossroads, Lifford, Co. Donegal

Civil Parish: **Donegal**
Map Grid: 48
RC Parish: Tawnawally Mts.
Diocese: RA
Earliest Record: b. 12.1872; m. 1.187
Parish Address: Rev. Andrew Carrabin, PP, Donegal, Co. Donegal

Civil Parish: **Drumhome**
Map Grid: 49
RC Parish: Drumhome (Ballintra)
Diocese: RA
Earliest Record: b. 6.1866; m. 8.1866
Parish Address: Rev. Augustine McCauley, PP, Ballintra, Co. Donegal

Civil Parish: **Fahan Lower**
Map Grid: 21
RC Parish: see Desertegny
Diocese: DE

Civil Parish: **Fahan Upper**
Map Grid: 22
RC Parish: see Burt
Diocese: DE

Civil Parish: **Gartan**
Map Grid: 14
RC Parish: Termon and Gartan
Diocese: RA
Earliest Record: b. 1862; m. 1862; d. 1862
Parish Address: Rev. P. McMahon, PP, Termon, Letterkenny, Co. Donegal

Civil Parish: **Glencolmbkille**
Map Grid: 42
RC Parish: Glencolumbkille
Diocese: RA
Earliest Record: b. 1860; m. 1860; d. 1860

Parish Address: Rev. James McDyer, PP, Carrick, Co. Donegal

Civil Parish: **Inch**
Map Grid: 24
RC Parish: see Burt
Diocese: DE

Civil Parish: **Inishkeel**
Map Grid: 28
RC Parish: Inishkeel (Glenties)
Diocese: RA
Earliest Record: b. 10.1866; m. 11.1866
Parish Address: Rev. Con Cunningham, PP, Glenties, Lifford, Co. Donegal

Civil Parish: **Inishmacsaint**
Map Grid: 52
RC Parish: see Co. Fermanagh
Diocese: CG

Civil Parish: **Inver**
Map Grid: 46
RC Parish: Inver
Diocese: RA
Earliest Record: b. 1.1861; m. 2.1861
Missing Dates: m. 6.1867-11.1875
Parish Address: Rev. Leo Moore, PP, Frosses, Co. Donegal

Civil Parish: **Kilbarron**
Map Grid: 51
RC Parish: Kilbarron
Diocese: RA
Earliest Record: b. 11.1854; m. 1.1858
Parish Address: Rev. D. Britton, PP, Ballyshannon, Co. Donegal

Civil Parish: **Kilcar**
Map Grid: 43
RC Parish: Kilcar
Diocese: RA
Earliest Record: b. 1.1848
Parish Address: Rev. D. McShane, PP, Kilcar, Co. Donegal

Civil Parish: **Killaghtle**
Map Grid: 45
RC Parish: see Killybegs
Diocese: CG

138 *Irish Records*

Civil Parish: **Killea**
Map Grid: 33
RC Parish: see Taughboyne
Diocese: RA

Civil Parish: **Killybegs Lower**
Map Grid: 41
RC Parish: Ardara
Diocese: RA
Earliest Record: b. 1.1869; m. 6.1867
Parish Address: Rev. Liam McCaul, PP, Ardara, Co. Donegal

Civil Parish: **Killybegs Upper**
Map Grid: 44
RC Parish: Killybegs and Killaghtee
Diocese: RA
Earliest Record: b. 1.1845; m. 9.1857
Missing Dates: b. 4.1847-10.1850, 10.1853-7.1857
Parish Address: Rev. Charles J. McGrenra, PP, Killybegs, Co. Donegal

Civil Parish: **Killygarvan**
Map Grid: 13
RC Parish: Killygarvan
Diocese: RA
Earliest Record: b. 10.1868; m. 2.1873
Parish Address: Rev. Patrick Muldoon, PP, Rathmullan, Co. Donegal

Civil Parish: **Killymard**
Map Grid: 47
RC Parish: Killymard
Diocese: RA
Earliest Record: b. 9.1874
Parish Address: Rev. Owen Friel, PP, Killymard, Co. Donegal

Civil Parish: **Kilmacrenan**
Map Grid: 15
RC Parish: Kilmacrenan
Diocese: RA
Earliest Record: b. 11.1862
Parish Address: Rev. Neil Boyle, PP, Kilmacrenan, Co. Donegal

Civil Parish: **Kilteevoge**
Map Grid: 37
RC Parish: Kilteevoge (Cloghan)
Diocese: RA

Earliest Record: b. 12.1855; m. 11.1855
Missing Dates: b. 4.1862-4.1870; m. 3.1862-5.1870
Parish Address: Rev. Austin Laverty, PP, Cloghan, Co. Donegal

Civil Parish: **Leck**
Map Grid: 30
RC Parish: see Conwal
Diocese: RA

Civil Parish: **Lettermacaward**
Map Grid: 27
RC Parish: Lettermacaward, see Templecrone
Diocese: RA

Civil Parish: **Mevagh**
Map Grid: 11
RC Parish: Mevagh
Diocese: RA
Earliest Record: b. 1.1871
Parish Address: Rev. Patrick Gallagher, PP, Downings, Co. Donegal

Civil Parish: **Mintiaghs** or **Barr of Inch**
Map Grid: 19
RC Parish: see Desertegny
Diocese: DE

Civil Parish: **Moville Lower**
Map Grid: 5
RC Parish: Moville Lower
Diocese: DE
Earliest Record: b. 11.1847; m. 11.1847; d. 11.1847
Missing Dates: d. ends 7.1854
Parish Address: Rev. Patrick McGoldrick, PP, Parochial House, Moville, Lifford, Co. Donegal

Civil Parish: **Moville Upper**
Map Grid: 6
RC Parish: Iskaheen and Moville Upper
Diocese: DE
Earliest Record: 9.1858
Parish Address: Rev. Laurence Keaveny, PP, Muff, Lifford, Co. Donegal

Civil Parish: **Muff**
Map Grid: 23
RC Parish: Iskaheen, see Moville Upper
Diocese: DE

Civil Parish: **Raphoe**
Map Grid: 34
RC Parish: Raphoe
Diocese: RA
Earliest Record: b. 2.1876; m. 2.1876
Parish Address: Rev. Canon Patrick Deegan,
    PP, Raphoe, Co. Donegal

Civil Parish: **Raymoghy**
Map Grid: 31
RC Parish: see Taughboyne
Diocese: RA

Civil Parish: **Raymunterdoney**
Map Grid: 9
RC Parish: part Clondahorky; part Tul-
    laghobegley
Diocese: RA

Civil Parish: **Stranorlar**
Map Grid: 38
RC Parish: Stranorlar
Diocese: RA
Earliest Record: b. 1860; m. 1860; d. 1860
Parish Address: Rev. Daniel McDyer, PP,
    Stranorlar, Ballybofey, Co. Donegal

Civil Parish: **Taughboyne**
Map Grid: 32
RC Parish: All Saints, Raymoghy, and Taugh-
    boyne
Diocese: RA
Earliest Record: b. 12.1843; m. 11.1843
Parish Address: Rev. D. G. Cunnea, PP, St.
    Johnston, Lifford, Co. Donegal

Civil Parish: **Templecarn** (see also Co. Fer-
    managh)
Map Grid: 50
RC Parish: Pettigo
Diocese: RA
Earliest Record: b. 3.1851; m. 1.1836
Parish Address: Rev. Gerard McSorley, Adm,
    Pettigo, Co. Donegal

Civil Parish: **Templecrone**
Map Grid: 26
RC Parish: Templecrone (Dungloe)
Diocese: RA
Earliest Record: b. 11.1876
Parish Address: Rev. Patrick McAteer, PP,
    Dungloe, Co. Donegal

Civil Parish: **Tullaghobegley (1)**
Map Grid: 8
RC Parish: Tullaghbegley East and Raymunter-
    doney; also Tullaghbegley West, see below
Diocese: RA
Earliest Record: b. 11.1849; m. 8.1861; d.
    11.1849
Missing Dates: 4.1861-11.1871; ends 8.1869
Parish Address: Rev. Michael Sweeney, PP,
    Derrybeg, Letterkenny, Co. Donegal

Civil Parish: **Tullaghobegley (2)**
Map Grid: 8
RC Parish: Tullaghbegley West
Diocese: RA
Earliest Record: b. 1.1868
Priest: see Tullaghobegley (1)

Civil Parish: **Tullyfern**
Map Grid: 12
RC Parish: see Killygarvan
Diocese: RA

Civil Parish: **Urney**
Map Grid: 40
RC Parish: Urney, see Co. Tyrone
Diocese: DE

Commercial and Social Directories

1824
J. Pigot's *City of Dublin & Hibernian Provincial Directory* includes traders, nobility,
gentry, and clergy lists of Ballybofey, Ballyshannon, Donegal, Letterkenny, Lifford,
Pettigo, Raphoe, and Stranorlar.

1839
*Directory of the Towns of Sligo, Enniskillen,
Ballyshannon . . . etc.,* gives an alphabetical
list of nobility, gentry, clergymen, and traders

listed by trades and alphabetically. Covers the towns of Ballyshannon, Donegal, Stranorlar, and Ballybofey.

1846

Slater's *National Commercial Directory of Ireland* lists nobility, clergy, traders, etc., in Ballyshannon and Bundoran, Buncrana, Donegal, Killybegs and Dunkineely, Letterkenny, Lifford and Castlefinn (the latter under Strabane, Co. Tyrone), Moville, Raphoe, Rathmelton, Stranorlar, and Ballybofey.

1854

Henderson's *Belfast & Province of Ulster Directory* covers the towns of Ballyshannon and Lifford. Further editions were issued in 1856, 1858, 1861, 1863, 1865, 1868, 1870, 1877, 1880, 1884, 1890, 1894, and 1900.

1870

Slater's *Directory of Ireland* contains trade, nobility, and clergy lists for Ballyshannon, Buncrana, Donegal, Dunfanaghy, Glenties and Ardara, Killybegs, Letterkenny and Manorcunningham, Lifford, Moville, Pettigoe, Raphoe and Convoy, Ramelton, and Stranorlar.

1881

Slater's *Royal National Commercial Directory of Ireland* contains lists of traders, clergy, nobility, and farmers in Ballyshannon, Buncrana and Clonmany, Donegal, Dunfanaghy, Glenties and Ardara, Killybegs, Letterkenny and Manorcunningham, Lifford, Moville, Pettigoe, Raphoe, Ramelton, Stranorlar and Ballybofey.

1891

The Derry Almanac & Directory has traders lists for the towns of Ardara, Ballintra, Ballybofey, Ballyshannon, Buncrana, Carndonagh, Carrigans, Castlefin, Donegal, Donemana, Dunfanaghy, Glenties, Killygordon, Letterkenny, Lifford, Manorcunningham, Milford, Mountcharles, Moville, Ramelton, Raphoe, Rathmullen, Stranorlar, and St. Johnstown. Produced annually from 1891.

1894

Slater's *Royal National Directory of Ireland* lists traders, police, teachers, farmers, and private residents in each of the towns, villages and parishes of the county.

Family History

"Abstracts of Some Boyd Wills." *Ir. Anc.* 9 (1) (1977): 53-55.

Crawford, R. *The Crawfords of Donegal and How They Came There.* Dublin, 1886.

"The Dickson and Connolly Families of Ballyshannon." *Donegal Annual* 4 (1959): 111-17.

"The Dills of Fanad." *Donegal Annual* 34 (see also Patton).

Doherty—see Co. Derry Family History section.

Downey—see Co. Sligo Family History section.

Early, Samuel S. *A History of the Family of Early in America: The Ancestors and Descendants of Jeremiah Early Who Came from Donegal.* New York, 1896.

Harvey, G.H. *The Harvey Families of Inishowen, Co. Donegal . . .* Folkestone, 1927.

Hewetson, John. "Hewetson of Ballyshannon, Donegal." *R.S.A.I.* 40 (1910): 238-43.

Irwin—see Co. Fermanagh Family History section

Nesbitt of Woodhill. Pedigree in *Swanzy Notebooks.* RCB Library, Dublin.

"Notes on the O'Peatains of Donegal, Mayo, and Roscommon." *Ir. Gen.* 4 (4) (1971): 303-07.

"O'Cannons of Tirchonaill." *Donegal Annual* 12 (2) (1978): 280-315.

"The Pattons and Dills of Springfield." *Donegal Annual* 11 (1) (1974).

Trench, C.V. *The Wrays of Donegal, Londonderry, and Antrim.* Oxford, 1945.

Young, A. *Three Hundred Years in Inishowen, Being More Particularly an Account of the Family of Young of Culdaff.* Belfast, 1929.

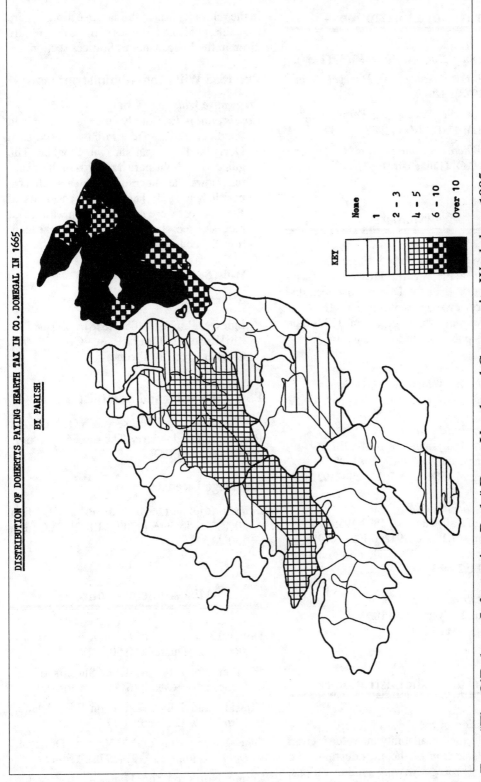

From "The O'Doherty Information Pack." Derry Youth and Community Workshop, 1985.

Gravestone Inscriptions

Assaroe Abbey: *Donegal Annual* 3(3) (1957).

Ballyshannon (St. Annes, CI): *Donegal Annual* 12(2) (1978): 320-58.

Ballyshannon (St. Annes, CI): *Family Links* 1 (2) (1981): 11-18; 1 (4) (1982): 31-39.

Finner: In *Where Erne and Drowes Meet the Sea,* by Rev. P.O. Gallachair, 1961.

Newspapers

The newspapers published within this county start relatively late. However, many biographical notices for Donegal are included in the Derry newspapers, particularly the *Londonderry Journal* which began in 1772. The newspapers published in the county are

Title: *Ballyshannon Herald*
Published in: Ballyshannon, 1831-73
BL Holdings: 1.1832-12.1873

Title: *Donegal Independent*
Published in: Ballyshannon, 1884-1927
NLI Holdings: 1.1885-6.1907; 8-9.1927
BL Holdings: 4.1884-6.1907; 2.1908-4.1921

Title: *Donegal Vindicator*
Published in: Ballyshannon, 1889-1956
NLI Holdings: 1.1906-5.1912; 6.1921-9.1956
BL Holdings: 2.1889-12.1920; odd numbers 1928; 10.1928-9.1956

Title: *The Liberator*
Published in: Ballyshannon, 1839
BL Holdings: 1-11.1839

Wills and Administrations

A discussion of the types of records, where they are held, their availability and value is given in the Wills section of the Introduction. The availability of prerogative wills, administrations, and marriage license records is also described in the relevant parts of the same section. Where available, published sources of these records are given in the Miscellaneous Sources section.

Pre-1858 Wills and Administrations

Prerogative Wills. see p. xli.
Consistorial Wills. County Donegal is mainly in the diocese of Raphoe, with two baronies in Derry and two parishes in Clogher. The guide to Catholic parish records in this chapter shows the diocese to which each civil parish belonged. The wills of residents of each diocese were usually proven within that diocese (see the Wills section for exceptions). The following records survive:

Wills. See p. xxxvii.

Abstracts. See p. xxxvii.

Indexes. Raphoe (1684-1858) published by Phillimore; Derry–see Co. Derry; Clogher–see Co. Tyrone.

Post-1858 Wills and Administrations

County Donegal was served by the District Registry of Londonderry. The surviving records are kept in the PRO.

Marriage Licenses

Indexes. Raphoe (1661-1750). PRO; SLC film 100872. Clogher (1709). PRO; SLC film 100861.

Miscellaneous Sources

Dolan, L. *Land War & Eviction in Derryveagh 1840-1865.* Dundalk, 1980.

"Further Notes on the High Sheriffs of Co. Donegal." *Ir. Gen.* 2 (6) (1948): 165-76.

"Kinship and Land Tenure on Tory Island." *Ulster Folk* 12 (1966): 1-17.

"The Muster Roll of c.1630: Co. Donegal." *Donegal Annual* 10 (2) (1972): 124-49.

"Some Notes on the High Sheriffs of Co. Donegal." *Ir. Gen.* 1 (6) (1939): 179-84.

Tory Island, 1841-1964. Parts 1 and 2. *Ir. J. Med. Sci.* 7th ser. 1 (1) (1968): 19-24, 63-72 (discusses trends in population size).

"Two Early Seventeenth Century Maps of Donegal." *R.S.A.I.* 94 (1964): 199-202.

"A Demographic Study of Tory Island and Rathlin Island, 1841-1964." *Ulster Folk* 17 (1971): 70-80.

Young, A.I. *300 Years in Inishowen.* Belfast, 1929.

O'Gallchobair. *History of Landlordism in Donegal.* Ballyshannon, 1975.

"Volunteer Companies of Ulster 1778-1793." *Irish Sword* 7 (1966) 29: 309-12 (officers names only).

Research Sources and Services

Journals

Donegal Annual published by County Donegal Historical Society (1947-present)

Libraries and Information Sources

Donegal County Library, Courthouse, Lifford, Co. Donegal Ph: (074) 41066 (local history section has some relevant holdings)

Research Services

Ramelton Heritage & Development Association, The Mall, Letterkenny, Ramelton, Co. Donegal

Donegal Genealogical Service, The Diamond, Lifford, Co. Donegal

See also research services in Dublin, p. xliv

Societies

County Donegal Historical Society (publishers of *Donegal Annual*), Mrs. Kathleen Emerson, 61 Cluain Barron, Ballyshannon, Co. Donegal

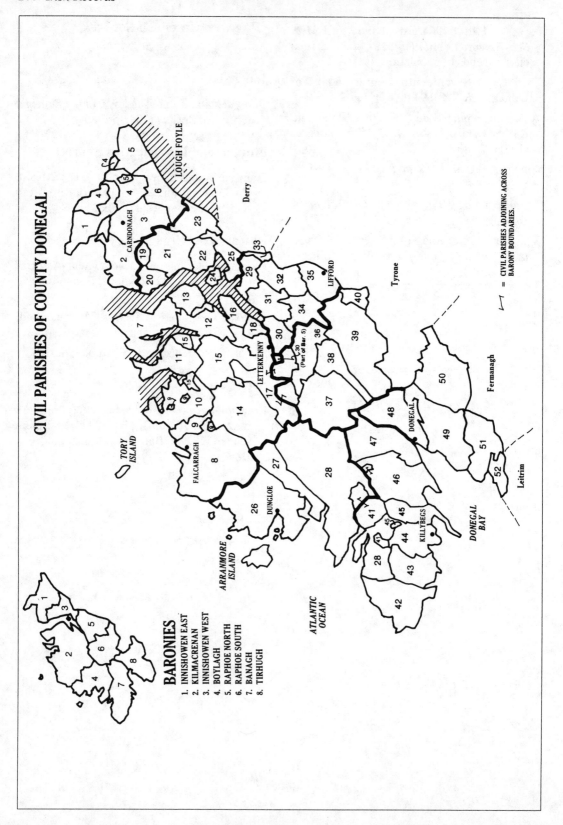

CIVIL PARISHES OF COUNTY DONEGAL

LOUGH FOYLE

Derry

Tyrone

Fermanagh

Leitrim

DONEGAL BAY

ATLANTIC OCEAN

ARRANMORE ISLAND

TORY ISLAND

FALCARRAGH

DUNGLOE

LETTERKENNY

LIFFORD

DONEGAL

KILLYBEGS

CARNDONAGH

30 (Part of Bar. 5)

⌐ = CIVIL PARISHES ADJOINING ACROSS BARONY BOUNDARIES.

BARONIES
1. INNISHOWEN EAST
2. KILMACRENAN
3. INNISHOWEN WEST
4. BOYLAGH
5. RAPHOE NORTH
6. RAPHOE SOUTH
7. BANAGH
8. TIRHUGH

County Down

A Brief History

County Down was the first Ulster county to be colonized by the Normans. The knight John de Courcy took the area around Downpatrick after the Norman invasion, and the county was formed around 1300. The county later came into the possession of the De Lacy's. Most of this county came to be known as the Earldom of Ulster during this period. One of the few Norman families who settled in the county is Savage. The major Gaelic families were O'Neill, McGuinness, McQuillan, McCartan, and MacGilmore.

In 1569 Sir Thomas Smith unsuccessfully attempted to bring English settlers into the Ards Peninsula and County Down. In 1594 a general rebellion in Ulster, led by the major Ulster chieftain Hugh O'Neill began (see Co. Tyrone). On the defeat of O'Neill, his lands and those of his allies were confiscated and divided among English and Scottish "adventurers." A well-planned plantation of Ulster began in 1609 involving the introduction to the province of thousands of settlers. These were brought in by adventurers who, in return for title to the land, agreed to bring in a specified number of settlers to their estates.

One Scottish adventurer, James Hamilton, brought over 10,000 Scots to northwest Down. Scots names such as Boyd, Fraser, Johnston, Lindsay, Morrison, Patterson, and Maxwell are consequently common in Down. English adventurers in Down who brought over English families included Annesley, Hill, and Montgomery. These settlers brought the names Wilson, Johnson, Young, Taylor, Walker, Jackson, Watson, Bradshaw, and Bradford to Ulster. The new settlers developed a prosperous linen industry in Down and surrounding counties. The industrial center of Belfast also grew rapidly during the eighteenth and nineteenth centuries.

The relative proportions of people of Irish/Norman, Scottish, and English extraction can, in very general terms, be estimated from the proportions of Catholic, Presbyterian, and Episcopalian (Protestant) respectively in the county. In 1841 the respective proportions were 32, 45, and 21 percent.

County Down was less badly affected by the Great Famine than many others. One of its effects, however, was a large exodus from the rural areas to the city of Belfast, part of which is in County Down. The population of Down in 1841 was 368,000. In 1851 this had reduced by around 11 percent. Of these, 46,000 died, mainly in the years 1847-50. The level of emigration from the county was among the lowest in Ireland, only 6 percent of the population against a national average of 11.4 percent.

During the remainder of the nineteenth century the town of Belfast and other towns in the county grew enormously. Some notes on the history of Belfast are included in the history of County Antrim. Belfast's prosperity attracted further immigration of workers from rural Ireland and Scotland to the city and to the outlying towns of the county. In 1921 Down was one of the six counties which remained part of the United Kingdom when an independent Irish state was formed.

Census and Census Substitutes

1642

Muster Roll for Parts of Co. Down. PRONI 7563; SLC film 897012.

1659

"Census" of Ireland. Edited by S. Pender. Dublin: Stationery Office, 1939; SLC film 924648.

1663

Subsidy Roll. SLC film 258621; PRONI T307, T1046; NLI 9584/5.

1698

Poll Tax Return: Newry and Mourne. PRONI T1046.

1708

"Householders in the Town of Downpatrick." In R.E. Parkinson, *The City of Downe.* 151-62.

1720

List of Landed Gentry in Co. Down and Antrim. RIA ms. 24 K 19.

1740

List of Protestants in Parishes of Kilbroney and Seapatrick. NLI ms. 4173.

1766

Religious Census of Parish of Kilbroney and Seapatrick. RCB Library; NLI ms. 4173; SLC film 258517

Parish of Shankill. PRO 1A 45 100.

1796

See Co. Mayo 1796 ("List of Catholics ").

1796-1811

List of Freeholders in Barony of Upper Iveagh. SLC film 258701.

1798

List of Persons Who Suffered Losses in '98 Rebellion. NLI JLB 94107 (approximately 180 names, addresses, and occupations).

1813-24

List of Freeholders in the County. SLC film 258701.

1821-51

Extracts from the Government Censuses (1821, 1831, 1841, and 1851) for the Parish of Anahilt, Mainly Referring to the Name "Hanna." SLC film 258608; PRONI.

1823-37

Tithe Applotment Survey (see p. xxvii).

1832

List of Freeholders on the Marquis of Londonderry's Estate. SLC film 258713.

1832-36

"Names of Holders of, and Applicants for, Licences to Sell Liquor in Downpatrick and Newry" (names and addresses). *Parl. Papers* 1837/38, 13 (2): Appendix 10.

1837

"Occupants of Newry, Arranged in 2 Lists" (valuations over and under £5 and by street). *Parl. Papers* 1837, 2 (1): Appendix G, 225-39.

1838

"Lists of Marksmen [illiterate voters] of Downpatrick and Newry" (names, occupations, and residences). *Parl. Papers* 1837, 2 (1): Appendix A3; 1837/38, 13 (2): Appendix 4.

1843

List of the Ballycopeland Presbyterian Congregation (Parish of Donaghadee). In *Millisle and Ballycopeland Presbyterian Church.* 117-21.

1851/61

Census of Presbyterian Parishoners in Loughlinisland Parish (names, addresses, relationships, and some comments). *Family Links* 1 (5) (1982): 5-11; 1 (7) (1983): 9-14.

Extract showing the principal tenants and sub-tenants, and descriptions of their properties, in the Irish Quarter of Downpatrick, 1708. From a "Survey of the Town of Downpatrick," an appendix to the *The City of Downe* by R. E. Parkinson. Belfast, 1927.

IRISH QUARTER
Irish Street on the West side

No	Denominations	No. of Feet in Front	Rear	Depth	Principall Tenants	Tenants in possession	Half year's Rent at May, 1708.	Nature of the Improvements and Observations.
1a	Old wall, orchard & garden	184	184	436				
1b	Bowling Green	192	square					
2a	Hutchinson's house & back side	42	38	78 } square	Seneca Hadzor	Do.	5 10 0	This with Prior's Island pays £20 ye ann.
2b	Hutchinson's Garden	184	square		Wash house		for building	
3	Wast Tent. unbuilt	44	44	78	Do. S. Hadzor has it for ye present			On it a tite mud wall House, now used as a Barn
4	McLeland's ½ Tent	30	30	84	Jno. McGrady &	Do.	0 10 0	An ordinary Mudd Wall Cabbin
5	Wm. Irwyn's Tent	64	53	90	Rob. McKewn			
6	Glencrosses Tent.	52	52	95	Waste unbuilt			
7	Margery Coots Tent.	60	34	448	Jno Curry & Jno McKeaten		1 8 0	A mudd wall Thatchd House, out of repair
8	Rider's Tenement	82	70	446	Francis Rider	Wm. Peery	1 3 4	A range of Clay and Stone wall thatchd Houses and 3 back Cabbins
9	Wm. McCrea's Tent.	42	42	440	Widow McCrea	Do.	1 3 4	A low Stone Wall House, Back House and Spring Well
10	Russell's Tenemt.	40	40	435	Wm. Thompson	Dr. Alex. Mercer	0 11 8	A stone wall slated House, 2½ story high, 2 back Houses, & a Wel
11	Widow Dounan's Tents.	44	44	436	Thos. Lautherdale	Do.	0 14 0	An old low stone wall thatchd House and 2 back houses
12					John Connor	Do.	0 11 8	
13	McKearly's Tent.	48	37	435	Pat Smith	Do.	1 0 0	A good stone wall house and new back house, all thatchd
14	Widow Eager's Tent.	43	37	436	Thos. Eager	{ Alex McCrery / John Coghran }	0 18 4	A strong stone wall thatched House with Malt House and Kiln backward
15								

1852-57

Poll-Books for Co. Down. PRONI D 671.

1856

"Tenants on Anglesey Estate" (parish of Newry; Townlands of Sheeptown, Derrylacka, Crobane, Dysert). *Louth Arch. J.* 12 (2) (1950): 151-53.

1863-64

Griffith's Valuation (see p. xxvii).

1901

Census. PRO.

1911

Census. PRO.

Church Records

Church of Ireland
(For Befast, see also appendix)
(Shows starting date of record)

Parish: **Aghaderry** (Loughbrickland)
Existing Records: b. 1816; m. 1814; d. 1816
Status: LC

Parish: **Annaduff**
Status: Lost

Parish: **Annahilt**
Status: Lost

Parish: **Annalong** (Castlewellan)
Existing Records: b. 1857; d. 1857
Status: LC

Parish: **Ardglass**
Status: Lost

Parish: **Ardkeen**
Existing Records: b. 1746; m. 1746; d. 1746
Status: LC

Parish: **Ardquin**
Status: Lost

Parish: **Ballee** (Downpatrick)
Existing Records: b. 1792; m. 1792; d. 1792
Status: LC

Parish: **Ballyculter**
Existing Records: b. 1777; m. 1812; d. 1812
Status: LC

Parish: **Ballyhalbert**
Existing Records: b. 1852; d. 1852
Status: LC

Parish: **Ballymacarret**
Existing Records: b. 1827; m. 1827
Status: LC

Parish: **Ballynahinch** (see Magheradrool)

Parish: **Ballyphilip** (Portsterry)
Existing Records: b. 1745; m. 1745; d. 1745
Status: LC

Parish: **Ballywalter** or **Whitechurch**
Existing Records: b. 1844; d. 1844
Status: LC

Parish: **Bangor**
Existing Records: b. 1803; m. 1805; d. 1815
Status: LC

Parish: **Castlewellan**
Status: Lost

Parish: **Clonallan**
Status: Lost

Parish: **Clonduff**
Existing Records: b. 1782; m. 1786; d. 1782
Status: LC

Parish: **Comber**
Existing Records: b. 1683; m. 1683; d. 1683
Status: LC

Parish: **Donaghadee**
Existing Records: b. 1778; m. 1778; d. 1778
Status: LC

Parish: **Donaghcloney**
Existing Records: b. 1697; m. 1697; d. 1697
Status: LC

Parish: **Donaghmore**
Existing Records: b. 1783; m. 1795; d. 1784
Status: LC

Parish: **Down** (Patrick)
Existing Records: b. 1750; m. 1752; d. 1752
Status: LC

Parish: **Dromara**
Status: Lost

Parish: **Dromore**
Existing Records: b. 1784; m. 1784; d. 1784
Status: LC

Parish: **Drumballyroney**
Existing Records: b. 1831; m. 1831; d. 1831
Status: LC

Parish: **Drumbeg**
Existing Records: b. 1823; m. 1823; d. 1823
Status: LC

Parish: **Drumbo**
Existing Records: b. 1791; m. 1791; d. 1791
Status: LC

Parish: **Drumgooland**
Existing Records: b. 1779; m. 1779; d. 1779
Missing Dates: d. 1791-1838
Status: LC

Parish: **Dundela**
Existing Records: b. 1864
Status: LC

Parish: **Dundonald**
Existing Records: b. 1811; m. 1811; d. 1823
Status: LC

Parish: **Dunsford**
Status: Lost

Parish: **Garvaghy**
Status: Lost

Parish: **Gilford**
Existing Records: b. 1869
Status: LC

Parish: **Glencraig**
Existing Records: b. 1858
Status: LC

Parish: **Grey Abbey**
Existing Records: b. 1807
Status: LC

Parish: **Groomsport**
Status: Lost

Parish: **Hillsborough**
Existing Records: b. 1777; m. 1782; d. 1823
Status: LC

Parish: **Hollymount**
Status: Lost

Parish: **Hollywood**
Existing Records: b. 1806; m. 1806; d. 1806
Status: LC

Parish: **Inch**
Existing Records: b. 1767; m. 1764; d. 1788
Missing Records: m. 1765-90
Status: LC

Parish: **Innishargy**
Existing Records: b. 1783; m. 1783; d. 1783
Status: LC

Parish: **Kilbroney**
Existing Records: b. 1814; m. 1818; d. 1814
Status: LC

Parish: **Kilclief**
Status: Lost

Parish: **Kilkeel**
Existing Records: b. 1816; m. 1816; d. 1816
Status: LC

Parish: **Killaney**
Existing Records: b. 1858; d. 1865
Status: LC

Parish: **Killinchy**
Existing Records: b. 1819; m. 1819; d. 1819
Status: LC

Parish: **Killyleagh**
Existing Records: b. 1830; m. 1830; d. 1836
Status: LC

Parish: **Kilmegan**
Existing Records: b. 1823; m. 1823; d. 1823
Status: LC

Parish: **Kilmood**
Existing Records: b. 1822; m. 1822; d. 1793
Status: LC

Parish: **Knockbreda**
Existing Records: b. 1784; m. 1784; d. 1784
Status: LC

Parish: **Knocknamuckley**
Existing Records: b. 1838; m. 1838; d. 1853
Status: LC

Parish: **Loughin Island**
Existing Records: b. 1760; m. 1760; d. 1760
Missing Dates: b. 1807-20; m. 1807-20; d. 1807-
  20
Status: LC

Parish: **Maghera**
Status: Lost

Parish: **Magheradrool**
Status: Lost

Parish: **Magherahamlet**
Status: Lost

Parish: **Magheralin**
Existing Records: b. 1692; m. 1692; d. 1692
Status: LC

Parish: **Magherally**
Status: Lost

Parish: **Moira**
Existing Records: b. 1845; d. 1845
Status: LC

Parish: **Newcastle**
Existing Records: b. 1843; d. 1845
Status: LC

Parish: **Newry**
Existing Records: b. 1822; m. 1784; d. 1824
Status: LC

Parish: **Newtownards**
Status: Lost

Parish: **Rathmullan**
Status: Lost

Parish: **St. John Kilwarlin**
Status: Lost

Parish: **St. Patricks, Newry** (see Newry)
Existing Records: b. 1847
Status: LC

Parish: **Saintfield**
Existing Records: b. 1724; m. 1724; d. 1798
Missing Dates: b. 1758-97; m. 1751-97
Status: LC

Parish: **Saul**
Status: Lost

Parish: **Scarvagh**
Status: Lost

Parish: **Seapatrick**
Existing Records: b. 1802; m. 1802; d. 1835
Status: LC

Parish: **Shankill**
Existing Records: b. 1681; m. 1676; d. 1675
Status: LC

Parish: **Tullynakill**
Status: Lost

Parish: **Tullylish**
Existing Records: b. 1820; m. 1820; d. 1849
Status: LC

Parish: **Tyrella**
Existing Records: b. 1839; m. 1844; d. 1839
Status: LC

Parish: **Warrenpoint**
Existing Records: b. 1825; m. 1826
Status: LC

Presbyterian
(For Belfast, see also appendix)

Parish: **Anaghlone** (Banbridge)
Starting Date: 1839

Parish: **Anahilt** (Hillsborough)
Starting Date: 1780

Parish: **Annalong**
Starting Date: 1840

Parish: **Ardaragh** (Newry)
Starting Date: 1804

Parish: **Ballydown** (Banbridge)
Starting Date: 1809

Parish: **Ballygilbert**
Starting Date: 1841

Parish: **Ballygraney** (Bangor)
Starting Date: 1838

Parish: **Ballynahinch**
Starting Date: 1841

Parish: **Ballyroney** (Banbridge)
Starting Date: 1831

Parish: **Ballywater**
Starting Date: 1824

Parish: **Banbridge**
Starting Date: 1756

Parish: **Bangor**
Starting Date: 1833

Parish: **Carrowdore** (Greyabbey)
Starting Date: 1843

Parish: **Clarkesbridge** (Newry)
Starting Date: 1833

Parish: **Clonduff** (Banbridge)
Starting Date: 1842

Parish: **Clough** (Downpatrick)
Starting Date: 1836

Parish: **Cloughey**
Starting Date: 1844

Parish: **Comber**
Starting Date: 1847

Parish: **Conligh** (Newtownards)
Starting Date: 1845

Parish: **Donaghadee**
Starting Date: 1822

Parish: **Downpatrick**
Starting Date: 1827

Parish: **Dromara**
Starting Date: 1823

Parish: **Dromore**
Starting Date: 1834

Parish: **Drumbanagher** (Derry)
Starting Date: 1832

Parish: **Drumgooland**
Starting Date: 1833

Parish: **Drumlee** (Banbridge)
Starting Date: 1826

Parish: **Edengrove** (Ballynahinch)
Starting Date: 1829

Parish: **Glastry**
Starting Date: 1728

Parish: **Groomsport**
Starting Date: 1841

Parish: **Hillsborough**
Starting Date: 1832

Parish: **Kilkeel**
Starting Date: 1842

Parish: **Killinchy**
Starting Date: 1835

Parish: **Killyleagh**
Starting Date: 1693

Parish: **Kilmore** (Crossgar)
Starting Date: 1833

Parish: **Kirkcubbin**
Starting Date: 1785

Parish: **Leitrim** (Banbridge)
Starting Date: 1837

Parish: **Lissera** (Crossgar)
Starting Date: 1809

Parish: **Loughagherry** (Hillsborough)
Starting Date: 1801

Parish: **Loughbrickland**
Starting Date: 1842

Parish: **Magherally** (Banbridge)
Starting Date: 1837

Parish: **Millisle**
Starting Date: 1773

Parish: **Mourne** (Kilkeel)
Starting Date: 1840

Parish: **Newry**
Starting Date: 1829

Parish: **Newtownards**
Starting Date: 1833

Parish: **Portaferry**
Starting Date: 1699

Parish: **Raffrey** (Crossgar)
Starting Date: 1843

Parish: **Rathfriland**
Starting Date: 1804

Parish: **Rostrevor**
Starting Date: 1851

Parish: **Saintfield**
Starting Date: 1831

Parish: **Scarva**
Starting Date:1807

Parish: **Seaforde**
Starting Date: 1826

Parish: **Strangford**
Starting Date: 1846

Parish: **Tullylish** (Gilford)
Starting Date: 1813

Parish: **Warrenpoint**
Starting Date: 1832

Roman Catholic

Civil Parish: **Aghaderg**
Map Grid: 50
RC Parish: Loughbrickland and Sisagade, see
   also Dromore
Diocese: DR
Earliest Record: b. 1.1816; m. 2.1816; d. 9.1838
Missing Dates: d. 11.1840-1.1843
Parish Address: Rev. Loughlin McAleavey, PP,
   25 Scarva Street, Loughbrickland, Co. Down

Civil Parish: **Annaclone**
Map Grid: 5
RC Parish: Annaclone
Diocese: DR
Earliest Record: b. 9.1834; m. 5.1851; d. 4.1851
Parish Address: Rev. James Fitzpatrick, PP,
   Annaclone, Banbridge, Co. Down

Civil Parish: **Annahilt**
Map Grid: 36
RC Parish: see Magheradrool
Diocese: DR

Civil Parish: **Ardglass**
Map Grid: 48
RC Parish: Ardglass, see Dunsfort
Diocese: DW

Civil Parish: **Ardkeen**
Map Grid: 13
RC Parish: Kircubbin
Diocese: DW
Earliest Record: b. 1.1828; m. 1.1828

Missing Dates: b. 11.1838-6.1852; m. 6.1839-
6.1852
Parish Address: Rev. A. Haughey, Ballycranbeg, Kircubbin, Newtownards, Co. Down

Civil Parish: **Ardquin**
Map Grid: 15
RC Parish: see Ballyphilip
Diocese: DW

Civil Parish: **Ballee**
Map Grid: 45
RC Parish: Ballee, see Saul
Diocese: DW

Civil Parish: **Ballyculter**
Map Grid: 44
RC Parish: part Saul; part Kilclief
Diocese: DW

Civil Parish: **Ballyhalbert** (St. Andrew)
Map Grid: 12
RC Parish: see Ballyphilip
Diocese: DW

Civil Parish: **Ballykinler**
Map Grid: 66
RC Parish: see Tyrella
Diocese: DW

Civil Parish: **Ballyphilip**
Map Grid: 18
RC Parish: Ballyphilip and Portaferry
Diocese: DW
Earliest Record: b. 3.1843
Parish Address: Rev. G. H. Laverty, PP,
Parochial House, Portaferry, Co. Down

Civil Parish: **Ballytrustan**
Map Grid: 16
RC Parish: see Ballyphilip
Diocese: DW

Civil Parish: **Ballywalter**
Map Grid: 10
RC Parish: Ballygalget
Diocese: DW
Earliest Record: b. 1.1828; m. 6.1852
Missing Dates: b. 4.1835-6.1852, 2.1864-
11.1866; m. 9.1866-3.1867

Parish Address: Rev. Bernard Armstrong, PP,
Parochial House, Ballygalget, Portaferry,
Co. Down

Civil Parish: **Bangor**
Map Grid: 7
RC Parish: see Newtownards
Diocese: DW

Civil Parish: **Blaris** (see also Co. Antrim)
Map Grid: 31
RC Parish: Lisburn
Diocese: CR
Parish Address: Rev. Joseph Cunningham, PP,
St. Patrick's Presbytery, 29 Chapel Hill, Lis-
burn, Co. Antrim

Civil Parish: **Bright**
Map Grid: 69
RC Parish: Bright, Rossglass, and Killough
Diocese: DW
Earliest Record: b. 11.1856; m. 11.1856
Parish Address: Rev. F. Glavin, PP, Parochial
House, 22 Castle, St. Killough, Co. Down

Civil Parish: **Castleboy**
Map Grid: 14
RC Parish: see Ardkeen
Diocese: DW

Civil Parish: **Clonallan**
Map Grid: 54
RC Parish: Clonallon, see Warrenpoint
Diocese: DR

Civil Parish: **Clonduff**
Map Grid: 62
RC Parish: Clonduff
Diocese: DR
Earliest Record: b. 9.1850; m. 8.1850; d. 7.1850
Parish Address: Rev. Mathhew O'Hare, PP, 17
Castlewellan Road, Hilltown, Newry, Co.
Down

Civil Parish: **Comber**
Map Grid: 4
RC Parish: see Newtownards
Diocese: DW

Civil Parish: **Donaghadee**
Map Grid: 8
RC Parish: see Newtownards
Diocese: DW

Civil Parish: **Donaghcloney**
Map Grid: 33
RC Parish: see Tullylish
Diocese: DR

Civil Parish: **Donaghmore**
Map Grid: 52
RC Parish: Donaghmore
Diocese: DR
Earliest Record: b. 5.1835; m. 9.1825; d. 10.1840
Missing Dates: d. ends 1871
Parish Address: Rev. F. Treanor, PP, 10 Barr Hill, Newry, Co. Down

Civil Parish: **Down**
Map Grid: 65
RC Parish: Downpatrick
Diocese: DW
Earliest Record: b. 10.1851; m. 2.1853; d. 8.1851
Parish Address: Rev. Joseph Maguire, PP, Parochial House, Downpatrick, Co. Down

Civil Parish: **Dromara**
Map Grid: 58
RC Parish: Dromara; part Ballynahinch, see Magheradrool
Diocese: DR
Earliest Record: b. 1.1844; m. 1.1844; d. 1.1844
Parish Address: Rev. Bernard Treanor, PP, 141 Rathfriland Road, Dromara, Dromore, Co. Down

Civil Parish: **Dromore**
Map Grid: 35
RC Parish: Dromore and Garvaghy (also contains marriages, 1827-1843, for Aghaderg, Seagoe, Tullylish, Shankill, etc.)
Diocese: DR
Earliest Record: b. 3.1843; m. 9.1821; d. 11.1821
Missing Dates: d. 1.1845-11.1847

Civil Parish: **Drumballyroney**
Map Grid: 59
RC Parish: see Annaclone
Diocese: DR

Civil Parish: **Drumbeg**
Map Grid: 22
RC Parish: Lisburn, see Blaris
Diocese: DW

Civil Parish: **Drumbo**
Map Grid: 23
RC Parish: Lisburn, see Blaris
Diocese: DW

Civil Parish: **Drumgath**
Map Grid: 53
RC Parish: Rathfryland, Drumgath, and Barnmeen
Diocese: DR
Earliest Record: b. 4.1829; m. 7.1837; d. 6.1837
Parish Address: Rev. Patrick McAnuff, PP, Barnmeen, Rathfriland, Co. Down

Civil Parish: **Drumgooland (1)**
Map Grid: 60
RC Parish: Drumgooland Upper (Leitrim); also Drumgooland lower, see below.
Diocese: DW
Earliest Record: b. 5.1827; m. 8.1827; d. 5.1828
Parish Address: Rev. J. Mooney, PP, 58 Ballydrummon Road, Ballyward, Castlewellan, Co. Down

Civil Parish: **Drumgooland (2)**
Map Grid: 60
RC Parish: Drumgooland Lower (Gargory)
Diocese: DW
Earliest Record: b. 3.1832; m. 4.1832; d. 3.1832
Parish Address: Rev. L. Boyle, 9 Gargory Road, Ballyward, Castlewellan, Co. Down

Civil Parish: **Dundonald**
Map Grid: 2
RC Parish: see Newtownards
Diocese: DW

Civil Parish: **Dunsfort**
Map Grid: 47
RC Parish: Dunsfort and Ardglass (also contains birth and marriages from 4.1845-2.1848 for Derraghy, Hannahstown, and Rockwilliam)
Diocese: DW
Earliest Record: b. 2.1848; m. 2.1848; d. 2.1848

Parish Address: Rev. Liam Mullan, PP, Parochial House, Ardglass, Co. Down

Civil Parish: **Garvaghy**
Map Grid: 57
RC Parish: part Dromore; part Annadone
Diocese: DR

Civil Parish: **Grey Abbey**
Map Grid: 9
RC Parish: Ballygalget, see Ballywalter
Diocese: DW

Civil Parish: **Hillsborough**
Map Grid: 30
RC Parish: see Blaris
Diocese: DW

Civil Parish: **Holywood**
Map Grid: 1
RC Parish: Holywood
Diocese: DW
Earliest Record: b. 11.1866; m. 5.1867
Parish Address: Rev. John Stewart, PP, Parochial House, 150 High Street, Holywood, Co. Down

Civil Parish: **Inch**
Map Grid: 42
RC Parish: see Kilmore
Diocese: DW

Civil Parish: **Inishargy**
Map Grid: 11
RC Parish: Kircubbin, see Ardkeen
Diocese: DW

Civil Parish: **Kilbroney**
Map Grid: 56
RC Parish: Kilbroney (Rostrevor)
Diocese: DR
Earliest Record: b. 1.1808; m. 1.1808; d. 1.1808
Parish Address: Rev. Thomas Mooney, PP, 44 Church Street, Rostrevor, Co. Down

Civil Parish: **Kilclief**
Map Grid: 46
RC Parish: Kilclief and Strangford
Diocese: DW
Earliest Record: b. 1.1866; m. 11.1865

Missing Dates: b. 7.1867-10.1870; m. 10.1868-1.1871
Parish Address: Rev. F. Toner, PP, Parochial House, Kilclief, Strangford, Co. Down

Civil Parish: **Kilcoo (1)**
Map Grid: 63
RC Parish: Kilcoo; also Ballymoney, see below; also part Maghera
Diocese: N and M
Earliest Record: b. 10.1832
Parish Address: Rev. Charles Denvir, PP, Parochial House, Kilcoo, Co. Down

Civil Parish: **Kilcoo (2)**
Map Grid: 63
RC Parish: Ballymoney
Diocese: N and M
Earliest Record: b. 3.1853; m. 4.1853
Parish Address: Rev. Christopher Dallat, PP, 81 Castle Street, Ballymoney, Co. Antrim

Civil Parish: **Kilkeel (1)**
Map Grid: 71
RC Parish: Lower Mourne (Glasdrummond); also Upper Mourne, see below
Diocese: DW
Earliest Record: b. 8.1842; m. 9.1839
Missing Dates: m. 11.1866-8.1867
Parish Address: Rev. Patrick McFerran, PP, Parochial House, Glasdrummon, Annalong, Newry, Co. Down

Civil Parish: **Kilkeel (2)**
Map Grid: F1
RC Parish: Upper Mourne (Kilkeel)
Diocese: DW
Earliest Record: b. 7.1839; m. 5.1839
Parish Address: Rev. Walter Larkin, PP, Parochial House, Kilkeel, Co. Down

Civil Parish: **Killaney**
Map Grid: 25
RC Parish: see Killinchy
Diocese: DW

Civil Parish: **Killinchy**
Map Grid: 26
RC Parish: Carrickmannan and Saintfield
Diocese: DW
Earliest Record: b. 10.1837; m. 10.1845

Parish Address: Rev. Ernest McCaughan, PP, Parochial House, 33 Crossgar Road, Saintfield, Ballynahinch, Co. Down

Civil Parish: **Killyleagh**
Map Grid: 27
RC Parish: see Kilmore
Diocese: DW

Civil Parish: **Kilmegan (1)**
Map Grid: 61
RC Parish: Kilmegan (Castlewellan); also Drumaroad, see below.
Diocese: N and M
Earliest Record: b. 1.1853; m. 5.1853
Parish Address: Rev. P. White, PP, Parochial House, Castlewellan, Co. Down

Civil Parish: **Kilmegan (2)**
Map Grid: G1
RC Parish: Drumaroad and Clannaraghan
Diocese: N and M
Earliest Record: b. 1.1853; m. 5.1853
Parish Address: Rev. P. White, PP, Parochial House, Castlewellan, Co. Down

Civil Parish: **Kilmood**
Map Grid: 5
RC Parish: see Newtownards
Diocese: DW

Civil Parish: **Kilmore**
Map Grid: 40
RC Parish: Kilmore (Crossgar)
Diocese: DW
Parish Address: Rev. Dominic McHugh, PP, Parochial House, Crossgar, Downpatrick, Co. Down

Civil Parish: **Knockbreda**
Map Grid: 20
RC Parish: see Holywood
Diocese: DW

Civil Parish: **Lambeg**
Map Grid: 21
RC Parish: see Blaris
Diocese: CR

Civil Parish: **Loughinisland**
Map Grid: 41
RC Parish: Loughinisland
Diocese: DW
Earliest Record: b. 1806; m. 11.1805; d. 11.1805
Missing Dates: all end 10.1852
Parish Address: Rev. Bernard Magee, PP, Parochial House, Loughinisland, Downpatrick, Co. Down

Civil Parish: **Maghera**
Map Grid: 64
RC Parish: Bryansford and Newcastle (Maghera)
Diocese: DW
Earliest Record: b. 2.1845; m. 3.1845; d. 4.1860
Parish Address: Rev. Hugh O'Neill, PP, 24 Downs Road, Newcastle, Co. Down

Civil Parish: **Magheradrool**
Map Grid: 38
RC Parish: Ballynahinch and Dunmore
Diocese: DR
Earliest Record: b. 5.1827; m. 3.1829
Parish Address: Rev. Patrick Smyth, PP, Church Street, Ballynahinch, Co. Down

Civil Parish: **Magherahamlet**
Map Grid: 39
RC Parish: Ballynahinch, see Magheradrool
Diocese: DR

Civil Parish: **Magheralin**
Map Grid: 32
RC Parish: Magheralin, Moira, and Aughalee
Diocese: DR
Earliest Record: b. 1815; m. 1815; d. 1815
Parish Address: Rev. Albert McGovern, PP, 25 Bottier Road, Moira, Lurgan, Co. Armagh

Civil Parish: **Magherally**
Map Grid: 37
RC Parish: see Tullylish
Diocese: DR

Civil Parish: **Moira**
Map Grid: 29
RC Parish: see Magheralin
Diocese: DR

Civil Parish: **Newry**
Map Grid: 70
RC Parish: Newry, see Co. Armagh
Diocese: N and M

Civil Parish: **Newtownards**
Map Grid: 3
RC Parish: Newtownards, Comber, and
   Donaghadee
Diocese: DW
Earliest Record: b. 6.1864
Parish Address: Rev. Francis McKenna, PP,
   Parochial House, North Street, New-
   townards, Co. Down

Civil Parish: **Rathmullan**
Map Grid: 68
RC Parish: see Bright
Diocese: DW

Civil Parish: **St. Andrews**
Map Grid: 12
RC Parish: see Ballyphilip
Diocese: DW

Civil Parish: **Saintfield**
Map Grid: 24
RC Parish: Saintfield, see Killinchy
Diocese: DW

Civil Parish: **Saul (1)**
Map Grid: 43
RC Parish: Saul and Ballee; also Ballyalter, see
   below
Diocese: DW
Earliest Record: b. 5.1868; m. 5.1868
Parish Address: Rev. M. McAleese, PP,
   Parochial House, Saul, Downpatrick, Co.
   Down

Civil Parish: **Saul (2)**
Map Grid: 43
RC Parish: Ballyculter and Ballee
Diocese: DW
Earliest Record: b. 1.1844; m. 8.1843
Missing Dates: b. 5.1864-11.1870
Parish Address: Rev. M. McAleese, PP,
   Parochial House, Saul, Downpatrick, Co.
   Down

Civil Parish: **Seapatrick**
Map Grid: 49
RC Parish: Banbridge; part Tullylish
Diocese: DR
Earliest Record: b. 1.1843; m. 7.1850; d. 7.1850
Parish Address: Rev. Michael O'Rourke, PP,
   Rosemount, Scarva Road, Banbridge, Co.
   Down

Civil Parish: **Shankill**
Map Grid: 28
RC Parish: see Magheralin
Diocese: DR

Civil Parish: **Slanes**
Map Grid: 17
RC Parish: see Ballyphilip
Diocese: DW

Civil Parish: **Tullylish**
Map Grid: 34
RC Parish: Tullylish, see also Dromore
Diocese: DR
Earliest Record: b. 1.1833; m. 1.1833; d. 1.1833
Missing Dates: b. 8.1844-4.1846; m. 4.1844-
   2.1845
Parish Address: Rev. John Treanor, PP, 4
   Holymount Road, Gilford, Portadown, Co.
   Armagh

Civil Parish: **Tullynakill**
Map Grid: 6
RC Parish: see Newtownards
Diocese: DW

Civil Parish: **Tyrella**
Map Grid: 67
RC Parish: Tyrella and Ballykinler
Diocese: DW
Earliest Record: b. 4.1854; m. 7.1854
Parish Address: Rev. Michael Blaney, PP,
   Parochial House, Dundrum, Newcastle, Co.
   Down

Civil Parish: **Warrenpoint**
Map Grid: 55
RC Parish: Warrenpoint (Clonallon)
Diocese: DR
Earliest Record: b. 11.1826; m. 11.1825
Missing Dates: b. ends 1.1869

Parish Address: Rev. Edward Hamill, PP, Warrenpoint, Co. Down

Civil Parish: Witter
Map Grid: 19
RC Parish: see Ballyphilip
Diocese: DW

Commercial and Social Directories

1819

Thomas Bradshaw's *General Directory of Newry, Armagh . . . etc.* gives an alphabetical listing of the traders in Banbridge, Newry, Rathfriland, Rostrevor, Kilkeel, and Warrenpoint.

1820

J. Pigot's *Commercial Directory of Ireland* contains information on the gentry, nobility, and traders in and around the town of Newry.

1824

J. Pigot's *City of Dublin & Hibernian Provincial Directory* includes traders, nobility, gentry, and clergy lists of Ballynahinch, Banbridge, Bangor, Castlewellan, Comber, Donaghadee, Downpatrick, Dromore, Gilford, Hillsborough, Killileigh, Loughbrickland, Newry, Newtownards, Portaferry, Rathfryland, Rosstrevor, Saintfield, Strangford, and Warrenpoint.

1841

Mathew Martin's *Belfast Directory* contains alphabetical lists of gentry, merchants, traders, street lists, and a list of noblemen, and gentry in and around the towns of Banbridge, Bangor, Comber, Downpatrick, Dromore, Hillsborough, Holywood, and Killileagh.

1842

Further edition of Martin's *Belfast Directory* covers Banbridge, Bangor, Castlewellan, Comber, Crawfordsburn, Donaghadee, Downpatrick, Dromore, Hillsborough, Holywood, Killileagh, Kircubbin, Newtownards, Portaferry, Rathfriland, Saintfield, and Strangford.

1846

Slater's *National Commercial Directory of Ireland* lists nobility, clergy, traders, etc., in Ballynahinch, Banbridge, Bangor, Castlewellan, Clough and Newcastle, Comber, Donaghadee, Downpatrick, Dromore, Gilford and Loughbrickland, Hillsborough, Killyleagh, Newry, Newtownards, Portaferry, Strangford and Kircubbin, Rathfryland, Saintfield, Warrenpoint, and Rosstrevor.

1852

Henderson's *Belfast & Province of Ulster Directory* has lists of inhabitants, traders, etc., in and around the towns of Ardglass, Ballynahinch, Banbridge, Bangor, Donaghadee, Downpatrick, Dromore, Hillsborough, Newry, Newtownards, and Saintfield.

1854

A further edition of Henderson's *Directory* covers Ardglass, Ballynahinch, Banbridge, Bangor, Castlewellan, Comber, Donaghadee, Downpatrick, Dromore, Gilford, Hillsborough, Holywood, Killyleagh, Loughbrickland, Newcastle, Newry, Newtownards, Rathfriland, Rosstrevor, Saintfield, and Strangford. Further editions in 1856, 1858, 1861 (Kilkeel included from this date), 1863, 1865, 1868 (Laurencetown included from this date), 1870, 1877, 1880, 1884, 1890, 1894, and 1900.

1856

Slater's *Royal National Commercial Directory of Ireland* lists nobility, gentry, clergy, traders, etc., in Ballynahinch, Banbridge, Bangor, Castlewellan, Comber, Donaghadee, Downpatrick, Dromore, Gilford, Loughbrickland and Laurencetown, Hillsborough, Kilkeel, Killyleagh, Newry, Newtownards and Grey Abbey, Portaferry, Strangford and Kircubbin, Rathfryland, Saintfield, Warrenpoint, and Rosstrevor.

1865

Wynne's *Directory of Ballynahinch, Banbridge, Bangor, Comber, Downpatrick, Donaghadee, Dromore, Hillsborough, Holywood, Newry, Newtownards, Rathfriland, and Warrenpoint.*

1870

Slater's *Directory of Ireland* contains trade, nobility, clergy lists for Ballynahinch, Banbridge, Bangor, Castlewellan, Comber, Donaghadee, Downpatrick, Dromore, Gilford, Hillsborough, Hollywood, Kilkeel, Killyleagh, Newry, Newtownards, Portaferry, Rathfryland, Saintfield, Warrenpoint, and Rosstrevor.

1881

Slater's *Royal National Commercial Directory of Ireland* contains lists of traders, clergy, nobility, and farmers in adjoining parishes of the towns of Ballynahinch and Saintfield, Banbridge, Bangor, Castlewellan, Donaghadee, Downpatrick, Dromore, Holywood, Kilkeel, Newry, Newtownards, Portaferry, Rathfryland, Warrenpoint, and Rosstrevor.

1883

S. Farrell's *County Armagh Directory & Alamanac* has a street directory for Newry.

1894

Slater's *Royal National Directory of Ireland* lists traders, police, teachers, farmers, and private residents in each of the towns, villages, and parishes of the county.

Family History

"A Quaker Wedding at Lisburn, Co. Down 1867" (Barcroft/Malcolmson). *Ir. Anc.* 1392 (1981): 90-92.

"The Bradshaws of Bangor and Mile-Cross, in the Co. of Down." *Ulster J. Arch.* 2nd Ser. 8 (1902): 4-6, 55-57.

"Clenlow of Co. Down." Pedigree in *Swanzy Notebooks*. RCB Library, Dublin.

"Cossett of Co. Down." Pedigree in *Swanzy Notebooks*. RCB Library, Dublin.

Danne, E.F. *Notes on the Family of Magennis, Formerly Lords of Iveagh, Newry and Mourne.* Salt Lake City, 1878.

Guinness, Henry S. "Magennis of Iveagh." *R.S.A.I.* 62 (1932): 96-102.

Hartigan, A.S. *The Family of Pollock of Newry.* Folkestone, n.d.

"Henry of Co. Down." Pedigree in *Swanzy Notebooks*. RCB Library, Dublin.

Linn, Richard. *Pedigree of the Magennis (Guinness) Family of North Ireland and of Dublin.* Christchurch, N.Z., 1897.

"Quinn of Newry." Pedigree in *Swanzy Notebooks*. RCB Library, Dublin.

"Smith of Co. Louth and Co. Down." Pedigree in *Swanzy Notebooks*. RCB Library, Dublin.

"Stothard of Co. Down." Pedigree in *Swanzy Notebooks*. RCB Library, Dublin.

"Surnames of the Upper Ards." *Family Links* 1 (1) (1981): 13-22.

"Waddell of Co. Down." Pedigree in *Swanzy Notebooks*. RCB Library, Dublin.

West – see Co. Wicklow.

Gravestone Inscriptions

Many of the graveyards in this county have been recorded in the series "Gravestone Inscriptions Series, Co. Down," edited by R.S Clarke and published by the Ulster-Scot Historical Foundation from 1966-81 in nineteen volumes.

Aghlisnafin: "Gravestone Inscription Series, Co. Down," No. 9.

Annahilt: "Gravestone Inscription Series, Co. Down," No.18.

Ardkeen: "Gravestone Inscription Series, Co. Down," No.13.

Ardglass: "Gravestone Inscription Series, Co. Down," No. 8.

Ardquin: "Gravestone Inscription Series, Co. Down," No. 18.

Baileysmill: "Gravestone Inscription Series, Co. Down," No. 2.

Ballee: "Gravestone Inscription Series, Co. Down," No. 8.

Balligan: "Gravestone Inscription Series, Co. Down," No. 14.

Balloo: "Gravestone Inscription Series, Co. Down," No. 17.

Ballyblack: "Gravestone Inscription Series, Co. Down," No. 12.

Ballycarn: "Gravestone Inscription Series, Co. Down," No. 3.

Ballycopeland: "Gravestone Inscription Series, Co. Down," No. 16.

Ballycranbeg: "Gravestone Inscription Series, Co. Down," No. 13.

Ballycruttle: "Gravestone Inscription Series, Co. Down," No. 8.

Ballyculter: "Gravestone Inscription Series, Co. Down," No. 8.

Ballygalget: "Gravestone Inscription Series, Co. Down," No. 13.

Ballygowan: "Gravestone Inscription Series, Co. Down," No. 5.

Ballyhalbert: "Gravestone Inscription Series, Co. Down," No. 15.

Ballyhemlin: "Gravestone Inscription Series, Co. Down," No. 14.

Ballykinler: "Gravestone Inscription Series, Co. Down," No. 9.

Ballymacashen: "Gravestone Inscription Series, Co. Down," No. 6.

Ballymageogh: "Gravestone Inscription Series, Co. Down," No. 10.

Ballymartin: "Gravestone Inscription Series, Co. Down," No. 10.

Ballynahinch: "Gravestone Inscription Series, Co. Down," No. 9.

Ballyphilip: "Gravestone Inscription Series, Co. Down," No. 13.

Ballytrustan: "Gravestone Inscription Series, Co. Down," No. 13.

Bangor: "Gravestone Inscription Series, Co. Down," No. 17.

Barr: J.D. Cowam. *An Ancient Irish Parish.* 1914.

Blaris: "Gravestone Inscription Series, Co. Down," No. 5.

Boardmills: "Gravestone Inscription Series, Co. Down," No. 2.

Breda: "Gravestone Inscription Series, Co. Down," No. 1.

Bright: "Gravestone Inscription Series, Co. Down," No. 8.

Cargacreevy: "Gravestone Inscription Series, Co. Down," No. 18.

Carrowdore: "Gravestone Inscription Series, Co. Down," No. 14.

Carryduff: "Gravestone Inscription Series, Co. Down," Nos. 1 and 18.

Castlereagh: "Gravestone Inscription Series, Co. Down," No. 1.

Clandeboye: "Gravestone Inscription Series, Co. Down," No. 17.

Cloghy: "Gravestone Inscription Series, Co. Down," No. 14.

Clough: "Gravestone Inscription Series, Co. Down," No. 9.

Comber: "Gravestone Inscription Series, Co. Down," No. 5.

Copeland Island: "Gravestone Inscription Series, Co. Down," No. 16.

Donaghadee: "Gravestone Inscription Series, Co. Down," No. 16.

Donaghcloney: Edward D. Atkinson. *An Ulster Parish.* 1898.

Donaghmore: J.D. Cowan. *An Ancient Irish Parish.* 1914.

Downpatrick: "Gravestone Inscription Series, Co. Down," No. 7.

Dromara: "Gravestone Inscription Series, Co. Down," No. 19.

Dromore: "Gravestone Inscription Series, Co. Down," No. 19.

Drumaroad: "Gravestone Inscription Series, Co. Down," No. 9.

Drumbeg: "Gravestone Inscription Series, Co. Down," No. 3.

Drumbo: "Gravestone Inscription Series, Co. Down," Nos. 1, 4, and 18.

Dundonald: "Gravestone Inscription Series, Co. Down," No. 2.

Dunsfort: "Gravestone Inscription Series, Co. Down," No. 8.

Edenderry: "Gravestone Inscription Series, Co. Down," No. 3.

Eglantine: "Gravestone Inscription Series, Co. Down," No. 18.

Gilnahirk: "Gravestone Inscription Series, Co. Down," No. 18.

Glasdrumman: "Gravestone Inscription Series, Co. Down," No. 10.

Glastry: "Gravestone Inscription Series, Co. Down," No. 15.

Gransha: "Gravestone Inscription Series, Co. Down," No. 1.

Greyabbey: "Gravestone Inscription Series, Co. Down," No. 12.

Groomsport: "Gravestone Inscription Series, Co. Down," No. 17.

Hillhall: "Gravestone Inscription Series, Co. Down," No. 1.

Hillsborough: "Gravestone Inscription Series, Co. Down," No. 18.

Holywood: "Gravestone Inscription Series, Co. Down," No. 14.

Inch: "Gravestone Inscription Series, Co. Down," No. 7.

Inishargy: "Gravestone Inscription Series, Co. Down," No. 14.

Kilcarn: "Gravestone Inscription Series, Co. Down," No. 5.

Kilclief: "Gravestone Inscription Series, Co. Down," No. 8.

Kilhorne: "Gravestone Inscription Series, Co. Down," No. 10.

Kilkeel: "Gravestone Inscription Series, Co. Down," No. 10.

Killarney: "Gravestone Inscription Series, Co. Down," No. 2.

Killaresy: "Gravestone Inscription Series, Co. Down," No. 6.

Killinakin: "Gravestone Inscription Series, Co. Down," No. 6.

Killinchy: "Gravestone Inscription Series, Co. Down," Nos. 5 and 6.

Killough: "Gravestone Inscription Series, Co. Down," No. 8.

Killybawn: "Gravestone Inscription Series, Co. Down," No. 1.

Killyleagh: "Gravestone Inscription Series, Co. Down," Nos. 6 and 7.

Killysuggan: "Gravestone Inscription Series, Co. Down," No. 5.

Kilmegan: "Gravestone Inscription Series, Co. Down," No. 9.

Kilmood: "Gravestone Inscription Series, Co. Down," No. 5.

Kilmore: "Gravestone Inscription Series, Co. Down," No. 3.

Kilwarlin: "Gravestone Inscription Series, Co. Down," No. 18.

Kircubbin: "Gravestone Inscription Series, Co. Down," No. 12.

Knock: "Gravestone Inscription Series, Co. Down," No. 4.

Knockbrecken: "Gravestone Inscription Series, Co. Down," Nos. 1 and 18.

Knockbreda: "Gravestone Inscription Series, Co. Down," No. 2.

Legacurry: "Gravestone Inscription Series, Co. Down," No. 2.

Lisbane: "Gravestone Inscription Series, Co. Down," No. 13.

Loughaghery: "Gravestone Inscription Series, Co. Down," No. 18.

Loughinisland: "Gravestone Inscription Series, Co. Down," Nos. 9 and 12.

Magheradrool: "Gravestone Inscription Series, Co. Down," Nos. 9 and 12.

Magherahamlet: "Gravestone Inscription Series, Co. Down," No. 9.

Magheralin: "Gravestone Inscription Series, Co. Down," No. 19.

Maze: "Gravestone Inscription Series, Co. Down," No. 18.

Millisle: "Gravestone Inscription Series, Co. Down," No. 16.

Moira: "Gravestone Inscription Series, Co. Down," No. 18.

Moneyrea: "Gravestone Inscription Series, Co. Down," No. 1.

Mourne: "Gravestone Inscription Series, Co. Down," No. 10.

Movilla: "Gravestone Inscription Series, Co. Down," No. 11.

Newtownards: "Gravestone Inscription Series, Co. Down," No. 11.

Old Court: "Gravestone Inscription Series, Co. Down," No. 8.

Portaferry: "Gravestone Inscription Series, Co. Down," No. 13.

Rademan: "Gravestone Inscription Series, Co. Down," No. 3.

Raffrey: "Gravestone Inscription Series, Co. Down," No. 5.

Saintfield: "Gravestone Inscription Series, Co. Down," No. 3.

Rathmullan: "Gravestone Inscription Series, Co. Down," No. 9.

Ravara: "Gravestone Inscription Series, Co. Down," No. 5.

Saul: "Gravestone Inscription Series, Co. Down," Nos. 7 and 8.

Seaforde: "Gravestone Inscription Series, Co. Down," No. 9.

Slanes: "Gravestone Inscription Series, Co. Down," No. 14.

Tamlaght: "Gravestone Inscription Series, Co. Down," No. 10.

Templepatrick: "Gravestone Inscription Series, Co. Down," No. 14.

Tullymacnous: "Gravestone Inscription Series, Co. Down," No. 6.

Tullynakill: "Gravestone Inscription Series, Co. Down," No. 1.

Waringstown: Edward D. Atkinson. *An Ulster Parish*. 1898.

Whitechurch: "Gravestone Inscription Series, Co. Down," No. 15.

Newspapers

The best early sources for this county are the *Newry Journal*(s) published in the 1770s and 1780s. However, there are few copies of this newspaper in existence. See the appendix for newspapers published in Belfast. Many of these covered events and carried notices of relevance to several of the surrounding counties.

Title: *Downpatrick Recorder*
Published in: Downpatrick, 1836-current
NLI Holdings: 12.1836-in progress
BL Holdings: 12.1836-in progress

Title: *Downshire Protestant*
Published in: Downpatrick, 1855-62
BL Holdings: 7.1855-9.1862

Title: *Newry Commercial Telegraph* (continued as *Newry Telegraph* in 1877)
Published in: Newry, 1812-1970
NLI Holdings: 1814-91 (odd numbers); 4.1858-12.1913; 1.1950-6.1970
BL Holdings: 1.1828-7.1877; 7.1877-9.1922; 1.1923-12.1927; 7.1928-6.1970

Title: *Newry Examiner* (continued as *Dundalk Examiner*)
Published in: Newry, 1830-80
NLI Holdings: 1.1852-12.1857
BL Holdings: 1.1832-8.1880

Title: *Newry Herald & Down, Armagh and Louth Journal*
Published in: Newry, 1858-64
BL Holdings: 1.1858-12.1864

Title: *Newry Journal* (Jones)
Published in: Newry, c.1770-c.1776

Title: *Newry Journal* (Stevenson)
Published in: Newry, c.1774-1788

Title: *Newry Reporter*
Published in: Newry, 1867-current
NLI Holdings: 6.1921-9.1922; 1.1923-in progress
BL Holdings: 11.1867-5.1901; 6.1901-9.1922; 1.1923-6.1925; 1.1926-in progress

Title: *Newry Standard* (continued as *Belfast and Newry Standard* in 1882 and as *Newry and Belfast Standard* in 1891)
Published in: Newry, 1879-99

NLI Holdings: 6.1879-4.1882; 5.1882-11.1891; 12.1891-6.1899
BL Holdings: 5.1889-6.1899

Title: *Newtownards Chronicle*
Published in: Newtownards, 1873-current
NLI Holdings: 6.1921-in progress
BL Holdings: 1.1874-in progress

Title: *North Down Herald* (continued as *Northern Herald* in 1926)
Published in: Bangor, c.1880-1957
NLI Holdings: 6.1921-2.1957
BL Holdings: 1.1898-12.1925; 1.1926-3.1939; 5.1952-1957

Wills and Administrations

A discussion of the types of records, where they are held, their availability, and value is given in the Wills section of the Introduction. The availability of prerogative wills, administrations, and marriage license records is also described in the relevant parts of the same section. Where available, published sources of these records are given in the Miscellaneous Sources section.

Pre-1858 Wills and Administrations

Prerogative Wills. See p. xli.
Consistorial Wills. County Down is in the dioceses of Down, Dromore, Newry, and Mourne (four parishes) and Connor (two parishes). The guide to Catholic Parish records in this chapter shows the diocese to which each civil parish belonged. The wills of residents of each diocese were usually proven within that diocese (see the Wills section for exceptions). The following records survive:

Wills. Connor (1818-20, 1853-58); Down (1850-58).

Abstracts. See p. xxxvii; Stewart-Kennedy notebooks – see Co. Antrim.

Indexes. Down (1646-1858) none published; Dromore (1678-1858); Newry and Mourne

(1727-1858) published in 1858 by Phillimore; Connor – see Co. Antrim.

Post-1858 Wills and Administrations

County Down was served by the District Registry of Belfast. The surviving records are kept in the PRONI. Other published records:

"Administrations from the Peculiar of Newry and Mourne." *Ir. Anc.* 1 (1) (1969): 41-42.

Marriage Licenses

Indexes. Down, Connor, and Dromore (1721-1845). PRO; SLC film 100867.

Miscellaneous Sources

"Administrations From the Peculiar of Newry and Mourne." *Ir. Anc.* 1 (1) (1969): 41-42.

"The Census of 1901 and 1911 for Copeland Island." *J. Bangor Hist. Soc.* 1 (1981).

"Maps of the Mountains of Mourne." *Ulster J. Arch.* 8 (1902): 133-37.

"Some Lists of Mid-18th Century Linen Drapers in S.E. Ulster." *Ir. Anc.* 11 (1) (1979): 9-14.

Stevenson, J. *Two Centuries of Life in County Down, 1600-1800.*

Young, R. *Historical Notices of Old Belfast.* 1896.

Research Sources and Services

Journals

Ards Upper Hist. Soc. Journal (1967-present)
Lecale Miscellany (published by Lecale Historical Society, 1983-present)
Old Newry Journal (published by Old Newry Society, 1977-present)

East Belfast Historical Society Journal (1981-present)

Saintfield Heritage (published by Saintfield Heritage Society in 1982)

Seanchas Ardmhacha (see Co. Armagh)

Libraries and Information Sources

Bangor Visitors and Heritage Centre, I.A. Wilson, Town Hall, Bangor, Co. Down

Down Museum, Southwell Building, The Mall, Downpatrick, Co. Down

South Eastern Education & Library Board, Library H.Q., Windmill Hill, Ballynahinch, Co. Down Ph: (0849) 562639

Research Services

See research services in Belfast, p. xlvi

Societies

Ards Historical Society, W.R. Plenderleith, 7 Burnside Park, Crawfordsburn, Co. Down

Ballynahinch Historical Society, D. Wightman, The Croft, 15 Dunmore Road, The Spa, Ballynahinch, Co. Down

Banbridge & District Historical Society, F. Downey, 64 Chinauley Park, Banbridge, Co. Down

Bangor Historical Society, J. McCormick, 282 Seacliff Road, Bangor, Co. Down

The Downe Society, Miss R. Baillie, 100 Ballynahinch Road, Crossgar, Co. Down

East Belfast Historical Society, Mr. Wm. Smith, 35 Belmont Avenue, Belfast

Killyleagh Family History Society, Miss J.O. Bain, 1A Net Walk, Killyleagh, Co. Down

Kingdom of Mourne Society, Mr. A. Doran, Springwell House, Mullartown, Annalong, Co. Down

Lecale Historical Society, Mr. R. Gifford, 5 The Quoile Brae, Downpatrick, Co. Down

Newcastle Field Club, Mr. T.P. Walsh, 41 Slievenamaddy Avenue, Newcastle, Co. Down

Old Newry Society, Mrs. G. McCoy, Homestead, Jonesboro, Newry, Co. Down

Poyntzpass and District Historical Society, Mrs. B. Heron, 'St. Jude,' William Street, Poyntzpass, Co. Down

Rathfriland Historical Society, Mrs. M. Harbinson, 34 Downpatrick Street, Rathfriland, Co. Down

Saintfield Heritage Society, Miss E. Minnis, 16 Moyra Drive, Saintfield, Co. Down

South Belfast Historical Society, E. Robinson, 47 Glenholm Avenue, Belfast BT8

Upper Ards Historical Society, Mr. R. Oram, Tara, Portaferry, Co. Down

Warrenpoint Historical Society, Miss E. Murray, 20 Pinewood Hill, Warrenpoint, Co. Down

West Belfast Historical Society, Miss M. Smith, 27 Cavendish Street, Belfast BT12

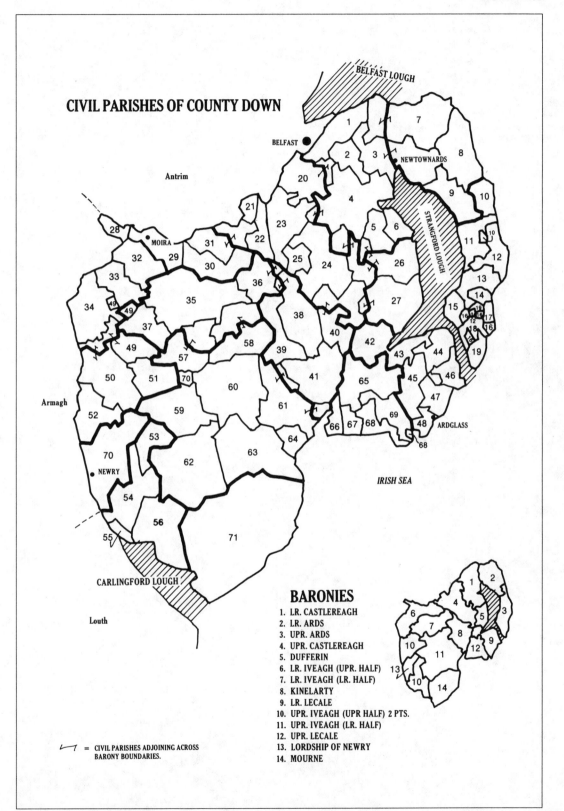

CIVIL PARISHES OF COUNTY DOWN

BELFAST LOUGH

BELFAST

Antrim

NEWTOWNARDS

STRANGFORD LOUGH

MOIRA

Armagh

NEWRY

ARDGLASS

IRISH SEA

CARLINGFORD LOUGH

Louth

BARONIES

1. LR. CASTLEREAGH
2. LR. ARDS
3. UPR. ARDS
4. UPR. CASTLEREAGH
5. DUFFERIN
6. LR. IVEAGH (UPR. HALF)
7. LR. IVEAGH (LR. HALF)
8. KINELARTY
9. LR. LECALE
10. UPR. IVEAGH (UPR HALF) 2 PTS.
11. UPR. IVEAGH (LR. HALF)
12. UPR. LECALE
13. LORDSHIP OF NEWRY
14. MOURNE

⌐1 = CIVIL PARISHES ADJOINING ACROSS
BARONY BOUNDARIES.

County Dublin

A Brief History

The earliest accounts of Dublin city go back as far as A.D. 140 when Ptolemy mentioned a settlement on this site. The major development of the city began in the eighth century when the Vikings or Norsemen established a settlement which developed into a powerful Viking base. The power of the Dublin Norsemen lasted until 1014 when they were defeated, at the Battle of Clontarf, by the native Irish, led by Brian Boru (see Co. Clare). However, the Vikings remained in much of the county, particularly north of the city. The Vikings did not use hereditary surnames or family names and therefore their influence is not obvious in the family names which exist in the county.

In 1169 the Normans made Dublin the center of their activities following their successful invasion of Ireland. It has remained the effective seat of government almost ever since. The north of the county was granted to the Norman Hugh de Lacy in the thirteenth century. Other Anglo-Norman families who settled in the county include those of Baggot, Sarsfield, Luttrell, Delahyde, Talbot, Barnewall, St. Lawrence, Cruise, Archbold, and Segrave. The city grew considerably during the fourteenth to sixteenth centuries, despite the continuing attacks by the O'Tooles and O'Byrnes of Wicklow (see Co. Wicklow) and the O'Moore and O'Carrolls (see counties Laois and Offaly).

As the seat of English administration of Ireland, Dublin was largely a Protestant city during the Middle Ages. In 1644 the total population of the city was only around 8,000. By 1682, when the rebellion of Irish Catholics (see Co. Kilkenny) had been defeated and English power was imposed on most of the country, the population of Dublin was estimated at 60,000. Extensive growth outside the walls of the old city was occurring at this time. By 1728 the population was 146,000, and by the end of the century it was over 170,000. The influx of people to Dublin included English administrators as well as people from all over Ireland. From abroad there have also been influxes of Huguenot, Jewish, and other peoples.

The eighteenth century was the great period of growth of Dublin city when the great streets were laid out and many of the great public buildings established. In this period Dublin was one of the great cities of Europe. In 1800, however, the Irish Parliament was amalgamated with the Westminster Parliament in London. As a consequence Dublin lost much of its glamour and many of the gentry moved to London. Although the administrative capital, the city did not develop extensive heavy industry as did Belfast, for instance. The population continued to grow, however, and by 1841 it had reached over 230,000.

During the Great Famine of 1845-47 the population expanded due to migration of people from other badly affected parts of the country. The population of Dublin county was 372,000 in 1841, and by 1851 this had grown to 405,000. There were, however, over 75,000 deaths in the city between 1845 and 1850, and thousands emigrated through Dublin port. The number of natives of the county who emigrated was relatively low, less than 4 percent of the population, compared to 18 percent in Tipperary and Clare. The city's population grew only slowly during the remainder of the century but has grown rapidly since the foundation of the Irish state. The current population is over 1 million.

Census and Census Substitutes

1468-85
Freemen of the City of Dublin. SLC film 100228.

1621
"List of Householders in St. John's Parish Who Were Rated for Parish Cess." Appendix 2 in the "Registers of St. John's, 1619-1699." *Parish Register Society* 1 (1906): 273; SLC film 82407.

1646
"List of Householders for St. John's Parish." *Parish Register Society* 1 (1906): 276; SLC film 824047.

1652
Inhabitants of the Baronies of Newcastle and Uppercross, districts of Ballyfermot, Balliowen, Ballidowde, Belgard, Bellemount, Blundestown, Butterfield, Carranstown, Crumlin, Dalkey, Deane Rath, Esker, Feddenstown, Finstown, Gallanstown, Great Katherins, Irishtown, Killnemanagh, Killiney, Kilmainham, Kilmatalway, Kilshock, Loughstown, Lucan, Milltown, Nanger, Nealstown, Newcastle, Newgrange, Newland, Oldbawn, Palmerstown, Rathgar, Rathfarnham, Rowlagh (Ranelagh), Rock-

stown, Shankill, Symon, Tallaght, Templeogue, and Terenure (gives names, ages, occupations, and relationships). PRO 1A 41 100.

1654-56
Civil Survey, Vol. 7. SLC film 973123.

1659
"Census" of Ireland. Edited by S. Pender. Dublin: Stationery Office, 1939. SLC film 924648.

1663-64
Hearth Money Roll. *Kildare Arch. Soc. J.* 10 (5): 245-54; 11 (1): 386-466 (also covers parts of Kildare).

1687
"List of Householders in St. John's Parish." *Parish Register Society* 1 (1906): 277; SLC film 824047.

1766
Religious Census of Parishes of Crumlin, Donnybrook, Castleknock, and Taney. RCB Library; SLC film 258517 (except Donnybrook).

1767
List of Freeholders in Co. Dublin. PRO film 4912.

1774-1824
"Alphabetical List of the Freemen of the City of Dublin." *Ir. Anc.* 15 (1) and (2) (1983): 2-133.

1775
Catholic Qualification Roll Extracts (ninety-eight names, addresses, and occupations). 59th Reprint DKPRI, 50-84.

1777-1830
"Brethren Admitted to the Guild of Smiths, Dublin, by Marriage Right, 1777-1830." Reports from Committees. *Parl. Papers* 1837, Vol. 2 (2): (480): 182.

1778-82
"The Catholic Merchants, Manufacturers and Traders of Dublin, 1778-1782." *Reportorium* 2 (2) (1960): 298-323 (compiled from Catholic qualification rolls – gives name, trade, and address).

1792-1837

"Names of All Persons Admitted to Dublin Trade Guilds (apothecaries, bakers, barbers, surgeons, carpenters, smiths, merchants, tailors, etc.), 1792-1837." *Parl. Papers* 1837, 11 (161-91): Appendix 3 (gives names, and some father's and father's-in-law names.

1793-1810

Census of Protestants in Castleknock. SLC film 100225.

1798

List of Persons who Suffered Losses in '98 Rebellion. NLI JLB 94107 (approximately 100 names, addresses, and occupations).

1820

Freemen of Dublin Who Voted at a Parliamentary Election (arranged alphabetically by candidate chosen with list of "neutral" freemen – gives name, residence, and occupation). NLI P734.

1821

Government Census Extracts for Dublin City and Tallaght for Selected Surnames. SLC film 100158; PRO.

1823-37

Tithe Applotment Survey (see p. xxvii).

1830

Dublin City and County Freeholders (contains names and addresses). NLI ms. 11.847.

1831

Householders in St. Bride's Parish (possibly based on 1831 government census). NLI P1994.

1832

"Number and Names of Freemen Registered as Voters, City of Dublin." *Parl. Papers* 1837, Vol. 2 (1): 159-75 (2,678 names only).

1832-36

"An Alphabetical List of the Registered Voters in Parliamentary Elections for the City of Dublin." *Parl. Papers* 1837, 12 (2) (480): 1-145 (names, occupations or "gent," residence, etc., given alphabetically by year of registration).

"Names and Residences of Persons in Dublin Receiving Liquor Licenses." *Parl. Papers* 1837, 11 (1) Appendix 11: 250.

1835-37

Dublin County Freeholders and Leaseholders 1835, 1837, and 1852. NLI ms. 9363.

1848-51

Griffith's Valuation, see p. xxvii (the parishes of Dublin city are not included in the Index to Surnames).

1852

see 1835-37.

1901

Census. PRO.

1911

Census. PRO.

Church Records

Church of Ireland
[Due to the scope of these records, they were not included here. Researchers are referred to James G. Ryan, *Tracing Your Dublin Ancestors* (Dublin, Flyleaf Press, 1988)]

Roman Catholic

Civil Parish: **Aderrig**
Map Grid: 49
RC Parish: see Lucan
Diocese: DU

Civil Parish: **Artaine**
Map Grid: 39
RC Parish: see Clontarf
Diocese: DU

Civil Parish: **Baldongan**
Map Grid: 5
RC Parish: Skerries
Diocese: DU

Civil Parish: **Baldoyle**
Map Grid: 36
RC Parish: Baldoyle
Diocese: DU
Earliest Record: b. 12.1784; m. 1.1785
Missing Dates: b. 12.1800-8.1806; m. 12.1800-
8.1806,11.1815-5.1818, 11.1824-1.1826
Parish Address: Rev. Canon G. Finnegan, PE,
76 Grange Road, Baldoyle, Dublin

Civil Parish: **Balgriffin**
Map Grid: 34
RC Parish: see Baldoyle
Diocese: DU

Civil Parish: **Ballyboghil**
Map Grid: 14
RC Parish: see Naul
Diocese: DU

Civil Parish: **Ballyfermot**
Map Grid: 59
RC Parish: part of Lucan, Palmerstown, and
Clondalkin
Diocese: DU

Civil Parish: **Ballymadun**
Map Grid: 10
RC Parish: see Garristown

Civil Parish: **Balrothery**
Map Grid: 2
RC Parish: Balrothery and Balbriggan
Diocese: DU
Earliest Record: b. 10.1816; m. 2.1817
Parish Address: Rev. James O'Sullivan, PP,
Parochial House, Balbriggan, Co. Dublin

Civil Parish: **Balscaddan**
Map Grid: 1
RC Parish: see Balrothery
Diocese: DU

Civil Parish: **Booterstown (1)**
Map Grid: 71

RC Parish: Booterstown; also Blackrock and
Dundrum, see below
Diocese: DU
Earliest Record: b. 1755; m. 1756
Parish Address: Rev. Jerome Curtin, PP,
Parochial House, Booterstown, Co. Dublin

Civil Parish: **Booterstown (2)**
Map Grid: F1
RC Parish: Blackrock
Diocese: DU
Earliest Record: b. 1850; m. 1922
Parish Address: Rev. D. Henry, CC, 35 New-
town Ave, Blackrock, Co. Dublin

Civil Parish: **Booterstown (3)**
Map Grid: F1
RC Parish: Dundrum
Diocese: DU
Earliest Record: b. 1861; m. 1861
Parish Address: Rev. J. Fagan, PP, The Pres-
bytery, Main St., Dundrum, Dublin 14

Civil Parish: **Castleknock**
Map Grid: 26
RC Parish: Blanchardstown
Diocese: DU
Earliest Record: b. 12.1774; m. 1.1775
Parish Address: Rev. S. McGeehan, PP,
Parochial House, Blanchardstown, Dublin
15

Civil Parish: **Chapelizod**
Map Grid: 27
RC Parish: Chapelizod, see Clondalkin for ear-
lier Records
Diocese: DU

Civil Parish: **Cloghran** (near Castleknock)
Map Grid: 23
RC Parish: see Castleknock
Diocese: DU

Civil Parish: **Cloghran** (near Santry)
Map Grid: 31
RC Parish: see Clontarf
Diocese: DU

Civil Parish: **Clondalkin**
Map Grid: 58

RC Parish: Clondalkin
Diocese: DU
Earliest Record: b. 5.1778; m. 6.1778
Missing Dates: b. 4.1800-8.1809; m. 2.1800-8.1812
Parish Address: Rev. M. Ryan, PP, St. Cecilia's, New Road, Clondalkin, Dublin 22

Civil Parish: **Clonmethan**
Map Grid: 12
RC Parish: Rolestown, see Killossery
Diocese: DU

Civil Parish: **Clonsilla**
Map Grid: 25
RC Parish: see Castleknock
Diocese: DU

Civil Parish: **Clontarf**
Map Grid: 46
RC Parish: Clontarf
Diocese: DU
Earliest Record: b. 1774; m. 1774
Parish Address: Rev. J. Gunning, 68 Clontarf Road, Clontarf, Dublin 3

Civil Parish: **Clonturk** (Drumcondra)
Map Grid: 38
RC Parish: Fairview, see Clontarf for earlier records
Diocese: DU
Earliest Record: b. 6.1879; m. 6.1879
Parish Address: Rev. W. Rogan, PP, Presbytery, Fairview, Dublin 3

Civil Parish: **Coolock**
Map Grid: 35
RC Parish: Coolock, see Clontarf for earlier records
Diocese: DU
Earliest Record: b. 1879; m. 1879
Parish Address: Rev. P. O'Farrell, PP, 36 St. Brendan's Ave., Coolock, Dublin 5

Civil Parish: **Cruagh**
Map Grid: 66
RC Parish: see Rathfarnham
Diocese: DU

Civil Parish: **Crumlin**
Map Grid: 62

RC Parish: see Rathfarnham
Diocese: DU

Civil Parish: **Dalkey**
Map Grid: 78
RC Parish: Dalkey
Diocese: DU
Earliest Record: b. 1861; m. 1894
Parish Address: Rev. J. Meagher, St. Joseph's, Dalkey Ave., Dalkey, Co. Dublin

Civil Parish: **Donabate**
Map Grid: 17
RC Parish: Donabate
Diocese: DU
Earliest Record: b. 11.1760; m. 1.1761
Missing Dates: b. 12.1807-7.1824; m. 6.1805-2.1869
Parish Address: Rev. D. O'Kane, PP, Parochial House, Donabate, Co. Dublin

Civil Parish: **Donnybrook**
Map Grid: 68
RC Parish: part Donnybrook, see Donnybrook Dublin City section; part Booterstown
Diocese: DU

Civil Parish: **Drimnagh**
Map Grid: 61
RC Parish: see Clondalkin
Diocese: DU

Civil Parish: **Dublin City**
RC Parish: see separate listing (p. 176) and map (p. 191).

Civil Parish: **Esker**
Map Grid: 50
RC Parish: see Lucan, Palmerstown, and Clondalkin
Diocese: DU

Civil Parish: **Finglas**
Map Grid: 24
RC Parish: Finglas and St. Margaret's
Diocese: DU
Earliest Record: b. 2.1784; m. 11.1757
Missing Dates: m. 7.1760-12.1784
Parish Address: Rev. W. Deasy, PE, Parochial House, Finglas, Dublin

Civil Parish: **Garristown**
Map Grid: 7
RC Parish: Garristown
Diocese: DU
Earliest Record: b. 1.1857; m. 7.1857
Parish Address: Rev. J. K. Dempsey, PP,
    Parochial House, Garristown, Co. Dublin

Civil Parish: **Glasnevin**
Map Grid: 37
RC Parish: part St. Michan's
Diocese: DU

Civil Parish: **Grallagh**
Map Grid: 8
RC Parish: see Garristown
Diocese: DU

Civil Parish: **Grangegorman**
Map Grid: 43
RC Parish: part St. Paul's
Diocese: DU

Civil Parish: **Hollywood**
Map Grid: 9
RC Parish: see Garristown or Balrothery
Diocese: DU

Civil Parish: **Holmpatrick**
Map Grid: 3
RC Parish: Skerries
Diocese: DU
Earliest Record: b. 10.1751; m. 6.1751
Parish Address: Rev. L. Shanahan, PP, Cuan
    Phadraig, South Strand, Skerries, Co. Dublin

Civil Parish: **Howth**
Map Grid: 42
RC Parish: Howth, see Baldoyle for earlier
    records
Diocese: DU
Earliest Record: b. 1890; m. 1890
Parish Address: Rev. Brian Kelly, PP, Mount
    Saint Mary's, Howth, Co. Dublin

Civil Parish: **Kilbarrack**
Map Grid: 41
RC Parish: see Baldoyle
Diocese: DU

Civil Parish: **Kilbride**
Map Grid: 53
RC Parish: see Lucan, Palmerstown, and Clon-
    dalkin
Diocese: DU

Civil Parish: **Kilgobbin**
Map Grid: 79
RC Parish: see Taney
Diocese: DU

Civil Parish: **Kill**
Map Grid: 77
RC Parish: Cabinteely, see also Booterstown
Diocese: DU
Earliest Record: b. 1859; m. 1859
Parish Address: Rev. George O'Sullivan, PP,
    Parochial House, Cabinteely, Co. Dublin

Civil Parish: **Killeek**
Map Grid: 20
RC Parish: see Finglas
Diocese: DU

Civil Parish: **Killester**
Map Grid: 45
RC Parish: see Finglas
Diocese: DU

Civil Parish: **Killiney**
Map Grid: 80
RC Parish: Kingstown
Diocese: DU

Civil Parish: **Killossery**
Map Grid: 15
RC Parish: Rowlestown
Diocese: DU
Earliest Record: b. 1.1857; m. 1.1857
Parish Address: Rev. P. Crowley, PP, Parochial
    House, Rolestown, Kilsallaghan, Co. Dublin

Civil Parish: **Kilmactalway**
Map Grid: 51
RC Parish: see Lucan, Palmerstown, and Clon-
    dalkin
Diocese: DU

Civil Parish: **Kilmacud**
Map Grid: 73
RC Parish: part Booterstown; part Kingstown
Diocese: DU

Civil Parish: **Kilmahuddrick**
Map Grid: 52
RC Parish: see Lucan, Palmerstown, and Clondalkin
Diocese: DU

Civil Parish: **Kilsallaghan**
Map Grid: 19
RC Parish: part Finglas; part Rowlestown, see Killossery
Diocese: DU

Civil Parish: **Kiltiernan**
Map Grid: 81
RC Parish: Sandyford, see Taney
Diocese: DU

Civil Parish: **Kilsaley**
Map Grid: 32
RC Parish: see Baldoyle
Diocese: DU

Civil Parish: **Leixlip**
Map Grid: 47
RC Parish: see Co. Kildare
Diocese: DU

Civil Parish: **Lucan**
Map Grid: 48
RC Parish: Lucan (part of Clondalkin)
Diocese: DU
Earliest Record: b. 9.1818; m. 9.1818
Missing Dates: b. 7.1834-8.1835, 8.1842-2.1849 ends 1.1862; m. 9.1842-2.1849
Parish Address: Rev. Donal Coghlan, PE, Main Road, Lucan, Co. Dublin

Civil Parish: **Lusk (1)**
Map Grid: 4
RC Parish: Lusk; also Rush, see below
Diocese: DU
Earliest Record: b. 9.1757; m. 11.1757
Missing Dates: b. 8.1801-3.1802, 12.1835-8.1856; m. 1.1801-3.1802, 12.1835-3.1856
Parish Address: Rev. William Warner, PE, Parochial House, Lusk, Co. Dublin

Civil Parish: **Lusk (2)**
Map Grid: 4
RC Parish: Rush
Diocese: DU
Earliest Record: b. 9.1785; m. 9.1785
Missing Dates: b. 12.1796-12.1799; m. 4.1810-8.1813
Parish Address: Rev. T. Randles, PP, St. Francis, Whitestown, Rush, Co.Dublin

Civil Parish: **Malahide**
Map Grid: 28
RC Parish: see Swords
Diocese: DU

Civil Parish: **Monkstown**
Map Grid: 75
RC Parish: Monkstown; also part Booterstown; also part Cabinteely, see Kill
Diocese: DU
Earliest Record: b. 1769; m. 1769
Parish Address: Rev. C. Mangan, PP, 4 Eblana Ave, Dun Laoghaire, Co. Dublin

Civil Parish: **Mulhuddart**
Map Grid: 22
RC Parish: see Castleknock
Diocese: DU

Civil Parish: **Naul**
Map Grid: 6
RC Parish: see Balrothery
Diocese: DU

Civil Parish: **Newcastle**
Map Grid: 54
RC Parish: see Saggart
Diocese: DU

Civil Parish: **Oldconnaught**
Map Grid: 83
RC Parish: Kingstown
Diocese: DU

Civil Parish: **Palmerston**
Map Grid: 11
RC Parish: Rowlestown, see Killossery
Diocese: DU

Civil Parish: **Palmerstown**
Map Grid: 57

RC Parish: Palmerstown (part of Clondalkin)
Diocese: DU
Earliest Record: b. 8.1798; m. 9.1837
Missing Dates: b. 12.1799-9.1837, ends 1862;
   m. ends 9.1857
Parish Address: Rev. V. Kelly, PP, Parochial
   House, Palmerstown, Dublin 20

Civil Parish: **Portmarnock**
Map Grid: 33
RC Parish: see Baldoyle
Diocese: DU

Civil Parish: **Portraine**
Map Grid: 18
RC Parish: see Donabate
Diocese: DU

Civil Parish: **Raheny**
Map Grid: 40
RC Parish: see Clontarf
Diocese: DU

Civil Parish: **Rathcoole**
Map Grid: 55
RC Parish: see Saggart
Diocese: DU

Civil Parish: **Rathfarnham (1)**
Map Grid: 69
RC Parish: Rathfarnham; also Terenure, see
   below
Diocese: DU
Earliest Record: b. 1771; m. 1771
Parish Address: Rev. P. Tuohy, PP, St. Mary's,
   Rathfarnham, Dublin 14

Civil Parish: **Rathfarnham (2)**
Map Grid: 69
RC Parish: Terenure
Diocese: DU
Earliest Record: b. 1870; m. 1894
Parish Address: Rev. John H. Greehy, PP, 83
   Terenure Road East, Dublin 6

Civil Parish: **Rathmichael**
Map Grid: 82
RC Parish: Sandyford, see Taney
Diocese: DU

Civil Parish: **Saggart**
Map Grid: 56
RC Parish: Saggart
Diocese: DU
Earliest Record: b. 10.1832; m. 5.1832
Parish Address: Rev. L. O'Sullivan, PP,
   Parochial House, Saggart, Co. Dublin

Civil Parish: **St. Mark's**
Map Grid: 67
RC Parish: Donnybrook, see Donnybrook,
   Dublin City section
Diocese: DU

Civil Parish: **St. Margaret's**
Map Grid: 29
RC Parish: see Finglas
Diocese: DU

Civil Parish: **St. Peter's (1)**
Map Grid: 64
RC Parish: Rathmines, see St. Nicholas
   Without, Dublin City section, for earlier
   records; also Rathgor, see below.
Diocese: DU
Earliest Record: b. 1823; m. 1823
Parish Address: Rev. Aidan Burke, PP, 54
   Lower Rathmines Road, Dublin 6

Civil Parish: **St. Peter's (2)**
Map Grid: 64
RC Parish: Rathgar, see Rathmines for earlier
   records
Diocese: DU
Earliest Record: b. 1874; m. 1874
Parish Address: Rev. John Molony, PP, 50
   Rathgar Road, Dublin 6

Civil Parish: **Santry**
Map Grid: 30
RC Parish: see Clontarf
Diocese: DU

Civil Parish: **Stillorgan**
Map Grid: 74
RC Parish: see Booterstown
Diocese: DU

Civil Parish: **Swords**
Map Grid: 16
RC Parish: Swords

212   1834 Feb.ᵇ

February first John Dawson & Ann Ellen Boynge.
Feb. first Christopher Searle & Peggy ... Kennedy.
Feb. 1 Thomas Donnelly & Ann Bradley.
Feb. 2 Richard Taylor & Eliza Bradon.
Feb. 2 Thomas Cavanagh & Ann Larvin.
Feb. 3 William Howe & Eliza McMullen.
Feb. 3 Edward Ellis & Jane Leslie.
Feb. 4 John Toole & Mary Walsh.
Feb. 4 Patrick McCabe & Catherine Lee.
Feb. 4 Michael Lawlor & Charlotte Farrell.
Feb. 4 Richard Mortin & Julia Byrne.
Feb. 4 George Grieve & Esther Connelly.
Feb. 5 Thomas Healy & Margaret Horigan.
Feb. 6 James White & Mary A. Beale.
Feb. 6 Mathew Noble & Eliza Smith.
Feb. 6 Michael Strub Ariw. 14 Kings Light Dn. Mary English.
Feb. 8 Michael Strub Ariw. 14 Kings Light Dn. Mary English.
Feb. 7 Wm Houldsworth P. 12 Reg. Laugh. Bridget McDermott.
Feb. 8 Edward Aitkeen Wright Esqr. & Miss Elizabeth Bateman.
Feb. 8 Abraham Fagan & Esther Gannon.
Feb. 8 Mr. Nathaniel Trust & Miss Amelia Gustafson.

213   1834

Feb. 9 Robert Barnett & Bridget Dolton.
Feb. 9 Gustav Melham Esqr. & Miss Elizabeth Calvert.
Feb. 9 Francis Shea & Anne Telford.
Feb. 10 Thomas Gannon & Ann Shaw.
Feb. 10 Henry Gordon & Catherine Winton.
Feb. 10 John Gore P. 10 Hussars & Catherine Barton.
Feb. 10 Thomas Barker & Jane Farley.
Feb. 10 John Catt Esq. 8 Dg. Mary A. Anderson.
Feb. 10 John Cullen & Mary Kelly Newmarket Kilkenny.
Feb. 11 John Cavanagh & Anne McLeod.
Feb. 11 John Fox & Rebecca Little.
Feb. 11 Mr. Miles Magrath & Mrs Hannah Kelly of an Esther.
Feb. 11 Mr. Nicholas Hopkins & Miss Mary A. Bateman.
Feb. 11 James Gray & Lydia Young.
Feb. 11 Edward Burke & Elizabeth Hopkins.
Feb. 11 Peter Norton & Elizabeth Lawrence.
Feb. 11 Michael Tegan & Betty Flanigan.
Feb. 11 James Kelly & Betty Leonard.
Feb. 11 Mr. Wm Buchanan & Miss Elizabeth Sampson.
Feb. 11 Mr. George Sutton & Miss Amelia Robinson.

Extract, from February 1834, of the Records of the German Church, Poolbeg Street, Dublin, showing marriages performed by the Rev. Shulze. The records of marriages and baptisms in this church (now extinct) from 1806 to 1835 are in the Office of the Registrar General, Dublin.

Diocese: DU
Earliest Record: b. 12.1763; m. 10.1763
Missing Dates: b. 7.1777-6.1802; m. 6.1777-
6.1802
Parish Address: Rev. M. O'Reilly, PP, Parochial
House, Seatown Road, Swords, Co. Dublin

Civil Parish: **Tallaght**
Map Grid: 65
RC Parish: see Rathfarnham
Diocese: DU

Civil Parish: **Taney**
Map Grid: 70
RC Parish: part Kingstown; part Booterstown
Diocese: DU
Earliest Record: b. 8.1856; m. 8.1856
Parish Address: Rev. Patrick Corridan, PP,
Parochial House, Sandyford, Co. Dublin

Civil Parish: **Tully**
Map Grid: 76
RC Parish: Kingstown
Diocese: DU

Civil Parish: **Ward**
Map Grid: 21
RC Parish: see Finglas
Diocese: DU

Civil Parish: **Westpalstown**
Map Grid: 13
RC Parish: see Naul
Diocese: DU

Civil Parish: **Whitechurch**
Map Grid: 72
RC Parish: see Garristown
Diocese: DU

Dublin City

Civil Parish: **Donnybrook (1)**
RC Parish: Sandymount, see Donnybrook (3)
for earlier records
Diocese: DU
Earliest Record: b. 1865; m. 1865
Parish Address: Rev. P. Rice, PP, 76 Tritonville
Road, Dublin 4

Civil Parish: **Donnybrook (2)**
RC Parish: Donnybrook
Diocese: DU
Earliest Record: b. 1871; m. 1877
Parish Address: Rev. Richard Sherry, PP, No. 2
Presbytery, Stillorgan Road, Dublin 4

Civil Parish: **Donnybrook (3)**
RC Parish: Haddington Road
Diocese: DU
Earliest Record: b. 1798; m. 1798
Parish Address: Rev. B. O'Sullivan, PP, The
Presbytery, Haddington Road, Dublin 4

Civil Parish: **Christ Church**
RC Parish: see St. Nicholas Without

Civil Parish: **St. Andrew (1)**
RC Parish: St. Andrew; also part St. Michael
and St. John
Diocese: DU
Earliest Record: b. 1.1742; m. 2.1742
Parish Address: Rev. Desmond Dockery, Adm,
47 Westland Row, Dublin 2

Civil Parish: **St. Andrew (2)**
RC Parish: St. Andrew
Diocese: DU
Earliest Record: b. 12.1778; m. 2.1787
Missing Dates: b. 12.1799-6.1800, 9.1856-
6.1878; m. 8.1785-1.1800
Parish Address: Rev. John Fitzpatrick, St.
Audoen, High Street, Dublin 8

Civil Parish: **St. Anne**
RC Parish: See Dublin: St. Andrew

Civil Parish: **St. Bartholomew**
RC Parish: part Donnybrook; part St. Peter

Civil Parish: **St. Bridget**
RC Parish: part Michael and John; part St.
Nicholas Without

Civil Parish: **St. Catherine**
RC Parish: St. Catherine
Diocese: DU
Earliest Record: b. 5.1740; m. 5.1740
Missing Dates: b. 2.1794-12.1979, 7.1866-
6.1871; m. 12.1792-2.1794, 7.1794-12.1799

Dublin 177

86   *Merchants and Traders.*   SAL

Rourke (John) Boot and Shoemaker, 4, S. gt. George's-street.
Rourke (Thomas) Watch and Clock-maker, 4, Inns-quay.
Rowan and Hamilton, Lace and Muslin-warehouse, 37, Abbey-street.
Rowe (Mary) Paper-maker, 17, Cook-street.
Roycraft (Thomas) Wine-cooper, 141, Abbey-street.
Roycroft (Michael) Cabinet-maker, 18, Fisher's-lane.
Russell and Taylor, Woollen-drapers, 24, Eustace-street.
Russell (Bernard) Whip-maker, 49, Bridgefoot-street.
Russell (Catherine) Haberdasher, 53, Stephen-street.
Russell (Christopher and Peter) Carpenters, Buckingham-street.
Russell (Henry) Merchant-tailor, 6, John's-lane.
Russell (James) Linen-printer and Dyer, Marrowbone-lane.
Russell (James F.) Clothier, 9, Ardee-street.
Russell (John) Builder and Carpenter, 11, Russel-place, Mountjoy-square.
Russell (John) Linen-manufacturer, 92, Coombe.
Russell (John) Cooper, 11, lit. Britain-street.
Russell (John and Co.) Merchants, 106, Townsend-street.
Russell (Newhold) Linen-draper, 8, low. Bridge-street.
Russell (Samuel) Painter, 8, gt. Strand-street.
Russell (Wm. and Francis) Merchants, 19, Meath-street.
†Rutherford (John) Merchant, 59, Abbey-street.
Ryan (Charles) Apothecary, 7, Church-street.
Ryan (Edward) Glover and Breeches-maker, 31, Denmark-street.
Ryan (Edward) Haberdasher, 36, Golden-lane.
Ryan (Edward) Tailor, 12, Crow-street.
Ryan (Denis) Stone-cutter, Swift's-alley.
Ryan (James and Edward) Linen-drapers, 14, low. Bridge-street.
†Ryan (James) Merchant, 77, Marlborough-street.
Ryan (John) Timber-merchant, 15, Hanbury-lane, & 6, S. Earl-street.
Ryan (Laurence) Perfumer, 109, Capel-street.
Ryan (Michael) Victualler, Cole's-lane-market.
Ryan (Pierce) Linen-draper, 99, Bride-street.
Ryan (Richard) Painter and Glazier, 7, N. King-street.
Ryan (Simon) Skinner, 17, Watling-street.
Ryan (Thomas) Silk-manufacturer, 42, Castle-street.
Ryan (Thomas) Baker, 161, Church-street.
Ryan (Tim.) Skinner, 59, Watling-street.
Ryan (William) Haberdasher, 10, Castle-street.
Ryder (Andrew) Silk-manufacturer, 5, W. Hanover-street.
Ryder (John) Grocer, 91, Dorset-street.
Ryder (Michael) Baker, 6, Moore-street.
Ryder (Patrick) Baker, 167, Abbey-street.

Extract from a List of the Merchants and Traders of Dublin 1808, in *Wilson's Dublin Directory for the Year 1808.*

SHA   *Merchants and Traders.*   131

Sankey (John) Sheriff's-peer and Merchant, 1, *Fitzwilliam-square, N.*
Sargent (Henry) Tailor, 37, *Bolton-street*
Satchwell (M.) Silk-manufacturer, 84, *Dame-street.*
Sattell (James) Fencing Academy, 34, *Bachelor's-walk.*
Saul (Edward) Merchant, 31, *gt. Britain-street*, and *Commercial-buildings.*
Saul (Francis) Silk, Poplin and Tabinet-manufacturer, 12, *Spitalfields.*
Saul (James) Woollen-draper, 4, *High-street.*
Saunders (George) Merchant-tailor, 10, *Cork-hill.*
Saunders (John) Slater, 4, *low. Digges-street.*
Saunders (William) Carpenter, 56, *Mecklenburgh-street.*
Savage (Andrew) Carpenter and Builder, 134, *N. King-street.*
Savage (Arthur and Son) Apothecaries and Druggists, 30, *Meath-street.*
Savage (Henry) Trimming & Ribbon-manufacturer, 11, *Wormwood-gt.*
Savage (Sylvester) Brazier, 105, *Thomas-street.*
Scaif, Willis and Co. Merchant-tailors, 11, *Kildare-street.*
Scallan (William) Carpenter and Builder, 3, *Pembroke-street.*
Scanlan (Daniel) Corn-chandler, 11, *Camden-street.*
Scanlan (M.) Paper-maker, 8, and 9, *Cook-street.*
Scanlan (Patrick) Merchant, 21, *Eustace-street.*
Scarlet (James) Iron-monger, 67, *Pill-lane.*
Schooles (Alexander) Apothecary, 107, *Capel-street.*
Scott & Co. Army-clothiers & Accoutrement-makers, 33, *Dawson-st.*
Scott and Son, Watch-makers, 41, *Grafton-street.*
Scott (John) Carpenter, 41, *Montgomery-street.*
Scott (John) Silk-throwster, 37, *New-street.*
Scott (John) Timber-merchant, 54, *Townsend-street.*
Scott (Samuel) Merchant, 37, *low. Gardiner-street.*
Scott (Thomas) Apothecary and Chymist, 8, *Kevin's-port,Camden-street.*
Scott (William) Cabinet-maker and Upholder, 44, *Stafford-street.*
Scully (E.) Tailor, 33, *Exchequer-street.*
Scully (James) Merchant-tailor, 4, *Pitt-street.*
Scully (John) Merchant-tailor, 58, *Dominick-street.*
Scully (M.) Broker, 40, *Tighe-street.*
Scully (Timothy) Turner, 22, and 8, *Ash-street.*
Scurlog (Gregory) Wine-merchant, 44, *Dominick-street.*
Seabrooke (Geo. & Co.) Fur and Straw-plat-warehouse, 11, *Crow-street.*
Seale (Edward) Baker, 13, *Smock-alley.*
Seaver (John) Currier, 29, *Back-lane.*
Seaver (Stev.) Dutch Consul & Merchant, 54, *Abbey-street.*
Seed (Richard) Watch-maker, 20, *Bride-street.*
Segrave (Nicholas) Delf and Glass-seller, 111, *Dorset-street.*
Segrave (Patrick) Manufacturing Jeweller, 87, *Dame-street.*
Segrave (Richard) Tallow-chandler, 110, *gt Britain-street.*
Segrave (Thomas) Tobacconist and Tallow-chandler, 1, *Kevin-street.*
Sellors (James) Wholesale Hardware-merchant, 19, *W. New-row.*
Semple (John) Sheriff's-peer and Builder, 21, *Marlborough-street.*
Shallow (Mathew) Dry-cooper, 14, *up. Liffey-street.*

Extract from the List of Merchants and Traders in *Wilson's Dublin Directory for the Year 1820.*

LINEN-HALL FACTORS.

Alexander and Garretts, Office, 4, *Lurgan-street.*
Bastiville (Richard) 16, *Bolton-street*
Beggs, Jameson and Co. Office, 6, *Lurgan-street.*
Brady (James and George) Office, 127, *Linen-hall.*
Chambers, Todd and Co. Office, entrance off *N. Fred.-street.*
Clarke (James) 4, *Granby-row.*
Christie (James M.) Office, *Linen-h.*
Clibborn (Edward) 42, *York-street.*
Coile(Bernard & Co.)10, *Linen-hall-s.*
Courtney (John) 10, *Linen-hall-str.*
Courtney (William) 1, *Yarn-hall-str*
Coulson(John & William)*Linen-hall.*
Dick (Sam. & Co.) 13, *Linen-hall-st.*
Egan (Constantine) 25, *Beresford-st*
Gardiner, Cusack & Co. *Linen-hall.*
Hall (Alexander) *Linen-hall.*
Harkness (W.&Co.) 22, *Dominick-s*
Hawthorne (Wm.) 5, *Lurgan-str.*

Johnston and Boyle, *Linen-hall.*
Knox (John) 5, *N. Anne-street.*
Knox (Wm.) 4, *Blessington-street.*
Leckey (John) 7, *N. Anne-street.*
Maguire (Alex.) Office, 58, *Bolton-st*
M'Kiernan (Hugh) 2, *Linen-hall.*
Mc. Mullen and Magrane, 20, *N. Anne-street.*
Meade (Mat.) 3, *Lisburn-street.*
Mills and Chambers, *Lisburn-str.*
Nicholson (John) *Linen-hall.*
Nolan and Taaffe, *Linen-hall.*
Ogilby (James & Son) 18, *Prussia-s*
Pepper and Locke, 26, *N. Anne-st.*
Pim (Tobias) 67, *Aungier-street.*
Richardson (R. & T.) 56, *Bolton-str.*
Salmon (Mich.) Office, *Linen-hall.*
Shaw and Carroll, 13, *Granby-row*
Stanley (John) *Linen-hall.*
Stott and Son, 36, *Dom.-str.*
Thompson (John) 167, *N.King-st*
Wolfenden (Wm.) 2, *up. Dorset-st*

PAWN-BROKERS.

Adams(Thomas)117, *Thomas-street.*
Anderson (John) 18, *gt. Longford-st*
Barnier (Jos.) 22, *Stephen-street.*
Bonham (Edw.) 199, *gt. Britain-str*
Booth (H.) 68, *Fleet-street,* and 49, *Bishop-street.*
Burrows (Robert) 25, *Denmark-str.*
Byrne (John) 28, *Townsend-street.*
Campbell (Pat) 28, *Chancery-lane.*
Carpenter (John) 76, *Bride-street.*
Cooney (James) 127, *Francis-street.*
Dillon (Robert) *Bride-street.*
Dooley (Timothy) 11, *Beresford-st.*
Douglass (Rich.) 16, *Meath-street*
Dunn (William) 13, *Phœnix-street.*
Eades (Wm. Geo.) 4, *Johnson's-pl*
Fannin (Thomas) 41, *York-street.*

Fenton (Joseph) 8, *Townsend-street*
Fox (Thomas) 46, *Francis-street.*
Gregor (George) 89, *Bride-street.*
Harris (Thomas) 43, *gt. Britain-str.*
Henderson (Prud.) 15, *Montague-st.*
Hickey (Laurence) 12, *Moore-str.*
Hunter (James) 3, *Smock-alley.*
Langan (John) 67, *Church-street.*
Locke (Henry) 34, *Coombe.*
M'Namara (J.) 12, *Usher's-court.*
M'Namara (John) 5, *Jervis-street.*
Miller (John H.) 11, *Exchequer-str.*
Muley (Thomas) 11, *Greek-street.*
Murphy (Thomas) 96, *Coombe.*
O'Hara (Mathias) 52, *King-str. S.*
Parker (Stephen) 2, *St. Andrew-str.*
Pearson (Eliza) 7, *Pitt-street.*

Extract from the List of Dublin Linen-Hall Factors and Pawnbrokers in *Wilson's Dublin Directory for the Year 1820.*

4 *Inspectors of Weights and Measures* —James Ryan and John M'Evoy, res. 6 Straudville avenue, 35*l.*
5 Bennett, M. tailor, 11*l.*
6 Ruins
7 Mooney, J. G. & Co. (limited), wine and spirit merchants, and 8, 40*l.*

.... *here Pitt-street intersects*.........

8 Mooney, J. G. & Co. (limited), wine and spirit merchants, and 7, 20*l.*

3 S.—Hatch-street, Lower.
From Leeson-street to Harcourt-street.
P. St. Peter.—Fitzwilliam W.

1 Duffy, Christopher, esq. 35*l.*
2 Andrews, Miss 45*l.*
3 Walsh, Miss, 40*l.*
4 Williams, Alexander, artist and musician, R.H.A. 40*l.*
5 Longfield, Mrs. George, 45*l.*
6 Macartney, Miss, 40*l.*
  „ Peebles, Miss
7 Trench, F. N. Le Poer, Q.C. 45*l.*
8 Geoghegan, Jacob T. barrister, 45*l.*
9 Hart, Henry Chichester, esq. 46*l.*
10 Carey, Mrs. 45*l.*
11 Bennett, Miss, professor of the pianoforte, 45*l.*
12 Wilson, Herbert, barrister, 45*l.*
13 Campion, Wm. Bennett, Q.C. 2nd Sergeant-at-law, 45*l.*
14 Stanley, Robert H. barrister, 45*l.*
  „ Stanley, Mrs.
15 Ryan, A. L. solicitor, commissioner for oaths, Offices—24 St. Andrew street 45*l.*
16 Roberts, Mrs.
  „ Roberts, William C. esq.

.... *here Earlsfort-terrace intersects*......

20 Murland, Mrs. 60*l.*
  „ Beckett, W. H. esq.
21 Verner, Miss Harriet, 48*l.*
22 Edge, J. Samuel, barrister, 48*l.*
  „ Edge, Miss
23 Sullivan, William, barrister, 48*l.*
24 Patton, Mrs. 36*l.*
  „ Patton, Miss C.
25 Murray, William D. esq. 35*l.*
26 Sheil, Richard H. barrister, 37*l.*
27 Leeper, Charles, esq. 35*l.*
28 Stubbs, William C. barrister, 38*l.*
29 Pierce, John, esq. 18*l.*
30 Archer, Mr. 18*l.*
31 Stubbs, Miss
31A McKnight, Mr. horse dealer, 18*l.*
32 Holland, Johnston, builder and contractor—res. Raglan house, Rathgar, 8*l.*
  „ Holland, George

3 S.—Hatch-street, Upper.
From Earlsfort-terrace to Harcourt-st.
P. St. Peter.—Fitzwilliam W.

1 Gilman, Daniel, esq. 60*l.*
  „ Gilman, Herbert R. esq.
  „ Gilman, Sylvester, esq.
2 Owen, Mrs. Frances, 50*l.*
  Bonded Stores—W. & A. Gilbey, 180*l.*

4 S.—Hawkins-street.
From D'Olier-street to Burgh-quay.
P. St. Mark.—Trinity W.

1 Gallaher & Co. tobacco manufacturers at Belfast. Branch house for south-west of Ireland—Wm. Hilles, agent, and 17 D'Olier-street, 43*l.*
2 Vacant, 24*l.*
3 Flynn, Mr. John, 24*l.*
  „ *Central Loan Office*—W. Watson, manager
4 Whelan, Mr. John,
5 Farrelly, John, & Son, saddlers & harness makers, 41*l.*
6, 7 and 8 Goods entrance, *Junior Army and Navy stores*, 28*l.* 26*l.*
9 Foran, Mrs. tobacconist, 11*l.*
  „ Dolan, J. shell-fish stores
  „ Penfold, William
10 *Alliance Gas Co.* stores, 22*l.*
.... *here Leinster Market intersects*......
11 Commins, Thomas, wine and spirit mer. & 10 Leinster-market, 40*l.*
12 Fry, O. and R. general commission agents, flour, cheese, ling, herring and butter stores, 100*l.*
  „ Matterson and Sons, Limerick
  „ Baron Liebig's Extract of Malt
  „ M'Call, John, & Co. London
  „ Moir, J. and Son
  „ Hay & Co. Lerwick
  „ *Edwards' Dessicated Soap*
  „ Libby, M'Neill & Libby, Chicago
  „ *Limerick Dairy Co.*
  „ White, T. H. and Co. and Belfast
  „ *Condensed Milk Co. of Ireland*
  „ Fry, Oliver, merchant—res. 7 Ailesbury-road, Merrion
  „ Fry, Richard, merchant—res. 8 Elton-park, Sandycove
13 MacMullen, Shaw, and Co. flour merchants, & 12 Burgh-quay
  „ Smyth, P. J. & Co.—office, 14
.... *here Burgh-quay intersects*........
14 Smyth, Patrick J. and Co. sacking merchants, 28*l.*
14A Gallagher, Alfred H. 28*l.*
.... *here Poolbeg-street intersects*......
16 *Alliance Gas Co.* 100*l.*
THE LEINSTER HALL (Concert Hall) —Michael Gunn, esq. proprietor —res. 69 Merrion-square
17A *Alliance and Consumers' Gas Co.* stove department
17 & 18 *Boys' Home* — Mrs. Macnamara, superintendent
19. Meagher, Philip, tea and wine merchant, and 1 & 2 Townsend-st.

1 E.—Hawthorn-avenue.
Off Church-road, North-strand.—North Dock W.
Nine small cottages

1 E.—Hawthorn-terrace.
Church-road, North-strand.—North Dock W.

1 Brough, Mr. John, 11*l.*
2 Smyth, Mrs. 8*l.*
3 Brownell, Mr. J. 8*l.*
4 Irwin, Mr. J. B. 10*l.*
5 Dempsey, Mr. Patrick, 10*l.*
6 Rocliffe, James, 10*l.*
7 Potter, James, engineer, 10*l.*
8 M'William, John, mariner, 10*l.*
9 M'William, Mr. Alexander, 8*l.*
10 O'Gier, Mr. A. V, 8*l.*

11 Hill, Mr. J. 8*l.*
12 Robertson, Mr. W. 8*l.*
13 Sanderson, Mr. T. 8*l.*
14 Buchanan, W. bottle maker, 8*l.*
15 M'Cormick, J. carpenter, 8*l.*
16 Rowe, Robert R. ship steward, 8*l.*
17 Vacant, 7*l.*
18 Vacant, 7*l.*
19 Walsh, Mrs. 7*l.*
20 Vance, Mr. W. 7*l.*
21 Willis, Mr. William, 10*l.*
22 Furlong, Mr. Michael, 9*l.*
23 Lynch, Mr. M. 9*l.*
24 Kennedy, Mr. T. 9*l.*
25 Casey, Mrs. 9*l.*
26 Cashmore, Robert, glass cutter, 9*l.*
27 M'Carthy, Bryan, late R.N. 9*l.*
28 Bratton, Mr. Henry James, 9*l.*
29 Harbron, Mr. W. J. 14*l.*
30 Tenements, 12*l.*
31 Adams, Mr. Harvey, 12*l.*
32 Tenements, 9*l.*

3 N.—Hay-market.
From Smithfield to Queen-street.
P. St. Michan.—Arran-quay W.

1 and 2 Petrie, Wm. sack merchant and sack hirer ; agents for Lipman and Co. hessian and sack manufacturers, Dundee—res. 30 North Summer-street, 26*l.* 7*l.*
3 Doyle, Gerald, stores, 5*l.*
4 M'Quaid, John, cattle exporter, and Stormanstown, Glasnevin
5 and 6 Tenements, each 13*l.*
.... *here Burgess-lane intersects*......
7 and 8 Vacant, 8*l.*, 13*l.*
9 Cullen, Mrs. dairy, 12*l.*
.... *here Queen-street intersects*.........
Weigh-house No. 5, 6*l.*
10 & 11 Doyle, James, and Son, coach factory
12 Hackett, William, & Son, farming implement manufacturers, 12*l.*
  „ Bergin, Jeremiah, factor
13 Vacant, 5*l.*
14 Tenements, 15*l.*
15 Osborne, G. T. & Co. corn, hay and potato factors, 6*l.*

3 N.—Hendrick-lane.
From Benburb-street to Hendrick-place.
P. St. Paul.—Arran-quay W.

1 and 2 Tenements, 6*l.* 10*l.*
3 O'Brien, James, car owner, 7*l.*
4 and 5 Vacant, 35*l.*
.... *here Hendrick-street intersects*......
6 Tenements, 2*l.*
7 Tenements
8 Tenements, 2*l.*
9 Devine, Mrs. provision dealer
10 and 11 M'Govern, M. grocer

3 N.—Hendrick-street.
From Queen-street to Hendrick-place.
P. St. Paul.—Arran-quay W.

1 to 4 Tenements, 12*l.*, 4*l.*, 9*l.*
5 Baird, Mr. John, 9*l.*
6 to 11 Tenements, 11*l.* to 15*l.*
12 Fletcher, Wm. upholsterer, 11*l.*
METHODIST CHURCH — Rev. R. Hazelton, minister
.... *here Hendrick-lane intersects*......
14 Tenements
15 Tenements, 12*l.*
16, 17, & 18 Judd, Brothers, hide and sheep skin tanners, 40*l.*
19 to 23 Tenements, 6*l.* to 21*l.*
24 Clarke, George, stores, 11*l.*

Extract from the Directory of Residents of Dublin Streets from *Thom's Official Directory of the United Kingdom of Great Britain and Ireland* for 1893. Also shown is the street location, the registration district for Birth, Deaths, and Marriages, and the house valuation.

1904

TRADES' DIRECTORY.

Benson, Charles W. 24 Rathmines road
Brown, Thomas, 48 Serpentine avenue, Sandymount
Catholic University School, 89 Leeson street, lower
Civil Service Academy, 15 Buckingham street, upper
Civil Service Academy, 46 George's st. gt. nth.—Hamilton Bell, principal
Civil Service College, 29 Gardiner's place
Collegiate Institute, 2 Leinster rd. Rathmines—W. H. Collison
Collegiate and General School, Roland Johnson, 53 Charles street, great
Crawley, William J. Chetwode, B.A., LL.D. (T.C.D.) Queen's Service Academy, 3 Ely place
Donne, Edward Wm. 157 Rathgar road
Dublin Civil Service College, 29 Gardiner's place—John Bates
French College, Castledawson, Williamstown
German School, 6 Wilton terrace
Hardwicke School, 33 Hardwicke st.— Samuel Bowden
Harricks, James T. 4 Leeson st. upper
High School of Erasmus Smith, 40 Harcourt street
Macklin's School, 41 Molesworth street
Military College, 30 Upper Merrion st.
Queen's Service Academy, 3 Ely place
Rice, Rev. James, Monkstown
Santry School, Santry
St. Columba College, Whitechurch, Rathfarnham
Smith, Erasmus, Brunswick street, great
Sullivan, Daniel T. A 79 Gardiner st. lower
Wesley College, 94 Stephen's green, sth.

Servants' Registry Offices.

Bates, Mrs. E. 17 Anne street, south
Bates, Mrs. jun. 11 Anne street, south
Blackwood, Mrs. 41 Mount street, lower
Clements, Mrs. 4 Anne street, south
English, Mrs. 22 Camden street, upper
Freeman's Journal, 96½ Grafton street
Hormell, Mrs. Elizabeth, 30 Dawson st.
Johnston, Mrs. 32 Aungier street
Leahy, M. 29 Pembroke street, lower
Louth, Sophia, 50 Aungier street
Malcolm, Mrs. 108 Abbey street, mid.
O'Donnell, Mrs. 31 Eccles street
Rippart, Miss M. 7 Gloucester street, lr.
Smith, Mrs. 13 Kildare street
Watson, Mrs. 19 Stephen's green, nth.
White, Mrs. 2 Lincoln place
Woods, Mrs. E. 1 Duke street

Sewed Muslin Manufacturers.

Chambers, Son, and Co. 4 Sackville st. up.
Cochrane, S. A. 21 D'Olier street
Cochrane, Robert, Skerries

Sewing Machine Agents.

Bradbury & Co. (limited), 5 Sth. Anne st.
Edmundson & Co. 33 to 36 Capel street
Howe Machine Co.
Hughes, Brothers, 23 Dawson street
Kinsley, Charles, 5 Whitefriar street
Murphy, Thomas, 24 Stafford street
Pim, Brothers, & Co. 75 George's st. sth.
Singer Company, 69 Grafton street
Todd, Burns & Co. 47 Mary street
Wheeler and Wilson, 139 Stephen's green, west

Ship Builders.

Bewley, Webb, and Co. North wall
Marshall, Henry, Ringsend
Pennie, Thomas. F. 143 Brunswick st. great

Ship Chandlers.

Eckford & Co. 3 and 4 City quay, and 24 Moss street
Merritt, Wm. J. 4 Rogerson's quay

Shipping Agents.

Baird, William, & Co. 16 Beresford pl.
Betson and Co. 20 Eden quay
Carolin and Egan, 30 Eden quay
Corvini, Signor Gustavo, 21 Eden quay
Gibbs, John and Son, 1 Eden quay
Graham, James, 6 Eden quay
Mackenzie, A. and Co. 204 Brunswick street, great
Murphy, Wm. 9 Sackville street
O'Dell, Thos. Sons, & Co. 12 Eden quay
O'Meara, John B. 16 Rogerson's quay
Wallace, Brothers, 32 City quay
Wells and Holahan, 6 Eden quay

Shirt Makers and Outfitters.

(See also Outfitters.)

Baker, Mrs., 33 Ormond quay, lower
Beattie, Andrew, 70 Grafton street
Bergin and Keogh, 19 Sackville st. low.
Buckham, Robert, 14 Sackville street lr.
Callaghan and Co. 10 Earl street, north
Clarke, B. J. 3 Lincoln pl. & 2 Henry st.
Duncan, W. 104 Talbot street
Grandy, George, 13 Stephen's green
Hawksby, F.W. & Co. 28 Sackville st. up.
Heather, George, 15 and 16 Arran quay, and 1 Lincoln lane
Hickey, John, 8 Earl street, north
M'Crea, Edward D. & Sons, 51 William street
M'Mahon & Co. 4 D'Olier st.
Seale, E. and W. 4 & 98 Grafton street
Sparrow & Co. 16 George's street, south
Taaffe and Cogswell, 81 Grafton street
Wilson, J. & W. Nassau street

Shoemakers.—(See Boot.)

Shoemakers' Grindery Shops.

Condon, Catherine, 16 Stephen street, up.
Delcambre and Co. 13 Capel street
Dillon, Owen, 78 Aungier street
Loug, R. J. 16 Capel street
Murphy, Edward, 37 Francis street
Stanley, Thomas and Sons, 17 Exchange street, lower

Shutters, Iron Revolving.

Carthy, Mrs. 10 St. Andrew street
O'Hara, Francis, 17 Aungier street

Silk Manufacturers.

Boland, Michael, 37 Chamber street
Ivers, Thomas, 51 Newmarket

Silk Mercers.

Arnott & Co. (limited), 11 to 15 Henry st.
Atkinson, Richard, & Co. 31 College gn.
Boyle, Thomas, 41 Grafton street
Brown, Thomas, & Co. 15 to 17 Grafton st.
Cameron, Alexander, 73 Grafton street
Clery and Co. (formerly M'Swiney and Co.), 23 to 27 Sackville street, lower
Foley, T. F. 30 Sackville street, lower
Forrest, James, & Sons, 101 Grafton st.
Henry Street Warehouse, The (ltd.), 59 to 62 Henry street
Manning, Alfred, 103 Grafton street
Matthews, George E. 49 Sackville st. up.
M'Birney & Co. 14 to 18 Aston's quay
M'Nally and Co. 105 George's street, up. Kingstown
Nickson, John, & Co. 10 Westmoreland st.
Ogilvy, Alexander, 13 Grafton street
O'Reilly, Dunne, & Co. 30 College green

Pim, Brothers, and Co. 70 to 88 George's street, great, south
Sims, Fred. 51 Dawson street
Stamp, J. 45 Grafton street
Switzer & Co. (limited), 92 Grafton street
Todd, Burns, and Co. 47 Mary street

Silversmiths.—(See Jewellers.)

Size and Glue Manufacturers.—(See Glue.)

Skinners.

(See Tanners.)

Slate, Flag, Brick, and Tile Merchants.

Brooks, Thomas, and Co. 4 Sackville pl.
Butler, Edward, 7 Cuffe lane
Byrne, John, 16 Bride street
Caffrey, J. A. Inchicore road, Chapelizod
Connolly, Thos. & Jas. 37 Dominick st. up.
Fitzsimon, Jas. & Son, 15 Bridgefoot st.
Flood, Michl. & Co. 105 Gloucester st. lr
Furlong, P. T. 138 Brunswick st. great
Graham, Wm. 3 Beresford place
Kelly, Joseph, 66 and 67 Thomas street
Lovely and Co. 150 Townsend street
M'Dowall, D. 22 to 28 Montgomery street
M'Ferran, J. and Co. 4 Beresford place
M'Kay, M'Donnell & Co. 7 Anglesea st.
Martin, T. and C. 76 North Wall quay
Monsell, Mitchell, & Co. 73 Townsend st.
Moyers, George, 47 Richmond st. south
O'Donohoe, Thomas, 12 Ross lane
O'Leary, E. M. 21 Townsend street
Robinson, W. J. 13 Eden quay
Tickell, Thomas, 193 King street, north

Slaters.

Collins, John, 61 Bridgefoot street
Donohoe, Arthur and Son, 5 Essex st. w.
Donohoe, James, 40 Cumberland st. nth.
Foster, William, 8 Peter street
Haskins, Wm. 3 St. Kevin's parade
Harrison, Wm. 7 Mercer street, lower
Keegan, James, 17 Harmony row
Lenehan, Thomas, 21 Braithwaite street
Moran, Patrick, 2 Phibsboro' avenue
Peake, Joseph, 11 Charlemont street
Pewris, Thomas, 26 Temple bar
Rutledge, Robert, 51 Francis street
Shannon, James, 7 Patrick street
Sherman, James, Little Bray
Short, J. 90 Dorset street, upper
Taaffe, J. 114 Seville place
White, John, 29 Dorset street, upper

Smiths and Bell Hangers.

Baker, P. 9 Forbes's street
Beddy, Henry, 22 Abbey street. up.
Cavanagh, John, 1 Tyrone place
Clarke and Byrne, 106 King street, north
Crooke, James, 22 Hanbury lane
Crosier, James, 25 Barrack street
Curtis, Bros. 10 Suffolk street
Daniel, Patrick & Sons, 44 Grafton street
Doyle, John, 7 Camden row
Edmundson and Co. 33 Capel street
Fagan, James, and Sons, 18 Brunswick street, great
Healy, T. 24 Commons street
Hopson, Edward and Son, 2 Yarnhall st.
M'Cann, Christopher, 39 Kevin st. upper
Maguire and Son, 10 Dawson street
O'Keeffe, Anthony, 65 Marlborough st.
Quinn, John, 36 Mountpelier hill
Quinn, Patrick, 7 Rathgar road

Extract from the Dublin Trade's Directory in *Thom's Official Directory of the United Kingdom of Great Britain and Ireland* for 1893.

Parish Address: Rev. Philip Kelly, PP, Parochial House, Meath Street, Dublin 8

Civil Parish: **St. George**
RC Parish: St. James
Diocese: DU
Earliest Record: b. 9.1742; m. 1754
Missing Dates: b. 9.1798-1.1803; m. 1755-10.1804
Parish Address: Rev. Gerald Healy, PP, Parochial House, James' Street, Dublin 8

Civil Parish: **St. John**
RC Parish: see St. Michael

Civil Parish: **St. Luke**
RC Parish: see St. Nicholas Without

Civil Parish: **St. Mark**
RC Parish: mainly St. Andrew

Civil Parish: **St. Mary (1)**
RC Parish: St. Mary's Pro-Cathedral; also part St. Michan
Diocese: DU
Earliest Record: b. 1734; m. 1734
Parish Address: Presbytery, 83 Marlboro Street, Dublin 1

Civil Parish: **St. Mary (2)**
RC Parish: Seville Place; also North William Street, see below (see St. Mary for earlier records)
Diocese: DU
Earliest Record: b. 7.1853; m. 6.1856
Parish Address: Rev. John Stokes, PP, Parochial House, Seville Place, Dublin 1

Civil Parish: **St. Mary (3)**
RC Parish: North William Street, see St. Mary for earlier records
Diocese: DU
Earliest Record: b. 12.1852; m. 1.1853
Parish Address: Rev. Michael Smythe, CC, Presbytery, North William Street, Dublin 1

Civil Parish: **St. Michael**
RC Parish: Michael and John
Diocese: DU
Earliest Record: (index from 1743 to 1842) b. 1.1768; m. 1.1784

Parish Address: Rev. Oscar O'Leary, PP, Adam and Eve, Merchant's Quay, Dublin 8

Civil Parish: **St. Michan**
RC Parish: St. Michan; also part St. Paul
Diocese: DU
Earliest Record: b. 1725; m. 1725
Parish Address: Rev. Donal O'Mahony, PP, Parochial House, Halston Street, Dublin 7

Civil Parish: **St. Nicholas Within**
RC Parish: part Michael and John, see St. Michael; part St. Nicholas Without

Civil Parish: **St. Nicholas Without (1)**
RC Parish: St. Nicholas Without; also Harrington St., see below
Diocese: DU
Earliest Record: b. 1.1742; m. 9.1767
Missing Dates: b. 8.1752-1.1767; m. 12.1801-11.1824
Parish Address: Rev. Desmond O' Beirne, PP, Parochial House, Francis Street, Dublin 8

Civil Parish: **St. Nicholas Without (2)**
RC Parish: Harrington St.
Diocese: DU
Earliest Record: b. 1865
Parish Address: Rev. D. O'Neill, PP, Parochial House, Harrington Street, Dublin 8

Civil Parish: **St. Patrick**
RC Parish: see St. Nicholas Without

Civil Parish: **St. Paul (1)**
RC Parish: St. Paul; also part St. Michan
Diocese: DU
Earliest Record: b. 1731; m. 1731
Parish Address: Rev. Donal O'Mahony, PP, Parochial House, Halston Street, Dublin 7

Civil Parish: **St. Paul (2)**
RC Parish: Cabra, see St. Paul for earlier records
Diocese: DU
Earliest Record: b. 1909; m. 1856
Parish Address: Rev. John Moroney, PP, 116 New Cabra Road, Dublin 7

Civil Parish: **St. Peter**
RC Parish: part St. Michael and St. John; part
St. Nicholas Without; part St. Andrew

Civil Parish: **St. Thomas'**
RC Parish: see St. Mary

Civil Parish: **St. Werburgh**
RC Parish: Michael and John, see St. Michael

Commercial and Social Directories

1751
Wilson's *Alphabetical List of Names and
Places of Abode of the Merchants and Traders
of the City of Dublin.*

1752
Similar list published as supplement to
Gentleman's & Citizen's Almanac. Further
edition in 1753.

1755
Merchants and traders list in *Gentlemans &
Citizens Almanac* (renamed the *Treble Almanac* in 1787). Lists of lawyers and medical
practitioners were also added and lists of city
officials, faculty of the College of Surgeons
and Physicians, clergy and city guild officers.
A list of nobility and gentry was added in 1815
and gradually enlarged from then on. Issued
annually to 1837.

1820
J. Pigot's *Commercial Directory of Ireland*
contains information on the gentry, nobility,
and traders in and around Dublin.

1824
J. Pigot's *City of Dublin & Hibernian Provincial Directory* includes traders, nobility,
gentry, and clergy lists of Dublin, Howth,
Lucan, and Swords.

1834
Pettigrew and Oulton's *Dublin Almanac &
General Register of Ireland* has lists of merchants and traders of various other
categories. It also has a list of residents of
each of the main streets . The residents of
rented houses, of which there were many,

were generally not listed, these premises
being referred to as tenements. The scope of
the directory was gradually increased over
the years to include the suburbs. Issued annually to 1849.

1844
Alexander Thom's *Irish Almanac & Official
Directory* has the same categories of lists as
Pettigrew and Oulton. It expanded annually
rapidly to include the Dublin suburbs. Issued
annually to present.

1846
Slater's *National Commercial Directory of
Ireland* lists nobility, clergy, traders, etc., in
Balbriggan and Skerries, Blackrock,
Booterstown, Dalkey, Dublin, Howth,
Kingstown (Dun Laoghaire), Monkstown,
Swords, Malahide, and Williamstown.

1850
Henry Shaw's *New City Pictorial Directory of
Dublin City* has a list of residents of the main
streets, an alphabetical list of residents, and
lists of attorneys and barristers. It also has
interesting line drawings of the street fronts
showing shop names, etc.

1856
Slater's *Royal National Commercial Direc-
tory of Ireland* lists nobility, gentry, clergy,
traders, etc., in Balbriggan and Skerries,
Dublin and Kingstown (Dun Laoghaire),
Howth, Swords, and Malahide.

1870
Slater's *Directory of Ireland* contains trade,
nobility, and clergy lists for Balbriggan and
Skerries, Dalkey, Dublin, Dundrum, Howth,
Rathfarnham, Swords, and Malahide.

1881
Slater's *Royal National Commercial Directory of Ireland* contains lists of traders, clergy, nobility, and farmers in adjoining
parishes of the towns of Balbriggan and Skerries, Donabate and Malahide, Dublin,
Howth and Baldoyle, Rathfarnham, and
Swords.

1894
Slater's *Royal National Directory of Ireland*
lists traders, police, teachers, farmers, and

private residents in Dublin city and in each of the towns, villages, and parishes of the county.

Family History

A Genealogical History of the Family of Sirr of Dublin. London, 1903.

"A Moorhouse Family of Dublin, Carlow, and Kildare." *Ir. Anc.* 9 (1) (1977): 15-18.

"Acton Papers" (Stradbrook, Co. Dublin). *Anal. Hib.* 25: 3-13.

"An Early Dublin Candlemaker: History of the Family of Rathborne, Chandlers, Dublin." *Dublin Hist. Record* 14 (1957): 66-73.

"Arnoldi of Dublin, 27 Entries in the Family Bible." *J. Ass. Pres. Mem. Dead* 8 (1910-12): 71.

"Barnewall." *Ir. Gen.* 5 (2) (1975): 181-85.

"The Barnewalls of Turvey." *Reportorium* 1 (2) (1956): 336-41.

"The Bathes of Drumcondra." *Reportorium* 1 (2) (1956): 328-30.

"The Brocas Family, Notable Dublin Artists." *University Review* 2 (6) (1959): 17-25.

"Cusack Family of Meath and Dublin." *Ir. Gen.* 5 (3) (1976): 298-313; 5 (4) (1977): 464-70; 5 (5) (1978): 591-600; 5 (6) 1979: 673-84; 6 (2) (1981): 130-53; 6 (3) (1982): 285-98.

"Dix Family of Dublin, Entries from Family Bible." *J. Ass. Pres. Mem. Dead* 11 (1921-25): 490.

"The Dexters of Dublin and Annfield, Co. Kildare." *Ir. Anc.* 2 (1) (1970): 31-42.

"Fagans of Feltrim." *Reportorium* 2 (1) (1958): 103-06.

"The Falkiners of Abbotstown, Co. Dublin." *J. Kildare Arch. Hist. Soc.* 8 (1915-17): 331-63.

"The Fitz Rerys, Welsh Lords of Cloghran, Co. Dublin." *J. Louth Arch. Soc.* 5 (1921): 13-17.

"The Fitzwilliams of Merrion." *Reportorium* 2 (1) 1958: 88-96.

Genealogical Memoir of the Family of Talbot of Malahide, Co. Dublin. 1829.

"King's Printers. Notes on the Family of Grierson of Dublin." *Ir. Gen.* 2 (1953): 303-37.

"The Hollywoods of Artane." *Reportorium* 1 (2) 1956: 341-44.

"Kingsbury of Dublin." Pedigree in *Swanzy Notebooks.* RCB Library, Dublin.

"Law Family of Dublin." Pedigree. *J. Ass. Pres. Mem. Dead* 11 (1921-25): 444.

"The Lawless Family." *Reportorium* 1 (2) (1956): 344-50.

Bigger, F. *The Magees of Belfast and Dublin.* Belfast, 1916.

"Moore of Rutland Square, Dublin." Pedigree in *Swanzy Notebooks.* RCB Library, Dublin.

"Notes on the Cooke, Ashe and Swift Families, All of Dublin." *J. Ass. Pres. Mem. Dead* 9 (1912-16): 503.

"Nottinghams of Ballyowen." *Reportorium* 1 (2) 1956: 323-24.

"Pemberton of Dublin." *Ir. Anc.* 11 (1) (1979): 14-26.

"The Plunketts of Dunsoghly." *Reportorium* 1 (2) (1956): 330-36.

"Plunketts of Portmarnock." *Reportorium* 2 (1) (1958): 106-08.

"The Scurlocks of Rathcredan." *Reportorium* 1 (1) (1955): 79-80.

"Segraves of Cabra." *Reportorium* 1 (2) (1956): 324-28.

"Talbot de Malahide." *Reportorium* 2 (1) (1958): 96-103.

"The Talbots of Belgard." *Reportorium* 1 (1) (1955): 80-83.

Tweedy, Owen. *The Dublin Tweedys: The Story of an Irish Family 1650-1882.* London, 1956.

Tyrrell, J.H. *Genealogical History of the Tyrrells of Castleknock in Co. Dublin, Fertullagh in Co. Westmeath, and Now of Grane Castle, Co. Meath.* London, 1904.

"The Tyrrells of Castleknock." *R.S.A.I.* 76 (1946): 151-54.

"The Wolverstons of Stillorgan." *Reportorium* 2 (2) (1960): 243-45.

Gravestone Inscriptions

Chapelizod: *Ir. Gen.* 5 (4) (1977): 490-505.

Cloghran: Adams, Rev. Benjamin W. *History and Description of Santry and Cloghran Parishes.* 1883.

Dalkey: *Ir. Gen.* 5 (2) (1975): 250-55.

Dublin City: Finlayson, Rev. *Inscriptions on the Monuments . . . in Christ Church Cathedral.* Dublin, 1878. "St. Andrew's, Westland Row" (names on coffin plates). *Ir. Gen.* 5 (1) (1974): 131-39. "SS. Michael & John" (names on coffin plates). *Ir. Gen.* 5 (3) (1976): 368-69. "St. Paul (CI)." *R.S.A.I.* 104 (1974).

Esker: *Ir. Gen.* 6 (1): 54-58.

Kilbride: *Ir. Gen.* 6 (3): 378-81.

Kilmactalway: *Ir. Gen.* 6 (3): 378-81.

Kilmahuddrick: *Ir. Gen.* 6 (3): 378-81.

Killiney (old Graveyard): *Ir. Gen.* 4 (6) (1973): 647-48.

Kill o' the Grange: *Ir. Gen.* 4 (5) (1972): 507-14.

Leixlip: *Ir. Gen.* 4 (2) (1969): 110-16.

Loughtown Lower: *Ir. Gen.* 6 (3): 378-81.

Lucan: *Ir. Gen.* 5 (6) (1976): 763-67.

Monkstown: *Ir. Gen.* 4 (3) (1970): 201-02; 4 (4) 1971.

Newcastle: *Ir. Gen.* 6 (2) (1981): 219-26.

Palmerstown: *Ir. Gen.* 4 (5) (1978): 650-53.

Rathcoole: *Ir. Gen.* 6 (4) (1983): 523-25.

Santry: Adams, Rev. Benjamin W. *History and Description of Santry and Cloghran Parishes.* 1883.

Tallaght: *Ir. Gen.* 4 (1) (1968): 29-36.

Taney: Ball, F. Elrington. *The Parish of Taney.* 1895.

Newspapers

Arguably the best Dublin newspapers for the eighteenth century are *Faulkner's Dublin Journal,* the *Freemans Journal, Dublin Hibernian Journal,* and the *Dublin Evening Post.* In the nineteenth century further useful papers began publication including the *Dublin Morning Post, Dublin Evening Herald,* and *Dublin Evening Mail.* A card index to biographical notices in *Faulkner's Dublin Journal* from 1763-71 is held in the National Library of Ireland.

Title: *Constitution and Church Sentinel*
Published in: Dublin, 1849-53
BL Holdings: 4.1849-5.1853

Title: *Dublin Courant*
Published in: Dublin, 1702-25; N.S. 1744-50
NLI Holdings: odd numbers 1703, 1705; 6.1744-2.1752; many issues missing
BL Holdings: odd numbers 1718-20, 22, 1.1723-12.1725; 4.1744-3.1750

Title: *Correspondent*
Published in: Dublin, 1806-61
Note: continued as *Dublin Correspondent* in 1822; *Evening Packet and Correspondent* in 1828; *Evening Packet* in 1860
NLI Holdings: 11.1806-12.1861
BL Holdings: 11.1806-4.1810; odd numbers 1810-11, 1813-16, 1820; 1-12.1823; odd numbers 1825, 26

Title: *Dublin Chronicle*
Published in: Dublin, 1762-1817
Note: breaks in publication
NLI Holdings: 1.1770-12.1771; 5.1787-12.1793; odd numbers 6.1815-1817
BL Holdings: 5.1787-4.1792; 5-12.1793

Title: *Dublin Evening Mail* (continued as *Evening Mail*)
Published in: Dublin, 1823-1962
NLI Holdings: 2.1823-7.1962
BL Holdings: 2.1823-2.1928

Title: *Dublin Evening Post*
Published in: Dublin, 1732-37 and 1778-1875
NLI Holdings: 6.1732-1.1737; 2.1778-8.1875
BL Holdings: 6.1732-7.1734; 7.1737-7.1741; 8.1778-7.1753; 10.1783-12.1785; 1787; 1789; 1792; 1794; 5-6.1795;1.1796-12.1797; 1.1804-12.1810; odd numbers 1813, 14; 1.1815-8.1875

Title: *Dublin Gazette* (continued as *Iris Oifiguil*)
Published in: Dublin, 1705-current
Note: government notices only
NLI Holdings: 11.1706-12.1727; 3.1729-4.1744;
   6.1756-12.1759; 1760; 1762; 1763; 1765; 1766;
   1767; 1-7.1775; 1776-88; 1790-1921

Title: *Dublin Gazette and Weekly Courant*
Published in: Dublin, 1703-28
NLI Holdings: odd numbers 1708

Title: *Dublin Intelligence*
Published in: Dublin, 1690-1725 (at various
   times under different managements)
NLI Holdings: 9.1690-5.1693
BL Holdigs: odd numbers 1708-12, 1723-25

Title: *Dublin Journal* (see *Faulkner's Dublin
   Journal*).

Title: *Dublin Mercury* (continued as *Hoey's
   Dublin Mercury* in 1770)
Published in: Dublin, 1704-75
NLI Holdings: 12.1722-5.1724; 1-9.1726; 1-
   9.1742; 3-9.1770; 9.1770-4.1773
BL Holdings: 1-9.1742; 3.1766-4.1773

Title: *Dublin Morning Post* (continued as *Car-
   ricks Morning Post* in 1804-21)
Published in: Dublin, c. 1804-32
NLI Holdings: 4.1814-1831
BL Holdings: odd numbers 1824-26; 1.1830-
   5.1832

Title: *Evening Freeman*
Published in: Dublin, 1831-71
NLI Holdings: 8.1831-7.1836; 4-12.1844; 1845-
   9.1847; odd numbers 1848; 2.1858-59
BL Holdings: 1.1831-6.1871

Title: *Evening Irish Times*
Published in: Dublin, c. 1860-1921
NLI Holdings: 4.1896-3.1900; 7.1900-3.1901;
   7.1901-1907; 1911-6.1915
BL Holdings: 10.1880-10.1921

Title: *Evening Herald*
Published in: Dublin, 1786-1814; new series
   1891-in progress
NLI Holdings: 5.1786-12.1789; 1.1806-12.1809;
   odd numbers 1810; 1.1812-6.1814

BL Holdings: 5.1786-12.1789; odd numbers
   1807, 1813; 12.1891-in progress

Title: *Evening Packet* (incorporated with *Dublin
   Evening Mail*)
Published in: Dublin, 1828-62
BL Holdings: 1.1828-4.1929; 9.1829-3.1862

Title: *Evening Telegraph*
Published in: Dublin, 1871-1924
NLI Holdings: 10.1884-12.1924
BL Holdings: 7.1871-11.1873; 8.1875-5.1916;
   1.1919-12.1924

Title: *Faulkner's Dublin Journal*
Published in: Dublin, 1725-1825
NLI Holdings: 1.1726-7.1735; 5.1736-1782;
   1787-90; 1.1791-4.1825
BL Holdings: odd numbers 1726, 1739-40;
   3.1741; 8-12.1744; 3.1748-3.1750; 3.1751-
   12.1764; 12.1765-12.1768; odd numbers
   1782-84, 1792; 1-12.1796; odd numbers 1798,
   99, 1803; 10.1804-12.1810; odd numbers
   1813-14, 1817; 12.1819-12.1821

Title: *Freeman's Journal* or *Public Register*
Published in: Dublin, 1763-1924
BL Holdings: odd numbers 1763-67; 9.1767-
   9.1775; 12.1775-6.1777; odd numbers 1779-
   1780; 9.1782-6.1753; 11.1783-12.1784; odd
   numbers 1823, 24; 1.1830-12.1833; 1.1837-
   12.1924

Title: *General Advertiser*
Published in: Dublin, 1804-1924
NLI Holdings: 9.1804-11.1820; odd numbers
   1837; 2.1841-12.1851; 1853-54, 1857-61;
   1864; 1866-67; 1869-70; 1874-12.1877;
   1.1880-1890; 1892-3.1924
BL Holdings: 10.1838-12.1840 (with gaps); odd
   numbers 1841, 1846; 12.1846-7.1914; 1.1915-
   12.1923

Title: *Impartial Occurrences* (continued as *Peu's
   Occurrences* in 1714)
Published in: Dublin, 1704-80
NLI Holdings: 12.1704-2.1706; 12.1718-1748;
   1751-1755; 1.1756-5.1757; 4-12.1768
BL Holdings: 1.1705-2.1706; odd numbers 1714,
   1719, 1740; 1.1741-12.1742; 1.1744-12.1749;
   1.1752-12.1753; 1.1756-12.1758; 1761

Title: *The Irish Times*
Published in: Dublin, 1859-current
Note: evening and weekly versions listed under
  Evening Irish Times and *Weekly Irish Times*
NLI Holdings: 3.1859-in progress
BL Holdings: 3.1859-in progress (except part of
  11.1871

Title: *Kingstown Gazette*
Published in: Kingstown Dun Laoghaire, old
  series 1857-58; new series 1868-69
BL Holdings: 12.1857-1.1858; 5.1868-7.1869

Title: *Magee's Weekly Packet*
Published in: Dublin, 1777-93
NLI Holdings: 6.1777-3.1895; 3.1787-8.1790;
  8.1792-8.1793
BL Holdings: 6-10.1777; 11.1777-3.1785; odd
  numbers to 1793

Title: *Morning Mail*
Published in: Dublin, 1870-1912
NLI Holdings: 2.1870-12.1883
BL Holdings: 3.1871-6.1880; 12.1896-8.1912
  (with gaps)

Title: *Morning Register*
Published in: Dublin, 1824-43
NLI Holdings: 10.1824-1.1843
BL Holdings: 10.1824-1.1843

Title: *Nation* (continued as *Daily Nation* and
  Weekly Nation)
Published in: Dublin, 1842-1900
NLI Holdings: 10.1842-7.1891; 6.1896-9.1900
BL Holdings: 10.1824-7.1848; 9.1849-7.1891;
  6.1896-9.1900

Title: *Patriot* (continued as *Statesman and
  Patriot* in 1828)
Published in: Dublin, c.1810-29
NLI Holdings: 7.1810-1815; 1818-10.1828;
  11.1829-5.1829
BL Holdings: 1.1823-10.1828

Title: *Saunder's Newsletter* (continued as
  Saunder's Irish Daily News in 1878)
Published in: Dublin, 1755-1879
NLI Holdings: odd numbers 1767-91; 3.1773-
  12.1787; 1.1789-3.1795; 2.1796-12.1802;

4.1804-12.1806; 1.1808-11.1809; 1812-18;
  1820-11.1879
BL Holdings: 3.1773-12.1787; 1789; 1.1793-
  12.1794; 1795; 1.1797-12.1811; 1.1813-
  12.1815; 1.1817-11.1879

Title: *The Warder* (continued as *Sport's Mail* and
  Irish Weekly Mail in 1921)
Published in: Dublin, 1821-1939
NLI Holdings: 3.1821-9.1938
BL Holdings: 3.1822-9.1939 (except 1930)

Title: *Weekly Freeman's Journal* (continued as
  Weekly Freeman, National Press, and *Irish
  Agriculturist* in 1892)
Published in: Dublin, c.1817-1924
NLI Holdings: 1-7.1818; 3-7.1830; 1.1834-
  4.1840; 6.1880-12.1882; 5.1883-3.1892;
  4.1892-12.1893; 1.1895-12.1913; 6.1914-
  12.1924
BL Holdings: 10.1821-12.1831; 1.1838-3.1892;
  4.1892-12.1924

Title: *Weekly Irish Times* (continued as *Times
  Pictorial* in 1941)
Published in: Dublin, 1875-1941
NLI Holdings: odd numbers 1875; 1.1883-
  6.1886; 1.1906-11.1941
BL Holdings: 6.1875-12.1920; 1.1922-11.1941

Wills and Administrations

A discussion of the types of records, where
they are held, their availability, and value is
given in the Wills section of the Introduction.
The availability of prerogative wills, administrations, and marriage license records is also
described in the relevant parts of the same section. Where available, published sources of
these records are given in the Miscellaneous
Sources section.

Pre-1858 Wills and Administrations

Prerogative Wills. see p. xli
Consistorial Wills. County Dublin is entirely in
  the diocese of Dublin. The guide to Catholic
  parish records in this chapter shows the

diocese to which each civil parish belonged. The wills of residents of each diocese were usually proven within that diocese (see the Wills section for exceptions). The following records survive:

Wills. see p. xxxvii
Abstracts. see p. xxxvii
Indexes. Dublin and Glendalough (1536-1858) published in the appendices to the 26th and 30th reports of the DKPRI of 1895 and 1899 respectively.

Post-1858 Wills and Administrations

Dublin County was served by the District Registry of Dublin (Principal Registry). The surviving records are kept in the PRO.

Other collections include:

Lane-Poole Papers Containing Dublin and Wicklow Abstracts. NLI Ms. 5359
Quaker Wills from Dublin and East Leinster. Society of Friends Library, Dublin.

Marriage Licenses

Indexes. Dublin (1672) PRO; SLC 100867 Original Bonds, Dublin (1749-1813) indexed by males, surnames beginning with A only. PRO; SLC 101770
Abstracts. Fisher's Abstracts (1638-1800), indexed separately for bride and groom, by surname, gives groom's name, address, bride's name and address, and date of marriage: GO MS 134-38. Listing of Dublin (1638-1800). Phillip's listing, by both bride and grooms' surnames of all marriage licenses granted, and intended place of marriage. GO MS 473-75. SLC 100227.

Miscellaneous Sources

Ball, F.E. *History of County Dublin.* 4 vols. Dublin, 1920. Reprint. 1979.
D'Alfon, J. *The History of Co. Dublin.* Dublin, 1838. Reprint. Cork, 1976.
Gilbert, J. *A History of the City of Dublin.* 3 vols. Reprint. Dublin, 1972.

"The Huguenots in Dublin." *Dublin Hist. Rec.* 8 (1945-46): 110-34.
"The Manor of Lucan and the Restoration Land Settlement, 1660-1688." *Dublin Hist. Rec.* 21 (1966-67): 139-43.
"Succession Lists of Parish Priests in Dublin Diocese 1771-1960." *Dublin Hist. Rec.* 3 (1) (1962): 178-90.
Warburton, J.W., Rev. J. Whitelaw, and Rev. R. Walsh. *A History of the City of Dublin.* 1818.

Research Sources and Services

Journals

Dublin Historical Record

Reportorium Novum (Dublin Diocesan History)

Libraries and Information Sources

Dublin Public Libraries (twenty-seven branches in Dublin city, and ten in Dublin County) Gilbert Library, Pearse Street, Dublin 2 Ph: (01) 777662 (has the best collection of books on Dublin)

Dun Laoghaire Public Library, Lower Georges Street, Dun Laoghaire, Co. Dublin Ph: (01) 801254

National Library, Kildare Street, Dublin 2

Research Services

See research services in Dublin, p. xliv

Societies

Balbriggan Historical and Cultural Society, Ms. May McKeon, Sheemore, Market Green, Balbriggan, Co. Dublin

Clondalkin History Society, Miss Aileen Gourley, 11 Lealand, Bawnogue, Clondalkin, Co. Dublin

Dublin Family History Society, Synod Hall, Christchurch, St Michael's Hill, Dublin 2

Dublin Archaeological Society, Ms. Jane Behan, 54 Meadowbrook, Baldoyle, Dublin 13

Dun Laoghaire Borough Historical Society, Mr. Dermot Dwyer, 35 Gleneageary Woods, Dun Laoghaire, Co. Dublin

Foxrock Local History Club, Mr. Geoffrey Johnson, 74 Clonkeen Drive, Foxrock, Dublin 18

Lucan Historical Society, Mr. Glascott Symes, c/o The King's Hospital, Palmerston, Co. Dublin

Old Dublin Society, City Assembly House, 58 South William Street, Dublin 2 (publishers of *Dublin Historical Record*)

Rathmichael Historical Society, Ms. Gwendoline Guildford, 4 Springfield Park, Foxrock, Dublin 18

CIVIL PARISHES OF COUNTY DUBLIN

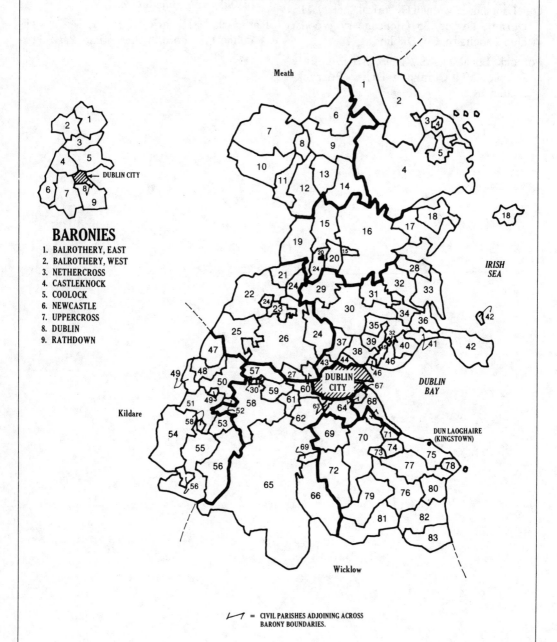

Meath

IRISH SEA

BARONIES

1. BALROTHERY, EAST
2. BALROTHERY, WEST
3. NETHERCROSS
4. CASTLEKNOCK
5. COOLOCK
6. NEWCASTLE
7. UPPERCROSS
8. DUBLIN
9. RATHDOWN

DUBLIN CITY

DUBLIN CITY

DUBLIN BAY

Kildare

DUN LAOGHAIRE
(KINGSTOWN)

Wicklow

= CIVIL PARISHES ADJOINING ACROSS
BARONY BOUNDARIES.

DUBLIN CITY AND ADJOINING PARISHES

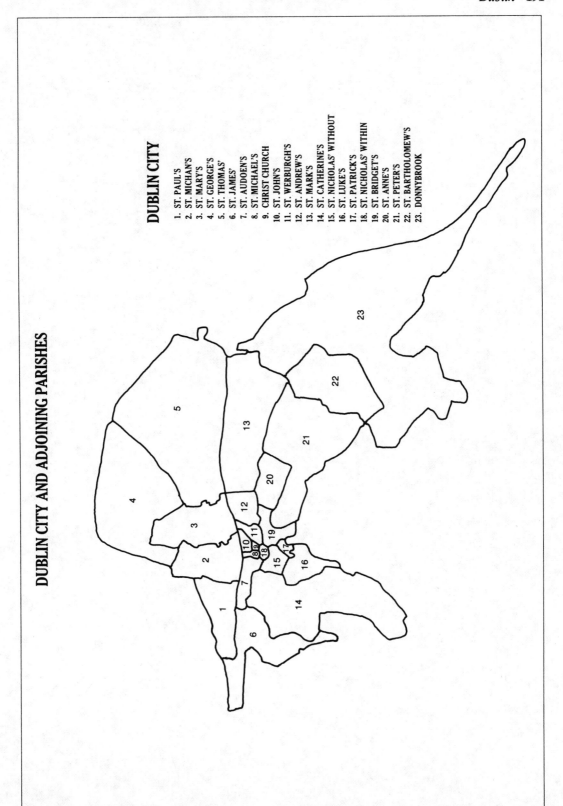

DUBLIN CITY

1. ST. PAUL'S
2. ST. MICHAN'S
3. ST. MARY'S
4. ST. GEORGE'S
5. ST. THOMAS'
6. ST. JAMES'
7. ST. AUDOEN'S
8. ST. MICHAEL'S
9. CHRIST CHURCH
10. ST. JOHN'S
11. ST. WERBURGH'S
12. ST. ANDREW'S
13. ST. MARK'S
14. ST. CATHERINE'S
15. ST. NICHOLAS' WITHOUT
16. ST. LUKE'S
17. ST. PATRICK'S
18. ST. NICHOLAS' WITHIN
19. ST. BRIDGET'S
20. ST. ANNE'S
21. ST. PETER'S
22. ST. BARTHOLOMEW'S
23. DONNYBROOK

County Fermanagh

A Brief History

This Ulster county contains the towns of Enniskillen, Kesh, Irvinestown, and Lisnaskea.

County Fermanagh was historically the territory of the Maguires and was partly in the Kingdom of Oriel. Other families associated with the county include Rooney (or Mulrooney), Muldoon, McKernan, Devine, McDonnell, Flanagan, Bannon, Owens, Fee, Corrigan, Hussey, Whelan, Corcoran, and Breslin.

In the twelfth and thirteenth centuries the Normans made several unsuccessful attempts to conquer Fermanagh. The Maguires and the other local chieftains allied themselves to the powerful O'Neills of Tyrone and remained independent for four centuries. From the beginning of the fourteenth century the Maguires dominated this territory. In the early sixteenth century they nominally submitted to the English crown, but in practice they retained control over the county.

Towards the end of the sixteenth century the English began making various administrative demands on the county and establishing administrators for various purposes. Accordingly, in 1593 the chief of the Maguires rebelled and expelled all the English from the county. He

later joined with O'Neill in the general Ulster rebellion.

After the defeat of the O'Neills and the emigration of most of the Ulster chieftains, Fermanagh was planted along with most of the Ulster counties. English and Scottish undertakers were appointed who obtained land in return for an "undertaking," to plant a specified number of English or Scottish famililes. Among the English undertakers were Flowerden, Blennerhassett, Archdale, Warde, Barton, Hunings, Wirral, Bogas, Calvert, and Sedborough. The Scottish undertakers included Hume, Hamilton, Gibb, Lindsey, Fowler, Dunbar, Balfour, Wishart, Moneypenny, Trayle, and Smelholme. Among the other families who obtained lands in the county at this time were ffoliot, Atkinson, Cole, Gore, Davys, Harrison, and Mistin. The O'Neills and Maguires and some of the other Gaelic families were also granted small portions of land.

Many of the native families either obtained lands in the county or else remained as tenants or servants on the planted lands. Many of those planted left again and the general picture was that the plantation was of mixed success in this county.

In 1641 the Maguires again led the county in support of the Catholic revolt and many of the new settlers were driven out or, in some cases, killed. Following the defeat of the rebellion, further lands in the county were confiscated and given to planters. The Brooke family got their lands at this time as well as Montgomery, Leonard, Wyatt, and Balfour.

Following the Williamite wars of the 1690s, the Fermanagh planters began to replace the native families with laborers from England and Scotland. Many of these left again, but nevertheless the county did gradually become more English and less Irish.

The 1609 plantation and the subsequent arrivals of laborers and farmers have introduced many English and Scottish names to the county. These include Johnson, Patterson, Armstrong, Morrison, Elliott, Graham, Irivine, Thompson, Noble, Carson, Forster, Hamilton, and Boyd.

In the eighteenth century the Penal Laws further deprived Catholics of lands and rights. Although primarily intended to restrict Catholic privileges, the laws also adversely affected the rights of Presbyterians. For this reason there was a steady emigration of Presbyterians, the so-called Scots-Irish, during this century. The origins of the inhabitants can, in very general terms, be shown by their religion as the natives are generally Catholic, the English Protestant, and the Scottish Presbyterian. In 1861, when religious persuasion was first determined in the census, the relative proportions of the three were 57, 38, and 2 percent respectively. Livingstone's history of the county gives an analysis of Fermanagh families from the voters list of 1962. The families are indicated as British(B), Gaelic (G), Gaelic names associated with Fermanagh (GF), or of mixed origin (M). The twenty-five most common families in 1962, in order of their abundance are: Maguire(GF), Johnston(B), Armstrong(B), MacManus(GF), Elliott(B), McCaffrey(GF), O'Reilly(G), Smith(M), Murphy(G), Graham(B), Irvine(B), Gallagher(G), Cassidy(GF), Owens(GF), Beatty(M), Thompson(B), MacBryan/Breen(GF), Noble(B), Duffy(G), Dolan(G), Morris(B), Woods(G), McElroy(GF), Monaghan(GF), and Corrigan(GF).

Census and Census Substitutes

1612-13
"Survey of Undertakers Planted in Fermanagh" (names, acreages allotted and account of the progress of each). *Hist. Mss. Comm. Rep.* (Hastings Mss.) 4 (1947): 159-82.

1625
"A Fermanagh Survey." *Clogher Record* 2 (2) (1958): 293-310 (account of the plantations; only major landholders named).

1631
Muster Roll. In *History of Enniskillen.* By W. C. Trimble, 198-219; SLC film 1341267; PRONI T934; BL add. ms. 4770.

1659
"Census" of Ireland. edited by S. Pender. Dublin:" Stationery Office, 1939; SLC film 924648.

1665
Hearth Money Roll. PRO film 2472; NLI ms. 9583.

The Roll for Barony of Lurg. *Clogher Record* 2 (1) (1957): 207-14.

1766
Religious Census of Parishes of Boho and Derryvullen. RCB Library; SLC film 100173, 258517.

Parishes of Devenish, Kinawley and Rossory. GO 536; SLC film 258517, 100173.

1770
Names of Resident Freeholders. NLI mss. 787-8.

1785
Male Protestants of 17 Years and Upwards in Clogher Diocese (civil parishes of Magheracloone and Trory). SLC film 258517.

1788
List of Freeholders. SLC film 100181; GO ms. 442; PRONI T543.

1796

See Co. Mayo 1796 (List of Catholics).

1821

Government Census Remnants: Parish of Aghalurcher (townlands of Altamartin, Altamullaboy, Altdark, Attyclenobrien, Aughavory, Augheetor, Carahoney, Cavanalack, Cleen, Colebrooke, Comaghy, Corlacky, Corrafat, Cran, Corkadreen, Currylongford, Derrintony, Derrychrum, Dordrany, Drumrock, Dunavoghy, Eshnasillog, Eshthomas, Feavanny, Foglish, Grogey, Killarbin, Killbawn, Lamphill, Legatillida, Lisavinick, Moughly, Mount Gibbon, Owenskerry, Ranult, Stripe, Tattenaheglish, Tattyreagh, Tereaghan, Tullaharney, Tullichanie, Tulnavarin), Parish of Derryvullen. PRO; SLC film 597733, 596418.

1823-37

Tithe Applotment Survey (see p. xxvii).

1832-37

"Voters (i.e., housholders and burgesses) in Enniskillen" (285 names). Reports from Committees. *Parl. Papers* 1837/38, 13 (2): Appendix 8.

"Names of £50, £20, and £10 Freeholders and Leaseholders in Fermanagh" (1,838 names). *Parl. Papers* 1837, 11 (1): Appendix A1, 7-21.

"List of Voters Registered in the Borough of Enniskillen." *Parl. Papers* 1837, 11 (2): 201-03. (284 names only).

1841 and 1851

Extracts from Government Census for Old Age Pension Claims. PRO; SLC film 258537.

1851

Extracts from Government Census for the Townland of Clonee, in Parish of Drumkeeran. PRO; SLC film 100858.

1862

Griffith's Valuation (see p. xxvii).

1901

Census. PRO.

1911

Census. PRO.

Church Records

Church of Ireland
(shows starting date of record)

Parish: **Aghadrum**
Existing Records: b. 1821; m. 1821; d. 1821
Status: LC

Parish: **Aghafurcher** (Lisnasken)
Existing Records: b. 1788; m. 1788; d. 1788
Status: LC

Parish: **Aghaveagh**
Existing Records: b. 1815; m. 1815; d. 1815
Status: LC

Parish: **Belleek**
Existing Records: b. 1822; m. 1822; d. 1822
Status: LC

Parish: **Bohoe**
Status: Lost

Parish: **Clabby**
Existing Records: b. 1862
Status: LC

Parish: **Cleenish**
Status: Lost

Parish: **Coolaghty**
Existing Records: b. 1835; m. 1844
Status: LC

Parish: **Derrybrusk**
Status: Lost

Parish: **Derryvullan North**
Existing Records: b. 1803; m. 1803; d. 1803
Status: LC

Parish: **Derryvullan South**
Statis: Lost

Parish: **Devenish**
Existing Records: b. 1800; m. 1800; d. 1800
Status: LC

Parish: **Drumkeeran**
Existing Records: b. 1801; m. 1801; d. 1801
Status: LC

Parish: **Drummully**
Existing Records: b. 1802; m. 1812; d. 1812
Status: LC

Parish: **Enniskillen**
Status: Lost

Parish: **Galloon**
Existing Records: b. 1798; m. 1798; d. 1798
Status: LC

Parish: **Garrison**
Status: Lost

Parish: **Garvary**
Status: Lost

Parish: **Innismacsaint**
Existing Records: b. 1813; m. 1813; d. 1813
Status: LC

Parish: **Killesher**
Existing Records: b. 1798; m. 1798; d. 1798
Status: LC

Parish: **Kiltumon**
Existing Records: b. 1861
Status: LC

Parish: **Kinawley**
Existing Records: b. 1761; m. 1761; d. 1761
Status: LC

Parish: **Lisbellaw**
Status: Lost

Parish: **Lisnaskea**
Existing Records: b. 1804; m. 1804; d. 1804
Status: LC

Parish: **Magheracross**
Existing Records: b. 1800; m. 1800; d. 1800
Status: LC

Parish: **Magheraculmoney**
Existing Records: b. 1767; m. 1767; d. 1767
Status: LC

Parish: **Maguires Bridge**
Existing Records: b. 1840; m. 1840; d. 1840
Status: LC

Parish: **Muckross**
Status: Lost

Parish: **Mullaghadun**
Status: Lost

Parish: **Mullaghfad**
Status: Lost

Parish: **Rossory**
Existing Records: b. 1799; m. 1799; d. 1799
Status: LC

Parish: **Sallaghy**
Status: Lost

Parish: **Slavin**
Status: Lost

Parish: **Templecarn**
Existing Records: b. 1825; m. 1825; d. 1825
Status: LC

Parish: **Tempo**
Existing Records: b. 1836; m. 1836; d. 1836
Status: LC

Parish: **Trory, St. Michael**
Existing Records: b. 1779; m. 1779; d. 1835
Status: LC

Presbyterian

Parish: **Enniskillen**
Starting Date: 1837

Parish: **Lisbellaw**
Starting Date: 1849

Parish: **Pettigo**
Starting Date: 1844

Roman Catholic

Civil Parish: **Aghalurcher**
Map Grid: 17
RC Parish: Aghalurcher (Lisnaskea)
Diocese: CG
Earliest Record: b. 10.1835
Parish Address: Rev. John McElroy, PP, Lisnaskea, Enniskillen, Co. Fermanagh

Civil Parish: **Aghavea**
Map Grid: 16
RC Parish: Aghavea or Aghintaine
Diocese: CG
Earliest Record: b. 3.1862; m. 5.1866
Parish Address: Rev. Patrick McCaughey, PP, Brookeboro, Enniskillen, Co. Fermanagh

Civil Parish: **Belleek**
Map Grid: 2
RC Parish: Templecarn (Pettigoe)
Diocese: CG
Earliest Record: b. 3.1851; m. 1.1836
Parish Address: Rev. Gerald McSorley, Pettigo, Co. Donegal

Civil Parish: **Boho**
Map Grid: 13
RC Parish: Derrygonnelly, see Devenish
Diocese: CG

Civil Parish: **Cleenish**
Map Grid: 14
RC Parish: Cleenish
Diocese: CG
Earliest Record: b. 12.1835; m. 4.1866
Missing Dates: b. 9.1839-2.1859
Parish Address: Rev. Kevin Slowey, PP, Arney, Enniskillen, Co. Fermanagh

Civil Parish: **Clones** (see also Co. Monaghan)
Map Grid: 18
RC Parish: Rosslea
Diocese: CG
Earliest Record: b. 1.1862; m. 1.1862
Parish Address: Rev. Eamonn Murphy, PP, Roslea, Enniskillen, Co. Fermanagh

Civil Parish: **Currin**
Map Grid: 19

RC Parish: Currin, Killeevan, and Aughabog
Diocese: CG
Parish Address: Rev. Hugh McCaughey, Newbliss, Co. Monaghan

Civil Parish: **Derrybrusk**
Map Grid: 11
RC Parish: part Enniskillen
Diocese: CG

Civil Parish: **Derryvullan**
Map Grid: 5
RC Parish: see Enniskillen
Diocese: CG

Civil Parish: **Devenish (1)**
Map Grid: 7
RC Parish: Devenish (Irvinestown); also Derrygonnelly, see below.
Diocese: CG
Earliest Record: b. 11.1846; m. 12.1851
Parish Address: Rev. Gerald Timoney, PP, Irvinestown, Enniskillen, Co. Fermanagh

Civil Parish: **Devenish (2)**
Map Grid: 7
RC Parish: Derrygonnelly (Botha)
Diocese: CG
Earliest Record: b. 2.1853
Parish Address: Rev. Patrick Gallagher, Derrygonnelly, Enniskillen, Co. Fermanagh

Civil Parish: **Drumkeeran**
Map Grid: 1
RC Parish: see Galloon
Diocese: CG

Civil Parish: **Drummully** (see also Co. Monaghan)
Map Grid: 23
RC Parish: part Galloon
Diocese: CG

Civil Parish: **Enniskillen (1)**
Map Grid: 12
RC Parish: Tempo (Pobal); also Enniskillen, see below
Diocese: CG
Earliest Record: b. 11.1845; m. 10.1845
Parish Address: Rev. Thomas Marron, PP, Tempo, Enniskillen, Co. Fermanagh

Civil Parish: **Enniskillen (2)**
Map Grid: 12
RC Parish: Enniskillen
Diocese: CG
Earliest Record: b. 1838; m. 2.1818
Missing Dates: b. 10.1870-8.1871
Parish Address: Rev. Sean Cahill, 1 Darling Street, Enniskillen, Co. Donegal

Civil Parish: **Galloon**
Map Grid: 22
RC Parish: Galloon
Diocese: CG
Earliest Record: b. 1.1853; m. 5.1847
Missing Dates: b. 2.1859-6.1863
Parish Address: Rev. Edward Murphy, PP, Newtownbutler, Enniskillen, Co. Fermanagh

Civil Parish: **Inishmacsaint** (see also Co. Donegal)
Map Grid: 6
RC Parish: Inishmacsaint; also part Derrygonnelly, see Devenish
Diocese: CG
Earliest Record: b. 7.1860; m. 1.1860
Parish Address: Rev. Patrick Lonergan, PP, Belleek, Enniskillen, Co. Fermanagh

Civil Parish: **Killesher**
Map Grid: 15
RC Parish: Killesher
Diocese: KM
Earliest Record: b. 9.1855; m. 9.1855; d. 9.1855
Parish Address: Rev. Brian McNamara, PP, Derrylester, Enniskillen, Co. Fermanagh

Civil Parish: **Kinawley**
Map Grid: 20
RC Parish: Kinawley
Diocese: KM
Earliest Record: b. 12.1835; m. 12.1835; d. 4.1853
Missing Dates: m. 3.1857-1.1870
Parish Address: Rev. Sean O'Reilly, PP, Kinawley, Enniskillen, Co. Fermanagh

Civil Parish: **Magheracross**
Map Grid: 9
RC Parish: see Enniskillen
Diocese: CG

Civil Parish: **Magheraculmoney**
Map Grid: 4
RC Parish: Culmaine or Magheraculmoney (Ederney)
Diocese: CG
Earliest Record: b. 8.1836; m. 11.1837
Parish Address: Rev. John Gilsenan, PP, Ederney, Enniskillen, Co. Fermanagh

Civil Parish: **Rossorry**
Map Grid: 8
RC Parish: see Enniskillen
Diocese: CG

Civil Parish: **Templecarn**
Map Grid: 3
RC Parish: see Belleek
Diocese: CG

Civil Parish: **Tomregan**
Map Grid: 21
RC Parish: see Co. Cavan
Diocese: KM

Civil Parish: **Trory**
Map Grid: 10
RC Parish: see Enniskillen

Commercial and Social Directories

1824
J. Pigot's *City of Dublin & Hibernian Provincial Directory* includes traders, nobility, gentry, and clergy lists of Churchill, Enniskillen, Irvinestown, and Maguiresbridge.

1846
Slater's *National Commercial Directory of Ireland* lists nobility, clergy, traders, etc., in Enniskillen, Lisnaskea, Maguiresbridge and Brookeborough, and Lowtherstown.

1852
Henderson's *Belfast & Province of Ulster Directory* has lists of inhabitants, traders, etc., in and around the town of Enniskillen. Further editions were issued 1854, 1856, 1858, 1861, 1863, 1865, 1868, 1870, 1877, 1880, 1884, 1890, 1894, and 1900.

1856

Slater's *Royal National Commercial Directory of Ireland* lists nobility, gentry, clergy, traders, etc., in Enniskillen, Lisnaskea, and Lowtherstown.

1870

Slater's *Directory of Ireland* contains trade, nobility, and clergy lists for Enniskillen, Lisnaskea, Maguiresbridge and Brookeborough, and Lowtherstown.

1881

Slater's *Royal National Commercial Directory of Ireland* contains lists of traders, clergy, nobility, and farmers in adjoining parishes of the towns of Enniskillen, Lisnaskea, and Lowtherstown.

1891

Derry Almanac & Directory has a list of traders in Enniskillen (published annually thereafter).

1894

Slater's *Royal National Directory of Ireland* lists traders, police, teachers, farmers, and private residents in each of the towns, villages, and parishes of the county.

Family History

Each of the Fermanagh families is briefly documented in *The Fermanagh Story*, by P. Livingstone, and *Cumann Seanchais Clochair*, 1969.

Belmore, Earl of. "Monea Castle: Co. Fermanagh, and the Hamiltons." *Ulster J. Arch.* 2nd ser. 1 (1895): 195-208, 256-77.

"Bredin of Drumcagh, Co. Fermanagh." Pedigree in *Swanzy Notebooks*. RCB Library, Dublin.

"Clogherici: the Connollys of Fermanagh and Co. Monaghan." *Clogher Record* 2 (1957): 172-76.

"Coulson of Belmont." Pedigree in *Swanzy Notebooks*. RCB Library, Dublin.

Downey – see Co. Sligo.

"Fawcett of Co. Fermanagh." Pedigree in *Swanzy Notebooks*. RCB Library, Dublin.

"Fiddes of Co. Fermanagh." Pedigree in *Swanzy Notebooks*. RCB Library, Dublin.

Fuller, J.F. *Pedigree of the Hamilton Family of Fermanagh and Tyrone*. London, 1889.

"The Irwins of Fermanagh and Donegal." *Ir. Gen.* 1 (1941): 278-83.

"The Johnstons of Correnney, Co. Fermanagh." *Ir. Gen.* 1 (1941): 321.

Moran, T. Whitley. *The Whitleys of Enniskillen*. Hoylake, 1962.

Nixon – see French under Co. Cavan.

"Ovens of Fermanagh." Pedigree in *Swanzy Notebooks*. RCB Library.

"Ramadge." *Clogher Record* 10 (1) 1979.

Swanzy, H.B. *Later History of the Family of Rosborough of Mullinagoan, Co. Fermanagh*. 1897.

Gravestone Inscriptions

Aghalurcher: *Clogher Record* 2 (2) (1958): 328-52.

Aghavea: *Clogher Record* 4 (1): 95-112; 4 (2) (1960-61).

Devenish (St. Molaise's and Devenish Abbey): MacKenna, Rev. J.E. and F. Bigger, *Devenish, Its History, Antiquities and Traditions*. 1897.

Donagh: *Clogher Record* 1 (3) (1955): 141-48.

Drumully: *Clogher Record* 1 (2) (1954): 35-38.

Enniskillen: Dundas, W.H. *Enniskillen Parish and Town*. 1913.

Galoon: *Clogher Record* 10 (2) (1980): 264-68.

Holywell: *Clogher Record* 2 (1) (1957): 138-47.

Kinawley: *Clogher Record* 1 (4) (1956): 161-65.

Monea: Steele, Rev. William B. *The Parish of Devenish, Co. Fermanagh*. 1937.

Templenafrin: *Clogher Record* 2 (1) (1957): 138-47.

Tullynageeran: *Clogher Record* 2 (3) (1959): 521-23.

Newspapers

Title: *Enniskillen Advertiser*
Published in: Enniskillen, 1864-76
BL Holdings: 7.1864-9.1876

Title: *Enniskillen Chronicle* (continued as *Fermanagh Mail and Enniskillen Chronicle* in 1885)
Published in: Enniskillen, 1808-93
NLI Holdings: odd numbers 1808-11; 1.1824-5.1849; odd numbers 1885; 1.1886-12.1892
BL Holdings: 1.1824-5.1849; 8.1849-11.1850; 3.1851-7.1893

Title: *Fermanagh News*
Published in: Enniskillen, 1894-1920
NLI Holdings: 1.1905-6.1907; 1.1972-in progress
BL Holdings: 7.1896-6.1907; 10.1907-5.1920

Title: *Fermanagh Times*
Published in: Enniskillen, 1880-1949
NLI Holdings: 9.1921-4.1949
BL Holdings: 3.1880-4.1949 (except 1930)

Title: *Impartial Reporter*
Published in: Enniskillen, 1825-current
NLI Holdings: 1.1894-12.1902
BL Holdings: 5.1825-5.1873; 4.1879-12.1925; 1.1927-in progress

Wills and Administrations

A discussion of the types of records, where they are held, their availability and value is given in the Wills section of the Introduction. The availability of prerogative wills, administrations, and marriage license records is also described in the relevant parts of the same section. Where available, published sources of these records are given in the Miscellaneous Sources section.

Pre-1858 Wills and Administrations

Prerogative Wills. see p. xli
Consistorial Wills. County Fermanagh is mainly in the diocese of Clogher, with three parishes in the diocese of Kilmore. The guide to Catholic parish records in this chapter shows the diocese to which each parish belonged. The wills of residents of each diocese were usually proven within that diocese (see the Wills section for exceptions). The following records survive:

Wills. see p. xxxvii

Abstracts. see p. xxxvii

Indexes. Clogher (1661-1858); Kilmore – see Co. Cavan

Post-1858 Wills and Administrations

County Fermanagh was served by the District Registry of Armagh. The surviving records are kept in the PRONI. Other collections are

"Upton Papers." Abstracts from Cavan, Longford, and Westmeath. RIA Library.

Marriage Licenses

Indexes. Clogher (1709-1866). PRO; SLC film 100862. Kilmore (1691-1845). PRO; SLC film 100869

Miscellaneous Sources

"English Settlement in Co. Fermanagh, 1610-1640." *Clogher Record* 10 (1) (1979): 137-43.

"The Scotch Settlement of Co. Fermanagh, 1610-30." *Clogher Record* 9 (2) (1976/78): 367-73.

"The Volunteer Companies of Ulster, 1778-1793, 6 Fermanagh." *Irish Sword* 8 (31): 92-94 (some officers names only).

Research Sources and Services

Journals

Clogher Record – see Co. Monaghan

Libraries and Information Sources

Fermanagh Divisional Library, Enniskillen, Co. Fermanagh, N. Ireland

Fermanagh County Museum, Castle Barracks, Enniskillen, Co. Fermanagh

Research Services

See research services in Belfast, p. xlvi

Irish World Citizen Organization, 3 Bilmore Street, Enniskillen, Co. Fermanagh

Societies

Clogher Historical Society – see Co. Monaghan

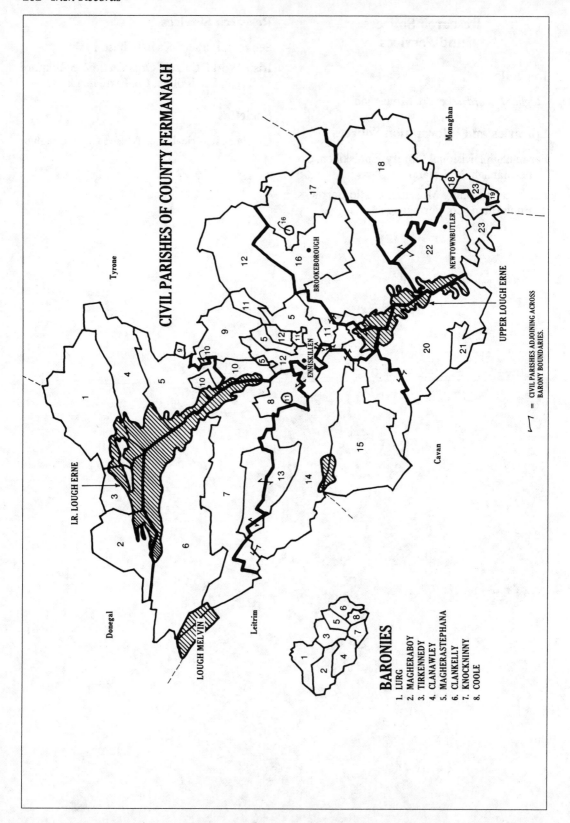

CIVIL PARISHES OF COUNTY FERMANAGH

Tyrone

Monaghan

LR. LOUGH ERNE

UPPER LOUGH ERNE

BROOKEBOROUGH

NEWTOWNBUTLER

ENNISKILLEN

Donegal

Cavan

Leitrim

LOUGH MELVIN

= CIVIL PARISHES ADJOINING ACROSS
BARONY BOUNDARIES.

BARONIES

1. LURG
2. MAGHERABOY
3. TIRKENNEDY
4. CLANAWLEY
5. MAGHERASTEPHANA
6. CLANKELLY
7. KNOCKNINNY
8. COOLE

County Galway

A Brief History

The county of Galway is on the west coast and contains the city of Galway and the towns of Tuam, Ballinasloe, Athenry, and Loughrea. The east of the county is relatively good farmland while the west, the area known as Connemara, is rocky and barren. In this area, and on the offshore islands, particularly the Aran islands, the Irish language is still the everyday language.

Before the redivision of the country into counties, the west of the county was the territory of Iar-Connacht. The major Gaelic families of the county were O'Halloran, O'Daly, O'Kelly, O'Flaherty, O'Malley, O'Madden, O'Fallon, O'Naughton, O'Mullaly, and O'Hynes.

The town of Galway was a prominent trading port from early times. It was also reputed to be one of the landmarks in the ancient division of Ireland (in the second century A.D.) into the northerly half, Leath-Cuin, controlled by Conn-Cead-Cathac, and the southerly Leath-Mogha, controlled by Eoghan, King of Munster. The fortunes of the town from earliest times have been documented in Hardiman's *History of Galway*. The city was destroyed on several occasions by local raids, fire, and by Danish Vikings, but was rebuilt. After the Norman invasion the whole Kingdom of Connaught, including Galway, was granted to Richard de Burgo, or Burke. However, because of the power of the existing chieftains, de Burgo only took control of part of the south of the county. One of the families who arrived with the Burkes were the Birminghams. Another family which settled in the north of the county was the Joyces. The part of the county in which they settled is still known as Joyce's country. The de Burgo's fortified the town of Galway and established it as a major center trading with Spain and Portugal. Gradually the Normans assimilated with the local people and, apart from the town of Galway itself, adopted Irish custom and dress.

The fourteen major merchant families in the city, known as the "Tribes of Galway" were Athy, Blake, Bodkin, Browne, Darcy, Deane, Font, French, Joyce, Kirwan, Lynch, Martin, Morris, and Skerrett. These families dominated Galway town which became a center of commercial activity in the province. As the power of the English receded in the province of Connaught, the town remained a bastion of English customs and language. The county of Galway and the other Connaught counties were established in 1584 by Sir Henry Sidney. Many of the native and Norman chieftains submitted at this time and promised their allegiance to the English crown.

The Catholics of Galway joined the general rebellion of the Catholic Confederacy (see Co. Kilkenny) in 1641. The city itself was a stronghold of the rebels but was finally taken by the Parliamentarians after a nine-month siege in 1652. In the aftermath of this rebellion the town and county suffered badly. It is calculated that over one third of the population perished though famine, disease, or at the hands of the victorious English parliamentary forces. In addition, over 1,000 people were taken and sold as slaves to the West Indies.

Although the estates of the leaders of this rebellion were confiscated and given to English adventurers and soldiers, many of these properties were returned after the restoration of King Charles.

County Galway was very badly affected by the Great Famine of 1845-47. The population, which in 1841 was 442,000, had fallen to 322,000 by 1851. Over 73,000 people died in the county between 1845 and 1850, and approximately 11 percent of the population emigrated in the succeeding five years. Through continued emigration the population fell to 215,000 by 1891 and today is approximately 172,000.

Census and Census Substitutes

1574
"Galway Castles and Owners in 1574." *J. Galway Arch. & Hist. Soc.* 1 (2) (1901): 109-23.

1599
Description of the County of Galway with the Names of the Principal Inhabitants. NLI P1707.

1640
"Irish Papist Proprietors in Galway Town." In *History of the Town and County of Galway* by James Hardiman, Dublin, 1820. Appendix 7; SLC film 990403.

1657
"English Protestant Proprietors." In *History of the Town and County of Galway* by James Hardiman, Dublin, 1820. Appendix 7; SLC film 990403.

1727
"A Galway Election List." *J. Galway Arch. & Hist. Soc.* 35 (1976): 105-28 (lists all entitled

to vote, i.e., Protestants, and also classified list according to trade; some comments, e.g., "Popish wife," etc.).

1749
"Census of Elphin Diocese; householders, occupations, number and religion of children and number of servants in parishes of Ahascragh, Athleague, Ballynakill, Drimatemple, Dunamon, Kilbegnet, Kilcroan, Killian, Killosolan." PRO film 2466; SLC film 101781.

1775
"Catholic Qualification Roll Extracts" (eighty-four names, addresses and occupations). 59th Report DKPRI: 50-84.

1791
"Survey of the Town of Loughrea." *J. Galway Arch. & Hist. Soc.* 23 (3) (1951): 95-110 (gives names of residents on each street and size of holding).

1794
"Names of Roman Catholic Freemen of Galway Town." *J. Galway Arch. & Hist. Soc.* 9 (1) (1915): 62-64 (gives list of 300 names only).

1798
"List of Convicted Rebels from Galway." *J. Galway Arch. & Hist. Soc.* 25 (3, 4) (1953): 104-33 (list of 130 names, occupations, addresses, and fate).

"List of Persons who Suffered Loss in '98 Rebellion." NLI JLB 94107 (approximately 100 names, addresses, and occupations).

1801-06
"Inhabitants of Killalaghten Catholic Parish." Included in parish records of Cappataggle. NLI P2431.

1806-10
"Catholic Householders in Each Townland of Killallaghten Parish." Included in parish registers of Killallaghten, p. 494.

1821
"Government Census Remnants: parishes of Athenry, Inishmore, Kilconickny, Kilconieran, Killimordaly, Kilreekil, Kiltullagh." PRO; SLC film 597734.

Houses, &c.	Proprieters in 1640, Irish Papists.	Proprietors in 1657, Eng. Protestants.	Yearly value, if to be let for years.

A SLHEDULE CONTAINING A SURVEY AND VALUATION OF SOE MANY OF THE HOUSES IN THE TOWN OF GALWAY, WITH THE GARDENS, ORCHARDS AND EDIFICES, AND THEIR APPURTENANCES, AS ARE SET OUT PURSUANT TO SAID ADDITIONAL ACT.

Houses, &c.	Proprieters in 1640, Irish Papists.	Proprietors in 1657, Eng. Protestants.	£. s. d.
A thatched house.	John Blake Fitz-Robert.	——	0 8 0
Do.	Thomas Browne.	Captain Bird.	1 5 0
A dwelling-house, covered with slate, three stories, with a yard.	Stephen Browne.	Thomas Williams.	7 10 0
Ditto, two stories,—a thatched house backward, one story high, with a back-side.	Thomas Nolan.	George Duffett.	12 0 0
Do. two stories, with do.	Do.	Thomas Marshell.	11 10 0
Two do. three stories, with do.	John Martin Fitz-Geffery.	Blanerhassett Wells.	13 0 0
Do. with back-house slated, one story	Do.	George Burwast.	16 0 0
Do. three stories,—a back-house slated, three stories, and a yard.	Mathew Martyn.	Thomas Symper.	14 0 0
A dwelling-house thatched, one story	James Lynch Fitz-Marcus.	Jarvis Hines.	1 15 0

An extract from a listing of houses in the town of Galway showing their proprietors ("Irish Papists") before the Catholic Rebellion of 1641, and in 1656 when most of the properties had been confiscated and given to English adventurers and soldiers, i.e., "English Protestants." From *The History of the Town and County of Galway from the Earliest Period to the Present Time* by James Hardiman. Dublin, 1820.

Extracts from government census for Galway City. *Utah Gen. and Hist. Mag.* 4 (1918): 75-79.

1824-44
Tithe Applotment Survey (p. xxvii).

1827
Protestant Parishoners of Aughrim (names of parents and children plus ages of latter in Aughrim CI parish register). PRO film 5359.

1832-36
"Names of Holders and of Applicants for Licenses to Sell Liquor in Galway" (names and addresses). *Parl. Papers* 1837/38, 13 (2): Appendix 10.

1837
"List of those Made Freemen of Galway Since 1831" (names, occupations and residences). *Parl. Papers* 1837, 2 (1): Appendix B1; 1837/38, 13 (2): Appendix 3.

The Names and Residences of Several Persons in the City of Galway who Were Discharged from Payment of Rates and Taxes. Reports from Committees. *Parl. Papers* 1837, 2 (1): (39) 206-10.

"Occupants of Galway, Arranged by Street Giving Property Values." *Parl. Papers* 1837, 2 (1): Appendix G, 206-10.

1839-46
"List of Subscribers to RC Chapel at Dunmore" (gives names, townlands, and subscription). In *Catholic Church Records of Dunmore*. NLI P4211.

1848-49
"Emigrants from Irvilloughter and Boughill" (parts of Ahascragh and Taghboy respectively–names, ages, and relationships of 410 people, dates of departure and arrival). In Ellis, E. *Emigrants from Ireland 1847-52*, 22-41. Baltimore: Genealogical Publishing Co., 1977.

1853-56
Griffith's Valuation (see p. xxvii).

1901
Census. PRO.

1911
Census. PRO.

Church Records

Church of Ireland
(shows starting date of record)

Parish: **Ahascragh**
Status: Lost

Parish: **Annaghdown**
Status: Lost

Parish: **Ardrahan**
Existing Records: b. 1804; m. 1804; d. 1804
Status: LC

Parish: **Arran**
Status: Lost

Parish: **Athenry**
Existing Records: b. 1796; m. 1796; d. 1795
Status: PRO

Parish: **Aughrim**
Existing Records: b. 1814; m. 1814; d. 1814
Status: LC

Parish: **Ballinacourty**
Existing Records: b. 1834
Status: LC

Parish: **Ballinakill**
Existing Records: b. 1852; d. 1852
Status: LC

Parish: **Ballymacward**
Status: Lost

Parish: **Castleblakeney**
Status: Lost

Parish: **Castlekirke**
Status: Lost

Parish: **Clonfert**
Status: Lost

Parish: **Clontuskart**
Status: Lost

Parish: **Creagh**
Existing Records: b. 1823; m. 1823; d. 1823
Status: LC

Parish: **Dononaughta**
Status: Lost

Parish: **Dunmore**
Status: Lost

Parish: **Errislanon**
Status: Lost

Parish: **Errismore**
Status: Lost

Parish: **Inniscaltra**
Existing Records: b. 1851; d. 1851
Status: LC

Parish: **Kilcolgan**
Status: Lost

Parish: **Kilconickny**
Status: Lost

Parish: **Kilconnell**
Status: Lost

Parish: **Kilcummin**
Existing Records: b. 1812; m. 1813; d. 1814
Status: LC

Parish: **Kilkerrin**
Status: Lost

Parish: **Killannin**
Existing Records: b. 1844
Status: LC

Parish: **Killererin**
Status: Lost

Parish: **Killinane**
Status: Lost

Parish: **Killyon** and **Kilroran**
Status: Lost

Parish: **Kilmacduagh**
Existing Records: b. 1787; m. 1811; d. 1827
Status: LC and PR

Parish: **Kilmoylan**
Status: Lost

Parish: **Kiltormer**
Status: Lost

Parish: **Lickmolassy**
Existing Records: b. 1766; m. 1762; d. 1800
Status: LC

Parish: **Loughrea**
Existing Records: b. 1747; m. 1747; d. 1747
Status: LC

Parish: **Monivea**
Status: Lost

Parish: **Moylough**
Status: LC

Parish: **Moyrus** (Beauchamp)
Status: Lost

Parish: **Moyrus** (Roundstone)
Existing Records: b. 1841; m. 1844; d. 1849
Status: LC

Parish: **Omey** or **Clifden**
Existing Records: b. 1831; m. 1831; d. 1832
Status: LC

Parish: **Rahoon**
Status: Lost

Parish: **Renvyle**
Status: Lost

Parish: **Ross**
Status: Lost

Parish: **St. Nicholas**
Existing Records: b. 1792; m. 1792; d. 1838
Status: LC

Parish: **Sellerna**
Status: Lost

Parish: **Taughmaconnell** (with Creagh)
Existing Records: b. 1855
Status: LC

Parish: **Tuam**
Existing Records: b. 1808; m. 1808; d. 1808
Status: LC

Parish: **Tynagh**
Status: Lost

Presbyterian

Parish: **Galway**
Starting Date: 1831

Roman Catholic

Civil Parish: **Abbeygormacan**
Map Grid: 112
RC Parish: Abbeygormacan and Killoran (Mullagh and Killoran)
Diocese: CF
Earliest Record: b. 2.1859; m. 4.1863
Parish Address: Rev. V. Twohig, PP, Mullagh, Loughrea, Co. Galway

Civil Parish: **Abbeyknockmoy**
Map Grid: 41
RC Parish: Abbeyknockmoy
Diocese: TU
Earliest Record: no register before 1880

Civil Parish: **Addergoole**
Map Grid: 10
RC Parish: Addergoole and Liskeevey
(Milltown)
Diocese: TU
Earliest Record: b. 8.1858; m. 1.1859
Parish Address: Rev. John Lowry, PP,
Milltown, Co. Galway

Civil Parish: **Ahascragh**
Map Grid: 78
RC Parish: Ahascragh (Caltra)
Diocese: EL
Earliest Record: b. 1.1840; m. 1.1866
Parish Address: Rev. J. Smyth, PP, Ahascragh,
Ballinasloe, Co. Galway

Civil Parish: **Annaghdown**
Map Grid: 36
RC Parish: Annaghdown (Corrandulla)
Diocese: TU
Earliest Record: b. 9.1834; m. 3.1834
Missing Dates: b. 9.1869-2.1875; m. 11.1868-
2.1875
Parish Address: Rev. P. O'Brien, PP, Corran-
dulla, Co. Galway

Civil Parish: **Ardrahan**
Map Grid: 66
RC Parish: Ardrahan
Diocese: KMC
Earliest Record: b. 5.1839; m. 3.1845
Missing Dates: b. 3.1846-11.1866; m. 2.1850-
2.1867
Parish Address: Rev. Joseph Kelly, PP,
Ardrahan, Co. Galway

Civil Parish: **Athenry**
Map Grid: 69
RC Parish: Athenry
Diocese: TU
Earliest Record: b. 8.1858; m. 8.1858
Parish Address: Rev. Mgr. Michael Mooney,
PP, Athenry, Co. Galway

Civil Parish: **Athleague** (see also Co. Roscom-
mon)
Map Grid: 49
RC Parish: Athleague and Fuerty
Diocese: EL
Earliest Record: b. 1.1808; m. 6.1808; d. 1.1807

Missing Dates: b. 5.1828-8.1834, 7.1864-1.1865;
m. 2.1834-3.1836; d. ends 1837
Parish Address: Rev Edward P. Jones, PP, Athleague, Co. Roscommon

Civil Parish: **Aughrim**
Map Grid: 77
RC Parish: Aughrim and Kilconnell
Diocese: CF
Earliest Record: b. 3.1828
Parish Address: Rev. P. Bruen, PP, Aughrim,
Ballinasloe, Co. Galway

Civil Parish: **Ballinchalla**
Map Grid: 6
RC Parish: see Co. Mayo
Diocese: TU

Civil Parish: **Ballindoon**
Map Grid: 4
RC Parish: Omey and Ballindoon (Clifden)
Diocese: CF
Earliest Record: b. 1.1838; m. 9.1839
Missing Dates: b. 10.1855-7.1856; m. 5.1855-
8.1858
Parish Address: Rev. Canon Thomas Heraty,
PP, Clifden, Co. Galway

Civil Parish: **Ballinrobe**
Map Grid: 5
RC Parish: see Co. Mayo
Diocese: TU

Civil Parish: **Ballymacward**
Map Grid: 46
RC Parish: Ballymacward and Clonkeenkerrill
Diocese: CF
Earliest Record: b. 10.1841
Missing Dates: b. 11.1843-5.1855
Parish Address: Rev. Peter Dunne, PP, Bal-
lymacward, Ballinasloe, Co. Galway

Civil Parish: **Ballynacourty**
Map Grid: 56
RC Parish: Ballynacourty, see Oranmore
Diocese: TU

Civil Parish: **Ballinakilly**
Map Grid: 50
RC Parish: Mountbellew, see Moylough
Diocese: TU

Civil Parish: **Ballynakill (1)** (Ballymoe)
Map Grid: 19
RC Parish: Glinsk and Kilbegnet (Creggs)
Diocese: CF
Earliest Record: b. 9.1836; m. 11.1836; d. 9.1836
Missing Dates: b. 6.1848-3.1849; m. 4.1865-7.1865; d. ends 9.1839
Parish Address: Rev. T. Garvey, CC, Glinsk, Castlerea, Co. Roscommon

Civil Parish: **Ballynakill (2)** (Ballynahinch)
Map Grid: 1
RC Parish: Ballynakill (Letterfrack); also part Kilbride and Ballynakill, see below
Diocese: TU
Earliest Record: b. 7.1869; m. 7.1869
Parish Address: Rev. Jos. Mcnamara, PP, Letterfrack, Co. Galway

Civil Parish: **Ballynakill (3)** (Ballynahinch)
Map Grid: 1
RC Parish: Kilbride
Diocese: TU
Earliest Record: b. 12.1853
Parish Address: Rev. W. P. Costelloe, Leenane, Co. Galway

Civil Parish: **Ballynakill (4)** (Leitrim)
Map Grid: 105
RC Parish: Ballinakill
Diocese: CF
Earliest Record: b. 4.1839
Missing Dates: b. 10.1851-6.1855, 12.1857-2.1859
Parish Address: Rev. C. Heenan, Ballinakill, Loughrea, Co. Galway

Civil Parish: **Ballynakill (5)** (Leitrim)
Map Grid: 105
RC Parish: Woodford
Diocese: CF
Earliest Record: b. 4.1821; m. 4.1821
Missing Dates: b. 11.1843-3.1851, 8.1861-4.1865, 9.1868-2.1869; m.10.1833-3.1851, 7.1861-7.1865, 2.1869-2.1871
Parish Address: Rev. P. Naughton, PP, Woodford, Co. Galway

Civil Parish: **Beagh**
Map Grid: 90
RC Parish: Beagh (Shanaglish)

Diocese: KMC
Earliest Record: b. 1.1855; m. 3.1849
Missing Dates: m. 2.1850-5.1860
Parish Address: Rev. R. J. Canavan, PP, Shanaglish, Gort, Co. Galway

Civil Parish: **Belclare**
Map Grid: 30
RC Parish: Kilmoylan and Cummer, see Cummer
Diocese: TU

Civil Parish: **Boyounagh**
Map Grid: 18
RC Parish: Boyounagh (Glenamaddy)
Diocese: TU
Earliest Record: b. 10.1838; m. 10.1838
Missing Dates: b. 6.1858-12.1859, 10.1863-10.1865
Parish Address: Rev. James Glynn, PP, Glenamaddy, Co. Galway

Civil Parish: **Bullaun**
Map Grid: 91
RC Parish: Bullaun, Grange, or Killaan
Diocese: CF
Earliest Record: b. 10.1827; m. 10.1827
Missing Dates: b. 4.1840-8.1841
Parish Address: Rev. Hubert Murray, PP, New Inn, Ballinasloe, Co. Galway

Civil Parish: **Cargin**
Map Grid: 31
RC Parish: Headford, see Killower

Civil Parish: **Claregalway**
Map Grid: 55
RC Parish: Claregalway
Diocese: TU
Earliest Record: b. 11.1849; m. 11.1849; d. 11.1849
Missing Dates: d. ends 11.1876
Parish Address: Rev. Canon Gerard F. Callanan, PP, Claregalway, Co. Galway

Civil Parish: **Clonbern**
Map Grid: 22
RC Parish: see Kilkerrin
Diocese: TU

Civil Parish: **Clonfert**
Map Grid: 111
RC Parish: Clonfert, Donanaghta, and Meelick
Diocese: CF
Earliest Record: b. 11.1849; m. 11.1849; d. 11.1849
Parish Address: Rev. C. Glynn, PP, Eyrecourt, Co. Galway

Civil Parish: **Clonkeen**
Map Grid: 45
RC Parish: see Ballymacward
Diocese: CF

Civil Parish: **Clonrush**
Map Grid: 107
RC Parish: see Co. Clare
Diocese: KL

Civil Parish: **Clontuskert**
Map Grid: 81
RC Parish: Clontuskert
Diocese: TU
Earliest Record: b. 10.1827; m. 10.1827; d. 10.1827
Missing Dates: b. 10.1868-3.1870; m. 10.1868-3.1870; d. ends 10.1868
Parish Address: Rev. J. Kelly, PP, Clontuskert, Ballinasloe, Co. Galway

Civil Parish: **Cong**
Map Grid: 8
RC Parish: Co. Mayo
Diocese: TU

Civil Parish: **Cummer**
Map Grid: 34
RC Parish: Kilmoylan and Cummer
Diocese: TU
Earliest Record: b. 12.1835; m. 10.1813
Missing Dates: b. 8.1860-8.1872
Parish Address: Rev. T. Concannon, PP, Cummer, Tuam, Co. Galway

Civil Parish: **Donaghpatrick**
Map Grid: 26
RC Parish: Donaghpatrick and Kilcoona
Diocese: TU
Earliest Record: b. 4.1844; m. 4.1844
Missing Dates: b. 6.1844-11.1849, 6.1861-8.1863; m. 12.1846-12.1849, 6.1861-9.1863

Parish Address: Rev. C. Kilkelly, PP, Caherlistrane, Co. Galway

Civil Parish: **Donanaghta**
Map Grid: 115
RC Parish: see Clonfert
Diocese: CF

Civil Parish: **Drumacoo**
Map Grid: 62
RC Parish: see Kilcolgan
Diocese: KMC

Civil Parish: **Drumatemple**
Map Grid: 17
RC Parish: see Ballintober, Co. Roscommon
Diocese: EL

Civil Parish: **Dunamon**
Map Grid: 21
RC Parish: Glinsk, etc., see Ballynakill (Ballymoe)
Diocese: CF

Civil Parish: **Duniry**
Map Grid: 103
RC Parish: Ballinakill, see Ballynakill (Leitrim)
Diocese: CF

Civil Parish: **Dunmore**
Map Grid: 11
RC Parish: Dunmore
Diocese: TU
Earliest Record: b. 3.1833; m. 3.1833
Missing Dates: b. 3.1846-12.1847, 10.1859-9.1877; m. 9.1860-1.1861
Parish Address: Rev. Canon Michael Walsh, PP, Dunmore, Co. Galway

Civil Parish: **Fahy**
Map Grid: 114
RC Parish: Fahy and Kilquain
Diocese: CF

Civil Parish: **Fohanagh**
Map Grid: 71
RC Parish: Fohenagh and Kilgerrill
Diocese: CF
Earliest Record: b. 8.1827; m. 8.1827; d. 8.1827
Parish Address: Rev. L. Moran, PP, Fohenagh, Ahascragh, Co. Galway

Civil Parish: **Grange**
Map Grid: 74
RC Parish: see Bullaun
Diocese: CF

Civil Parish: **Inishbofin**
Map Grid: 106
RC Parish: see Ballynakill (Ballynahinch)
Diocese: TU

Civil Parish: **Inisheer**
Map Grid: 84
RC Parish: Aran Islands
Diocese: TU
Earliest Record: b. 11.1874; m. 2.1872
Parish Address: Rev. Padraic O. Tuairisg, PP, Kilronan, Aran Islands, Co. Galway

Civil Parish: **Inishmaan**
Map Grid: 83
RC Parish: Aran Islands; see Inisheer
Diocese: TU

Civil Parish: **Inishmore**
Map Grid: 82
RC Parish: Aran Islands, see Inisheer
Diocese: KMC

Civil Parish: **Isertkelly**
Map Grid: 93
RC Parish: see Kilchreest
Diocese: CF

Civil Parish: **Kilbeacanty**
Map Grid: 89
RC Parish: Kilbeacanty
Diocese: KMC
Earliest Record: b. 8.1854
Parish Address: Rev. Bernard Duffy, PP, Kilbeacanty, Gort, Co. Galway

Civil Parish: **Kilbegnet**
Map Grid: 20
RC Parish: Glinsk and Kilbegnet, see Ballynakill (Ballymoe)
Diocese: EL

Civil Parish: **Kilbennon**
Map Grid: 13
RC Parish: Kilconly and Kilbennon
Diocese: TU

Earliest Record: b. 3.1872
Parish Address: Rev. John Jennings, PP, Kilbannon, Tuam, Co. Galway

Civil Parish: **Kilchreest**
Map Grid: 95
RC Parish: Kilchreest
Diocese: CF
Earliest Record: b. 2.1855; m. 2.1865
Parish Address: Rev. Liam Power, PP, Kilchreest, Loughrea, Co. Galway

Civil Parish: **Kilcloony**
Map Grid: 80
RC Parish: Kilcloony (Ballinasloe, Creagh, and Kilclooney)
Diocese: CF
Earliest Record: b. 3.1872
Parish Address: Rev. D. Gordon, St. Michael's, Ballinasloe, Co. Galway

Civil Parish: **Kilcolgan**
Map Grid: 63
RC Parish: Kilcolgan, Drumacoo, and Killeenavara
Diocese: KMC
Earliest Record: b. 11.1854; m. 1.1871
Parish Address: Rev. A. J. O'Halloran, PP, Ballindereen, Kilcolgan, Co. Galway

Civil Parish: **Kilconickny**
Map Grid: 68
RC Parish: Kilconickny, etc., see Kilconieran
Diocese: CF

Civil Parish: **Kilconieran**
Map Grid: 61
RC Parish: Kilconickny (Kiconickny, Kilconieran, and Lickerrig)
Diocese: CF
Earliest Record: b. 7.1831; m. 7.1831
Parish Address: Rev. W. Naughton, PP, Carrabane, Loughrea, Co. Galway

Civil Parish: **Kilconly**
Map Grid: 12
RC Parish: see Kilbennon
Diocese: TU

Civil Parish: **Kilconnell**
Map Grid: 72
RC Parish: see Aughrim
Diocese: CF

Civil Parish: **Kilcooly**
Map Grid: 100
RC Parish: Kilcooly and Leitrim
Diocese: CF
Earliest Record: b. 5.1815; m. 5.1815; d. 5.1815
Missing Dates: b. 6.1829-9.1850; m. 6.1829-
12.1846; d. 6.1829-12.1846
Parish Address: Rev. T. Kennedy, PP, Leitrim,
Loughrea, Co. Galway

Civil Parish: **Kilcoona**
Map Grid: 33
RC Parish: see Donaghpatrick
Diocese: TU

Civil Parish: **Kilcroan**
Map Grid: 16
RC Parish: Glinsk, see Ballynakill (Ballymoe)
Diocese: EL

Civil Parish: **Kilcummin (1)**
Map Grid: 23
RC Parish: Rosmuck; also Killeen and
Oughterard, see below
Diocese: TU
Earliest Record: b. 8.1840
Parish Address: Rev. C. Leo Morohan, PP, Ros
Muc, Co. Galway

Civil Parish: **Kilcummin (2)**
Map Grid: 23
RC Parish: Killeen
Diocese: TU
Earliest Record: b. 8.1853
Parish Address: Rev. Martin Lang, PP, Car-
raroe, Co. Galway

Civil Parish: **Kilcummin (3)**
Map Grid: 23
RC Parish: Oughterard
Diocese: TU
Earliest Record: b. 6.1809; m. 7.1809; d. 3.1827
Missing Dates: b. 8.1821-3.1827; m. 2.1816-
3.1827; d. ends 2.1874
Parish Address: Rev. Patrick Eaton, PP,
Oughterard, Co. Galway

Civil Parish: **Kilgerrill**
Map Grid: 79
RC Parish: see Fohanagh
Diocese: CF

Civil Parish: **Kilkerrin**
Map Grid: 39
RC Parish: Kilkerrin and Clonberne
Diocese: TU
Earliest Record: b. 8.1853
Parish Address: Rev. T. Lynch, PP, Kilkerrin,
Ballinasloe, Co. Galway

Civil Parish: **Kilkilvery**
Map Grid: 29
RC Parish: Killursa, etc., see Killower
Diocese: TU

Civil Parish: **Killaan**
Map Grid: 75
RC Parish: see Bullaun
Diocese: CF

Civil Parish: **Killalaghten**
Map Grid: 76
RC Parish: Killalaghten and Kilriekhill (Cap-
patagle)
Diocese: CF
Earliest Record: b. 1.1809; m. 1.1809; d. 1.1809
Missing Dates: b. 5.1827-9.1827, ends 9.1869;
m. 5.1827-9.1827, ends 7.1863; d. 5.1827-
9.1827, ends 9.1869
Parish Address: Rev. A. Cummins, PP, Cap-
patagle, Ballinasloe, Co. Galway

Civil Parish: **Killannin**
Map Grid: 24
RC Parish: Killanin (Rosscahill)
Diocese: TU
Earliest Record: b. 1.1875; m. 1.1875
Parish Address: Rev. Patrick Woods, PP,
Rosscahill, Co. Galway

Civil Parish: **Killeany**
Map Grid: 32
RC Parish: Killursa, etc., see Killower
Diocese: KMC

Civil Parish: **Killeely**
Map Grid: 58
RC Parish: see Kinvarradoorus
Diocese: KMC

Civil Parish: **Killeenadeema**
Map Grid: 96
RC Parish: Kilnadeema and Kilteskil
Diocese: CF
Earliest Record: b. 5.1836; m. 4.1836
Parish Address: Rev. E. Melody, PP, Kil-
nadeema, Loughrea, Co. Galway

Civil Parish: **Killeenavarra**
Map Grid: 65
RC Parish: see Kilcolgan
Diocese: KMC

Civil Parish: **Killeeney**
Map Grid: 59
RC Parish: Castlegar
Diocese: KMC
Earliest Record: b. 11.1864; m. 11.1864;
d. 11.1864
Parish Address: Rev. Canon Brendan Helly, PP,
Castlegar, Co. Galway

Civil Parish: **Killererin**
Map Grid: 35
RC Parish: Killererin
Diocese: TU
Earliest Record: b. 6.1870; m. 2.1851
Missing Dates: m. 8.1858-10.1870
Parish Address: Ven. Conor Heaney, PP, Kil-
lererin, Barnderg, Tuam, Co. Galway

Civil Parish: **Killeroran**
Map Grid: 48
RC Parish: see Killian
Diocese: EL

Civil Parish: **Killian**
Map Grid: 47
RC Parish: Killian and Killeroran
Diocese: EL
Earliest Record: b. 4.1804; m. 4.1804; d. 5.1804
Missing Dates: b. 7.1833-10.1844; m. 2.1843-
10.1844; d. 9.1829-10.1844, ends 1859
Parish Address: Rev. G. Donnelly, PP, Ballygar,
Co. Galway

Civil Parish: **Killimorbologue**
Map Grid: 116
RC Parish: Killimorbologue and Tiranascragh
Diocese: CF

Civil Parish: **Killimordaly**
Map Grid: 73
RC Parish: Killimordaly and Kiltullagh
Diocese: CF
Earliest Record: b. 9.1839; m. 8.1839
Missing Dates: m. 4.1874-1.1877
Parish Address: Rev. John Glynn, PP, Kiltulla,
Athenry, Co. Galway

Civil Parish: **Killinan**
Map Grid: 94
RC Parish: see Kilchreest
Diocese: CF

Civil Parish: **Killinny**
Map Grid: 86
RC Parish: Killursa, etc., see Killower
Diocese: TU

Civil Parish: **Killogilleen**
Map Grid: 67
RC Parish: Killogilleen, etc., see Killora
Diocese: CF

Civil Parish: **Killora**
Map Grid: 60
RC Parish: Killogilleen and Killora (Craugh-
well)
Diocese: KMC
Earliest Record: b. 11.1847; m. 7.1856
Parish Address: Rev. Laurence Bane, PP,
Craughwall, Co. Galway

Civil Parish: **Killoran**
Map Grid: 109
RC Parish: see Abbeygormacan
Diocese: CF

Civil Parish: **Killoscobe**
Map Grid: 42
RC Parish: Killascobe
Diocese: TU
Earliest Record: b. 7.1867; m. 6.1807
Missing Dates: m. 7.1819-11.1825, 6.1847-
7.1849

Parish Address: Rev. Jarlath Canney, PP, Menlough, Ballinasloe, Co. Galway

Civil Parish: **Killosolan**
Map Grid: 43
RC Parish: Caltra, see Ahascragh
Diocese: EL

Civil Parish: **Killower**
Map Grid: 27
RC Parish: Killursa and Killower
Diocese: TU
Earliest Record: no register pre-1880
Parish Address: Rev. William Clarke, PP, Claran, Ower, Co. Galway

Civil Parish: **Killursa**
Map Grid: 28
RC Parish: see Killower
Diocese: TU

Civil Parish: **Kilmacduagh**
Map Grid: 88
RC Parish: Kilmacduagh
Diocese: KMC
Earliest Record: b. 2.1848; m. 12.1853
Parish Address: Rev. Christopher Walsh, PP, Gort, Co. Galway

Civil Parish: **Kilmalinoge**
Map Grid: 120
RC Parish: Kilmalinoge and Lickmolassey (Portumna)
Diocese: CF
Earliest Record: b. 10.1830; m. 10.1830
Parish Address: Rev. Patrick Egan, PP, St. Brigid's, Portumna, Co. Galway

Civil Parish: **Kilmeen**
Map Grid: 99
RC Parish: see Kilcooly
Diocese: TU

Civil Parish: **Kilmoylan**
Map Grid: 37
RC Parish: see Cummer
Diocese: TU

Civil Parish: **Kilquain**
Map Grid: 113

RC Parish: see Fahy
Diocese: CF

Civil Parish: **Kilreekil**
Map Grid: 98
RC Parish: see Killalaghten
Diocese: CF

Civil Parish: **Kiltartan**
Map Grid: 87
RC Parish: Kiltartan, see Kilmacduagh
Diocese: KMC

Civil Parish: **Kilteskil**
Map Grid: 101
RC Parish: see Killeenadeema
Diocese: CF

Civil Parish: **Kilthomas**
Map Grid: 97
RC Parish: Peterswell
Diocese: KMC
Earliest Record: b. 1.1884; m. 1.1856
Parish Address: Rev. Vincent Jennings, PP, Peterswell, Co. Galway

Civil Parish: **Kiltormer**
Map Grid: 110
RC Parish: Kiltormer and Oghill
Diocese: CF
Earliest Record: b. 3.1834; m. 2.1834
Missing Dates: b. 7.1860-5.1862; m. 5.1860-9.1860
Parish Address: Rev. Martin Walsh, PP, Laurencetown, Ballinasloe, Co. Galway

Civil Parish: **Kiltullagh**
Map Grid: 70
RC Parish: see Killimordaly
Diocese: CF

Civil Parish: **Kinvarradoorus**
Map Grid: 85
RC Parish: Kinvarra
Diocese: KMC
Earliest Record: b. 6.1831; m. 7.1831
Missing Dates: b. 5.1837-6.1843, 8.1853-7.1854; m. 5.1837-6.1843, 8.1853-7.1854
Parish Address: Rev. Michael O'Connor, PP, Kinvara, Co. Galway

Civil Parish: **Lackagh**
Map Grid: 38
RC Parish: Lackagh
Diocese: TU
Earliest Record: b. 7.1842; m. 9.1841
Missing Dates: b. 9.1847-3.1848; m. 12.1847-9.1853
Parish Address: Rev. Michael Lyons, PP, Turloughmore, Co. Galway

Civil Parish: **Leitrim**
Map Grid: 102
RC Parish: see Kilcooly
Diocese: CF

Civil Parish: **Lickmolassy**
Map Grid: 119
RC Parish: see Kilmalinoge
Diocese: CF

Civil Parish: **Liskeevy**
Map Grid: 9
RC Parish: see Addergoole
Diocese: TU

Civil Parish: **Loughrea**
Map Grid: 92
RC Parish: Loughrea (St. Brendan's Cathedral)
Diocese: CF
Earliest Record: b. 4.1827; m. 5.1827
Parish Address: Rev. E. Stankard, The Presbytery, Loughrea, Co. Galway

Civil Parish: **Meelick**
Map Grid: 118
RC Parish: see Clonfert
Diocese: CF

Civil Parish: **Monivea**
Map Grid: 44
RC Parish: part Athenry; part Abbeyknockmoy
Diocese: TU

Civil Parish: **Moycullen (1)**
Map Grid: 25
RC Parish: Moycullen; also Spiddal, see below
Diocese: CF
Earliest Record: b. 1.1786; m. 1.1786; d. 1.1786
Missing Dates: b. 3.1823-1.1837, 5.1841-10.1843, m. 1.1823-10.1843, 10.1848-2.1849; d. 1.1823-11.1848

Parish Address: Rev. E. McInerney, PP, Moycullen, Co. Galway

Civil Parish: **Moycullen (2)**
Map Grid: 25
RC Parish: Spiddal
Diocese: CF
Earliest Record: b. 2.1861; m. 4.1873; d. 4.1873
Parish Address: Rev. Thomas Kyne, PP, Spiddal, Co. Galway

Civil Parish: **Moylough**
Map Grid: 40
RC Parish: Moylough
Diocese: TU
Earliest Record: b. 1.1848; m. 11.1848
Missing Dates: b. 7.1870-1.1871
Parish Address: Rev. Michael Tobin, PP, Mountbellew, Ballinasloe, Co. Galway

Civil Parish: **Moyrus**
Map Grid: 3
RC Parish: Moyrus (Carna)
Diocese: TU
Earliest Record: b. 12.1853; m. 9.1852
Missing Dates: 9.1873-10.1874
Parish Address: Rev. P. Delaney, PP, Kilkerrin, Carna, Co. Galway

Civil Parish: **Omey**
Map Grid: 2
RC Parish: see Ballindoon
Diocese: CF

Civil Parish: **Oranmore**
Map Grid: 52
RC Parish: Oranmore
Diocese: TU
Earliest Record: b. 3.1833; m. 5.1833; d. 1.1833
Missing Dates: m. 7.1838-8.1848; d. ends 12.1837
Parish Address: Rev. Martin O'Connor, PP, Oranmore, Co. Galway

Civil Parish: **Rahoon**
Map Grid: 53
RC Parish: Rahoon
Diocese: TU
Earliest Record: b. 1.1819; m. 1.1819; d. 1.1819
Missing Dates: b. 1.1845-4.1845; m. ends 12.1832; d. ends 7.1826

Parish Address: Rev. Patrick Tully, PP, Barna, Co. Galway

Civil Parish: **Ross**
Map Grid: 7
RC Parish: Clonbur (Ross); see also Cong, Co. Mayo
Diocese: TU
Earliest Record: b. 12.1853
Missing Dates: b. 4.1871-1.1873
Parish Address: Rev. James Heaney, PP, Clonbur, Claremorris, Co. Galway

Civil Parish: **St. Nicholas**
Map Grid: 54
RC Parish: St. Nicholas Cathedral
Diocese: TU
Earliest Record: b. 3.1723
Missing Dates: b. 3.1725-2.1814
Parish Address: Rev. James McLoughlin, PP, The Cathedral Presbytery, Co. Galway

Civil Parish: **Stradbally**
Map Grid: 57
RC Parish: Kilcornan or Clarenbridge
Diocese: KMC
Earliest Record: b. 8.1854; m. 6.1837
Parish Address: Rev. Dermot Higgins, PP, Clarenbridge, Co. Galway

Civil Parish: **Taghboy**
Map Grid: 51
RC Parish: Dysart and Tisara, see Dysart, Co. Roscommon
Diocese: EL

Civil Parish: **Templetogher**
Map Grid: 15
RC Parish: see Boyounagh
Diocese: TU

Civil Parish: **Tiranascragh**
Map Grid: 117
RC Parish: see Killimorebologue
Diocese: CF

Civil Parish: **Tuam**
Map Grid: 14
RC Parish: Tuam
Diocese: TU
Earliest Record: b. 3.1790; m. 1.1799

Missing Dates: b. 7.1804-10.1811, 10.1857-10.1858; m. 3.1832-10.1832
Parish Address: Rev. Dominick Grealy, Tuam, Co. Galway

Civil Parish: **Tynagh**
Map Grid: 104
RC Parish: Tynagh
Diocese: CF
Earliest Record: b. 5.1809; m. 5.1816
Missing Dates: b. 12.1842-9.1846; m. 12.1842-9.1846
Parish Address: Rev. Kevin Ryle, PP, Tynagh, Loughrea, Co. Galway

Commercial and Social Directories

1820
J. Pigot's *Commercial Directory of Ireland* contains information on the gentry, nobility, and traders in and around the city of Galway.

1824
J. Pigot's *City of Dublin & Hibernian Provincial Directory* includes traders, nobility, gentry, and clergy lists of Ballinasloe, Eyrecourt, Galway, Gort, Loughrea, and Tuam.

1846
Slater's *National Commercial Directory of Ireland* lists nobility, clergy, traders, etc., in Athenry, Ballinasloe, Castleblakeney, Clifden, Dunmore, Eyrecourt, Galway, Gort, Headford, Loughrea, Portumna, and Tuam.

1856
Slater's *Royal National Commercial Directory of Ireland* lists nobility, gentry, clergy, traders, etc., in Athenry, Ballinasloe, Clifden, Dunmore, Eyrecourt, Galway, Gort, Headford, Loughrea, Portumna, and Tuam.

1870
Slater's *Directory of Ireland* contains trade, nobility, and clergy lists for Athenry, Ballinasloe, Clifden, Dunmore, Eyrecourt, Galway, Gort, Headford, Loughrea, Portumna, and Tuam.

1881

Slater's *Royal National Commercial Directory of Ireland* contains lists of traders, clergy, nobility, and farmers in adjoining parishes of the towns of Athenry, Ballinasloe, Clifden, Eyrecourt, Galway, Gort, Loughrea, Portumna, and Tuam.

1894

Slater's *Royal National Directory of Ireland* lists traders, police, teachers, farmers, and private residents in each of the towns, villages, and parishes of the county.

Family History

Blake, Martin J. "Families of Daly of Galway with Tabular Pedigrees." *J. Galway Arch. & Hist. Soc.* 13 (1926-27): 140.

_____. "Pedigree of Lynch of Lavally, County Galway." *J. Galway Arch. & Hist. Soc.* 10 (1917-18): 66-69.

"The Burkes of Marble Hill." *J. Galway Arch. & Hist. Soc.* 8 (1913-14): 1-11.

"The De Burgo Clans of Galway." *J. Galway Arch. & Hist. Soc.* 1 (1900-01): 123-31; 3 (1903-04): 46-58; 4 (1905-06): 55-62.

Genealogy of the O'Malleys of the Owals. Philadelphia, 1913.

Hartigan, A.S. *A Short Account of the Eyre Family of Eyre Court, and Eyre of Eyreville, in Co. Galway.* Reading, n.d.

Hayes-McCoy, Marguerite. "The Eyre Documents in University College, Galway." *J. Galway Arch. & Hist. Soc.* 20: 57-74; 21: 71-95; 23: 147-53 (1942-49).

Kenney, J.F. *Pedigree of the Kenney Family of Kilclogher, Co. Galway.* Dublin, 1868.

Knox, H. "The Bermingham Family of Athenry." *J. Galway Arch. & Hist. Soc.* 10 (1917-18): 139-54.

Lynch, E. *Genealogical Memoranda Relating to the Family of Lynch.* London, 1883.

Lynch Record, containing biographical sketches of men of the name Lynch, 16th century to 20th century. New York, 1925.

Lynch, John. "Account of the Lynch Family and of the Memorable Events of the Town of Galway." *J. Galway Arch. & Hist. Soc.* 8 (1913-14): 76-93.

"Mahon Papers" (Castlebar, Co. Galway). *Anal. Hib.* 25: 77-93.

"Notes on the Mills Family of Headford, Co. Galway and Roscommon." *J. Ass. Pres. Mem. Dead* 10: 241.

O'Malley, Sir Owen. "Note on the O'Malley Lordship at the Close of the XVIth Century." *J. Galway Arch. & Hist. Soc.* 24 (1950-51): 27-57.

"O'Malleys Between 1607 and 1725." *J. Galway Arch. & Hist. Soc.* 25 (1952): 32-46.

"The O'Maolconaire Family." *J. Galway Arch. & Hist. Soc.* 29 (1940-41): 118-46.

"The O'Maolconaire Family." *J. Galway Arch. & Hist. Soc.* 20 (1942-43): 82-88.

Orpen, Goddard H. "Notes on the Bermingham Pedigree." *J. Galway Arch. & Hist. Soc.* 9 (1915-16): 195-205.

"O'Shaughnessy of Gort (1543-1783): Tabular Pedigree." *J. Galway Arch. & Hist. Soc.* 7 (1911-12): 53.

"Portumna and the Burkes." *J. Galway Arch. & Hist. Soc.* 6 (1909): 107-09.

"Seanchus nam Burcach and Historia et Genealogia Familae De Burgo." *J. Galway Arch. & Hist. Soc.* 13 (1926-27): 50-60, 101-37; 14 (1928-29): 310-51, 142-66.

"Some Notes on the Burkes." *J. Galway Arch. & Hist. Soc.* 1 (1900-01): 1966-67.

Walsh, Rev. Paul. "The Learned Family of O'Maelconaire." Chapter 4 of *Irish Men of Learning.* Dublin, 1947.

Gravestone Inscriptions

Kilmacduagh: *Irish Ancestor* 7 (1) (1975): 26-34.

Newspapers

Unfortunately, there were not very many newspapers published in Galway and surviving copies of those published are rare. The *Connaught Journal* is the best of the early (1813) surviving papers.

Title: *Ballinasloe Independent* (see *Western Argus*)

Title: *Connaught Journal*
Published in: Galway, 1793-1840
NLI Holdings: 1793; 1795; 1823-36; odd numbers 1839, 1840
BL Holdings: 1.1823-12.1836; 2-12.1840

Title: *Connaught Patriot*
Published in: Tuam, 1859-69
BL Holdings: 8.1859-12.1864; 10.1865-3.1869

Title: *Connaught People*
Published in: Ballinasloe, 1882-86
BL Holdings: 4.1884-9.1886

Title: *Galway Express*
Published in: Galway, 1853-1920
NLI Holdings: 1.1853-10.1918; 3.1919-9.1920
BL Holdings: 1.1853-12.1918; 3.1919-9.1920

Title: *Galway Free Press*
Published in: Galway, 1832-35
NLI Holdings: 1.1832-3.1835
BL Holdings: 1.1832-3.1835

Title: *Galway Independent Paper*
Published in: Galway, ca. 1825-32
NLI Holdings: 1.1829-3.1832
BL Holdings: 1.1829-3.1832

Title: *Galway Mercury*
Published in: Galway, 1844-60
NLI Holdings: 10.1844-3.1860
BL Holdings: 10.1844-3.1860

Title: *Galway Observer*
Published in: Galway, 1881-1966
NLI Holdings: 1902; 1917-21; 8.1927-10.1966

BL Holdings: odd numbers 1882-84; 6.1889-8.1923; 2.1925-10.1966

Title: *Galway Packet*
Published in: Galway, 1852-54
NLI Holdings: 4.1852-12.1854
BL Holdings: 4.1852-12.1854

Title: *Galway Patriot*
Published in: Galway, 1835-39
NLI Holdings: 7.1835-10.1839
BL Holdings: 7.1835-10.1839

Title: *Galway Vindicator*
Published in: Galway, 1841-99
NLI Holdings: 7.1841-12.1844; 3-12.1845; 1846-55; 2.1856-12.1858; 1.1859-12.1898; 1-11.1899
BL Holdings: 7.1841-12.1844; 3.1845-12.1855; 2.1856-1.1876; 2.1876-11.1899

Title: *Galway Weekly Advertiser*
Published in: Galway, 1823-43
NLI Holdings: 1.1823-5.1843
BL Holdings: 1.1823-5.1843

Title: *Tuam Herald* (continued as *Herald and Western Advertiser* in 1955)
Published in: Tuam, 1837-1955
NLI Holdings: 5.1837-9.1955 (with gaps)
BL Holdings: 5.1837-9.1955 (with gaps)

Title: *Tuam News and Western Advertiser*
Published in: Tuam, 1871-1904
NLI Holdings: 1.1882-12.1904 (with gaps)
BL Holdings: 6.1871-7.1873; 4.1884-1.1896

Title: *Western Argus & Ballinasloe Independent*
Published in: Ballinasloe, 1828-33
NLI Holdings: 4.1828-12.1829; 2.1830-1.1833
BL Holdings: 4.1828-10.1829; odd numbers 1830; 7.1830-1833

Title: *Western News*
Published in: Ballinasloe, 1877-1926
NLI Holdings: 10-12.1898; 3.1901-7.1903; 7.1904-12.1926
BL Holdings: 11.1878-11.1877; 2.1888-1.1892; 12.1899-12.1902

Title: *Western Star & Ballinasloe Advertiser*
Published in: Ballinasloe, 1845-1902
NLI Holdings: 10.1845-12.1866; 1.1867-8.1869; 12.1888-5.1902
BL Holdings: 10.1845-8.1869; 12.1888-5.1902

Marriage Licenses

Indexes. Tuam (1661-1750). PRO; SLC film 100872. Elphin (1740-1850). PRO; SLC film 100868. Clonfert (1691-1845). PRO; SLC film 100869

Wills and Administrations

A discussion of the types of records, where they are held, their availability and value is given in the Wills section of the Introduction. The availability of prerogative wills, administrations, and marriage license records is also described in the relevant parts of the same section. Where available, published sources of these records are given in the Miscellaneous Sources section.

Pre-1858 Wills and Administrations

Prerogative Wills. see p. xli
Consistorial Wills. County Galway is mainly in the diocese of Tuam, but also in Elphin, Kilmacduagh, and Clonfert. The guide to Catholic parish records in this chapter shows the diocese to which each civil parish belonged. The wills of residents of each diocese were usually proven within that diocese (see the Wills section for exceptions). The following records survive:

Wills. see p. xxxvii

Abstracts. see p. xxxvii; also GO ms. 707 has many abstracts from Diocese of Tuam, Clonfert, and Kilmacduagh.

Indexes. Tuam (1648-1858), Elphin (1650-1858), Kilmacduagh and Clonfert (1663-1858) published to 1800 by Phillimore; also in *Clonfert and Kilmacduagh* by P. Smythe-Wood. 1977.

Post-1858 Wills and Administrations

County Galway was served by the District Registry of Tuam. The surviving records are kept in the PRO.

Miscellaneous Sources

"The Ethnography of the Aran Islands, Co. Galway." *R. Ir. Acad. Proc.* 3rd ser., 2 (1891-93): 827-29.

"The Ethnography of Inishbofin and Inishshark, Co. Galway." *R. Ir. Acad. Proc.* 3 (1893-96): 360-80.

"The Ethnography of Carna and Mweenish in the Parish of Moyruss, Connemara." *R. Ir. Acad. Proc.* 6 (1900-02): 503-34.

Hardiman, J. *History of the Town and County of Galway.* Dublin, 1820. Reprint. 1978.

Kavanagh, M.A. *Bibliography of the County Galway.* Galway, 1965.

"Mayors, Sheriffs and other Public Officials of Galway Town. 1274-1820." In *History of the Town & County of Galway* by J. Hardiman (Dublin, 1820), 197-232.

McLochlainn, J. *A Historical Summary of the Parish of Ahascragh, Caltra & Castleblakeny.* Ballinalsoe, 1979.

O'Sullivan, M.D. *Old Galway.* Cambridge, 1942.

"Tenants of J.P. Smyth at Gort, Co. Galway in 1805." *Ir. Anc.* 14 (1) (1982): 20-21.

"The Tribes of Galway." *Ir. Gen.* 2 (4) (1946): 99-106.

Tuam RC Diocese. Register of marriages in each Deanery for parts of 1821 and 1822, with additions in many parishes to 1829. NLI film P4222.

Research Sources and Services

Journals

Journal of the Galway Archaeological and Historical Society

Libraries and Information Sources

Galway County Library, Galway Ph: (091) 62471

Research Services

See research services in Dublin, p. xliv

Galway-Mayo Family History Research Society (see Co. Mayo)

Galway Heritage Society, c/o 46 Maunsells Park, Galway (in the process of indexing local parish records)

Societies

Old Galway Society, Mrs. D. Crambie, Garraun Lower, Maree, Oranmore, Co. Galway

Kilbegnet-Ballinakill Historical Society, Mr. Lawrence, Kilcommons, Creggs, Co. Galway

Galway Archaeological and Historical Society, c/o Galway County Library, Galway

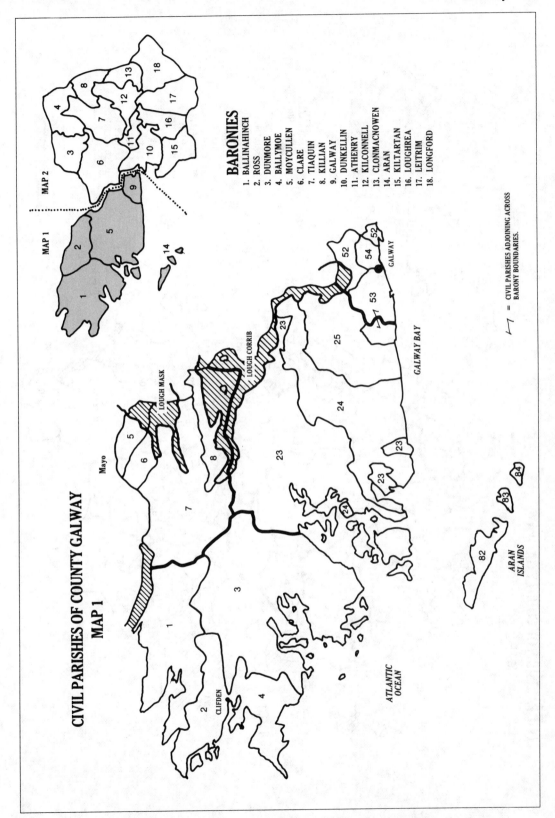

CIVIL PARISHES OF COUNTY GALWAY
MAP 1

BARONIES
1. BALLINAHINCH
2. ROSS
3. DUNMORE
4. BALLYMOE
5. MOYCULLEN
6. CLARE
7. TIAQUIN
8. KILLIAN
9. GALWAY
10. DUNKELLIN
11. ATHENRY
12. KILCONNELL
13. CLONMACNOWEN
14. ARAN
15. KILTARTAN
16. LOUGHREA
17. LEITRIM
18. LONGFORD

⌐ = CIVIL PARISHES ADJOINING ACROSS BARONY BOUNDARIES.

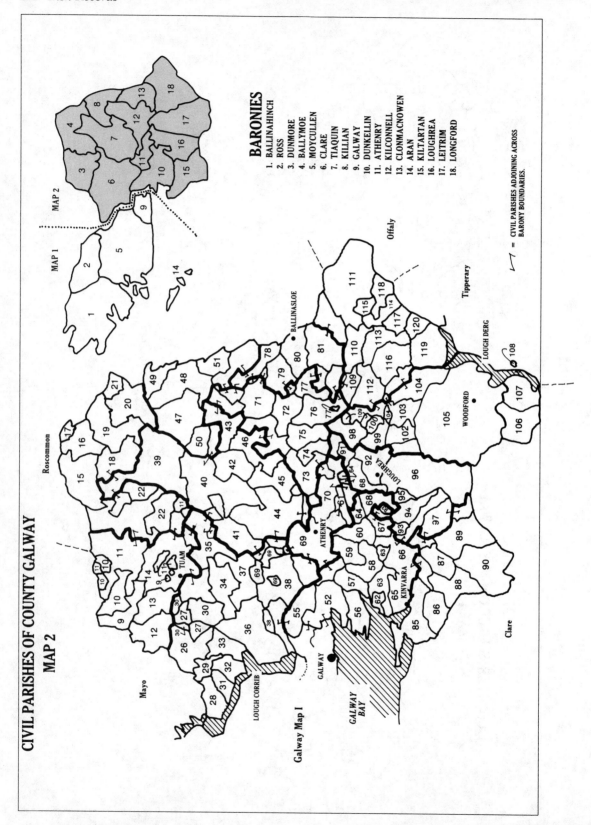

CIVIL PARISHES OF COUNTY GALWAY
MAP 2

BARONIES

1. BALLINAHINCH
2. ROSS
3. DUNMORE
4. BALLYMOE
5. MOYCULLEN
6. CLARE
7. TIAQUIN
8. KILLIAN
9. GALWAY
10. DUNKELLIN
11. ATHENRY
12. KILCONNELL
13. CLONMACNOWEN
14. ARAN
15. KILTARTAN
16. LOUGHREA
17. LEITRIM
18. LONGFORD

⌐ = CIVIL PARISHES ADJOINING ACROSS
      BARONY BOUNDARIES.

County Kerry

A Brief History

The county of Kerry is on the south-western coast of Ireland. Its major towns are Tralee, Listowel, Castleisland, Killarney, Caherciveen, Dingle, and Ballybunion. Before the division of Ireland into counties, this area formed part of the Gaelic territory of Desmond. The major Gaelic families included O'Connor Kerry, O'Driscoll, O'Donoghue, O'Falvey, O'Shea, O'Kelleher, Moriarty, O'Mahoney, and O'Connell. Following the Norman invasion the county was granted to Robert Fitzstephen and Milo de Cogan. However, because of the power of the native chieftains, they were unable to take possession of the county.

The Norman conquest of the more easterly parts of Munster, however, drove the McCarthys and O'Sullivans of those parts to Kerry, displacing some of the resident families. Although the chief of the McCarthys nominally submitted to Henry II in 1172, the McCarthys and the other chieftains effectively retained their lands and control of much of the county.

Parts of the county did come under the chieftainship of Norman families by other means. Raymond Fitzgerald, ancestor of the present Fitzmaurice family, was granted the area around Lixnaw (or Clanmaurice) by one of the McCarthys in return for assistance in a dispute.

John Fitzthomas also obtained large parts of Kerry by marriage. Apart from Fitzgerald and Fitzmaurice, the other families which became established in Kerry after the Norman invasion were Cantillon, Stack, Ferriter, Brown, Clifford, Cromwell, Hussey, and Trant. Fitzthomas was an ancestor of the Fitzgeralds who were made Earls of Desmond in 1329 and maintained control of Desmond for centuries.

By the mid-fourteenth century the three major families in the county were Fitzgerald, Fitzmaurice, and McCarthy.

By the late sixteenth century the lands of Kerry and Cork began to attract the attention of English "adventurers" who approached the English crown to give them title to these lands. A huge scheme of confiscation of Munster lands was planned. This alarmed the Irish and Norman chieftains who protested against the scheme. Their formal protests about the scheme failed, and in 1580 the Earl of Desmond rebelled against the English. He was eventually defeated after a bloody war which devastated much of Desmond. The people of Munster suffered greatly after this rebellion both from the savagery of the troops and from the famine which resulted from their destruction of crops and property. The power of the Fitzgeralds never recovered after this. Thousands of those made homeless during this rebellion were gathered together and transported to the West

Indies. After the rebellion the estates of all the rebels were confiscated and distributed among English adventurers, in particular Blennerhassett, Browne, Herbert, Champion, Holly, Denny, and Conway. Among the settlers who obtained grants from these adventurers were the families of Spring, Rice, Morris, and Gunn.

Following the defeat of the 1641 rebellion further parts of the county were granted to English adventurers, in particular Sir William Petty. Many of the settlers brought in at this time (the 1670s) left again during the Williamite wars when the Irish forces again took control of the county. The names of the pre-1641 and post-1641 owners of land are listed in the Book of Survey of Distribution and in the Civil Survey.

The county was relatively badly affected by the Great Famine of 1845-47. The population was 294,000 in 1841 and had dropped by 19 percent in 1851. During the main years of the famine, 1845-50, around 32,000 people died. Furthermore, between 1851 and 1855, 44,000 people, or 17 percent of the population, emigrated.

The eastern part of the county, particularly the northeast, is rich agricultural land while the more westerly parts are mountainous.

The major industries are agriculture, fishing, and tourism. The lakes of Killarney, for instance, have been a tourist attraction since the early nineteenth century.

Census and Census Substitutes

1641

List of Proprietors of Land: Books of Survey and Distribution. NLI ms. 970.

1657

"Parishes of Dysart, Killurry, Rathroe." *Civil Survey.* Vol. 4; also in *Kerry Arch. Mag.* 1 (6) (1911): 357-68; SLC film 973122.

1659

"Census" of Ireland. Edited by S. Pender. Dublin: Stationery Office, 1939. SLC film 924648.

1666-68

"New Grantees of Lands" (see source listed in 1641 above).

1775

"Catholic Qualification Roll Extracts" (103 names, addresses, and occupations). 59th Report *DKPRI,* 50-84.

1821

Government Census Remnants: Parish of Kilcummin. RIA; McSwiney Papers (Parcel F, No. 3); SLC film 596418.

1824-37

Tithe Applotment Survey. (see p. xxvii).

1834

"Census of the Parishes of Prior and Killenlagh." *J. Kerry Arch. Hist. Soc.* 8 (1975): 114-35.

1835

"A Census of the Catholic Parish of Ferriter" (comprising civil parishes of Dunquin, Dunurlin, Kilmalkedar, Kilquane, and Marhin). *J. Kerry. Arch. Hist. Soc.* 7 (1974): 37-70 (both above list householders in each townland, and total males and females in each household).

1852

Griffith's Valuation. (p. xxvii)

1901

Census. PRO.

1911

Census. PRO.

Church Records

Church of Ireland
(shows starting date of record)

Parish: **Aghavallin**
Existing Records: b. 1802; m. 1804; d. 1803
Status: LC

Population returun of the Parish of Keelimila Barony of Iueragh County of Kerry as enumerated in the month of December 1834

Townlands	M.	F.	Tot.		M.	F.	Tot.
BOLUS				John Goggin	4	3	7
William Cronin	5	4	9	Michael Shea	1	3	4
Daniel Leary	4	6	10	James FitzGerald	3	4	7
William Casey	3	2	5				
John Sullivan	3	2	5		25	23	48
Daniel Hartnett	5	2	7		[all Catholics]		
Cornelius Kelly	3	2	5				
Michael Burke	2	1	3		Houses		7
Darby Currane	2	2	4				
Maurice Currane	2	2	4				
John Currane	2	2	4				
Denis Currane	3	1	4	**TUREEN**			
Daniel Gallivan	2	2	4	Daniel Foley	5	1	6
John Sughrue	5	2	7	Timothy Foley	2	3	5
Thomas Moore	2	3	5	Patrick Casey	2	2	4
				Michael Burke	5	4	9
	43	33	76	Daniel Connor	1	1	2
	[all Catholics]						
					15	11	26
	Houses		14		[all Catholics]		
					Houses		5
DUCALLA							
Darby Murphy	2	2	4				
Daniel Murphy	2	3	5	**KEELŌNCAH**[38]			
John Murphy	2	2	4	Daniel Murphy	4	3	7
Daniel Sullivan	1	2	3	Maurice Sullivan	3	3	6
Maurice Sullivan	1	1	2	Eugene Sullivan	3	2	5[39]
John Keating	4	1	5	Cornelius Sullivan	2	2	4
Denies Sullivan	1	1	2	Darby Sullivan	2	3	5
Daniel Sullivan	1	2	3	Cornelius Connor	1	1	2
William Goggin	1	2	3				
					15	14	29
	15	16	31		[all Catholics]		
	[all Catholics]						
					Houses		6
	Houses		9				
				AHERT			
ALAHEE[37]				Patrick Sullivan	7	3	10
John Sullivan	5	4	9	Thomas Currane	4	3	7
William Murphy	2	4	6	Michael Connell	4	4	8
Barth[w] Murphy	6	1	7	Michael Keary	3	5	8
Patrick Mahoney	4	4	8	Thomas Currane	4	3	7

37. Allaghee More in Ordnance Survey; see also note 44.
38. *Sic*; also spelt thus in totals. Cf. note 84.
39. Corrected from '3'.

Extract from a census of the County Kerry, Parishes of Prior and Killemlagh in December, 1834. From *J. Kerry Arch. & Hist. Soc.* 8 (1975).

Parish: **Aghlish**
Status: Lost

Parish: **Ardfert**
Status: Lost

Parish: **Ballincuslane** (see Ballycuslane)

Parish: **Ballycuslane**
Status: Lost

Parish: **Ballyheige**
Status: Lost

Parish: **Ballymacelligot**
Existing Records: b. 1817; m. 1817; d. 1817
Status: LC

Parish: **Ballynacourty**
Existing records: b. 1803; m. 1803; d. 1803
Status: LC

Parish: **Ballynahaglish**
Status: Lost

Parish: **Ballyseedy**
Existing Records: b. 1830; d. 1831
Status: LC

Parish: **Caher**
Status: Lost

Parish: **Castleisland**
Existing Records: b. 1835; m. 1836; d. 1836
Status: LC

Parish: **Cloghane**
Status: Lost

Parish: **Dromod** and **Prior**
Existing Records: b. 1820; m. 1827; d. 1833
Status: LC and PRO

Parish: **Duagh**
Status: Lost

Parish: **Glenbeigh**
Status: Lost

Parish: **Kenmare**
Existing Records: b. 1799; m. 1799; d. 1799
Status: LC

Parish: **Kilbonane** (see Mollahiffe)

Parish: **Kilconly** (see Aghavallin)

Parish: **Kilcrohane** (see also Templenoe)
Status: Lost

Parish: **Kilcummin** (see Killarney)

Parish: **Kilflynn**
Status: Lost

Parish: **Kilgarrylander** (see Kiltallagh)

Parish: **Kilgarvan**
Existing Records: b. 1811; m. 1811; d. 1811
Status: LC

Parish: **Kilgobbin**
Existing Records: b. 1713; m. 1713; d. 1713
Missing Dates: b. 1755; m. 1755; d. 1755
Status: LC

Parish: **Killarney**
Status: Lost

Parish: **Killemlogh**

Parish: **Killeentierna** or **Disert**
Status: Lost

Parish: **Killeny**
Status: Lost

Parish: **Killorglin**
Status: Lost

Parish: **Killury** and **Rattoo**
Existing Records: b. 1803; m. 1803; d. 1802
Status: LC

Parish: **Kilmackelogue** or **Tuosist** (see Kenmare)

Parish: **Kilmalkedar**
Status: Lost

Parish: **Kilmoiley** (see also Ballyheige)
Status: Lost

Parish: **Kilnaughtin**
Existing Records: b. 1793; m. 1793; d. 1793
Status: LC

Parish: **Kilshenane** (see Kilflynn)

Parish: **Kiltallagh**
Status: Lost

Parish: **Knockane**
Status: Lost

Parish: **Lisselton** (see also Listowel)
Existing Records: b. 1840; d. 1840
Status: LC

Parish: **Listowel**
Existing Records: b. 1790; m. 1790; d. 1790
Status: LC

Parish: **Mollahiffe**
Status: Lost

Parish: **Rattoo** (see also Killury)
Existing Records: b. 1868; d. 1870
Status: LC

Parish: **St. Anne** (see also Ballynahaglish)
Status: Lost

Parish: **Templenoe** (see also Kilcrohane)
Status: Lost

Parish: **Tralee**
Existing Records: b. 1771; m. 1771; d. 1771
Status: LC

Parish: **Ventry**
Status: Lost

Presbyterian

Parish: **Tralee**
Starting Date: 1840

Roman Catholic

Civil Parish: **Aghadoe**
Map Grid: 79
RC Parish: Killarney (Fossa); also part
  Glenflesk, see Killaha
Diocese: A and A
Earliest Record: b. 1.1857; m. 1.1858
Parish Address: Rev. James Galvin, PP, Fossa,
  Killarney, Co. Kerry

Civil Parish: **Aghavallen**
Map Grid: 2
RC Parish: Ballylongford
Diocese: A and A
Earliest Record: b. 3.1823; m. 6.1826
Missing Dates: b. 5.1838-10.1869; m. few
  Records to 1837
Parish Address: Rev. T. McMahon, PP, Bal-
  lylongford, Co. Kerry

Civil Parish: **Aglish**
Map Grid: 75
RC Parish: Fieries, see Kilnanare
Diocese: A and A

Civil Parish: **Annagh**
Map Grid: 53
RC Parish: part Tralee; part Ballymacelligott
Diocese: A and A

Civil Parish: **Ardfert**
Map Grid: 25
RC Parish: Ardfert
Diocese: A and A
Earliest Record: (only scattered records to
  1835) b. 3.1819; m. 2.1825
Missing Dates: b. 1846-1859; m. 1846-1859
Parish Address: Rev. Arthur Moynihan, PP,
  Ardfert, Co. Kerry

Civil Parish: **Ballincuslane**
Map Grid: 56
RC Parish: Knocknagoshel; also part Castleis-
  land

Civil Parish: **Ballinvoher**
Map Grid: 40
RC Parish: Annascaul, see Kilgobban
Diocese: A and A

Civil Parish: **Ballyconry**
Map Grid: 8
RC Parish: see Lisselton
Diocese: LK

Civil Parish: **Ballyduff**
Map Grid: 28
RC Parish: Castlegregory, see Killiney
Diocese: A and A

Civil Parish: **Ballyheigue**
Map Grid: 16
RC Parish: Ballyheigue
Diocese: A and A
Earliest Record: b. 12.1857; m. 1.1858
Parish Address: Rev. P. Scott, PP, Ballyheigue, Tralee, Co. Kerry

Civil Parish: **Ballymacelligott**
Map Grid: 49
RC Parish: Ballymacelligott
Diocese: A and A
Earliest Record: b. 10.1868; m. 11.1868
Parish Address: Rev. D. O'Doherty, PP, Ballymacelligott, Co. Kerry

Civil Parish: **Ballynacourty**
Map Grid: 39
RC Parish: Annascaul, see Ballinvoher
Diocese: A and A

Civil Parish: **Ballynahaglish**
Map Grid: 45
RC Parish: Spa
Diocese: A and A
Earliest Record: b. 11.1866; m. 1.1867
Parish Address: Rev. E. O'Connor, PP, Fenit, Tralee, Co. Kerry

Civil Parish: **Ballyseedy**
Map Grid: 54
RC Parish: see Ballymacelligott
Diocese: A and A

Civil Parish: **Brosna**
Map Grid: 52
RC Parish: Brosna
Diocese: A and A
Earliest Record: b. 3.1868
Parish Address: Rev. D. Griffin, PP, Brosna via Abbeyfeale, Co. Limerick

Civil Parish: **Caher**
Map Grid: 65
RC Parish: Cahirciveen
Diocese: A and A
Earliest Record: b. 11.1846
Parish Address: Rev. D. Curtin, PP, Cahirciveen, Co. Kerry

Civil Parish: **Castleisland**
Map Grid: 51
RC Parish: Castleisland
Diocese: A and A
Earliest Record: b. 4.1823; m. 10.1822
Missing Dates: b. 8.1869-2.1870; m. 8.1858-2.1859
Parish Address: Rev. Canon M. Herlihy, PP, Castleisland, Co. Kerry

Civil Parish: **Cloghane**
Map Grid: 27
RC Parish: part Castlegregory, see Killiney; part Dingle
Diocese: A and A

Civil Parish: **Clogherbrien**
Map Grid: 46
RC Parish: Mainly Tralee; part Spa, see Ballynahaglish
Diocese: A and A

Civil Parish: **Currans**
Map Grid: 59
RC Parish: see Killeentierna
Diocese: A and A

Civil Parish: **Dingle**
Map Grid: 35
RC Parish: Dingle
Diocese: A and A
Earliest Record: b. 2.1825; m. 5.1821
Missing Dates: b. 4.1837-9.1837
Parish Address: Rev. Canon J. Colbert, PP, Dingle, Co. Kerry

Civil Parish: **Dromod**
Map Grid: 70
RC Parish: Dromod (Waterville)
Diocese: A and A
Earliest Record: b. 2.1850; m. 1.1850
Parish Address: Rev. E. O'Riordan, PP, Waterville, Killarney, Co. Kerry 0667-4151

Civil Parish: **Duagh**
Map Grid: 15
RC Parish: Duagh
Diocese: A and A
Earliest Record: (some gaps in early 1850s)
   b. 1.1819; m. 1.1832
Parish Address: Rev. T. O'Sullivan, PP, Duagh,
   Kilmorna, Co. Kerry

Civil Parish: **Dunquin**
Map Grid:
RC Parish: Ballyferriter, see Kilmalkedar
Diocese: A and A

Civil Parish: **Dunurlin**
Map Grid: 32
RC Parish: Ballyferriter, see Kilmalkedar
Diocese: A and A

Civil Parish: **Dysert** (Trughenackmy)
Map Grid: 13
RC Parish: see Killeentierna
Diocese: A and A

Civil Parish: **Dysart** (Clanmaurice)
Map Grid: 61
RC Parish: part Lixnaw, see Kilcarragh; part
   Listowel
Diocese: A and A

Civil Parish: **Fenit**
Map Grid: 44
RC Parish: Ardfert and Spa, see Ballynahaglish
Diocese: A and A

Civil Parish: **Finuge**
Map Grid: 14
RC Parish: see Listowel
Diocese: A and A

Civil Parish: **Galey**
Map Grid: 6
RC Parish: part Listowel; part Lisselton
Diocese: A and A

Civil Parish: **Garfinny**
Map Grid: 36
RC Parish: see Dingle
Diocese: A and A

Civil Parish: **Glanbehy**
Map Grid: 67
RC Parish: Glenbeigh
Diocese: A and A
Earliest Record: b. 3.1830; m. 3.1830
Missing Dates: b. 8.1837-6.1841; m. ends 2.1835
Parish Address: Rev. B. Kelly, PP, Glenbeigh,
   Co. Kerry

Civil Parish: **Kenmare**
Map Grid: 84
RC Parish: Kenmare
Diocese: A and A
Earliest Record: b. 1.1819; m. 1.1819
Missing Dates: m. 3.1824-1.1826, 7.1838-1.1839
Parish Address: Rev. D. Long, PP, Kenmare,
   Co. Kerry

Civil Parish: **Kilbonane**
Map Grid: 74
RC Parish: Milltown
Diocese: A and A
Earliest Record: b. 10.1825; m. 10.1821
Missing Dates: b. 9.1840-10.1841; m. 11.1832-
   10.1842
Parish Address: Rev. J. Kissane, PP, Milltown,
   Co. Kerry

Civil Parish: **Kilcarragh**
Map Grid: 19
RC Parish: Lixnaw
Diocese: A and A
Earliest Record: b. 8.1810; m. 1.1810
Missing Dates: b. 2.1845-6.1848; m. 6.1852-
   8.1856
Parish Address: Rev. J. McGrath, PP, Lixnaw,
   Co. Kerry

Civil Parish: **Kilcaskan** (see Co. Cork)
Map Grid: 87
RC Parish: Glengarriffe
Diocese: RO

Civil Parish: **Kilcolman**
Map Grid: 62
RC Parish: Milltown, see Kilbonane
Diocese: A and A

Civil Parish: **Kilconly**
Map Grid: 1
RC Parish: see Lisselton
Diocese: A and A

Civil Parish: **Kilcredane**
Map Grid: 76
RC Parish: Firies, see Kilnanare
Diocese: A and A

Civil Parish: **Kilcrohane (1)**
Map Grid: 82
RC Parish: Sneem; also Cahirdaniel, see below
Diocese: A and A
Earliest Record: b. 8.1845; m. 2.1858
Missing Dates: b. 11.1848-11.1857
Parish Address: Rev. Michael J. Murphy, PP,
    Sneem, Co. Kerry

Civil Parish: **Kilcrohane (2)**
Map Grid: 82
RC Parish: Cahirdaniel
Diocese: A and A
Earliest Record: b. 2.1831; m. 5.1831
Parish Address: Rev. David McElligott, PP,
    Cahirdaniel, Co. Kerry

Civil Parish: **Kilcummin**
Map Grid: 77
RC Parish: Kilcummin
Diocese: A and A
Earliest Record: b. 1.1821; m. 1.1823
Missing Dates: b. 8.1859-11.1859; m. 9.1859-
    2.1873
Parish Address: Rev. J. O'Sullivan, Kilcummin,
    Killarney, Co. Kerry

Civil Parish: **Kildrum**
Map Grid: 43
RC Parish: see Dingle
Diocese: A and A

Civil Parish: **Kilfeighny**
Map Grid: 20
RC Parish: Abbeydorney
Diocese: A and A

Civil Parish: **Kilflyn**
Map Grid: 24
RC Parish: Abbeydorney
Diocese: A and A

Civil Parish: **Kilgarrylander**
Map Grid: 57
RC Parish: Castlemaine, see Kiltallagh
Diocese: A and A

Civil Parish: **Kilgarvan**
Map Grid: 85
RC Parish: Kilgarvan
Diocese: A and A
Earliest Record: b. 4.1818; m. 11.1818
Missing Dates: m. 4.1864-9.1864
Parish Address: Rev. J. Dillon, PP, Kilgarvan,
    Killarney, Co. Kerry

Civil Parish: **Kilgobban**
Map Grid: 31
RC Parish: Cappaclough
Diocese: A and A
Earliest Record: b. 4.1829; m. 5.1829
Missing Dates: b. 3.1834-3.1837, 3.1839-
    10.1857; m. 6.1835-5.1837, 10.1837-9.1855
Parish Address: Rev. J. O'Keeffe, PP, Annas-
    caul, Co. Kerry

Civil Parish: **Killaha**
Map Grid: 81
RC Parish: Glenflesk
Diocese: A and A
Earliest Record: b. 9.1821; m. 2.1831
Parish Address: Rev. S. O'Leary, PP, Station
    Road, Headford, Co. Kerry

Civil Parish: **Killahan**
Map Grid: 17
RC Parish: Abbeydorney
Diocese: A and A

Civil Parish: **Killarney**
Map Grid: 80
RC Parish: Killarney
Diocese: A and A
Earliest Record: b. 8.1792; m. 8.1792
Missing Dates: b. 3.1854-5.1854; m. 5.1851-
    1.1858
Parish Address: Rev. T. Egan, Adm, Killarney,
    Co. Kerry

Civil Parish: **Killeentierna**
Map Grid: 60
RC Parish: Killeentierna
Diocese: A and A

Earliest Record: b. 6.1801; m. 6.1803
Missing Dates: b. 12.1809-7.1823; m. 2.1828-6.1830
Parish Address: Rev. R. Flavin, PP, Killeentierna, Farranfore, Co. Kerry

Civil Parish: **Killehenny**
Map Grid: 4
RC Parish: Ballybunion
Diocese: A and A
Earliest Record: b. 11.1831; m. 2.1837
Parish Address: Rev. Michael Galvin, PP, Ballybunion, Co. Kerry

Civil Parish: **Killemlagh**
Map Grid: 68
RC Parish: see Prior
Diocese: A and A

Civil Parish: **Killinane**
Map Grid: 66
RC Parish: see Caher
Diocese: A and A

Civil Parish: **Killiney**
Map Grid: 30
RC Parish: Castlegregory
Diocese: A and A
Earliest Record: b. 12.1828; m. 2.1829
Parish Address: Rev. Canon D. Murphy, PP, Castlegregory, Co. Kerry

Civil Parish: **Killorglin**
Map Grid: 63
RC Parish: Killorglin
Diocese: A and A
Earliest Record: no records before 1880
Parish Address: Rev. Canon M. Keane, PP, Killorglin, Co. Kerry

Civil Parish: **Killury**
Map Grid: 11
RC Parish: Causeway
Diocese: A and A
Earliest Record: b. 12.1782; m. 2.1809
Missing Dates: b. 7.1786-11.1806, 11.1819-7.1820; m. 5.1845-2.1846
Parish Address: Rev. John B. Daly, PP, Causeway, Co. Kerry

Civil Parish: **Kilmalkedar**
Map Grid: 34
RC Parish: Ballyferriter
Diocese: A and A
Earliest Record: b. 1.1807; m. 1.1808
Parish Address: Rev. Michael O'Ciosain, Ballyferriter, Dingle, Co. Kerry

Civil Parish: **Kilmoyly**
Map Grid: 22
RC Parish: see Ardfert
Diocese: A and A

Civil Parish: **Kilnanare**
Map Grid: 73
RC Parish: Firies
Diocese: A and A
Earliest Record: b. 1.1871; m. 1.1830
Parish Address: Rev. D. Curran, PP, Firies, Killarney, Co. Kerry

Civil Parish: **Kilnaughtin**
Map Grid: 3
RC Parish: Tarbert and Ballylongford; see also Aghavallen
Diocese: A and A
Earliest Record: b. 10.1859; m. 7.1859
Parish Address: Rev. M. Leahy, PP, Tarbert, Listowel, Co. Kerry

Civil Parish: **Kilquane**
Map Grid: 26
RC Parish: Ballyferriter, see Kilmalkedar
Diocese: A and A

Civil Parish: **Kilshinane**
Map Grid: 21
RC Parish: part Lixnaw, see Kilcarragh; part Listowel
Diocese: A and A

Civil Parish: **Kiltallagh**
Map Grid: 58
RC Parish: Castlemaine
Diocese: A and A
Earliest Record: b. 2.1804; m. 2.1804
Missing Dates: b. 7.1813-1.1815, 10.1817-4.1818
Parish Address: Rev. L. Kelly, PP, Castlemaine, Co. Kerry

Civil Parish: **Kiltomy**
Map Grid: 18
RC Parish: Lixnaw, see Kilcarragh
Diocese: A and A

Civil Parish: **Kinard**
Map Grid: 37
RC Parish: see Dingle
Diocese: A and A

Civil Parish: **Knockane**
Map Grid: 71
RC Parish: Tuogh
Diocese: A and A
Earliest Record: b. 3.1844; m. 1.1843
Parish Address: Rev. Noel Moran, PP, Beaufort, Co. Kerry

Civil Parish: **Knockanure**
Map Grid: 10
RC Parish: Newtownsandes
Diocese: A and A

Civil Parish: **Lisselton**
Map Grid: 5
RC Parish: Ballydonohoe and Ballybunion, see Killehenny
Diocese: A and A

Civil Parish: **Listowel**
Map Grid: 9
RC Parish: Listowel
Diocese: A and A
Earliest Record: (many gaps to 1856) b. 8.1802; m. 1.1837
Parish Address: Rev. M. Leahy, PP, Listowel, Co. Kerry

Civil Parish: **Marhin**
Map Grid: 33
RC Parish: Ballyferriter, see Kilmalkedar
Diocese: A and A

Civil Parish: **Minard**
Map Grid: 38
RC Parish: see Dingle
Diocese: A and A

Civil Parish: **Molahiffe**
Map Grid: 72

RC Parish: Fieries, see Kilnanare
Diocese: A and A

Civil Parish: **Murhir**
Map Grid: 7
RC Parish: Moyvane
Diocese: A and A
Earliest Record: b. 7.1855; m. 10.1855
Parish Address: Rev. Michael O'Leary, Moyvane, Listowel, Co. Kerry

Civil Parish: **Nohaval**
Map Grid: 55
RC Parish: see Ballymacelligott
Diocese: A and A

Civil Parish: **Nohavaldal**
Map Grid: 78
RC Parish: Boherboy
Diocese: A and A
Earliest Record: b. 7.1833; m. 3.1863
Missing Dates: b. 12.1860-2.1863
Parish Address: Rev. D. O'Donovan, PP, Boherbue, Mallow, Co. Cork

Civil Parish: **O'Brennan**
Map Grid: 50
RC Parish: see Ballymacelligot
Diocese: A and A

Civil Parish: **O'Dorney**
Map Grid: 23
RC Parish: Abbeydorney
Diocese: A and A
Earliest Record: b. 10.1835; m. 1.1837
Missing Dates: b. 9.1844-2.1851; m. 7.1859-11.1859
Parish Address: Rev. D. Hickey, PP, Abbeydorney, Co. Kerry

Civil Parish: **Prior**
Map Grid: 69
RC Parish: Prior (Ballinskelligs)
Diocese: A and A
Earliest Record: b. 1.1832; m. 1.1832
Parish Address: Rev. T. Hickey, PP, St. Michael's, Ballinskelligs, Killarney, Co. Kerry

Civil Parish: **Ratass**
Map Grid: 48
RC Parish: part Ballymacelligott; part Tralee
Diocese: A and A

Civil Parish: **Rattoo**
Map Grid: 12
RC Parish: Causeway, see Killury
Diocese: A and A

Civil Parish: **Stradbally**
Map Grid: 29
RC Parish: Castlegregory, see Killiney
Diocese: A and A

Civil Parish: **Templenoe**
Map Grid: 83
RC Parish: see Kenmare
Diocese: A and A

Civil Parish: **Tralee**
Map Grid: 47
RC Parish: Tralee (St. John's)
Diocese: A and A
Earliest Record: b. 1.1772; m. 2.1774
Parish Address: Rev. John O'Keeffe, PP, St. John's Presbytery, Tralee, Co. Kerry

Civil Parish: **Tuosist**
Map Grid: 86
RC Parish: Tuosist
Diocese: A and A
Earliest Record: b. 4.1844
Parish Address: Rev. D. Quirke, PP, St. Joseph's, Lauragh, Killarney, Co. Kerry

Civil Parish: **Valentia**
Map Grid: 64
RC Parish: Valentia
Diocese: A and A
Earliest Record: b. 3.1825; m. 2.1827
Missing Dates: b. 7.1864-5.1867; m. 4.1856-1880
Parish Address: Rev. D. Costello, PP, Valentia Island, Co. Kerry

Civil Parish: **Ventry**
Map Grid: 42
RC Parish: see Dingle
Diocese: A and A

Commercial and Social Directories

1824
J. Pigot's *City of Dublin & Hibernian Provincial Directory* includes traders, nobility, gentry, and clergy lists of Dingle, Kenmare, Killarney, Listowel, Tarbert, and Tralee.

1846
Slater's *National Commercial Directory of Ireland* lists nobility, clergy, traders, etc., in Castleisland, Dingle, Kenmare, Killarney, Listowel, Milltown, Tarbert, and Tralee.

1856
Slater's *Royal National Commercial Directory of Ireland* lists nobility, gentry, clergy, traders, etc., in Cahirciveen and Valentia, Castleisland, Dingle, Kenmare, Killarney, Listowel, Milltown, Tarbert, Tralee, and Blennerville.

1870
Slater's *Directory of Ireland* contains trade, nobility, and clergy lists for Cahirciveen and Valentia, Castleisland, Dingle, Kenmare, Killarney, Listowel, Milltown and Castlemaine, Tarbert and Ballylongford, and Tralee.

1881
Slater's *Royal National Commercial Directory of Ireland* contains lists of traders, clergy, nobility, and farmers in adjoining parishes of the towns of Cahirciveen and Valentia, Castleisland, Dingle, Kenmare, Killarney, Listowel, Milltown and Castlemaine, Tarbert and Ballylongford, and Tralee.

1886
Francis Guy's *Postal Directory of Munster* lists gentry, clergy, traders, principal farmers, teachers, and police in each postal district and a listing of magistrates, clergy, and the professions for the county.

1893
Francis Guy's *Postal Directory of Munster* lists traders and farmers in each of the postal districts of the county, and a general alphabetical index to persons in the whole county.

A Handbook of

County Kerry Family History, Biography, &c.,

BY

The Rev. H. L. L. DENNY, M.A., F.S.G.,

Author of 'Anglo-Irish Genealogy,' 'Memorials of an Ancient House,'
'The Manor of Hawkesbury,' Etc. Etc.

(Ancient Seal of the Borough of Tralee.)

Compiled for the Archæological Group

OF

The County Kerry Society.

MCMXXIII.

SELECTIONS

FROM

OLD KERRY RECORDS,

Historical and Genealogical,

WITH

INTRODUCTORY MEMOIR, NOTES, AND APPENDIX.

BY

MARY AGNES HICKSON

London

PRINTED BY WATSON & HAZELL,
28, CHARLES STREET, HATTON GARDEN.
1872.

Title pages from two major sources of Kerry family history.

1894

Slater's *Royal National Directory of Ireland* lists traders, police, teachers, farmers, and private residents in each of the towns, villages, and parishes of the county.

Family History

Bernard, J.H. *The Bernards of Kerry*. Dublin, 1922.

"The Blennerhassets of Kerry: Earlier English Stock." *Kerry Arch. Mag.* 5 (1919): 34-39.

Conway–see Mahony

"The Conways of Kerry." S. *Kerry Arch. Mag.* 5 (1920): 71-91.

Denny, H.L.L. *A Handbook of County Kerry Family History, Biography, etc.* Co. Kerry Society, Tralee, 1923.

Eagar, F. *The Eagar Family of Co. Kerry*. Dublin, 1860.

"The Fitzmaurices of Duagh, Co. Kerry." *Ir. Gen.* 3 (1): 25-35.

"The Fitzmaurices, Lords of Kerry." *J. Cork. Arch. Hist. Soc.* N.S., 26 (1920): 10-18.

"The Fitzmaurices of Kerry." *Kerry Arch. Mag.* 3 (1970): 23-42.

Fuller, J.F. *Some Descendents of the Kerry Branch of the Fuller Family*. Dublin, 1880.

_____. *Pedigree of the Family of Fuller of Cork, Kerry, and Halstead*. 1909.

Hewson, John. *Hewsons of Finuge, Kerry, of Royal Descent*. 1907.

King, J. "The Fuller Family." In the *History of Co. Kerry,* Dublin, 1910, 208-11, 346-52.

_____. "The O'Moriarty Family." In *History of Co. Kerry*. Dublin, 1935, 265-79.

_____. "The Trant Family." *History of Co. Kerry*. Dublin, 1911.

MacCarthy, S. "Three Kerry Families: O'Mahony, Conway and Spotswood." *Folkestone* (1923).

"The Mahonys of Kerry." *Kerry Arch. Mag.*, 4 (1917-18): 171-90, 223-35.

"Markham of Nunstown and Callinafercy, Co. Kerry." *Ir. Anc.* 16 (2) (1984): 60.

Marquis of Ruvigny and Raineval. *Morris of Ballybeggan and Castle Morris, Co. Kerry.* 1904.

Marquis of Lansdowne. *Glanerought and the Petty-Fitzmaurices*. London, 1937.

McCarthy, S. "The Trant Family." *Folkestone* 1924 and Supplement 1926.

"Murphys of Muskerry." *J. Cork Hist. Arch. Soc.* 219 (1969): 1-19.

"Notes on the Families of . . . Denny of Tralee." *J. Ass. Pres. Mem. Dead* 7 (1907-09): 373.

"Richard Cantillon de Ballyheigue." *Studies* 11 (1932): 105-22.

Orpen, G.H. *The Orpen Family: Richard Orpen of Killowen, Co. Kerry, with Some Researches into the Early History of his Forebears*. Frome, 1930.

Palmer, A.H. *Genealogical and Historical Account of the Palmer Family of Kenmare, Co. Kerry.* 1872.

Pielou, P.L. *The Leslies of Tarbert, Co. Kerry and their Forbears*. Dublin, 1935.

"The Pierse Family of Co. Kerry." *Kerry Arch. Mag.* 5 (1972): 14-32.

Spotswood–see Mahony

"Trant Family." *Kerry Arch. Mag.* 2 (1914): 237-62; 3 (1914): 20-38; 5 (1919): 18-26.

Gravestone Inscriptions

The major series of gravestone inscriptions in this county are those included in volumes 6 and 8 of the series, *O'Kief, Coshe Mang & Slieve Luachra* by Albert Casey. Seven graveyards have also been indexed by the Finuge Heritage Survey (see Research Sources and Services) from whom they are available.

Aghadoe: *O'Kief, Coshe Mang, etc.* 6 (1963).

Aglish: *O'Kief, Coshe Mang, etc.* 6 (1963).

Ardfert: *O'Kief, Coshe Mang, etc.* 8 (1965).

Ballymacelligott: *O'Kief, Coshe Mang, etc.* 8 (1965).

Castleisland: *O'Kief, Coshe Mang, etc.* 6 (1963).

Clogherbrien: *O'Kief, Coshe Mang, etc.* 8 (1963).

Currans: *O'Kief, Coshe Mang, etc.* 6 (1963).

Duagh: Finuge Heritage Survey.

Dysert: *O'Kief, Coshe Mang, etc.* 6 (1963).

Finuge: Finuge Heritage Survey.

Galey: Finuge Heritage Survey.

Kilcummin: *O'Kief, Coshe Mang, etc.* 6 (1963).

Killarney and Muckross Abbey: *O'Kief, Coshe Mang, etc.* 6 (1963).

Kilshanane: Finuge Heritage Survey.

Kilnanare: *O'Kief, Coshe Mang, etc.* 6 (1963).

Killorglin: *O'Kief, Coshe Mang, etc.* 8 (1965).

Kiltoney: Finuge Heritage Survey.

Lisselton: Finuge Heritage Survey.

Listowel: Finuge Heritage Survey.

Nohoval: *O'Kief, Coshe Mang, etc.* 8 (1965).

O'Brennan: *O'Kief, Coshe Mang, etc.* 8 (1965).

Rathmore: *O'Kief, Coshe Mang, etc.* 6 (1963).

Tralee: *O'Kief, Coshe Mang, etc.* 8 (1965).

Newspapers

A card index to biographical notices in Cork and Kerry newspapers from 1754 to 1827 is held in the Library of University College, Cork. Microfiche copies of this are held in the NLI, the library of University College, Dublin, and the New York Public Library. Microfiche copies are also available from the compiler, Ms. R. ffolliott, Glebe House, Fethard, Co. Tipperary. Biographical notices from the *Kerry Evening Post* (1828-64) are listed in Dr. Albert Casey's publication *O'Keif, Coshe Mang, etc.*, Vol. 6.

Title: *Chute's Western Herald* (continued as *Western Herald* in 1828)
Published in: Tralee, 1791-1835
NLI Holdings: 1791-1823 (with gaps); 1.1824-9.1829; 10.1828-5.1835

BL Holdings: 1-9.1828; 10.1828-3.1830; 3.1830-5.1835

Title: *Kerry Evening Post*
Published in: Tralee, 1813-1917
NLI Holdings: odd numbers 1813-24; 1.1828-9.1917
BL Holdings: odd numbers 1813-24; 1.1828-9.1917 (see also card-index above)

Title: *Kerry Examiner and Munster General Observer*
Published in: Tralee, 1840-56
NLI Holdings: 8.1840-3.1856 (with gaps)
BL Holdings: 8.1840-10.1849; 3.1850-8.1854; 1.1855-3.1856

Title: *Kerry Independent*
Published in: Tralee, 1880-84
NLI Holdings: 10.1880-7.1884 (with gaps)
BL Holdings: 10.1880-7.1884 (with gaps)

Title: *Kerry News*
Published in: Tralee, 1894-1939
NLI Holdings: 8.1927-6.1941
BL Holdings: 1.1894-8.1920; 8.1927-12.1929; 1.1931-7.1939

Title: *Kerry Star*
Published in: Tralee, 1861-63
NLI Holdings: 5.1861-3.1863
BL Holdings: 5.1861-3.1863

Title: *Kerry Weekly Reporter and Commercial Advertiser* (continued as *Kerry Reporter* in 1927)
Published in: Tralee, 1883-1936
NLI Holdings: 2.1883-8.1920; 8.1927-12.1935
BL Holdings: 2.1883-8.1920; 8.1927-2.1936

Title: *Tralee Chronicle* (continued as *Tralee Chronicle and Killarney Echo* in 1857)
Published in: Tralee, 1843-81
NLI Holdings: 3.1843-5.1881
BL Holdings: 3.1843-10.1848; 1849-5.1881

Title: *Tralee Mercury*
Published in: Tralee, 1829-39
NLI Holdings: 2.1829-12.1836; 2.1837-7.1839
BL Holdings: 2.1829-12.1836; 2.1837-7.1839

Wills and Administrations

A discussion of the types of records, where they are held, their availability and value is given in the Wills section of the Introduction. The availability of prerogative wills, administrations, and marriage license records is also described in the relevant parts of the same section. Where available, published sources of these records are given in the Miscellaneous Sources section.

Pre-1858 Wills and Administration

Prerogative Wills. see p. xli

Consistorial Wills. County Kerry is mainly in the diocese of Ardfert with one parish in each of Limerick and Ross dioceses. The guide to Catholic parish records in this chapter shows the diocese to which each civil parish belonged. The wills of residents of each diocese were usually proven within that diocese (see the Wills section for exceptions). The following records survive:

Wills. See p. xxxvii

Abstracts. See p. xxxvii

Indexes. Ardfert (1690-1858) published to 1800 by Phillimore, and to 1858 in *O'Kief, Coshe Mange, etc.* 5 (1962) (see also counties Limerick and Cork).

Post-1858 Wills and Administrations

County Kerry was served by the District Registries of Limerick (Baronies of Clanmaurice and Iraghticonnor) and Cork (rest of county). The surviving records are kept in the PRO.

Marriage Licenses

Indexes. Limerick (1691-1845). PRO; SLC film 100869. Ross (1623-1845). PRO; SLC film 100864-66

Miscellaneous Sources

Cusack, N. *History of the Kingdom of Kerry.* London, 1871.

Hickson, M.A. *Selections from Old Kerry Records Historical and Genealogical.* 2 vols. London, 1872-74.

King, J. *County Kerry, Past and Present — Handbook to Local and Family History.* Dublin, 1931.

"Land Tenure in Kenmare and Tuosist 1696-1716," *Kerry Arch. Hist. Soc. J.* 10 (1977).

O'Casey, O'Kief, Coshe Mang & Slieve Luachra. 16 vols.

Smith, C. *The Ancient and Present State of the County of Kerry.* Dublin, 1756.

"Some Kerry Wild Geese." *Ir. Gen.* 2 (8) (1950): 250-54.

"A View of the State of Agriculture in the County of Kerry" (1800). *Kerry Arch. Hist. Soc. J.* 1 (1968): 81-100.

Research Sources and Services

Journals

Kerry Archaeological Magazine

Journal of Kerry Archaeological & Historical Society

Kenmare Literary & Historical Society Journal

Libraries and Information Sources

Kerry County Library, Moyderwell, Tralee, Co. Kerry Ph: (066) 21200

Research Services

See research services in Dublin, p. xliv

Mr. J. McCarthy and Mr. E. Myers, Muckross House, Killarney, Co. Kerry

Finuge Heritage Survey, c/o Gene O'Carroll, Teach Siamsa, Finuge, Lixnaw, Co. Kerry (index of parish registers and gravestones for Listowel and Lixnaw)

Kerry Genealogical Center, c/o John Griffin, Town Hass, Princes Quay, Trallee, Co. Kerry

Kerry Archaeological and Historical Society, c/o Kerry Co. Library, Moyderwell, Tralee, Kerry

Oidhreacht Corca Dhuibne (Dingle Peninsula Heritage Society), c/o Mr. Ted Creedon, Ballyferriter, Co. Kerry

Societies

Kenmare Library and Historical Society

Killorglin History & Folklore Society, Mrs. Jo Scanlon, Sun Hill, Killorglin, Co. Kerry

CIVIL PARISHES OF COUNTY KERRY

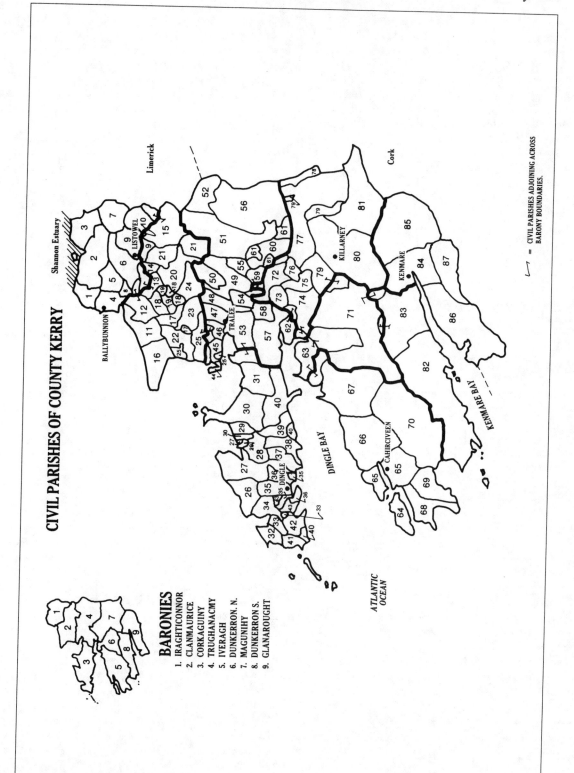

BARONIES

1. IRAGHTICONNOR
2. CLANMAURICE
3. CORKAGUINY
4. TRUGHANACMY
5. IVERAGH
6. DUNKERRON. N.
7. MAGUNIHY
8. DUNKERRON S.
9. GLANAROUGHT

⌐┐ = CIVIL PARISHES ADJOINING ACROSS
      BARONY BOUNDARIES.

Shannon Estuary

Limerick

Cork

BALLYBUNNION

LISTOWEL

TRALEE

DINGLE

CAHIRCIVEEN

KILLARNEY

KENMARE

DINGLE BAY

KENMARE BAY

ATLANTIC
OCEAN

County Kildare

A Brief History

Kildare is a relatively small inland county in Leinster. It is forty-two miles from north to south and twenty-six miles from east to west, and contains the towns of Naas, Newbridge, Maynooth, Kildare, and Athy. The county derives its name from Cill-Dara, the Church of Oak, which is said to have been built in the fifth century. In pre-Norman times the county was partly the territory of Hy-Kaelan, which was the territory of the O'Byrnes, and Hy-Murray, the territory of the O'Tooles. The Cullens, Dowlings, and Mc-Kellys were also families of this county.

During the peak of their power in the tenth century, the Vikings of Dublin extended their territory to the northeast of Kildare. The town of Leixlip, meaning Salmon Leap in old Norse, derives its name from the Vikings.

Following the Norman invasion, the county was granted to the Fitzgeralds. The O'Byrnes and O'Tooles were displaced into Wicklow where they continued to raid the Norman oc-cupied area called the "Pale" (see Co. Wicklow) for centuries. Other Norman families who set-tled in Kildare included Birmingham, Sutton, Aylmer, Wogan, Sherlock, White, and Eustace. The Fitzgeralds became a major force in Ireland in the Middle Ages. Their base was at Maynooth castle in the county. The family's power was reduced by an ill-conceived rebellion by "Silken Thomas" Fitzgerald in 1536.

Following the defeat of the rebellion of the Catholic Confederacy of 1641 (see Co. Kilken-ny), Cromwell confiscated the lands of many of the Norman families in the county in 1654. Some of these estates were restored by Charles II in 1662-64. Following the Williamite war of 1689-91, many of these landholders again lost their lands, some of which were planted with settlers.

The county was less badly affected by the Great Famine of 1845-47 than many others. A relatively high proportion of the county was in pasture rather than in potato crops at this time. The population in 1841 was 114,000, and by 1851 it had fallen to 96,000. Of the difference, about 14,000 died and the remainder emigrated.

The county is mainly agricultural and is also a major center of the horse-racing and bloodstock industry.

Census and Census Substitutes

1641
"Book of Survey and Distribution." *Kildare Arch. Soc. J.* 10 (1918-21): 197-205, 221-30.

1654-55
Civil Survey. Vol. 8. SLC film 973123.

1659

"Census" of Ireland. Edited by S. Pender. Dublin: Stationery Office, 1939. SLC film 924648

1663

"Hearth Money Roll" (for some areas). *Kildare Arch. Soc. J.* 10 (5): 245-54; 11 (1): 386-466.

1700

"Claimants of Lands in Co. Kildare." *Kildare Arch. Soc. J.* 9 (1918-21): 331-57.

1766

"Religious Census of Parishes of Ballybought, Ballymore-Eustace, Coghlanstown, Tipperkevin." SLC film 258517.

"Parish of Ballycommon." *Kildare Arch. Soc. J.* 7 (1912): 274-76.

1775

"Catholic Qualification Roll Extracts" (forty-five names, addresses, and occupations). 59th Report DKPRI: 50-84.

1779

"Persons Willing to Join Naas Volunteers." *Kildare Arch. Soc. J.* 11 (1) (1930): 467-68.

1798

List of Persons Who Suffered Loss in '98 Rebellion. NLI JLB 94107 (approximately 320 names, occupations, and addresses).

1804

"Yeomanry Order Book (Millicent, Co. Kildare)." *J. Kildare Arch. Soc.* 13 (4) (1953): 211-19 (gives names and addresses of officers and men).

1808

"Grand Jury Panel for Kildare." *Kildare Arch. Soc. J.* 12 (3) (1938): 128-30 (names and address).

1821

Extracts from the Government Census for Naas, Mainly Dealing with the Surname Tracey. SLC film 100158.

1823-37

Tithe Applotment Survey (see p. xxvii).

1837

Alphabetical List of Registered Voters. NLI ms. 1398.

1840

Census of Castledermot Parish. Names of householders and families (not age) in each townland or street of Castledermot parish. NLI P 3511.

1851

Griffith's Valuation (see p. xxvii).

1859-63

"Tenants on Aylmer Estate, Donadea Castle." *Kildare Arch. Soc. J.* 7 (1912): 411-16 (eighty-three names and addresses).

1901

Census. PRO.

1911

Census. PRO.

Church Records

Church of Ireland
(shows starting date of record)

Parish: **Athy**
Existing Records: b. 1669; m. 1669; d. 1669
Status: LC

Parish: **Attanagh**
Status: Lost

Parish: **Ballaghmoon** (see Castledermot)

Parish: **Ballymore-Eustace**
Existing Records: b. 1838; m. 1840; d. 1832
Status: LC

Parish: **Ballysax**
Existing Records: b. 1830; m. 1830; d. 1834
Status: LC

Parish: **Ballysonnon**
Status: Lost

468

The following persons are willing to serve as Volunteers in the District of Naas and to associate themselves in a troop of Dragoons and to arm, mount and acoutre themselves :—

1. Lord Visc. Allen
2. Hon. Richard Allen.
3. William Eustace.
4. John Mt. Gomery.
5. William Mt. Gomery.
6. David Burtchel.
7. Bartholomew Callan.
8. Richard Archbold.
9. Charles Geoghagan.
10. Henry Haydon.
11. Thomas Dunn.
12. James Martin.
13. Martin Dunty.
14. Laurence Dunty.
15. Andrew Carthy.
16. Gerald Archbold.
17. Grantham Gale.
18. John Plunket.
19. James Moilsey.
20. John Highland.
21. William Tracy.
22. Edward Dunn.
23. Edward Wilson.
24. Samuel Whelan.
25. Christopher Nagle.
26. Maurice Fitzgerald.
27. William Moore.
28. James Ennis.
29. Thomas Browne.
30. Robert Day.
31. Pat. Cosgrave.
32. Edward Scully.
33. Bart. Martin.
34. Pat Lyons.
35. ....
36. James Meaghan.
37. Pat Corcoran.
38. James O'Reilly.
39. Charles Fitzgerald.
40. Mathew Dodd.
41. Dennis Rafter.
42. Timothy Holden.
43. James Owens.
44. Edward Collogan.
45. James Magee.
46. .... Renolds.
47. Terence Dunn.
48. John Fennel.
49. Theady Kilroy.
50. John Burke.
51. Richard Mooney.
52. James Eustace.
53. Robert Graydon.

We approve of the above list, and are willing and desirous to serve and associate with them. However, we express a doubt whether it be legal to arm some of them above gentleman who profess the roman catholick Religion.

Sept. 20th, 1779.

ROBERT GRAYDON.
WILLIAM EUSTACE.

In the troop of light horse the following persons have associated since the former lists were approved by your Grace, and have been approved of by Mr. Nevill and your humble Servant :—viz.,

Arthur Wolfe.
James Cusack.
Maurice Peppard Warren.
William S. Wolfe.

John Wolfe.

THESE LISTS APPROVED OF BY ME.
LEINSTER, G.

A listing of the persons in the District of Naas, Co. Kildare, who declared themselves willing to serve as volunteers in 1779. From *J. Kildare Arch. Soc.* 11(1) 1930.

Parish: **Carnalway**
Existing Records: b. 1805; m. 1805; d. 1805
Status: LC

Parish: **Carogh**
Status: Lost

Parish: **Castlecarbery**
Existing Records: b. 1814; m. 1814; d. 1814
Status: LC

Parish: **Castledermot**
Status: Lost

Parish: **Celbridge** or **Kildrought**
Existing Records: b. 1777; m. 1779; d. 1787
Status: LC

Parish: **Clane**
Existing Records: b. 1863; d. 1863
Status: PRO

Parish: **Clonaslee**
Status: Lost

Parish: **Clonsast** (Newbridge)
Existing Records: b. 1805; m. 1805; d. 1805
Status: LC

Parish: **Donadea**
Status: Lost

Parish: **Feighcullen**
Status: Lost

Parish: **Fontstown**
Status: Lost

Parish: **Great Connell** and **Ladytown**
Status: Lost

Parish: **Harristown**
Existing Records: b. 1666; m. 1666; d. 1666
Status: LC

Parish: **Kilberry**
Status: Lost

Parish: **Kilcock**
Status: Lost

Parish: **Kilcullen**
Existing Records: b. 1778; m. 1819; d. 1779
Status: LC

Parish: **Kildare**
Existing Records: b. 1801; m. 1801; d. 1801
Status: LC

Parish: **Kill**
Existing Records: b. 1814; m. 1814; d. 1814
Status: LC

Parish: **Killishee**
Status: Lost

Parish: **Kilmeague** or **Lullymore**
Status: Lost

Parish: **Lackagh**
Existing Records: b. 1830; m. 1830; d. 1829
Status: LC

Parish: **Leixlip**
Existing Records: b. 1669; m. 1669; d. 1669
Status: LC

Parish: **Maynooth** or **Laraghbryan**
Existing Records: b. 1774; m. 1792; d. 1792
Status: LC

Parish: **Monasteroris**
Existing Records: b. 1698; m. 1698; d. 1698
Status: LC and PRO

Parish: **Morristownbiller** and **Old Connell**
Status: Lost

Parish: **Naas**
Existing Records: b. 1679; m. 1679; d. 1679
Status: LC

Parish: **Narraghmore**
Status: Lost

Parish: **Nurney**
Status: Lost

Parish: **Rathangan**
Status: Lost

Parish: **Rathmore**
Status: Lost

Parish: **Straffan** (see also Celbridge)
Existing Records: b. 1838; m. 1838; d. 1841
Status: LC

Parish: **Taghadoe** (see Maynooth)

Parish: **Thomastown**
Status: Lost

Parish: **Timahoe** and **Ballinfagh**
Status: Lost

Parish: **Tipperkevin**
Status: Lost

Roman Catholic

Civil Parish: **Ardkill**
Map Grid: 10
RC Parish: see Carbury
Diocese: KD

Civil Parish: **Ardree**
Map Grid: 104
RC Parish: see Churchtown
Diocese: DU

Civil Parish: **Ballaghmoon**
Map Grid: 115
RC Parish: see Castledermot
Diocese: DU

Civil Parish: **Ballybrackan**
Map Grid: 86
RC Parish: see Monastervin
Diocese: KD

Civil Parish: **Ballymany**
Map Grid: 63
RC Parish: Newbridge, see Greatconnell
Diocese: KD

Civil Parish: **Ballymore Eustace**
Map Grid: 77
RC Parish: Ballymore Eustace

Diocese: DU
Earliest Record: b. 3.1779; m. 10.1779
Missing Dates: b. 4.1796-1.1797; m. 6.1796-5.1797
Parish Address: Rev. Laurence O'Donoghue, PP, The Presbytery, Ballymore Eustace, Naas, Co. Kildare

Civil Parish: **Ballynadrumny**
Map Grid: 1
RC Parish: Balyna
Diocese: KD
Earliest Record: b. 10.1785; m. 11.1797
Missing Dates: b. 7.1803-8.1807, 10.1811-1.1815, 2.1815-1.1818; m. 4.1799-11.1801, 1.1802-10.1807, 10.1811-1.1815, 2.1815-3.1818
Parish Address: Rev. Barry O'Connell, PP, Balyna, Broadford, Co. Kildare

Civil Parish: **Ballynafagh**
Map Grid: 30
RC Parish: Downings, see Carragh
Diocese: KD

Civil Parish: **Ballysax**
Map Grid: 64
RC Parish: Suncroft, see Carn (for Army Camp records see Curragh Camp)
Diocese: KD

Civil Parish: **Ballyshannon**
Map Grid: 92
RC Parish: Suncroft, see Carn
Diocese: KD

Civil Parish: **Balraheen**
Map Grid: 16
RC Parish: see Clane
Diocese: KD

Civil Parish: **Belan**
Map Grid: 107
RC Parish: see Castledermot
Diocese: KD

Civil Parish: **Bodenstown**
Map Grid: 36
RC Parish: see Kill
Diocese: KD

Civil Parish: **Brannockstown**
Map Grid: 78
RC Parish: see Kilcullen
Diocese: DU

Civil Parish: **Brideschurch**
Map Grid: 35
RC Parish: see Carragh
Diocese: KD

Civil Parish: **Cadamstown**
Map Grid: 4
RC Parish: Balyna, see Ballynadrumny
Diocese: KD

Civil Parish: **Carbury**
Map Grid: 9
RC Parish: Carbury
Diocese: KD
Earliest Record: b. 10.1821; m. 11.1821; d. 2.1869
Parish Address: Rev. Eugene Shine, PP, Carbury, Co. Kildare

Civil Parish: **Carn**
Map Grid: 65
RC Parish: Suncroft
Diocese: KD
Earliest Record: b. 3.1805; m. 5.1805
Parish Address: Rev. Thomas O'Donnell, PP, Suncroft, Curragh Camp, Co. Kildare

Civil Parish: **Carnalway**
Map Grid: 75
RC Parish: Newbridge, see Greatconnell
Diocese: DU

Civil Parish: **Carragh**
Map Grid: 34
RC Parish: Carragh (Downings)
Diocese: KD
Earliest Record: b. 6.1849; m. 2.1850
Parish Address: Rev. Jeremiah Bennett, PP, Caragh, Naas, Co. Kildare

Civil Parish: **Carrick**
Map Grid: 5
RC Parish: Balyna, see Ballynadrumny
Diocese: KD

Civil Parish: **Castledermot**
Map Grid: 111
RC Parish: Castledermot
Diocese: DU
Earliest Record: b. 11.1789; m. 11.1789
Parish Address: Rev. John Duff, PP, Parochial House, Castledermot, Co. Kildare

Civil Parish: **Castledillon**
Map Grid: 46
RC Parish: Celbridge, see Straffan
Diocese: DU

Civil Parish: **Churchtown**
Map Grid: 96
RC Parish: Athy
Diocese: DU
Earliest Record: b. 3.1837; m. 4.1837
Parish Address: Rev. Philip Dennehy, PP, Parochial House, Athy, Co. Kildare

Civil Parish: **Clane**
Map Grid: 33
RC Parish: Clane
Diocese: KD
Earliest Record: b. 3.1785; m. 4.1825
Missing Dates: b. 9.1785-2.1786, 7.1786-12.1788, 4.1789-2.1825; m. 6.1828-11.1829
Parish Address: Rev. Richard Kelly, PP, Clane, Naas, Co. Kildare

Civil Parish: **Clonaghlis**
Map Grid: 48
RC Parish: see Kill
Diocese: DN

Civil Parish: **Cloncurry** (near Kilcock)
Map Grid: 12
RC Parish: see Kilcock
Diocese: KD

Civil Parish: **Cloncurry** (near Rathangan)
Map Grid: 56
RC Parish: see Kildare
Diocese: KD

Civil Parish: **Clonshanbo**
Map Grid: 15
RC Parish: see Kilcock
Diocese: DU

Civil Parish: **Coghlanstown**
Map Grid: 76
RC Parish: see Ballymore Eustace
Diocese: DU

Civil Parish: **Confey**
Map Grid: 21
RC Parish: Maynooth, see Laraghbryan
Diocese: DU

Civil Parish: **Curragh Camp** (Civil Parish of
  Ballysax)
Map Grid: 64
RC Parish: Curragh Camp
Earliest Record: b. 8.1855; m. 9.1855
Parish Address: Parish Priest, Curragh Camp,
  Newbridge, Co. Kildare

Civil Parish: **Davidstown**
Map Grid: 99
RC Parish: see Narraghmore
Diocese: DU

Civil Parish: **Donadea**
Map Grid: 18
RC Parish: Maynooth, see Laraghbryan
Diocese: KD

Civil Parish: **Donaghcumper**
Map Grid: 44
RC Parish: Celbridge, see Straffan
Diocese: KD

Civil Parish: **Donaghmore**
Map Grid: 22
RC Parish: Celbridge, see Straffan
Diocese: KD

Civil Parish: **Downings**
Map Grid: 31
RC Parish: Caragh, see Carragh
Diocese: KD

Civil Parish: **Duneany**
Map Grid: 84
RC Parish: see Monasterevin
Diocese: KD

Civil Parish: **Dunfierth**
Map Grid: 7

RC Parish: see Carbury
Diocese: KD

Civil Parish: **Dunmanoge**
Map Grid: 110
RC Parish: see Castledermot
Diocese: DU

Civil Parish: **Dunmurraghill**
Map Grid: 17
RC Parish: Maynooth, see Laraghbryan
Diocese: KD

Civil Parish: **Dunmurry**
Map Grid: 59
RC Parish: see Kildare
Diocese: KD

Civil Parish: **Feighcullen**
Map Grid: 68
RC Parish: see Kilmeage
Diocese: KD

Civil Parish: **Fontstown**
Map Grid: 93
RC Parish: see Narraghmore
Diocese: KD

Civil Parish: **Forenaghts**
Map Grid: 52
RC Parish: see Kill
Diocese: DU

Civil Parish: **Gilltown**
Map Grid: 79
RC Parish: part Kilcullen; part Ballymore Eus-
  tace
Diocese: DU

Civil Parish: **Graney**
Map Grid: 113
RC Parish: part Castledermot; part Baltinglass,
  Co. Wicklow
Diocese: DU

Civil Parish: **Grangeclare**
Map Grid: 58
RC Parish: see Kildare
Diocese: KD

Civil Parish: **Grangerosnolvan**
Map Grid: 106
RC Parish: see Castledermot
Diocese: DU

Civil Parish: **Greatconnell**
Map Grid: 72
RC Parish: Newbridge
Diocese: KD
Earliest Record: b. 8.1786; m. 8.1786
Missing Dates: b. 1.1795-1.1820, 8.1832-1.1834;
    m. 1.1795-1.1820
Parish Address: Rev. Laurence T. Newman, PP,
    Newbridge, Co. Kildare

Civil Parish: **Harristown**
Map Grid: 89
RC Parish: Athy, see Churchtown
Diocese: KD

Civil Parish: **Haynestown**
Map Grid: 53
RC Parish: see Kill
Diocese: DU

Civil Parish: **Johnstown**
Map Grid: 41
RC Parish: see Kill
Diocese: KD

Civil Parish: **Kerdiffstown**
Map Grid: 39
RC Parish: part Newbridge, see Greatconnell;
    part Kill

Civil Parish: **Kilberry**
Map Grid: 95
RC Parish: see Churchtown
Diocese: DU

Civil Parish: **Kilcock**
Map Grid: 13
RC Parish: Kilcock
Diocese: KD
Earliest Record: b. 7.1771; m. 8.1816
Missing Dates: b. 12.1786-8.1816, 12.1826-
    10.1831; m. 9.1822-7.1834
Parish Address: Rev. John McWey, PP, Kil-
    cock, Co. Kildare

Civil Parish: **Kilcullen**
Map Grid: 94
RC Parish: Kilcullen
Diocese: DU
Earliest Record: b. 10.1777; m. 5.1786
Missing Dates: b. 9.1818-4.1829, 9.1840-1.1857;
    m. 11.1806-4.1810, 10.1816-5.1829, 11.1831-
    4.1836, 6.1840-1.1857
Parish Address: Rev. William Dunlea, PP,
    Parochial House, Kilcullen, Co. Kildare

Civil Parish: **Kildangan**
Map Grid: 87
RC Parish: see Monasterevin
Diocese: KD

Civil Parish: **Kildare**
Map Grid: 61
RC Parish: Kildare (for Army Camp records
    see Curragh Camp)
Diocese: KD
Earliest Record: b. 11.1815; m. 11.1815
Parish Address: Rev. Robert Prendergast, PP,
    Kildare, Co. Kildare

Civil Parish: **Kildrought**
Map Grid: 26
RC Parish: Celbridge, see Straffan
Diocese: DU

Civil Parish: **Kilkea**
Map Grid: 109
RC Parish: see Castledermot
Diocese: DU

Civil Parish: **Kill**
Map Grid: 50
RC Parish: Kill and Lyons; also part Newbridge,
    see Greatconnell
Diocese: DU
Earliest Record: b. 11.1840; m. 2.1843
Parish Address: Rev. Paul Maher, PP, Naas,
    Co. Kildare

Civil Parish: **Killadoon**
Map Grid: 27
RC Parish: Celbridge, see Straffan
Diocese: DU

Civil Parish: **Kilashee** (or Killishy)
Map Grid: 73
RC Parish: Newbridge, see Greatconnel

Civil Parish: **Killelan**
Map Grid: 108
RC Parish: see Castledermot
Diocese: DU

Civil Parish: **Killybegs**
Map Grid: 32
RC Parish: see Carragh
Diocese: KD

Civil Parish: **Kilmacredock**
Map Grid: 23
RC Parish: Maynooth, see Laraghbryan
Diocese: DU

Civil Parish: **Kilmeage**
Map Grid: 66
RC Parish: Allen and Milltown
Diocese: KD
Earliest Record: b. 10.1820; m. 10.1820
Missing Dates: b. ends 10.1852
Parish Address: Rev. Liam Merrigan, CC, Allen, Kilmeague, Naas, Co. Kildare

Civil Parish: **Kilmore**
Map Grid: 8
RC Parish: part Carbury; part Balyna, see Ballynadrumny
Diocese: KD

Civil Parish: **Kilpatrick**
Map Grid: 11
RC Parish: see Carbury
Diocese: KD

Civil Parish: **Kilrainy**
Map Grid: 2
RC Parish: Balyna, see Ballynadrumny
Diocese: DU

Civil Parish: **Kilrush**
Map Grid: 91
RC Parish: Suncroft, see Carn
Diocese: KD

Civil Parish: **Kilteel**
Map Grid: 51

RC Parish: Blessington, see Co. Wicklow
Diocese: DU

Civil Parish: **Kineagh**
Map Grid: 112
RC Parish: part Castledermot; part Rathvilly, see Co. Carlow
Diocese: DU

Civil Parish: **Knavinstown**
Map Grid: 83
RC Parish: see Kildare
Diocese: KD

Civil Parish: **Lackagh**
Map Grid: 82
RC Parish: part Monasterevin; part Kildare
Diocese: KD

Civil Parish: **Ladytown**
Map Grid: 71
RC Parish: see Carragh
Diocese: KD

Civil Parish: **Laraghbryan**
Map Grid: 20
RC Parish: Maynooth and Leixlip
Diocese: DU
Earliest Record: b. 8.1814; m. 1.1806
Parish Address: Rev. Brendan Supple, PP, St. Mary's Maynooth, Co. Kildare

Civil Parish: **Leixlip**
Map Grid: 24
RC Parish: Maynooth
Diocese: DU

Civil Parish: **Lullymore**
Map Grid: 54
RC Parish: see Kildare
Diocese: DU

Civil Parish: **Lyons**
Map Grid: 47
RC Parish: see Kill
Diocese: DU

Civil Parish: **Mainham**
Map Grid: 19
RC Parish: see Clane
Diocese: KD

Civil Parish: **Monasterevin**
Map Grid: 85
RC Parish: Monasterevin and Kildangan
Diocese: KD
Earliest Record: b. 1.1819; m. 9.1819
Parish Address: Rev. Denis O'Sullivan, PP,
    Monasterevin, Co. Kildare

Civil Parish: **Moone**
Map Grid: 103
RC Parish: see Castledermot
Diocese: DU

Civil Parish: **Morristownbiller**
Map Grid: 69
RC Parish: Newbridge, see Greatconnell
Diocese: DU

Civil Parish: **Mylerstown**
Map Grid: 3
RC Parish: Balyna, see Ballynadrumny
Diocese: DU

Civil Parish: **Naas**
Map Grid: 40
RC Parish: Naas
Diocese: KD
Earliest Record: b. 3.1813; m. 2.1813; d. 3.1861
    Missing Dates: d. ends 12.1868
Parish Address: Rev. M. Lennon, PP, Sallins
    Road, Naas, Co. Kildare

Civil Parish: **Narraghmore**
Map Grid: 101
RC Parish: Narraghmore
Diocese: DU
Earliest Record: b. 4.1827; m. 10.1827
Missing Dates: b. 7.1846-5.1853; m. 8.1840-
    7.1842, 7.1846-1.1853
Parish Address: Rev. Henry O'Connor, PP,
    Crookstown, Athy, Co. Kildare

Civil Parish: **Nurney (1)** (near Carrick)
Map Grid: 6
RC Parish: Balyna, see Ballynadrumny
Diocese: KD

Civil Parish: **Nurney (2)** (near Harristown)
Map Grid: 90

RC Parish: Monasterevin and Kildangan, see
    Monasterevin
Diocese: KD

Civil Parish: **Oldconnell**
Map Grid: 70
RC Parish: Newbridge, see Greatconnell
Diocese: KD

Civil Parish: **Oughterard**
Map Grid: 49
RC Parish: see Kill
Diocese: DU

Civil Parish: **Painestown**
Map Grid: 114
RC Parish: Painestown, Co. Carlow
Diocese: LE

Civil Parish: **Pollardstown**
Map Grid: 62
RC Parish: Allen and Milltown, see Kilmeage
Diocese: KD

Civil Parish: **Rathangan**
Map Grid: 55
RC Parish: see Kildare
Diocese: KD

Civil Parish: **Rathernan**
Map Grid: 67
RC Parish: Allen and Milltown, see Kilmeage
Diocese: KD

Civil Parish: **Rathmore**
Map Grid: 43
RC Parish: Blessington, see Co. Wicklow
Diocese: DU

Civil Parish: **St. John's** (also Co. Offaly)
Map Grid: 98
RC Parish: Athy, see Churchtown
Diocese: DU

Civil Parish: **St. Michaels**
Map Grid: 97
RC Parish: Athy, see Churchtown
Diocese: DU

Civil Parish: **Scullogestown**
Map Grid: 14
RC Parish: see Kilcock
Diocese: KD

Civil Parish: **Sherlockstown**
Map Grid: 38
RC Parish: Kill and Lyons, see Kill
Diocese: KD

Civil Parish: **Stacumny**
Map Grid: 45
RC Parish: Celbridge, see Straffan
Diocese: DU

Civil Parish: **Straffan**
Map Grid: 28
RC Parish: Straffan
Diocese: DU
Earliest Record: b. 1.1857
Parish Address: Rev. P. Walsh, The Presbytery,
    12 Coarse Moor, Straffan, Co. Kildare

Civil Parish: **Taghadoe**
Map Grid: 25
RC Parish: Maynooth, see Laraghbryan
Diocese: DU

Civil Parish: **Tankardstown** (also Co. Laois)
Map Grid: 105
RC Parish: Athy, see Churchtown
Diocese: DU

Civil Parish: **Thomastown**
Map Grid: 57
RC Parish: see Kildare
Diocese: KD

Civil Parish: **Timahoe**
Map Grid: 29
RC Parish: see Clane
Diocese: KD

Civil Parish: **Timolin**
Map Grid: 102
RC Parish: see Castledermot
Diocese: DU

Civil Parish: **Tipper**
Map Grid: 42

RC Parish: part Naas; part Kill
Diocese: DU

Civil Parish: **Tipperkevin**
Map Grid: 74
RC Parish: see Ballymore Eustace
Diocese: DU

Civil Parish: **Tully**
Map Grid: 60
RC Parish: Kildare and Rathangan, see Kildare
Diocese: DU

Civil Parish: **Usk**
Map Grid: 100
RC Parish: see Narraghmore
Diocese: DU

Civil Parish: **Walterstown**
Map Grid: 88
RC Parish: see Kildare
Diocese: KD

Civil Parish: **Whitechurch**
Map Grid: 37
RC Parish: see Kill
Diocese: KD

Commercial and Social Directories

1788
Richard Lucas's *General Directory of the Kingdom of Ireland* contains lists of traders in Athy. Reprinted in *Ir. Gen.* 3 (10) (1965): 392-416.

1824
J. Pigot's *City of Dublin & Hibernian Provincial Directory* includes traders, nobility, gentry, and clergy lists of Athy, Celbridge, Kilcock, Kilcullen, Kildare, Leixlip, Maynooth, Monasterevin, Naas, and Rathangan.

1846
Slater's *National Commercial Directory of Ireland* lists nobility, clergy, traders, etc., in Athy, Celbridge, Leixlip and Lucan, Kilcullen, Kildare, Maynooth and Kilcock, Monasterevin, Naas, and Rathangan.

1856

Slater's *Royal National Commercial Directory of Ireland* lists nobility, gentry, clergy, traders, etc., in Athy, Celbridge, Leixlip and Lucan, Kilcullen, Kildare, Maynooth and Kilcock, Monasterevin, Naas and Newbridge, and Rathangan.

1870

Slater's *Directory of Ireland* contains trade, nobility, and clergy lists for Athy, Kilcullen, Kildare, Maynooth and Kilcock, Monasterevin, Naas, Newbridge, and Rathangan.

1881

Slater's *Royal National Commercial Directory of Ireland* contains lists of traders, clergy, nobility, and farmers in adjoining parishes of the towns of Athy, Celbridge, Kildare, Maynooth and Kilcock, and Naas.

1894

Slater's *Royal National Directory of Ireland* lists traders, police, teachers, farmers, and private residents in each of the towns, villages, and parishes of the county.

Family History

"Alen of St. Wolstan's." *J. Kildare Arch. & Hist. Soc.* 1 (1892-95): 340-41.

"An Account of the Family of Alen, of St. Wolstan's, Co. Kildare." *J. Kildare Arch. & Hist. Soc.* 4 (1903-05): 95-110; 5 (1906-08): 344-47.

"The Aylmer Family." *J. Kildare Arch. & Hist. Soc.* 1 (1893-95): 295-307; 3 (1899-1902): 169-78; 4 (1903-05): 179-83.

"The Boylan Family of Carbury Area." *J. Kildare Arch. & Hist. Soc.* 14 (3) 1968.

"The Breretons of Co. Carlow and Co. Kildare." *Ir. Anc.* 3 (1971): 10-26, 124.

Dexter – see Co. Dublin.

Dundrum, E. O'H. *The O'Reillys of Templemills, Celbridge . . . with a Note on the History of the Clann Ui Raghallaigh in General.* Dublin, 1941.

"The Eustace Family and Their Lands in Co. Kildare." *J. Kildare Arch. & Hist. Soc.* 13 (6): 270-87; 13 (7): 307-41; 13 (8): 364-413.

"The Eustaces of Co. Kildare." *J. Kildare Arch. & Hist. Soc.* 1 (1891-95): 115-30.

"The Extinct Family of Young of Newtown-O'More, Co. Kildare." *J. Kildare Arch. & Hist. Soc.* 3 (1899-1902): 338.

The Family of Fish of Castlefish, Co. Kildare." *Ir. Anc.* 14 (1) 1982.

The Family of Flatesbury, of Ballynascullogue and Johnstown, Co. Kildare." *J. Kildare Arch. & Hist. Soc.* 4 (1903): 87-94.

"The Family of Tone." *J. Kildare Arch. & Hist. Soc.* 12 (1935-45): 326-29.

"The Fitzgeralds of Ballyshannon (Co. Kildare), and Their Successors Thereat." *J. Kildare Arch. Hist. Soc.* 3 (1899-1902): 425-52.

"The Hewetsons of Co. Kildare." *R.S.A.I.* 39 (1909): 146-63.

"The House of Eustace." *Reportorium* 2 (2) (1960): 245-56.

"Kilcullen New Abbey and the FitzEustaces." *J. Kildare Arch. & Hist. Soc.* 12 (1935-45): 217-21

"Ladytown and the Allens." *J. Kildare Arch. & Hist. Soc.* 9 (1918-21): 60-69.

"The Lattin and Mansfield Families, in the Co. Kildare." *J. Kildare Arch. & Hist. Soc.* 3 (1899-1902): 186-90.

"The La Touche Family of Harristown, Co. Kildare." *J. Kildare Arch. & Hist. Soc.* 7 (1912-14): 33-40.

"Lawe of Leixlip." *J. Kildare Arch. & Hist. Soc.* 6 (1909-11): 730-39.

"The Lockes of Athgoe." *Reportorium* 1 (1) (1955): 76-79.

"Mansfield Papers (Co. Kildare)." *Anal. Hib.* 20: 92-125.

McCann, P.D. *The Dooney Family of Co. Kildare and New Zealand.* 1977, 64 (c/o De la Salle Provincialate, 121 Howth Road, Dublin).

Moorhouse – see Co. Dublin.

"Notes on the Family of Sherlock: from State

Papers and Official Documents." *J. Kildare Arch. & Hist. Soc.* 2 (1896-99): 33-47; 6 (1909-11): 155-59.

"The Nuttalls of Co. Kildare." *J. Kildare Arch. & Hist. Soc.* 8 (1915-17): 180-84.

"The O'More Family of Balyna in the Co. Kildare, ca. 1774." *J. Kildare Arch. & Hist. Soc.* 9 (1918-21): 227-91, 318-30.

Prince, T. *Account of the Palmer Family of Rahan, Co. Kildare.* New York, 1903.

"Patrick Sarsfield, Earl of Lucan, with an Account of His Family and Their Connection with Lucan and Tully." *J. Kildare Arch. & Hist. Soc.* 4 (1903-05): 114-47.

Wolfe, George. "The Wolfe Family of Co. Kildare." *J. Kildare Arch. & Hist. Soc.* 3 (1899-1902): 361-67.

Wolfe, R. *Wolfes of Forenaghts, Blackhall, Baronrath, Co. Kildare, and Tipperary.* Guildford, 1893.

Gravestone Inscriptions

Clane: Index to seven local graveyards available from Mr. J.N.S. Reid, Kilmurray Place, Clane, Co. Kildare.

Newspapers

There are no early newspapers published within this county. Those from the surrounding counties, especially Dublin, should be consulted depending on their proximity to the area of interest.

Title: *Kildare Observer*
Published in: Naas, 1879-1935
NLI Holdings: 4.1879-6.1890; 1.1892-3.1897 (with gaps); 1.1899-5.1935
BL Holdings: 10.1880-1.1921; 5.1921-12.1924; 1.1926-12.1929; 1.1931-5.1935

Title: *Leinster Express*
Published in: Naas, 1868-73 and 1874-1947

Title: *Leinster Leader*
Published in: Naas, 1880-current
NLI Holdings: 1.1881-in progress
BL Holdings: 11.1882-in progress

Wills and Administrations

A discussion of the types of records, where they are held, their availability and value is given in the Wills section of the Introduction. The availability of prerogative wills, administrations, and marriage license records is also described in the relevant parts of the same section. Where available, published sources of these records are given in the Miscellaneous Sources section.

Pre-1858 Wills and Administrations

Prerogative Wills. see p. xli
Consistorial Wills. County Kildare is partly in the diocese of Kildare and partly in Dublin. One parish is in Leighlin. The guide to Catholic parish records in this chapter shows the diocese to which each civil parish belonged. The wills of residents of each diocese were usually proven within that diocese (see the Wills section for exceptions). The following records survive:

Wills. see p. xxxvii

Abstracts. see p. xxxvii; also the Betham Collection (PRO) has abstracts of most wills from 1661 to 1826 for names beginning A-K, and to 1824 for those beginning K-S. PRO 1A 44 22.

Indexes. Dublin–see Co. Dublin; Kildare (1661-1858) published in *J. Kildare Arch. Hist. Soc.* 1905; also to 1800 by Phillimore.

Post-1858 Wills and Administrations

This county was served by the District Registry of Dublin. The surviving records are kept in the PRO.

Marriage Licenses

Original Marriage Records. Kildare (1845-65).
PRO; SLC film 100873.

Indexes. Kildare (1740-1850). PRO; SLC film
100868; Dublin–see Co. Dublin.

"Index to Kildare Marriage License Bonds." *J.
Kildare Arch. Hist. Soc.* 11 (2) (1932): (A-C)
43-58, (D-I) 114-33; 12 (1) (1935): (J-O).

Miscellaneous Sources

"The High Sheriffs of Co. Kildare (1286-1897)."
J. Kildare Arch. Hist. Soc. 2 (1896-99): 253-
76.

O'Loan, J. "The Manor of Cloncurry, Co. Kildare, and the Feudal System of Land Tenure
in Ireland." *Ir. Dept. Agric. J.* 58 (1961): 14-
36.

"The Pre-famine Population of Some Kildare
Towns, with an Additional Note on the
Population of Some Rural Areas." *J. Kildare
Arch. Hist. Soc.* 14 (4) (1969): 444-51.

Research Sources and Services

Journals

Kildare Archaeological Society Journal, edited
by Lt. Col. C. Costello, Tullig, Dublin Road,
Naas, Co. Kildare

Libraries and Information Sources

Kildare County Library, Athgarvan Road,
Newbridge, Co. Kildare Ph: (045)
31486/31109

Research Services

Liam A. Ryan, 2320 Maryville, Kildare, Co. Kildare Ph: (045) 21124; Telex: 30971 E.I.

See also research services in Dublin, p. xliv

Societies

Kildare Archaeological Society, Mrs. M.
Grehan, Oakfield, Naas, Co. Kildare
Ph: (045) 97702

Naas Local History Group, Brian McCabe, Ivy
Cottage, Johnstown, Naas, Co. Kildare

CIVIL PARISHES OF COUNTY KILDARE

BARONIES

1. CARBURY
2. IKEATHY & OUGHTERANY
3. NORTH SALT
4. CLANE
5. NORTH NAAS
6. SOUTH SALT
7. EAST OFFALY
8. CONNELL
9. SOUTH NAAS
10. WEST OFFALY
11. KILCULLEN
12. NARRAGH & REBAN WEST
13. NARRAGH & REBAN EAST
14. KILKEA & MOONE

⌐ = CIVIL PARISHES ADJOINING ACROSS
BARONY BOUNDARIES.

County Kilkenny

A Brief History

In the old Gaelic territorial system, this county formed the bulk of the Kingdom of Ossory. The major Gaelic families in the county were the Walshes, the O'Brennans, and the O'Dunphys. After the Norman invasion a number of Norman families settled in Kilkenny and have been associated with the county ever since. These include Archer, Grace, Forestal, Comerford, Cantwell, Shortall, Wandesford, Rothe, Archdeacon ("Gaelicized" as Cody), and Butler. As elsewhere, these Normans became "more Irish than the Irish." The Sweetman family, which is of Norse origin, is also associated with the county.

Kilkenny City was probably founded by the establishment of a monastery there in 1052. The Norman invaders built a large castle on this site in 1195. The city acted as the parliamentary seat for Ireland on many occasions from the thirteenth to sixteenth centuries. In 1366 the English-controlled Parliament passed the infamous "Statutes of Kilkenny" in an attempt to prevent the adoption of the Irish life-style by the Normans. These statutes made it treasonable for a Norman to marry an Irishwoman or to adopt the dress, language, or customs of the Irish. The native Irish were also prohibited from living in walled towns. These statutes failed completely in their aims.

In the early seventeenth century, when English power had greatly receded in Ireland, Kilkenny City became the meeting-place of an independent Irish government, called the Confederation of Kilkenny, set up in opposition to the English-controlled Dublin Parliament. A general rebellion by those represented at this parliament, which began in 1641 and lasted until 1650, resulted in confiscation of the lands of these rebels and their redistribution to English soldiers and adventurers.

The county has very good agricultural soils and had a generally well developed system of agriculture in the early nineteenth century, including a large dairy industry. In the Great Famine, Kilkenny was relatively badly hit. The population in 1841 was 202,400 and in 1861 had fallen to 124,500. There were some 27,000 deaths in the county between 1845 and 1850.

The current population of the county is approximately 71,000. The major towns are Kilkenny, Callan, Graiguenamanagh, Thomastown, and Castlecomer. The county is still a major dairying area while Kilkenny City now has many industries and is the center of Irish design because of the establishment there by the government of the Kilkenny Design Centre. In regard to records, the county has a long-established local history society, the Kilkenny Archaeological and Historical Society, whose library is a valuable local archive.

Census and Census Substitutes

1537-1628

"Corporation Book of Irish Town of Kilkenny." *Anal. Hib.* 28 (1978): 1-78 (lists public officials, corporation members, etc.).

1569

Names of Gentlemen of Co. Kilkenny. Lambeth Palace Library, London. ms. 611; NLI P1699.

1654-56

Kilkenny City. Civil Survey, Vol. 6. SLC film 973123.

1659

"Census" of Ireland. Edited by S. Pender. Dublin: Stationery Office, 1939. SLC film 924648.

1664

Hearth Money Roll for parishes of Agherney, Aghavillar, Bellaghtobin, Belline, Burnchurch, Callan, Castleinch, Clone, Coolaghmor, Coolcashin, Danganmore, Derrinahinch, Dunkitt, Earlstown, Eynk, Fartagh, Inishnagg and Stonecarthy, Jerpoint, Kells, Kilbecon and Killahy, Kilcolm, Kilferragh, Kilkredy, Killamerry, Killaloe, Killree, Kilmoganny, Kiltacaholme, Knocktopher and Kilkerchill, Mucklee and Lismatigue, Outrath, Rathbach, Rathpatrick, Tullaghanbrogue, Tullaghmaine, Tullahaght, Urlingford. Transcript in the Carrigan Mss., Kilkenny. In *Ir. Gen.* 5 (1) (1974): 33-47 (Baronies of Ida, Knocktopher and Kells); 5 (2) (1975): 169-80 (rest of the county).

1702

List of Male Householders in Kilkenny City, comprising Catholics of St. Mary's Hightown Ward, and both Catholics and Protestants of St. Canice's Ingate and Outgate, city of Kilkenny. PRO 1A 55 82.

1766

Religious Census of Catholics in Portnascully. SLC film 100158.

1775

Names of Co. Kilkenny Land Holders. GO ms. 443; SLC film 100181.

Catholic Qualification Roll Extracts (189 names, addresses, and occupations). 59th Report DKPRI: 50-84.

1797

"Chief Inhabitants of the Parishes of Graiguenemanagh and Knocktopher." *Ir. Anc.* 10 (2) (1978): 73-76.

1798

List of Persons Who Suffered Loss in '98 Rebellion. NLI JLB 94107 (approximately 250 names, addresses, and occupations).

1809-19

A List of Co. Kilkenny Freeholders, 1809-1819. NLI ms. 14181.

1821

"Government Census Remnants": Parishes of Aglish and Portnascully. *Ir. Anc.* 8 (2) (1976): 113-24; *Ir. Gen.* 5 (3) (1976): 383-93. Parish of Pollrone. *Ir. Gen.* 5 (4) (1977): 522-26; SLC film 100158. Parishes of Clonmore, Fiddown, Kilmacow, Muckalee, Owning, Rathkieran, Tubrid, Tybroughney, Ullid and Whitechurch. *Ir. Gen.* 5 (5) (1978): 643-49.

1822-30

Lists of Applicants for the Vote. Division of Kilkenny (1,285 names) and Thomastown (2,525 names). (gives names, occupations, residence, description of property, etc.). NLI ILB 324 Kilkenny.

1823-38

Tithe Applotment Survey (see p. xxvii).

1832-36

"Names of Holders and Applicants for Licenses to Sell Liquor in Kilkenny" (names and addresses). *Parl. Papers* 1837/38, 13 (2): Appendixes 10 and 13.

1837

"List of those Made Freemen of Kilkenny Since 1831" (names, addresses, and occupations). *Parl. Papers* 1837, Vol. 11 (1): Appendix B1; 1837/38, 13 (2): Appendix 3.

Praysers: Thomas Phelan, Thomas Dwygine, Thomas Carran.
Porters; Dennis Caghell, William Longe, Donogheh O'Loghman.
The rates of vittles to continue as the last yere.
Free burgesses admitted: David Pembroke, Thomas Corran.

(This yere uppon the seccond of July, 1574, the Lord Deputy directed his letters unto Master Robert Poore, then being Portrive of the Irishtoune, therein requyring him to repayre unto his Honour to show what he had in the mayntenance of that xorporaction of meetre land commonly called the cross of meetre land; which thing he performed accordingly. The proceedings of this suite you shall find in sixte leaf of this booke).[1]

fol. 35b. Thomas Seix, Portrive, the 11th of Octobre, 1574.
Sargente: Robert Roth.
Constables: Micholas Lawles, Thomas Carran, Edmund Browne, William Hoyne.
Bayliffs: Walter Roth, fitz Oliver, Dennise Carran.
(Free burgess admitted: Nicholas Fleming).[2]
Proctors: Geffry Roth, Thomas Dullany.
Auditors: Morgan Kealy, Richard Poore, Thomas Dullany, John Hoyne.
Praysers: John Dywy, Robert Roth, fitz David, Thomas Deegin.
Porters: Dennise Caghell, Patrick Brenen, Dennise Loghman, James Stackboll.
The rates of all kinde of vittles of beefe, bread, and ale, fish, tallow, (the wages of) laborers and artificers, to continue as affore is concluded the yere John Busher was Portrive.
David Pembrocke, sworne Portrive the 11th of Octobre, 1575.
Officers appointed:
Sargente: Robert Roth.
Constables: William Donogh, John Morphy, Thomas Hoyne, William Breckley.
Bayliffs: Dennise Kelly, John Fleming.
Proctors: James Kenedy, Edward Browne.
Auditors: Richard Poore, John Dowly, Richard Mooney, Thomas Dullany.
Prayers: William Brenagh, Derby Pysan, Thomas Dwigin.
Porters: John Galvan, Dennise Davyn Loghman.
(Free burgesses admitted: Thomas Raghtor, William Donogho, Lawrence Walsh, Dennise Call.)
Sessors: Dennise Davyne, Robert Kyvan, Danyell O'Teyne, Robert Kelly.

[1] Matter within brackets is in margin in a later hand.
[2] The words between brackets inserted in different ink.

An extract from a copy of the "Corporation Book of the Irish Town of Kilkenny, 1537-1628" giving the names of various corporation officers. *Analecta Hibernica* 28 (1978).

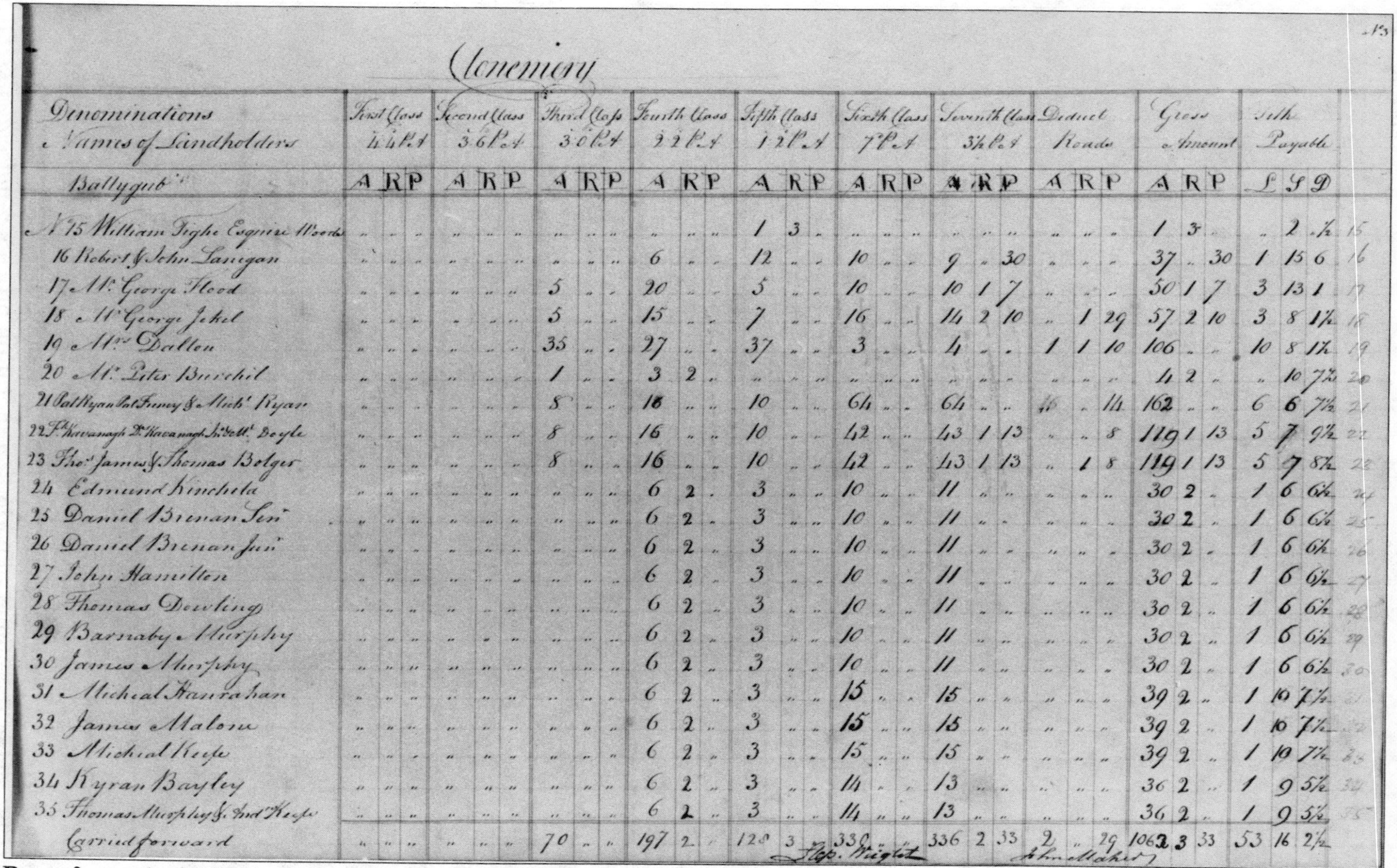

Clonemery

Denominations & Names of Landholders	First Class 4/4 P. A. (A R P)	Second Class 3/6 P. A. (A R P)	Third Class 3/0 P. A. (A R P)	Fourth Class 2/2 P. A. (A R P)	Fifth Class 1/2 P. A. (A R P)	Sixth Class 7 P. A. (A R P)	Seventh Class 3½ P. A. (A R P)	Deduct Roads (A R P)	Gross Amount (A R P)	Tithe Payable (£ S D)
Ballygub										
No. 15 William Fighe Esquire Woods					1 3				1 3	2 ½
16 Robert & John Lanigan				6	12	10	9 . 30		37 . 30	1 15 6
17 Mr George Flood			5	20	5	10	10 1 7		50 1 7	3 13 1
18 Mr George Jekel			5	15	7	16	14 2 10	. 1 29	57 2 10	3 8 1½
19 Mrs Dalton			35	27	37	3	4	1 1 10	106	10 8 1½
20 Mr Peter Burchil			1	3 2					4 2	10 7½
21 Pat Ryan Pat Finney & Michl Ryan			8	16	10	64	64	16 . 14	162	6 6 7½
22 Ths Kavanagh Dn Kavanagh Jn & Wm Doyle			8	16	10	42	43 1 13	. . 8	119 1 13	5 7 9½
23 Thos James & Thomas Bolger			8	16	10	42	43 1 13	. 1 8	119 1 13	5 7 8½
24 Edmund Kinchela				6 2	3	10	11		30 2	1 6 6½
25 Daniel Brenan Senr				6 2	3	10	11		30 2	1 6 6½
26 Daniel Brenan Junr				6 2	3	10	11		30 2	1 6 6½
27 John Hamilton				6 2	3	10	11		30 2	1 6 6½
28 Thomas Dowling				6 2	3	10	11		30 2	1 6 6½
29 Barnaby Murphy				6 2	3	10	11		30 2	1 6 6½
30 James Murphy				6 2	3	10	11		30 2	1 6 6½
31 Michael Hanrahan				6 2	3	15	15		39 2	1 10 7½
32 James Malone				6 2	3	15	15		39 2	1 10 7½
33 Michael Keefe				6 2	3	15	15		39 2	1 10 7½
34 Kyran Bayley				6 2	3	14	13		36 2	1 9 5½
35 Thomas Murphy & Andw Keefe				6 2	3	14	13		36 2	1 9 5½
Carried forward			70	197 2	120 3	330	336 2 33	2 . 29	1062 3 33	53 16 2½

Page from the *Tithe Applottment Survey* showing the tithe-payers of the townland of Ballygub, Parish of Clonamery, Co. Kilkenny, in 1829.

1841
"Government Census Remnants: Townlands of Aglish North and South and Portnascully, Parish of Aglish." *Ir. Anc.* 9 (1) (1977): 44-47; SLC film 100158

1849-50
Griffith's Valuation (see p. xxvii).

1851
"Government Census Remnants: Parishes of Aglish, Portnascully and Rathkieran." *Ir. Anc.* 9 (2) (1977): 129-33.

1901
Census. PRO.

1911
Census. PRO.

Church Records

Church of Ireland
(shows starting date of record)

Parish: **Aghour** or **Freshford**
Status: Lost

Parish: **Ballinamare**
Status: Lost

Parish: **Blackrath**
Existing Records: b. 1811; d. 1845
Status: LC

Parish: **Burnchurch**
Status: Lost

Parish: **Callan**
Status: Lost

Parish: **Castlane** or **Whitechurch** (Castle Archdall)
Status: Lost

Parish: **Castlecomer**
Existing Records: b. 1799; m. 1799; d. 1799
Status: LC

Parish: **Castlecomer Colliery**
Existing Records: b. 1838; m. 1839; d. 1861
Status: LC

Parish: **Clara** (see St. John Kilkenny)

Parish: **Clonmantagh**
Status: Lost

Parish: **Clonmore**
Existing Records: b. 1817; m. 1820; d. 1822
Status: LC

Parish: **Donoughmore** (see Odagh)

Parish: **Dunkitt** (including Gaulskill and Kilcollum)
Status: Lost

Parish: **Dunmore**
Existing Records: b. 1839; m. 1838; d. 1842
Status: LC

Parish: **Eirke**
Status: Lost

Parish: **Ennisnag**
Status: Lost

Parish: **Fertagh**
Existing Records: b. 1797; m. 1797; d. 1797
Status: LC

Parish: **Fiddown**
Status: Lost

Parish: **Gowran**
Status: Lost

Parish: **Graigue**
Existing Records: b. 1827; m. 1827; d. 1827
Status: LC

Parish: **Grangesylvae** (Gowran)
Existing Records: b. 1803; m. 1803; d. 1806
Status: LC

Parish: **Inchyolaghan**
Status: Lost

Parish: **Innistiogue**
Existing Records: b. 1797; m. 1797; d. 1797
Status: LC

Parish: **Jerpoint** (with Thomastown)
Status: Lost

Parish: **Kells**
Status: Lost

Parish: **Kilbecon**
Status: Lost

Parish: **Kilfane**
Status: Lost

Parish: **Killamery**
Status: Lost

Parish: **Kilmacow**
Status: Lost

Parish: **Kilmanagh**
Existing Records: b. 1784; m. 1784; d. 1784
Status: LC

Parish: **Kilmocahill** (see also Shankill)
Status: Lost

Parish: **Kilmoganny**
Existing Records: b. 1782; m. 1782; d. 1782
Status: LC

Parish: **Knocktopher**
Status: Lost

Parish: **Listerlin**
Status: Lost

Parish: **Macully** or **Kilculliheen**
Status: Lost

Parish: **Mothel**
Status: Lost

Parish: **Odagh**
Status: Lost

Parish: **Powerstown**
Status: Lost

Parish: **Rathkieran Church**
Status: Lost

Parish: **Rower, The**
Status: Lost

Parish: **St. Canice**
Existing Records: b. 1789; m. 1789; d. 1789

Parish: **St. John Kilkenny**
Status: Lost

Parish: **St. Mary's** and **St. Patrick, Kilkenny**
Existing Records: b. 1732; m. 1732; d. 1732
Status: LC

Parish: **Shankill** or **St. Kill** and **Kilmocahill**
Status: Lost

Parish: **Stamcarty** (see Kells)

Parish: **Tiscoffin**
Status: Lost

Parish: **Thomastown**
Existing Records: b. 1825; m. 1825; d. 1825
Status: LC

Parish: **Treadingstown**
Status: Lost

Parish: **Ullard** (Graigue up to ca. 1833)
Status: Lost

Roman Catholic

Civil Parish: **Abbeyleix**
Map Grid: 14
RC Parish: part Abbeyleix, Co. Laois; part Ballyragget, see Donaghmore
Diocese: LE

Civil Parish: **Aghaviller**
Map Grid: 104
RC Parish: Danesfort
Diocese: OS
Earliest Record: b. 10.1847; m. 2.1848

Parish Address: Rev. Joseph Gallavan, PP, Newmarket, Hugginstown, Co. Kilkenny

Civil Parish: **Aghlish**
Map Grid: 140
RC Parish: Mooncoin, see Pollrone
Diocese: OS

Civil Parish: **Aharney** (see also Co. Laois)
Map Grid: 10
RC Parish: Lisdowney
Diocese: OS
Earliest Record: b. 5.1817; m. 9.1771
Missing Dates: b. 10.1853-4.1854; m. 4.1778-11.1828, 8.1853-11.1853
Parish Address: Rev. Seamus McEvoy, PP, Lisdowney, Ballyragget, Co. Kilkenny

Civil Parish: **Arderra**
Map Grid: 136
RC Parish: Mooncoin, see Pollrone
Diocese: OS

Civil Parish: **Attanagh** (see also Co. Laois)
Map Grid: 13
RC Parish: Ballyraggett, see Donaghmore
Diocese: OS

Civil Parish: **Balleen**
Map Grid: 7
RC Parish: Lisdowney, see Aharney
Diocese: OS

Civil Parish: **Ballinamara**
Map Grid: 38
RC Parish: see Freshford
Diocese: OS

Civil Parish: **Ballybur**
Map Grid: 52
RC Parish: part Danesfort; part St. Canice's
Diocese: OS

Civil Parish: **Ballycallan**
Map Grid: 41
RC Parish: Ballycallan
Diocese: OS
Earliest Record: b. 5.1845; m. 7.1845
Parish Address: Rev. Patrick Brennan, PP, Kilmanagh, Co. Kilkenny

Civil Parish: **Ballygurrum**
Map Grid: 119
RC Parish: Slievrue, see Rathpatrick
Diocese: OS

Civil Parish: **Ballylarkin**
Map Grid: 32
RC Parish: see Freshford
Diocese: OS

Civil Parish: **Ballylinch**
Map Grid: 83
RC Parish: see Thomastown
Diocese: OS

Civil Parish: **Ballytarsney**
Map Grid: 135
RC Parish: Mooncoin, see Pollrone
Diocese: OS

Civil Parish: **Ballytobin**
Map Grid: 97
RC Parish: see Dunnamaggan
Diocese: OS

Civil Parish: **Blackrath**
Map Grid: 66
RC Parish: part St. John's, part Gowran
Diocese: OS

Civil Parish: **Blanchvilleskill**
Map Grid: 74
RC Parish: see Gowran
Diocese: OS

Civil Parish: **Borrismore**
Map Grid: 6
RC Parish: see Urlingford
Diocese: OS

Civil Parish: **Burnchurch**
Map Grid: 56
RC Parish: part Danesfort; part Freshford; part Mooncoin, see Pollrone; part Ballyhale, see Derrynahinch
Diocese: OS

Civil Parish: **Callan**
Map Grid: 47
RC Parish: part Callan; see also Ballycallan
Diocese: OS

Earliest Record: b. 1.1821; m. 1.1821
Parish Address: Rev. John Brennan, PP, Callan,
    Co. Kilkenny

Civil Parish: **Castlecomer**
Map Grid: 15
RC Parish: Clogh and Castlecomer
Diocese: OS
Earliest Record: b. 1.1812; m. 8.1831
Missing Dates: b. 10.1818-12.1828
Parish Address: Rev. T. Bowden, PP, Clogh,
    Castlecomer, Co. Kilkenny; and Rev. M. Kir-
    wan, PP, Castlecomer, Co. Kilkenny

Civil Parish: **Castleinch** (or Incholaghan)
Map Grid: 51
RC Parish: see St. Patrick's
Diocese: OS

Civil Parish: **Clara**
Map Grid: 70
RC Parish: see Gowran
Diocese: OS

Civil Parish: **Clashacrow**
Map Grid: 36
RC Parish: see Freshford
Diocese: OS

Civil Parish: **Clomantagh**
Map Grid: 28
RC Parish: part Urlingford; part Freshford
Diocese: OS

Civil Parish: **Clonamery**
Map Grid: 112
RC Parish: see Inistioge
Diocese: OS

Civil Parish: **Clonmore**
Map Grid: 131
RC Parish: Mooncoin, see Pollrone
Diocese: OS

Civil Parish: **Columkille**
Map Grid: 89
RC Parish: see Thomastown
Diocese: OS

Civil Parish: **Coolaghmore**
Map Grid: 93
RC Parish: see Callan
Diocese: OS

Civil Parish: **Coolcashin**
Map Grid: 8
RC Parish: Lisdowney, see Aharney
Diocese: OS

Civil Parish: **Coolcraheen**
Map Grid: 22
RC Parish: part Conahy; part Muckalee
Diocese: OS

Civil Parish: **Danesfort**
Map Grid: 57
RC Parish: Danesfort and Cuffe's Grange
Diocese: OS
Earliest Record: b. 1.1819; m. 1.1824
Parish Address: Rev. Eamonn O'Gorman, CC,
    Danesfort, Co. Kilkenny

Civil Parish: **Derrynahinch**
Map Grid: 106
RC Parish: Ballyhale; also Mullinavat, see Kil-
    beacon
Diocese: OS
Earliest Record: b. 8.1823
Parish Address: Rev. Michael Morrissey, PP,
    Ballyhale, Co. Kilkenny

Civil Parish: **Donaghmore**
Map Grid: 18
RC Parish: Ballyragget
Diocese: OS
Earliest Record: b. 8.1857; m. 4.1856
Parish Address: Rev. Peter Grant, PP, Ballyrag-
    get, Co. Kilkenny

Civil Parish: **Dunbell**
Map Grid: 73
RC Parish: see Gowran
Diocese: OS

Civil Parish: **Dungarvan**
Map Grid: 81
RC Parish: see Gowran
Diocese: OS

Civil Parish: **Dunkitt**
Map Grid: 121
RC Parish: see Kilmacow
Diocese: OS

Civil Parish: **Dunmore**
Map Grid: 26
RC Parish: see Muckalee (1)
Diocese: OS

Civil Parish: **Dunnamaggan**
Map Grid: 98
RC Parish: Dunnamaggan
Diocese: OS
Earliest Record: b. 9.1826; m. 10.1826
Missing Dates: b. 6.1840-4.1843; m. 6.1842-2.1843
Parish Address: Rev. James Brennan, PP, Dunamaggan, Co. Kilkenny

Civil Parish: **Durrow** (see also Co. Laois)
Map Grid: 11
RC Parish: part Ballyragget, see Donaghmore
Diocese: OS

Civil Parish: **Dysart**
Map Grid: 21
RC Parish: see Muckalee (1)
Diocese: OS

Civil Parish: **Dysartmoon**
Map Grid: 113
RC Parish: see Rosbercon
Diocese: OS

Civil Parish: **Earlstown**
Map Grid: 59
RC Parish: see Callan
Diocese: OS

Civil Parish: **Ennisnag**
Map Grid: 60
RC Parish: see Danesfort
Diocese: OS

Civil Parish: **Erke** (see also Co. Laois)
Map Grid: 1
RC Parish: Johnstown, see Fertagh
Diocese: OS

Civil Parish: **Famma**
Map Grid: 91
RC Parish: see Thomastown
Diocese: OS

Civil Parish: **Fertagh (1)**
Map Grid: 4
RC Parish: Johnstown
Diocese: OS
Earliest Record: b. 8.1814; m. 2.1851
Parish Address: Rev. Patrick Greene, PP, Johnstown, Co. Kilkenny

Civil Parish: **Fertagh (2)**
Map Grid: 4
RC Parish: Galmoy
Diocese: OS
Earliest Record: b. 6.1861; m. 9.1861
Parish Address: Rev. Michael Purcell, PP, Galmoy, Crosspatrick, via Thurles, Co. Kilkenny

Civil Parish: **Fiddown**
Map Grid: 128
RC Parish: Owning and Templeorum
Diocese: OS
Earliest Record: b. 10.1803; m. 8.1815; d. 9.1803
Missing Dates: m. 11.1849-1.1851; d. 3.1806-8.1808, ends 6.1815
Parish Address: Rev. John Woods, PP, Piltown, Co. Kilkenny

Civil Parish: **Freshford**
Map Grid: 33
RC Parish: part Freshford; part Ballyragget, see Donaghmore
Diocese: OS
Earliest Record: b. 1.1773; m. 8.1775
Missing Dates: b. 8.1797-3.1800; m. 11.1779-2.1801
Parish Address: Rev. Martin Comerford, PP, Freshford, Co. Kilkenny

Civil Parish: **Garranamanagh**
Map Grid: 29
RC Parish: see Freshford
Diocese: OS

Civil Parish: **Gaulskill**
Map Grid: 122
RC Parish: see Kilmacow
Diocese: OS

Civil Parish: **Glashare** (see also Co. Laois)
Map Grid: 2
RC Parish: Johnstown, see Fertagh (1)

Civil Parish: **Gowran**
Map Grid: 71
RC Parish: Gowran and Clara
Diocese: OS
Earliest Record: b. 1.1809; m. 1.1810
Parish Address: Rev. Philip Madigan, PP, Gowran, Co. Kilkenny

Civil Parish: **Graiguenamanagh**
Map Grid: 86
RC Parish: Graignamanagh
Diocese: LE
Earliest Record: b. 4.1838; m. 7.1818
Parish Address: Rev. William Gavin, PP, Graiguenamanagh, Co. Kilkenny

Civil Parish: **Grange**
Map Grid: 50
RC Parish: see St. Patrick's
Diocese: OS

Civil Parish: **Grangekilree**
Map Grid: 58
RC Parish: see Dunnamaggan
Diocese: OS

Civil Parish: **Grangemaccomb**
Map Grid: 19
RC Parish: Conahy
Diocese: OS
Earliest Record: b. 6.1832; m. 6.1832
Parish Address: Rev. Peter Hoyne, PP, Conahy, Jenkinstown, Co. Kilkenny

Civil Parish: **Grangesilvia**
Map Grid: 76
RC Parish: Paulstown, see Kilmacahill
Diocese: LE

Civil Parish: **Inistioge**
Map Grid: 92
RC Parish: Inistioge and Clodiagh
Diocese: OS
Earliest Record: b. 12.1810 (2 registers); m. 1.1827
Parish Address: Rev. Patrick Grace, PP, Inistioge, Co. Kilkenny

Civil Parish: **Jerpointabbey**
Map Grid: 88
RC Parish: see Thomastown
Diocese: OS

Civil Parish: **Jerpointchurch**
Map Grid: 102
RC Parish: see Thomastown
Diocese: OS

Civil Parish: **Jerpointwest**
Map Grid: 108
RC Parish: part Thomastown; part Mullinavat, see Kilbeacon

Civil Parish: **Kells**
Map Grid: 95
RC Parish: part Danesfort; part Ballyhale, see Derrynahinch
Diocese: OS

Civil Parish: **Kilbeacon**
Map Grid: 110
RC Parish: Mullinavat
Diocese: OS
Earliest Record: b. 2.1843; m. 5.1843
Parish Address: Rev. Thomas Maher, PP, Mullinavat, Waterford

Civil Parish: **Kilbride**
Map Grid: 117
RC Parish: Slieverue, see Rathpatrick
Diocese: OS

Civil Parish: **Kilcoan**
Map Grid: 118
RC Parish: Slieverue, see Rathpatrick
Diocese: OS

Civil Parish: **Kilcolumb**
Map Grid: 123
RC Parish: Sliverue, see Rathpatrick
Diocese: OS

Civil Parish: **Kilculliheen**
Map Grid: 140a
RC Parish: Slieverue, see Rathpatrick
Diocese: OS

Civil Parish: **Kilcooly**
Map Grid: 34

RC Parish: Gortnahoe, see Buolick, Co. Tipperary
Diocese: CA

Civil Parish: **Kilderry**
Map Grid: 67
RC Parish: see St. John
Diocese: OS

Civil Parish: **Kilfane**
Map Grid: 85
RC Parish: see Thomastown
Diocese: OS

Civil Parish: **Kilferagh**
Map Grid: 54
RC Parish: see St. Patrick's
Diocese: OS

Civil Parish: **Kilkeasy**
Map Grid: 105
RC Parish: Ballyhale, see Derrynahinch
Diocese: OS

Civil Parish: **Kilkieran**
Map Grid: 63
RC Parish: Templeorum, see Fiddown
Diocese: OS

Civil Parish: **Killahy (1)** (Barony of Cranagh)
Map Grid: 35
RC Parish: see Freshford
Diocese: OS

Civil Parish: **Killahy (2)** (Barony of Knocktopher)
Map Grid: 109
RC Parish: see Kilmacow
Diocese: OS

Civil Parish: **Killaloe**
Map Grid: 48
RC Parish: see Ballycallan
Diocese: OS

Civil Parish: **Killamery**
Map Grid: 96
RC Parish: Windgap
Diocese: OS
Earliest Record: b. 8.1822; m. 9.1822

Parish Address: Rev. Garrett Phelan, PP, Windgap, Thomastown, Co. Kilkenny

Civil Parish: **Killarney**
Map Grid: 79
RC Parish: see Thomastown
Diocese: OS

Civil Parish: **Kilmacahill**
Map Grid: 72
RC Parish: Paulstown and Goresbridge
Diocese: LE
Earliest Record: b. 7.1824; m. 1.1824
Missing Dates: b. 4.1846-5.1852; m. 11.1869-2.1870
Parish Address: Rev. John O'Leary, PP, Paulstown, Gowran, Co. Kilkenny

Civil Parish: **Kilmocar**
Map Grid: 20
RC Parish: part Ballyragget, see Donaghmore; part Conahy, see Grangemaccomb
Diocese: OS

Civil Parish: **Kilmacow**
Map Grid: 138
RC Parish: Kilmacow
Diocese: OS
Earliest Record: b. 7.1858; m. 8.1858; d. 6.1858
Parish Address: Rev. William Daly, PP, Kilmacow, Waterford

Civil Parish: **Kilmademoge**
Map Grid: 27
RC Parish: see Muckalee
Diocese: OS

Civil Parish: **Kilmadum**
Map Grid: 62
RC Parish: see St. John
Diocese: OS

Civil Parish: **Kilmaganny**
Map Grid: 100
RC Parish: see Dunnamaggan
Diocese: OS

Civil Parish: **Kilmakevoge**
Map Grid: 124
RC Parish: Glenmore

Diocese: OS
Earliest Record: b. 3.1831; m. 1.1831
Parish Address: Rev. Timothy O'Connor, PP,
  Glenmore, Waterford

Civil Parish: **Kilmanagh**
Map Grid: 40
RC Parish: see Ballycallan
Diocese: OS

Civil Parish: **Kilmenan**
Map Grid: 17
RC Parish: Ballyragget, see Donaghmore
Diocese: OS

Civil Parish: **Kilree**
Map Grid: 99
RC Parish: see Dunnamaggan
Diocese: OS

Civil Parish: **Knocktopher**
Map Grid: 103
RC Parish: Ballyhale, see Derrynahinch
Diocese: OS

Civil Parish: **Lismateige**
Map Grid: 107
RC Parish: part Templeorum, see Fiddown;
  part Aghaviller
Diocese: OS

Civil Parish: **Listerlin**
Map Grid: 115
RC Parish: see Rosbercon
Diocese: OS

Civil Parish: **Mallardstown**
Map Grid: 94
RC Parish: see Callan
Diocese: OS

Civil Parish: **Mayne**
Map Grid: 23
RC Parish: Conahy, see Grangemaccomb
Diocese: OS

Civil Parish: **Mothell**
Map Grid: 24
RC Parish: see Muckalee
Diocese: OS

Civil Parish: **Muckalee (1)** (Barony of Fas-
  sadinin)
Map Grid: 25
RC Parish: Muckalee
Diocese: OS
Earliest Record: b. 10.1801; m. 4.1809
Missing Dates: b. 9.1806-6.1840; m. 11.1857-
  2.1858
Parish Address: Rev. John Loughrey, PP,
  Muckalee, Ballyfoyle, Co. Kilkenny

Civil Parish: **Muckalee (2)** (Barony of Knock-
  topher)
Map Grid: 130
RC Parish: part Mooncoin, see Pollrone; part
  Aghaviller
Diocese: OS

Civil Parish: **Odagh**
Map Grid: 39
RC Parish: part Freshford; part Conahy, see
  Grangemaccomb
Diocese: OS

Civil Parish: **Outrath**
Map Grid: 53
RC Parish: see St. Patrick's
Diocese: OS

Civil Parish: **Owning**
Map Grid: 127
RC Parish: Templeorum, see Fiddown
Diocese: OS

Civil Parish: **Pleberstown**
Map Grid: 90
RC Parish: see Thomastown
Diocese: OS

Civil Parish: **Pollrone**
Map Grid: 134
RC Parish: Mooncoin
Diocese: OS
Earliest Record: b. 12.1797; m. 1.1772
Missing Dates: m. 3.1783-1.1789, 2.1814-2.1816,
  9.1836-1.1837
Parish Address: Rev. Francis Grace, PP, Moon-
  coin, Waterford

Civil Parish: **Portnascully**
Map Grid: 139
RC Parish: Mooncoin, see Pollrone
Diocese: OS

Civil Parish: **Powerstown**
Map Grid: 82
RC Parish: see Graiguenamanagh
Diocese: LE

Civil Parish: **Rathaspick**
Map Grid: 16
RC Parish: see Co. Laois
Diocese: LE

Civil Parish: **Rathbeagh**
Map Grid: 30
RC Parish: Lisdowney, see Aharney
Diocese: OS

Civil Parish: **Rathcoole**
Map Grid: 64
RC Parish: see St. John
Diocese: OS

Civil Parish: **Rathkieran**
Map Grid: 133
RC Parish: Mooncoin, see Pollrone
Diocese: OS

Civil Parish: **Rathlogan**
Map Grid: 5
RC Parish: Johnstown, see Fertagh
Diocese: OS

Civil Parish: **Rathpatrick**
Map Grid: 125
RC Parish: Slieverue
Diocese: OS
Earliest Record: b. 11.1766; m. 2.1766; d. 12.1766
Missing Dates: m. 5.1778-5.1791, 7.1801-10.1801; d. ends 11.1799
Parish Address: Rev. Joseph Delaney, PP, Slieverue, Waterford

Civil Parish: **Rosbercon**
Map Grid: 116
RC Parish: Rosbercon
Diocese: OS
Earliest Record: b. 4.1817; m. 1.1835

Missing Dates: b. 6.1819-1.1821, 3.1825-1.1830
Parish Address: Rev. John Carey, PP, Rosbercon, New Ross, Co. Wexford

Civil Parish: **Rosconnell** (see also Co. Laois)
Map Grid: 12
RC Parish: Ballyragget, see Donaghmore
Diocese: OS

Civil Parish: **Rossinan**
Map Grid: 111
RC Parish: see Kilmacow
Diocese: OS

Civil Parish: **The Rower**
Map Grid: 114
RC Parish: see Inistioge
Diocese: OS

Civil Parish: **St. Canice's**
Map Grid: 42
RC Parish: St. Canice's, Kilkenny
Diocese: OS
Earliest Record: b. 4.1768; m. 6.1768
Parish Address: Rev. Paul Fitzgerald, Adm, St. Canice's, Kilkenny

Civil Parish: **St. John (1)**
Map Grid: 43
RC Parish: St. John's, Kilkenny; also Kilkenny Workhouse, see below
Diocese: OS
Earliest Record: b. 1.1809; m. 6.1809
Missing Dates: b. 7.1830-2.1842; m. 7.1830-4.1842
Parish Address: Rev. Laurence Dunphy, PP, St. John's Presbytery, Kilkenny

Civil Parish: **St. John (2)**
Map Grid: 43
RC Parish: Kilkenny Workhouse
Earliest Record: b. 4.1876

Civil Parish: **St. Martin's**
Map Grid: 69
RC Parish: see St. Patrick's
Diocese: OS

Civil Parish: **St. Mary's**
Map Grid: 44
RC Parish: St. Mary's Kilkenny

Diocese: OS
Earliest Record: b. 1.1754; m. 1.1754; d. 1.1754
Missing Dates: b. 8.1782-8.1784; d. ends 7.1787
Parish Address: Rev. Patrick Duggan, Adm, St.
  Mary's Presbytery, Kilkenny

Civil Parish: **St. Maul's**
Map Grid: 45
RC Parish: see St. Canice's
Diocese: OS

Civil Parish: **St. Patrick's**
Map Grid: 46
RC Parish: St. Patrick's, Kilkenny
Diocese: OS
Earliest Record: b. 8.1800; m. 7.1801
Parish Address: Rev. Brian Flynn, Adm, St.
  Patrick's, Kilkenny

Civil Parish: **Shanbogh**
Map Grid: 120
RC Parish: see Rosbercon
Diocese: OS

Civil Parish: **Shankill**
Map Grid: 68
RC Parish: Paulstown; see Kilmacahill
Diocese: LE

Civil Parish: **Sheffin**
Map Grid: 9
RC Parish: Lisdowney; see Aharney
Diocese: OS

Civil Parish: **Stonecarthy**
Map Grid: 61
RC Parish: see Dunnamaggan
Diocese: OS

Civil Parish: **Thomastown**
Map Grid: 84
RC Parish: Thomastown and Tullaherin
Diocese: OS
Earliest Record: b. 6.1782; m. 1.1786
Missing Dates: b. 9.1809-1.1810; m. 8.1806-
  5.1810
Parish Address: Rev. Michael Carroll, PP,
  Thomastown, Co. Kilkenny

Civil Parish: **Tibberraghny**
Map Grid: 129
RC Parish: Templeorum, see Fiddown
Diocese: OS

Civil Parish: **Tiscoffin**
Map Grid: 65
RC Parish: see Gowran
Diocese: OS

Civil Parish: **Treadingstown**
Map Grid: 77
RC Parish: see Danesfort
Diocese: OS

Civil Parish: **Tubbrid**
Map Grid: 132
RC Parish: Mooncoin, see Pollrone
Diocese: OS

Civil Parish: **Tubbridbritain**
Map Grid: 31
RC Parish: see Urlingford
Diocese: OS

Civil Parish: **Tullaghanbrogue**
Map Grid: 49
RC Parish: see St. Patrick's
Diocese: OS

Civil Parish: **Tullaherin**
Map Grid: 80
RC Parish: see Thomastown
Diocese: OS

Civil Parish: **Tullahought**
Map Grid: 101
RC Parish: Windgap, see Killamery
Diocese: OS

Civil Parish: **Tullamaine**
Map Grid: 55
RC Parish: see Callan
Diocese: OS

Civil Parish: **Tullaroan**
Map Grid: 37
RC Parish: Tullaroan
Diocese: OS
Earliest Record: b. 3.1843; m. 4.1843

Parish Address: Rev. Andrew O'Dwyer, PP, Tullaroan, Co. Kilkenny

Civil Parish: **Ullard** (see also Co. Carlow)
Map Grid: 87
RC Parish: see Graiguenamanagh
Diocese: LE

Civil Parish: **Ullid**
Map Grid: 137
RC Parish: see Kilmacow
Diocese: OS

Civil Parish: **Urlingford**
Map Grid: 3
RC Parish: Urlingford (Graine)
Diocese: OS
Earliest Record: b. 5.1805; m. 5.1805
Missing Dates: m. 9.1870-2.1871
Parish Address: Rev. Joseph Langton, PP, Urlingford, Co. Kilkenny

Civil Parish: **Wells**
Map Grid: 75
RC Parish: Leighlinbridge, see Agha, Co. Carlow
Diocese: LE

Civil Parish: **Whitechurch**
Map Grid: 126
RC Parish: Templeorum, see Fiddown
Diocese: OS

Civil Parish: **Woolengrange**
Map Grid: 78
RC Parish: see Danesfort
Diocese: OS

Commercial and Social Directories

1788
Richard Lucas's *General Directory of the Kingdom of Ireland* contains lists of traders in Kilkenny and Thomastown.

1820
J. Pigot's *Commercial Directory of Ireland* contains information on the gentry, nobility, and traders in and around the town of Kilkenny.

1824
J. Pigot's *City of Dublin & Hibernian Provincial Directory* includes traders, nobility, gentry, and clergy lists of Ballyragget, Callan, Castlecomer, Kilkenny, and Thomastown.

1839
T. Shearman's *New Commercial Directory for the Cities of Waterford and Kilkenny, Towns of Clonmel, Carrick on Suir, New Ross and Carlow* lists traders, gentry, etc.

1840
F. Kinder's *New Triennial & Commercial Directory for the Years 1840, '41 and '42.* Lists traders, nobility, etc., in Kilkenny city (very rare volume).

1846
Slater's *National Commercial Directory of Ireland* lists nobility, clergy, traders, etc., in Ballyragget, Callan, Castlecomer, Durrow, Kilkenny, and Thomastown.

1856
Slater's *Royal National Commercial Directory of Ireland* lists nobility, gentry, clergy, traders, etc., in Ballyragget, Callan, Castlecomer, Durrow, Kilkenny, and Thomastown.

1870
Slater's *Directory of Ireland* contains trade, nobility, and clergy lists for Ballyragget, Callan, Castlecomer, Durrow, Kilkenny, and Thomastown.

1881
Slater's *Royal National Commercial Directory of Ireland* contains lists of traders, clergy, nobility, and farmers in adjoining parishes of the towns of Callan, Castlecomer, Durrow, Kilkenny, and Thomastown.

1884
G.H. Bassett's *Kilkenny City & County Guide and Directory* of Ballyhale, Ballyragget, Bennett's Bridge, Callan, Castlecomer, Clonmantagh, Cuff's Grange, Dungarvan, Ferrybank, Freshford, Glenmore, Goresbridge, Gowran, Graigue, Inistioge,

Jenkinstown, Johnstown, Johnswell, Kells, Kilfane, Kilkenny, Kilmacow, Kilmanagh, Kilmoganny, Knocktopher, Luke's Well, Mooncoin, Mullinavat, Piltown and Fiddown, Rosbercon, Slieverue, Stonyford, The Rower, Thomastown, Three Castles, Tullaroan, Tullogher, Urlingford, Whitehall, and Windgap.

1894

Slater's *Royal National Directory of Ireland* lists traders, police, teachers, farmers, and private residents in each of the towns, villages, and parishes of the county.

Family History

Anderson, A.L.B. *The Andersons of Co. Kilkenny.* Simla, 1931.

"The Bourchier Tablet in the Cathedral Church of St. Canice, Kilkenny, with Some Account of That Family." *R.S.A.I.* 34 (1904): 365-79; 35 (1905): 21-33.

Brennan, T.A. *A History of the O'Brennan's of Idough, Co. Kilkenny.* New York, 1975.

"Bryan's of Jenkinstown." *Old Kilkenny Review* 2 (3) 1981.

"Edwards of Newtown, Co. Kilkenny." *J. Cork Hist. Arch. Soc.* N.S. 34 (1929): 100-05.

"The Family of Gall Burke, of Gallstown, in the Co. of Kilkenny." *R.S.A.I.* 6 (1860): 97-120.

"The Family of Rothe of Kilkenny." *R.S.A.I.* 17 (1886): 501-37, 620-54.

Fitzgerald – see Geraldines.

"Fitzpatricks of Ossory." *Old Kilkenny Review* 2 (3) 1981.

"The Geraldines of the Co. Kilkenny." *R.S.A.I.* 22 (1892): 358-76; 23 (1893): 179-86, 408-20; 32 (1902): 128-31.

"The Helshams of Kilkenny." *Old Kilkenny Review* 2 (4) (1982): 319-27.

"Hewetson of the Co. Kilkenny." *R.S.A.I.* 39 (1909): 369-92.

Hogan, W. *History and Antiquities of Kilkenny County & City.* Kilkenny, 1893.

"An Inquiry into the Origin of the Family of Archer in Kilkenny, with Notices of Other Families of the Name in Ireland." *R.S.A.I.* 9 (1867): 220-32.

"Loftus Papers (Cos. Kilkenny and Wexford)." *Anal. Hib.* 25: 31-55.

"The Manor of Erley or Erlestown, Co. Kilkenny." *R.S.A.I.* 36 (1906): 154-65.

McCall, H.B. *The Story of the Family of Wandesforde of Kirklington and Castlecomer.* London, 1904.

"Memorials of the Family of Langton of Kilkenny." *R.S.A.I.* 8 (1864): 59-108.

O'Kelly, O. *A History of Co. Kilkenny.* Donegal, 1969.

"The Origin of the Grace Family of Courtstown, Co. Kilkenny, and of Their Title to the Tullaroan Estate." *R.S.A.I.* 30 (1900): 319-24; 32 (1902): 64-67.

"Some Notice of the Family of Cowley in Kilkenny." *R.S.A.I.* 2 (1852): 102-14.

"The Sullivans: a Notable Nineteenth Century Kilkenny Family." *Old Kilkenny Review* 16 (1954): 23-32.

"Tobin of Caherlesk." *Ir. Gen.* 5 (6) (1979): 760-62.

Gravestone Inscriptions

St. Canice's Cathedral: Graves, Rev. James, and J.G.A. Prim. *The History, Architecture and Antiquities of the Cathedral Church of St. Canice, Kilkenny.* 1857.

St. Mary's, Kilkenny: *Old Kilkenny Review* (1979-81).

Tullawaine: held by Kilkenny Archaeological Society. (see Research Sources and Services section)

Newspapers

The best early source for this county is *Finn's Leinster Journal,* although this newspaper did not contain many detailed local biographical notices.

Title: *Finn's Leinster Journal*
Published in: Kilkenny, 1767-1965
NLI Holdings: 1.1767-12.1776; 1778-89; 12.1789-1799; 1801-08; 1.1818-1828

Title: *Kilkenny and Wexford Express* (see also Co. Wexford, *County of Wexford Express*)
Published in: Kilkenny, 1878-1907
BL Holdings: 2.1878-4.1905; 6-11.1907

Title: *Kilkenny Journal*
Published in: Kilkenny, 1830-1965
NLI Holdings: 5.1830-12.1845; 1.1847-11.1851; 1.1859-12.1965
BL Holdings: 1.1832-3.1924; 5.1935-12.1965 (except 12.1849-12.1893)

Title: *Kilkenny People*
Published in: Kilkenny, 1892-current
NLI Holdings: odd numbers 1922; 8.1927-in progress
BL Holdings: 10.1895-12.1922; 1.1924-12.1925; 1.1927-12.1929; 3-11.1930; 1.1931-in progress

Title: *Moderator* (continued as *Kilkenny Moderator* in 1829 and as *Moderator* in 1920)
Published in: Kilkenny, ca. 1775-1924
NLI Holdings: 1814-19; 7.1815-8.1822; 12.1832-11.1843; 1845 (with gaps); 4.1849-11.1851 (with gaps); 1905-19
BL Holdings: 2.1825; 1.1828-12.1919; 1.1920-12.1924

Wills and Administrations

A discussion of the types of records, where they are held, their availability and value is given in the Wills section of the Introduction. The availability of prerogative wills, administrations, and marriage license records is also described in the relevant parts of the same section. Where available, published sources of these records are given in the Miscellaneous Sources section.

Pre-1858 Wills and Administrations

Prerogative Wills. see p. xli
Consistorial Wills. County Kilkenny is mainly in the diocese of Ossory, with nine parishes in Leighlin and one in Cashel diocese. The guide to Catholic parish records in this chapter shows the diocese to which each civil parish belonged. The wills of residents of each diocese were usually proven within that diocese (see the Wills section for exceptions). The following records survive:

Wills. see p. xxxvii

Abstracts. See p. xxxvii. The Walsh Kelly Papers in the GO include mainly Ossory wills. GO ms. 683-6. Carrigan Manuscripts: Administration Wills and Abstracts from Ossory and Leighlin Dioceses. NLI P903; indexed in *Ir. Gen.* 4 (3) (1970): 221-42. Also, the intestate administrations from Ossory (1660-1803) and Leighlin (1702-1802) were published in *Ir. Gen.* 4 (5) (1972): 477-89.

Indexes. Ossory (1536-1858) published to 1800 by Phillimore. Leighlin—see Co. Carlow.

Post-1858 Wills and Administrations

This county was served by the District Registry of Kilkenny. The surviving records are kept in the PRO.

Marriage Licenses

Original Marriage Records. Kildare (1845-65). PRO; SLC film 100873.
Indexes. Kildare (1740-1850). PRO; SLC film 100868. Dublin—see Co. Dublin.

Miscellaneous Sources

Burtchaell, G.D. *Genealogical Memoirs of the Members of Parliament for the County and City of Kilkenny.* Dublin, 1888.

Comerford, Patrick. "The Early Society of Friends and Their History in Kilkenny." *Old Kilkenny Review* 25 (1973): 68-75.

"Kilkenny Deeds, 1785-1779." (list of deeds recently deposited in PRO). *Old Kilkenny Review* 2 (4) (1982): 393-400.

Research Sources and Services

Journals

Old Kilkenny Review

Deenside

Libraries and Information Sources

Kilkenny County Library, 6 Johns Quay, Kilkenny Ph: (056) 22021/22606 (local history section)

Research Services

See research services in Dublin, p. xliv

Irish Origins, College Road, Kilkenny Ph: (056) 21483; Telex: 265871 EIM434 (Genealogical research service, specializing in counties Kilkenny, Wexford, Waterford, and Tipperary)

Societies

Kilkenny Archaeological Society (publishers of *Old Kilkenny Review*), Rothe House, Parliament Street, Kilkenny

Tullaherin Parish Heritage Society, Ms. Peggy Walpole, Thomastown Road, Bennettsbridge, Co. Kilkenny

Callan Local History Society, Mr. Joe Kennedy, Moonarch, Callan, Co. Kilkenny

Castlecomer Local History Society, Georgian Mews, The Square, Castlecomer, Co. Kilkenny

CIVIL PARISHES OF COUNTY KILKENNY

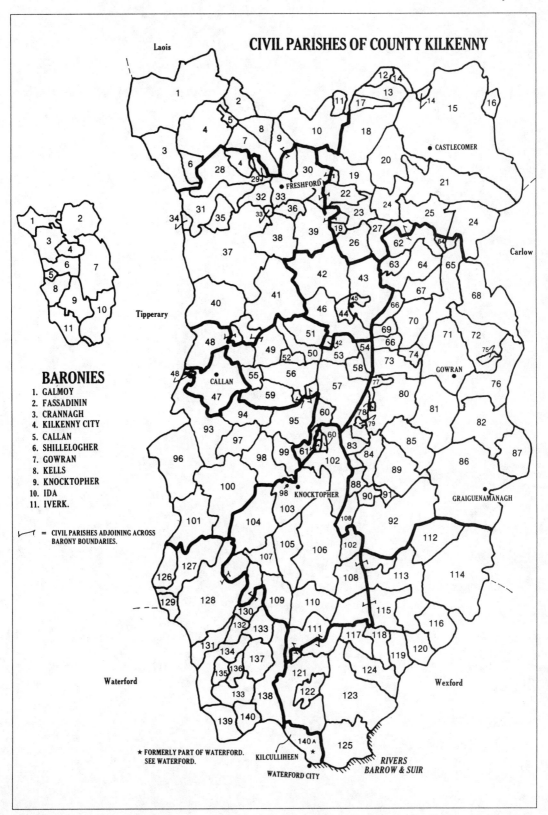

Laois

Tipperary

Carlow

• CASTLECOMER

FRESHFORD

GOWRAN
•

• KNOCKTOPHER

GRAIGUENAMANAGH
•

Wexford

Waterford

BARONIES

1. GALMOY
2. FASSADININ
3. CRANNAGH
4. KILKENNY CITY
5. CALLAN
6. SHILLELOGHER
7. GOWRAN
8. KELLS
9. KNOCKTOPHER
10. IDA
11. IVERK.

⌐ = CIVIL PARISHES ADJOINING ACROSS
BARONY BOUNDARIES.

★ FORMERLY PART OF WATERFORD.
SEE WATERFORD.

CALLAN

KILCULLIHEEN ★

WATERFORD CITY

*RIVERS
BARROW & SUIR*

County Laois (Leix)

A Brief History

This small county is in the midlands of Ireland and contains the towns of Portlaoise (formerly Maryborough), Mountmellick, Portarlington, Abbeyleix, Rathdowney, and Durrow. In ancient times the present county was partly in the Kingdom of Laois and partly in Ossory. The county was formed by the English in 1547 and named Queen's County. Its name was changed back to Laois (sometimes also called Leix) in 1922 after the formation of the Irish Free State.

The major families in this area were the O'Moores and O'Dunnes. Other families included the Lawlors, (O')Dowlings, (O')Deevys or Devoys, (O')Dorans, McEvoys, (O')Dempseys, (O')Brophys, (O')Deegans, (O')Tynans, (Mc)Cashins, (O')Mulhalls, and (Mac)Crossons.

After the Norman conquest the area was granted to the Fitzpatricks. Although the Fitzpatricks maintained control over a small part of the county, the O'Moores gradually regained power over much of the present County Laois and were undisputed rulers during the fifteenth and early sixteenth centuries. The tribes of Laois and Offaly continued to raid the English controlled area around Dublin during this time. As a result, the English decided to invade the counties in 1547.

After the successful invasion a major fort was built at Portlaoise on the site of an O'Moore stronghold. This was first named Fort Protector and later Maryborough. Because of continued resistance to English rule and attacks on the fort, it was decided to clear the counties of natives and bring in English settlers. This was begun in 1556, making it the first plantation of Ireland. The plantation was fiercely resisted by the native tribes and was only partially successful. The seven families which were most influential in this settlement were those of Cosby, Hartpole, Barrington, Bowen, Hetherington, Ruish, and Ovington.

In the early seventeenth century the families of Piggott, Parnell, Coote, Prior, and Pole settled in the county, and later in the century the families Vesey, Johnson, Dawson, Staples, and Burrowes were granted lands in the county.

The town of Mountmellick had a considerable Quaker population in the eighteenth and nineteenth centuries. There was also a large Huguenot population in the county, particularly in Portarlington. In 1696 this town and surrounding area were granted by King William to one of his victorious Huguenot generals. A colony of Huguenot soldiers were subsequently planted there and developed a thriving town. The county was relatively badly affected by the Great Famine of 1845-47. The population was 154,000 in 1841 and had dropped by 28 percent in 1851. Over 18,000 people died of disease and starvation between 1845 and 1850, and many thousands emigrated. The current population of the county is around 52,000.

Census and Census Substitutes

1599

Names of Principal Inhabitants. Lambeth Palace Library, London. ms. 635; NLI film P1707.

1659

"Census" of Ireland. Edited by S. Pender. Dublin: Stationery Office, 1939; SLC film 924648.

1758-75

"List of Freeholders of Co. Leix." GO ms. 443; SLC film 100181; published in *Kildare Arch. Soc. J.* 8 (1915): 309-27 (gives name, address, and date of registration).

1766

Religious Census of Parish of Lea. RCB Library; SLC film 258517.

1775

Catholic Qualification Roll Extracts (948 names, addresses, and occupations). 59th Report DKPRI: 59-84.

1779

"List of High Sheriffs, Grand Jury, and Gentlemen of Queen's Co." *Freeman's J.* 17 (13) 23 Sept. 1779; SLC film 993912.

1821

Extracts from Government Census for the Parish of Aghaboe, Mainly Dealing with the Name Kelly. PRO; SLC film 100158.

1823-38

Tithe Applotment Survey (see p. xxvii).

1844

List of Persons Having Licenses to Keep Arms, Division of Ballinakill (Baronies of Cullenagh, Upper Ossory and Maryborough West (gives 433 names arranged alphabetically, occupations, residences, and types of arms). NLI ILB 04 P12.

1847

List of Voters in Queen's Co. up to 1847 (mainly 1838-47) (gives approximately 1,000 names arranged alphabetically by barony, with occupation, residence, location of freehold, etc.). NLI ILB 04 P12.

1850-51

Griffith's Valuation (see p. xxvii).

1901

Census. PRO.

1911

Census. PRO.

Church Records

Church of Ireland
(shows starting date of record)

Parish: **Abbeyleix**
Existing Records: b. 1781; m. 1781; d. 1781
Status: LC

Parish: **Aghavoe** (District Church in Aghavoe Parish)
Status: Lost

Parish: **Aghmacart** and **Bordwell**
Status: Lost

Parish: **Attanagh**
Status: Lost

Parish: **Ballyadams**
Status: Lost

Parish: **Ballyfinn** (with Cloneagh)
Existing Records: b. 1821; m. 1821; d. 1821
Status: LC

Parish: **Ballyroan**
Status: Lost

Parish: **Bordwell** (see Aghmacart)

QUEEN'S COUNTY.

DIVISION OF BALLINAKILL.

A LIST OF PERSONS WHO HAVE OBTAINED

LICENSES TO KEEP ARMS,

AT A GENERAL QUARTER SESSIONS OF THE PEACE, HELD AT

ABBEYLEIX, ON THE 1st & 15th JANUARY, 1844.

No.	Name, Addition, Residence, and Barony.	No. and Description of Arms Registered.
1	Abbott Francis of the Swan, farmer, barony of Upper Ossory	one gun and one pistol.
2	Atkinson Richard of Rathdowney, do.	one gun.
3	Alley Peter T. of Donamore, gentleman, do.	2 guns, 1 double-barrelled gun, 2 pistols, 2 blunderbuses, 1 sword and 1 bayonet
4	Abbott Thomas K. of Borris-in-Ossory, yoeman, do.	two pistols.
5	Brennan, William O of Knockbawn, barony of Cullenagh	one gun.
6	Bailey Thomas A. of Thornbury, gentleman, do.	3 guns, 2 pistols, and 1 blunderbuss.
7	Bowe Timothy of Clonking, do.	one gun.
8	Bonte Mary of Boley, do.	one gun and one pistol.
9	Bland John Thomas of Blandsfort, gentleman, do.	3 guns, 3 pistols, blunderbuses, 2 swords and two bayonets.
10	Bannon John of Scotchrath, farmer, barony of Maryborough West	one gun and two pistols.
11	Brownlow William of Knapton, esquire, barony of Cullenagh	1 double gun, 4 muskets and 2 swords.
12	Betts Clement of Abbeyleix, tailor, do.	one gun.
13	Bolton George, jun., of Abbeyleix, gentleman, do.	one gun, one pistol, and one cane sword.
14	Ball Wellington of Ballymagh, esquire, do.	three guns and two pistols.
15	Bolton George of Abbeyleix, attorney at law, do.	one gun, two pistols and one sword.
16	Bergin James of Ballyking, farmer, do.	4 guns, 2 pistols, three swords, 2 bayonets
17	Bagnall John H. of Attian, clerk, barony of Upper Ossory,	6 blunderbuses, and 1 rifle.
18	Bergin John of Tubberboes, farmer, do.	one single-barrel fowling-piece.
19	Bond Robert of Rathdowney, do.	one gun.
20	Bergin Timothy of Bishopwood, farmer, do.	two guns.
20½	Byrne Edward of Abbeyleix, shopkeeper, barony of Cullenagh	one gun.
21	Bolton Pepper of Pinfield, gentleman, barony of Upper Ossory	one gun, two pistols, and one blunderbuss
22	Biggs William of Borris Castle, esquire, do.	seven guns, 1 double & 2 single pistols.
23	Bate Robert of Borris-in-Ossory, do.	one flint gun.
24	Boland James of Borris-in-Ossory, bacon merchant, do.	two pistols
25	Boud George of Spring-hill, farmer, do.	one gun and two pistols
26	Boud William of Lisduffe, do.	two pistols.
27	Bond William of Lisduffe, do.	one pistol
28	Brophy Michael of Donaghmore, do.	three guns, one pistol and one blunderbuss
29	Beresford Rev. James Isaac, Rector of Donaghmore, do.	
30	Comerford Edward of Ballyrakill, gentleman, barony of Cullenagh	three guns and one sword.
31	Campion, John of Derry, farmer, do.	one gun.
32	Campion, John of Corbally, farmer, barony of Maryborough West	two guns.
33	Case Thomas of Rahemabrogue, farmer, barony of Cullenagh	two guns, two pistols, and one sword.
34	Case William of Rahemabrogue, farmer, do.	one gun.
35	Case Allen of Newtown, farmer, do.	one gun and one case of pistols.
36	Carrick Robert of Rathdowney, barony of Upper Ossory	one pistol.
37	Caldbeck Richard of Clonkeen, gentleman, do.	two guns, two pistols, and three swords
38	Conway William of Ballincolla, inn-keeper, do.	one gun.
39	Coolgan Michael of Oldglass, farmer, do.	one gun and one pistol.
40	Coolgan Michael of Ballymaddy, farmer, do.	one gun.
41	Cooper Mathew of Coolrain, farmer, do.	one gun.
42	Connor Denis of Mountealam, farmer, do.	one gun.
43	Campion James of Badger-hill, farmer, do.	two guns.
44	Cornelius Henry C. of Coldblow, esquire, do.	one gun.
45	Coady Edward of Marymount, farmer, barony of Upper Ossory	two guns.
46	Cuddy Martin of Conrea, farmer, barony of Upper Ossory	two guns.
47	Cuddy Martin of Conrea, farmer, barony of Cullenagh	one gun.
48	Case Allen of Newtown, farmer, barony of Upper Ossory	one pistol.
49	Case Joseph of Rahemabrogue, farmer, do.	
50	Case Henry of Ballyvickas, farmer,	
51	Coyle Mary of C. of Cullenagh, farmer, barony of Cullenagh	one pistol and two blunderbusses.
52	Case Thomas of Abbeyleix, shopkeeper, do.	one gun two pistols and one bayonet.
53	Crowley Mattias Morgan, of Durrow, barony of Upper Ossory	1 double and 1 single gun and two pistols.
54	Cantwell Joseph of Ellis, farmer, do.	two pistols.
55	Dwyer Patrick of Kyleeg, farmer, do.	two pistols and one bayonet.
56	Cantwell Jacob of Kyleeg, farmer, do.	one gun.
57	Cantwell George of Knockanoras, farmer, do.	one gun two pistols and one blunderbuss.
58	Chaplain Samuel of Woodview, farmer, do.	one gun and two pistols.
59	Clarke Benjamin T. of Durrow, do.	one gun.
60	Cole Samuel of Dairyhill, farmer, do.	2 guns two pistols and two blunderbusses.
61	Chamberlain Joseph of Millamore, farmer, do.	one gun.
62	Chamberlain Joseph of Knockdom, farmer,	one gun and one pistol.
63	Chrystal George of Charleville, do.	one gun and two pistols.
64	Claxton Langley of Cloocoures, farmer, do.	one gun.
65	Carroll Charles of Graigansallia, do.	one gun and two pistols.
66	Carter John d. of Killadooley, farmer, do.	one gun.
67	Carter Isaac of Rathmakelly, farmer, do.	one gun and two pistols.
68	Comerford John of Bawnaghra, farmer,	
70	Dobbs James of Abbeyleix, gentleman, barony of Cullenagh	one gun.
71	Dunne Francis of Moyadd, farmer, do.	gun and one pistol.
72	Dunne Peter of Rathleague, farmer, do.	one gun.
73	Delany Patrick of Ballyrakill, do.	two pistols.
74	Deegan Lawrence of Ballyrakill, do.	one gun one blunderbuss and one dagger.
75	Doran Michael of Cashel, farmer, do.	one gun.
76	Dowling James of Cappanaclongh, farmer, barony of Maryborough West	one gun.
77	Dunning Patrick of Copanadough, farmer, do.	one gun.
78	Duggan gydon of Ballinakill, gentleman, barony of Cullenagh	two guns and one dagger.
79	Duffe Henry of Aughnacross, farmer, do.	one gun.
80	Dagge Thomas of Bonlyhawn, farmer, do.	one gun one pistol and one dagger.
81	Dooley Sylvester of Kill, farmer, barony of Upper Ossory	one pistol.
82	Dooley John jun. of Raltuh, farmer, barony of Cullenagh	one gun.
83	Dooley John senior of Millwood, do.	one pistol.
84	Dooley Thomas of Millwood, gentleman, M.D. & J.P. do.	three guns, pistols.
85	Dobbs Henry of Cullenagh, caretaker, do.	one gun and two pistols.
86	Dundas William John of Farmley, esquire, do.	one gun three pistols and one blunderbuss.
87	Delany William of Durrow, esquire J.P., barony of Upper Ossory	one gun four pistols and one blunderbuss.
88	Delany John of Cappanellan, farmer, barony of Upper Ossory	one gun.
89	Dagge Robert of Castlewood, farmer, do.	one gun and two pistols
90	Delany Edward of Abamey, farmer, do.	one gun.
91	Dunne Edward of Abamey, farmer, do.	one gun.
92	Delany Edmund Scully of Durrow, gentleman, do.	one double and one single barrelled gun.
93	Dunne Mathew of Castledaming, farmer, do.	one gun.
94	Dugdale John of Donamore, miller, do.	4 guns 2 pistols and 2 blunderbusses
95	Dunn Edward of Coolrain, farmer, do.	two pistols.
96	Dunne Martin of Coolrain, farmer, do.	one gun.
97	Dunne James of Castletown, gentleman, do.	one gun.
98	Despard William W. of Donore, esquire, justice of the peace, do.	two guns.
99	Despard Richard of Donore, esquire, same barony	one gun.
100	Dunn Robert of Coolrain, farmer,	one gun, one pistol, and one blunderbuss.
101	Delaney Denis of Strahard, farmer, do.	one gun.
102	Delaney John of Strahard, farmer, do.	one pistol.
103	Delaney Michael of Coalamacurragh, farmer, do.	one pistol.
104	Delaney John of Borris-in-Ossory, shopkeeper, do.	one gun and two pistols.
105	Deegan Joseph of Kiledelig, farmer.	one gun and two pistols.

List of persons in Queen's County (now County Laois) who were licensed to keep arms in 1844.

Parish: **Borris-in-Ossory**
Stauts: Lost

Parish: **Castlebrack** (see Oregan)

Parish: **Castletown** (Killeban)
Existing Records: b. 1802; m. 1802; d. 1802
Status: LC

Parish: **Clonenagh** (union including Ballyfin,
    Mountrath, and Roskelton)
Existing Records: b. 1749; m. 1749; d. 1749
Status: LC

Parish: **Coolbanagher**
Existing Dates: b. 1802; m. 1802; d. 1802
Status: LC

Parish: **Corclone**
Status: Lost

Parish: **Donoughmore**
Status: Lost

Parish: **Durrow**
Existing Records: b. 1731; m. 1731; d. 1731
Status: LC

Parish: **Dysertgallen**
Status: Lost

Parish: **Graigue** (see Killeshin, RC section)

Parish: **Killeban** (Castletown District)
Existing Records: b. 1802; m. 1802; d. 1802
Status: LC

Parish: **Killeban** (Mayo District)
Existing Records: b. 1830; m. 1826; d. 1828
Status: LC

Parish: **Killermagh**
Status: Lost

Parish: **Lea**
Existing Records: b. 1801; m. 1801; d. 1801
Status: LC

Parish: **Maryborough** (Portlaoise)
Existing Records: b. 1793; m. 1793; d. 1793
Status: LC

Parish: **Mayo**
Existing Records: b. 1830; m. 1826; d. 1828
Status: LC

Parish: **Mountmellick** (see also Coolbanagher
    and Oregan)
Existing Records: b.1840; m. 1840; d. 1840
Status: LC

Parish: **Mountrath** (with Clonenagh)
Existing Records: b. 1749; m. 1749; d. 1749
Status: LC

Parish: **Offerlane**
Existing Records: b. 1807; m. 1807; d. 1807
Status: LC

Parish: **Oregan** (Rosenallis)
Existing Records: b. 1801; m. 1801; d. 1801
Status: LC

Parish: **Rathaspect**
Status: Lost

Parish: **Rathdowney**
Existing Records: b. 1756; m. 1756; d. 1756
Status: LC

Parish: **Rathsaran**
Existing Records: b. 1810; m. 1810; d. 1810
Status: LC

Parish: **Roscrea**
Existing Records: b. 1784; m. 1784; d. 1784
Status: LC

Parish: **Roskelton** (with Clonenagh)
Existing Records: b. 1826; m 1826; d. 1826
Status: LC

Parish: **St. Michael Portarlington**
Status: Lost

Parish: **St. Paul's** (French Church, Portar-
    lington)
Existing Records: b. 1694; m. 1694; d. 1694
Status: LC

Parish: **Skeirke**
Status: Lost

Parish: **Straboe** (see Maryborough)

Parish: **Stradbally**
Existing Records:b. 1772; m. 1776; d. 1826
Status: LC

Parish: **Timahoe**
Existing Records: b. 1845; m. 1850; d. 1856
Status: LC

Parish: **Timogue**
Status: Lost

Presbyterian

Parish: **Mountmellick**
Starting Date: 1849

Roman Catholic

Civil Parish: **Abbeyleix**
Map Grid: 41
RC Parish: Abbeyleix; also part Ballyragget, see Donaghmore, Co. Kilkenny
Diocese: LE
Earliest Record: b. 6.1824; m. 7.1824
Missing Dates: b. 8.1830-1.1838, 12.1849-4.1850; m. 7.1830-1.1838
Parish Address: Rev. Patrick Kehoe, Abbeyleix, Co. Laois

Civil Parish: **Aghaboe**
Map Grid: 23
RC Parish: Aghaboe
Diocese: OS
Earliest Record: b. 1795; m. 7.1794
Missing Dates: b. 1802-1803, 1813, 6.1825-6.1826; m. 2.1807-11.1816, 8.1824-8.1825, 8.1846-6.1850
Parish Address: Rev. James Carrigan, PP, Ballacolla, Portlaoise, Co. Laois

Civil Parish: **Aghmacart**
Map Grid: 32

RC Parish: see Durrow
Diocese: OS

Civil Parish: **Aharney**
Map Grid: 36
RC Parish: Lisdowney, see Aharney, Co. Kilkenny
Diocese: OS

Civil Parish: **Ardea**
Map Grid: 5
RC Parish: see Rosenallis
Diocese: KD

Civil Parish: **Attanagh**
Map Grid: 37
RC Parish: Ballyraggett, see Donaghmore, Co. Kilkenny
Diocese: KD

Civil Parish: **Ballyadams**
Map Grid: 43
RC Parish: Ballyadams
Diocese: LE
Earliest Record: b. 1.1820; m. 1.1820
Parish Address: Rev. L. Fleming, PP, Luggacurren, Stradbally, Co. Laois

Civil Parish: **Ballyroan**
Map Grid: 38
RC Parish: part Ballinakill, see Dysartgallen; part Abbeyleix
Diocese: LE

Civil Parish: **Bordwell**
Map Grid: 29
RC Parish: see Aghaboe
Diocese: OS

Civil Parish: **Borris** or **Maryborough**
Map Grid: 10
RC Parish: Maryborough (Portlaoise)
Diocese: LE
Earliest Record: b. 5.1826; m. 4.1826
Parish Address: Rev. Gregory Brophy, PP, Parochial House, Portlaoise, Co. Laois

Civil Parish: **Castlebrack**
Map Grid: 1
RC Parish: Rosenallis and Mountmellick, see Rosenallis

Civil Parish: **Clonenagh** and **Clonagheen (1)**
Map Grid: 9
RC Parish: Ballyfin (Cappinrush); also Mountrath and Raheen, see below
Diocese: LE
Earliest Record: b. 10.1824; m. 8.1819
Parish Address: Rev. Joseph Meaney, PP, Ballyfin, Portlaoise, Co. Laois

Civil Parish: **Clonenagh** and **Clonagheen (2)**
Map Grid: 9
RC Parish: Mountrath
Diocese: LE
Earliest Record: b. 10.1823; m. 6.1827
Parish Address: Rev. Gerard O'Mahony, PP, Mountrath, Co. Laois

Civil Parish: **Clonenagh** and **Clonagheen (3)**
Map Grid: 9
RC Parish: Raheen
Diocese: LE
Earliest Record: b. 4.1819; m. 1.1820
Parish Address: Rev. John Carter, PP, Raheen, Abbeyleix, Co. Laois

Civil Parish: **Cloydagh**
Map Grid: 53
RC Parish: Leighlin Bridge, see Agha, Co. Carlow
Diocese: LE

Civil Parish: **Coolbanagher**
Map Grid: 6
RC Parish: part Portarlington, see Lea; part Mountmellick, see Rosenallis
Diocese: KD

Civil Parish: **Coolkerry**
Map Grid: 31
RC Parish: part Aghaboe; part Rathdowney
Diocese: OS

Civil Parish: **Curraclone**
Map Grid: 18
RC Parish: see Stradbally
Diocese: LE

Civil Parish: **Donaghmore**
Map Grid: 25
RC Parish: see Rathdowney
Diocese: OS

Civil Parish: **Durrow** (see also Co. Kilkenny)
Map Grid: 33
RC Parish: Durrow
Diocese: OS
Earliest Record: b. 1.1789; m. 7.1811
Parish Address: Rev. T. Marnell, PP, Durrow, Portlaoise, Co. Laois

Civil Parish: **Dysartenos**
Map Grid: 14
RC Parish: Maryborough, see Borris
Diocese: LE

Civil Parish: **Dysartgallen**
Map Grid: 42
RC Parish: Ballinakill
Diocese: LE
Earliest Record: b. 10.1794; m. 10.1794
Missing Dates: b. 3.1815-1.1820, 5.1820-11.1820, 9.1872-4.1877; m. 2.1815-1.1820, 7.1820-11.1820, 11.1875-5.1877
Parish Address: Rev. Michael Gleeson, PP, Ballinakill, Co. Laois

Civil Parish: **Erke**
Map Grid: 27
RC Parish: see Co. Kilkenny
Diocese: OS

Civil Parish: **Fossy** (or Timahoe)
Map Grid: 40
RC Parish: part Ballyadams; part Stradbally
Diocese: LE

Civil Parish: **Glashare**
Map Grid: 35
RC Parish: see Co. Kilkenny
Diocese: LE

Civil Parish: **Grangemonk** (see Monksgrange)

Civil Parish: **Kilcolmanbane**
Map Grid: 13
RC Parish: Maryborough, see Borris
Diocese: LE

Civil Parish: **Kilclonbrook** or **Kilcolmanbrack**
Map Grid: 39
RC Parish: see Stradbally
Diocese: LE

Civil Parish: **Kildellig**
Map Grid: 28
RC Parish: see Aghaboe
Diocese: OS

Civil Parish: **Killaban**
Map Grid: 49
RC Parish: Arles; also part Ballyadams; and
  part Doonane, see Rathaspick
Diocese: LE
Earliest Record: (entries from 1821 to 1856 are
  arranged by townland) b. 1821; m. 1821;
  d. 1821
Parish Address: Rev. Edward Kennedy, PP,
  Arles, Ballickmoyler, Carlow

Civil Parish: **Killenny**
Map Grid: 15
RC Parish: Maryborough, see Borris
Diocese: LE

Civil Parish: **Killermagh**
Map Grid: 30
RC Parish: see Aghaboe
Diocese: OS

Civil Parish: **Killeshin**
Map Grid: 51
RC Parish: Graigue and Killeshin
Diocese: LE
Earliest record: b. 11.1819; m. 1.1822
Missing Dates: b. 10.1845-8.1846
Parish Address: Rev. Sean Kelly, CC,
  Graiguecullen, Carlow

Civil Parish: **Kilmanman**
Map Grid: 2
RC Parish: Clonaslee
Diocese: KD
Earliest Record: b. 1.1849; m. 2.1849
Parish Address: Rev. Joseph Shortall, PP,
  Clonaslee, Co. Laois

Civil Parish: **Kilteale**
Map Grid: 12
RC Parish: Maryborough, see Borris
Diocese: LE

Civil Parish: **Kyle**
Map Grid: 21
RC Parish: Kyle and Knock

Diocese: OS
Earliest Record: b. 1.1845; m. 2.1846
Parish Address: Rev. Timothy Tuohy, PP, Kil-
  martin, Borris-in-Ossory, Co. Laois

Civil Parish: **Lea**
Map Grid: 7
RC Parish: Portarlington
Diocese: KD
Earliest Record: b. 1.1820; m. 11.1822
Parish Address: Rev. Michael Noonan, PP, Por-
  tarlington, Co. Laois

Civil Parish: **Maryborough** (see Borris)
Map Grid: 19
RC Parish: Maryborough (Portlaoise)
Diocese: LE

Civil Parish: **Monksgrange** (or Grangemonk)
Map Grid: 48
RC Parish: Arles, see Killaban
Diocese: LE

Civil Parish: **Moyanna**
Map Grid: 16
RC Parish: see Stradbally
Diocese: LE

Civil Parish: **Offerlane (1)**
Map Grid: 8
RC Parish: Castletown; also Cormorass, see
  below
Diocese: OS
Earliest Record: b. 9.1772; m. 9.1784
Missing Dates: b. 5.1816-5.1831; m. 5.1816-
  2.1831, 2.1855-9.1857
Parish Address: Rev. Eamonn Rhatigan, PP,
  Castletown, Portlaoise, Co. Laois

Civil Parish: **Offerlane (2)**
Map Grid: 8
RC Parish: Cormorass or Comeris
Diocese: OS
Earliest Record: b. 5.1816; m. 1.1820
Missing Dates: b. 3.1830-10.1838, gaps 1838-
  1850; m. 3.1830-8.1839, 2.1842-8.1846
Parish Address: Rev. Dominic O'Hanlon, PP,
  Camross, Portlaois, Co. Laois

Civil Parish: **Rathaspick** (see also Co. Kilkenny)
Map Grid: 47
RC Parish: Ballyadams; also part Doonane
Diocese: LE
Earliest Record: b. 6.1843; m. 5.1843
Parish Address: Rev. Joseph Fleming, PP, Tolerton, Ballickmoyler, Co. Carlow

Civil Parish: **Rathdowney**
Map Grid: 24
RC Parish: Rathdowney
Diocese: OS
Earliest Record: b. 7.1763; m. 5.1769
Missing Dates: b. 11.1781-9.1782, 7.1789-5.1790, 11.1791-4.1810, 9.1810-6.1839; m. 11.1781-9.1782, 7.1789-9.1789, 11.1791-1.1808, 5.1808-10.1839
Parish Address: Rev. John Holohan, PP, Rathdowney, Portlaoise, Laois

Civil Parish: **Rathsaran**
Map Grid: 26
RC Parish: see Rathdowney
Diocese: OS

Civil Parish: **Rearymore**
Map Grid: 3
RC Parish: part Clonaslee, see Kilmanman; part Rosenallis
Diocese: KD

Civil Parish: **Rosconnell**
Map Grid: 34
RC Parish: Ballyraggett, see Donaghmore, Co. Kilkenny
Diocese: LE

Civil Parish: **Rosenallis (1)**
Map Grid: 4
RC Parish: Rosenallis; also Mountmellick, see below
Diocese: KD
Earliest Record: b. 10.1765; m. 10.1765; d. 10.1824
Missing Dates: b. 1.1777-2.1782, 8.1782-8.1823; m. 6.1777-2.1782, 6.1782-7.1823, 7.1859-1.1865; d. ends 9.1827
Parish Address: Rev. Thomas Donohoe, PP, Rosenallis, Portlaoise, Co. Laois

Civil Parish: **Rosenallis (2)**
Map Grid: 4
RC Parish: Mountmellick
Diocese: KD
Earliest Record: b. 1.1814; m. 2.1814
Missing Dates: m. 4.1843-7.1843
Parish Address: Rev. C. Crowley, PP, Mountmellick, Co. Laois

Civil Parish: **St. John** (see Co. Kildare)
Map Grid: 44
RC Parish: Athy, see Churchtown, Co. Kildare
Diocese: LE

Civil Parish: **Shrule**
Map Grid: 50
RC Parish: Arles, see Killaban
Diocese: LE

Civil Parish: **Skirk** (Skeirke)
Map Grid: 52
RC Parish: see Rathdowney
Diocese: OS

Civil Parish: **Sleaty**
Map Grid: 52
RC Parish: Graigue and Killeshin, see Killeshin
Diocese: LE

Civil Parish: **Straboe**
Map Grid: 11
RC Parish: Maryborough, see Borris
Diocese: LE

Civil Parish: **Stradbally**
Map Grid: 17
RC Parish: Stradbally
Diocese: LE
Earliest Record: b. 1.1820; m. 1.1820
Missing Dates: m. 6.1849-2.1851
Parish Address: Rev. John Gahan, PP, Stradbally, Co. Laois

Civil Parish: **Tankardstown**
Map Grid: 46
RC Parish: Athy, see Churchtown, Co. Kildare
Diocese: LE

Civil Parish: **Tecolm**
Map Grid: 45

RC Parish: see Ballyadams
Diocese: LE

Civil Parish: **Timogue**
Map Grid: 19
RC Parish: see Stradbally
Diocese: LE

Civil Parish: **Tullomoy**
Map Grid: 20
RC Parish: see Ballyadams
Diocese: LE

Commercial and Social Directories

1788
   Richard Lucas's *General Directory of the Kingdom of Ireland* contains lists of traders in Mountmellick and Portarlington. Reprinted in Ir. Gen. 3 (10) (1965): 392-416.

1824
   J. Pigot's *City of Dublin & Hibernian Provincial Directory* includes traders, nobility, gentry, and clergy lists of Ballinakill, Durrow, Maryborough, Mountrath, Mountmellick, Portarlington, and Stradbally.

1846
   Slater's *National Commercial Directory of Ireland* lists nobility, clergy, traders, etc., in Ballinakill, Maryborough, Mountmellick, Mountrath, Portarlington, and Stradbally.

1856
   Slater's *Royal National Commercial Directory of Ireland* lists nobility, gentry, clergy, traders, etc., in Ballinakill, Maryborough, Mountmellick, Mountrath, Portarlington, Rathdowney and Donaghmore, and Stradbally.

1870
   Slater's *Directory of Ireland* contains trade, nobility, and clergy lists for Abbeyleix, Maryborough, Mountmellick, Mountrath, Portarlington, Rathdowney, and Stradbally.

1881
   Slater's *Royal National Commercial Directory of Ireland* contains lists of traders, clergy, nobility, and farmers in adjoining parishes of the towns of Abbeyleix, Ballinakill, and Ballyroan, Maryborough and Stradbally, Mountmellick, Mountrath, Portarlington, and Rathdowney.

1894
   Slater's *Royal National Directory of Ireland* lists traders, police, teachers, farmers, and private residents in each of the towns, villages, and parishes of the county.

Family History

"The Autobiography of Pole Cosby, of Stradbally, Queen's Co" (1703-1737). *J. Kildare Arch. Hist. Soc.* 5 (1906-08).

Baldwin, William. *The Genealogy of Baldwins from Queen's County.* New York, 1918.

"Ballyadams in the Queen's County, and the Bowen Family." *J. Kildare Arch. Hist. Soc.* 7 (1912-14): 3-32.

"The Chetwoods of Woodbrook in the Queen's Co." *J. Kildare Arch. Hist. Soc.* 9 (1918-21): 205-26.

"Historical Notes on the O'Mores and Their Territory of Leix, to the End of the Sixteenth Century." *J. Kildare Arch. Hist. Soc.* 6 (1909-11): 1-88.

Houston, J.R. *A History of the Standish Family in Ireland and Canada.* Toronto: Houston Publication Trust, 1979.

Impey, E. Adeir. *A Roberts Family, Quondam Quakers of Queen's Co.* London, 1939.

Jolly, M.A. *Jolly–a Portarlington Settler and His Descendants.* London, 1935.

"Notes on an Old Pedigree of the O'More Family of Leix." *R.S.A.I.* 35 (1905): 53-59.

"Notes on Some Portarlington Families 1860-1893." *Ir. Anc.* 17 (2) (1985): 82-95.

Newspapers

There are few papers which are specific to this county. Those in the surrounding counties should be consulted depending on the area of interest. Note that the county was previously known as Queen's county and that the town of Portlaoise was also officially known as Maryborough until 1922.

Title: *Leinster Express*
Published in: Portlaoise, 1831-current
NLI Holdings: 9.1831-in progress
BL Holdings: 9.1831-12.1927; 1.1929-3.1941; 6.1941-in progress

Title: *Leinster Independent*
Published in: Portlaoise, 1834-40
NLI Holdings: 12.1834-12.1840 (with gaps)
BL Holdings: 12.1834-12.1835; 7.1836-5.1839; 10.1839-4.1840

Miscellaneous Sources

Coote, Charles. *General View of Agriculture and Manufactures of the Queen's County.* 1801.

"The Huguenots of Portarlington." *Studies* 61 (1972): 343-53.

"Huguenot Officers and Soldiers Settled at Portarlington." *J. Kildare Arch. Hist. Soc.* 11 (4): 177-200 (gives names, biography, and holdings on attached map). Addendum 12 (5) (1940/41): 227-29.

MacCaba, S. *Historical Notes on Laois.* Portlaoise, 1963.

MacSuibhne, P. *Parish of Killeshin, Graigcullen.* Naas, 1972.

O'Byrne, D. *History of the Queen's County.* Dublin, 1856.

O'Hanlon, J. and E. O'Leary. *History of the Queen's County.* 4 vols. Dublin, 1907-14. Reprint. Kilkenny, 1981.

Research Sources and Services

Journals

Laois Heritage (bulletin of Laois Heritage Society)

Libraries and Information Sources

Laois County Library, County Hall, Portlaoise, Co. Laois Ph: (0502) 22044

Research Services

Offaly Heritage Society – see Co. Offaly

See also research services in Dublin, p. xliv

Societies

Laois Heritage Society, Mrs. Matilda Cooney, Monamanry, Luggacurran, Portlaoise, Co. Laois

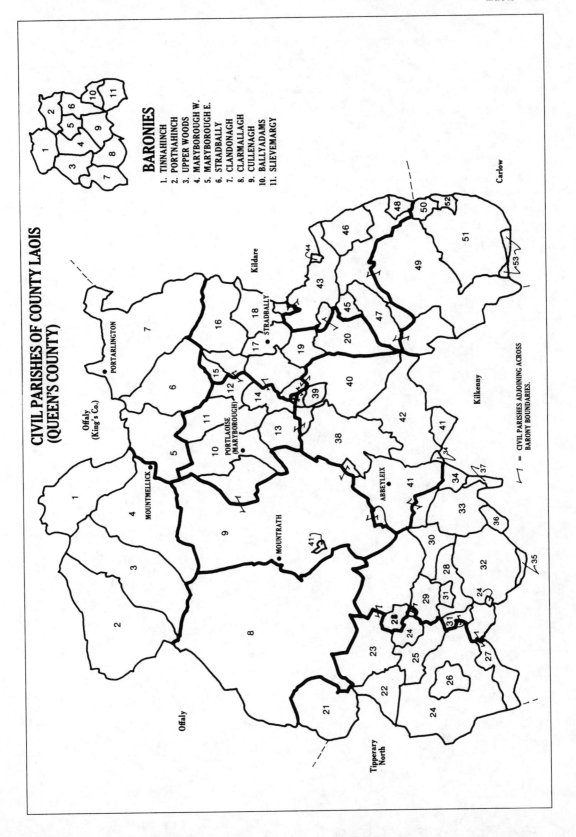

CIVIL PARISHES OF COUNTY LAOIS
(QUEEN'S COUNTY)

BARONIES

1. TINNAHINCH
2. PORTNAHINCH
3. UPPER WOODS
4. MARYBOROUGH W.
5. MARYBOROUGH E.
6. STRADBALLY
7. CLANDONAGH
8. CLARMALLAGH
9. CULLENAGH
10. BALLYADAMS
11. SLIEVEMARGY

= CIVIL PARISHES ADJOINING ACROSS
BARONY BOUNDARIES.

County Leitrim

A Brief History

This Connaught county contains the towns of Dromahaire, Manorhamilton, Drumshanbo, Carrick-on-Shannon, and Ballinamore.

The northern and western parts of the county were once part of the old Gaelic kingdom of Breffni which was ruled by the O'Rourkes. Other families associated with this part of the county are the McClancys and O'Meehans. In the southerly part of the county the major families are the McRannals (often anglicized Reynolds) and McMorrows. The other families of the county are McGilheely, O'Gallon, O'Mulvey, McShanley, McColgan, McSharry, McWeeney, and McGovern.

Up to the Middle Ages this county was densely wooded. The woods were gradually felled to provide charcoal and timber for local iron mining operations. The county is now generally boggy and has a large proportion of wetlands and lakes.

The county was invaded by the Normans in the thirteenth century. Although they succeeded in taking the south of the county, they failed to conquer the northern portion. This remained under the control of the O'Rourkes until the sixteenth century.

Large portions of the county were confiscated from their owners in 1620 and given to English adventurers, including Villiers and Hamilton, who founded the town of Manorhamilton. The objective was to plant the county with English settlers, but this was largely unsuccessful. Further confiscations followed the unsuccessful 1641 rebellion of the Catholic Irish, when the Gaelic and Norman families of Leitrim joined the Catholic Confederacy (see Co. Kilkenny).

As the Gaelic and Norman families were very predominantly Catholic, and the English of the Protestant faith, the proportions of these religions among the population can, in very general terms, be used to estimate the origins of the inhabitants of the county and the success of the various attempts to "plant" the county. When religious affiliation was first determined in the census of 1861, the respective proportions of Catholic and Protestant were 90 percent and 9 percent.

The county was very badly affected by the Great Famine of 1845-47. The population was 155,000 in 1841, and by 1851 it had fallen to 112,000. Of this reduction almost 20,000 people died between 1845 and 1850, and the remainder emigrated to the cities or, more usually, abroad. Because of the poor agricultural productivity of the county, it has been a high-emigration county ever since these times, and the population is currently around 28,000.

Census and Census Substitutes

1659
"Census" of Ireland. Edited by S. Pender. Dublin: Stationery Office, 1939. SLC film 924648.

1791
Names of the Registered Freeholders of Co. Leitrim, 1791. GO ms.. 665; SLC film 100213.

1792
"List of the Protestants in the Barony of Mohill." *Ir. Anc.* 16 (1): 35-36.

1798
List of Persons who Suffered Loss in '98 Rebellion. NLI JLB 94107 (approximately eighty names, addresses, and occupations).

1820
A List of the Freeholders or Voters in Co. Leitrim, c. 1820. NLI ms. 3830.

1821
Census of Parish of Carrigallen. NLI 4646; SLC film 596418.

1823-38
Tithe Applotment Survey (see p. xxvii).

1852
"Leitrim Voters in Oughteragh and Cloonclare Parishes." *Breifne* 5 (20): 459-66.

1856
Griffith's Valuation (see p. xxvii).

1901
Census. PRO.

1911
Census. PRO.

Church Records

Church of Ireland
(shows starting date of record)

Parish: **Annaduff**
Status: Lost

Parish: **Aughavass**
Status: Lost

Parish: **Ballymeehan**
Status: Lost

Parish: **Carrigallen**
Status: Lost

Parish: **Cloon** (see also Aughavass)
Status: Lost

Parish: **Corawollen**
Status: Lost

Parish: **Drumlease** (Dromahavre)
Existing Records: b. 1828; m. 1828; d. 1828
Status: LC

Parish: **Drumreilly**
Status: Lost

Parish: **Drumshanbo**
Status: Lost

Parish: **Feenagh**
Status: Lost

Parish: **Glenlough** (Killasnett Parish)
Status: Lost

Parish: **Innismagrath**
Status: Lost

Parish: **Killargue**
Status: Lost

Parish: **Killasnett** (see also Glenlough)
Status: Lost

COUNTY of LEITRIM,

And who have given in their Claims on or before the 6th of April, 1799, to the Commissioners for enquiring into the Losses sustained by such of his Majesty's *Loyal Subjects*, as have suffered in their Property by the Rebellion.

☞ This LIST is published for the Purpose of calling the Attention of all Persons well acquainted with the County of Leitrim, to the several Claims therein specified; and all such Persons are requested to communicate, as soon as possible, to the Commissioners (or any one of them) under Cover, to the Right Hon. the Chancellor of the Exchequer, Parliament House, Dublin, such Observations respecting the *Loyalty or Losses* of the several Persons mentioned therein, as may enable the Commissioners to ascertain their Title to Compensation.

CLAIMANT'S NAME.	ADDITION.	RESIDENCE.	County in which they reside	Place where Loss was sustained.	NATURE OF LOSS.	AMOUNT CLAIMED.
						£. s. d.
Abraham, Richard	—	Carrickban	Leitrim	Residence.	A mare	6 16 6
Acheson, John	—	Derrinacrery	ditto	ditto	Cloaths, furniture, and provisions	5 2 2
Acheson, Mary	Widow	Dininoran	ditto	ditto	Provision, cloaths, furniture	8 9 0½
Acheson, George	—	Lavagh	ditto	ditto	Furniture, fowl, hay, and flax	4 7 4
Baker, Farrell	—	Drumahair	ditto	ditto	Cash, cloaths, a watch, linen, and arms	61 6 2½
Blair, James	—	Drumleafe	ditto	ditto	Cloaths, and shoebuckles	13 14 1½
Bragdon, David	—	Drumahair	ditto	ditto	A mare	2 10 0
Buchanan, Andrew	—	Shevdella	ditto	ditto	Cattle, fowl, and cloaths	15 4 5
Carty, George	—	Drumleafe	ditto	ditto	Cloaths and linen	2 4 7½
Carter, Thomas	—	Ditto	ditto	ditto	Wearing apparel	58 14 10½
Carter, Anne	—	Ditto	ditto	ditto	Cloaths, jewellery, and cash	14 2 3
Carter, John	—	Ditto	ditto	ditto	Cloaths, jewellery, and cash	92 2 3½
Carter, Patrick	Esquire	Ditto	ditto	ditto	Cash, wine, spirits, cloaths, and linen, &c.	849 19 10½
Carney, Martin	—	Drumahair	ditto	ditto	Spirits, wine, cloaths, and provisions	18 7 6
Clarke, Patrick	Yeoman	Ditto	ditto	ditto	Cloaths, provision, fowl, and books	10 13 0
Clarke, Hugh	—	Bawn	ditto	ditto	A horse, saddle and bridle, cloaths, and provisions	10 14 2
Cunhoy, Michael	—	Ardvarney	ditto	ditto	Yarn, furniture, cloaths	3 8 8
Crawford, Ann	—	Drumleafe	ditto	ditto	Cloaths, linen, and a saddle and bridle	50 1 1½
Cunian, John	—	Drumahair	ditto	ditto	A mare	6 16 6
Dodd, Roger	—	Ditto	ditto	ditto	Furniture, cloaths, plate, and watches	73 7 10½
Dogherty, Mary	—	Ditto	ditto	ditto	Cloaths	2 11 7
Elliott, John	—	Ardvardney	ditto	ditto	Furniture, cloaths, and provision	32 2 6
Elliotte, James	—	Ditto	ditto	ditto	A horse, saddle and bridle, windows broke, furniture, cloaths	33 19 10½
Gaffry, Patrick John	—	Ballinamore	ditto	ditto	Cloaths, and fire-arms	26 9 10
Gallagher, Hannah	Widow	Drumkerin	ditto	ditto	Watch, fowl, cloaths, and furniture	4 0 5
Hamilton, John	—	Ditto	ditto	ditto	Cloaths, furniture, provision, and a horse	55 7 7½
Hamilton, Wm. on behalf the children of Edw. Hamilton of Drumkerin, deceased.	—	Blackrock	ditto	Drumkerin, Co. Leitrim	Horses, spirits, oats, hay, and potatoes	71 10 3½
Hutton, Joseph	—	Cornougher	ditto	Residence	Saddle and bridle, cloaths, furniture	23 3 4½
Johnston, John	—	Ardvarney	ditto	ditto	A horse, and cloaths	7 1 1
Johnston, Robert	—	Aughnagallop	ditto	ditto	A horse	4 0 0
Johnston, Andrew	—	Addergold.	ditto	Lands of Bawn, Co. Leitrim	A horse, and a mare	22 0 0
Johnston, Andrew	—	Lodge	ditto	ditto	Cloaths, furniture, and groceries	44 10 4
Johnston, James	—	Gurtermore	ditto	Lands of Belbovil, Co. Leitrim	17 Sheep	17 0 0
Kelly, Ann	—	Drumleafe	ditto	Residence.	Cloaths, jewellery, and books	45 10 0
Keys, William	—	Derr'noran	ditto	ditto	Provision, fowl, and a saddle	4 3 2
Killcollum, Eleanor	Widow	Deubrisk	ditto	ditto	A horse and saddle	46 12 9
M'Connell, Edward	—	Tullydall	ditto	ditto	Cloaths, furniture, fowl, and a gun	5 9 2
M'Loughlin, Farrell	—	Drumkerin	ditto	ditto	Oats, spirits, furniture, and cloaths	42 9 4
M'Mullen, James	—	Drincroora	ditto	ditto	A mare	5 13 9
M'Sharry, Patrick	—	Drumahair	ditto	ditto	A horse, oats, and cloaths	12 17 2
M'Tenan, Charles	—	Corroder	ditto	ditto	Two saddles, and cloaths	9 19 1
Morrison, John	—	Chen	ditto	ditto	A horse, cavalry saddle and bridle, and cloaths	17 3 4½
Moystyn, William	Yeoman	Drumahair	ditto	ditto	Cloaths, plate, fire-arms, fruit of orchard	29 4 5½
Moystyn, Henry	—	Glenmore	ditto	ditto	Cloaths, furniture, and fowl	9 4 3½
Munroe, Thomas	—	Drumahair	ditto	ditto	Furniture, and cloaths	7 4 1
Murray, William	—	Ditto	ditto	ditto	Wearing apparel	2 19 8½
Nevill, Ann	—	Carrick-on-Shannon	ditto	Great road, leading from Dublin to Carrick-on-Shannon.	Millinery	46 14 11½
Newland, William	—	Gurteen	ditto	Residence	A horse, cloaths, damage to house	16 0 4
Palmer, John	—	Shibdella	ditto	ditto	Damage to windows, cloaths, furniture, and fowl	21 11 2
Palmer, William	—	Killargy	ditto	ditto	Horse, butter, meal, and cloaths	17 17 1
Patterson, William,	—	Kilmore	ditto	ditto	Cloaths, furniture, bank note, linen	10 6 4½
Patterson, George	—	Grouslodge	ditto	ditto,	Fruit, furniture, hay, and butter	10 14 1½
Peyton, Tobias	—	Kefscarigan	ditto	ditto	Cloaths, furniture, provisions, and windows broke	30 7 10½
Peyton, William	Gent.	Ditto	ditto	ditto	Damage to house, furniture, cloaths, and horse	16 15 1
Raycroft, Gilbert	—	Streamstown	ditto	Lands of Cashill, Co. Leitrim	Six bullocks	54 12 0
Roarke, Bryan	—	Tullicooly	ditto	Residence	A colt	3 6 0
Rue, Pat. M'Dermott	—	Barough	ditto	ditto	Tools, cloaths, furniture, and oats	6 11 5
Ross, George	—	Drumahair	ditto	ditto	Oats, hay, cloaths, a pocket-book, and helmet	5 13 6½
Rutledge, Mary	Widow	Drumkerrin	ditto	ditto	Oats, furniture, cloaths, and crop	10 0 1
					Carried forward —	£ 2140 19 10

Extract from "A List of Persons Who Have Suffered Losses in Their Property in the County of Leitrim." The losses referred to are those which occurred during the Rebellion of 1798. NLI JLB 94107.

Parish: **Killenumery**
Status: Lost

Parish: **Killigar**
Status: Lost

Parish: **Kiltoghert** (see also Drumshanbo)
Existing Records: b. 1810; m. 1810; d. 1810
Status: LC

Parish: **Kiltubrid**
Status: Lost

Parish: **Kiltyclogher** (for earlier entries see Manorhamilton)
Status: Lost

Parish: **Manorhamilton** or **Cloonclare** (see also Killasnett)
Existing Records: b. 1816 ; m. 1816; d. 1816
Status: LC

Parish: **Mogarban**
Status: Lost

Parish: **Newtown Gore**
Status: Lost

Parish: **Outragh**
Existing Records: b. 1833; m. 1833; d. 1833
Status: LC

Parish: **Rossinver**
Status: Lost

Presbyterian

Parish: **Carrigallen**
Starting Date: 1844

Roman Catholic

Civil Parish: **Annaduff**
Map Grid: 13
RC Parish: Annaduff

Diocese: AD
Earliest Record: b. 2.1849; m. 2.1849; d. 2.1849
Parish Address: Rev. Kevin Sullivan, PP, Annaduff, Carrick-on-Shannon, Co. Leitrim

Civil Parish: **Carrigallen (1)**
Map Grid: 15
RC Parish: Aughavas; also Carrigallen, see below
Diocese: KM
Earliest Record: b. 6.1845; m. 8.1845; d. 5.1845
Parish Address: Rev. James Prunty, PP, Aughavas, via Cavan, Co. Leitrim

Civil Parish: **Carrigallen (2)**
Map Grid: 15
RC Parish: Carrigallen
Diocese: KM
Earliest Record: b. 11.1829; m. 1.1841; d. 3.1842
Missing Dates: b. gaps 2.1830-12.1838; m. gaps 4.1848-1854; d. ends 6.1860
Parish Address: Rev. John Young, PP, Carrigallen, Co. Leitrim

Civil Parish: **Cloone (1)**
Map Grid: 17
RC Parish: Cloone
Diocese: AD
Earliest Record: b. 2.1820; m. 1.1823; d. 1.1823
Missing Dates: b. 3.1820-1.1834, 1.1841-1.1843, 10.1849-1.1850; m. 1.1839-1.1843; d. 9.1845-1.1850
Parish Address: Rev. Peter Bohan, PP, Cloone, Carrick-on-Shannon, Co. Leitrim

Civil Parish: **Cloone (2)**
Map Grid: 17
RC Parish: Gortletteragh
Diocese: AD
Earliest Record: b. 4.1830; m. 1.1826; d. 1.1826
Missing Dates: b. 8.1840-7.1848; m. 9.1827-2.1830, 4.1835-5.1848; d. 9.1826-3.1830, 2.1831-3.1839, 7.1839-8.1851, ends 7.1869
Parish Address: Rev. Sean Rooney, PP, Gortletteragh, Carrick-on-Shannon, Co. Leitrim

Civil Parish: **Clooneclare**
Map Grid: 5
RC Parish: Clooneclare
Diocese: KM

Earliest Record: b. 4.1841; m. 11.1850

Parish Address: Rev. Fintan McKiernan, CC, East Bars, Glenfarne, Co. Leitrim

Civil Parish: **Cloonlogher**
Map Grid: 4
RC Parish: part Drumlease; part Killarga
Diocese: KM

Civil Parish: **Drumlease**
Map Grid: 3
RC Parish: Drumlease or Drumlish
Diocese: KM
Earliest Record: b. 8.1859; m. 9.1859
Parish Address: Rev. Joseph Skelly, CC, St. Mary's, Drumlish, Co. Longford

Civil Parish: **Drumreilly (1)**
Map Grid: 9
RC Parish: Ballinglera; also Drumreilly Upper and Corlough, see below (2 and 3)
Diocese: KM
Earliest Record: b. 1883; m. 1887
Parish Address: Rev. James Duffy, PP, Ballinglera, Carrick-on-Shannon

Civil Parish: **Drumreilly (2)**
Map Grid: 9
RC Parish: Drumreilly Upper
Diocese: KM
Earliest Record: b. 1878; m. 1870
Parish Address: Fr. Patrick J. Flynn, CC, Corawaken, Co. Leitrim

Civil Parish: **Drumreilly (3)**
Map Grid: 9
RC Parish: Corlough and Drumreilly Lower
Diocese: KM
Earliest Record: b. 3.1867
Parish Address: Rev. Sean McDermott, CC, Derradda, Ballinamore, Co. Leitrim

Civil Parish: **Fenagh**
Map Grid: 12
RC Parish: Fenagh
Diocese: AD
Earliest Record: b. 6.1825; m. 10.1826
Missing Dates: b. 10.1829-11.1834; m. 2.1832-1.1835, 3.1842-1.1844
Parish Address: Rev. Francis Doyle, PP, Fenagh, Carrick-on-Shannon, Co. Longford

Civil Parish: **Inishmagrath**
Map Grid: 8
RC Parish: Inishmagrath (Drumkeerin)
Diocese: KM
Earliest Record: b. 1834; m. 1834; d. 1834
Missing Dates: b. 1839-1880; m. 1839-1880; d. 1839-1880
Parish Address: Rev. Edward Lynch, PP, Drumkeerin, Co. Leitrim

Civil Parish: **Killanummery**
Map Grid: 6
RC Parish: Killenumerry and Ballintogher
Diocese: AD
Earliest Record: b. 5.1828; m. 6.1827; d. 5.1829
Missing Dates: b. 8.1846-11.1848; m. 8.1846-11.1848; d. ends 4.1846
Parish Address: Rev. Timothy Foran, PP, Killenummery, Dromahair, via Sligo, Co. Leitrim

Civil Parish: **Killarga**
Map Grid: 7
RC Parish: Killarga and Dromahair
Diocese: KM
Earliest Record: b. 9.1852; m. 11.1853
Parish Address: Rev. John Phair, CC, Killargue, Dromahaire, Co. Leitrim

Civil Parish: **Killasnet**
Map Grid: 2
RC Parish: Killasnet
Diocese: KM
Earliest Record: b. 3.1852; m. 3.1852; d. 3.1852
Missing Dates: b. 1.1869-11.1878; m. 5.1871-11.1878; d. ends 3.1868
Parish Address: Rev. Patrick Brady, PP, Gurteen, P.O. Manorhamilton, Co. Leitrim

Civil Parish: **Kiltoghert (1)**
Map Grid: 10
RC Parish: Murhaun; also Kiltoghert and Bornacoola, see below (2 and 3)
Diocese: AD
Earliest Record: b. 5.1861; m. 6.1868
Parish Address: Rev. Thomas MacHale, Drumshanbo, Co. Leitrim

Civil Parish: **Kiltoghert (2)**
Map Grid: 10
RC Parish: Kiltoghert

Diocese: AD
Earliest Record: b. 8.1826; m. 7.1832; d. 8.1832
Missing Dates: m. 6.1854; d. 6.1854-12.1866
Parish Address: Rev. Michael Ryan, PP, Carrick-on-Shannon, Co. Leitrim

Civil Parish: **Kiltoghert (3)**
Map Grid: 10
RC Parish: Bornacoola
Diocese: AD
Earliest Record: b. 1.1824; m. 6.1824; d. 6.1824
Missing Dates: m. 9.1837-5.1850
Parish Address: Rev. Thomas O'Brien, PP, Bornacoola, Carrick-on-Shannon, Co. Leitrim

Civil Parish: **Kiltubrid**
Map Grid: 11
RC Parish: Kiltubrid
Diocese: AD
Earliest Record: b. 1.1841; m. 1.1841; d. 1.1847
Parish Address: Rev. Michael Killian, PP, Drumcong, Carrick-on-Shannon, Co. Leitrim

Civil Parish: **Mohill** (see also Co. Longford)
Map Grid: 16
RC Parish: Mohill-Manachain
Diocese: AD
Earliest Record: b. 8.1836 (includes workhouse baptisms 1846-55); m. 7.1836; d. 7.1836
Missing Dates: m. 5.1854-8.1854
Parish Address: Rev. Hubert Fee, PP, St. Patrick's, Mohill, Co. Leitrim

Civil Parish: **Oughteragh**
Map Grid: 14
RC Parish: Oughteragh (Ballinamore)
Diocese: KM
Earliest Record: b. 11.1841; m. 1.1841
Parish Address: Rev. Terence McManus, PP, Ballinamore, Co. Leitrim

Civil Parish: **Rossinver (1)**
Map Grid: 1
RC Parish: Kinlough; also Glenade and Rossinver, see below (2 and 3)
Diocese: KM
Earliest Record: b. 7.1835; m. 11.1840
Parish Address: Rev. Thomas Curran, PP, Kinlough, Co. Leitrim

Civil Parish: **Rossinver (2)**
Map Grid: 1
RC Parish: Glenade
Diocese: KM
Earliest Record: b. 11.1867; m. 11.1867
Parish Address: see Rossinver (1) above

Civil Parish: **Rossinver (3)**
Map Grid: 1
RC Parish: Rossinver (Ballaghameehan)
Diocese: KM
Earliest Record: b. 8.1851; m. 8.1844
Parish Address: Rev. Patrick J. Corrigan, PP, Rossinver, Co. Leitrim

Commercial and Social Directories

1824

J. Pigot's *City of Dublin & Hibernian Provincial Directory* includes traders, nobility, gentry, and clergy lists of Ballinamore, Carrick-on-Shannon, Drumsna, Jamestown, and Manorhamilton.

1846

Slater's *National Commercial Directory of Ireland* lists nobility, clergy, traders, etc., in Carrick-on-Shannon, Dromahaire, Drumsna and Jamestown, Manorhamilton, and Mohill.

1856

Slater's *Royal National Commercial Directory of Ireland* lists nobility, gentry, clergy, traders, etc., in Ballinamore, Carrick-on-Shannon, Dromahaire, Drumsna and Jamestown, Manorhamilton, and Mohill.

1870

Slater's *Directory of Ireland* contains trade, nobility, and clergy lists for Ballinamore, Carrick-on-Shannon and Leitrim, Dromahaire, Drumsna, Manorhamilton, and Mohill.

1881

Slater's *Royal National Commercial Directory of Ireland* contains lists of traders, clergy, nobility, and farmers in adjoining parishes of the towns of Ballinamore,

Carrick-on-Shannon, Manorhamilton and Dromahaire, and Mohill.

1894

Slater's *Royal National Directory of Ireland* lists traders, police, teachers, farmers, and private residents in each of the towns, villages, and parishes of the county.

Family History

Breen, Fr. Mark. *The Gray Family of Co. Leitrim.* 1980.

Downey – see Co. Sligo.

"The Descendants of Col. Miles O'Reilly in Co. Leitrim (1650-1830) from Tradition." *Breifne* 2 (1) (1923): 15-19.

Hawksby – see Co. Sligo.

"The Morans and the Mulveys of South Leitrim." *Ardagh and Clonmacnois Antiq. J.* 1 (3) (1932): 14-19.

"Notes on the MacRannals of Leitrim and Their Country: Being Introductory to a Diary of James Reynolds, Lough Scur, Co. Leitrim, for the Years 1658-1660." *R.S.A.I.* 35 (1905): 139-51.

Reynolds – see MacRannal.

Newspapers

There are few papers which only cover this county. Those in the surrounding counties should be consulted depending on the area of interest. All the papers listed below are also held in Leitrim County Library.

Title: *Leitrim and Longford Advertiser* (continued as *Leitrim Advertiser* in 1870)
Published in: Mohill, 1867-1924
NLI Holdings: 10.1867-12.1916; 6.1921-12.1924
BL Holdings: 10.1867-12.1916

Title: *Leitrim Gazette*
Published in: Mohill, 1858-67
NLI Holdings: 1858-67

Title: *Leitrim Journal*
Published in: Carrick-on-Shannon, 1850-72
NLI Holdings: 10.1850-3.1860; 11.1861-12.1872
BL Holdings: 10.1850-12.1857 (with gaps); 2.1858-3.1860; odd numbers 1861, 1870, and 1872

Title: *Leitrim Observer*
Published in: Carrick-on-Shannon, ca. 1890-current
NLI Holdings: 1904-in progress
BL Holdings: 1.1904-11.1920; 7.1959-in progress

Wills and Administrations

A discussion of the types of records, where they are held, their availability and value is given in the Wills section of the Introduction. The availability of prerogative wills, administrations, and marriage license records is also described in the relevant parts of the same section. Where available, published sources of these records are given in the Miscellaneous Sources section.

Pre-1858 Wills and Administrations

Prerogative Wills. see p. xli.
Consistorial Wills. County Leitrim is in the dioceses of Ardagh and Kilmore. The guide to Catholic parish records in this chapter shows the diocese to which each civil parish belonged. The wills of residents of each diocese were usually proven within that diocese (see the Wills section for exceptions). The following records survive:

Wills. see p. xxxvii.

Abstracts. see p. xxxvii.

Indexes. Ardagh (1695-1858). *Ir. Anc.* (1971). Kilmore – see Co. Cavan

Post-1858 Wills and Administrations

This county was served by the District Registries of Ballina (Baronies of Rosclogher and Dromahaire) and Cavan (rest of the county).

Marriage Licenses

Indexes. Ardagh and Kilmore (1691-1845). PRO; SLC film 100869

Miscellaneous Sources

Clancy, E., and P. Forde. *Ballinaglera Parish, Co. Leitrim: Aspects of its History and Traditions.* Dublin, 1980.

Clancy, P.S. *Historical Notices of the Parish of Inishmagrath, Co. Leitrim.* Carrick-on-Shannon, 1958.

"List of Sheriffs, Sub-Sheriffs, Jury Foremen, Lieutenants and M.P.s 1600-1868." Pub. 1869; NLI 2179.

MacParlan, J. *Statistical Survey of the County of Leitrim.* Royal Dublin Society, 1802.

O'Flynn, T. *History of Leitrim.* Dublin, 1937.

"Some Notes on the High Sheriffs of Co. Leitrim, 1701-1800." *Ir. Gen.* 1 (10) (1941): 301-09.

Research Sources and Services

Journals

Breifne (see Co. Cavan)

Libraries and Information Sources

Leitrim County Library, The Courthouse, Ballinamore, Co. Leitrim Ph: (078) 44012/44424/44425

Research Services

Leitrim Heritage Centre in County Library (see above): Full time genealogical service provided on Leitrim families (facilities include indexed church records)

See also research services in Dublin, p. xliv

LEITRIM HERITAGE CENTRE

TRACING ANCESTORS IN LEITRIM

Leitrim Heritage Centre has been set up to deal with enquiries from people who want to trace their Leitrim ancestors. The difficulty faced by many people who travelled from many lands to trace their Leitrim ancestors was that the source material was scattered throughout the County and elsewhere. All the available sources have now been gathered in the one place and Leitrim Heritage Centre and Leitrim County Library have now combined to provide a full time professional geneaological service for County Leitrim.

ENQUIRIES

Enquiries can be dealt with by calling to the Centre or by writing giving all available details.

SOURCES

All the major sources are now available at the Centre. Registers of baptisms, marriages and deaths for County Leitrim have all been indexed, and Griffiths Valuation, Tithe Books, maps and many other sources are available.

CHARGES

Enquiry fees depend on the amount of work involved. Staff will advise on the probability of positive or negative results before any charge is made. Obviously the more information the enquirer can provide the better the chance of positive results.

LOCATION

The address of the Centre is:-
Leitrim Heritage Centre,
County Library,
Ballinamore,
Co. Leitrim.
Ireland.
Tel: (078) 44012.

TIMES OF OPENING

Monday to Friday 10 am - 1 pm. 2 pm - 5 pm.

Leitrim Heritage Centre acknowledges the assistance of Leitrim County Council, County Library, County Development Team, AnCo and Clergy throughout the County in establishing the Centre.

Printed by Leitrim Observer Ltd.

Pamphlet for the Leitrim Heritage Centre.

Societies

Breifne Historical Society (see Co. Cavan, mainly covers Cavan and West Leitrim)

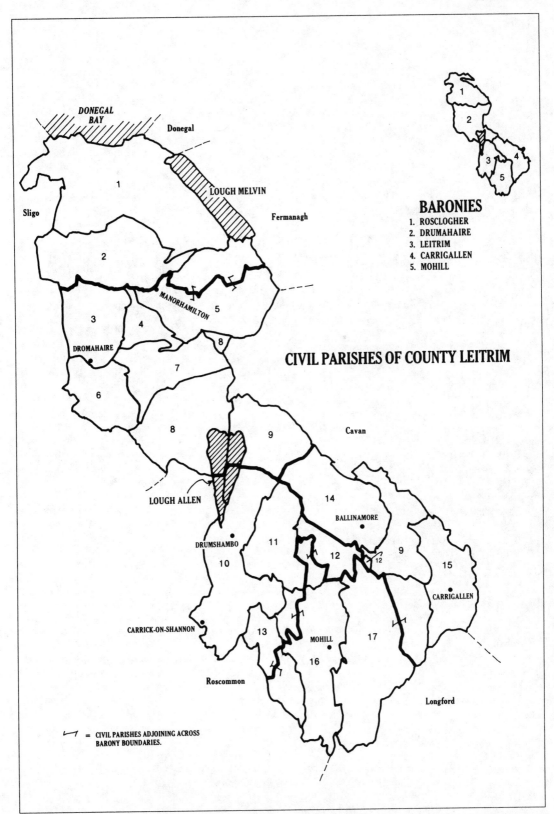

DONEGAL BAY

Donegal

LOUGH MELVIN

Sligo

Fermanagh

MANORHAMILTON

DROMAHAIRE

LOUGH ALLEN

DRUMSHAMBO

Cavan

BALLINAMORE

CARRICK-ON-SHANNON

CARRIGALLEN

MOHILL

Roscommon

Longford

BARONIES
1. ROSCLOGHER
2. DRUMAHAIRE
3. LEITRIM
4. CARRIGALLEN
5. MOHILL

CIVIL PARISHES OF COUNTY LEITRIM

= CIVIL PARISHES ADJOINING ACROSS BARONY BOUNDARIES.

County Limerick

A Brief History

Much of this county was part of the old Gaelic Kingdom of Thomond, while parts of the west of the county were in the Kingdom of Desmond. The major families in the county were the O'Briens, O'Ryans, O'Donovans, and O'Sheehans. Other families in the area included O'Hurley, Mac-Sheehy, O'Gorman, O'Scanlan, and O'Hallinan.

In the mid-ninth century the Vikings took control of Limerick city and retained it until the eleventh century when they were defeated by the O'Brien chieftain, Brian Boru. From that time it became the seat of the O'Briens, rulers of Thomond. Because the Norse people did not use surnames, there is little evidence of the Viking heritage among the family names in the area. However, one of the few Norse names found in Ireland, Harold, is found in Limerick.

Following the Norman invasion the county was granted to the De Burgos, ancestors of the Burkes, and to Fitzwalters and Fitzgeralds. The Norman influence is still evident in the names which are now common in Limerick, including Fitzgerald, Fitzgibbon, de Lacy, Woulfe, and Wall.

At the end of the sixteenth century a rebellion by Fitzgerald, the Earl of Desmond (see Co. Kerry), led to a very bloody war, which devastated much of this area of Munster. Following the defeat of Desmond, his estates, some of which were in western Limerick, were granted to various adventurers and were planted with English settlers. The Plantation of Munster in 1598, which also included parts of Limerick, was largely a failure. Many of the settlers left during the O'Neill march through Munster in 1601 and others simply adopted Irish customs and assimilated into the native population. Further confiscations, which followed the 1641 and 1688 wars, increased the numbers of English landowners but did not greatly increase the numbers of English settlers.

In 1709 families of German settlers from the Rhine Palatinate were brought to Limerick and settled around Rathkeale. These people were of the Moravian faith and came to be known as Palatines. Of the original 800 families who were brought to the county, only 200 (around 1,200 people) remained in Ireland. Later in the century, groups of the remaining Palatine families moved to other colonies in Adare and in Castleisland in County Kerry. The commoner names among these people included Shouldice, Switzer and Cole (see Miscellaneous Sources section for further references).

The county was badly affected by a local famine in 1820 caused by an outbreak of potato blight, and by the Great Famine of 1845-47. Almost 17 percent of the county's population emigrated between 1851 and 1855, and almost 30,000 died between 1847 and 1850. The population was 330,000 in 1841, and by 1851 had fallen by 21 percent. By 1891 it had fallen to around 160,000 and is currently around 122,000.

Limerick is now an important industrial city and port. The other major towns in the county include Kilmallock, Newcastle West, Rathkeale, Abbeyfeale, and Adare.

Census and Census Substitutes

1570
List of the Freeholders and Gentlemen in Co. Limerick. NLI P1700; *N. Munster Arch. and Hist. Soc. J.* 9 (3) (1964): 108-12.

1654-56
Civil Survey. Vol. 4. SLC film 973122

1659
"Census" of Ireland. Edited by S. Pender. Dublin: Stationery Office, 1939; SLC film 924648.

1746-1836
"Index of Freemen of Limerick." *N. Munster Antiq. J.* 4 (3) (1945): 103-30 (gives name, address, occupation in some cases, and date freedom attained).

1761
Names and Addresses of Freeholders Voting in a Parliamentary Election. NLI ms. 16093.

1766
Religious Census of Parishes of Abington, Cahircomey, Cahirelly, Carrigparson, Clonkeen, Kilkellane, Tuough. PRO 1A 46 49.

Protestants in the Parishes of Croagh, Kilscannel, Nantinan and Rathkeale. *Ir. Anc.* 9 (2) (1977): 77-78; SLC film 258517.

1776
Names of the Owners of Freeholds Entitled to Vote. PRO film 1321-22.

1793
"Two Lists of Persons Resident in the Vicinity of Newcastle in 1793 and 1821." *Ir. Anc.* 16 (1) (1984): 40-44.

1798
"List of Rebel Prisoners in Limerick Gaol." *N. Munster Antiq. J.* 10 (1) (1966): 79-82.

1799
"Gentlemen of the Counties Clare and Limerick Who Were in Favour of the Union in 1799." *Ir. Anc.* 14 (1) (1982): 30-35.

1813
"The Chief Inhabitants of the Parishes of St. Mary's and St. John's Limerick in 1813." *Ir. Anc.* 17 (2) (1985): 75-76.

1816-28
"List of Freeholders for the County of Limerick." SLC film 100224; GO M623.

1817
"Voters in the Limerick City Election of 1817." NLI IR324L1; *Ir. Anc.* 17 (1) (1985): 49-57.

1821
Newcastle – see 1793.

"Fragments of Census Returns for Kilfinane District." *N. Munster Antiq. J.* 17 (1975): 83-90.

1823-38
Tithe Applotment Survey (see p. xxvii).

1829
Limerick's Freeholders with Addresses and Occupations. GO M623.

1834
"Heads of Households in the Parish of Templebredin and Numbers in Each. *N. Munster Arch. and Hist. Soc. J.* 17 (1975): 91-101.

1836
Freemen – see 1746.

1840
List of Freeholders in the Barony of Coshlea. NLI ms. 9452.

1846
Survey of Households in Connection with Famine Relief. NLI ms. 582 (Loughill, Foynes, and Shangolden area).

Delivery he is Intitled to 13s. 4d. fees on each Man for such Crimes. The following is a list disposed of as underneath mentioned—

Death, Executed

No. 1 Mathew Kennedy
2 John Moore
3 Stephen Dundon
4 Thomas Mullanny
5 John Hayes
6 Thomas McInerney
7 Thomas Kennedy
8 William Ryan Stephens
9 Patrick O Neill
10 Patrick Wallace

Transported

No. 1 Owen Ryan
2 Thomas Gorman
3 James Ryan
4 Edmond Ryan
5 James Keagh
6 John Dwyer
7 Thomas Dwyer
8 Charles Nolan
9 David Leahy
10 James Kennedy
11 John Moroney
12 Richard Kelly
13 Michael McInerney
14 Owen Ryan
15 James Brohane
16 John Cunningham
17 Wm. Higgins Enlisted in 54th Regt.
18 Andrew Ryan
19 Philip Hogan
20 John Cowney
21 Daniel Carroll
22 James Ryan Stephens
23 Daniel Hayes
24 James Kelly
25 Thomas Frost
26 John Connor
27 John Mawn
28 James Casey
29 Maurice Shea
30 Francis Arthur
31 John Kerin
32 Michael Conry
33 Ell^s. Allum
34 John Abraham

35 James Mahon
36 Thomas Lawler
37 Michael Timmen
38 Michael Daley
39 Michael Mulconry
40 Rich^d. Robinson Enlisted in the 54th Reg^t. Foot

Persons discharged on Bail

No. 1 Joseph O Loughlin
2 John FitzGerald
3 Daniel Bohan
4 James Hillard
5 Patrick Carroll
6 Michael Callaghan
7 Thomas Butler
8 Denis Halloran
9 Patrick Halloran
10 John Ryan
11 Darby Ward
12 Mathew Hayes
13 David Twohy
14 Michael Callaghan
15 Thomas Ryan
16 Michael Donegan
17 James Dundon
18 Martin Kelly
19 George Murphy
20 Wm. Gleeson
21 John Flinn
22 Hugh Dwyer
23 James Crough
24 George Hardgrove
25 Robert Cross
26 Martin Howard
27 Thomas Collopy
28 Wm. Tubbs
29 Richard Welsh
30 John Murphy
31 John O Hogan
32 Wm. Crowe
33 Edmond Dunn
34 Andrew Kennedy
35 Michael Considine
36 Mathew Dea
37 John Twohy
38 Thomas McKnight
39 Theobald Barry

40 Wm. Healy
41 Thomas Dunn
42 John Murphy
43 Wm. Gorman
44 James Grant
45 David Callon
46 Rich^d. McElligott
47 Wm. Hannabury
48 John Sullivan
49 Edward Riely
50 Edmond Sheehan
51 James Hackett
52 Daniel O Brien
53 Denis McNamara
54 John Meade
55 James Hayes

Prisoners discharged by the Court Martial

No. 1 Peter O Keeffe
2 Denis Ryan
3 John Clume
4 Edmond Ryan
5 Patrick Ryan
6 James Cowney
7 Thomas Lane
8 Charles Small
9 Michael McCormack
10 John Coraghan
11 John Ryan
12 Fran^s. McNamara
13 Martin Kelly
14 Patrick Connor
15 Barth^w. Clanchy
16 Lieu^t. Harrass
17 Lieut. Rice
18 John Sullivan
19 Quarter Master Holmes
20 Thomas Doe
21 John Burke
22 Lieu^t. O Dwyer
23 Thomas Madagan
24 Chas. Strudgeon
25 Timothy Tierney
26 John Cloghessy
27 Danl. Shaughnessy
28 John McInerney
29 Edward Hastings
30 Michael Hastings
31 John Garvey

The Petition

To his Excellency Lord Marquis of Cornwallis,
Lieutenant General and General Governor & Commander in Chief of the Kingdom of Ireland—

A list of the Rebel prisoners held in Limerick Jail following the Rebellion of 1798, with their sentences. From *North Munster Antiquarian Journal* 10 (1) (1966).

1851

Kilfinane – see 1821.

1851-52

Griffith's Valuation (see p. xxvii).

1867

"List of Active Fenians in Co. Limerick." *N. Munster Antiq. J.* 10 (2) (1967): 169-72.

"Persons Attending Fenian Memorial Procession" (437 people named with occupation and residence). *N. Munster Antiq. J.* 10 (2) (1967): 173-205.

1901

Census. PRO.

1911

Census. PRO.

Church Records

Church of Ireland
(shows starting date of record)

Parish: **Abington**
Existing Records: b. 1811; m. 1811; d. 1811
Status: LC

Parish: **Adare**
Existing Records: b. 1806; m. 1806; d. 1806
Status: LC

Parish: **Aney**
Status: Lost

Parish: **Ardcanny**
Existing Records: b. 1802; m. 1802; d. 1805
Status: LC and PRO

Parish: **Askeaton**
Status: Lost

Parish: **Athlacca** and **Dromin**
Status: Lost

Parish: **Ballingarry**
Existing Records: b. 1785; m. 1786; d. 1785
Status: LC

Parish: **Ballinlanders**
Status: Lost

Parish: **Ballybrood**
Status: Lost

Parish: **Ballycahane**
Status: Lost

Parish: **Caherconlish**
Status: Lost

Parish: **Cahercorney**
Status: Lost

Parish: **Cahernarry** (also see St. Mary)
Status: Lost

Parish: **Cappamore** and **Tuogh** (see also Abington)
Existing Records: b. 1858; d. 1859
Status: LC

Parish: **Chapelrussell**
Existing Records: b. 1822; m. 1824; d. 1823
Status: LC and PRO

Parish: **Croagh**
Status: Lost

Parish: **Croom**
Status: Lost

Parish: **Doon**
Existing Records: b. 1804; m. 1812; d. 1812
Status: LC and PRO

Parish: **Drehidtarsna** (see also St. Munchen)
Status: Lost

Parish: **Dromkeen**
Status: Lost

Parish: **Fedamore**
Existing Records: b. 1811; m. 1809; d. 1810
Status: LC and PRO

Parish: **Grean**
Status: Lost

Parish: **Kilbeheney**
Status: Lost

Parish: **Kilcornan**
Status: Lost

Parish: **Kildimo**
Existing Records: b. 1809; m. 1809; d. 1809
Status: LC

Parish: **Kilfergus** and **Kilmoylan**
Existing Records: b. 1812; m. 1812; d. 1812
Status: LC

Parish: **Kilfinane**
Existing Records: b. 1804; m. 1804; d. 1804
Status: LC

Parish: **Kilflyn**
Existing Records: b. 1813; m. 1813; d. 1813
Status: LC

Parish: **Kilkeedy**
Existing Records: b. 1799; m. 1799; d. 1799
Status: LC

Parish: **Killaliathan**
Status: Lost

Parish: **Killeedy**
Status: Lost

Parish: **Killeely**
Status: Lost

Parish: **Kilmallock**
Status: Lost

Parish: **Kilmurry**
Status: Lost

Parish: **Kilpeacon** (also see Rathkeale)
Existing Records: b. 1824; m. 1825; d. 1860
Status: LC

Parish: **Kilscaddel**
Existing Records: b. 1824; m. 1825; d. 1860
Status: PRO

Parish: **Lounghill**
Status: Lost

Parish: **Mungret** (no records forthcoming, see
St Michael)
Status: LC and PRO

Parish: **Nantinan**
Status: Lost

Parish: **Newcastle**
Existing Records: b. 1709; m. 1708; d. 1709
Status: LC

Parish: **Particles** (with Kilflyn)
Existing Records: b. 1841
Status: LC

Parish: **Rathkeale**
Existing Records: b. 1742; m. 1742; d. 1742
Status: PRO

Parish: **Kilscannell**
Existing Records: b. 1824; m. 1825; d. 1860
Status: PRO

Parish: **Rathronan** and **Ardagh**
Existing Records: b. 1720; m. 1722; d. 1722
Status: LC and PRO

Parish: **St. John**
Existing Records: b. 1697; m. 1697; d. 1697
Status: LC

Parish: **St. Laurence**
Existing Records: b. 1863; d. 1697
Status: LC

Parish: **St. Mary**
Existing Records: b. 1726; m. 1726; d. 1726
Status: LC

Parish: **St. Michael**
Existing Records: b. 1801; m. 1801; d. 1835
Status: LC

Parish: **St. Munchin**
Existing Records: b. 1700; m. 1700; d. 1700
Missing Dates: b. 1705-34; m. 1769-97; d. 1705-
34
Status: LC

Parish: **St. Patrick** and **Kilquane**
Status: Lost

Parish: **Shanagolden**
Status: Lost

Parish: **Stradbally**
Existing Records: b. 1850; m. 1787; d. 1787
Status: LC and PRO

Parish: **Tullybracky**
Status: Lost

Roman Catholic

Civil Parish: **Abbeyfeale**
Map Grid: 74
RC Parish: Abbeyfeale
Diocese: LK
Earliest Record: b. 2.1829; m. 11.1856
Missing Dates: b. 10.1843-8.1856 (records for these dates exist but are not on microfilm)
Parish Address: Rev. Daniel Gallagher, PP, Abbeyfeale, Co. Limerick

Civil Parish: **Abington** (see also Co. Tipperary)
Map Grid: 61
RC Parish: Murroe and Boher
Diocese: EM
Earliest Record: b. 6.1814; m. 11.1815
Parish Address: Rev. Denis O'Meara, PP, Murroe, Co. Limerick

Civil Parish: **Adare**
Map Grid: 89
RC Parish: Adare
Diocese: LK
Earliest Record: b. 7.1832; m. 7.1832
Parish Address: Rev. John Browne, PP, Adare, Co. Limerick

Civil Parish: **Aglishcormick**
Map Grid: 60
RC Parish: see Kilteely
Diocese: EM

Civil Parish: **Anhid**
Map Grid: 93

RC Parish: see Croom
Diocese: LK

Civil Parish: **Ardagh**
Map Grid: 11
RC Parish: Ardagh
Diocese: LK
Earliest Record: b. 3.1845; m. 10.1841
Parish Address: Rev. James Power, PP, Ardagh, Co. Limerick

Civil Parish: **Ardcanny**
Map Grid: 17
RC Parish: see Kildimo
Diocese: LK

Civil Parish: **Ardpatrick**
Map Grid: 121
RC Parish: Ardpatrick
Diocese: LK
Earliest Record: b. 7.1861; m. 8.1861
Parish Address: Rev. Timothy Greene, PP, Ardpatrick, Kilmallock, Co. Limerick

Civil Parish: **Askeaton**
Map Grid: 14
RC Parish: Askeaton (previously part of Kilfinane)
Diocese: LK
Earliest Record: b. 1.1829; m. 1.1829
Missing Dates: m. 7.1861-10.1861
Parish Address: Rev. Michael O'Connor, PP, Askeaton, Co. Limerick

Civil Parish: **Athlacca**
Map Grid: 95
RC Parish: see Dromin
Diocese: LK

Civil Parish: **Athneasy**
Map Grid: 116
RC Parish: Bulgaden, see Kilbreedy Major
Diocese: LK

Civil Parish: **Ballinard**
Map Grid: 109
RC Parish: see Hospital
Diocese: EM

Civil Parish: **Ballingaddy**
Map Grid: 122

RC Parish: Kilmallock, see SS Peter and Paul
Diocese: LK

Civil Parish: **Ballingarry (1)**
Map Grid: 81
RC Parish: Ballingarry
Diocese: LK
Earliest Record: b. 1.1825; m. 1.1825
Missing Dates: b. 5.1828-12.1849; m. 2.1836-
    1.1850
Parish Address: Rev. Gerard MacNamee, PP,
    Ballingarry, Co. Limerick

Civil Parish: **Ballingarry (2)**
Map Grid: 125
RC Parish: see Knocklong
Diocese: EM

Civil Parish: **Ballinlough**
Map Grid: 111
RC Parish: see Hospital
Diocese: EM

Civil Parish: **Ballybrood**
Map Grid: 57
RC Parish: see Caherconlish
Diocese: EM

Civil Parish: **Ballycahane**
Map Grid: 38
RC Parish: see Fedamore
Diocese: LK

Civil Parish: **Ballylanders**
Map Grid: 126
RC Parish: Ballylanders
Diocese: EM
Earliest Record: b. 3.1849; m. 1.1857
Parish Address: Rev. Patrick O'Gorman, PP,
    Ballylanders, Kilmallock, Co. Limerick

Civil Parish: **Ballynaclogh**
Map Grid: 66
RC Parish: Pallasgreen, see Grean
Diocese: EM

Civil Parish: **Ballynamona**
Map Grid: 110
RC Parish: see Hospital
Diocese: EM

Civil Parish: **Ballyscaddan**
Map Grid: 119
RC Parish: see Emly, Co. Tipperary
Diocese: EM

Civil Parish: **Bruff**
Map Grid: 96
RC Parish: Bruff
Diocese: LK
Earliest Record: b. 11.1781; m. 2.1781
Missing Dates: b. 9.1792-12.1807
Parish Address: Rev. James Culhane, PP, Bruff,
    Kilmallock, Co. Limerick

Civil Parish: **Bruree**
Map Grid: 84
RC Parish: Rockhill
Diocese: LK
Earliest Record: b. 1.1842; m. 7.1861
Parish Address: Rev. Joseph Moran, PP, Rock-
    hill, Bruree, Co. Limerick

Civil Parish: **Cahervally**
Map Grid: 50
RC Parish: see Donaghmore
Diocese: LK

Civil Parish: **Caherconlish**
Map Grid: 53
RC Parish: Caherconlish
Diocese: EM
Earliest Record: b. 1.1841; m. 2.1841
Parish Address: Rev. Denis Keogh, PP, Caher-
    conlish, Co. Limerick

Civil Parish: **Cahercorney**
Map Grid: 106
RC Parish: see Hospital
Diocese: EM

Civil Parish: **Caherelly**
Map Grid: 55
RC Parish: Ballybricken, see Ludden
Diocese: EM

Civil Parish: **Cahernarry**
Map Grid: 51
RC Parish: see Donaghmore
Diocese: LK

Civil Parish: **Cappagh**
Map Grid: 17
RC Parish: Cappagh, see also Kilcornan
Diocese: LK
Earliest Record: b. 1.1841; m. 1.1841
Parish Address: Rev. Peadar de Burca, Cappagh, Askeaton, Co. Limerick

Civil Parish: **Carrigparson**
Map Grid: 49
RC Parish: part Caherconlish; part Ballybricken, see Ludden
Diocese: EM

Civil Parish: **Castletown**
Map Grid: 64
RC Parish: see Doon
Diocese: CA

Civil Parish: **Chapelrussel**
Map Grid: 26
RC Parish: see Kildimo
Diocese: LK

Civil Parish: **Clonagh**
Map Grid: 19
RC Parish: see Kilcolman
Diocese: LK

Civil Parish: **Cloncagh**
Map Grid: 80
RC Parish: Knockaderry and Cloncagh
Diocese: LK
Earliest Record: b. 2.1838; m. 2.1838
Parish Address: Rev. Timothy Lyons, PP, Cloncagh, Ballingarry, Co. Limerick

Civil Parish: **Cloncrew**
Map Grid: 86
RC Parish: see Dromcolliher
Diocese: LK

Civil Parish: **Clonelty**
Map Grid: 73
RC Parish: see Cloncagh
Diocese: LK

Civil Parish: **Clonkeen**
Map Grid: 47
RC Parish: Murroe, see Abington
Diocese: EM

Civil Parish: **Clonshire**
Map Grid: 18
RC Parish: see Adare
Diocese: LK

Civil Parish: **Colmanswell**
Map Grid: 87
RC Parish: Ballyagran
Diocese: LK
Earliest Record: b. 9.1841; m. 9.1841
Missing Dates: b. 11.1844-1.1847, 8.1847-9.1850; m. 9.1844-1.1847, 10.1847-1.1851, 11.1859-9.1860
Parish Address: Rev. John Burke, PP, Ballyagran, Kilmallock, Co. Limerick

Civil Parish: **Corcomohide**
Map Grid: 83
RC Parish: Ballyagran, see Colmanswell
Diocese: LK

Civil Parish: **Crecora**
Map Grid: 35
RC Parish: Crecora, see Mungret
Diocese: LK

Civil Parish: **Croagh**
Map Grid: 22
RC Parish: Croagh and Kilfinny
Diocese: LK
Earliest Record: b. 8.1836; m. 1.1844
Missing Dates: b. 6.1843-11.1843
Parish Address: Rev. L. Kelly, PP, Croagh, Rathkeale, Co. Limerick

Civil Parish: **Croom**
Map Grid: 91
RC Parish: Croom
Diocese: LK
Earliest Record: b. 10.1828; m. 12.1770; d. 12.1770
Missing Dates: m. 7.1794-8.1807; d. ends 7.1794
Parish Address: Rev. Liam Boyle, PP, Croom, Co. Limerick

Civil Parish: **Darragh**
Map Grid: 129
RC Parish: Glenroe and Ballyorgan
Diocese: LK
Earliest Record: b. 6.1853; m. 8.1853

Parish Address: Rev. C. O'Neill, PP, Glenroe, Kilmallock, Co. Limerick

Civil Parish: **Derrygalvin**
Map Grid: 46
RC Parish: Limerick, St. Patrick's; part Fedamore.
Diocese: LK

Civil Parish: **Donaghmore**
Map Grid: 48
RC Parish: Donaghmore and Knockea
Diocese: LK
Earliest Record: b. 1.1830; m. 7.1827
Parish Address: Rev. Denis Browne, PP, Donaghmore, Co. Limerick

Civil Parish: **Doon**
Map Grid: 63
RC Parish: part Doon; part Cappamore, see Tuogh
Diocese: EM
Earliest Record: b. 3.1824; m. 1.1839
Parish Address: Rev. John McGrath, PP, Doon, Co. Limerick

Civil Parish: **Doondonnell**
Map Grid: 20
RC Parish: Coolcappa, see Clonagh
Diocese: LK

Civil Parish: **Drehidtarsna**
Map Grid: 90
RC Parish: see Adare
Diocese: LK

Civil Parish: **Dromin**
Map Grid: 97
RC Parish: Dromin and Athlacca
Diocese: LK
Earliest Record: b. 5.1817; m. 6.1817
Missing Dates: b. 9.1837-3.1849; m. 12.1837-11.1849
Parish Address: Rev. J. O'Beirne, PP, Athlacca, Kilmallock, Co. Limerick

Civil Parish: **Dromkeen**
Map Grid: 58
RC Parish: part Kilteely; part Pallasgreen, see Grean
Diocese: EM

Civil Parish: **Dromcolliher**
Map Grid: 85
RC Parish: Drumcolliher and Broadford
Diocese: LK
Earliest Record: b. 3.1830; m. 1.1830
Missing Dates: b. 9.1850-11.1851; m. 9.1850-10.1851, 10.1864-5.1866
Parish Address: Rev. John Liston, PP, Drumcollogher, Co. Limerick

Civil Parish: **Dunmoylan**
Map Grid: 7
RC Parish: Coolcappa, see Clonagh
Diocese: LK

Civil Parish: **Dysert**
Map Grid: 92
RC Parish: see Croom
Diocese: LK

Civil Parish: **Effin**
Map Grid: 102
RC Parish: Effin
Diocese: LK
Earliest Record: b. 3.1843; m. 4.1843
Parish Address: Rev. Edmond Houlihan, PP, Effin, Kilmallock, Co. Limerick

Civil Parish: **Emlygreenan**
Map Grid: 117
RC Parish: Ballinvana, see Kilbreedy Major
Diocese: LK

Civil Parish: **Fedamore**
Map Grid: 104
RC Parish: Fedamore, see also Monasteranenagh
Diocese: LK
Earliest Record: b. 10.1806; m. 10.1806
Missing Dates: b. 7.1813-1.1814, 1.1822-7.1854; m. 7.1813-1.1814, 11.1825-8.1854
Parish Address: Rev. A. Elliott, PP, Fedamore, Co. Limerick

Civil Parish: **Galbally**
Map Grid: 120
RC Parish: Galbally
Diocese: EM
Earliest Record: b. 3.1810; m. 10.1809
Missing Dates: b. 7.1820-7.1821, 7.1812-12.1828; m. 3.1820-7.1821

Parish Address: Rev. John Hennessy, PP, Lis-vernane, Aherlow, Co. Tipperary

Civil Parish: **Glenogra**
Map Grid: 105
RC Parish: part Dromin; part Bruff
Diocese: LK

Civil Parish: **Grange**
Map Grid: 72
RC Parish: see Bruff
Diocese: LK

Civil Parish: **Grean**
Map Grid: 65
RC Parish: Pallasgreen
Diocese: EM
Earliest Record: b. 1.1811; m. 1.1811
Parish Address: Rev. Philip Hickey, PP, Pallasgreen, Co. Limerick

Civil Parish: **Hackmys** (see Co. Cork)
Map Grid: 100
RC Parish: Charleville, see Rathgoggan, Co. Cork
Diocese: LK

Civil Parish: **Hospital**
Map Grid: 112
RC Parish: Hospital
Diocese: EM
Earliest Record: b. 1.1810; m. 2.1812
Parish Address: Rev. James Bacon, PP, Hospital, Co. Limerick

Civil Parish: **Inch St. Laurence** or **Isertlawrence**
Map Grid: 56
RC Parish: see Caherconlish
Diocese: EM

Civil Parish: **Iveruss**
Map Grid: 24
RC Parish: see Askeaton
Diocese: LK

Civil Parish: **Kilbeheny**
Map Grid: 130
RC Parish: mainly Kilbehenny; part Mitchelstown, see Brigown, Co. Cork
Diocese: EM
Earliest Record: b. 12.1824; m. 1.1825

Missing Dates: m. 2.1843-5.1843
Parish Address: Rev. John P. Ryan, PP, Kilbehenny, Mitchelstown, Co. Cork

Civil Parish: **Kilbolane**
Map Grid: 88
RC Parish: see Co. Cork
Diocese: CY

Civil Parish: **Kilbradran**
Map Grid: 9
RC Parish: Coolcappa, see Clonagh
Diocese: LK

Civil Parish: **Kilbreedy Major**
Map Grid: 115
RC Parish: Bulgaden and Ballinvana
Diocese: LK
Earliest Record: b. 3.1812; m. 6.1812
Missing Dates: m. 11.1853-2.1854
Parish Address: Rev. P. Kelly, PP, Bulgaden, Kilmallock, Co. Limerick

Civil Parish: **Kilbreedy Minor**
Map Grid: 101
RC Parish: see Effin
Diocese: LK

Civil Parish: **Kilcolman**
Map Grid: 8
RC Parish: Kilcolman (Coolcappa)
Diocese: LK
Earliest Record: b. 10.1827; m. 1.1828
Parish Address: Rev. Michael Lane, CC, Coolcappa, Ardagh, Co. Limerick

Civil Parish: **Kilcornan**
Map Grid: 25
RC Parish: Kilcornan, Stonehall, and Cappagh
Diocese: LK
Earliest Record: b. 4.1825; m. 4.1825
Missing Dates: m. 3.1848-9.1848
Parish Address: Rev. John Irwin, PP, Kilcornan, Co. Limerick

Civil Parish: **Kilcullane**
Map Grid: 108
RC Parish: see Hospital
Diocese: EM

Civil Parish: **Kildimo**
Map Grid: 28
RC Parish: Kildimo
Diocese: LK
Earliest Record: b. 1.1831; m. 1.1831
Parish Address: Rev. David Crowley, PP, Kildimo, Co. Limerick

Civil Parish: **Kilfergus**
Map Grid: 2
RC Parish: Glin
Diocese: LK
Earliest Record: b. 10.1851; m. 10.1851
Parish Address: Rev. Cornelius Collins, PP, Glin, Co. Limerick

Civil Parish: **Kilfinane**
Map Grid: 124
RC Parish: Kilfinane
Diocese: LK
Earliest Record: b. 6.1832; m. 8.1832
Parish Address: Rev. Patrick O'Dea, PP, Kilfinane, Co. Limerick

Civil Parish: **Kilfinny**
Map Grid: 79
RC Parish: see Croagh
Diocese: LK

Civil Parish: **Kilflyn**
Map Grid: 128
RC Parish: see Darragh
Diocese: LK

Civil Parish: **Kilfrush**
Map Grid: 113
RC Parish: see Hospital
Diocese: EM

Civil Parish: **Kilkeedy**
Map Grid: 29
RC Parish: Patrickswell (Lurriga)
Diocese: LK
Earliest Record: b. 10.1801; m. 4.1802
Parish Address: Rev. Michael Frawley, PP, Patrickswell, Co. Limerick

Civil Parish: **Killagholehane** (Killaliathan)
Map Grid: 78
RC Parish: see Drumcolliher
Diocese: LK

Civil Parish: **Killeedy**
Map Grid: 77
RC Parish: part Newcastle; part Tournafulla
Diocese: LK
Earliest Record: b. 8.1840; m. 12.1840
Parish Address: Rev. Daniel Murphy, PP, Tournafulla, Co. Limerick

Civil Parish: **Killeely**
Map Grid: 30
RC Parish: see Co. Clare
Diocese: LK

Civil Parish: **Killeengarriff**
Map Grid: 43
RC Parish: see Fedamore
Diocese: LK

Civil Parish: **Killeenoghty**
Map Grid: 37
RC Parish: see Mungret
Diocese: LK

Civil Parish: **Killonahan** (Killelonahan)
Map Grid: 34
RC Parish: see Mungret
Diocese: LK

Civil Parish: **Kilmeedy**
Map Grid: 82
RC Parish: Feenagh (Kilmeedy)
Diocese: LK
Earliest Record: b. 8.1833; m. 7.1854
Parish Address: Rev. Edward Looby, Kilmeedy, Co. Limerick

Civil Parish: **Kilmoylan**
Map Grid: 6
RC Parish: see Shanagolden
Diocese: LK

Civil Parish: **Kilmurry**
Map Grid: 42
RC Parish: see Limerick: St. Patrick's
Diocese: LK

Civil Parish: **Kilpeacon**
Map Grid: 103
RC Parish: part Fedamore; part Loughmore
Diocese: LK

Civil Parish: **Kilquane** (see also Co. Cork)
Map Grid: 127
RC Parish: Kilmallock, see SS Peter and Paul
Diocese: LK

Civil Parish: **Kilscannell**
Map Grid: 23
RC Parish: part Ardagh; part Rathkeale
Diocese: LK

Civil Parish: **Kilteely**
Map Grid: 69
RC Parish: Kilteely
Diocese: EM
Earliest Record: b. 12.1815; m. 11.1832
Missing Dates: b. 4.1829-9.1832
Parish Address: Rev. John Sweeny, PP, Kilteely, Co. Limerick

Civil Parish: **Knockaney** or **Aney**
Map Grid: 107
RC Parish: Knockaney
Diocese: EM
Earliest Record: b. 3.1808; m. 4.1808; d. 6.1819
Missing Dates: m. 10.1821-1.1822, 2.1841-5.1841; d. ends 3.1821
Parish Address: Rev. Michael Meagher, PP, Knockaney, Kilmallock, Co. Limerick

Civil Parish: **Knocklong**
Map Grid: 118
RC Parish: Knocklong and Glenbrohane
Diocese: EM
Earliest Record: b. 4.1809; m. 4.1809
Missing Dates: b. 6.1819-9.1823, 6.1830-1.1832, 7.1854-11.1854; m. 10.1819-1.1824, 10.1831-1.1836, 2.1854-8.1854
Parish Address: Rev. George Bourke, CC, Knocklong, Kilmallock, Co. Limerick

Civil Parish: **Knocknagaul**
Map Grid: 36
RC Parish: see Mungret
Diocese: LK

Civil Parish: **Limerick: St. John's**
Map Grid: 1
RC Parish: St. John's
Diocese: LK
Earliest Record: b. 5.1788; m. 7.1821
Missing Dates: b. 12.1797-1.1825

Parish Address: Rev. James Ambrose, Adm, St. John's Presbytery, Limerick

Civil Parish: **Limerick: St. Lawrence's**
Map Grid: 44
RC Parish: see St. John's
Diocese: LK

Civil Parish: **Limerick: St. Mary's** (see Limerick: St. Nicholas)

Civil Parish: **Limerick: St. Michael's**
Map Grid: 33
RC Parish: St. Michael; also part St. John's
Diocese: LK
Earliest Record: b. 8.1776; m. 2.1772
Missing Dates: b. 10.1801-1.1803, 2.1807-10.1807, 4.1813-1.1814, 9.1819-1.1820; m. 9.1802-3.1803, 7.1804-10.1807, 5.1813-6.1814, 11.1819-5.1821, 10.1861-1.1863
Parish Address: Rev. Francis Moriarty, PP, St. Michael's, Denmark Street, Limerick

Civil Parish: **Limerick: St. Munchin's** (see also Co. Clare)
Map Grid: 31
RC Parish: St. Munchin; also St. Mary's, see St. Nicholas
Diocese: LK
Earliest Record: b. 11.1764; m. 11.1764
Missing Dates: b. 5.1792-10.1798; m. 5.1792-10.1798, 5.1819-9.1819
Parish Address: Rev. Michael Manning, PP, Clancy Strand, Limerick

Civil Parish: **Limerick: St. Nicholas**
Map Grid: 45
RC Parish: St. Mary's; also part St. Munchin's
Diocese: LK
Earliest Record: b. 1.1745; m. 10.1745
Parish Address: Rev. Brendan Connellan, PP, St. Mary's, Limerick

Civil Parish: **Limerick: St. Patrick's** (see also Co. Clare)
Map Grid: 41
RC Parish: St. Patrick's
Diocese: LK
Earliest Record: b. 1.1812; m. 1.1812
Missing Dates: m. 9.1840-2.1841
Parish Address: Rev. James Sadlier, PP, St. Patrick's, Dublin Road, Limerick

Civil Parish: **Lismakeery**
Map Grid: 15
RC Parish: see Askeaton
Diocese: LK

Civil Parish: **Loughill**
Map Grid: 3
RC Parish: Loughill (previously part of Glin)
and Balyhahill (previously part of Shanagolden)
Diocese: LK
Earliest Record: b. 10.1855; m. 11.1855
Parish Address: see Shanagolden

Civil Parish: **Ludden**
Map Grid: 52
RC Parish: Ballybricken and Bohermore
Diocese: EM
Earliest Record: b. 11.1800; m. 8.1805
Parish Address: Rev. John Dwyer, PP, Ballybricken, Grange, Kilmallock, Co. Limerick

Civil Parish: **Mahoonagh**
Map Grid: 76
RC Parish: Mahoonagh
Diocese: LK
Earliest Record: b. 3.1812; m. 8.1810
Missing Dates: b. 8.1830-6.1832, 7.1838-11.1839; m. 5.1839-2.1840
Parish Address: Rev. Michael Kelly, PP, Castlemahon, Co. Limerick

Civil Parish: **Monagay (1)**
Map Grid: 75
RC Parish: Newcastle (Monagea); also part Templeglantine, see below.
Diocese: LK
Earliest Record: b. 1.1809; m. 1.1777
Missing Dates: b. 7.1813-3.1829, 12.1831-8.1833; m. 2.1792-1.1829
Parish Address: Rev. Patrick Howard, PP, Monagea, Newcastle West, Co. Limerick

Civil Parish: **Monagay (2)**
Map Grid: 75
RC Parish: Templeglantine
Diocese: LK
Earliest Record: b. 12.1864; m. 1.1865
Parish Address: Rev. James Galvin, PP, Templeglantine, Co. Limerick

Civil Parish: **Monasteranenagh**
Map Grid: 39
RC Parish: Manister
Diocese: LK
Earliest Record: b. 1.1826; m. 1.1826
Parish Address: Rev. James Costelloe, PP, Manister, Croom, Co. Limerick

Civil Parish: **Morgans**
Map Grid: 12
RC Parish: see Shanagolden
Diocese: LK

Civil Parish: **Mungret**
Map Grid: 32
RC Parish: Mungret and Crecora
Diocese: LK
Earliest Record: b. 11.1844; m. 11.1844
Parish Address: Rev. Eamonn Dillane, PP, The Presbytery, Raheen, Co. Limerick

Civil Parish: **Nantinan**
Map Grid: 16
RC Parish: see Cappagh
Diocese: LK

Civil Parish: **Newcastle**
Map Grid: 71
RC Parish: Newcastle
Diocese: LK
Earliest Record: b. 5.1815; m. 4.1815 (also workhouse records from 11.1852)
Missing Dates: m. 11.1831-2.1834
Parish Address: Rev. Edmond O'Dea, PP, Newcastle West, Co. Limerick

Civil Parish: **Oola**
Map Grid: 68
RC Parish: Oola and Solohead
Diocese: EM
Earliest Record: b. 10.1809; m. 1.1810
Missing Dates: b. 4.1828-2.1837; m. 11.1828-10.1832
Parish Address: Rev. Eamonn Hackett, CC, Oola, Co. Tipperary

Civil Parish: **Particles**
Map Grid: 123
RC Parish: see Kifinane
Diocese: LK

Civil Parish: **Rathjordan**
Map Grid: 59
RC Parish: see Hospital
Diocese: EM

Civil Parish: **Rathkeale**
Map Grid: 21
RC Parish: Rathkeale
Diocese: LK
Earliest Record: b. 1.1811; m. 1.1811
Missing Dates: b. 7.1823-9.1831
Parish Address: Rev. Thomas Costello, PP, Rathkeale, Co. Limerick

Civil Parish: **Rathronan (1)**
Map Grid: 10
RC Parish: Ardagh; also part Athea; also part Cratloe, see below
Diocese: LK
Earliest Record: b. 4.1830; m. 11.1827
Parish Address: Rev. Thomas O'Donnell, PP, Athea, Co. Limerick

Civil Parish: **Rathronan (2)**
Map Grid: 10
RC Parish: Cratloe
Diocese: LK
Earliest Record: b. 11.1802; m. 1.1822
Parish Address: Rev. Ronald Costello, PP, Cratloe, Co. Clare

Civil Parish: **Robertstown**
Map Grid: 5
RC Parish: see Shanagolden
Diocese: LK

Civil Parish: **Rochestown**
Map Grid: 54
RC Parish: Ballybricken, see Ludden
Diocese: EM

Civil Parish: **St. John's**
Map Grid: 1
RC Parish: see Limerick
Diocese: LK

Civil Parish: **St. Lawrence's**
Map Grid: 44
RC Parish: see Limerick
Diocese: LK

Civil Parish: **St. Mary's**
Map Grid: between 41 and 45
RC Parish: see Limerick
Diocese: LK

Civil Parish: **St. Michael's**
Map Grid: 33
RC Parish: see Limerick
Diocese: LK

Civil Parish: **St. Munchin's**
Map Grid: 31
RC Parish: see Limerick
Diocese: LK

Civil Parish: **St. Nicholas**
Map Grid: 45
RC Parish: see Limerick
Diocese: LK

Civil Parish: **St. Patrick's**
Map Grid: 41
RC Parish: see Limerick
Diocese: LK

Civil Parish: **St. Peter's and St. Paul's**
Map Grid: 114
RC Parish: Kilmallock
Diocese: LK
Earliest Record: b. 10.1837; m. 11.1837
Parish Address: Rev. Gerard Wall, PP, Kilmallock, Co. Limerick

Civil Parish: **Shanagolden**
Map Grid: 4
RC Parish: Shanagolden and Foynes
Diocese: LK
Earliest Record: b. 4.1824; m. 4.1824
Parish Address: Rev. Gerard Enright, PP, Shanagolden, Co. Limerick

Civil Parish: **Stradbally**
Map Grid: 40
RC Parish: Castleconnell
Diocese: KL
Earliest Record: b. 2.1850; m. 8.1863
Parish Address: Rev. John Cooney, PP, Castleconnell, Co. Limerick

Civil Parish: **Tankardstown**
Map Grid: 99

RC Parish: Killmallock, see SS Peter and Paul
Diocese: LK

Civil Parish: **Templebredon** (see also Co. Tip-
perary)
Map Grid: 70
RC Parish: Pallasgreen, see Grean
Diocese: EM

Civil Parish: **Tomdeely**
Map Grid: 13
RC Parish: see Askeaton
Diocese: LK

Civil Parish: **Tullabracky**
Map Grid: 94
RC Parish: see Bruff
Diocese: LK

Civil Parish: **Tuogh**
Map Grid: 62
RC Parish: Cappamore
Diocese: EM
Earliest Record: b. 4.1845; m. 2.1843
Parish Address: Rev. William Whyte, Cap-
pamore, Co. Limerick

Civil Parish: **Tuoghcluggin**
Map Grid: 67
RC Parish: part Pallasgreen, see Grean; part
Doon
Diocese: EM

Civil Parish: **Uregare**
Map Grid: 98
RC Parish: part Dromin; part Bruff
Diocese: LK

Commercial and Social Directories

1769

John Ferrar's *Directory of Limerick* contains
an alphabetical list of merchants, traders, city
officials, military personnel, Anglican clergy,
and church-wardens; also lists of revenue officers at Limerick, Scattery, Kilrush, and
Tarbert; lists of barristers, attorneys, and
public notaries; a list of guilds officers,
physicians, surgeons, and apothecaries; and
a list of Freemason officers. Also published
in *Ir. Gen.* 3 (9) (1964): 329-40.

1788

Richard Lucas's *General Directory of the
Kingdom of Ireland* contains lists of traders
in Limerick. Also reprinted in *The Irish
Genealogist* 3 (12) (1967): 529-37.

1809

Holden's *Triennial Directory* has alphabetical
lists of traders in Limerick city.

1820

J. Pigot's *Commercial Directory of Ireland*
contains information on the gentry, nobility,
and traders in and around the city of
Limerick.

1824

J. Pigot's *City of Dublin & Hibernian Provincial Directory* includes traders, nobility,
gentry, and clergy lists of Castleconnell, Kilmallock, Limerick, Newcastle, and Rathkeale.

1840

F. Kinder's *New Triennial & Commercial
Directory for 1840, '41 and '42* gives traders,
nobility, etc., for Limerick city (rare volume).

1846

Slater's *National Commercial Directory of
Ireland* lists nobility, clergy, traders, etc., in
Adare, Bruff, Castleconnell and O'Brien's
Bridge, Croom, Kilmallock, Limerick, New-
castle, and Rathkeale.

1856

Slater's *Royal National Commercial Directory of Ireland* lists nobility, gentry, clergy,
traders, etc., in Adare, Bruff, Castleconnell
and O'Brien's Bridge, Croom, Kilmallock,
Limerick, Newcastle, and Rathkeale.

1866

G.H. Bassett's *Directory of the City and
County of Limerick and of the Principal
Towns in the Cos. of Tipperary and Clare* has
traders lists for Adare, Castleconnell, Kilmallock, Limerick, Newcastle, and Rathkeale and an alphabetical list of the gentry in
the county.

1870

Slater's *Directory of Ireland* contains trade, nobility, and clergy lists of Adare, Askeaton, Bruff, Castleconnell, Croom, Kilmallock, Limerick, Newcastle, and Rathkeale.

1879

G. H. Bassett's *Limerick Directory* has a list of residents, professions, and traders in Limerick city and a list of traders in the towns of Abbeyfeale, Adare, Ardagh, Ashford, Askeaton, Athea, Broadford, Bruff, Caherconlish, Castleconnell, Croom, Drumcollogher, Foynes, Glin, Hospital, Kilmallock, Murroe, Newcastle West, Oola, Pallaskenry, Rathkeale, Shanagolden, and Tournafulla. There is also a list of gentlemen in the county.

1881

Slater's *Royal National Commercial Directory of Ireland* contains lists of traders, clergy, nobility, and farmers in adjoining parishes of the towns of Adare and Croom, Askeaton, Castleconnell and O'Brien's Bridge, Foynes (see Tarbert, Commercial and Social Directories section, Co. Kerry), Kilmallock, Limerick, Newcastle West, and Rathkeale.

1886

Francis Guy's *Postal Directory of Munster* lists gentry, clergy, traders, principal farmers, teachers, and police sergeants in each postal district of the county and has a listing of magistrates, clergy, and the professions.

1893

Francis Guy's *Directory of Munster* lists traders and farmers in each of the postal districts of the county and a general alphabetical index to persons in the whole county.

1894

Slater's *Royal National Directory of Ireland* lists traders, police, teachers, farmers, and private residents in each of the towns, villages, and parishes in the county.

Note also that there are national directories for some of the professions including medicine and clergy.

Family History

"Bevan of Co. Limerick." *Ir. Anc.* 6 (1) (1974): 1-5.

"Carrigogunnell Castle and the O'Briens of Pubblebrien in the Co. Limerick." *R.S.A.I.* 37 (1907): 374-92; 38 (1908): 141-59.

"The Desmonds Castle at Newcastle Oconyll, Co. Limerick." *R.S.A.I.* 39 (1909): 42-58, 350-68.

"The Family Bible of John Ganley, William St., Limerick." *Ir. Anc.* 9 (2) (1979): 84-85.

Going – see Co. Tipperary.

"O'Grady of Cappercullen (Co. Limerick)." *N. Munster Antiq. J.* 7 (4) (1957): 20-22.

"O'Grady Papers (Kilballyowen, Co. Limerick)." *Anal. Hib.* 15: 35-62.

"Harte of Co. Limerick." Pedigree in *Swanzy Notebooks.* RCB Library, Dublin.

"Families of Hodges and Morgan of Old Abbey, Co. Limerick." *Ir. Anc.* 11 (2) (1979): 77-84.

Ferrar, Michael Lloyd. *The Limerick Huntingdon Ferrars by One of Them.* Plymouth, n.d.

"The MacSheehys of Connelloe, Co. Limerick." *Ir. Gen.* 4 (1970): 560-77.

"Monckton of Co. Limerick." *Ir. Anc.* 4 (1) (1972): 15-21.

Morgan – see Hodges.

"Nihell of Clare and Limerick." *Ir. Gen.* 4 (5) (1972): 496-506.

"The Peppards of Cappagh, Co. Limerick." *Ir. Anc.* 16 (2) (1984): 68-70.

"Roches of Newcastlewest, Co. Limerick." *Ir. Gen.* 2 (1950): 244-45.

"Scanlan of the Barony of Upper Connello, Co. Limerick." *Ir. Anc.* 4 (2) (1972): 71-80.

Tuthill, P.B. *Pedigrees of Families of Tuthill and Villiers of Co. Limerick* (with notes). London, 1907-08.

Tuthill, P.B. *Pedigree of the Family of Villiers of Kilpeacon, Co. Limerick.* London, 1907.

Villiers – see Tuthill.

"The Vincent Family of Limerick and Clare." *Ir. Gen.* 4 (4) (1971): 347-48.

White, J.D. *The History of the Family of White of Limerick, Cappawhite.* Cashel, 1887.

Gravestone Inscriptions

Ardcanny: *Ir. Anc.* 9 (1) (1977): 3-5.

Ardpatrick: Fleming, John. *Reflections, Historical and Topographical on Ardpatrick, Co. Limerick.* 1979.

Athlacca: Seoighe, Mainchin. *Dromin & Athlacca.* 1978.

Ballingarry: Hamilton, Rev. G.F. *Records of Ballingarry.* 1930.

Bruree: Seoighe, Mainchin. *Bru Ri: the History of the Bruree District.* 1973.

Corrigenda: *Ir. Anc.* 16(1) 1984: 53.

Dromin: Seoighe, Mainchin. *Dromin & Athlacca.* 1978.

Grange: *Ir. Anc.* 10 (1) (1978): 49-51.

Kilbehenny: *Ir. Gen.* 2 (11) (1954): 349-54.

Knockainey (Lough Gur): *L. Gur. Hist. Soc. J.* 1 (1985): 51-61.

Knockainey (Patrickswell): *L. Gur. Hist. Soc. J.* 2 (1986): 71-79.

Limerick City Cemetery: Indexed by Midwest Regional Archives (see Research Services section).

Lough Gur – see Knockainey.

Nantinan: *Ir. Anc.* 7 (1980).

Patrickswell – see Knockainey.

Rathkeale, CI: *Ir. Anc.* 14 (2) (1982): 105-20.

St. Mary's Cathedral: Talbot, Very Rev. M. *The Monuments of St. Mary's Cathedral, Limerick.* 1976 (available from Cathedral).

Tankardstown: Seoighe, Mainchin. *Bru Ri: the History of the Bruree District.* 1973.

Newspapers

A card index to biographical notices in Limerick, Ennis, Clonmel, and Waterford newspapers up to 1821 (50,000 items) is available on microfiche from Ms. R. ffolliott, Glebe House, Fethard, Co. Tipperary. A copy of this is held by the Library of University College, Dublin.

Title: *General Advertiser* or *Limerick Gazette*
Published in: Limerick, 1804-20
NLI Holdings: 9.1809-9.1818
BL Holdings: 9.1804-11.1820

Title: *Limerick and Clare Examiner*
Published in: Limerick, 1846-55
BL Holdings: 1.1846-6.1855

Title: *Limerick Chronicle*
Published in: Limerick, 1766-current
NLI Holdings: odd numbers 1768-1831; 1841-42; 1844-45; 1847-48; 1852; 1855; 1859-8.1921; 8.1927-12.1981; 1.1982- in progress
BL Holdings: odd numbers 1768-1825; 1.1826-12.1829; 1.1832-7.1869; 1.1879-in progress

Title: *Limerick Evening Post* (continued as *Limerick Evening Post and Clare Sentinel* in 1828)
Published in: Limerick, 1811-33
NLI Holdings: 10.1811-12.1813; 3.1814-12.1818; 3.1828-12.1833
BL Holdings: 1-4.1828; 10.1832-3.1833; 8-12.1833

Title: *Limerick Gazette* – see *General Advertiser*

Title: *Limerick Herald* (continued as *Limerick Evening Herald* in 1833)
Published in: Limerick, 1831-35
NLI Holdings: 4.1831-4.1835
BL Holdings: 4.1831-4.1835

Title: *Limerick Journal* (continued as *Munster Journal* in 1774)
Published in: Limerick, 1739-44
NLI Holdings: 11.8.1741 (one issue)
BL Holdings: odd numbers 1761; 1766-77

Title: *Limerick Leader*
Published in: Limerick, 1889-current
NLI Holdings: 6.1893-in progress
BL Holdings: 6.1893-12.1925; 8.1926-in progress
Other Holdings: *The Limerick Leader,* a current Limerick newspaper, has an almost complete run of this paper.

Title: *Limerick Reporter* (continued as *Limerick Reporter & Tipperary Vindicator* in 1850)
Published in: Limerick, 1839-99
NLI Holdings: 7.1839-12.1855; 4.1856-12.1895
BL Holdings: 7.1839-10.1871; 1.1872-1.1896

Title: *Munster Journal*
Published in: Limerick, ca. 1737-77
NLI Holdings: 5.1749-1.1755
BL Holdings: 5.1749-1.1755

Title: *Munster News*
Published in: Limerick, 1851-1935
NLI Holdings: 6.1851-1.1871; 6.1873-8.1922; 2.1925-6.1935
BL Holdings: 6.1851-1.1871; 5.1873-6.1920; 1.1921-12.1925; 1.1927-6.1935

Title: *Southern Advertiser*
Published in: Limerick, c.1889-93
BL Holdings: 4.1889-3.1893

Title: *Southern Chronicle* (called *Limerick Southern Chronicle* from 1864 and *Bassett's Chronicle* from 1875)
Published in: Limerick, 1863-85
NLI Holdings: 1.1865-12.1867; 1871-72
BL Holdings: 4.1863-5.1873; 4.1874-8.1875; 10.1875-12.1885

Wills and Administrations

A discussion of the types of records, where they are held, their availability and value is given in the Wills section of the Introduction. The availability of prerogative wills, administrations, and marriage license records is also described in the relevant parts of the same section. Where available, published sources of these records are given in the Miscellaneous Sources section.

Pre-1858 Wills and Administrations

Prerogative Wills. see p. xli.
Consistorial Wills. County Limerick is in the dioceses of Emly and Limerick with a few parishes in Cashel, Killaloe, and Cloyne. The guide to Church of Ireland parish records in this chapter shows the diocese to which each civil parish belonged. The wills of residents of each diocese were usually proven within that diocese (see the Wills section for exceptions). The following records survive:

Wills. see p. xxxvii.

Abstracts. see p. xxxvii. The Westropp manuscripts in the RIA have many abstracts of wills and administrations from counties Clare and Limerick.

Indexes. Limerick (1615-1858). up to 1800 published by Phillimore. Killaloe – see Co. Clare. Cloyne – see Co. Cork.

Post-1858 Wills and Administrations

This county was served by the District Registry of Limerick. The surviving records are kept in the PRO and are on microfilm in Mid-West Regional Archives (see Research Sources and Services section).

Marriage Licenses

Indexes. Emly (1664-1857). PRO; SLC film 100861. Limerick (1691-1845). PRO; SLC film 100869. Cashel – see Co. Tipperary. Killaloe – see Co. Clare.

Miscellaneous Sources

"The Arthur Manuscripts" (medical records, wills and mortgages, accounts, and other records kept by Dr. Arthur of Limerick, 1590-1675). *N. Munster Antiq. J.* 6 (2) (1950): 29-40; continued in 6 (3) (1951): 67-82; 7 (1) (1953): 168-82; 7 (4) (1957): 4-10; 8 (1) (1958): 2-19.

"An Elizabethan Map of Kilmallock." *N. Munster Antiq. J.* 11 (1968): 27-35.

"Emigration from Kilmallock Workhouse, 1848-1860." *L. Gur Hist. Soc. J.* 3 (1987).

"Emigration from the Limerick Workhouse 1848-1860." *Ir. Anc.* 14 (2) (1982): 83-94.

"Emigration to North America from Limerick Port, 1841." *N. Munster Antiq. J.* 23 (1981): 67-76 (includes the passenger list for the *Shelmalere,* 26 May 1841 to New York).

Ferrar, J. *The History of Limerick to the Year 1787.* Limerick, 1787.

Fitzgerald, P., and J. McGregor. *The History, Topography and Antiquities of the County and City of Limerick.* 2 vols. Limerick, 1825-27.

"The German Colony in Co. Limerick." *N. Munster Antiq. J.* 1 (2) (1937): 42-53.

"Limerick Shop Signs of the 18th Century." *N. Munster Antiq. J.* 2 (4) (1941): 156-66 (lists proprietors names, occupations, and relationships in some cases).

"The Silvermakers of Limerick." *Ir. Anc.* 10 (2) (1978): 99-1907.

"The Trade Guilds of Limerick." *N. Munster Antiq. J.* 2 (3) (1941): 121-34 (names officials and members in some cases).

Research Sources and Services

Journals

North Munster Antiquarian Journal
Old Limerick Journal

Libraries and Information Sources

Limerick County Library, 58 O'Connell Street, Limerick Ph: (061) 318692/318477 (has local history section and bibliography of Limerick)

Limerick City Library, The Granary, Limerick Ph: (061) 44668 (local history section)

Research Services

Mid-West Regional Archives, 104 Henry Street, Limerick Ph: (061) 313898; contact: Dr. Chris O'Mahony (genealogical research service in parish records, census records, estate papers, newspapers, etc., for Limerick and Tipperary)

See also research services in Dublin, p. xliv

Societies

Thomond Archaeological Society, Rev. John Leonard, 9 Castletroy Heights, Limerick (publishers of *North Munster Antiquarian Journal*)

Newcastle West Historical Society, Mr. John Cussen, Newcastle West, Co. Limerick

Old Limerick Society (publishers of *Old Limerick Journal*), c/o 33 Greenhill Road, Garryowen, Limerick

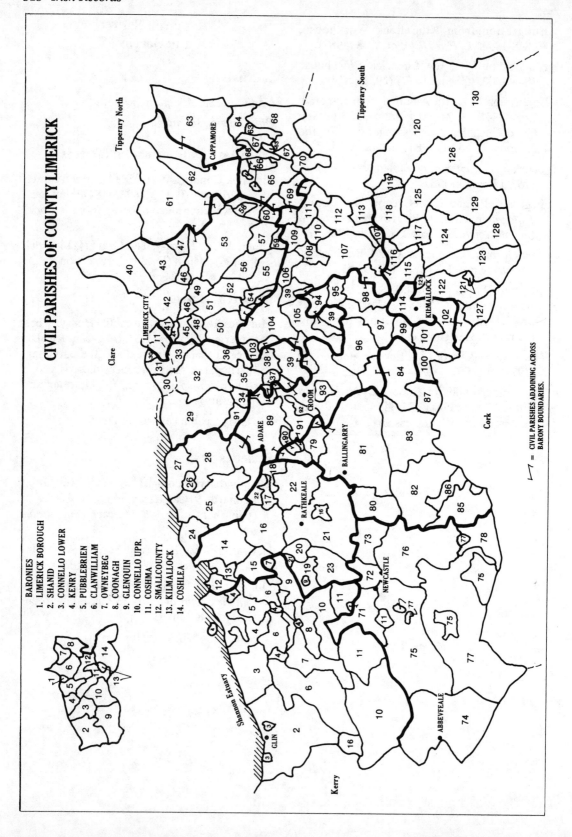

CIVIL PARISHES OF COUNTY LIMERICK

BARONIES
1. LIMERICK BOROUGH
2. SHANID
3. CONNELLO LOWER
4. KENRY
5. PUBBLEBRIEN
6. CLANWILLIAM
7. OWNEYBEG
8. COONAGH
9. GLENQUIN
10. CONNELLO UPR.
11. COSHMA
12. SMALLCOUNTY
13. KILMALLOCK
14. COSHLEA

⌐ = CIVIL PARISHES ADJOINING ACROSS
    BARONY BOUNDARIES.

County Longford

A Brief History

This Leinster county contains the towns of Longford, Granard, Ballymahon, Edgeworthstown, and Ballinamuck.

At the beginning of the Christian era, the area now forming County Longford was part of the Kingdom of Conmaicne. From the ninth to the fifteenth centuries it was known as "Annaly." The county was mainly the territory of the O'Farrells. Other Irish families associated with the county are O'Quinns, (Mc) Gilna, Leavy, Mulroy, and (Mac) Gaynor.

Although Longford was nominally granted to Hugh de Lacy after the Norman conquest in the twelfth century, there was little real Norman influence in the county because of the power of the O'Farrells. The family of Tuite was one of the few to establish a settlement in the county.

In the sixteenth and early seventeenth century, parts of Longford were planted with English settlers including Aungier, Forbes, Newcomen, King, Harman, Lane, and Edgeworth. The Edgeworths were major landowners in the county and were very popular because of their efforts on the tenant's behalf.

In 1641 the O'Farrells joined the rebellion by the Catholic Confederacy (see Co. Kilkeny). On its defeat by Cromwell in 1649, they lost their remaining estates and influence in the county.

This largely agricultural county was badly affected by the Great Famine of 1845-47. The population, which was 115,000 in 1841, had fallen by 29 percent in 1851. Over 14,000 Longford people died between 1845 and 1850 of starvation and disease, and the remainder emigrated to the cities or, more usually, abroad. The county continued to have a high rate of emigration throughout the remainder of the century and beyond. The current population is 31,000.

Census and Census Substitutes

1659
"Census" of Ireland. Edited by S. Pender. Dublin: Stationery Office, 1939; SLC film 924648.

1731
Protestants in the Parish of Shrule. RCB Library.

1766
Protestants in the Parishes of Abbeylara and Russough. RCB Library. Abbeylara on SLC film 258517.

1790
Names of the Owners of Freeholds in Co. Longford, ca. 1790. PRO film 2486-88; SLC film 100888.

1800-35

Printed List of Co. Longford Freeholders. GO ms. 444; SLC film 100181.

1823-38

Tithe Applotment Survey (see p. xxvii).

1834

List of Heads of Households in the Parish of Granard, showing numbers of males and of females of each religion (i.e., Catholic, Protestant, or Presbyterian) in each household. In the Catholic parish register for Granard; SLC film 926027.

1838

"Householders in the Catholic Parish of Mullinalaghta [part of civil parish of Scrabby and Columbkille East]" (gives names of householders in each of twelve townlands who contributed to a new church at Cloonagh). In Mullinalaghta parish records; *Teathbha* 1 (3) (1973): 244-51.

1854

Griffith's Valuation (see p. xxvii).

1901

Census. PRO.

1911

Census. PRO.

Church Records

Church of Ireland
(shows starting date of record)

Parish: **Ardagh**
Existing Records: b. 1811; m. 1811; d. 1811
Status: LC

Parish: **Ballymacormick**
Status: Lost

Parish: **Cashel**
Status: Lost

Parish: **Clonbroney**
Existing Records: b. 1821; m. 1821; d. 1821
Status: Lost

Parish: **Clonguish and Clongishkilloe**
Existing Records: b. 1820; m. 1820; d. 1820
Status: LC

Parish: **Columbkille**
Status: Lost

Parish: **Forgney**
Existing Records: b. 1803; m. 1804; d. 1804
Status: LC

Parish: **Granard**
Existing Records: b. 1820; m. 1820; d. 1820
Status: LC

Parish: **Kilcommick**
Existing Records: b. 1795; m. 1795; d. 1795
Status: LC

Parish: **Kilglass**
Status: Lost

Parish: **Mothel**
Status: Lost

Parish: **Moydow**
Existing Records: b. 1821; m. 1821; d. 1821
Status: LC

Parish: **Rathcline**
Existing Records: b. 1846; d. 1847
Status: LC

Parish: **Shrule**
Status: Lost

Parish: **Templemichael** (see also Killoe, RC section)
Existing Records: b. 1795; m. 1795; d. 1795
Status: LC and PRO

Presbyterian

Parish: **Tully** (Edgeworthstown)
Starting Date: 1844

Roman Catholic

Civil Parish: **Abbeylara**
Map Grid: 7
RC Parish: Abbeylara
Diocese: AD
Earliest Record: b. 1854; m. 1854; d. 1854
Parish Address: Rev. Michael Egan, Granard,
   Co. Longford

Civil Parish: **Abbeyshrule**
Map Grid: 23
RC Parish: see Taghshinny
Diocese: AD

Civil Parish: **Agharra**
Map Grid: 24
RC Parish: see Kilglass
Diocese: AD

Civil Parish: **Ardagh**
Map Grid: 9
RC Parish: Ardagh and Moydow
Diocese: AD
Earliest Record: b. 1793; m. 1793; d. 1822
Missing Dates: b. 1.1816-10.1822
Parish Address: Rev. Patrick Kearney, PP, Ar-
   dagh, Co. Longford

Civil Parish: **Ballymacormick**
Map Grid: 14
RC Parish: see Templemichael
Diocese: AD

Civil Parish: **Cashel**
Map Grid: 19
RC Parish: Cashel (Newtowncashel)
Diocese: AD
Earliest Record: not on microfilm
Parish Address: Rev. Jeremian Macaulay, PP,
   Newtowncashel, Co. Longford

Civil Parish: **Clonbroney**
Map Grid: 5
RC Parish: Clonbroney
Diocese: AD
Earliest Record: b. 1849; m. 1854; d. 1854
Parish Address: Rev. Patrick Lane, PP, Bal-
   linalee, Co. Longford

Civil Parish: **Clongesh**
Map Grid: 3
RC Parish: Clonguish (Newtownforbes)
Diocese: AD
Earliest Record: b. 1829; m. 1829; d. 1829
Parish Address: Rev. F. Prunty, PP, St. Mary's
   Newtownforbes, Co. Longford

Civil Parish: **Columbkille (1)**
Map Grid: 4
RC Parish: Columbkille; also Scrabby, see
   below
Diocese: AD
Earliest Record: b. 1845; m. 1845; d. 1845
Parish Address: Rev. Canon John Corkery, PP,
   Aughnacliffe, Co. Longford

Civil Parish: **Columbkille (2)**
Map Grid: 4
RC Parish: Scrabby and Columbkille East
Diocese: AD
Earliest Record: b. 1870; m. 1877
Parish Address: see Columbkille (1)

Civil Parish: **Forgney**
Map Grid: 25
RC Parish: Moyvore
Diocese: ME

Civil Parish: **Granard**
Map Grid: 6
RC Parish: Granard
Diocese: AD
Earliest Record: b. 1779; m. 1782; d. 1818
Parish Address: Rev. Francis Gilfillan, PP,
   Granard, Co. Longford

Civil Parish: **Kilcommock**
Map Grid: 20
RC Parish: Kilcomogue or Kenagh
Diocese: AD
Earliest Record: b. 1859; m. 1859; d. 1859
Parish Address: Rev. M. Lane, PP, Kenagh, Co.
   Longford

Civil Parish: **Kilglass**
Map Grid: 16
RC Parish: Kilglass and Rathreagh (Legan and
   Ballycloughan)
Diocese: AD
Earliest Record: b. 1855; m. 1855; d. 1855

Parish Address: Rev. Brendan Tyrrell, PP, Lenamore, Co. Longford

Civil Parish: **Killashee**
Map Grid: 13
RC Parish: Killashee (and Cluain-a-Donald from 1864)
Diocese: AD
Earliest Record: b. 1826; m. 1826; d. 1826
Missing Dates: b. 12.1843-4.1848; m. 10.1843-6.1848; d. 8.1843-11.1858
Parish Address: Rev. David Kelly, PP, Killashee, Co. Longford

Civil Parish: **Killoe (1)**
Map Grid: 1
RC Parish: Drumlish; also Killoe, see below
Diocese: AD
Earliest Record: b. 1834; m. 1834; d. 1834
Missing Dates: b. 3.1868-3.1874; m. 3.1868-1.1870, 6.1872-1.1870; d. 3.1868-2.1870, 7.1872-8.1876
Parish Address: see Killoe (2)

Civil Parish: **Killoe (2)**
Map Grid: 1
RC Parish: Killoe
Diocese: AD
Earliest Record: b. 1826; m. 1826; d. 1826
Missing Dates: b. 8.1852-2.1853, 10.1868-4.1869; m. 10.1852-9.1854; d. 6.1853-8.1853
Parish Address: Rev. Thomas Leavy, PP, Ennybegs, Drumlish, Co. Longford

Civil Parish: **Mohill**
Map Grid: 2
RC Parish: see Co. Leitrim
Diocese: AD

Civil Parish: **Mostrim**
Map Grid: 10
RC Parish: Mostrim (Edgeworthstown)
Diocese: AD
Earliest Record: b. 1838; m. 1838; d. 1838
Parish Address: Rev. James Kaughnan, PP, St. Mary's, Mostrim, Co. Longford

Civil Parish: **Moydow**
Map Grid: 15
RC Parish: see Ardagh
Diocese: AD

Civil Parish: **Noughaval**
Map Grid: 26
RC Parish: see Drumraney, Co. Westmeath
Diocese: ME

Civil Parish: **Rathcline**
Map Grid: 18
RC Parish: Rathcline (Lanesboro)
Diocese: AD
Earliest Record: not on microfilm
Parish Address: Rev. Laurence O'Grady, PP, Lanesboro, Co. Longford

Civil Parish: **Rathreagh**
Map Grid: 12
RC Parish: see Kilglass
Diocese: AD

Civil Parish: **Shrule**
Map Grid: 21
RC Parish: Ballymahon or Shrule
Diocese: AD
Earliest Record: b. 1820; m. 1829; d. 1820
Missing Dates: b. 11.1830; d. 10.1830
Parish Address: Rev. James Bland, Adm, Ballymahon, Co. Longford

Civil Parish: **Street**
Map Grid: 11
RC Parish: Streete
Diocese: AD
Earliest Record: b. 1820; m. 1820; d. 1823
Missing Dates: b. 7.1827-11.1831, 12.1831-12.1834; m. 1.1828-1.1835; d. 8.1829-12.1834, 1.1841-7.1842
Parish Address: Rev. Michael Reid, PP, Lismacaffrey, Mullingar, Co. Westmeath

Civil Parish: **Taghsheenod**
Map Grid: 17
RC Parish: see Taghshinny
Diocese: AD

Civil Parish: **Taghshinny**
Map Grid: 22
RC Parish: Taghshinney, Taghshinod, and Abbeyshrule
Diocese: AD
Earliest Record: b. 1835; m. 1835; d. 1835
Missing Dates: b. 3.1844-5.1848; m. 8.1842-5.1848; d. 11.1842-5.1848

Parish Address: Rev. Christopher Lynch, PP, Carrickedmond, Colehill, Co. Longford

Civil Parish: **Templemichael**
Map Grid: 8
RC Parish: Templemichael and Ballymacormack
Diocese: AD
Earliest Record: b. 1802; m. 1802; d. 1802
Missing Dates: b. 1.1808-6.1808
Parish Address: Rev. Patrick Earley, The Presbytery, St. Mel's Cathedral, Longford

Commercial and Social Directories

1824
J. Pigot's *City of Dublin & Hibernian Provincial Directory* includes traders, nobility, gentry, and clergy lists of Granard, Lanesborough, and Longford.

1846
Slater's *National Commercial Directory of Ireland* lists nobility, clergy, traders, etc., in Ballymahon, Granard, Longford, and Mostrim (Edgeworthstown).

1856
Slater's *Royal National Commercial Directory of Ireland* lists nobility, gentry, clergy, traders, etc., in Ballymahon, Granard, Longford and Newtown-Forbes, and Mostrim (Edgeworthstown).

1870
Slater's *Directory of Ireland* contains trade, nobility, and clergy lists for Ballymahon, Edgeworthstown, Granard, and Longford.

1881
Slater's *Royal National Commercial Directory of Ireland* contains lists of traders, clergy, nobility, and farmers in adjoining parishes of the towns of Ballymahon, Edgeworthstown, Granard, and Longford.

1894
Slater's *Royal National Directory of Ireland* lists traders, police, teachers, farmers, and private residents in each of the towns, villages, and parishes of the county.

Family History

"Burrowes of Fernsborough." Pedigree in *Swanzy Notebooks*. RCB Library, Dublin.

"Entries from the Family Bible of James Hyde of Longford." *Ir. Anc.* 2 (1) (1970): 23.

"The Fetherton Family of Ardagh." *Teathbha* 2 (1) (1980): 17-32.

Forbes, John. *Memoirs of the Earls of Granard.* London, 1868.

"Grier of Gurteen." Pedigree in *Swanzy Notebooks*. RCB Library, Dublin.

Lefroy, Sir J.H. *Notes and Documents Relating to Lefroy of Carrickglass, Co. Longford.* 1868.

Newspapers

There were no early papers published within the county. Those in the surrounding counties should be consulted depending on the area of interest.

Title: *Longford Independent*
Published in: Longford, 1868-1918
NLI Holdings: 1888-1913; 1921-1.1925
BL Holdings: 9.1869-12.1918

Title: *Longford Journal*
Published in: Longford, 1839-1914
NLI Holdings: odd numbers 1842-66
BL Holdings: 1.1839-7.1869; 1.1870-9.1888; odd numbers 1889, 1890; 1.1899-8.1914

Title: *Longford Leader and Cavan, Leitrim, Roscommon & Westmeath News*
Published in: Longford, 1897-current
NLI Holdings: 4.1907-7.1910; 7.1927-in progress
BL Holdings: 4.1907-in progress (except 1-2.1926)

Title: *Midland Counties Gazette*
Published in: Longford, 1853-63
BL Holdings: 6.1853-4.1863

Wills and Administrations

A discussion of the types of records, where they are held, their availability and value is given in the Wills section of the Introduction. The availability of prerogative wills, administrations, and marriage license records is also described in the relevant parts of the same section. Where available, published sources of these records are given in the Miscellaneous Sources section.

Pre-1858 Wills and Administrations

Prerogative Wills. see p. xli.
Consistorial Wills. County Longford is mainly in the diocese of Ardagh with two parishes in Meath. The guide to Catholic parish records in this chapter shows the diocese to which each civil parish belonged. The wills of residents of each diocese were usually proven within that diocese (see the Wills section for exceptions). The following records survive:

Wills. see p. xxxvii.

Abstracts. see p. xxxvii. The RIA's Upton Papers also contain abstracts to Longford wills. RIA Library.

Indexes: Ardagh (1695-1858) *Ir. Anc.* (1971). Meath – see Co. Meath.

Post-1858 Wills and Administrations

This county was served by the District Registry of Cavan. The surviving records are kept in the PRO.

Marriage Licenses

Indexes. Meath (1691-1845). PRO; SLC film 100869

Miscellaneous Sources

Farrell, J.P. *Historical Notes and Stories of the County Longford.* Longford, 1979.

Murray, C. *Bibliography of Co. Longford.* Longford, 1961.

"Some Notes on the High Sheriffs of Co. Longford 1701-1800." *Ir. Gen.* 2 (1) (1943): 13-21.

Research Sources and Services

Journals

Teathbha (Journal of Longford Historical Society)

Libraries and Information Sources

Longford/Westmeath Joint Library, Dublin Road, Mullingar, Co. Westmeath Ph: (044) 40781/2/3 (has indexes to six Longford parishes and answers research queries)

Research Services

See research services in Dublin, p. xliv

Societies

Longford Historical Society (publishers of *Teathbha*), Mr. Jude Flynn, Aughadegnan, Longford

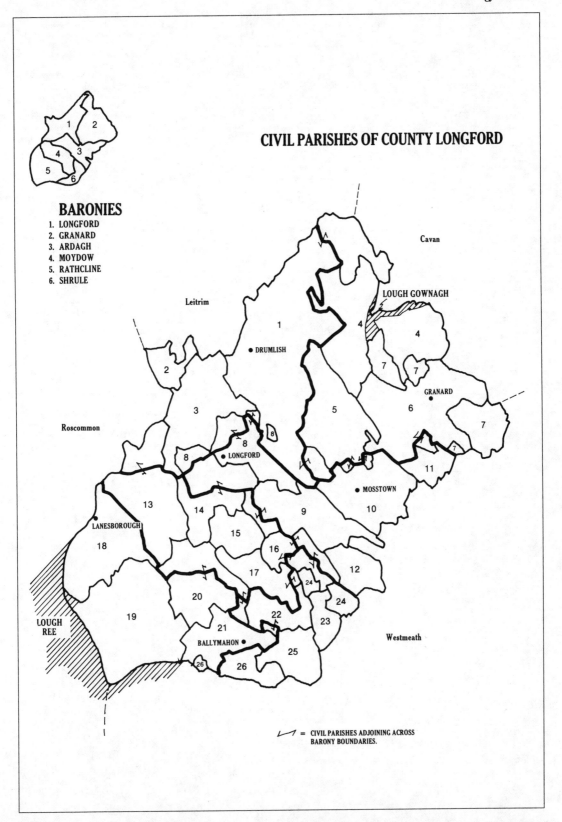

CIVIL PARISHES OF COUNTY LONGFORD

BARONIES
1. LONGFORD
2. GRANARD
3. ARDAGH
4. MOYDOW
5. RATHCLINE
6. SHRULE

Cavan

Leitrim

LOUGH GOWNAGH

• DRUMLISH

Roscommon

GRANARD •

• LONGFORD

Westmeath

LANESBOROUGH •

• MOSSTOWN

LOUGH
REE

BALLYMAHON •

⌐╱ = CIVIL PARISHES ADJOINING ACROSS
BARONY BOUNDARIES.

County Louth

A Brief History

Louth is the smallest county in Ireland comprising only 200,000 acres. It contains the towns of Drogheda, Dundalk, Ardee, Carlingford, and Castlebellingham.

Before the arrival of the Normans it formed part of the Kingdom of Oriel. The territory within the present county of Louth was then ruled by the O'Carrolls. Other Gaelic families in the area included McArdle, McSorly, (Mc)Barron, and McScanlan. The main town in the county, Drogheda, was founded by the Norse Vikings under Turgesius in 911.

Following the Norman invasion this area was overtaken in 1183 by John de Courcey, and the area now forming the county of Louth was immediately settled with English farmers. Among these were the families of Verdon, Bellew, Taaffe, Dowdall, Peppard, and Plunkett. The county was one of the first four established in 1210 by King John of England.

Louth was part of the "Pale," the English controlled part of Ireland, for most of the succeeding centuries and was fortified against attack from the surrounding areas. In the rebellion of O'Neill and the Ulster chieftains in the 1590s the county was overrun but reverted to English control afterwards.

In the rebellion of the Catholic Confederacy of 1641 (see Co. Kilkenny), Drogheda was one of the rebel strongholds. In 1649 it was besieged by the army of Oliver Cromwell who, on its surrender, massacred 2,000 of the garrison of the town and transported the few survivors to the Barbadoes.

The county was less affected than many by the Great Famine of 1845-47. The population was 128,000 in 1845 and by 1851 it had fallen to 108,000. Around 14,000 people died between 1845 and 1850. Further thousands emigrated in this period and in the succeeding decades.

The county is agriculture-based and also has major brewing, fishing, cement, and shipping industries. The current population is around 90,000.

Census and Census Substitutes

1600

"Gentlemen of Co. Louth." *Louth Arch. J.* 4 (4) (1919/20): 308-10 (names, residence, and some biographical details).

1659

"Census" of Ireland. Edited by S. Pender. Dublin: Stationery Office, 1939; SLC film 924648.

"Rent Roll of Some Parts of Dundalk Town and Adjoining Lands." *Louth Arch. J.* 19 (1)

(1977): 24-58 (lists tenants, subtenants, description of property, and rent).

1659-60

"Census of Louth County and Drogheda" (based on Poll money returns). *Louth Arch. J.* 1 (2) (1905): 61-73 (gives townlands, tituladoes, numbers of English and Irish, and principal Irish names in each barony).

1663-64

"Hearth Money Rolls – Baronies of Ferrard, Ardee, Louth, and Dundalk" (part). *Louth Arch. J.* 6 (4) (1928): 181-89.

"Hearth Money Roll for Drogheda." *Louth Arch. J.* 6 (2) (1926): 79-88.

"Hearth Money Roll for Orior Barony." *Louth Arch. J.* 7 (3) (1931): 419-31.

1664-66

"Hearth Money Roll for Barony of Dundalk." *Louth. Arch. J.* 7 (4) (1932): 500-15; SLC film 990411. Supplement in *Louth Arch. J.* 12 (4): 276-77.

1666-67

"Hearth Money Roll of Dunleer Parish." *Ir. Gen.* 4 (2) (1969): 142-44.

1683

"Co. Louth Brewers and Retailers." *Louth Arch. J.* 3 (3) (1914): 261-66 (names and barony/town of residence).

"Drogheda Trade and Customs Records." *Louth Arch. J.* 3 (1) (1912): 83-104; 3 (3) (1914): 250-58 (lists names of merchants).

1715

"Freemen of the Corporation of Dunleer." *Ir. Gen.* 4 (1): 10-13; SLC film 100225.

1739-41

"Corn Census of Co. Louth." *Louth. Arch. J.* 11 (4) (1948): 254-86; SLC film 990411 (lists over 1,600 persons, with addresses and their stock of corn).

1760

"Census of Ardee Parish." *Ir. Gen.* 3 (5): 179-84.

1765

"Tenants of Bayly Estate, Lordship of O'Meath." *Louth Arch. J.* 18 (1) (1973): 43-45 (ninety names with notes in text).

1766

"Catholic and Protestants in Ardee and United Parishes" (parishes of Ardee, Ballymachkinny, *Beaulieu, Carlingford,* Charlestown, Clonkeehan, *Darver,* Drogheda, *Dromiskin,* Kildemock, Killeshiel, *Louth,* Mapestown, *Phillipstown,* Shanlis, Smarmore, Stickallen, *Tallonstown* and *Termonfecken*). PRO 1A 41 100; SLC film 990411 (except Charlestown, Clonkeehan, Killeshiel and Mapestown).

Parish of Creggan. In Rev. L. P. Murray, *History of the Parish of Creggan.* Dundalk, 1940; *Louth Arch. J.* 8 (2) (1934): 156-62; PRO 1A 46 49.

"Census of Louth Parishes" (parishes *italicized* above). *Louth Arch. J.* 14 (2) (1958): 103-17.

"Families Around Ardee" (census of parishes of Ardee, Kildemock, Shanlis, Smarmore, Stichillen). *Louth Arch. J.* 10 (1) (1941): 72-76.

1775

"Catholic Qualification Roll Extracts" (forty-nine names, addresses, and occupations). 59th Report DKPRI: 50-84.

1777

"Jurors of Co. Louth." *Louth Arch. J.* 6 (4) (1928): 275-76 (thirty-seven names and addresses).

1779-81

"Rental and Accounts of Collon Estate (Hon. John Foster)." *Louth Arch. J.* 10 (3) (1943): 222-29 (lists tenants by townland, holdings, etc.).

1782-88

"Tenants on 2 Clanbrassil Estate Maps of Dundalk." *Louth Arch. J.* 15 (1) (1961): 39-87 (gives tenants on 425 holdings in twenty-five townlands around Dundalk and tenants of 305 holdings in the town with description of holdings).

1786-92

"Cess Payers in Dunleer Union" (i.e., parishes of Dunleer, Cappagh, Drumcar, Dysart, Moylary and Monasterboice). *Louth Arch. J.* 9 (1) (1937-40): 42-45.

1791

"Names of Landholders in the Parish of Dromiskin." In Rev. J. B. Leslie, *History of Kilsaran Union of Parishes.* Dundalk, 1908.

1798-1802

"Voters List of Drogheda." *Louth Arch. J.* 20: 319-33.

1801

"Tithe Applotment Survey of the Parishes of Stabannon and Roodstown." In Rev. J. B. Leslie, *History of Kilsaran Union of Parishes.* Dundalk, 1908.

1802

"Protestant Parishioners of Carlingford." *Louth Arch. J.* 16 (3) (1967): 161-62.

1809

"Tenants in Culver House Park, Drogheda." *Louth Arch. J.* 11 (3) (1947): 206-08 (lists thirty tenants and addresses, with map).

1810

"Tenants List for Anglesey Estate" (17 townlands in parish of Carlingford (name, townland, lease status, etc.). *Louth Arch. J.* 12 (2) (1950): 136-43.

1810-17

"Tenants on Caraher of Cardistown Potato Land." *Louth Arch. J.* 16 (3) (1967): 177-83.

1821

Registered Freeholders of Co. Louth. Dublin, 1820; NLI (gives name, residence, location of freehold, and landlords name).

1823-38

Tithe Applotment Survey (see p. xxvi).

1830

"Subscribers to School at Drakestown" (parish of Kildemock). *Louth Arch. J.* 12 (1) (1949): 38 (fifty-two names and addresses).

1832-36

"List of Holders of, and Applicants for, Licenses to Sell Liquor in Drogheda and Dundalk" (names and addresses). *Parl. Papers* 1837, 13 (2): Appendix 10.

1834

"Census of the Parish of Tallanstown." *Louth Arch. J.* 14 (1) (1957): 14-25; SLC film 990411 (gives householders in each townland and number of Catholics and Protestants in each house).

1837

"Occupants of Drogheda, Arranged by Street Within Each Parish, Giving Description of Premises and Valuation." *Parl. Papers* 1837, 11 (2): 265-71.

"Tithe Census of Parishes of Kilsaran and Gormanstown." *Louth Arch J.* 12 (3) (1951): 197-204 (landlords names in each townland). Addendum in 12 (4) (1952): 281.

"Occupants of Dundalk Arranged by Street, Giving Valuation of Property." *Parl. Papers* 1837, 11 (2): 272-79.

"List of Those Made Freemen of Drogheda and Dundalk Since 1831" (names, occupations, and addresses). *Parl. Papers* 1837, 11 (1): Appendix B1; 1837/38, 13 (2): Appendix 3.

1838

"Lists of Marksmen (illiterate voters) in Drogheda and Dundalk" (names, addresses, and occupations). *Parl. Papers* 1837, 11 (1): Appendix A3; 1837/38, 13 (2): Appendix 4.

"Tenants on Balfour Estates" (part of Ardee; townlands of Dromin, Dunbin, Hacklim, Listulk, Keeron, Little Grange, Mellifont, Sheepgrange). *Louth Arch. J.* 12 (3) (1951): 188-90.

1847

"Voters Lists for Borough of Dundalk." *Louth Arch. J.* 16 (4) (1968): 224-32 (names, addresses, occupations, and political persuasion).

1852

"Tenants on McClintock Estate, Drucear." *Louth Arch. J.* 16 (4) (1968): 230-32 (114 names and addresses; mainly townlands of

Drumcar, Greenmount, Adamstown, Annagassan, and Dillonstown).

"Families in the Townlands of Mosstown and Phillipstown (parish of Mosstown)." *Louth Arch. J.* 18 (3) (1975): 232-37; SLC film 990411 (lists thirty-eight families including names, ages, and notes on each).

List of Electors of Co. Louth who voted in the general election of 1852. NLI ms. 1660.

1854
Griffith's Valuation (See p. xxvii).

1856
"Tenants on Anglesey Estate" (parish of Carlingford: twenty-two townlands). *Louth Arch. J.* 12 (2) (1950): 143-51.

1865
Parliamentary Register of Workers for Co. Louth, Showing Landlords and Their Tenants on the Register. Dublin, 1865; NLI (gives tenants name, address, and landlord in each Barony).

1901
Census. PRO.

1911
Census. PRO.

Church Records

Church of Ireland
(shows starting date of record)

Parish: **Ardee**
Existing Records: b. 1735; m. 1744; d. 1732
Status: LC

Parish: **Ballymakenny**
Status: Lost

Parish: **Barronstown**
Status: Lost

Parish: **Beaulieu**
Status: Lost

Parish: **Carlingford**
Status: Lost

Parish: **Carlingford Rathcorr**
Status: Lost

Parish: **Carrick** or **Carrick-baggot** (see Rathdrumin)

Parish: **Charlestown**
Existing Records: b. 1822; m. 1822; d. 1822 (b.1822-36, m. 1824-1911, d. 1823-1912 in printed index)
Status: LC

Parish: **Clonkeen**
Status: Lost

Parish: **Clonmore**
Status: Lost

Parish: **Collon**
Existing Records: b. 1790; m. 1790; d. 1790
Status: LC

Parish: **Dromiskin**
Status: Lost

Parish: **Drumcar**
Existing Records: b. 1841; m. 1841; d. 1841
Status: LC

Parish: **Dunany**
Status: Lost

Parish: **Dundalk**
Existing Records: b. 1729; m. 1755; d. 1727
Status: LC

Parish: **Dunleer**
Status: Lost

Parish: **Faughart**
Status: Lost

Parish: **Haggardstown**
Status: Lost

Parish: **Haynestown**
Status: Lost

Parish: **Killanney**
Existing Records: b. 1825; m. 1825; d. 1825
Status: LC

Parish: **Killencoole**
Status: Lost

Parish: **Louth**
Status: Lost

Parish: **Mansfieldstown**
Status: Lost

Parish: **Moylary**
Status: Lost

Parish: **Omeath**
Status: Lost

Parish: **Rathdrumin**
Status: Lost

Parish: **St. Mary, Drogheda**
Existing Records: b. 1763; m. 1763; d. 1763
Missing Dates: b. 1775-1820; m. 1775-1820; d. 1775-1820

Parish: **St. Peter, Drogheda**
Existing Records: b. 1654; m. 1654; d. 1654
Missing Dates: b. 1747-1772; m. 1747-1772; d. 1747-1772
Status: LC

Parish: **Stabannon**
Status: Lost

Parish: **Stoneborough**
Existing Records: b. 1802; m. 1821; d. 1826
Status: LC

Parish: **Termonfeckin**
Status: Lost

Parish: **Tullyallen** and **Mellifont**
Existing Records: b. 1812; m. 1815; d. 1814

Presbyterian

Parish: **Corvally** (Dundalk)
Starting date: 1840

Parish: **Dundalk**
Starting date: 1819

Roman Catholic

Civil Parish: **Ardee**
Map Grid: 29
RC Parish: Ardee
Diocese: AM
Earliest Record: b. 4.1763; m. 8.1769; d. 7.1802
Missing Dates: b. 10.1810-4.1821; m. 10.1810-4.1821, ends 2.1826; d. 10.1810-3.1821, ends 2.1825
Parish Address: Rev. Peter Shields, PP, Ardee, Co. Louth

Civil Parish: **Ballybarrack**
Map Grid: 14
RC Parish: Kilkerley, see Dunbin
Diocese: AM

Civil Parish: **Ballyboys**
Map Grid: 3
RC Parish: Lordship, see Ballymascanlon
Diocese: AM

Civil Parish: **Ballymakenny**
Map Grid: 62
RC Parish: part Monasterboice; part Termonfeckin
Diocese: AM

Civil Parish: **Ballymascanlon**
Map Grid: 1
RC Parish: Lordship and Ballymascanlon; also part Faughart
Diocese: AM
Earliest Record: b. 1.1838; m. 1.1838
Parish Address: Rev. John Keelan, PP, Ravensdale, Dundalk, Co. Louth

Civil Parish: **Barronstown**
Map Grid: 10
RC Parish: Kilkerley, see Dunbin
Diocese: AM

Civil Parish: **Beaulieu**
Map Grid: 61
RC Parish: see Termonfeckin
Diocese: AM

Civil Parish: **Cappoge**
Map Grid: 38
RC Parish: see Dunleer
Diocese: AM

Civil Parish: **Carlingford**
Map Grid: 2
RC Parish: Carlingford and Cloghorny
Diocese: AM
Earliest Record: b. 4.1835; m. 4.1835; d. 4.1835
Missing Dates: d. 8.1848-10.1867
Parish Address: Rev. Patrick McVeigh, PP, Carlingford, Co. Louth

Civil Parish: **Carrickbaggot**
Map Grid: 51
RC Parish: Clogherhead, see Clogher
Diocese: AM

Civil Parish: **Castletown**
Map Grid: 11
RC Parish: see Dundalk
Diocese: AM

Civil Parish: **Charlestown**
Map Grid: 27
RC Parish: see Tallanstown
Diocese: AM

Civil Parish: **Clogher**
Map Grid: 57
RC Parish: Clogherhead (Walshestown and Clogher)
Diocese: AM
Earliest Record: b. 11.1744; m. 2.1742
Missing Dates: b. 10.1777-4.1780, 12.1799-3.1833, 10.1836-8.1837; m. 8.1771-4.1780, 9.1799-4.1833, 10.1836-8.1837
Parish Address: Rev. William Murtagh, PP, Clogherhead, Drogheda, Co. Louth

Civil Parish: **Clonkeehan**
Map Grid: 21
RC Parish: see Tallanstown
Diocese: AM

Civil Parish: **Clonkeen**
Map Grid: 26
RC Parish: see Tallanstown
Diocese: AM

Civil Parish: **Clonmore**
Map Grid: 46
RC Parish: Togher
Diocese: AM
Earliest Record: b. 11.1791; m. 7.1791
Missing Dates: b. 4.1828-8.1869; m. 3.1828-2.1873
Parish Address: Rev. Turlough Connolly, PP, Togher, Drogheda, Co. Louth

Civil Parish: **Collon**
Map Grid: 48
RC Parish: Collon
Diocese: AM
Earliest Record: b. 4.1789; m. 1.1789
Missing Dates: b. 3.1807-8.1819; m. 2.1807-12.1817, 9.1845-3.1848
Parish Address: Rev. P. McDonnell, PP, Collon, Drogheda, Co. Louth

Civil Parish: **Creggan**
Map Grid: 6
RC Parish: see Co. Armagh
Diocese: AM

Civil Parish: **Darver**
Map Grid: 20
RC Parish: see Dromiskin
Diocese: AM

Civil Parish: **Dromin**
Map Grid: 37
RC Parish: see Dunleer
Diocese: AM

Civil Parish: **Dromiskin**
Map Grid: 19
RC Parish: Darver (Dromiskin)
Diocese: AM
Earliest Record: b. 6.1787; m. 7.1787
Missing Dates: m. 6.1836-5.1837

Parish Address: Rev. Michael Dorman, PP, Dromiskin, Dundalk, Co. Louth

Civil Parish: **Drumcar**
Map Grid: 35
RC Parish: Togher, see Clonmore
Diocese: AM

Civil Parish: **Drumshallon**
Map Grid: 55
RC Parish: part Monasterboice; part Termonfeckin
Diocese: AM

Civil Parish: **Dunany**
Map Grid: 43
RC Parish: Togher, see Clonmore
Diocese: AM

Civil Parish: **Dunbin**
Map Grid: 13
RC Parish: Kilkerley (Haggardstown)
Diocese: AM
Earliest Record: b. 1.1752; m. 1.1752; d. 1.1752
Missing Dates: d. 3.1806-9.1831, ends 8.1838
Parish Address: Rev. Michael Murtagh, PP, Kilkerley, Dundalk, Co. Louth

Civil Parish: **Dundalk**
Map Grid: 12
RC Parish: Dundalk
Diocese: AM
Earliest Record: b. 8.1790; m. 8.1790; d. 8.1790
Missing Dates: b. 9.1802-5.1814; m. 11.1802-10.1817, ends 8.1831; d. ends 11.1802
Parish Address: Rev. S. McCartan, PP, St. Patrick's Presbytery, Roden Place, Dundalk, Co. Louth

Civil Parish: **Dunleer**
Map Grid: 44
RC Parish: Dunleer
Diocese: AM
Earliest Record: b. 10.1847; m. 1.1848; d. 12.1847
Missing Dates: d. 12.1858-1.1877
Parish Address: Rev. John Mulgrew, PP, Parochial House, Dunleer, Co. Louth

Civil Parish: **Dysart**
Map Grid: 45

RC Parish: Togher, see Clonmore
Diocese: AM

Civil Parish: **Faughart**
Map Grid: 5
RC Parish: Faughart
Diocese: AM
Earliest Record: b. 4.1851; m. 4.1851
Parish Address: Rev. Sean Quinn, PP, St. Brigids, Kilcurry, Dundalk, Co. Louth

Civil Parish: **Gernonstown**
Map Grid: 32
RC Parish: see Kilsaran
Diocese: AM

Civil Parish: **Haggardstown**
Map Grid: 15
RC Parish: Kilkerley, see Dunbin
Diocese: AM

Civil Parish: **Haynestown**
Map Grid: 16
RC Parish: Kilkerley, see Dunbin
Diocese: AM

Civil Parish: **Inishkeen**
Map Grid: 9
RC Parish: see Co. Monaghan
Diocese: AM

Civil Parish: **Kane**
Map Grid: 8
RC Parish: see Dundalk
Diocese: AM

Civil Parish: **Kildemock**
Map Grid: 40
RC Parish: see Ardee
Diocese: AM

Civil Parish: **Killincoole**
Map Grid: 18
RC Parish: Darver, see Dromiskin
Diocese: AM

Civil Parish: **Kilsaran**
Map Grid: 31
RC Parish: Kilsaran
Diocese: AM
Earliest Record: b. 1.1809; m. 1.1809

Missing Dates: b. 5.1824-8.1831, 6.1836-7.1853;
    m. 10.1826-8.1831, 11.1836-9.1853
Parish Address: Rev. Francis Donnelly, PP, Kil-
    saran, Castlebellingham, Co. Louth

Civil Parish: **Louth**
Map Grid: 17
RC Parish: Louth
Diocese: AM
Earliest Record: b. 3.1833; m. 4.1833
Missing Dates: b. 9.1871-10.1873
Parish Address: Rev. John Finn, PP, Parochial
    House, Louth, Dundalk, Co. Louth

Civil Parish: **Mansfieldstown**
Map Grid: 22
RC Parish: Darver, see Dromiskin
Diocese: AM

Civil Parish: **Mapastown**
Map Grid: 28
RC Parish: see Ardee
Diocese: AM

Civil Parish: **Marlestown**
Map Grid: 50
RC Parish: Clogherhead, see Clogher
Diocese: AM

Civil Parish: **Mayne**
Map Grid: 56
RC Parish: Clogherhead, see Clogher
Diocese: AM

Civil Parish: **Monasterboice**
Map Grid: 54
RC Parish: Monasterboice
Diocese: AM
Earliest Record: b. 1.1834; m. 10.1830; d. 9.1830
Missing Dates: d. ends 1.1850
Parish Address: Rev. John Hanratty, PP,
    Fieldstown, Monasterboice, Drogheda, Co.
    Louth

Civil Parish: **Mosstown**
Map Grid: 41
RC Parish: see Dunleer
Diocese: AM

Civil Parish: **Mullary**
Map Grid: 49

RC Parish: see Monasterboice
Diocese: AM

Civil Parish: **Parsonstown**
Map Grid: 53
RC Parish: Clogherhead, see Clogher
Diocese: AM

Civil Parish: **Philipstown (1) (near Bar-
    ronstown)**
Map Grid: 7
RC Parish: Kilkerley, see Dunbin
Diocese: AM

Civil Parish: **Philipstown (2) (near Clonkeen)**
Map Grid: 24
RC Parish: see Tallanstown
Diocese: AM

Civil Parish: **Philipstown (3) (near Drogheda)**
Map Grid: 59
RC Parish: see St. Peter's, Drogheda
Diocese: AM

Civil Parish: **Port**
Map Grid: 47
RC Parish: Togher, see Clonmore
Diocese: AM

Civil Parish: **Rathdrumin**
Map Grid: 52
RC Parish: Clogherhead, see Clogher
Diocese: AM

Civil Parish: **Richardstown**
Map Grid: 34
RC Parish: see Dunleer
Diocese: AM

Civil Parish: **Roche**
Map Grid: 4
RC Parish: see Dundalk
Diocese: AM

Civil Parish: **St. Mary's, Drogheda** (see also Co.
    Meath)
Map Grid: 64
RC Parish: Drogheda
Diocese: AM

Civil Parish: **St. Peter's, Drogheda**
Map Grid: 63
RC Parish: Drogheda
Diocese: AM
Earliest Record: b. 1.1744; m. 11.1815
Missing Dates: b. 5.1757-8.1764, 10.1771-
4.1777, 2.1778-6.1781, 4.1795-10.1803,
12.1804-11.1815
Parish Address: Rev. James Lennon, PP, St.
Peter's, Drogheda, Co. Louth

Civil Parish: **Salterstown**
Map Grid: 42
RC Parish: Togher, see Clonmore
Diocese: AM

Civil Parish: **Shanlis**
Map Grid: 36
RC Parish: see Ardee
Diocese: Am

Civil Parish: **Smarmore**
Map Grid: 39
RC Parish: see Ardee
Diocese: AM

Civil Parish: **Stabannon**
Map Grid: 30
RC Parish: see Kilsaran
Diocese: AM

Civil Parish: **Stickillin**
Map Grid: 33
RC Parish: see Ardee
Diocese: AM

Civil Parish: **Tallanstown**
Map Grid: 25
RC Parish: Tallanstown
Diocese: AM
Earliest Record: b. 11.1817; m. 4.1804
Missing Dates: b. 4.1825-9.1830; m. 6.1863-
8.1867
Parish Address: Rev. Shane Cullen, PP,
Reaghstown, Ardee, Co. Louth

Civil Parish: **Termonfeckin**
Map Grid: 60
RC Parish: Termonfeckin
Diocese: AM
Earliest Record: b. 4.1823; m. 4.1823; d. 1.1827

Missing Dates: d. ends 10.1833
Parish Address: Rev. Patrick Morgan, PP, Termonfeckin, Drogheda, Co. Louth

Civil Parish: **Tullyallen (1)** (see also Co. Meath)
Map Grid: 58
RC Parish: Tullyallen, Kilichel, Donoghmore
and Killishall, see also Mellifont below
Diocese: AM
Earliest Record: b. m. and d. 1.1816
Missing Dates: b. 1.1834-3.1837, 8.1844-8.1845;
m. 1.1834-4.1837, 7.1844-9.1845; d. 5.1834-
3.1837, 8.1844-8.1845
Parish Address: Rev. Padraic O'Kelly, PP,
Parochial House, Tullyallen, Drogheda, Co.
Louth

Civil Parish: **Tullyallen (2)**
Map Grid: 58
RC Parish: Mellifont
Diocese: AM
Earliest Record: b. 12.1821; m. 12.1821
Parish Address: see Tullyallen (1)

Commercial and Social Directories

1820
J. Pigot's *Commercial Directory of Ireland*
contains information on the gentry, nobility,
and traders in and around the towns of
Drogheda and Dundalk.

1824
J. Pigot's *City of Dublin & Hibernian Provincial Directory* includes traders, nobility,
gentry, and clergy lists of Ardee, Carlingford,
Castlebellingham, Drogheda, and Dundalk.

1830
McCabe's *Directory of Drogheda.*

1846
Slater's *National Commercial Directory of
Ireland* lists nobility, clergy, traders, etc., in
Ardee and Louth, Carlingford, Castlebellin-
gham and Dunleer, Drogheda, and Dundalk.

1856
Slater's *Royal National Commercial Directory of Ireland* lists nobility, gentry, clergy,

traders, etc., in Ardee and Louth, Carlingford, Castlebellingham and Dunleer, Drogheda, and Dundalk.

1886
G.H. Bassett's *Louth County Guide and Directory.*

1870
Slater's *Directory of Ireland* contains trade, nobility, and clergy lists for Ardee, Carlingford, Castlebellingham, Drogheda, and Dundalk.

1881
Slater's *Royal National Commercial Directory of Ireland* contains lists of traders, clergy, nobility, and farmers in adjoining parishes of the towns of Ardee and Louth, Carlingford, Castlebellingham and Dunleer, Drogheda, and Dundalk.

1894
Slater's *Royal National Directory of Ireland* lists traders, police, teachers, farmers, and private residents in each of the towns, villages, and parishes of the county.

1896
Tempest's *Almanac and Directory of Dundalk.* The 1890-95 editions have no lists of traders. Published annually from 1896.

Family History

Amory, T.C. *Materials for a History of the Family of Sullivan . . . of Ardee, Ireland.* Cambridge, Mass., 1893.

"The Byrnes of Co. Louth." *J. Louth Arch. & Hist. Soc.* 2 (1908-11): 45-49.

"The Clinton Family of Co. Louth." *J. Louth Arch. & Hist. Soc.* 3 (1912): 1-15.

"Clinton Records." *J. Louth Arch. & Hist. Soc.* 12 (1950): 109-16.

"The Dawsons of Ardee." *J. Louth. Arch. Hist. Soc.* 8 (1933): 22-33.

"The De Verdons of Louth." *R.S.A.I.* 25 (1895): 317-28.

"The De Verdons of Louth." *R.S.A.I.* 29 (1899): 417-19.

"Family Names in Louth." *J. Louth Arch. & Hist. Soc.* 1 (3) (1906): 64-76.

"Genealogy of a North Louth Family (Murphy)." *J. Louth Arch. & Hist. Soc.* 18 (2) (1974): 105-09.

"In Search of a Louth Family, the Nearys." *J. Louth Arch. & Hist. Soc.* 15 (1968): 239-50.

"Moore of Mooremount." Pedigree in *Swanzy Notebooks.* RCB Library, Dublin.

"The Moores of the City of Drogheda." *Gen.* 33, N.S. (1916): 127-28.

O'Boyle, Edward. *The Warren Saga.* Londonderry, 1947.

"Potters of Ardee." *J. Louth Arch. & Hist. Soc.* 18 (2) (1974): 165-70.

"Smiths of Cos. Louth and Down." Pedigree in *Swanzy Notebooks.* RCB Library, Dublin.

"Some Early Documents Relating to English Uriel, and the Towns of Drogheda and Dundalk." In Charles McNeill, *The Draycott Family;* and *J. Louth Arch. Hist. Soc.* 5 (1924): 270-75.

"Some Notes on the Family of Bellew of Thomastown, Co. Louth." *J. Louth Arch. & Hist. Soc.* 5 (1923): 193-97.

"Some Notes on the Family of Warren of Warrenstown, Co. Louth." *J. Louth Arch. & Hist. Soc.* 4 (1916): 26-34.

"Taaffe of Co. Louth." *J. Louth Arch. & Hist. Soc.* 14 (1960): 55-67.

Warren, Thomas. *History of the Warren Family.* 1902.

Gravestone Inscriptions

Ardee: *Ir. Gen.* 3 (1) (1956): 36-40.

Ballymakenny: *Seanchas Ardmhacha* 2 (1) (1983/84): 107-27.

Ballymascanlon: *Louth Arch. J.* 17 (4) (1972): 215-27.

Ballypousta (Kildemock, CI): *Louth Arch. J.* 12 (1) (1949): 37.

Bannteale – see Rathdrummin.

Beaulieu: *Louth Arch. J.* 10 (1): 1981.

Cappoge – see Dysart.

Carlingford: *Louth Arch. J.* 19 (2) (1978): 149-65.

Castlebellingham: Leslie, Rev. James B. *History of Kilsaran Union of Parishes in the Co. of Louth.* 1908.

Charlestown: L'Estrange, G.W. *Notes and Jottings Concerning the Parish of Charlestown Union.* 1912.

Clonkeen: L'Estrange, G.W. *Notes and Jottings Concerning the Parish of Charlestown Union.* 1912.

Clonmore (near Dunleer): *Louth Arch. J.* 20 (2) 1982.

Dromiskin: Leslie, Rev. James B. *History of Kilsaran Union of Parishes in the Co. of Louth.* 1908.

Dundalk (St. Leonard's Garden): *Irish American Genealogist* (1978): 174-75, 179-80.

Dysart, Cappoge, and Drumshallon: *Louth Arch. J.* 19 (3) (1979): 240-48.

Drumshallon – see Dysart.

Faughart: *Tombstone Inscriptions from Fochart.* Dundalgan Press, 1968.

Faughart: Maciomhair, Rev. D. *Urnai.* Dundalk: Dundalgan Press, 1969; SLC 94.5 A150 (cemetery).

Kildemock: *Louth Arch J.* 13 (1) (1953): 81-82.

Killanny: *Clogher Record* 6 (1) 1966.

Kilsaran: Leslie, Rev. James B. *History of Kilsaran Union of Parishes in the Co. of Louth.* 1908.

Louth Village: "St. Mary's Abbey." *Louth Arch. J.* 19 (4) (1980): 297-317.

Manfieldstown: Leslie, Rev. James B. *History of Kilsaran Union of Parishes in the Co. of Louth.* 1908.

Newtownstalaban: *Louth Arch. J.* 17 (2) 1970.

Rathdrumin and Banntaaffe (Glebe Townland): *Louth Arch. J.* 19 (1) (1977): 74-76.

Seatown, Dundalk: *Tempest's Annual Directory and Guide for the Town of Dundalk.* Dundalgan Press, 1967, 1971-72.

Stabannon: Leslie, Rev. James B. *History of Kilsaran Union of Parishes in the Co. of Louth.* 1908.

Stagrennan: *J. Old Drogheda Soc.* 2 (1977): 31-36.

Tullyallen: *Seanchas Ardmhacha* 8 (2) (1977): 308-43.

Newspapers

Title: *Drogheda Argus* (continued as *Argus* in 1951)
Published in: Drogheda, 1835-current
NLI Holdings: 1.1859-12.1913; 7.1927-in progress
BL Holdings: 9.1835-12.1921; 1.1923-11.1936

Title: *Drogheda Conservative Journal*
Published in: Drogheda, 1837-48
NLI Holdings: 6.1837-12.1848
BL Holdings: 6.1837-12.1848

Title: *Drogheda Independent*
Published in: Drogheda, 1884-current
NLI Holdings: odd numbers 12.1884-8.1889; 1889-in progress
BL Holdings: 1.1890-in progress

Title: *Drogheda Journal*
Published in: Drogheda, 1788-1843
NLI Holdings: 1.1823-5.1840; 7.1841-3.1843
BL Holdings: 1.1823-5.1840; 7.1841-3.1843

Title: *Dundalk and Newry Express*
Published in: Dundalk, 1860-70
BL Holdings: 6-10.1860; 10-11.1861; 12.1861-1.1870

Title: *Dundalk Democrat*
Published in: Dundalk, 1849-current

NLI Holdings: 10.1849-in progress
BL Holdings: 10.1849-10.1948 (except 1926)

Title: *Dundalk Examiner*
Published in: Dundalk, 1881-1960
NLI Holdings: odd numbers 1920; 1929-30
BL Holdings: 1.1881-6.1930

Title: *Dundalk Herald*
Published in: Dundalk, 1868-1921
NLI Holdings: 1880 (two issues)
BL Holdings: 10.1868-1.1921

Title: *The Conservative* (continued as *Drogheda Conservative* in 1864)
Published in: Drogheda, 1849-1908
NLI Holdings: odd numbers 4.1855-3.1901
BL Holdings: 6.1849-10.1908

Wills and Administrations

A discussion of the types of records, where they are held, their availability and value is given in the Wills section of the Introduction. The availability of prerogative wills, administrations, and marriage license records is also described in the relevant parts of the same section. Where available, published sources of these records are given in the Miscellaneous Sources section.

Pre-1858 Wills and Administrations

Prerogative Wills. see p. xli.
Consistorial Wills. County Louth is mainly in the diocese of Armagh with two parishes in Clogher. The guide to Catholic parish records in this chapter shows the diocese to which each civil parish belonged. The wills of residents of each diocese were usually proven within that diocese (see the Wills section for exceptions). The following records survive:

Wills. see p. xxxvii. There are eighty-six wills in the Townley Hall papers. NLI D 15093-15178 .

"Indexed List of Wills of Dundalk Residents." *Louth Arch. J.* 10 (2) (1942): 113-

15 (some 250 names, addresses, dates, and few occupations).

Abstracts. see p. xxxvii.

Indexes. Armagh – see Co. Armagh. Clogher – see Co. Monaghan.

Post-1858 Wills and Administrations

This county was served by the District Registry of Armagh. The surviving records are kept in the PRONI.

Marriage Licenses

Indexes. Armagh (1727-1845). PRO; SLC film 100859-860. Clogher (1709-1866). PRO; SLC film 100862; see also Miscellaneous Sources below.

Miscellaneous Sources

"A Census of Ardee, Co. Louth in 1760." *Ir. Gen.* 3 (5): 179-84.

"Clergy and Churchwardens of Termonfeckin Parish (1725-1804)." *Louth Arch. J.* 17 (2) (1970): 84-86.

D'Alton, John. *A History of Drogheda.* 2 vols. 1844.

"Dowdall Deeds." Irish Manuscripts Commission. Dublin: Stationery Office, 1960.

"Drogheda Census, 1798" (numbers on each street). *Louth Arch. J.* 17 (2) (1970): 91-95.

"Farm Account Books from Gaulstown, Monasterboice 1802-1860." *Louth Arch. J.* 17 (4) (1972): 235-49 (lists over 200 names of labourers, tenants, etc., and financial dealings – including loans to send family members to America).

"Life and Times of Fr. Edmund Murphy, Killeavy 1680." *Louth Arch. J.* 7 (3) (1931): 336-81 (lists many residents of Killeavy RC parish).

"Old Title Deeds of Co. Louth." *Louth Arch. J.* 7 (2) (1930): 168-74; 7 (3) (1931): 402-05; 7 (4) (1932): 488-96; 8 (1) (1933): 52-60; 8 (2)

(1934): 193-209; 8 (3) (1935): 283-88; 10 (1) (1941): 63-66; 10 (3) (1943): 245-50; 11 (1) (1945): 58-62.

"Roll of the Sovereigns and Burgesses of Carlingford 1706-1828." *Louth Arch. J.* 3 (3) (1914): 273-82.

"Some (19) Dundalk leases (1715-1815)." *Louth Arch. J.* 6 (4) (1928): 213-28 (gives 1,544 tenants on the primates lands in Clonfeacle, Kilmore, O'Neilland, Deanery of Dundalk, Drumyskyn (Dromiskin), Primatestown, Kilmone, and the Newton of Monasterboyde).

"Title Deed Extracts: Drakestown and Kilpatrick (part of Kildemock) 1669-1852." *Louth Arch. J.* 12 (1) (1949): 61-81.

"Title Deed Extracts: Paughanstown, Hacklim and Roestown." *Louth Arch. J.* 12 (3) (1951): 157-96.

"Title Deed Extracts: Millockstown and Blakestown." *Louth Arch. J.* 13 (1) (1953): 102-23.

The Landless in Mid-nineteenth Century Louth." *Louth Arch. J.* 16 (2) (1966): 103-10.

"Volunteers, Militia, Yeomanry, and Orangemen (1726-1825)." *Louth Arch. J.* 18 (4) (1976): 279-94 (officers names).

Research Sources and Services

Journals

Co. Louth Archaeological & Historical Journal

Seanchas Ardmhacha

Clogher Record

Tempest's Annual

Libraries and Information Sources

Louth County Library, Chapel Street, Dundalk, Co. Louth Ph: (042) 35457

Research Services

See research services in Dublin, p. xliv

Societies

County Louth Archaeological & Historical Society, Mr. Noel Ross, 5 Oliver Plunkett Park, Dundalk, Co. Louth

Old Drogheda Society, Mrs. Moira Corcoran, 5 Brushrod Avenue, Drogheda, Co. Louth

Old Dundalk Society, Miss M. Wilson, 13 St. Mary's Road, Dundalk, Co. Louth

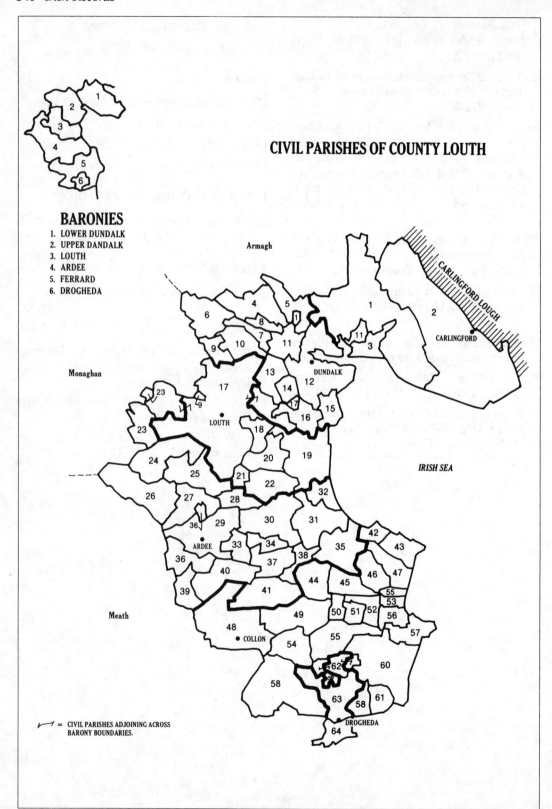

CIVIL PARISHES OF COUNTY LOUTH

BARONIES
1. LOWER DUNDALK
2. UPPER DANDALK
3. LOUTH
4. ARDEE
5. FERRARD
6. DROGHEDA

Armagh

Monaghan

Meath

CARLINGFORD LOUGH

CARLINGFORD

DUNDALK

LOUTH

IRISH SEA

ARDEE

COLLON

DROGHEDA

╱▔ = CIVIL PARISHES ADJOINING ACROSS
        BARONY BOUNDARIES.

County Mayo

A Brief History

Situated on the northwestern shore of Connaught, County Mayo contains the towns of Killala, Castlebar, Crossmolina, Westport, and Ballina.

The main Gaelic families in the area were O'Malley, O'Flaherty, McEvilly, O'Henaghan, and O'Flannery. Among the Norman families who settled in this county were the Burkes, Barretts, Nangles, Costelloes, and Jordans. Other septs related to these Norman families and now found in the county, include the McPhilbins, McAndrews, Prendergasts, and Fitzmaurice.

After the seventeenth-century redistribution of Mayo land to English adventurers, the major estate-holders included Browne, Altamont, and Cuffe. During the seventeenth century there were a few attempts to settle parts of Mayo with people from England or northern Ireland. One such settlement was that of the Mullett Peninsula with families from Ulster. Several of these, including the Dixons, established themselves in the area. Many families who were forced to leave the northern counties because of the sectarian fighting of the 1790s also settled in Mayo. These incidents have been relatively well documented.

In 1798 the French landed 1100 men in Mayo under General Humbert to assist the rebellion of United Irishmen. This invasion was too late to be effective, however, as the main rebellion had been defeated earlier in the year. Assisted by local rebels, this army took control of Mayo but was eventually defeated at Ballinamuck.

The land in Mayo is relatively poor. In spite of that the county was one of the most densely populated at the beginning of the nineteenth century when there were 474 people per square mile of arable land in the county. This dense population was very badly affected by the Great Famine of 1845-47. The population dropped from almost 390,000 in 1841 to 274,000 in 1851. Around 45,000 people died between 1845 and 1850, and huge numbers emigrated. Between 1850 and 1855 alone, over 21,000 people emigrated. By 1891 the population had dropped to 219,000 and is currently around 115,000.

Census and Census Substitutes

1641
Books of Survey & Distributions. Vol 2; SLC film 962524.

1783
"Register of the Householders of the Parish of Ballinrobe Showing Residence. *Anal. Hib.* 14: 113-17.

which they remained from the 26th of August to the 26th of September. The Earl of Lucan, the owner of the town, has a residence in the suburbs, but it does not possess any particular attractions.

It was market day at Castlebar when I arrived there, and I strolled for a couple of hours among the market people. Great numbers of women, holding a hank or two of yarn of their own spinning, stood in the streets and offered their trifling commodities for sale. Very few of those whom I addressed could speak English; but some of the men about, seeing the disadvantages under which I laboured, very obligingly stepped forward, and offered assistance as interpreters. This sort of politeness is common to the Irish. I ascertained that the women could not earn by spinning more than a penny or two-pence a day, and hundreds of them attended the market whose earnings for the whole week did not exceed sixpence or ninepence; yet notwithstanding this inadequate reward of long and hard labour, their honest countenances wore the habi-

tual impress of cheerfulness and perfect good humour. Scarcely any of the women had shoes, and I felt considerable alarm while threading my way through a dense crowd, lest I should step upon their feet.

The corn and meal were brought into the town by horses, mules, and asses, many of which remained in the market with their loads upon their backs. Oats were selling at 5d. and 6d. per stone. But little wheat is produced in the neighbourhood, nor is barley much grown, except to supply the potheen manufactories in the mountains. Rents are about 20s. an acre ; and wages from 6d. to 8d. a day ; but if regular work is afforded, 6d., without diet, is the usual amount. Although their agriculture and customs seem better adapted to the last century, yet if we may draw a comparison between their present practises, and the account given by Arthur Young in 1779, some improvement has actually taken place. "To Castlebar," says he, "over an indifferent country and a vile stony road ; about that town the husbandry is admirable. They have three customs,

A description of Fair Day in Castlebar, Co. Mayo, in 1835. From *The Miseries and Beauties of Ireland* by Jonathan Binns. London, 1837.

1796

"Lists of Catholics Emigrating from Ulster to Mayo" (arranged by parish and counties of origin, i.e., Antrim, Armagh, Cavan, Down, Fermanagh, Derry, Monaghan, and Tyrone). *Seanchas Ardmhacha* 3 (1) (1958): 17-50.

"Lists of Northern Catholics Recently Settled in Mayo Compiled by Landlords Browne, Altamont, and Cuffe" (gives 1,074, 116, and 167 names respectively). SPO Reb. Papers 620 (series for 1796).

1798

List of Persons Who Suffered Loss in '98 Rebellion. NLI JLB 94107 (approximately 650 names, addresses, and occupations).

1823-38

Tithe Applotment Survey (see p. xxvii).

1826-27

Mayo Assizes Quaere Book. NLI IR 94123 M3 (names contractors, public employees, jurymen, etc.).

1856-57

Griffith's Valuation (see p. xxvii).

1901

Census. PRO.

1911

Census. PRO.

Church Records

Church of Ireland
(shows starting date of record)

Parish: **Achill**
Existing Records: b. 1854; m. 1854; d. 1854
Status: LC

Parish: **Aghaslee**
Status: Lost

Parish: **Aughagower**
Existing Records: b. 1825; m. 1828; d. 1828
Status: PRO

Parish: **Balla**
Status: Lost

Parish: **Ballina** (see Kilmoremoy, RC section)

Parish: **Ballinakill**
Existing Records: b. 1852; d. 1852
Status: LC

Parish: **Ballincholla** or **The Neale**
Existing Records: b. 1811; m. 1810; d. 1813
Status: LC

Parish: **Ballinrobe**
Existing Records: b. 1796; m. 1796; d. 1796
Status: LC

Parish: **Ballycroy** (Kilcommon Erris)
Status: Lost

Parish: **Ballyhane**
Status: Lost

Parish: **Ballyovie**
Staus: Lost

Parish: **Ballysakeery**
Existing Records: b. 1802; m. 1802; d. 1802
Status: LC

Parish: **Belcarra Church** (Drum Parish)
Status: Lost

Parish: **Belmullet** (see Kilcommon Erris)

Parish: **Binghamstown** (see Kilcommon Erris)

Parish: **Burriscarra** (see Ballyhane)

Parish: **Burrishoole**
Status: Lost

Parish: **Castlebar**
Status: Lost

Parish: **Castlemore**
Status: Lost

Parish: **Cong**
Existing Records: b. 1811; m. 1811; d. 1811
Status: LC

Parish: **Crossboyne**
Status: Lost

Parish: **Crossmolina**
Existing Records: b. 1768; m. 1768; d. 1768
Status: LC

Parish: **Drum** (see Belcarra)

Parish: **Dugort** (Achill)
Existing Records: b. 1838 (1866 missing);
   m. 1838; d. 1838
Status: LC

Parish: **Dunfeeny** and **Kilbride**
Status: Lost

Parish: **Kilcolman**
Status: Lost

Parish: **Kilcommon Erris**
Status: Lost

Parish: **Kilcommon** or **Hollymount Union**
Status: Lost

Parish: **Kilconduff**
Status: Lost

Parish: **Killala**
Existing Records: b. 1757; m. 1757; d. 1757
Status: LC

Parish: **Killedan**
Status: Lost

Parish: **Kilmainemore**
Existing Records: b. 1744; m. 1744; d. 1774; also
   Vestry Book, 1812-19, containing some
   entries of baptisms, marriages, and burials.
   1811-23
Missing Dates: b. 1779-1820; m. 1779-1820; d.
   1779-1820
Status: LC

Parish: **Kilmina**
Status: Lost

Parish: **Kilmore Erris** and **Kilcommon**
Status: Lost

Parish: **Knappagh**
Existing Records: b. 1855; d. 1855
Status: LC

Parish: **Lackan**
Status: Lost

Parish: **Louisburgh** (Burnlahinch)
Status: Lost

Parish: **Mayo**
Status: Lost

Parish: **Moygounagh** (see also Crossmolina)
Existing Records: b. 1856
Status: LC

Parish: **Straid** (see Templemore)

Parish: **Swineford** (see Kilconduff)

Parish: **Toomore** (see Straid)

Parish: **Templemore**
Existing Records: b. 1755; m. 1758; d. 1755
Status: LC

Parish: **Turlough** (see also Castlebar)
Existing Records: b. 1821; m. 1822; d. 1822
Status: LC

Parish: **Westport** or **Aughaval**
Existing Records: b. 1801; m. 1801; d. 1801
Status: LC

Presbyterian

Parish: **Dromore** (Ballina)
Starting Date: 1849

Roman Catholic

Civil Parish: **Achill**
Map Grid: 19
RC Parish: Achill
Diocese: TU
Earliest Record: b. 12.1867; m. 10.1867
Parish Address: Rev. Patrick Williams, PP, Achill Sound, Co. Mayo

Civil Parish: **Addergoole**
Map Grid: 16
RC Parish: Addergoole (Lahardane)
Diocese: KA
Earliest Record: b. 1.1840; m. 1.1840
Parish Address: Rev. James Boland, PP, Lahardane, Ballina, Co. Mayo

Civil Parish: **Aghagower**
Map Grid: 48
RC Parish: Aghagower (Westport)
Diocese: TU
Earliest Record: b. 4.1828; m. 11.1854
Missing Dates: b. 5.1836-3.1842
Parish Address: Rev. John Fitzgerald, PP, Aughagower, Westport, Co. Mayo

Civil Parish: **Aghamore**
Map Grid: 70
RC Parish: Aghamore
Diocese: TU
Earliest Record: b. 2.1864; m. 12.1864
Parish Address: Rev. Joseph Moran, PP, Aghamore, Ballyhaunis, Co. Mayo

Civil Parish: **Aglish**
Map Grid: 24
RC Parish: Aglish, Ballyheane, and Breaghwy
Diocese: TU
Earliest Record: b. 1.1838; m. 6.1824
Parish Address: Rev. Sean Blake, PP, Castlebar, Co. Mayo

Civil Parish: **Annagh**
Map Grid: 73
RC Parish: Ballyhaunis
Diocese: TU
Earliest Record: b. 11.1851; m. 6.1852
Parish Address: Rev. Patrick Costelloe, PP, Ballyhaunis, Co. Mayo

Civil Parish: **Ardagh**
Map Grid: 14
RC Parish: Ardagh
Diocese: KA
Earliest Record: b. 2.1870
Parish Address: Rev. James Nallen, PP, Ardagh, Ballina, Co. Mayo

Civil Parish: **Athymass**
Map Grid: 36
RC Parish: Attymass
Diocese: KA
Earliest Record: b. 6.1875; m. 2.1874
Parish Address: Rev. Thomas Gavigan, PP, Attymass, Ballina, Co. Mayo

Civil Parish: **Balla**
Map Grid: 59
RC Parish: Balla and Manulla
Diocese: TU
Earliest Record: b. 5.1837; m. 7.1837
Parish Address: Rev. Charles Scahill, PP, Balla, Co. Mayo

Civil Parish: **Ballinchalla**
Map Grid: 52
RC Parish: see Cong
Diocese: TU

Civil Parish: **Ballinrobe**
Map Grid: 50
RC Parish: Ballinrobe
Diocese: TU
Earliest Record: b. 8.1843; m. 10.1850
Missing Dates: 4.1856-1.1861; 4.1856-1.1861
Parish Address: Rev. Thomas Shannon, PP, Ballinrobe, Co. Mayo

Civil Parish: **Ballintober**
Map Grid: 30
RC Parish: Burriscarra and Ballintubber
Diocese: TU
Earliest Record: b. 9.1839; m. 9.1839
Parish Address: Rev. James Fitzsimon, PP, Carnacon, Claremorris, Co. Mayo

Civil Parish: **Ballyhean**
Map Grid: 27
RC Parish: see Aglish, etc.
Diocese: TU

Civil Parish: **Ballynahaglish**
Map Grid: 18
RC Parish: Backs (Rathduff)
Diocese: KA
Earliest Record: b. 8.1848; m. 12.1848
Missing Dates: b. 1860; m. 4.1860-1.1865,
12.1869-2.1874
Parish Address: Rev. James Gilvarry, Adm,
Knockmore, Ballina, Co. Mayo

Civil Parish: **Ballyovey**
Map Grid: 34
RC Parish: Partry, see Ballinrobe for pre-1869
Records
Diocese: TU
Earliest Record: b. 10.1869; m. 1.1870
Parish Address: Rev. Jarlath Waldron, PP,
Partry, Claremorris, Co. Mayo

Civil Parish: **Ballysakeery**
Map Grid: 12
RC Parish: Ballysakeery (Cooneal)
Diocese: KA
Earliest Record: b. 11.1843; m. 10.1843
Parish Address: Rev. George Curry, PP,
Cooneal, Ballina, Co. Mayo

Civil Parish: **Bekan**
Map Grid: 72
RC Parish: Bekan
Diocese: TU
Earliest Record: b. 8.1832; m. 5.1832
Missing Dates: b. 2.1844-12.1844; m. pages
missing
Parish Address: Rev. Edward McEllin, PP,
Bekan, Claremorris, Co. Mayo

Civil Parish: **Bohola**
Map Grid: 43
RC Parish: Bohola
Diocese: AC
Earliest Record: b. 10.1857; m. 10.1857
Parish Address: Rev. Padraic O'Fionnain, PP,
Bohola, Claremorris, Co. Mayo

Civil Parish: **Breaghwy**
Map Grid: 26
RC Parish: see Aglish, etc.
Diocese: TU

Civil Parish: **Burriscarra**
Map Grid: 31
RC Parish: Burriscarra, etc., see Ballintober
Diocese: TU

Civil Parish: **Burrishoole**
Map Grid: 20
RC Parish: Burrishoole (Newport)
Diocese: TU
Earliest Record: b. 1.1872
Parish Address: Rev. Michael Moran, PP, New-
port, Co. Mayo

Civil Parish: **Castlemore**
Map Grid: 69
RC Parish: see Balla
Diocese: TU

Civil Parish: **Cong** (see also Co. Galway)
Map Grid: 55
RC Parish: Cong and Neale
Diocese: TU
Earliest Record: b. 2.1870
Parish Address: Rev. Brendan Kavanagh, PP,
Cong, Co. Mayo

Civil Parish: **Crossboyne**
Map Grid: 63
RC Parish: Crossboyne and Tagheen
Diocese: TU
Earliest Record: b. 7.1862; m. 1.1877
Parish Address: Rev. John Glynn, PP,
Crossboyne, Claremorris, Co. Mayo

Civil Parish: **Crossmolina**
Map Grid: 13
RC Parish: Crossmolina
Diocese: KA
Earliest Record: b. 8.1831; m. 11.1832
Missing Dates: b. 8.1841-4.1845; m. 2.1841-
3.1846
Parish Address: Rev. Gerard Moore, PP,
Crossmolina, Ballina, Co. Mayo

Civil Parish: **Doonfeeny**
Map Grid: 3
RC Parish: Kilbride and Doonfeeny (Bal-
lycastle)
Diocese: KA
Earliest Record: b. 8.1864; m. 1.1869

Parish Address: Rev. William Moyles, PP, Ballycastle, Co. Mayo

Civil Parish: **Drum**
Map Grid: 29
RC Parish: see Balla
Diocese: TU

Civil Parish: **Islandeady**
Map Grid: 23
RC Parish: Islandeady
Diocese: TU
Earliest Record: b. 9.1839; m. 9.1839
Parish Address: Rev. Anthony O'Toole, PP, Islandeady, Castlebar, Co. Mayo

Civil Parish: **Kilbeagh**
Map Grid: 66
RC Parish: Kilbeagh (Charlestown)
Diocese: AC
Earliest Record: b. 1.1855; m. 5.1845
Parish Address: Rev. Andrew Kelly, PP, Charlestown, Co. Mayo

Civil Parish: **Kilbelfad**
Map Grid: 17
RC Parish: Backs, see Ballynahaglish
Diocese: KA

Civil Parish: **Kilbride**
Map Grid: 4
RC Parish: see Doonfeeny
Diocese: KA

Civil Parish: **Kilcolman (1)** (near Crossboyne)
Map Grid: 61
RC Parish: Kilcolman (Claremorris)
Diocese: TU
Earliest Record: b. 4.1835; m. 6.1806
Missing Dates: b. 1.1838-3.1839; m. 2.1830-1.1835, 3.1836-12.1838
Parish Address: Rev. John Sweeney, PP, Claremorris, Co. Mayo

Civil Parish: **Kilcolman (2)**
Map Grid: 67
RC Parish: see Co. Sligo
Diocese: TU

Civil Parish: **Kilcommon (1)** (near Kilmore)
Map Grid: 2

RC Parish: Belmullet
Diocese: KA
Earliest Record: b. 2.1841; m. 1.1836
Missing Dates: m. 5.1845-8.1857
Parish Address: Rev. John Gilroy, PP, Belmullet, Co. Mayo

Civil Parish: **Kilcommon (2)** (near Crossboyne)
Map Grid: 51
RC Parish: Kilcommon, see also Robeen
Diocese: TU
Earliest Record: b. 12.1865; m. 11.1865
Parish Address: Rev. William Walsh, Roundfort, Hollymount, Co. Mayo

Civil Parish: **Kilconduff**
Map Grid: 41
RC Parish: Kilconduff and Meelick
Diocese: AC
Earliest Record: b. 9.1850; m. 7.1846
Parish Address: Rev. Paul Cryan, PP, Swinford, Co. Mayo

Civil Parish: **Kilcummin**
Map Grid: 5
RC Parish: see Lackan
Diocese: KA

Civil Parish: **Kildacommoge**
Map Grid: 42
RC Parish: Keelogues
Diocese: TU
Earliest Record: b. 8.1847; m. 8.1847
Parish Address: Rev. William Fair, PP, Keelogues, Ballyvary, Co. Mayo

Civil Parish: **Kilfian**
Map Grid: 7
RC Parish: Kilfian
Diocese: KA
Earliest Record: b. 10.1826; m. 7.1826; d. 10.1826
Missing Dates: b. ends 7.1836; m. ends 10.1844; d. ends 2.1832
Parish Address: Rev. Patrick Guckian, PP, Kilfian, Killala, Co. Mayo

Civil Parish: **Kilgarvan**
Map Grid: 35
RC Parish: Kilgarvan (Bonniconlon)
Diocese: KA

Earliest Record: b. 8.1870; m. 11.1844
Parish Address: Rev. Martin McManus, PP, Conniconlon, Ballina, Co. Mayo

Civil Parish: **Kilgeever (1)**
Map Grid: 47
RC Parish: Clare Island; also Kilgeever, see below.
Diocese: TU
Earliest Record: b. 10.1851
Parish Address: Rev. Denis Carney, Adm, Clare Island, Westport, Co. Mayo

Civil Parish: **Kilgeever (2)**
Map Grid: 47
RC Parish: Kilgeever (Louisburgh)
Diocese: TU
Earliest Record: b. 2.1850
Missing Dates: b. 3.1869-8.1872
Parish Address: Rev. T. O. Morain, PP, Lousiburgh, Co. Mayo

Civil Parish: **Killala**
Map Grid: 10
RC Parish: Killala
Diocese: KA
Earliest Record: b. 4.1852; m. 12.1873
Parish Address: Rev. Edward McHale, PP, Killala, Co. Mayo

Civil Parish: **Killasser**
Map Grid: 38
RC Parish: Killasser
Diocese: AC
Earliest Record: b. 11.1847; m. 12.1847; d. 11.1847
Missing Dates: d. ends 6.1848
Parish Address: Rev. Sean Leonard, PP, Killasser, Swinford, Co. Mayo

Civil Parish: **Killedan**
Map Grid: 44
RC Parish: Killedan (Kiltimagh)
Diocese: AC
Earliest Record: b. 2.1861; m. 5.1834
Parish Address: Rev. Michael Cryan, PP, Kiltimagh, Co. Mayo

Civil Parish: **Kilmaclasser**
Map Grid: 22
RC Parish: Kilmeena

Diocese: TU
Earliest Record: not on microfilm
Parish Address: Rev. Eamonn O'Malley, PP, Kilmeena, Westport, Co. Mayo

Civil Parish: **Kilmainebeg**
Map Grid: 56
RC Parish: Kilmaine (Kilmeine)
Diocese: TU
Earliest Record: b. 6.1854; m. 5.1855
Parish Address: Rev. Thomas Rushe, PP, Kilmaine, Claremorris, Co. Mayo

Civil Parish: **Kilmainemore**
Map Grid: 54
RC Parish: Kilmaine, see Kilmainbeg
Diocese: TU

Civil Parish: **Kilmeena**
Map Grid: 21
RC Parish: Kilmeena, see Kilmaclasser
Diocese: TU

Civil Parish: **Kilmolara**
Map Grid: 53
RC Parish: Neale, see Cong
Diocese: TU

Civil Parish: **Kilmore**
Map Grid: 1
RC Parish: Kilmore-Erris
Diocese: KA
Earliest Record: b. 6.1860; m. 9.1860
Parish Address: Rev. Anthony Rea, PP, Carne, Belmullet, Co. Mayo

Civil Parish: **Kilmoremoy**
Map Grid: 15
RC Parish: Kilmoremoy
Diocese: KA
Earliest Record: b. 5.1823; m. 5.1823; d. 4.1823
Missing Dates: b. 10.1836-5.1849, 7.1849-7.1857; m. 10.1842-10.1850; d. 8.1836-9.1840, ends 5.1844
Parish Address: Rev. P. Gallagher, PP, Ballina, Co. Mayo

Civil Parish: **Kilmovee**
Map Grid: 68
RC Parish: Kilmovee
Diocese: AC

Earliest Record: b. 2.1854 (2 registers); m. 11.1824
Missing Dates: m. 8.1848-10.1854
Parish Address: Rev. Thomas Lynch, PP, Kilmovee, Ballaghaderreen, Co. Roscommon

Civil Parish: **Kilturra** (see also Co. Sligo)
Map Grid: 65
RC Parish: Kilshalvey, Kilturra, and Cloonoghill
Diocese: AC
Earliest Record: b. 1.1842; m. 4.1833
Missing Dates: b. incomplete pre-1852
Parish Address: Rev. Gerard Henry, PP, Bunninadden, Ballymote, Co. Sligo

Civil Parish: **Kilvine**
Map Grid: 64
RC Parish: Kilvine
Diocese: TU
Earliest Record: no registers pre-1880
Parish and priest: Rev. John Colleran, PP, Ballindine, Co. Mayo

Civil Parish: **Knock**
Map Grid: 71
RC Parish: Knock
Diocese: TU
Earliest Record: b. 12.1868; m. 9.1875
Parish Address: Parish Priest, Knock, Co. Mayo

Civil Parish: **Lackan**
Map Grid: 6
RC Parish: Lackan
Diocese: KA
Earliest Record: b. 8.1852; m. 3.1854
Parish Address: Rev. Mark Diamond, PP, Carrowmore, Ballina, Co. Mayo

Civil Parish: **Manulla**
Map Grid: 28
RC Parish: Balla and Manulla, see Balla
Diocese: TU

Civil Parish: **Mayo**
Map Grid: 60
RC Parish: Mayo and Roslea, see also Balla
Diocese: TU
Earliest Record: b. 4.1841; m. 9.1841
Parish Address: Rev. Patrick McDermott, PP, Mayo Abbey, Claremorris, Co. Mayo

Civil Parish: **Meelick**
Map Grid: 40
RC Parish: Kilconduff and Meelick, see Kilconduff
Diocese: AC

Civil Parish: **Moorgagagh**
Map Grid: 57
RC Parish: Kilmaine, see Kilmainebeg
Diocese: TU

Civil Parish: **Moygownagh**
Map Grid: 11
RC Parish: Moygownagh
Diocese: KA
Earliest Record: no pre-1880 registers
Missing Dates: Rev. Seamus Heverin, PP, Moygownagh, Ballina, Co. Mayo

Civil Parish: **Oughaval**
Map Grid: 45
RC Parish: Aughaval (Westport)
Diocese: TU
Earliest Record: b. 7.1845 (2 registers); m. 4.1823
Missing Dates: m. 5.1857-1.1959
Parish Address: Rev. Anthony King, Adm, Westport, Co. Mayo

Civil Parish: **Rathreagh**
Map Grid: 8
RC Parish: Kilfian, see Kilfian
Diocese: KA

Civil Parish: **Robeen**
Map Grid: 49
RC Parish: Kilcommon and Robeen
Diocese: TU
Earliest Record: b. 10.1857; m. 10.1857
Parish Address: Rev. Patrick Henry, PP, Robeen, Hollymount, Co. Mayo

Civil Parish: **Rosslee**
Map Grid: 32
RC Parish: Mayo and Rosslea, see Mayo
Diocese: TU

Civil Parish: **Shrule**
Map Grid: 58
RC Parish: Shrule
Diocese: TU

Earliest Record: b. 7.1831; m. 7.1831
Missing Dates: b. ends 8.1864; m. 6.1848-
10.1855, ends 5.1864
Parish Address: Rev. Colman O'Halloran, PP,
Shrule, Co. Galway

Civil Parish: **Tagheen**
Map Grid: 62
RC Parish: Crossboyne and Tagheen, see
Crossboyne
Diocese: TU

Civil Parish: **Templemore**
Map Grid: 39
RC Parish: Templemore (Straide)
Diocese: KA
Earliest Record: b. 5.1872
Parish Address: Rev. Padraig McGovern, PP,
Straide, Foxford, Co. Mayo

Civil Parish: **Templemurry**
Map Grid: 9
RC Parish: Killala, see Killala
Diocese: AC

Civil Parish: **Toomore**
Map Grid: 37
RC Parish: part Toomore (Foxford); part Kil-
turra
Diocese: AC
Earliest Record: b. 4.1833; m. 12.1871
Missing Dates: b. 3.1840-1.1870
Parish Address: Rev. Michael F. McGuinn, PP,
Foxford, Co. Mayo

Civil Parish: **Touaghty**
Map Grid: 33
RC Parish: Burriscarra, etc., see Ballintober
Diocese: TU

Civil Parish: **Turlough**
Map Grid: 25
RC Parish: Turlough (Parke)
Diocese: TU
Earliest Record: b. 8.1847; m. 8.1847
Parish Address: Rev. Martin Jennings, PP,
Parke, Castlebar, Co. Mayo

Commercial and Social Directories

1824
J. Pigot's *City of Dublin & Hibernian Provincial Directory* includes traders, nobility,
gentry, and clergy lists of Ballina, Ballinrobe,
Castlebar, Killala, Swinford, and Westport.

1846
Slater's *National Commercial Directory of
Ireland* lists nobility, clergy, traders, etc., in
Ballina, Ballinrobe, Castlebar, Claremorris,
Killala, Newport, Swinford, and Westport.
1856.

Slater's *Royal National Commercial Directory of Ireland* lists nobility, gentry, clergy,
traders, etc., in Ballina, Ballinrobe,
Castlebar, Claremorris, Killala, Newport,
Swinford, and Westport.

1870
Slater's *Directory of Ireland* contains trade,
nobility, and clergy lists for Ballina, Ballinrobe and Hollymount, Castlebar, Claremorris and Ballyhaunis, Killala, Newport,
Swinford, and Westport.

1881
Slater's *Royal National Commercial Directory of Ireland* contains lists of traders, clergy, nobility, and farmers in adjoining
parishes of the towns of Ballina and Killala,
Ballinrobe and Hollymount, Castlebar,
Claremorris, Ballyhaunis and Knock, Swinford and Bellaghy, Westport, and Newport.

1894
Slater's *Royal National Directory of Ireland*
lists traders, police, teachers, farmers, and
private residents in each of the towns, villages, and parishes of the county.

Family History

Burtchaell, G.D. "The Moore Family of Brize
Castle, Co. Mayo." *R.S.A.I.* (1901).

"The Elwood Family." *Ir. Gen.* 6 (4) (1983): 477-
86.

"The MacDonalds of Mayo." *J. Galway Arch. Hist. Soc.* 17 (1936-37): 65-82.

Morris – see Co. Tipperary

"Notes on the Lineage of Lambert of Brookhill, Co. Mayo." *Ir. Gen.* 3 (10) (1965): 372-79.

"O'Malley Papers (Co. Mayo)." *Anal. Hib.* 25: 185-202.

"O'Malleys Between 1651 and 1725." *J. Galway Arch. Hist. Soc.* 25 (1952).

"The Ormsbys of Tobervaddy (Co. Mayo)." *Ir. Gen.* 1 (1941): 284-86.

"Sir Thomas More: Descendants in the Male Line: the Moores of Moorehall, Co. Mayo." *R.S.A.I.* 36 (1906): 224-30.

Gravestone Inscriptions

Transcriptions available from Mr. Ian Cantwell, 5 Seafield Ave., Monkstown, Co. Dublin are as follows:

Aasleagh

Aughagower (RC; CI)

Aughavale

Castlebar, Old

Holy Trinity (CI; New CI)

Churchfield

Clare Island

Clogher Lough

Cushlough

Drummin

Islandeady

Kilbride

Kilgeever

Killeen

Kilmeena, Old (CI)

Knappagh (CI)

Louisburgh

St. Catherines (CI)

Murrisk Abbey and Church

Newport, Old (CI; RC; Presbyterian)

Partry

Raheen (private graveyard)

Toormakeady (RC; CI)

Westport, Old (CI)

Newspapers

Title: *Ballina Advertiser*
Published in: Ballina, 1840-43
NLI Holdings: 1.1840-11.1843
BL Holdings: 1.1840-11.1843

Title: *Ballina Chronicle*
Published in: Ballina, 1849-51
BL Holdings: 5.1849-8.1851

Title: *Ballina Herald* (incorporated with *Western People*)
Published in: Ballina, ca. 1866-1962
NLI Holdings: 8.1927-4.1962
BL Holdings: 10.1891-11.1892; 4.1913-4.1962

Title: *Ballina Impartial* or *Tyrawly Advertiser*
Published in: Ballina, 1823-35
NLI Holdings: 1.1823-12.1825; 1.1827-11.1835
BL Holdings: 1.1823-12.1825; 1.1827-11.1835

Title: *Ballina Journal & Connaught Advertiser*
Published in: Ballina, 1882-95
BL Holdings: 11.1882-3.1895

Title: *Ballinrobe Chronicle* (and *Mayo Advertiser*)
Published in: Ballinrobe, 1866-1903
NLI Holdings: 9.1866-10.1903 (none published 12.1867-4.1868)
BL Holdings: 9.1866-10.1903 (none published 12.1867-4.1868)

Title: *Connaught Telegraph*
Published in: Castlebar, 1828-current
NLI Holdings: 6.1879-12.1913; 6.1919-in progress
BL Holdings: 5.1876-in progress

Title: *Connaught Watchman*
Published in: Ballina, 1851-63
BL Holdings: 8.1851-10.1863

Title: *Mayo Constitution* (and *Roscommon Intelligencer*)
Published in: Castlebar, 1812-72
NLI Holdings: 1.1828-11.1871
BL Holdings: 1.1828-11.1871

Title: *Mayo Examiner*
Published in: Castlebar, 1868-1903
BL Holdings: 7.1868-6.1903

Title: *Mayo News*
Published in: Westport, 1893-current
BL Holdings: 1.1893-in progress

Title: *Telegraph* or *Connaught Ranger*
Published in: Castlebar, 1830-70
BL Holdings: 8.1830-12.1855; 2.1856-12.1869, odd numbers 1870

Title: *Tyrawly Herald* or *Mayo & Sligo Intelligencer*
Published in: Ballina, 1844-70
NLI Holdings: 1.1844-9.1870
BL Holdings: 1.1844-9.1870

Title: *Western Gem*
Published in: Ballina, 1843
NLI Holdings: 4.-12.1843
BL Holdings: 4.-12.1843

Title: *Western People*
Published in: Ballina, 1883-current
NLI Holdings: 5.1889-in progress
BL Holdings: 5.1889-in progress

Wills and Administrations

A discussion of the types of records, where they are held, and their availability and value is given in the Wills section of the Introduction. The availability of wills, administrations, and marriage license records is also described in the relevant parts of the same section. Where available, published sources of these records are given in the Miscellaneous Sources section.

Pre-1858 Wills and Administrations

Prerogative Wills. see p. xli.

Consistorial Wills. County Mayo is in the dioceses of Killala, Achonry, and Tuam. The guide to Catholic parish records in this chapter shows the diocese to which each civil parish belonged. The wills of residents of each diocese were usually proven within that diocese (see the Wills section for exceptions). The following records survive:

Wills. see p. xxxvii.

Abstracts. see p. xxxvii.

Indexes. "Killala and Achonry: 1698-1838." *Ir. Gen.* 3 (12): 506-19.

Tuam – see Co. Galway.

Post-1858 Wills and Administrations

This county was served by the District Registry of Ballina. The surviving records are kept in the PRO.

Marriage Licenses

Indexes. Tuam (1661-1750). PRO; SLC film 100872

Miscellaneous Sources

"A Map of Part of the County of Mayo in 1584; With Notes Thereon, and an Account of the Author (John Browne), and His Descendants." *J. Galway Arch. Hist. Soc.* 5 (1907-08): 145-58.

"Crossmolina – An Historical Survey." Available from Crossmolina Historical & Archaeological Society.

D'Alton, Rev. M. *A Short History of Ballinrobe Parish.* Browne & Nolan, 1931.

"The Ethnography of Ballycroy, Co. Mayo." *Pro. R. Ir. Acad.* 3rd ser. 4 (1896-98): 110-11.

"The Ethnography of Clare Island and Inishturk, Co. Mayo." *Proc. R. Ir. Acad.* 5 (1898-1900): 72.

"The Ethnography of The Mullet, Inishkea Islands and Portnacloy, Co. Mayo." *Proc. R. Ir. Acad.* 3 (1893-96): 648-49.

"Mayo Landowners in the Seventeenth Century." *R.S.A.I.* 95 (1965): 237-47.

Knox, H. *History of Co. Mayo from Earliest Times to the Close of the 16th Century.* Dublin, 1915.

"A List of the Yeomanry Corps of Connaught, 1803." *Irish Sword* 3 (12) 1958.

Research Sources and Services

Journals

Cathair na Mairt (Journal of the Westport Historical Society)

North Mayo Historical & Archaeological Society Journal

Libraries and Information Sources

Mayo County Library, Mountain View, Castlebar, Co. Mayo Ph: (094) 21342

Research Services

Mayo Family History Research Society, Bushfield House, Hollymount, Co. Mayo

See also research services in Dublin, p. xliv

Societies

Westport Historical Society, Mr. Peadar O'Flanagan, Bridge Street, Westport, Co. Mayo

Mayo Historical Society, John Clarke, Moneen, Castlebar, Co. Mayo

North Mayo Historical & Archaeological Society, Ms. Carmel Hughes, Rehins, Ballina, Co. Mayo

Crossmolina Historical & Archaeological Society, Enniscoe, Castlehill, Ballina, Co. Mayo

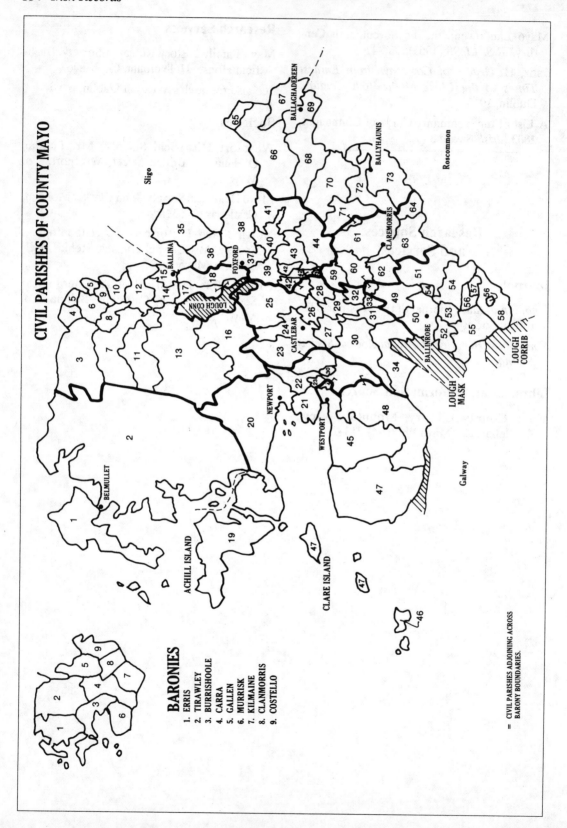

CIVIL PARISHES OF COUNTY MAYO

Sligo

Roscommon

BALLAGHADEREEN
67
65
69
66
68
BALLYHAUNIS
70
72
73
71
35
36
38
41
40
44
61
63
CLAREMORRIS
37
FOXFORD
39
42
43
59
60
62
64
51
BALLINA
15
14
18
42
28
54
49
54
LOUGH CONN
17
25
26
29
32
33
56
57
CASTLEBAR
24
27
30
31
50
52
53
55
58
10
12
23
34
BALLINROBE
16
13
5
4
6
8
7
11
22
21
48
LOUGH
MASK
LOUGH
CORRIB
Galway
3
NEWPORT
20
45
WESTPORT
2
47
BELMULLET
1
19
ACHILL ISLAND
47
46
CLARE ISLAND
47

BARONIES

1. ERRIS
2. TIRAWLEY
3. BURRISHOOLE
4. CARRA
5. GALLEN
6. MURRISK
7. KILMAINE
8. CLANMORRIS
9. COSTELLO

= CIVIL PARISHES ADJOINING ACROSS
 BARONY BOUNDARIES.

County Meath

A Brief History

This Leinster county contains the towns of Navan, Trim, Kells, Oldcastle, and Athboy.

In the old Irish system of administration, the present county of Meath was part of a larger area of the same name which was the territory of the High King of Ireland. The High King's residence was situated on the Hill of Tara which is within the present county of Meath.

The major Irish families in the county were O'Melaghlin or McLoughlin, McGogarty, O'Loughnane, Hayes, (O')Kelly, (O')Hennessy, and O'Reilly.

Following the Norman conquest of Leinster, the county was given to Hugh de Lacy, who built an extensive castle on the site of the present town of Trim. The Normans also built castles at Navan and Kells. Over the succeeding centuries, however, the effective control of the English administration in the county waned as the Normans assimilated into the Irish way of life, and the native families became more powerful. The area controlled by England gradually shrunk to an area around Dublin, the Pale, which included the eastern parts of the present County Meath. It was in this area of rich farmland that many Norman families settled. The main families which settled were those of Preston, Plunkett, Cusack, Darcy, Dillon, Nangle, Dowdall, Fleming, and Barnewall.

Some of the native families migrated from the county as a result of the Norman conquest, but most remained either as tenants or servants of the Normans or on their own lands.

During the 1641 rebellion most of the Irish and Norman families of the county, led by a Preston, rebelled against English rule. This rebellion was defeated and the lands of many of the rebels were confiscated and given to soldiers and officers of Cromwell's army.

Once described as "the great grazing ground" of Ireland, County Meath has an abundance of pastureland. Large farms prospered on these lands, but few small farmers were able to earn a sufficient living.

The population of the county dramatically dropped during the 1840s, the period of the Great Famine. The population was 183,000 in 1841, making Meath one of the least densely populated counties in the country (200 people per square mile). By 1857 this population had dropped to 141,000. Almost 20,000 died between 1845 and 1850 from starvation and disease, and further thousands emigrated. The population is currently around 96,000.

MEATH

(*The following persons, in the baronies of Upper and Lower Duleek, have this day taken the Oath of Allegiance):

Richard Aylward (*Aylmer), Par. Pr. & Vic. Genl. Diocese Meath, Stamullin residg. therein.

Wm. Coleman	Balltray	Farmer
James Mackey	Ninch	,,
Ignatius Farrell	Balloy	,,
Geo. Ennis	Claristown	,,
John Murphy	Rogerstn.	,,
John Tuite	Minnetstown	,,
Richd. Callaghan	Smithstn.	,,
Wm. Boylan	Legdoory	,,
Corns. Dempsey	Stamulon (*Stamullen)	,,
Nichs. Pentony	Gormanstn.	,,
Patt. Caulfield	Dananestn. (*Demanestown)	,,
Nichs. Rafferty	Millmurderry	,,
Thos. Caulief	Demanestn.	,,
Bryan McEnally	Bryerlays	,,
Patrick McEnally	Sarsfieldstn.	,,

Before James Brabazon—11 Dec. 1775. (*Mornington).

An extract from the "Catholic Qualification Rolls" for County Meath, 1775. The persons listed were Catholics who took an Oath of Allegiance to the British Sovereign and thereby qualified for certain benefits which had previously been denied under the Penal Laws. From the 59th Report of the Deputy Keeper of Public Records of Ireland.

Census and Census Substitutes

1654-56

Civil Survey. Vol. 5. SLC film 973122.

1659

"Census" of Ireland. Edited by S. Pender. Dublin: Stationery Office, 1939. Covers parishes of Abbey, Athlumney, Ardcath, Ardmulchan, Ballygart, Ballymagarvey, Ballymaglassan, Brownstown, Clonalvy, Colpe, Crookstown, Donoghmore, Dowestown, Duleek, Dunshaughlin, Dunowre, Dunsany, Fennor, Grenock, Julianstown, Kentstown, Kilbrew, Kilcarne, Kilkervan, Killeen, Killegan, Kilmoon, Knockamon, Macestown, Moorchurch, Monkstown, Paynstown, Rathbeggan, Rathfeagh, Rathregan, Ratoath, Skryne, Staffordstown, Stamullen, Tara, Trevett, and Templekeran. SLC film 924648.

1766

Religious Census Giving Protestants in the Parish of Ardbraccan, and All Religions in the Parishes of Churchtown, Liscartan, Martry, and Rataine. RCB Library; SLC film 258517.

1770

List of Freeholders of Co. Meath, Compiled for Election Purposes. NLI ms. 787/8; SLC film 100181.

1775

"Catholic Qualification Roll Extracts" (seventy names, addresses, and occupations). 59th Report DKPRI: 50-84.

1781

List of Voters. PRO film 4878, 4910-12.

1794

List of the Freeholders of Co. Meath. RIA; Upton Papers No. 12.

1798

List of Persons who Suffered Loss in '98 Rebellion. NLI JLB 94107 (approximately 120 names, addresses, and occupations).

1802-03

"Protestants in Parishes of Agher, Ardagh, Clonard, Clongill, Drumconrath, Duleek, Emlagh, Julianstown, Kells, Kentstown, Kilbeg, Kilmainhamwood, Kilskyre, Laracor, Moynalty, Navan, Robertstown, Raddenstown, Rathcore, Rathkenny, Rathmolyan, Ratoath, Skryne, Slane, Syddan, Tara, and Trim." *Ir. Anc.* 5 (1) (1973): 37-53.

1813

"Protestant Children at Ardbraccan School." *Ir. Anc.* 5 (1) (1973): 38.

1816

"Tenants of the Wellesley Estates at Dengan, Ballymaglossan, Moyare, Mornington, and Trim." *Riocht na Midhe* 4 (4) (1967): 10-25.

1821

Government Census Remnants for... Parishes of Ardbraccan, Ardsallagh, Balrathboyne, Bective, Churchtown, Clonmacduff, Donaghmore, Donaghpatrick, Kilcooly, Liscartan, Martry, Moymet, Navan, Newtownclonbun, Rathkenny, Rataine, Trim, Trimlestown, Tullaghanoge. PRO; SLC film 597735.

1823-38

Tithe Applotment Survey (See p. xxvii).

1830

"Census of Landowners in Julianstown, Moorchurch, Stamullen, and Clonalvy." *Riocht na Midhe* 3 (4) (1966): 354-58 (gives name and holding in each townland of each parish except townlands of Ballygarth, Corballis, and Whitecross).

1833

"List of Protestant Parishioners Paying Church Cess in Colpe and Kilsharvan Parishes." *Riocht na Midhe* 4 (3) (1969): 61-62.

1838

"Balfour Tenants in Townlands of Belustran, Cloughmacow, and Doe and Hurtle." *Louth Arch. J.* 12 (3) (1951): 190.

1854

Griffith's Valuation (See p. xxvii).

1871

Census of the Parishes of Drumcondra and Loughbracken. Included in the Catholic Parish Register.

1901

Census. PRO.

1911

Census. PRO.

Church Records

Church of Ireland
(shows starting date of record)

Parish: **Agher**
Status: Lost

Parish: **Ardagh**
Status: Lost

Parish: **Ardbraccan**
Status: Lost

Parish: **Ardmulchan** (see Painestown)

Parish: **Athboy**
Existing Records: b. 1736; m. 1737; d. 1738
Missing Dates: b. 1749-97; m. 1748-98; d. 1740-98
Status: LC

Parish: **Athlumney** (see Navan)

Parish: **Ballymaglasson**
Existing Records: b. 1851; d. 1835
Status: LC

Parish: **Balrathboyne**
Status: Lost

Parish: **Bective**
Existing Records: b. 1853; d. 1853
Status: LC

Parish: **Castlerickard**
Existing Records: b. 1836; m. 1837; d. 1844
Status: LC

Parish: **Churchtown** (see Ardbraccan)

Parish: **Clonard**
Existing Records: b. 1792; m. 1793; d. 1793 (on
    temporary deposit in PRO 1944)
Status: LC

Parish: **Clongill**
Status: Lost

Parish: **Colpe**
Status: Lost

Parish: **Donoghpatrick**
Status: Lost

Parish: **Drakestown**
Status: Lost

Parish: **Drumconrath**
Existing Records: b. 1799; m. 1822; d. 1822
Status: LC

Parish: **Duleek**
Status: Lost

Parish: **Dunboyne**
Status: Lost

Parish: **Dunshaughlin**
Existing Records: b. 1839; m. 1846; d. 1839
Status: LC

Parish: **Galtrim**
Status: Lost

Parish: **Girley**
Status: Lost

Parish: **Julianstown**
Status: Lost

Parish: **Kells**
Existing Records: b. 1773; m. 1773; d. 1773
Status: LC

Parish: **Kentstown**
Status: Lost

Parish: **Kilbrew** (see also Kilmoon)
Status: Lost

Parish: **Kilbride** (see Dunboyne)

Parish: **Kilbride, Castlecor**
Status: Lost

Parish: **Kildalkey**
Status: Lost

Parish: **Killallon**
Status: Lost

Parish: **Killeagh**
Status: Lost

Parish: **Killochonagan** (Trim)
Status: Lost

Parish: **Kilmainhamnood**
Status: Lost

Parish: **Kilmessan**
Status: Lost

Parish: **Kilmoon**
Status: Lost

Parish: **Kilmore**
Existing Records: b. 1859; d. 1859
Status: LC

Parish: **Kilskeer**
Status: Lost

Parish: **Knockmark**
Existing Records: b. 1825; m. 1837; d. 1825
Status: LC

Parish: **Laracor**
Status: Lost

Parish: **Loughan** or **Castlekieran**
Existing Records: b. 1836; d. 1865
Status: LC

Parish: **Loughcrewe**
Status: Lost

Parish: **Moyglare**
Status: Lost (a few entries of baptisms 1803-1815 not belonging to Moyglare Parish)

Parish: **Moynalty**
Status: Lost

Parish: **Navan**
Existing Records: b. 1766; m. 1766; d. 1772
Status: LC

Parish: **Newtown**
Status: Lost

Parish: **Nobber**
Existing Records: b. 1800; m. 1805; d. 1803
Status: LC

Parish: **Oldcastle**
Existing Records: b. 1814; m. 1814; d. 1814
Status: LC

Parish: **Painestown**
Existing Records: b. 1.8.1698-6.1.1706/07 (one entry baptism 11.5.1744 found on removal of books to Slane); m. 1.8.1698-6.1.1706/07; d. 1.8.1698-6.1.1706/07
Status: LC

Parish: **Piercetown** (see Kilmoon)
Status: Lost

Parish: **Rathbeggan**
Existing Records: b. 1821; m. 1837; d. 1836
Status: LC

Parish: **Rathcore**
Existing Records: b. 1810; m. 1811; d. 1810
Status: LC

Parish: **Rathkenny**
Status: Lost

Parish: **Rathmolyon**
Status: Lost

Parish: **Ratoath**
Status: Lost

Parish: **Robertstown** (see Newtown)

Parish: **St. Mary, Drogheda**
Existing Records: b. 1763; m. 1763; d. 1763
Missing Dates: b. 1776-1801; m. 1776-1801; d. 1776-1801
Status: LC

Parish: **Skryne**
Status: Lost

Parish: **Slane**
Status: Lost

Parish: **Stackallen**
Status: Lost

Parish: **Syddan**
Existing Records: b. 1720; m. 1721; d. 1725
Status: LC

Parish: **Tara**
Status: Lost

Parish: **Tessauran**
Existing Records: b. 1819; m. 1820; d. 1819
Status: LC

Parish: **Trim**
Existing Records: b. 1836; d. 1849
Status: LC

Roman Catholic

Civil Parish: **Agher**
Map Grid: 138
RC Parish: see Laracor
Diocese: ME

Civil Parish: **Ardagh**
Map Grid: 17
RC Parish: see Drumcondra
Diocese: ME

Civil Parish: **Ardbraccan**
Map Grid: 50
RC Parish: Bohermeen
Diocese: ME
Earliest Record: b. 6.1832; m. 4.1831; d. 1.1833
Missing Dates: 5.1842-1.1865, ends 3.1868
Parish Address: Rev. Patrick A. Mackin, PP, Parochial House, Bohermeen, Navan, Co. Meath

Civil Parish: **Ardcath**
Map Grid: 102
RC Parish: Ardcath
Diocese: ME
Earliest Record: b. 10.1795; m. 6.1797
Parish Address: Rev. P. Mulvany, PP Ardcath, Garristown, Co. Dublin.

Civil Parish: **Ardmulchan**
Map Grid: 79
RC Parish: Blacklion or Beaupark
Diocese: ME
Earliest Record: b. 12.1815; m. 1.1816
Parish Address: Rev. Patrick Bartley, Beauparc, Navan, Co. Meath

Civil Parish: **Ardsallagh**
Map Grid: 57
RC Parish: see Navan
Diocese: ME

Civil Parish: **Assey**
Map Grid: 116
RC Parish: Dunsany and Kilmessan, see Kilmessan
Diocese: ME

Civil Parish: **Athboy**
Map Grid: 70
RC Parish: Athboy
Diocese: ME
Earliest Record: b. 4.1794; m. 5.1794; d. 4.1794
Missing Dates: b. 11.1799-3.1807, 5.1826-1.1827; m. 11.1799-3.1807, 10.1864-2.1865; d. 3.1798-3.1807, 2.1826-1.1827, 1.1848-1.1865
Parish Address: Rev. Joseph Kelly, PP, Athboy, Co. Meath

Civil Parish: **Athlumney**
Map Grid: 80
RC Parish: Johnstown, see Monkstown
Diocese: ME

Civil Parish: **Balfeaghan**
Map Grid: 141
RC Parish: Kilcloon, see Rathregan
Diocese: ME

Civil Parish: **Ballyboggan**
Map Grid: 110
RC Parish: see Castlejordan, Co. Offaly
Diocese: ME

Civil Parish: **Ballygarth**
Map Grid: 100
RC Parish: see Stamullin
Diocese: ME

Civil Parish: **Ballymagarvey**
Map Grid: 68
RC Parish: Blacklion, see Ardmulchan
Diocese: ME

Civil Parish: **Ballymaglassan**
Map Grid: 135
RC Parish: Kilcloon, see Rathregan
Diocese: ME

Civil Parish: **Balrathboyne**
Map Grid: 36
RC Parish: Bohermeen, see Ardbraccan
Diocese: ME

Civil Parish: **Balsoon**
Map Grid: 117
RC Parish: Dunsany and Kilmessan, see Kilmessan
Diocese: ME

Civil Parish: **Bective**
Map Grid: 76
RC Parish: see Navan
Diocese: ME

Civil Parish: **Brownstown**
Map Grid: 84
RC Parish: Blacklion, see Ardmulchan
Diocese: ME

Civil Parish: **Burry**
Map Grid: 35
RC Parish: see Kells
Diocese: ME

Civil Parish: **Castlejordan**
Map Grid: 111
RC Parish: see Castlejordan, Co. Offaly
Diocese: ME

Civil Parish: **Castlekeeran**
Map Grid: 32
RC Parish: see Loughan
Diocese: ME

Civil Parish: **Castlerickard**
Map Grid: 108
RC Parish: Killyon and Longwood
Diocese: ME
Earliest Record: b. 1.1829; m. 1.1829; d. 1.1829
Missing Dates: d. ends 2.1855
Parish Address: Rev. Patrick Carberry, Longwood, Co. Meath

Civil Parish: **Castletown**
Map Grid: 11
RC Parish: Castletown Kilpatrick
Diocese: ME
Earliest Record: b. 12.1805; m. 5.1816
Missing Dates: b. 5.1822-1.1826; m. 5.1822-1.1824; 4.1841-11.1842
Parish Address: Rev. Kevin Cuffe, PP, Castletown, Kilpatrick, Co. Meath

Civil Parish: **Churchtown**
Map Grid: 55
RC Parish: Dunderry
Diocese: ME
Earliest Record: b. 10.1837; m. 10.1841
Missing Dates: b. 7.1869-5.1870; m. 5.1869-5.1871

Parish Address: Rev. Joseph McCarthy, Churchtown, Navan, Co. Meath

Civil Parish: **Clonalvy**
Map Grid: 106
RC Parish: see Ardcath
Diocese: ME

Civil Parish: **Clonard**
Map Grid: 109
RC Parish: part Kinnegad; part Longwood, see Castlerickard
Diocese: ME
Earliest Record: b. 6.1827; m. 7.1844; d. 2.1869
Parish Address: Rev. Eamonn Marron, PP, Kinnegad, Co. Westmeath

Civil Parish: **Clongil**
Map Grid: 15
RC Parish: Castletown-Kilpatrick, see Castletown
Diocese: ME

Civil Parish: **Clonmacduff**
Map Grid: 73
RC Parish: see Churchtown
Diocese: ME

Civil Parish: **Collon**
Map Grid: 43
RC Parish: see Collon, Co. Louth
Diocese: AM

Civil Parish: **Colp**
Map Grid: 61
RC Parish: St. Mary's, Co. Louth
Diocese: ME

Civil Parish: **Cookstown**
Map Grid: 129
RC Parish: see Ratoath
Diocese: ME

Civil Parish: **Crickstown**
Map Grid: 128
RC Parish: Curraha
Diocese: ME
Earliest Record: b. 4.1802; m. 6.1802; d. 6.1802
Missing Dates: d. 4.1823-11.1833, ends 4.1863
Parish Address: Rev. Edward Daly, PP, Ashbourne, Co. Meath

Civil Parish: **Cruicetown**
Map Grid: 5
RC Parish: see Nobber
Diocese: ME

Civil Parish: **Culmullin**
Map Grid: 137
RC Parish: see Dunshaughlin
Diocese: ME

Civil Parish: **Cushinstown**
Map Grid: 99
RC Parish: see Duleek
Diocese: ME

Civil Parish: **Danestown**
Map Grid: 88
RC Parish: Blacklion, see Ardmulchan
Diocese: ME

Civil Parish: **Derrypatrick**
Map Grid: 123
RC Parish: Moynalvy and Galtrim
Diocese: ME
Earliest Record: b. 10.1811; m. 11.1783; d.
   10.1811
Missing Dates: b. 10.1828-3.1831; m. 11.1786-
   10.1811, 9.1828-4.1831; d. 9.1828-10.1877
Parish Address: Rev. Patrick Stewart, PP,
   Moynalvy, Summerhill, Co. Meath

Civil Parish: **Diamor**
Map Grid: 29
RC Parish: Kilskyre, see Kilskeer
Diocese: ME

Civil Parish: **Donaghmore** (near Navan)
Map Grid: 52
RC Parish: see Navan
Diocese: ME

Civil Parish: **Donaghmore** (near Ratoath)
Map Grid: 133
RC Parish: see Crickstown
Diocese: ME

Civil Parish: **Donaghpatrick**
Map Grid: 38
RC Parish: Kilberry and Telltown, see Kilberry
Diocese: ME

Civil Parish: **Donore**
Map Grid: 59
RC Parish: Rosnaree or Donore
Diocese: ME
Earliest Record: b. 1.1840; m. 4.1840
Missing Dates: m. 7.1841-11.1850
Parish Address: Rev. Terence Caffrey, PP,
   Donore, Drogheda, Co. Louth

Civil Parish: **Dowdstown**
Map Grid: 85
RC Parish: Skryne, see Skreen
Diocese: ME

Civil Parish: **Dowth**
Map Grid: 48
RC Parish: see Slane
Diocese: AM

Civil Parish: **Drakestown**
Map Grid: 12
RC Parish: see Castletown
Diocese: ME

Civil Parish: **Drumcondra**
Map Grid: 18
RC Parish: Drumcondra (Drumconrath)
Diocese: ME
Earliest Record: b. 10.1811; m. 9.1811; d. 8.1811
Parish Address: Rev. Eamonn Butler, PP,
   Parochial House, Drumconrath, Navan, Co.
   Meath

Civil Parish: **Drumlargan**
Map Grid: 139
RC Parish: Summerhill, see Laracor
Diocese: ME

Civil Parish: **Dulane**
Map Grid: 33
RC Parish: Carnaross, see Loughan
Diocese: ME

Civil Parish: **Duleek**
Map Grid: 64
RC Parish: Duleek
Diocese: ME
Earliest Record: b. 2.1852; m. 2.1852
Parish Address: Rev. Patrick Tully, PP,
   Parochial House, Duleek, Co. Meath

Civil Parish: **Duleek Abbey**
Map Grid: 103
RC Parish: see Duleek
Diocese: ME

Civil Parish: **Dunboyne**
Map Grid: 145
RC Parish: Dunboyne
Diocese: ME
Earliest Record: b. 9.1798; m. 6.1787; d. 6.1787
Parish Address: Rev. Edward Rispin, PP, Dunboyne, Co. Meath

Civil Parish: **Dunmoe**
Map Grid: 53
RC Parish: see Slane
Diocese: ME

Civil Parish: **Dunsany**
Map Grid: 95
RC Parish: see Kilmessan
Diocese: ME

Civil Parish: **Dunshaughlin**
Map Grid: 126
RC Parish: Dunshaughlin
Diocese: ME
Earliest Record: b. 1.1789; m. 10.1800; d. 1.1789
Missing Dates: b. 1.1843-1.1849; m. 2.1834-2.1849; d. 1.1828-1.1863, ends 12.1872
Parish Address: Rev. Brendan Caffrey, PP, Parochial House, Dunshaughlin, Co. Meath

Civil Parish: **Emlagh**
Map Grid: 7
RC Parish: Stahalmock, see Kilbeg
Diocese: ME

Civil Parish: **Enniskeen**
Map Grid: 9
RC Parish: Kingscourt, see Enniskeen, Co. Cavan
Diocese: ME

Civil Parish: **Fennor**
Map Grid: 58
RC Parish: see Slane
Diocese: ME

Civil Parish: **Follistown**
Map Grid: 82

RC Parish: Johnstown, see Monkstown
Diocese: ME

Civil Parish: **Gallow**
Map Grid: 140
RC Parish: Summerhill, see Laracor
Diocese: ME

Civil Parish: **Galtrim**
Map Grid: 121
RC Parish: Moynalvy, see Derrypatrick
Diocese: ME

Civil Parish: **Gernonstown**
Map Grid: 41
RC Parish: see Slane
Diocese: ME

Civil Parish: **Girley**
Map Grid: 39
RC Parish: see Kells
Diocese: ME

Civil Parish: **Grangegeeth**
Map Grid: 42
RC Parish: see Slane
Diocese: ME

Civil Parish: **Greenoge**
Map Grid: 134
RC Parish: see Crickstown
Diocese: ME

Civil Parish: **Inishmot**
Map Grid: 20
RC Parish: Lobinstown, see Killary
Diocese: ME

Civil Parish: **Julianstown**
Map Grid: 66
RC Parish: see Stamullen
Diocese: ME

Civil Parish: **Kells**
Map Grid: 34
RC Parish: Kells
Diocese: ME
Earliest Record: b. 7.1791; m. 8.1791; d. 6.1794
Missing Dates: b. 12.1827-7.1828; d. ends 3.1824
Parish Address: Rev. John Shortall, PP, Parochial House, Kells, Co. Meath

Civil Parish: **Kentstown**
Map Grid: 67
RC Parish: Blacklion
Diocese: ME

Civil Parish: **Kilbeg**
Map Grid: 4
RC Parish: Kilbeg or Stahalmog
Diocese: ME
Earliest Record: b. 12.1817; m. 1.1810
Missing Dates: b. 1.1852-3.1858; m. 6.1813-
1.1830, 5.1852-5.1858
Parish Address: Rev. Patrick Adams, PP, Kells,
Co. Meath

Civil Parish: **Kilberry**
Map Grid: 16
RC Parish: Kilberry and Teltown
Diocese: ME
Earliest Record: b. 12.1757; m. 11.1763; d. 1771
Missing Dates: b. 7.1784-4.1797, 5.1814-2.1831,
12.1840-11.1847; m. 5.1780-1.1783, 6.1784-
4.1797, 4.1801-9.1801, 8.1842-3.1848;
d. various dates to 1881

Civil Parish: **Kilbrew**
Map Grid: 125
RC Parish: see Crickstown
Diocese: ME

Civil Parish: **Kilbride (1)** (near Oldcastle)
Map Grid: 24
RC Parish: Killeagha and Kilbride (Mount
Nugent), see also Co. Cavan
Diocese: ME
Earliest Record: b. 1.1832; m. 1.1832
Parish Address: Rev. John Molloy, PP,
Parochial House, Moutnugent, Co. Meath.

Civil Parish: **Kilbride (2)** (near Dunboyne)
Map Grid: 146
RC Parish: Dunboyne and Kilbride, see Dun-
boyne
Diocese: ME

Civil Parish: **Kilcarn**
Map Grid: 81
RC Parish: Johnstown, see Monkstown
Diocese: ME

Civil Parish: **Kilclone**
Map Grid: 143
RC Parish: Kilcloon, see Rathregan
Diocese: ME

Civil Parish: **Kilcooly**
Map Grid: 78
RC Parish: see Churchtown
Diocese: ME

Civil Parish: **Kildalkey**
Map Grid: 71
RC Parish: Ballivor, see Killaconnigan
Diocese: ME

Civil Parish: **Killaconnigan**
Map Grid: 72
RC Parish: Ballivor
Diocese: ME
Earliest Record: b. 2.1837; m. 4.1837; d. 2.1837
Parish Address: Rev. Christopher Gaffney, PP,
Ballivor, Co. Meath

Civil Parish: **Killallon**
Map Grid: 30
RC Parish: Clonmellon, see Killua, Co.
Westmeath
Diocese: ME

Civil Parish: **Killary**
Map Grid: 23
RC Parish: Lobinstown
Diocese: ME
Earliest Record: b. 10.1823; m. 9.1823
Parish Address: Rev. Leonard Moran, PP,
Lobinstown, Navan, Co. Meath

Civil Parish: **Killeagh**
Map Grid: 26
RC Parish: see Kilbride
Diocese: ME

Civil Parish: **Killeen**
Map Grid: 94
RC Parish: Dunsany, see Kilmessan
Diocese: ME

Civil Parish: **Killegland**
Map Grid: 130
RC Parish: see Ratoath
Diocese: ME

Civil Parish: **Killyon**
Map Grid: 107
RC Parish: Longwood, see Castlerickard
Diocese: ME

Civil Parish: **Kilmainham**
Map Grid: 2
RC Parish: Kilmainhamwood and Moybologue
Diocese: ME
Earliest Record: b. 1.1869; m. 1.1869
Parish Address: Rev. Noel McIntyre, PP, Kilmainhamwood, Kells, Co. Meath

Civil Parish: **Kilmessan**
Map Grid: 120
RC Parish: Kilmessan
Diocese: ME
Earliest Record: b. 7.1742; m. 7.1742; d. 10.1756
Missing Dates: b. 8.1750-10.1756, 6.1768-1.1791; m. 8.1750-10.1756, 6.1768-1.1791
Parish Address: Rev. James Bird, PP, Kilmessan, Navan, Co. Meath

Civil Parish: **Kilmoon**
Map Grid: 98
RC Parish: see Crickstown
Diocese: ME

Civil Parish: **Kilmore**
Map Grid: 136
RC Parish: Moynalvy, see Derrypatrick
Diocese: ME

Civil Parish: **Kilsharvan**
Map Grid: 65
RC Parish: St. Mary's, Drogheda, see St. Mary's
Diocese: ME

Civil Parish: **Kilshine**
Map Grid: 14
RC Parish: Castletown-Kilpatrick, see Castletown
Diocese: ME

Civil Parish: **Kilskeer**
Map Grid: 31
RC Parish: Kilskeer
Diocese: ME
Earliest Record: b. 4.1784; m. 1.1784; d. 1.1784
Missing Dates: m. 11.1790-6.1808, 7.1841-1.1842; d. 8.1790-11.1859

Parish Address: Rev. Conor McGreevy, PP, Kilskyre, Kells, Co. Meath

Civil Parish: **Kiltale**
Map Grid: 122
RC Parish: Moynalvy, see Derrypatrick
Diocese: ME

Civil Parish: **Knock**
Map Grid: 13
RC Parish: Castletown-Kilpatrick, see Castletown
Diocese: ME

Civil Parish: **Knockcommon**
Map Grid: 63
RC Parish: see Donore
Diocese: ME

Civil Parish: **Knockmark**
Map Grid: 124
RC Parish: see Dunshaughlin
Diocese: ME

Civil Parish: **Laracor**
Map Grid: 113
RC Parish: Summerhill
Diocese: ME
Earliest Record: b. 4.1812; m. 4.1812; d. 4.1812
Missing Dates: m. 2.1854-7.1854; d. ends 11.1836
Parish Address: Rev. Joseph Abbott, PP, Summerhill, Co. Meath

Civil Parish: **Liscartan**
Map Grid: 51
RC Parish: see Ardbraccan
Diocese: ME

Civil Parish: **Lismullin**
Map Grid: 90
RC Parish: see Skreen
Diocese: ME

Civil Parish: **Loughan** or **Castlekeeran** (see also Co. Cavan)
Map Grid: 32
RC Parish: Carnaross
Diocese: ME
Earliest Record: b. 8.1806; m. 6.1805; d. 6.1805
Missing Dates: b. 10.1807-5.1808, 9.1815-

6.1827; m. 2.1820-2.1823, 2.1825-1.1828,
4.1861-7.1861; d. ends 9.1856
Parish Address: Rev. Patrick Casey, PP, Carnaross, Kells, Co. Meath

Civil Parish: **Loughbrackan**
Map Grid: 19
RC Parish: see Drumcondra
Diocese: ME

Civil Parish: **Loughcrew**
Map Grid: 28
RC Parish: see Oldcastle
Diocese: ME

Civil Parish: **Macetown**
Map Grid: 97
RC Parish: see Skreen
Diocese: ME

Civil Parish: **Martry**
Map Grid: 49
RC Parish: see Ardbraccan
Diocese: ME

Civil Parish: **Mitchelstown**
Map Grid: 21
RC Parish: Lobinstown, see Killary
Diocese: ME

Civil Parish: **Monknewtown**
Map Grid: 47
RC Parish: see Grangegeeth
Diocese: ME

Civil Parish: **Monkstown**
Map Grid: 87
RC Parish: Johnstown
Diocese: ME
Earliest Record: b. 1.1839; m. 1.1839
Parish Address: Rev. Finian O'Connor, PP,
Johnstown, Navan, Co. Meath

Civil Parish: **Moorechurch**
Map Grid: 101
RC Parish: see Stamullen
Diocese: ME

Civil Parish: **Moybolgue** (see also Co. Cavan)
Map Grid: 1

RC Parish: see Kilmainham
Diocese: ME

Civil Parish: **Moyglare**
Map Grid: 144
RC Parish: Kilcloon, see Rathregan
Diocese: ME

Civil Parish: **Moylagh**
Map Grid: 27
RC Parish: see Oldcastle
Diocese: ME

Civil Parish: **Moymet**
Map Grid: 75
RC Parish: see Churchtown
Diocese: ME

Civil Parish: **Moynalty**
Map Grid: 3
RC Parish: Moynalty
Diocese: ME
Earliest Record: b. 7.1830; m. 12.1829; d. 3.1830
Parish Address: Rev. Patrick A. Reilly, PP,
Parochial House, Moynalty, Kells, Co.
Meath

Civil Parish: **Navan**
Map Grid: 54
RC Parish: Navan
Diocese: ME
Earliest Record: b. 1.1782; m. 2.1852; d. 6.1868
Missing Dates: b. 5.1813-9.1842
Parish Address: Rev. Andrew Farrell, PP, St.
Mary's, Navan, Co. Meath

Civil Parish: **Newtown**
Map Grid: 6
RC Parish: Stahalmog, see Kilbeg
Diocese: ME

Civil Parish: **Newtownclonbun**
Map Grid: 77
RC Parish: see Trim
Diocese: ME

Civil Parish: **Nobber**
Map Grid: 10
RC Parish: Nobber
Diocese: ME

Earliest Record: b. 7.1754; m. 2.1757; d. 1.1757
Missing Dates: records end 1865
Parish Address: Rev. Patrick O'Reilly, PP, Nobber, Co. Meath

Civil Parish: **Oldcastle**
Map Grid: 25
RC Parish: Oldcastle
Diocese: ME
Earliest Record: b. 1.1789; m.. 4.1789; d. 3.1789
Missing Dates: b. 2.1807-11.1808; m. 2.1807-11.1808; d. 2.1807-11.1808, ends 1.1809
Parish Address: Rev. Eugene Conlan, PP, Oldcastle, Co. Meath

Civil Parish: **Painestown**
Map Grid: 62
RC Parish: Blacklion, see Ardmulchan
Diocese: ME

Civil Parish: **Piercetown**
Map Grid: 105
RC Parish: see Ardcath
Diocese: ME

Civil Parish: **Rataine**
Map Grid: 56
RC Parish: Dunderry, see Churchtown
Diocese: ME

Civil Parish: **Rathbeggan**
Map Grid: 132
RC Parish: see Ratoath
Diocese: ME

Civil Parish: **Rathcore**
Map Grid: 115
RC Parish: see Rathmolyon
Diocese: ME

Civil Parish: **Rathfeigh**
Map Grid: 92
RC Parish: see Skreen
Diocese: ME

Civil Parish: **Rathkenny**
Map Grid: 40
RC Parish: see Slane
Diocese: ME

Civil Parish: **Rathmolyon**
Map Grid: 114
RC Parish: Summerhill, see Laracor
Diocese: ME

Civil Parish: **Rathmore**
Map Grid: 69
RC Parish: see Athboy
Diocese: ME

Civil Parish: **Rathregan**
Map Grid: 131
RC Parish: Kilcloon, see Dunboyne for pre-1836 records
Diocese: ME
Earliest Record: b. 2.1836; m. 4.1836
Parish Address: Rev. G. Stanley, PP, Dunboyne, Co. Meath

Civil Parish: **Ratoath**
Map Grid: 127
RC Parish: Ratoath
Diocese: ME
Earliest Record: b. 8.1818; m. 8.1818
Parish Address: Rev. Francis McNamara, PP, Parochial House, Ratoath, Co. Meath

Civil Parish: **Radonstown** (Rabonstown)
Map Grid: 142
RC Parish: Kilcloon, see Rathregan
Diocese: ME

Civil Parish: **St. Mary's**
Map Grid: 60
RC Parish: see St. Mary's, Drogheda, Co. Louth
Diocese: ME

Civil Parish: **Scurlockstown**
Map Grid: 119
RC Parish: see Kilmessan
Diocese: ME

Civil Parish: **Siddan**
Map Grid: 22
RC Parish: Lobinstown, see Killary
Diocese: ME

Civil Parish: **Skreen**
Map Grid: 91
RC Parish: Skryne
Diocese: ME

Earliest Record: b. 11.1841; m. 1.1842
Parish Address: Rev. John Healy, PP, Parochial House, Skryne, Tara, Co. Meath

Civil Parish: **Slane**
Map Grid: 44
RC Parish: Slane
Diocese: ME
Earliest Record: b. 11.1784; m. 11.1784
Missing Dates: b. 12.1815-7.1818, 2.1861-8.1866; m. 1.1788-8.1818, 12.1844-5.1846, 11.1857-10.1866
Parish Address: Rev. Joseph Dooley, PP, Parochial House, Slane, Co. Meath

Civil Parish: **Stackallan**
Map Grid: 46
RC Parish: part Rathkenny; part Slane, see Slane
Diocese: ME

Civil Parish: **Staffordstown**
Map Grid: 83
RC Parish: Johnstown, see Monkstown
Diocese: ME

Civil Parish: **Staholmog**
Map Grid: 8
RC Parish: Stahalmog, see Kilbeg
Diocese: ME

Civil Parish: **Stamullin**
Map Grid: 104
RC Parish: Stamullen
Diocese: ME
Earliest Record: b. 1.1831; m. 5.1830; d. 1.1834
Parish Address: Rev. Michael Daly, PP, Preston Hill, Stamullen, Co. Meath

Civil Parish: **Tara**
Map Grid: 89
RC Parish: see Skreen
Diocese: ME

Civil Parish: **Teltown**
Map Grid: 37
RC Parish: see Kilberry
Diocese: ME

Civil Parish: **Templekeeran**
Map Grid: 86

RC Parish: see Skreen
Diocese: ME

Civil Parish: **Timoole**
Map Grid: 93
RC Parish: Blacklion, see Ardmulchan
Diocese: ME

Civil Parish: **Trevet**
Map Grid: 96
RC Parish: see Skreen
Diocese: ME

Civil Parish: **Trim**
Map Grid: 112
RC Parish: Trim
Diocese: ME
Earliest Record: b. 7.1829; m. 7.1829; d. 1.1831
Missing Dates: d. ends 4.1841
Parish Address: Rev. Sean Kenny, PP, Trim, Co. Meath

Civil Parish: **Trubley** (Tubberville)
Map Grid: 118
RC Parish: Dunsany, see Kilmessan
Diocese: ME

Civil Parish: **Tullaghanoge**
Map Grid: 74
RC Parish: see Churchtown
Diocese: ME

Civil Parish: **Tullyallen**
Map Grid: 45
RC Parish: see Tullyallen (1), Co. Louth
Diocese: AM

Commercial and Social Directories

1824

J. Pigot's *City of Dublin & Hibernian Provincial Directory* includes traders, nobility, gentry, and clergy lists of Athboy, Duleek, Kells, Navan, Ratoath, Summerhill, and Trim.

1846

Slater's *National Commercial Directory of Ireland* lists nobility, clergy, traders, etc., in

Athboy, Duleek, Kells, Navan, Ratoath, Ashbourne and Dunshaughlin, Trim, and Summerhill.

1856

Slater's *Royal National Commercial Directory of Ireland* lists nobility, gentry, clergy, traders, etc., in Athboy, Duleek, Kells, Navan, Oldcastle, Ratoath, Ashbourne and Dunshaughlin, Slane, Trim, and Summerhill.

1870

Slater's *Directory of Ireland* contains trade, nobility, and clergy lists for Athboy, Duleek, Kells, Navan, Oldcastle, Ratoath, Slane, and Trim.

1881

Slater's *Royal National Commercial Directory of Ireland* contains lists of traders, clergy, nobility, and farmers in adjoining parishes of the towns of Duleek, Kells, Navan, Oldcastle, Ratoath, Ashbourne and Dunshaughlin, Trim, and Athboy.

1894

Slater's *Royal National Directory of Ireland* lists traders, police, teachers, farmers, and private residents in each of the towns, villages, and parishes of the county.

Family History

"Barnewall of Rowestown Co. Meath." *Ir. Gen.* 4 (1978): 174-82.

"The Barnwalls." *Riocht na Midhe* 1 (1957): 64-68.

"Barnwell of Kilbrew, Co. Meath." *Ir. Gen.* 6 (1) (1980): 9-17.

"The Berfords of Kilrue." *Riocht na Midhe* 6 (4) (1978/79): 89-118.

"The Briens of Brawney." *Riocht na Midhe* 7 (4) (1980/81): 80-98.

"The MacCoghlans of Delvin." *Ir. Gen.* 4 (6) (1973): 534-46; 5 (1) (1974): 21-32.

"The Cusacks of Killeen, Co. Meath." *Riocht na Midhe* 7 (4) (1980/81): 3-35.

Cusack – see Co. Dublin.

"The Cusacks of Portraine and Rathaldron." *Riocht na Midhe* 4 (4) (1970): 58-61.

"Darcy of Platten." *Ir. Gen.* 6 (4) (1983): 403-22.

"Dowdalls of Athlumney." *Riocht na Midhe* 3 (3) (1965): 205-10.

"Draycott of Mornington." *Riocht na Midhe* 6 (3).

"ffolliott of Co. Meath." *Ir. Anc.* 1 (1): 27-33.

"The Family of Barnewall." *Ir. Gen.* 3 (1959-66): 124-35, 173-76, 198-209, 249-56, 311-21, 384-88, 445-54.

"Fleming & Conyngham of Slane." *Riocht na Midhe* 7 (2) (1982/83): 69-75.

"The Foxes of Muintir Thaidgean." *Riocht na Midhe* 4 (4) (1970): 6-23.

"The Griersons of Co. Meath." *Ir. Gen.* 3 (4) (1959): 136-43.

"The Mageoghans." *Riocht na Midhe* 4 (3) (1969): 63-86.

"The Molloy Family of Kells." *Ir. Gen.* 3 (1961): 187-89.

"O'Molloys of Fircall." *Riocht na Midhe* 5 (3) (1973): 14-45.

"Piers of Tristernagh." *Riocht na Midhe* 7 (4) (1980/81): 52-76.

"Plunkett of Loughcrew." *Ir. Gen.* 5 (4) (1977): 422-27.

"The Plunkett Family of Loughcrew." *Riocht na Midhe* 1 (4) (1958): 49-53.

"Tandy of Drewstown." Pedigree in *Swanzy Notebooks*. RCB Library, Dublin.

"Tandy of Johnsbrook." Pedigree in *Swanzy Notebooks*. RCB Library, Dublin.

"Tucker of Petersville." Pedigree in *Swanzy Notebooks*. RCB Library, Dublin.

Tyrrell – see Co. Dublin.

"The Wakelys of Navan and Ballyburly." *Riocht na Midhe* 5 (4) (1974): 3-19.

Gravestone Inscriptions

A series of records of gravestone inscriptions made by the late Dr. Beryl Moore are held in

Meath Co. Library. These are denoted below as "Moore Transcriptions."

Agher: Moore Transcriptions; *Ir. Anc.* 10 (2) (1978): 129-38.

Arodstown: *Riocht na Midhe* 6 (1) (1975): 38-49; Moore Transcriptions.

Athboy: *Ir. Anc.* 13 (1), (2): 113-24.

Athlumney: Moore Transcriptions.

Balfeaghan: Moore Transcriptions.

Balsoon: *Ir. Anc.* 8 (2) (1976): 94-95.

Castlejordan: Moore Transcriptions.

Castlekieran: Moore Transcriptions.

Clonabreany: Moore Transcriptions; *Riocht na Midhe* 6 (2) (1976): 16-36.

Clady (Parish of Bective): *Ir. Anc.* 16 (1) (1984): 9-13.

Clonmacduff (alias Courtown or Blackchurch): *Riocht na Midhe* 7 (4) (1980/81): 111-28.

Courtown: Moore Transcriptions.

Danestown: *Riocht na Midhe* 5 (4) (1974): 87-97; Moore Transcriptions.

Drumlargan: *Ir. Anc.* 12 (1), (2): 1980; Moore Transcriptions.

Duleek: *Ir. Gen.* 3 (12) (1967): 538-40.

Dunboyne, CI: *Ir. Anc.* 11 (1) (1979): 54-68; (2): 137-53.

Gallow: Moore Transcriptions.

Kells: *Ir. Gen.* 3 (12) (1966): 439-44.

Kilbride: *Riocht na Midhe* 6 (3) (1977): 23-38; Moore Transcriptions.

Killaconnigan: *Ir. Anc.* 16 (2) (1984): 107-17.

Killeen: *Riocht na Midhe* 4 (4) (1970): 24-29.

Loughcrew: *Ir. Anc.* 9 (2) (1977): 85-101

Loughcrew, Old: Moore Transcriptions.

Macetown: Moore Transcriptions.

Moy: Moore Transcriptions; *Ir. Anc.* 6 (2) (1974): 85-96.

Moyagher: Moore Transcriptions; *Ir. Anc.* 8 (1) (1976): 9-12.

Oldcastle: *Riocht na Midhe* 4 (2) (1968): 11-19.

Rathmore: *Ir. Anc.* 7 (2) (1975): 70-82; Moore Transcriptions.

Scullockstown: Moore Transcriptions.

St. Fechin's Church: Moore Transcriptions.

St. Kilmore: *Riocht na Midhe* 6 (1) (1975): 38-49; Moore Transcriptions.

St. Mary's, Killeen: Moore Transcriptions.

Tyrcogan: Moore Transcriptions.

Newspapers

There were no newspapers published in this county before 1845. Papers from the surrounding counties should be searched, starting with those in the county adjacent to the area of interest.

Title: *Meath Chronicle*
Published in: Navan, 1897-current
BL Holdings: 5.1906-9.1907; 1.1909-1.1924
Co. Library: 1904-in progress

Title: *Meath Herald & Cavan Advertiser*
Published in: Kells, 1845-1936
NLI Holdings: 2.1845-9.1913; 1.1928-11.1936
BL Holdings: 2.1845-12.1921; 4.1924-9.1933

Title: *Meath People*
Published in: Navan, 1857-63
NLI Holdings: 8.1857-11.1863
BL Holdings: 8.1857-11.1863

Title: *Meath Reporter*
Published in: Trim, 1870-1901
NLI Holdings: 1.1888-6.1901
BL Holdings: 3-10.1871

Wills and Administrations

A discussion of the types of records, where they are held, their availability and value is given in the Wills section of the Introduction. The availability of prerogative wills, administrations, and marriage license records is also described in the relevant parts of the same section. Where available, published sources of these records are given in the Miscellaneous Sources section.

Pre-1858 Wills and Administrations

Prerogative Wills. see p. xli.

Consistorial Wills. County Meath is mainly in the diocese of Meath with three parishes in Armagh. The guide to Catholic parish records in this chapter shows the diocese to which each civil parish belonged. The wills of residents of each diocese were usually proven within that diocese (see the Wills section for exceptions). The following records survive:

Wills. see p. xxxvii.

Abstracts. see p. xxxvii.

Indexes. Meath (fragment of 1572-1858 with index). PRO. A transcript for 1635-1838 provides name of testator and year of probate only. Kilmore – see Co. Cavan; Armagh – see Co. Armagh.

Post-1858 Wills and Administrations

This county was served by the District Registry of Dublin. The surviving records are kept in the PRO.

Marriage Licenses

Indexes. Meath and Kilmore (1691-1845). PRO; SLC film 100869. Armagh – see Co. Armagh.

Miscellaneous Sources

"Aspects of Navan History." *Riocht na Midhe* 3 (1) (1963): 33-56.

Cogan, A. *The Ecclesiastical History of the Diocese of Meath.* 3 vols. Dublin, 1874.

Connell, P. *Changing Forces Shaping a Nineteenth Century Town: A Case Study of Navan.* Maynooth, 1978.

Fitzsimons, J. *The Parish of Kilbeg.* Kells, 1979.

"The Great Landowners of Meath 1879." *Riocht na Midhe* 7 (4) (1980/81): 99-110.

"Land Tenure in East Westmeath and Agriculture 1820-4." *Riocht na Midhe* 5 (4) (1978/79): 33-48.

"Register of Pupils at Donacarney School, Co. Meath, 1873." *Ir. Anc.* 16 (2) (1984): 75-77.

"State of the Poor in Oldcastle 1834." *Riocht na Midhe* 1 (4) (1958): 69-74.

"Yeomanry, Militia, and Orangemen of Co. Meath." *Riocht na Midhe* 5 (4) (1978/79): 3-32 (names of officers only).

Research Sources and Services

Journals

Riocht na Midhe (published by Meath Archaeological and Historical Society)

Annala Dhamhliag (The Annals of Duleek)

Libraries and Information Sources

Meath County Library, Railway Street, Navan, Co. Meath Ph: (046) 21134/21451 (local studies section has all standard sources plus other local material and an index to *Riocht na Midhe*).

Research Services

See research services in Dublin, p. xliv

Societies

Meath Archaeological & Historical Society (publishers of *Riocht na Midhe*), Mr. William Battersby, 5 Ludlow Street, Navan, Co. Meath

Duleek Historical Society (publishers of *Annala Dhamhliag*), Mr. Enda O'Boyle, "Endevere," Dunleek, Co. Meath

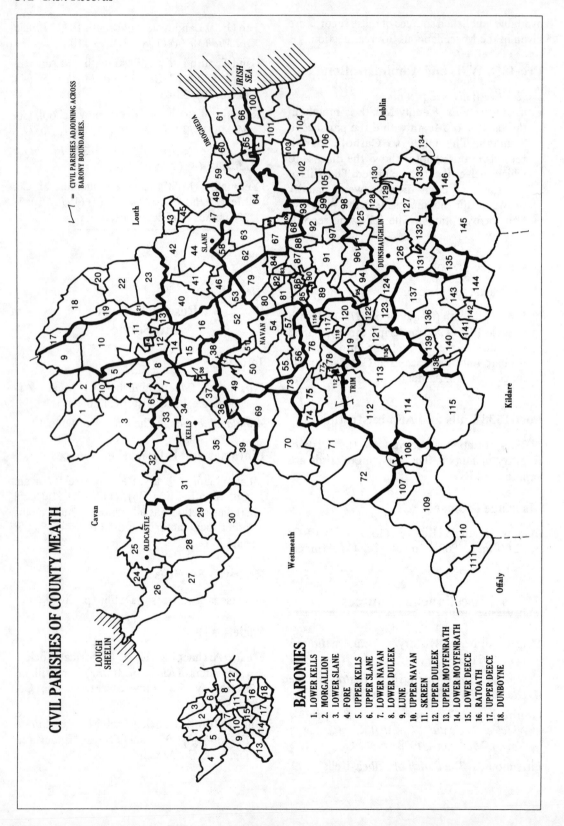

CIVIL PARISHES OF COUNTY MEATH

LOUGH SHEELIN

Cavan

Louth

DROGHEDA

IRISH SEA

Dublin

Westmeath

Kildare

Offaly

OLDCASTLE

KELLS

SLANE

NAVAN

TRIM

DUNSHAUGHLIN

= CIVIL PARISHES ADJOINING ACROSS BARONY BOUNDARIES.

BARONIES

1. LOWER KELLS
2. MORGALLION
3. LOWER SLANE
4. FORE
5. UPPER KELLS
6. UPPER SLANE
7. LOWER NAVAN
8. LOWER DULEEK
9. LUNE
10. UPPER NAVAN
11. SKREEN
12. UPPER DULEEK
13. UPPER MOYFENRATH
14. LOWER MOYFENRATH
15. LOWER DEECE
16. RATOATH
17. UPPER DEECE
18. DUNBOYNE

County Monaghan

A Brief History

This Ulster county contains the towns of Monaghan, Clones, Castleblayney, and Carrickmacross.

In the old Gaelic system of land division, Monaghan was part of the Kingdom of Oriel. It was also known as McMahon's country after the dominant family in the area. The McMahons and their allies, the McKennas and O'Connollys, maintained effective domination of the county even after the arrival of the Normans in the twelfth century. The county boundaries were not established by the English administration until the late sixteenth century.

After the defeat of the rebellion of O'Neill and the Ulster chieftains in 1603, the county was not planted like the other counties of Ulster. The lands were instead left in the hands of the native chieftains. In 1641 the McMahons and their allies joined the general rebellion of Irish Catholics, and following their defeat there was some plantation of the county with Scottish and English families.

Analysis of the Hearth Money Rolls of 1663 shows that the commonest names in the county at the time (in descending order) were McMahon, McKenna, O'Duffy, O'Connolly, McCabe, McWard, McArdle, McIlmartin, O'Byrne, O'Callan, McCallan, O'Kelly, O'Murphy, McNaney, McTreanor, O'Gowan or McGowan, O'Boylan, McIlcollin, O'Finnegan, O'Cassidy, and McPhilip.

The McCabes were a Gallowglass, or mercenary, family probably brought into the county by the McMahons following the Norman invasion. The O'Byrnes, who are relatively numerous in the county, are probably descendants of the Kildare or Wicklow O'Byrnes. This family was driven from its Kildare territories by the Normans in the late twelfth century. It is suggested that part of this clan may have migrated into Monaghan.

The major settlers in the county were Scottish farmers brought over from the area of Strathclyde. Common names among these settlers were McAndrew, Mackay, Sinclair, Stewart, Buchanan, McKenzie, Davidson, Ferguson, Blackshaw, McCaig, Walker, Cameron, Gordon, Patterson, and McCutcheon.

A general indication of the proportions of the population of Irish or Norman extraction, or of English or Scottish descent, can be derived from the statistics on religious persuasions of the inhabitants. These groups were, respectively, predominantly Catholic, Church of Ireland, or Presbyterian. In 1861, when the census first determined religion, the respective proportions were 73, 14, and 12 percent.

In the late eighteenth and early nineteenth centuries the county became increasingly more densely populated. In 1841 there were 428 people per square mile, making the county one of the most densely populated in the country. The Great Famine of 1845-47 very badly affected the county. In 1841 the population was 200,000, but by 1851 it had fallen by 30 percent to 142,000. Over 25,000 people died in the same decade and a further 30,000 emigrated.

The county is currently mainly dependent on agriculture and related industry and has a population of around 52,000.

Census and Census Substitutes

1632-36
"The Balfour Rentals of 1632 and 1636" (with tenants list). *Clogher Record* 12 (1) (1985): 92-109.

1659
"Census" of Ireland. Edited by S. Pender. Dublin: Stationery Office, 1939; SLC film 924648.

1666
Hearth Money Roll. In D. Rushe. *A History of Monaghan*. pp. 291-338.

1738
"Some Clones Inhabitants." *Clogher Record* 2 (3) (1959): 512-14.

1772
"Castleblayney Rent Book 1772." *Clogher Record* 11 (1) (1982): 414-18.

1777
"Some Protestant Inhabitants of Carrickmacross 1777." *Clogher Record* 6 (1) (1966): 119-25.

1778-96
"Catholic Qualification Rolls Index: Fermanagh and Monaghan." *Clogher Record* 2 (3) (1959): 544-51 (Catholics taking oath of loyalty; gives name, occupation, and residence).

1784-89
"A Rental of the Anketell Estate, Co. Monaghan 1784-89" (with indexed list of tenants). *Clogher Record* 11 (3) (1984): 403-20.

1785
Male Protestants of 17 Years and Over in the Diocese of Clogher (i.e., parishes of Errigal, Trough, and Magheracloone). SLC film 258517.

1786
"The Ballybay Estate 1786" (including list of tenants). *Clogher Record* 11 (1) (1982): 71-76.

1790-c.1830
"The Ker Estate, Newbliss, Co. Monaghan 1790-ca.1830" (with list of landholders). *Clogher Record* 12 (1) (1985): 110-26.

1796
See Mayo 1796 (List of Catholics).

1823-38
Tithe Applotment Survey (see p. xxvii).

1847
"Castleblayney Poor Law Rate Book (1847)." *Clogher Record* 5 (1) (1963): 131-48 (ratepayers in each townland in Castleblayney Poor Law Union).

1858-60
Griffith's Valuation (see p. xxvii).

1901
Census. PRO.

1911
Census. PRO.

Church Records

Church of Ireland
(shows starting date of record)

Parish: **Aghadrumsee**
Existing Records: b. 1821; m. 1821; d. 1822
Status: LC

Parish: **Ardragh** (St. Patrick's)
Status: Lost

Parish: **Aughnamullen**
Status: Lost

Parish: **Ballybay**
Existing Records: b. 1813; m. 1813; d. 1813
Status: LC

Parish: **Carrickmacross** or **Magheross**
Existing Records: b. 1796; m. 1798; d. 1798
Status: LC

Parish: **Castleblayney** (see Mucknoe)

Parish: **Clones**
Existing Records: b. 1682; m. 1682; d. 1682
Status: LC

Parish: **Clontibret**
Existing Records: b. 1799; m. 1799; d. 1799
Status: LC

Parish: **Clough**
Existing Records: b. 1811; m. 1811; d. 1811
Status: LC

Parish: **Crossduff** (Aughnamullen East)
Status: Lost

Parish: **Currin** (Rockcorry)
Existing Records: b. 1810; m. 1812; d. 1810
Status: LC

Parish: **Currin Drum**
Existing Records: b. 1828; m. 1828; d. 1828
Status: LC

Parish: **Donagh**
Existing Records: b. 1796; m. 1796; d. 1796
Status: LC

Parish: **Donaghmoyne**
Status: Lost

Parish: **Drumsnat**
Existing Records: b. 1825; m. 1825; d. 1825
Status: LC

Parish: **Errigle-Shanco**
Status: Lost

Parish: **Errigle-Trough**
Existing Records: b. 1809; m. 1803; d. 1802
Status: LC

Parish: **Inniskeen**
Status: Lost

Parish: **Killanney**
Existing Records: b. 1825; m. 1825; d. 1825
Status: LC

Parish: **Killeevan**
Existing Records: b. 1811; m. 1811; d. 1811
Status: LC

Parish: **Kilmore** (also see St. Ranoodan)
Existing Records: b. 1796; m. 1796; d. 1796
Status: LC

Parish: **Magheracloone**
Existing Records: b. 1806; m. 1806; d. 1806
Status: LC

Parish: **Mucknoe** or **Castleblayney**
Existing Records: b. 1810; m. 1810; d. 1810
Status: LC

Parish: **Mullaghfad**
Existing Records: b. 1836; m. 1837 (four entries
    of marriages 1868-69 in burial register);
    d. 1850
Status: LC

Parish: **Newbliss**
Existing Records: b. 1841; d. 1837
Status: LC

Parish: **Rockcorry**
Status: Lost

Parish: **St. Mark, Augher**
Existing Records: b. 1866
Status: LC

Parish: **St. Ranoodan** (see also Kilmore)
Existing Records: b. 1861; d. 1867
Status: LC

Parish: **Tullycorbet**
Status: Lost

Parish: **Tydavnet**
Existing Records: b. 1822; m. 1822; d. 1822
Status: LC

Parish: **Tyholland**
Existing Records: b. 1806; m. 1806; d. 1806
Status: LC

Presbyterian

Parish: **Ballyalbany**
Starting Date: 1802

Parish: **Ballybay**
Starting Date: 1833

Parish: **Ballyhobridge** (Clones)
Starting Date: 1846

Parish: **Broomfield** (Castleblaney)
Starting Date: 1841

Parish: **Cahans** (Ballybay)
Starting Date: 1752

Parish: **Castleblaney**
Starting Date: 1832

Parish: **Clones**
Starting Date: 1856

Parish: **Clontibret**
Starting Date: 1825

Parish: **Corlea**
Starting Date: 1835

Parish: **Derryvalley** (Ballybay)
Starting Date: 1816

Parish: **Drumkeen** (Newbliss)
Starting Date: 1856

Parish: **Frankford** (Castleblaney)
Starting Date: 1820

Parish: **Glennan** (Glasslough)
Starting Date: 1829

Parish: **Middletown** (Glasslough)
Starting Date: 1829

Parish: **Monaghan**
Starting Date: 1824

Parish: **Newbliss**
Starting Date: 1856

Parish: **Scotstown**
Starting Date: 1856

Parish: **Stonebridge** (Newbliss)
Starting Date: 1821

Roman Catholic

Civil Parish: **Aghabog**
Map Grid: 12
RC Parish: Aghabog, see Killevan
Diocese: CG

Civil Parish: **Aghnamullen (1)**
Map Grid: 18
RC Parish: Aghnamullen East; also Aghnamullen West, see below
Diocese: CG
Earliest Record: b. 7.1857; m. 7.1857; d. 7.1857
Missing Dates: b. 10.1876-8.1878; m. 10.1876-8.1878
Parish Address: Rev. James Brennan, PP, Shantonagh, Castleblayney, Co. Monaghan

Civil Parish: **Aghnamullen (2)**
Map Grid: 18
RC Parish: Aghnamullen West
Diocese: CG
Earliest Record: b. 2.1841; m. 2.1841
Parish Address: Rev. Sean Clerkin, PP, Castleblaney, Co. Monaghan

Civil Parish: **Ballybay**
Map Grid: 17

RC Parish: part Tallcorbet; part Aughwamullen East
Diocese: CG

Civil Parish: **Clones** (see also Co. Fermanagh)
Map Grid: 9
RC Parish: Clones
Diocese: CG
Earliest Record: b. 7.1848; m. 5.1821
Missing Dates: b. 4.1854-4.1855; m. 3.1840-10.1840
Parish Address: Rev. Sean McNaboe, PP, Clones, Co. Monaghan

Civil Parish: **Clontibret**
Map Grid: 15
RC Parish: Clontibret
Diocese: CG
Earliest Record: b. 2.1861
Parish Address: Rev. Philip Connolly, PP, Annyalla, Castleblayney, Co. Monaghan

Civil Parish: **Currin**
Map Grid: 13
RC Parish: see Killeevan
Diocese: CG

Civil Parish: **Donagh**
Map Grid: 2
RC Parish: Donagh
Diocese: CG
Earliest Record: b. 5.1836; m. 5.1836
Parish Address: Rev. Enda McCormack, PP, Glaslough, Monaghan

Civil Parish: **Donaghmoyne**
Map Grid: 20
RC Parish: Donaghmoyne
Diocese: CG
Earliest Record: b. 1.1863; m. 10.1872
Parish Address: Rev. Augustine Duffy, PP, Donaghmoyne, Carrickmacross, Co. Monaghan

Civil Parish: **Drummully** (see also Co. Fermanagh)
Map Grid: 11
RC Parish: see Galloon, Co. Fermanagh; see also Killeevan
Diocese: CG

Civil Parish: **Drumsnat**
Map Grid: 5
RC Parish: Drumsnat and Kilmore
Diocese: CG
Earliest Record: b. 2.1836; m. 2.1836; d. 2.1836
Missing Dates: b. 6.1872-3.1875; m. 6.1872-3.1875; d. 6.1872-3.1875
Parish Address: Rev. Kevin Cassidy, PP, Corcaghan, Monaghan

Civil Parish: **Ematris**
Map Grid: 14
RC Parish: Ematris
Diocese: CG
Earliest Record: b. 5.1848; m. 2.1850
Missing Dates: b. 3.1860-3.1861
Parish Address: Rev. Gerard Ferguson, PP, Rockcorry, Monaghan

Civil Parish: **Errigal Trough** (see also Co. Tyrone)
Map Grid: 1
RC Parish: Errigal Trough
Diocese: CG
Earliest Record: b. 11.1835; m. 12.1837
Missing Dates: b. 3.1852-3.1861; m. 7.1849-1.1862
Parish Address: Rev. Thomas McCarvill, PP, St. Joseph's, Emyvale, Monaghan

Civil Parish: **Inishkeen**
Map Grid: 21
RC Parish: Inishkeen
Diocese: CG
Earliest Record: b. 7.1837; m. 4.1839
Missing Dates: b. 10.1862-7.1863; m. ends 11.1850
Parish Address: Rev. Vincent McDonald, PP, Inniskeen, Dundalk, Co. Louth

Civil Parish: **Killanny**
Map Grid: 23
RC Parish: see Co. Louth
Diocese: CG

Civil Parish: **Killeevan**
Map Grid: 10
RC Parish: Killeevan
Diocese: CG
Earliest Record: b. 1.1871; m. 1.1871

Parish Address: Rev. Hugh McCaughey, PP, Newbliss, Co. Monaghan

Civil Parish: **Kilmore**
Map Grid: 6
RC Parish: see Drumsnat
Diocese: CG

Civil Parish: **Magheracloone**
Map Grid: 22
RC Parish: Magheracloone
Diocese: CG
Earliest Record: b. 5.1836; m. 10.1826
Missing Dates: b. 11.1863-1.1865; m. 3.1959-4.1866
Parish Address: Rev. T. Mohan, Drumgossatt, Carrickmacross, Co. Monaghan

Civil Parish: **Magheross**
Map Grid: 19
RC Parish: Carrickmacross
Diocese: CG
Earliest Record: b. 1.1858; m. 2.1838
Missing Dates: m. 1.1844-1.1858
Parish Address: Rev. S. Morris, PP, St. Joseph's, Carrickmacross, Co. Monaghan

Civil Parish: **Monaghan**
Map Grid: 7
RC Parish: Monaghan
Diocese: CG
Earliest Record: b. 11.1835; m. 2.1827
Missing Dates: b. 12.1847-6.1849, 4.1850-1.1857; m. 6.1850-1.1857
Parish Address: Rev. Sean Nolan, Adm, The Presbytery, Park Street, Monaghan

Civil Parish: **Muckno**
Map Grid: 16
RC Parish: Muckno
Diocese: CG
Earliest Record: b. 11.1835; m. 10.1835
Parish Address: Rev. Canon Morris, PP, Castleblayney, Co. Monaghan

Civil Parish: **Tedavnet**
Map Grid: 3
RC Parish: Tydavnet
Diocese: CG
Earliest Record: b. 11.1835; m. 4.1825
Missing Dates: m. 10.1865-1.1876

Parish Address: Rev. Bernard Maguire, PP, Scotstown, Monaghan

Civil Parish: **Tehallan**
Map Grid: 4
RC Parish: Tyholland
Diocese: CG
Earliest Record: b. 5.1835; m. 1.1827; d. 1.1851
Missing Dates: b. 12.1863-12.1863; m. 12.1865-2.1866; d. ends 12.1863
Parish Address: Rev. Denis Dolan, Adm, Silverstream, Monaghan

Civil Parish: **Tullycorbet**
Map Grid: 8
RC Parish: Tullycorbet
Diocese: CG
Earliest Record: b. 4.1862; m. 5.1862
Parish Address: Rev. Eugene Lennon, PP, Ballybay, Co. Monaghan

Commercial and Social Directories

1824
J. Pigot's *City of Dublin & Hibernian Provincial Directory* includes traders, nobility, gentry, and clergy lists of Ballybay, Carrickmacross, Castleblayney, Clones, and Monaghan.

1846
Slater's *National Commercial Directory of Ireland* lists nobility, clergy, traders, etc., in Ballybay, Carrickmacross, Castleblayney, Clones and Newtown-Butler, and Monaghan.

1852
Henderson's *Belfast and Province of Ulster Directory* has lists of inhabitants, traders, etc., in and around the towns of Ballybay, Clones, and Monaghan.

1854
Further edition of the above extended to cover Carrickmacross and Castleblayney. Further editions were issued in 1856, 1858, 1861, 1863, 1865, 1868, 1870, 1877, 1880, 1884, 1890, 1894, 1900.

1856

Slater's *Royal National Commercial Directory of Ireland* lists nobility, gentry, clergy, traders, etc., in Ballybay, Carrickmacross, Castleblayney, Clones and Newtown-Butler, and Monaghan.

1865

R. Wynne's *Business Directory of Belfast* covers Clones and Monaghan.

1870

Slater's *Directory of Ireland* contains trade, nobility, and clergy lists for Ballybay, Carrickmacross and Shercock, Castleblayney, Clones, and Monaghan.

1881

Slater's *Royal National Commercial Directory of Ireland* contains lists of traders, clergy, nobility, and farmers in adjoining parishes of the towns of Ballybay, Carrickmacross and Shercock, Castleblayney, Clones, and Monaghan.

1894

Slater's *Royal National Directory of Ireland* lists traders, police, teachers, farmers, and private residents in each of the towns, villages, and parishes of the county.

Family History

Belfast, G.S. *A Family History of Montgomery of Ballyleck, Co. Monaghan*. Belfast, 1887.

"Campbell of Co. Monaghan." Pedigree in *Swanzy Notebooks*. RCB Library.

Carson, T.W. *Carson of Shanroe, Co. Monaghan*. Dublin, 1879.

Carson, James. *A Short History of the Carson Family of Monanton, Co. Monaghan*. Belfast, 1879.

"Dawson of Co. Monaghan." Pedigree in *Swanzy Notebooks*. RCB Library.

"Families of Medieval Clones." *Clogher Record* 2 (3) (1959): 385-414.

"The MacMahons of Monaghan (1500-1603)." *Clogher Record* 1 (1955-62): 22-38, 85-107; 2: 490-503; 4: 190-94.

"Noble of Co. Monaghan." Pedigree in *Swanzy Notebooks*. RCB Library.

"Notes on the Families of Blaney, Co. Monaghan, and Denny of Tralee, Co. Kerry." *J. Ass. Pres. Mem. Dead* 7 (1907-09): 373.

"Pockrick of Co. Monaghan." Pedigree in *Swanzy Notebooks*. RCB Library.

"Rogers of Co. Monaghan." Pedigree in *Swanzy Notebooks*. RCB Library.

Williams, J.F. *The Groves and Lappan; Monaghan County, Ireland. An account of...the Genealogy of the Williams*. Saint Paul, 1889.

"Wray of Co. Monaghan." Pedigree in *Swanzy Notebooks*. RCB Library.

"Wright of Co. Monaghan." Pedigree in *Swanzy Notebooks*. RCB Library.

Gravestone Inscriptions

Aghabog: see Killeevan.

Clones Abbey and Round Tower Graveyard: *Clogher Record* 11 (3) (1984): 421-48.

Clontibret: *Clogher Record* 8 (2) 1974.

Donagh: *Clogher Record* 2 (1) (1957): 192-204.

Drumsnat: *Clogher Record* 6 (1) (1966): 71-103.

Drumswords: *Clogher Record* 12 (1): 18-22.

Glaslough: *Clogher Record* 9 (3) (1978): 77-85.

Killanny: *Clogher Record* 6 (1) (1966): 191-96.

Killeevan and Aghabog: *Clogher Record* 11 (1) (1982): 119-49.

Kilmore: *Clogher Record* 11 (3) (1983): 184-86; 12 (1) (1985): 127-31.

Macalla, *Clogher Record* 3 (4) 1978.

Magheross: *Clogher Record* 5 (1) (1963): 123-30.

Rackwallace: *Clogher Record* 4 (3) (1962): 155-62.

Roslea (St. Tierneys R.): *Clogher Record* 13 (1) (1984): 421-48.

Tydavnet (old Cemetery): *Clogher Record* 1 (2) (1954): 43-55.

Newspapers

There were no newspapers published in this county before 1839. Papers from the surrounding counties should be searched, starting with those in the county adjacent to the area of interest.

Title: *The Argus*
Published in: Monaghan, 1875-81
BL Holdings: odd numbers 1875; 10.1875-11.1877; 2.1878-7.1881

Title: *Northern Standard*
Published in: Monaghan, 1839-current
NLI Holdings: 1.1885-12.1913; 6.1921-in progress
BL Holdings: 1.1839- in progress

Title: *People's Advocate*
Published in: Monaghan, 1876-1906
NLI Holdings: 12.1904-4.1906
BL Holdings: 2.1876-4.1906

Title: *Weekly Chronicle*
Published in: Clones, 1883
BL Holdings: 7-11.1883

Wills and Administrations

A discussion of the types of records, where they are held, their availability and value is given in the Wills section of the Introduction. The availability of prerogative wills, administrations, and marriage license records is also described in the relevant parts of the same section. Where available, published sources of these records are given in the Miscellaneous Sources section.

Pre-1858 Wills and Administrations

Prerogative Wills. see p. xli.
Consistorial Wills. County Monaghan is entirely in the diocese of Clogher. The guide to Catholic parish records in this chapter shows the diocese to which each civil parish belonged. The wills of residents of each diocese were usually proven within that diocese (see the Wills section for exceptions). The following records survive:

Wills. see p. xxxvii.

Abstracts. Swanzy Will Abstracts (mainly from Clogher and Kilmore) are in the RCB Library.

Indexes. Clogher (1661-1858). Published by Phillimore. PRO.

Post-1858 Wills and Administrations

This county was served by the District Registry of Armagh. The surviving records are kept in the PRO.

Marriage Licenses

Indexes. Clogher (1709-1866). PRO; SLC film 100862

Miscellaneous Sources

"Clogherici: Catholic Clergy of the Diocese of Clogher (1535-1835): The McMahon Clergy." *Clogher Record* 11 (1) (1982): 43-59.

"Farney in 1634: an Examination of John Raven's Survey of the Essex Estate." *Clogher Record* 11 (3) (1983): 245-56 (no residents).

Moffett, Rev. B. *A List of Pupils of Viscount Weymouth's School, Carrickmacross, Who Entered Trinity College, Dublin, from 1706 to 1909.* Dundalk: Tempest, 1911.

Rushe, D. *Monaghan in the 18th Century.* Dundalk, 1919.

Rushe, D. *History of Monaghan for 200 Years: 1660-1860.* Dundalk, 1921.

Shirley, E.P. *The History of the County of Monaghan.* London, 1879.

"The Volunteer Companies of Ulster 1778-1793: 7, Monaghan." *Irish Sword* 8 (31) (1967): 95-97 (some officer's and prisoner's names only).

Research Sources and Services

Journals

Clogher Record (published by Clogher Historical Society, 1953-present), c/o Theo McMahon, 6 Tully, Monaghan

Libraries and Information Sources

Monaghan County Library, The Diamond, Clones, Co. Monaghan Ph: Clones 143

Monaghan County Museum, The Courthouse, Monaghan

Research Services

See research services in Dublin, p. xliv

Societies

Clogher Historical Society (publishers of *Clogher Record*), Mr. J.I.D. Johnston, Corick, Clogher, Co. Tyrone

CIVIL PARISHES OF COUNTY MONAGHAN

Tyrone

Fermanagh

Armagh

1

2
GLASLOUGH

3

4

MONAGHAN

5

7

9

CLONES

6

10

12

8

15

16
CASTLEBLANEY

13

14

6

17

11 +

13
10

18

Cavan

20

21

19

CARRICKMACROSS

BARONIES

1. TROUGH
2. MONAGHAN
3. DARTREE
4. CREMORNE
5. FARNEY

★ PART OF BARONY 2. BUT OF PARISH 10.
+ PART OF PARISH OF COOLE, CO. FERMANAGH

1

2

3

4

5

22

23

Louth

⊢─┐ = CIVIL PARISHES ADJOINING ACROSS
     BARONY BOUNDARIES.

County Offaly

A Brief History

Located in the midlands of Ireland, this small county contains the towns of Tullamore, Birr, Portarlington, Ferbane, and Daingean. In the old Gaelic system the county was part of the Kingdom of Ui Failghe, or Offaly. In the English redivision of the country into counties it was named King's County in 1547. The name was changed back to Offaly on the foundation of the Irish state in 1922.

Within the ancient territory the major Gaelic families were the O'Carrolls, O'Delaneys, Mac-Coghlans, O'Molloys, and O'Connors. Although conquered by the Normans in the twelfth century, English rule gradually waned in the county. In the fifteenth and sixteenth centuries, Offaly and neighbouring Laois were among the most rebellious counties in the country. Continued raids by the Irish from these counties on the English-controlled area around Dublin finally caused the English to invade Laois and Offaly in 1547. The native families were driven back, and several garrisons and forts were built. In Offaly the O'Connor's fort of Daingean was garrisoned by the English and renamed Philipstown (now renamed Daingean). The lands confiscated from the native families were granted to officers and settlers.

However, as resistance to the English garrisons by the native population continued, the English authorities decided to clear the counties of the native people and bring in settlers from England. This was begun in 1556, making it the first plantation of Ireland. Two-thirds of tribal lands were confiscated at this time. The plantation was fiercely resisted and only partially successful. However, it did result in the introduction of a large number of English families to the area.

Since the native population is predominantly Catholic, and English settlers mainly of the Protestant faith, the proportions of these religions among the population can, in very general terms, be used to estimate the origins of the inhabitants of the county. When religious affiliation was first determined in the census of 1861, the proportions of Catholic and Protestant in County Offaly were 89 and 10 percent respectively.

The county was badly affected by the Great Famine of 1845-47. The population, which was 147,000 in 1841, fell to 112,000 in 1851. Of this, some 22,000 died between 1845 and 1851, and a high proportion emigrated. The population continued to fall for the rest of the century and beyond and is now around 58,000.

Census and Census Substitutes

1659

"Census" of Ireland. Edited by S. Pender. Dublin: Stationery Office, 1939; SLC film 924648.

1766

Religious Census of the "Parish of Ballycommon." *J. Kildare Arch. Hist. Soc.* 7: 274-76; GO ms. 537; SLC film 100173, 258517.

1802

"Protestants in Parishes of Ballyboggan, Ballyboy, Castlejordan, Clonmacnoise, Drumcullen, Eglish, Gallen, Killoughey, Lynally, Reynagh, Tullamore-Kilbride." *Ir. Anc.* 5 (2) (1973): 113-20.

1821

Government Census of Parishes of Aghacon, Birr, Ettagh, Kilcolman, Kinnitty, Letterluna, Roscomroe, Roscrea, Seirkieran. PRO; SLC film 100818.

1823-38

Tithe Applotment Survey (see p. xxvii).

1824

List of Catholic Householders in Each Townland of Lusmagh Parish on November 1st. Included in the Catholic registers of Lusmagh (see Roman Catholic records section).

1830

List of Contributors to a New Catholic Church at Wherry (gives only townland and sum subscribed by each person). Included in the Catholic registers of Lusmagh Church.

1835

Census of Tubber Parish (arranged by townland, giving age, occupation, and religion of each person, but no relationships). NLI P 1994.

1840

Census of Parishes of Eglish and Drumcullen. Arranged by townland, gives heads of households, occupations, numbers of males and females in each household, numbers over and under 15, numbers of male and female servants. Included in the Catholic

parish register of Eglish (see Roman Catholic records section). Another undated census is also included in the register.

1852

"Emigrants from Kilconcouse (parish of Kinnity)" (names, ages, and relationships of fifty-six people with dates of departure, arrival, etc). In E. Ellis, *Migrants from Ireland 1847-52*. Baltimore: Genealogical Publishing Co., 1977: 57-59.

1854

Griffith's Valuation (see p. xxvii).

1901

Census. PRO.

1911

Census. PRO.

Church Records

Church of Ireland
(shows starting date of record)

Parish: **Aghancon**
Status: Lost

Parish: **Ballyboy** (Frankford)
Existing Records: b. 1710
Status: PRO

Parish: **Ballyburley** (see Primult)

Parish: **Ballycommon**
Status: Lost

Parish: **Ballykean**
Status: Lost

Parish: **Ballymacwilliam** (see Monasteroris, RC records section)

Parish: **Birr**
Existing Records: b. 1772; m. 1772; d. 1772
Status: LC

Parish: **Borrisnafarney**
Existing Records: b. 1827; m. 1827; d. 1827
Status: LC

Parish: **Castlejordan**
Existing Records: (including curacy of Ballyboggan: register of b.m.d. for 1702-68 also exists) b. 1823; m. 1823; d. 1823
Status: LC

Parish: **Clara** and **Kilmonaghan**
Status: Lost

Parish: **Cloneyburke**
Existing Records: b. 1847; d. 1847
Status: LC

Parish: **Clonmacnois**
Existing Records: b. 1828; m. 1830; d. 1818
Status: LC

Parish: **Drumraney**
Status: Lost

Parish: **Dunkerrin**
Existing Records: b. 1825; m. 1826; d. 1825
Status: LC

Parish: **Durrow**
Existing Records: b. 1706; m. 1797; d. 1706
Missing Records: b. 1801-15; m. 1802-15; d. 1801-15

Parish: **Eglish**
Status: Lost

Parish: **Ettagh**
Existing Records: b. 1825; m. 1820; d. 1826
Status: LC

Parish: **Ferbane** (see also Gallen)
Existing Records: b. 1819; m. 1819; d. 1821
Status: LC

Parish: **Gallen** (see also Reynagh)
Existing Records: b. 1842; m. 1842; d. 1844
Status: LC

Parish: **Geashill**
Existing Records: b. 1713; m. 1713; d. 1713
Status: LC

Parish: **Kilbride** (see Clara)

Parish: **Kilbride, Tullamore**
Existing Records: b. 1805; m. 1805; d. 1805
Status: LC

Parish: **Kilcoleman**
Status: Lost

Parish: **Killaderry** or **Philipstown**
Status: Lost

Parish: **Killeigh** (see also Geashill)
Existing Records: b. 1835; m. 1835; d. 1835 (PRO copy is incomplete)
Status: LC

Parish: **Killoughy**
Existing Records: b. 1818; m. 1816; d. 1877
Status: LC

Parish: **Kilmurryely** (see Shinrone)

Parish: **Kilnegarenagh** or **Lemanaghan**
Status: Lost

Parish: **Kinnitty**
Existing Records: (transferred to Co. Meath) b. 1800; m. 1801; d. 1802
Status: LC

Parish: **Lynally**
Status: Lost

Parish: **Primult** or **Ballybarley**
Status: Lost

Parish: **Rahan**
Status: Lost

Parish: **Reynagh**
Status: Lost

Parish: **Roscrea**
Existing Records: b. 1784; m. 1784; d. 1784
Status: LC

Parish: **Seirkieran**
Status: Lost

Parish: **Shinrone**
Existing Records: b. 1741; m. 1741; d. 1741
Status: LC

Parish: **Templeharry**
Existing Records: b. 1800; m. 1800; d. 1800
Status: LC

Roman Catholic

Civil Parish: **Aghancon**
Map Grid: 38
RC Parish: see Seirkieran
Diocese: K and K

Civil Parish: **Ardnurcher** (or Horseleap, see also Co. Westmeath)
Map Grid: 3
RC Parish: Clara, see Kilbride
Diocese: ME

Civil Parish: **Ballyboy**
Map Grid: 27
RC Parish: Ballyboy and Killoughy (Kilcormac)
Diocese: ME
Earliest Record: b. 1.1821; m. 6.1821; d. 2.1826
Parish Address: Rev. Thomas Mullen, PP, Kilcormac, Co. Offaly

Civil Parish: **Ballyburly**
Map Grid: 6
RC Parish: Rhode
Diocese: KD
Earliest Record: b. 1.1829; m. 8.1829
Missing Dates: m. gaps 2.1878 12.1880
Parish Address: Rev. James Kaye, PP, Tullamore, Co. Offaly

Civil Parish: **Ballycommon**
Map Grid: 21
RC Parish: see Killaderry
Diocese: KD

Civil Parish: **Ballykean**
Map Grid: 29
RC Parish: Portarlington, see Clonyhurk
Diocese: KD

Civil Parish: **Ballymacwilliam**
Map Grid: 7
RC Parish: Edenderry, see Monasteroris
Diocese: KD

Civil Parish: **Ballynakill**
Map Grid: 24
RC Parish: Ballynakill
Diocese: KD
Earliest Record: b. 10.1794; m. 10.1794; d. 10.1794
Missing Dates: b. 3.1815-1.1820, 5.1820-11.1820; m. 2.1815-1.1820, 7.1820-11.1820; d. 2.1815-1880
Parish Address: Rev. Michael Gleeson, PP, Ballinakill, Co. Laois

Civil Parish: **Birr**
Map Grid: 34
RC Parish: Birr and Loughkeen
Diocese: K and K
Earliest Record: b. 5.1838 (2 record books in some periods); m. 5.1838
Missing Dates: 12.1846
Parish Address: Rev. Patrick J. Hammell, PP, Birr, Co. Offaly

Civil Parish: **Borrisnafarney** (see also Co. Tipperary)
Map Grid: 51
RC Parish: Couraganeen (Bourney and Corbally)
Diocese: K and K
Earliest Record: b. 7.1836; m. 6.1836
Missing Dates: b. 8.1866-1.1867, 1873; m. 12.1866-1.1867, 1873
Parish Address: Rev. Patrick Whelan, PP, Bournea, Roscrea, Co. Tipperary

Civil Parish: **Castlejordan** (see also Co. Meath)
Map Grid: 5
RC Parish: Ballinabrackey; also Rhode, see Ballyburly
Diocese: ME
Earliest Record: b. 11.1826; m. 11.1826; d. 11.1848
Missing Dates: d. 7.1849-1880
Parish Address: Rev. Edward Flynn, PP, Ballinbrackey, Kinnegad, Co. Westmeath

Civil Parish: **Castletownely**
Map Grid: 48
RC Parish: see Dunkerrin
Diocese: K and K

Civil Parish: **Clonmacnoise**
Map Grid: 8
RC Parish: Clonmacnoise
Diocese: ME
Earliest Record: b. 4.1826 (2 separate record books for some periods); m. 4.1826; d. 2.1841
Missing Dates: b. 7.1842-2.1848; m. 2.1842-2.1848; d. 2.1842-2.1848
Parish Address: Rev. Donal O'Lehane, PP, Shannonbridge, Athlone, Co. Westmeath

Civil Parish: **Clonsast**
Map Grid: 25
RC Parish: Clonbulloge
Diocese: KD
Earliest Record: b. 11.1819; m. 1.1808
Parish Address: Rev. Michael J. Foynes, PP, Clonbullogue, Tullamore, Co. Offaly

Civil Parish: **Clonyhurk**
Map Grid: 30
RC Parish: Portarlington
Diocese: KD
Earliest Record: b. 1.1820; m. 11.1822
Parish Address: Rev. M. Noonan, PP, Portarlington, Co. Laois

Civil Parish: **Corbally** (see also Co. Tipperary)
Map Grid: 40
RC Parish: Couraganeen, see Borrisnafarney
Diocese: K and K

Civil Parish: **Croghan**
Map Grid: 19
RC Parish: Edenderry, see Monasteroris
Diocese: K and K

Civil Parish: **Cullenwaine**
Map Grid: 50
RC Parish: see Dunkerrin
Diocese: K and K

Civil Parish: **Drumcullen**
Map Grid: 32
RC Parish: see Eglish
Diocese: ME

Civil Parish: **Dunkerrin**
Map Grid: 46
RC Parish: Dunkerrin (Moneygall and Barna)
Diocese: K and K
Earliest Record: b. 1.1820; m. 1.1820
Parish Address: Rev. Patrick O'Meara, PP, Dunkerrin, Birr, Co. Offaly

Civil Parish: **Durrow** (see also Co. Westmeath)
Map Grid: 15
RC Parish: Tullamore, see Kilbride
Diocese: ME

Civil Parish: **Eglish**
Map Grid: 31
RC Parish: Eglish and Drumcullen
Diocese: ME
Earliest Record: b. 1.1809; m. 2.1819; d. 1.1819
Missing Dates: b. 12.1810-2.1819; m. 3.1829-6.1829; d. 4.1829-6.1837, 5.1846-1.1848
Parish Address: Rev. Michael Daly, PP, Eglish, Birr, Co. Offaly

Civil Parish: **Ettagh**
Map Grid: 43
RC Parish: see Kilcolman
Diocese: K and K

Civil Parish: **Finglass**
Map Grid: 49
RC Parish: see Dunkerrin
Diocese: K and K

Civil Parish: **Gallen**
Map Grid: 12
RC Parish: Gallen and Reynagh
Diocese: ME
Earliest Record: b. 11.1811; m. 10.1797; d. 11.1803
Missing Dates: b. several gaps 1812-1829 (2 record books for saome periods); m. 7.1837-2.1838; d. few records to 1820
Parish Address: Rev. Brendan Hynds, PP, Banagher, Co. Offaly

Civil Parish: **Geashill**
Map Grid: 28
RC Parish: part Tullamore, see Kilbride (2); part Portarlington

Civil Parish: **Horseleap** (see Ardnurcher)
Map Grid: 3
RC Parish: Clara, see Kilbride (1)

Civil Parish: **Kilbride (1)** (near Kilmanaghan)
Map Grid: 4
RC Parish: Clara
Diocese: ME
Earliest Record: b. 2.1845; m. 11.1821; d. 1.1825
Missing Dates: d. 2.1854-10.1864, ends 10.1868
Parish Address: Rev. James Deignan, PP, Clara, Co. Offaly

Civil Parish: **Kilbride (2)** (near Lynally)
Map Grid: 17
RC Parish: Tullamore
Diocese: ME
Earliest Record: b. 6.1809; m. 4.1801
Missing Dates: b. 2.1810-11.1820, 2.1822-2.1827, 2.1836; m. 10.1807-11.1820, 2.1822-2.1827
Parish Address: Rev. Patrick Fallon, PP, Tullamore, Co. Offaly

Civil Parish: **Kilclonfert**
Map Grid: 20
RC Parish: see Killaderry
Diocese: KD

Civil Parish: **Kilcolman**
Map Grid: 41
RC Parish: Kilcolman
Diocese: K and K
Earliest Record: b. 3.1830; m. 4.1830
Missing Dates: b. 11.1869-1880; m. 2.1868-1880
Parish Address: Rev. E. Gilmartin, PP, Coolderry, Brosna, Birr, Co. Offaly

Civil Parish: **Kilcomin**
Map Grid: 45
RC Parish: see Shinrone
Diocese: K and K

Civil Parish: **Kilcumreragh**
Map Grid: 1
RC Parish: Tobber, see Kilmanaghan
Diocese: ME

Civil Parish: **Killaderry**
Map Grid: 22
RC Parish: Philipstown

Diocese: KD
Earliest Record: (there are 2 separate books for Daingean in the period 1850-55) b. 8.1795; m. 1.1820
Missing Dates: b. 9.1798-1.1820; m. 12.1866-2.1867
Parish Address: Rev. William O'Byrne, PP, Daingean, Co. Offaly

Civil Parish: **Killagally** (Wherry)
Map Grid: 11
RC Parish: see Wherry
Diocese: ME

Civil Parish: **Killoughy**
Map Grid: 26
RC Parish: Kilcormac, see Ballyboy
Diocese: ME

Civil Parish: **Kilmanaghan** (see also Co. Westmeath)
Map Grid: 2
RC Parish: Tobber
Diocese: ME
Earliest Record: b. 11.1821; m. 11.1824
Parish Address: Rev. Michael Walsh, PP, Springlawn, Tubber, Athlone, Co. Westmeath

Civil Parish: **Kilmurryely**
Map Grid: 42
RC Parish: Shinrone
Diocese: K and K

Civil Parish: **Kinnitty**
Map Grid: 36
RC Parish: Kinnitty
Diocese: K and K
Earliest Record: b. 2.1833; m. 1.1833
Missing Dates: m. 12.1871-1.1872
Parish Address: Rev. Dermot Kenny, PP, Kinnitty, Birr, Co. Offaly

Civil Parish: **Lemanaghan**
Map Grid: 9
RC Parish: Balnahowen and Lemanaghan
Diocese: ME
Earliest Record: b. 8.1821; m. 1.1830; d. 11.1829
Missing Dates: b. 12.1824-2.1826, 2.1839-2.1841, 9.1845-7.1854; m. 8.1845-10.1854; d. 9.1845-9.1854

Parish Address: Rev. Patrick McKeown, PP, Ballinahowen, Athlone, Co. Westmeath

Civil Parish: **Letterluna**
Map Grid: 33
RC Parish: see Kinnitty
Diocese: K and K

Civil Parish: **Lusmagh**
Map Grid: 14
RC Parish: Lusmagh
Diocese: ME
Earliest Record: b. 12.1827; m. 1824; d. 1.1837
Missing Dates: b. 5.1829-4.1833; m. 3.1829-7.1832
Parish Address: Rev. Michael Geoghegan, PP, Lusmagh, Banagher, Co. Offaly

Civil Parish: **Lynally**
Map Grid: 18
RC Parish: see Rahan
Diocese: ME

Civil Parish: **Monasteroris** or **Castropetre**
Map Grid: 23
RC Parish: Edenderry
Diocese: KD
Earliest Record: b. 1.1820; m. 1.1820
Missing Dates: m. 11.1837-9.1838
Parish Address: Rev. Dermot McDermott, PP, Edenderry, Co. Offaly

Civil Parish: **Rahan**
Map Grid: 16
RC Parish: Rahan
Diocese: ME
Earliest Record: b. 7.1810; m. 7.1810
Missing Dates: b. 5.1816-1.1822; m. 3.1816-1.1822
Parish Address: Rev. J. Mooney, PP, Killina, Blueball, Tullamore, Co. Offaly

Civil Parish: **Reynagh**
Map Grid: 13
RC Parish: see Gallen
Diocese: ME

Civil Parish: **Roscomroe**
Map Grid: 37
RC Parish: see Kinnitty
Diocese: K and K

Civil Parish: **Roscrea**
Map Grid: 39
RC Parish: see Roscrea, Co. Tipperary
Diocese: KL

Civil Parish: **Seirkieran**
Map Grid: 35
RC Parish: Seirkieran
Diocese: OS
Earliest Record: b. 4.1830; m. 7.1830
Parish Address: Rev. Sean Collier, PP, Seir Kieran, Clareen, Birr, Co. Offaly

Civil Parish: **Shinrone**
Map Grid: 44
RC Parish: Shinrone and Ballinagarry
Diocese: K and K
Earliest Record: b. 2.1842; m. 4.1842
Parish Address: Rev. Francis Bergin, PP, Shinrone, Co. Offaly

Civil Parish: **Templeharry**
Map Grid: 47
RC Parish: see Dunkerrin
Diocese: K and K

Civil Parish: **Tisaran**
Map Grid: 10
RC Parish: see Wherry
Diocese: ME

Civil Parish: **Wherry** or **Killagally**
Map Grid: 11
RC Parish: Wherry
Diocese: ME
Earliest Record: b. 10.1819; m. 11.1819; d. 12.1821
Missing Dates: b. 7.1865-6.1876; m. ends 11.1833; d. 8.1835-3.1855
Parish Address: Rev. Sean O'Rourke, PP, Ferbane, Co. Offaly

Commercial and Social Directories

1824
J. Pigot's *City of Dublin & Hibernian Provincial Directory* includes traders, nobility, gentry, and clergy lists of Banagher, Birr,

Cloghan, Edenderry, Frankford, Philipstown, and Tullamore.

1846

Slater's *National Commercial Directory of Ireland* lists nobility, clergy, traders, etc., in Banagher, Birr, Clara, Cloghan, Edenderry, Frankford and Ballyboy, Philipstown, and Tullamore.

1856

Slater's *Royal National Commercial Directory of Ireland* lists nobility, gentry, clergy, traders, etc., in Banagher, Birr, Clara, Cloghan and Ferbane, Edenderry, Frankford and Ballyboy, Philipstown, and Tullamore.

1870

Slater's *Directory of Ireland* contains trade, nobility, and clergy lists for Banagher, Birr, Cloghan and Ferbane, Clara, Edenderry, Frankford, Philipstown, and Tullamore.

1881

Slater's *Royal National Commercial Directory of Ireland* contains lists of traders, clergy, nobility, and farmers in adjoining parishes of the towns of Banagher, Cloghan and Ferbane, Birr, Edenderry, Frankford, and Tullamore.

1890

King's County Directory contains lists of electors for each polling district; residents (by street) of Parsonstown (Birr) with occupations, and Tullamore; also tradesmen for other towns. Also lists of jurymen, etc., and notes on the principal families and parishes, published in Parsonstown, 1890. NLI I655l.

1894

Slater's *Royal National Directory of Ireland* lists traders, police, teachers, farmers, and private residents in each of the towns, villages, and parishes of the county.

Family History

"The Fitzgeralds, Barons of Offaly." *R.S.A.I.* 44 (1914): 99-113.

The Hopper Family. *Ir. Anc.* 149 (2) (1982): 13-19, 59-73.

Smith – see Co. Tipperary.

Memoir of the Warburton Family of Garryhinch, Kings Co. Dublin, 1848. 2nd ed. 1881.

Stone, M.E. *Some Notes on the Fox Family of Kilcoursey in King's Co.* Chicago, 1890.

"The Turpin Family of Tullamore, Co. Offaly." *Ir. Anc.* 16 (1) (1984): 1-5.

"The Ushers of Birr." *Ir. Gen.* 5 (5) (1978): 606-24.

Gravestone Inscriptions

Offaly Tombstone Inscription Series (numbers 1-4) published by Offaly Historical Society (see Research Sources and Services):

Daingean: (No. 4).

Kilclonfert: In *Towards a History of Kilclonfert.* Offaly Historical Society, 1984.

Lusmagh: (No. 3).

Monasteroris: (No. 2).

Rahan: (No. 1).

Newspapers

There were no newspapers published in this county before 1839. Papers from the surrounding counties should be searched, starting with those in the county adjacent to the area of interest. Part of the *Kings County Chronicle* has been indexed by the Offaly Historical Society (see Research Sources and Services).

Title: *Kings County Chronicle* (continued as *Offaly Chronicle,* then *Midland Chronicle*)
Published in: Birr, 1845-1922
NLI Holdings: 9.1845-2.1920; 10.1921-6.1963
BL Holdings: 9.1845-6.1963 (except 1-3.1926; 1930)

Title: *Leinster Reporter & Midland Counties Advertiser*
Published in: Tullamore, 1859-1929
BL Holdings: 1.1859-11.1881; 6.1889-11.1892; 1.1893-12.1914; 1.1916-1.1920; 3.1920-12.1925; 1.1927-12.1929

Title: *Midland Tribune*
Published in: Birr, 1881-current
NLI Holdings: 8.1882-in progress
BL Holdings: odd numbers 9.1881; 8.1882-in progress (except 1926)

Wills and Administrations

A discussion of the types of records, where they are held, their availability, and value is given in the Wills section of the Introduction. The availability of prerogative wills, administrations, and marriage license records is also described in the relevant parts of the same section. Where available, published sources of these records are given in the Miscellaneous Sources section.

Pre-1858 Wills and Administrations

Prerogative Wills. see p. xli.
Consistorial Wills. County Offaly is in the dioceses of Meath, Kildare, Killaloe, and one parish in each of Clonfert and Ossory. The guide to Catholic parish records in this chapter shows the diocese to which each civil parish belonged. The wills of residents of each diocese were usually proven within that diocese (see Wills section for exceptions). The following records survive:

Wills. see p. xxxvii.

Abstracts. see p. xxxvii.

Indexes. Meath: fragments from 1572 to 1858. Killaloe – see Co. Clare. Clonfert – see Co. Galway. Ossory – see Co. Kilkenny.

Post-1858 Wills and Administrations

This county was served by the District Registry of Kilkenny. The surviving records are kept in the PRO.

Marriage Licenses

Original Records. Kildare – see Co. Kildare
Indexes. Kildare (1740-1850). PRO; SLC film 100868. Meath, Killaloe, and Clonfert (1691-1845). PRO; SLC film 100869. Ossory – see Co. Kilkenny

Miscellaneous Sources

Byrne, Michael. *Sources for Offaly History.* Tullamore: Offaly Research Library, 1978.

Feehan, J. *The Landscape of Slieve Bloom – A Study of its Natural and Human Heritage.* Dublin, 1979.

"High Sheriffs of Kings Co. 1655-1915" (with biographical notes to 1860). *J. Kildare Arch. Hist. Soc.* 8 (1) (1915): 30-50.

"Register of Tenants who Planted Trees: Geashill Parish 1793-1907; Eglish Parish 1809-1837." *J. Kildare Arch. Hist. Soc.* 15 (3) (1973/74): 310-18.

Research Sources and Services

Libraries and Information Sources

Offaly County Library, O'Connor Square, Tullamore, Co Offaly Ph: (0506) 21419/21113

Research Services

Tullamore Heritage Centre, Charleville Road, Tullamore, Co. Offaly Ph: (0506) 21199 (research services for Offaly and parts of Westmeath and Leix)

See also research services in Dublin, p. xliv

Societies

Offaly Historical Society (journal in preparation), Mr. James Scully, St. Rynagh's National School, Banagher, Co. Offaly: (Banagher Branch) Mrs. Margaret Barton, Lusmagh, Banagher, Co. Offaly; (Birr Branch) Mrs. Margaret Hogan, Hillside, Birr, Co. Offaly; (Edenderry Branch) Mr. Michael Collins, Edenderry, Co. Offaly; (Tullamore Branch) Mr. Michael Byrne, Convent View, Tullamore, Co. Offaly.

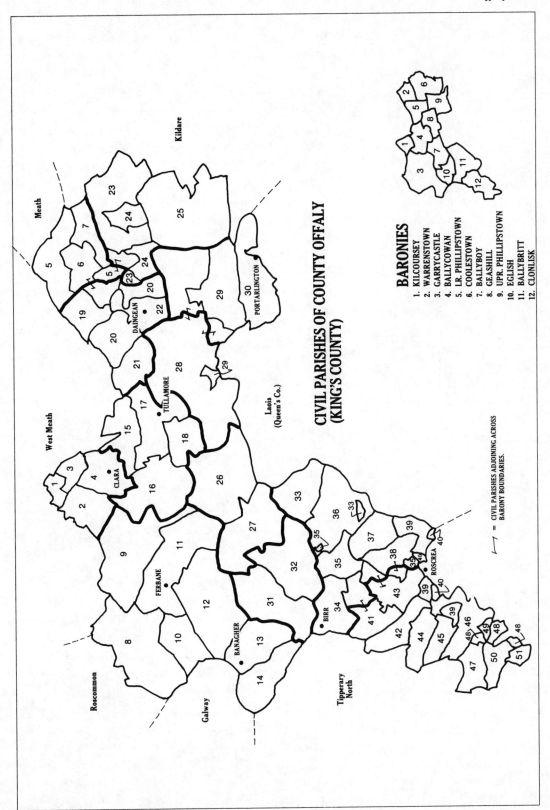

CIVIL PARISHES OF COUNTY OFFALY
(KING'S COUNTY)

BARONIES

1. KILCOURSEY
2. WARRENSTOWN
3. GARRYCASTLE
4. BALLYCOWAN
5. LR. PHILLIPSTOWN
6. COOLESTOWN
7. BALLYBOY
8. GEASHILL
9. UPR. PHILLIPSTOWN
10. EGLISH
11. BALLYBRITT
12. CLONLISK

〜 = CIVIL PARISHES ADJOINING ACROSS
BARONY BOUNDARIES.

Meath

Kildare

West Meath

Roscommon

Galway

Tipperary
North

Laois
(Queen's Co.)

CLARA

DAINGEAN

TULLAMORE

PORTARLINGTON

FERBANE

BANAGHER

BIRR

ROSCREA

County Roscommon

A Brief History

This Connaught county contains the towns of Boyle, Roscommon, Strokestown, and Castlerea.

Under the old Gaelic system the ruling families in this area were the O'Connors and McDermotts in the north, and O'Kellys in the south. Other names associated with the county include McGreevy, O'Beirne, Duignan, O'Gormley, O'Cooney, McAneeny, Hayes, O'Clabby, and McDockery.

The Norman invasion had little effect on this county due to the power of the native inhabitants.

The boundaries of the county were established in 1565 by Sir Henry Sidney. In 1641 the Gaelic families joined the Rebellion of the Catholic Confederacy but were defeated; their lands were confiscated and granted to English and Scottish settlers. In the Cromwellian resettlement of Ireland, the county was one of those set aside for occupation by the "delinquent proprietors," i.e., those landowners who had been dispossessed of their land in other parts of the country. The number of non-native settlers in the county has therefore been very low. As a rough indication of this, the Roman Catholic proportion of the population has been over 96 percent since census records began.

In the Middle Ages the county was densely wooded. Most of these woods were gradually cut down and used for charcoal in local iron mining operations during this time, and also in an iron works established in the county in 1788. The county has generally wet and marshy land which is not ideally suited to agriculture. The major agricultural produce of the county was cattle and sheep, and it was famed for the quality of its cattle in the eighteenth century.

The county suffered relatively badly during the Great Famine of 1845-47. There were 13,000 deaths in the county in these three years and further thousands emigrated. From a peak of 253,000 in 1841, the population in 1851 had dropped by 80,000. Because of the poor agricultural nature of the area and the tradition of emigration which remained in the county the population continued to decrease for the remainder of the century. In 1891 the population had fallen to only 114,000 and is currently around 54,000.

Census and Census Substitutes

1659
"Census" of Ireland. Edited by S. Pender. Dublin: Stationery Office, 1939; SLC film 962524.

1749

Religious Census of Elphin Diocese: Householders, occupations, religion, number of children and number of servants: Parishes of Aughrim, Ardcarne, Athleague, Ballintober, Ballynakill, Baslick, Boyle, Bumlin, Cam, Clontuskert, Clooncraff, Cloonfinlough, Cloonygormican, Creive, Drimatemple, Donamon, Dysart, Eastersnow, Elphin, Fuerty, Kilbride, Kilbryan, Kilcolagh, Kilcooley, Kilcorkey, Kilgefin, Kilglass, Kilkeevin, Killinvoy, Killuken, Killumod, Kilmacallan, Kilmacumsy, Kilmore, Kilnamanagh, Kilronan, Kiltoom, Kiltrustan, Lissonuffy, Ogulla, Oran, Rahara, Roscommon, St. John's Athlone, St. Peter's Athlone, Shankill, Taghboy, Termonbarry, Tibohine, Tisrara, and Tumna. PRO 1A 3613; SLC film 101781.

1780

List of Freeholders. SLC film 100181.

1813-21

Registers of Freeholders (alphabetically arranged within each barony; gives names, addresses, location of freehold, etc.). NLI ILB 324.

1823-38

Tithe Applotment Survey (see p. xxvii).

1836-44

List of Qualified Voters (arranged alphabetically within each barony; gives address). NLI IR 32341 R 20.

1847-48

"Tenants From Ballykilcline (Kilglass parish) Who Emigrated Under State-aided Scheme" (names, ages, and relationships of 336 people, and dates of departure, arrival, and name of ship). In E. Ellis, *Emigrants from Ireland 1847-52.* 10-21. Baltimore: Genealogical Publishing Co., 1977.

1857-58

Griffith's Valuation (see p. xxvii).

1901

Census. PRO.

1911

Census. PRO.

Church Records

Church of Ireland
(shows starting date of record)

Parish: **Ahanagh**
Existing Records: b. 1856
Status: LC

Parish: **Ardcarne**
Existing Records: b. 1820; m. 1813; d. 1820
Status: LC

Parish: **Ardclare**
Status: Lost

Parish: **Athleague**
Status: Lost

Parish: **Aughrim**
Status: Lost

Parish: **Boyle**
Existing Records: b. 1793; m. 1793; d. 1793
Status: LC

Parish: **Bumlin** (Smokestown)
Existing Records: b. 1811; m. 1811; d. 1811
Status: LC

Parish: **Battlebridge** (see Toomna)

Parish: **Croghan**
Existing Records: b. 1862; d. 1860
Status: LC

Parish: **Donamon** and **Fuerty** (Donamon and Fuerty united in 1866)
Status: Lost

Parish: **Eastersnow**
Existing Records: b. 1800; m. 1800; d. 1800
Status: LC

Parish: **Elphin**
Status: Lost

Parish: **Fuerty** (see also Donamon)
Status: Lost

Parish: **Kilbride** (see Roscommon)

Parish: **Kilbryan**
Existing Records: b. 1852
Status: LC

Parish: **Kilcorkey** (no inventory)

Parish: **Kilgeffin**
Status: Lost

Parish: **Kilglass**
Existing Records: b. 1842; m. 1842; d. 1845
 (doubt exists as to dates of transcripts)
Status: LC

Parish: **Kilkeevin**
Existing Records: b. 1748; m. 1748; d. 1748
Status: LC

Parish: **Killenvoy**
Status: Lost

Parish: **Killukin** (see Ardclare)
Status: Lost

Parish: **Kilmore**
Status: Lost

Parish: **Kilronan**
Status: Lost

Parish: **Kiltoom**
Existing Records: b. 1797; m. 1797; d. 1797
Status: LC

Parish: **Kiltullagh**
Existing Records: b. 1822; m. 1822; d. 1822
Status: LC

Parish: **Loughglinn**
Status: Lost

Parish: **Moore and Drum**
Status: Lost

Parish: **Roscommon** and **Kilbride**
Status: Lost

Parish: **St. John** (see Killenvoy)

Parish: **St. Peter, Athlone**
Status: Lost

Parish: **Strokestown** (see Bumlin)

Parish: **Tarmonbarry**
Status: Lost

Parish: **Tessaragh, Taughboy,** and **Dysart**
Status: Lost

Parish: **Tibohine**
Existing Records: b. 1811; m. 1811; d. 1811
Status: LC

Parish: **Toomna** (Battlebridge Church)
Status: Lost

Roman Catholic

Civil Parish: **Ardcarn**
Map Grid: 4
RC Parish: Ardcarn (Cootehall)
Diocese: EL
Earliest Record: b. 3.1843; m. 3.1843
Missing Dates: m. 6.1860-4.1861
Parish Address: Rev. Henry Harte, PP, Cootehall, Boyle, Co. Roscommon

Civil Parish: **Athleague**
Map Grid: 44
RC Parish: Athleague and Fuerty
Diocese: EL
Earliest Record: b. 1.1808; m. 7.1808; d. 1.1807
Missing Dates: b. 5.1828-8.1834, 7.1864-1.1865; m. 2.1834-3.1836; d. ends 1837
Parish Address: Rev. Edward P. Jones, PP, Athleague, Co. Roscommon

Civil Parish: **Aughrim**
Map Grid: 19
RC Parish: Aughrim (see also Kilmore)
Diocese: EL
Earliest Record: b. 8.1816; m. 8.1816
Missing Dates: b. 12.1837-1.1865; m. 12.1837-1.1865

Parish Address: Rev. Patrick McHugh, PP, Aughrim, Hillstreet, Carrick-on-Shannon, Co. Roscommon

Civil Parish: **Ballintober**
Map Grid: 18
RC Parish: Ballintober
Diocese: EL
Earliest Record: b. 12.1831; m. 7.1831
Parish Address: Rev. Sean Kelly, PP, Ballintubber, Castlerea, Co. Roscommon

Civil Parish: **Ballynakill**
Map Grid: 35
RC Parish: see Ballynakill (Ballymoe), Co. Galway
Diocese: EL

Civil Parish: **Baslick**
Map Grid: 16
RC Parish: see Ogulla
Diocese: EL

Civil Parish: **Boyle**
Map Grid: 2
RC Parish: Boyle
Diocese: EL
Earliest Record: b. 9.1827; m. 9.1828; d. 7.1848
Missing Dates: m. 6.1846-10.1864; d.ends 11.1864
Parish Address: Rev. Kevin Dodd, PP, Boyle, Co. Roscommon

Civil Parish: **Bumlin**
Map Grid: 26
RC Parish: see Lissonuffy
Diocese: EL

Civil Parish: **Cam** or **Camma**
Map Grid: 51
RC Parish: see Kiltoom
Diocese: EL

Civil Parish: **Castlemore**
Map Grid: 9b
RC Parish: Castlemore and Kilcolman
Diocese: AC
Earliest Record: b. 11.1851; m. 8.1830
Missing Dates: m. 10.1867-2.1868

Parish Address: Rev. John Doherty, Adm, The Presbytery, Ballaghadereen, Co. Roscommon

Civil Parish: **Clooncraff**
Map Grid: 21
RC Parish: Kiltrustan, etc., see Lissonuffy
Diocese: EL

Civil Parish: **Cloonfinlough**
Map Grid: 28
RC Parish: Lissonuffy, see Lissonuffy
Diocese: EL

Civil Parish: **Cloontuskert**
Map Grid: 40
RC Parish: Cloontuskert
Diocese: EL
Earliest Record: b. 1.1865; m. 2.1865
Parish Address: Rev. Thomas Martin, PP, Kilrooskey, Roscommon

Civil Parish: **Cloonygormican**
Map Grid: 34
RC Parish: Glinsk; see Ballynakill (Ballymoe), Co. Galway
Diocese: EL

Civil Parish: **Creagh**
Map Grid: 57
RC Parish: see Kilcloony, Co. Galway
Diocese: CF

Civil Parish: **Creeve**
Map Grid: 13
RC Parish: Creeve, see Elphin

Civil Parish: **Drum**
Map Grid: 56
RC Parish: see St. Peter's (Athlone)
Diocese: TU

Civil Parish: **Drumatemple** (see also Co. Galway)
Map Grid: 33
RC Parish: see Ballintober
Diocese: EL

Civil Parish: **Dunamon**
Map Grid: 37
RC Parish: Kilbegnet, see Ballynakill (Bal-
lymoe), Co. Galway
Diocese: EL

Civil Parish: **Dysart**
Map Grid: 53
RC Parish: Dysart and Tissara
Diocese: EL
Earliest Record: b. 7.1850 (2 registers); m.
12.1862; d. 12.1862
Missing Dates: d. ends 1.1867
Parish Address: Rev. Joseph McElhone, PP,
Ballyforan, Ballinasloe, Co. Galway

Civil Parish: **Elphin**
Map Grid: 22
RC Parish: Elphin and Creeve
Diocese: EL
Earliest Record: b. 6.1807; m. 5.1807
Missing Dates: b. 12.1808-5.1810, 7.1860-
1.1866; m. 10.1830-3.1864
Parish Address: Rev. Patrick Gearty, PP, El-
phin, Co. Roscommon

Civil Parish: **Eastersnow**
Map Grid: 6
RC Parish: part Killukin (1); part Kilnamanagh
Diocese: EL

Civil Parish: **Fuerty**
Map Grid: 43
RC Parish: see Athleague
Diocese: EL

Civil Parish: **Kilbride**
Map Grid: 38
RC Parish: Kilbride
Diocese: EL
Earliest Record: b. 7.1835; m. 9.1838
Missing Dates: b. 9.1849-4.1868; m. ends 1846
Parish Address: Rev. Thomas Moran, PP, Four-
milehouse, Roscommon

Civil Parish: **Kilbryan**
Map Grid: 3
RC Parish: see Boyle
Diocese: EL

Civil Parish: **Kilcolagh**
Map Grid: 11
RC Parish: see Killukin (1)
Diocese: EL

Civil Parish: **Kilcolman** (see also Co. Mayo and
Co. Sligo)
Map Grid: 9a
RC Parish: see Castlemore
Diocese: AC

Civil Parish: **Kilcooly**
Map Grid: 25
RC Parish: see Ogulla
Diocese: EL

Civil Parish: **Kilcorkey**
Map Grid: 14
RC Parish: Kilcorkey and Frenchpark
Diocese: EL
Earliest Record: b. 1.1865
Parish Address: Rev. Michael Martin, PP,
French Park, Castlerea, Co. Roscommon

Civil Parish: **Kilgefin**
Map Grid: 39
RC Parish: see Cloontuskert, etc.
Diocese: EL

Civil Parish: **Kilglass**
Map Grid: 31
RC Parish: Kilglass and Rooskey
Diocese: EL
Earliest Record: b. 10.1865
Parish Address: Rev. Thomas Devine, CM,
Kilglass, Co. Roscommon

Civil Parish: **Kilkeevan**
Map Grid: 15
RC Parish: Kilkeevan
Diocese: EL
Earliest Record: b. 11.1804; m. 11.1804; d.
2.1805
Missing Dates: b. 5.1809-1.1816, 8.1819-1.1826;
m. 7.1809-1.1816, 4.1820-10.1838; d. 5.1809-
1.1816, 10.1819-1.1852, ends 1855
Parish Address: Rev. Patrick Collins, PP,
Castlerea, Co. Roscommon

Civil Parish: **Killinvoy**
Map Grid: 46
RC Parish: see St. John's
Diocese: EL

Civil Parish: **Killukin (1)** (Barony of Boyle)
Map Grid: 77
RC Parish: Killukin and Killumod
Diocese: EL
Earliest Record: b. 6.1811; m. 4.1825; d. 10.1820
Missing Dates: d. ends 3.1826
Parish Address: Rev. Roger Leonard, PP, Croghan, Boyle, Co. Roscommon

Civil Parish: **Killukin (2)** (Roscommon)
Map Grid: 27
RC Parish: part Ogulla; part Cloonfinlough, see Lissonuffy
Diocese: EL

Civil Parish: **Killumod**
Map Grid: 8
RC Parish: Killumod, see Killukin (1)
Diocese: EL

Civil Parish: **Kilmacumsy**
Map Grid: 12
RC Parish: see Elphin
Diocese: EL

Civil Parish: **Kilmeane**
Map Grid: 45
RC Parish: see St. John's
Diocese: EL

Civil Parish: **Kilmore**
Map Grid: 30
RC Parish: Kilmore
Diocese: EL
Earliest Record: b. 2.1825; m. 3.1825
Missing Dates: b. 2.1860-1.1865; m. 11.1859-2.1865
Parish Address: see Aughrim

Civil Parish: **Kilnamanagh**
Map Grid: 9
RC Parish: Kilnamanagh (Breedogue and Ballinameen)
Diocese: EL
Earliest Record: b. 11.1859; m. 2.1860

Parish Address: Rev. James Tighe, PP, Ballinameen, Boyle, Co. Roscommon

Civil Parish: **Kilronan**
Map Grid: 1
RC Parish: Kilronan (Keadue, Arigna, and Ballyfarnon)
Diocese: TU
Earliest Record: b. 1.1824; m. 10.1823; d. 6.1835
Missing Dates: b. 7.1829-1.1835; m. 6.1829-1.1835
Parish Address: Rev. John P. Masterson, PP, Keadue, Boyle, Co. Roscommon

Civil Parish: **Kilteevan**
Map Grid: 42
RC Parish: see Roscommon
Diocese: EL

Civil Parish: **Kiltoom**
Map Grid: 52
RC Parish: Kiltoom (Ballybay)
Diocese: EL
Earliest Record: b. 10.1835; m. 10.1835; d. 7.1837
Missing Dates: b. 5.1845-4.1848; m. 7.1846-1.1848; d. 3.1845-1.1857, ends 1865
Parish Address: Rev. Edward Higgins, PP, Kiltoom, Athlone, Co. Roscommon

Civil Parish: **Kiltrustan**
Map Grid: 23
RC Parish: see Lissonuffy
Diocese: EL

Civil Parish: **Kiltullagh**
Map Grid: 17
RC Parish: Kiltullagh
Diocese: TU
Earliest Record: b. 9.1839; m. 8.1839
Missing Dates: m. 4.1874-1.1877
Parish Address: Rev. John Ball, PP, Ballinlough, Co. Roscommon

Civil Parish: **Lissonuffy**
Map Grid: 29
RC Parish: Kiltrustan, Lissonuffy, and Cloonfinlough (Strokestown)
Diocese: EL
Earliest Record: b. 10.1830 (several different registers); m. 10.1830

Missing Dates: b. 1.1846-12.1851; m. 11.1852-
11.1853
Parish Address: Rev. Desmond McLoughlin,
PP, Strokestown, Co. Roscommon

Civil Parish: **Moore**
Map Grid: 58
RC Parish: Moore
Diocese: TU
Earliest Record: b. 9.1876; m. 1.1877
Parish Address: Rev. Richard Horan, PP, Bal-
lydangan, Athlone, Co. Roscommon

Civil Parish: **Ogulla**
Map Grid: 24
RC Parish: Ogulla and Baslic (Tulsk)
Diocese: EL
Earliest Record: b. 1.1865; m. 1.1864
Parish Address: Rev. Enda Farrell, PP, Tulsk,
Castlerea, Co. Roscommon

Civil Parish: **Oran**
Map Grid: 36
RC Parish: Oran (Cloverhill)
Diocese: EL
Earliest Record: b. 1.1845; m. 1.1845
Parish Address: Rev. Michael Dunning, PP,
Cams, Roscommon

Civil Parish: **Rahara** or **Raharrow**
Map Grid: 48
RC Parish: see St. John's
Diocese: EL

Civil Parish: **Roscommon**
Map Grid: 41
RC Parish: Roscommon and Kilteevan
Diocese: EL
Earliest Record: b. 10.1837; m. 1.1820
Parish Address: Rev. Thomas A. Finnegan, PP,
Parochial House, Roscommon, Co. Ros-
common

Civil Parish: **St. John's** or **Ivernoon**
Map Grid: 49
RC Parish: St. John's
Diocese: EL
Earliest Record: b. 7.1841 (several different
registers); m. 7.1841; d. 1854
Missing Dates: d. 1858-1859

Parish Address: Rev. Joseph Fitzgerald, CC, St.
John's, Lecarrow, Roscommon

Civil Parish: **St. Peter's** (Athlone)
Map Grid: 55
RC Parish: St. Peter's Athlone
Diocese: EL
Earliest Record: b. 1.1789; m. 1.1789; d. 1.1789
Parish Address: Rev. Patrick Murray, SS, Peter
and Paul's, Athlone

Civil Parish: **Shankill**
Map Grid: 20
RC Parish: see Elphin
Diocese: EL

Civil Parish: **Taghboy** (see also Co. Galway)
Map Grid: 50
RC Parish: see Dysart
Diocese: EL

Civil Parish: **Taghmaconnell**
Map Grid: 54
RC Parish: Taghmaconnell
Diocese: CF
Earliest Record: b. 7.1842; m. 1.1863
Parish Address: Rev. J. Egan, PP, Taghmacon-
nell, Ballinasloe, Co. Galway

Civil Parish: **Termonbarry**
Map Grid: 32
RC Parish: Rooskey, see Kilglass
Diocese: EL

Civil Parish: **Tibohine (1)**
Map Grid: 10
RC Parish: Tibohine; also Loughglynn, see
below; also part Frenchpark, see Kilcorkey
Diocese: EL
Earliest Record: b. 1.1833; m. 1.1833
Missing Dates: b. 9.1864-5.1875; m. 6.1864-
2.1865
Parish Address: Rev. Thomas Beirne, PP,
Fairymount, Castlerea, Co. Roscommon

Civil Parish: **Tibohine (2)**
Map Grid: 10
RC Parish: Loughglynn and Lisacul
Diocese: EL
Earliest Record: b. 3.1817; m. 4.1817; d. 1.1850

Missing Dates: b. 11.1826-12.1829, 4.1863-1.1865; m. 3.1827-2.1836, 4.1837-12.1849, 2.1858-1.1865; d. 6.1854-1.1868

Parish Address: Rev. Peter Feely, PP, Loughglynn, Castlerea, Co. Roscommon

Civil Parish: **Tisrara**
Map Grid: 47
RC Parish: see Dysart
Diocese: EL

Civil Parish: **Tumna**
Map Grid: 5
RC Parish: part Killukin (1); also part Ardcarne
Diocese: EL

Commercial and Social Directories

1824

J. Pigot's *City of Dublin & Hibernian Provincial Directory* includes traders, nobility, gentry, and clergy lists of Boyle, Castlerea, Elphin, Roscommon, and Strokestown.

1846

Slater's *National Commercial Directory of Ireland* lists nobility, clergy, traders, etc., in Boyle, Castlerea, Elphin, Roscommon, and Strokestown.

1856

Slater's *Royal National Commercial Directory of Ireland* lists nobility, gentry, clergy, traders, etc., in Boyle, Castlerea, Elphin, Roscommon, and Strokestown.

1870

Slater's *Directory of Ireland* contains trade, nobility, and clergy lists for Boyle, Castlerea, Elphin, Roscommon, and Strokestown.

1881

Slater's *Royal National Commercial Directory of Ireland* contains lists of traders, clergy, nobility, and farmers in adjoining parishes of the towns of Boyle, Castlerea, Elphin, Roscommon, and Strokestown.

1894

Slater's *Royal National Directory of Ireland* lists traders, police, teachers, farmers, and private residents in each of the towns, villages, and parishes of the county.

Family History

Crofton, H. *Crofton Memoirs: Account of John Crofton of Ballymurray, Co. Roscommon, his Ancestors and Descendants and Others Bearing his Name.* York, 1911.

"The Irwins of Roxborough, Co. Roscommon and Streamstown, Co. Sligo." *Ir. Gen.* 1 (2) (1937): 19-24.

"Mahon of Strokestown, Co. Roscommon." *Ir. Anc.* 10 (2) (1978): 77-80.

Mills – see Co. Galway.

"Nicholas Mahon and 17th Century Roscommon." *Ir. Gen.* 3 (6) (1963): 228-35.

"Notes on the Dodwells of Manor Dodwell, Co. Roscommon." *Ir. Gen.* I (1941): 315-17.

"Notes on the Lloyd Family of Ardnagowen, Co. Roscommon." *J. Ass. Pres. Mem. Dead* 6 (1904-06): 403.

O'Conor, Don C. *The O'Connors of Connaught.* Dublin, 1891.

O'Conor, R. *Memoir of the O'Connors of Ballintubber, Co. Roscommon.* Dublin, 1859.

O'Connor, Roderic. *Lineal Descent of the O'Connors of Co. Roscommon.* Dublin, 1862.

O'Connor, R. *Historical and Genealogical Memoir of the O'Connors, Kings of Connaught.* Dublin, 1861.

"The O'Connor Papers: their Significance to Genealogists." *Eire-Ir* 2 (2) (1976): 104-18.

"O'Hanly and the Townland of Kilmacough." *Ir. Gen.* 3 (3) (1963): 101-08.

"Pedigree of Walsh of Crannagh, Co. Roscommon." *J. Ass. Pres. Mem. Dead* 7 (1907-09): 700.

Newspapers

There were no newspapers published in this county before 1828. Papers from the surrounding counties should be searched, starting with those in the county adjacent to the area of interest.

Title: *Boyle Gazette*
Published in: Boyle, 1891
NLI Holdings: 1-7.1891
BL Holdings: 2-7.1891

Title: *Roscommon and Leitrim Gazette*
Published in: Boyle, 1822-82
NLI Holdings: 1.1841-12.1844
BL Holdings: 4.1822-6.1882

Title: *Roscommon Constitutionalist*
Published in: Boyle, 1886-ca. 1891
NLI Holdings: 1.1889-11.1891
BL Holdings: 4.1889-11.1891

Title: *Roscommon Herald*
Published in: Boyle, 1859-current
NLI Holdings: 1.1882-11.1920; 1.1921-in progress
BL Holdings: 4.1859-11.1920; 1921-in progress

Title: *Roscommon Journal*
Published in: Roscommon, 1828-1927
NLI Holdings: 11.1841-12.1927 (with gaps)
BL Holdings: 7.1828-9.1832; 11.1832-10.1848; 8.1849-12.1918; 3.1919-12.1925

Title: *Roscommon Reporter*
Published in: Roscommon, 1850-60
BL Holdings: 3.1850-3.1851; 2.1856-3.1859; 10.1860

Title: *Roscommon Weekly Messenger* (continued as *Roscommon Messenger* in 1861)
Published in: Roscommon, 1848-1935
NLI Holdings: 1.1902-12.1935
BL Holdings: 5.1845-12.1886; 1.1888-12.1935

Wills and Administrations

A discussion of the types of records, where they are held, their availability and value is given in the Wills section of the Introduction. The availability of prerogative wills, administrations, and marriage license records is also described in the relevant parts of the same section. Where available, published sources of these records are given in the Miscellaneous Sources section.

Pre-1858 Wills and Administrations

Prerogative Wills. see p. xli.
Consistorial Wills. County Roscommon is in the dioceses of Elphin, Achonry, Clonfert, Tuam, and Ardagh. The guide to Catholic parish records in this chapter shows the diocese to which each civil parish belonged. The wills of residents of each diocese were usually proven within that diocese (see the Wills section for exceptions). The following records survive:

Wills. see p. xxxvii.

Abstracts. see p. xxxvii.

Indexes. Elphin (1650-1858); Tuam (1648-1858); Clonfert – see Co. Galway; Achonry – see Co. Mayo; Ardagh – see Co. Longford.

Post-1858 Wills and Administrations

This county was served by the District Registry of Tuam. The surviving records are kept in the PRO.

Marriage Licenses

Indexes. Elphin and Achonry (1740-1850). PRO; SLC 100868. Clonfert and Ardagh (1691-1845). PRO; SLC film 100869. Tuam (1661-1750). PRO; SLC film 100872.

Miscellaneous Sources

Burke, F. *Loch Ce, and Its Annals, North Roscommon and the Diocese of Elphin in Times of Old.* Dublin, 1895.

Carthy, P. *Landholding and Settlement in Co. Roscommon.* M.A. Thesis, University College Dublin, 1970 (unpublished).

Dunleavy, J.E., and W.G. Dunleavy. "Catalogue of the O'Connor Papers." *Studies* (Autumn/Winter 1973).

Weld, I. *Statistical Survey of the County of Roscommon.* Dublin: Royal Dublin Society, 1832.

―――――――――――――――――――

Research Sources and Services

Journals

J. Co. Roscommon Hist. & Arch. Soc. (1986-present)

Libraries and Information Sources

Roscommon County Library, Abbey Street, Roscommon Ph: (0903) 6203

Research Services

County Heritage Centre, St John's, Strokestown, Co. Roscommon Ph: (078) 33380 (conducts a research service and has an index to parish records)

See also research services in Dublin, p. xliv

Societies

County Roscommon Historical & Archaeological Society, Mr. Michael Kelly, Edenaun, Elphin, Co. Roscommon

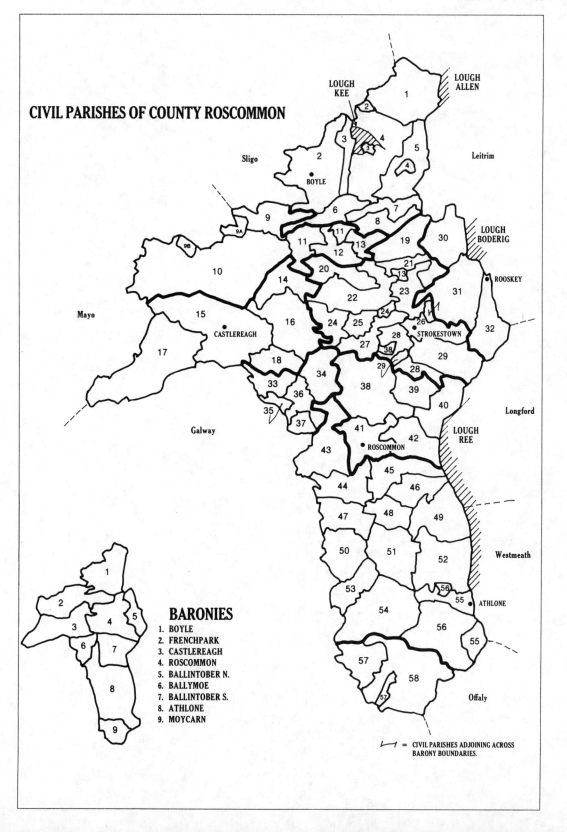

CIVIL PARISHES OF COUNTY ROSCOMMON

LOUGH KEE

LOUGH ALLEN

Sligo

BOYLE

Leitrim

LOUGH BODERIG

ROOSKEY

Mayo

CASTLEREAGH

STROKESTOWN

Longford

LOUGH REE

Galway

ROSCOMMON

Westmeath

ATHLONE

Offaly

BARONIES

1. BOYLE
2. FRENCHPARK
3. CASTLEREAGH
4. ROSCOMMON
5. BALLINTOBER N.
6. BALLYMOE
7. BALLINTOBER S.
8. ATHLONE
9. MOYCARN

⌐┐ = CIVIL PARISHES ADJOINING ACROSS
     BARONY BOUNDARIES.

County Sligo

A Brief History

This Connaught county contains the towns of Sligo, Ballymote, Collooney, Ballysodare, and Enniscrone.

Sligo was the ancestral territory of a branch of the O'Connors, called O'Connor Sligo. Other Gaelic families associated with the county include O'Dowd, O'Hara, O'Hart, McDonagh, Mac Firbis, and O'Colman. The site of the town of Sligo has been of strategic importance since ancient times as all traffic on the coastal route between South and North had to ford the river here. A fortress which guarded this ford was plundered by Norse pirates as early as A.D. 807.

After the Norman invasion of Connacht in 1235, Sligo was granted to Maurice Fitzgerald who effectively founded Sligo town by building a castle there in 1245 and making it his residence. The Taaffe family was among the Norman families who settled in the county. Further settlers were brought into the county at various periods, including weavers from the north of Ireland brought in by Lord Shelbourne in 1749.

As the native Irish and Norman population were predominantly Catholic, the Scottish usually Presbyterian, and the English of the Protestant faith, the proportions of these religions among the population can, in very general terms, be used to estimate the origins of the inhabitants of the county. When religious affiliation was first determined in the census of 1861, the respective proportions of Catholic, Presbyterian, and Protestant in Sligo were 90, 8, and 1 percent. Apart from the weaving industry and some mining operations, Sligo is basically an agricultural county. The town of Sligo was an important port in the eighteenth and nineteenth centuries, particularly as the River Erne and its lake systems facilitated inland trading and transport. It was also an important port of emigration. The peak of population was reached in 1841 at 181,000. The Great Famine of 1845-47 badly affected the county and the population had dropped by 52,000 in ten years, including some 20,000 deaths. By 1901 the population had fallen to 84,000 and is currently 56,000.

Census and Census Substitutes

1659
"Census" of Ireland. Edited by S. Pender. Dublin: Stationery Office, 1939; SLC film 924648.

1665
Hearth Money Rolls. Printed by Stationery

Office for the Irish Manuscripts Commission, 1967; also in *Anal. Hib.* 24.

1749

Religious Census of Elphin Dioceses: lists householders, occupation, religion, number of children, and servants: Parishes of Aghanagh, Ahamlish, Ballynakill, Ballysumaghan, Drumcliff, Drumcolumb, Killadoon, Kilmacallan, Kilmactranny, Kilross, Shancough, Sligo, Tawnagh. PRO 1A 3613; SLC film 101781.

1795-97

Voters List for Co. Sligo (transcribed from NLI ms. 3075). McDonagh Ms. No. 21, Sligo Co. Library.

1798

List of Persons who Suffered Loss in '98 Rebellion. NLI JLB 94107 (approximately 250 names, addresses, and occupations).

1823-37

Tithe Applotment Survey (see p. xxvii).

1832-37

"List of Voters Registered in the Borough of Sligo." *Parl. Papers* 1837, 11 (2): 205-16 (835 names, occupations, and addresses).

1858

Griffith's Valuation (see p. xxvii).

1860

Rental of the Estate of Viscount Palmerston for 1860, 1879, 1888, 1902, and 1911.

1876

Owners of Land in Co. Sligo, compiled by Local Government Board (lists owners of land of one acre and over). Sligo Co. Library.

1901

Census. PRO.

1911

Census. PRO.

SLIGO (or 22d) Batt.		
Col.	John Irwin	4 June 1807
Lt. Col.	Roger Parke	20 July do.
Majors	Alex. Perceval	12 Feb 1807
	Chas. K. O'Hara	23 July do.
Capts.	Rob. Lindfay	13 May 1801
	John Tyler	21 May 1803
	Wm. Lindfey	18 Aug. 1803
	Rob. Powell	1 Dec. do.
	James Jones	26 Apr. 1804
	Wm. Furey	30 Sept. 1805
Lieuts.	Wm. Clarke	26 Oct. 1798
	Tho. Trumble	13 May 1801
	Booth Jones	25 Oct. 1803
	Harloe Elwood	30 Sept. 1805
	Wm. Barrett	1 Oct. do.
	John Coen	20 Feb. 1806
	James Burrowes	do.
	James Light	do.
	Geo. Powell	5 May do.
	Hen. Fawcett	18 Nov. do.
	Francis Knox	do.
	Jones T. Irwin	4 May 1807
	Thos. P. Jones	24 June do.
Enfigns	Wm. Hamilton	18 Nov. 1806
	John Ormfby	do.
	Richard Eagar	do.
	Andw. Parke	4 May 1807
	Wm. Dennis	24 June do.
Paym.	Rob. Ormfby	1 Apr. 1799
Adjut.	Capt. S. Goodwin	10 July 1798
Q. Maf.	Ja. Burrowes	22 Aug. 1803
Surg.	John Fawcett	15 July 1793
Affift. do.	Geo. Smith	5 Aug. 1807
Agents	Cane and Son	

The Officers of the Sligo Militia, or 22nd Battalion, in 1808. Extract from *The Gentlemans and Citizens Almanack* compiled by John Watson Stewart. Dublin, 1808.

Church Records

Church of Ireland
(shows starting date of record)

Parish: **Ahamlish**
Status: Lost

Parish: **Ballysodare**
Status: Lost

Parish: **Ballysodare, CE**
Status: Lost

Parish: **Ballysumaghan**
Existing Records: (volume for 1828-48 destroyed by fire in church, two other volumes since rebound as one) b. 1849; d. 1850
Status: LC

Parish: **Castleconnor**
Existing Records: b. 1834; m. 1834; d. 1834
Status: LC

Parish: **Kilglass**
Existing Records: b. 1821; m. 1821; d. 1821
Status: LC

Parish: **Drumard** (including Beltra)
Status: Lost

Parish: **Drumcliff**
Existing Records: b. 1805; m. 1805; d. 1805
Status: LC and PRO

Parish: **Easkey**
Existing Records: b. 1822; m. 1822; d. 1822
Status: LC

Parish: **Emlafad**
Existing Records: b. 1831; m. 1831; d. 1831
Status: LC

Parish: **Kilglass** (see also Castleconnor)
Status: Lost

Parish: **Killaraght**
Status: Lost

Parish: **Killaspicbrone** (see St. John, Sligo)

Parish: **Killerry**
Status: Lost

Parish: **Killoran**
Status: Lost

Parish: **Kilmacowen** (see St. John, Sligo)

Parish: **Kilmacteige**
Status: Lost

Parish: **Kilmactranny**
Existing Records: b. 1816; m. 1816; d. 1816
Status: LC

Parish: **Knocknarea**
Existing Records: b. 1842; d. 1842
Status: LC

Parish: **Lissadill**
Existing Records: b. 1836; m. 1842
Status: LC

Parish: **Rosses**
Status: Lost

Parish: **St. John, Sligo**
Existing Records: b. 1802; m. 1802; d. 1802
Status: LC

Parish: **Skreen**
Status: Lost

Parish: **Taunagh** (including Riverstown, Kilmacalane, Drumcollum)
Status: LC

Parish: **Tobbercurry**
Status: Lost

Parish: **Toomour-Sligo** (see Emlafad)

Roman Catholic

Civil Parish: **Achonry (1)**
Map Grid: 19
RC Parish: Clonacool; also Achonry and Curry, see below
Diocese: AC
Earliest Record: b. 10.1859; m. 10.1859
Parish Address: Rev. J. Higgins, PP, Tubbercurry, Co. Sligo

Civil Parish: **Achonry (2)**
Map Grid: 19
RC Parish: Achonry

Diocese: AC
Earliest Record: b. 1878; m. 8.1865
Parish Address: Rev. P. O'Grady, PP, Lavagh, Ballymote, Co. Sligo

Civil Parish: **Achonry (3)**
Map Grid: 19
RC Parish: Curry
Diocese: AC
Earliest Record: b. 10.1867; m. 11.1867
Parish Address: Rev. J. Lafferty, PP, Ballymote, Co. Sligo

Civil Parish: **Aghanagh**
Map Grid: 38
RC Parish: Aghanagh
Diocese: EL
Earliest Record: b. 6.1803; m. 1.1800; d. 3.1800
Missing Dates: b. 1.1808-10.1816, 1.1819-1.1821, 11.1841-1.1844; m. 6.1802-4.1829, 3.1850-11.1858; d. 3.1802-11.1822, 9.1846-11.1858
Parish Address: Rev. P. Brady, PP, Ballinafad, Boyle, Co. Roscommon

Civil Parish: **Ahamlish**
Map Grid: 1
RC Parish: Ahamlish
Diocese: EL
Earliest Record: b. 11.1796; m. 12.1796; d. 11.1796
Missing Dates: b. 5.1829-1.1831, 11.1835-9.1836; d. 10.1822-1.1827, ends 7.1845
Parish Address: Rev. P. Healy, PP, Clifoney, Co. Sligo

Civil Parish: **Ballynakill**
Map Grid: 31
RC Parish: Sowey, see Kilmacallan
Diocese: EL

Civil Parish: **Ballysadare**
Map Grid: 16
RC Parish: Balysodare and Kilvarnet
Diocese: AC
Earliest Record: b. 4.1842; m. 1.1858
Missing Dates: b. 8.1853-2.1858
Parish Address: Rev. J. Duffy, PP, Ballisodare, Co. Sligo

Civil Parish: **Ballysumaghan**
Map Grid: 30
RC Parish: Sowey, see Kilmacallan
Diocese: EL

Civil Parish: **Calry**
Map Grid: 4
RC Parish: Sligo, see St. John's
Diocese: EL

Civil Parish: **Castleconor**
Map Grid: 14
RC Parish: Castleconor
Diocese: KA
Earliest Record: b. 1.1855; m. 10.1854
Parish Address: Rev. M. Halloran, PP, Corballa, Ballina, Co. Mayo

Civil Parish: **Cloonoghil**
Map Grid: 23
RC Parish: Kilshalvey, etc., see Kilturra, Co. Mayo
Diocese: AC

Civil Parish: **Dromard**
Map Grid: 13
RC Parish: see Skreen
Diocese: KA

Civil Parish: **Drumcliff**
Map Grid: 3
RC Parish: Drumcliff
Diocese: EL
Earliest Record: b. 5.1841; m. 1.1865
Parish Address: Rev. K. McDermott, PP, Drumcliff, Sligo

Civil Parish: **Drumcolumb**
Map Grid: 32
RC Parish: Riverstown, see Kilmacallan
Diocese: EL

Civil Parish: **Drumrat**
Map Grid: 27
RC Parish: Drumrat
Diocese: AC
Earliest Record: b. 11.1843; m. 1.1842
Missing Dates: b. 3.1855-1.1874; m. 5.1851-12.1872
Parish Address: Rev. C. McLoughlin, PP, Keash, Ballymote, Co. Sligo

Civil Parish: **Easky**
Map Grid: 9
RC Parish: Easkey
Diocese: KA
Earliest Record: b. 6.1864
Parish Address: Rev. P. Clarke, PP, Easkey, Ballina, Co. Mayo

Civil Parish: **Emlaghfad**
Map Grid: 21
RC Parish: Emlefad and Kilmorgan
Diocese: AC
Earliest Record: b. 7.1856; m. 8.1824
Parish Address: Rev. R. Flynn, PP, Ballymote, Co. Sligo

Civil Parish: **Kilcolman** (see also Co. Roscommon and Co. Mayo)
Map Grid: 40
RC Parish: see Castlemore, Co. Roscommon
Diocese: AC

Civil Parish: **Kilfree**
Map Grid: 39
RC Parish: see Killaraght
Diocese: AC

Civil Parish: **Kilglass**
Map Grid: 8
RC Parish: Kilglass
Diocese: KA
Earliest Record: b. 10.1825; m. 11.1825; d. 11.1825
Missing Dates: m. 5.1867-11.1867; d. ends 6.1867
Parish Address: Rev. Thomas Clarke, PP, Ballyglass, Enniscrone, Ballina, Co. Mayo

Civil Parish: **Killadoon**
Map Grid: 35
RC Parish: Geevagh; see Kilmactranny
Diocese: EL

Civil Parish: **Killaraght**
Map Grid: 41
RC Parish: Kilfree and Killaraght
Diocese: AC
Earliest Record: b. 5.1873; m. 2.1844
Parish Address: Rev. Patrick Towey, PP, Gurteen, Co. Sligo

Civil Parish: **Killaspugbrone**
Map Grid: 5
RC Parish: Sligo, see St. John's
Diocese: EL

Civil Parish: **Killerry**
Map Grid: 28
RC Parish: see Killanummery, Co. Leitrim
Diocese: AD

Civil Parish: **Killoran**
Map Grid: 17
RC Parish: Killoran
Diocese: AC
Earliest Record: b. 4.1878; m. 4.1846
Parish Address: Rev. John MacNicholas, PP, Coolaney, Co. Sligo

Civil Parish: **Kilmacallan**
Map Grid: 34
RC Parish: Riverstown (Taunagh)
Diocese: EL
Earliest Record: b. 11.1803; m. 11.1803
Missing Dates: b. 12.1834-5.1836; m. 1.1829-5.1836
Parish Address: Rev. Matthew McLoughlin, PP, Riverstown, Boyle, Co. Roscommon

Civil Parish: **Kilmacowen**
Map Grid: 7
RC Parish: Sligo, see St. John's
Diocese: EL

Civil Parish: **Kilmacshalgan**
Map Grid: 10
RC Parish: Kilmacshalgan (see Templeboy for pre-1808 records)
Diocese: KA
Earliest Record: b. 6.1868; m. 1.1868
Parish Address: Rev. John Durcan, PP, Dromore West, Ballina, Co. Mayo

Civil Parish: **Kilmacteige**
Map Grid: 20
RC Parish: Kilmacteige (Tourlestrane)
Diocese: AC
Earliest Record: b. 4.1845; m. 1.1848
Parish Address: Rev. Seamus Colleary, CC, Kilmacteigue, Aclare, Co. Sligo

Civil Parish: **Kilmactranny**
Map Grid: 37
RC Parish: Geevagh
Diocese: EL
Earliest Record: b. 2.1873; m. 1.1851
Parish Address: Rev. Thomas Sharkey, PP, Geevagh, Ballyfarnon, Boyle, Co. Roscommon

Civil Parish: **Kilmoremoy**
Map Grid: 15
RC Parish: see Kilmoremoy, Co. Mayo
Diocese: KA

Civil Parish: **Kilmorgan**
Map Grid: 22
RC Parish: see Emlaghfad
Diocese: AC

Civil Parish: **Kilross**
Map Grid: 29
RC Parish: Sowey, see Kilmacallan
Diocese: EL

Civil Parish: **Kilshalvy**
Map Grid: 26
RC Parish: see Kilturra, Co. Mayo
Diocese: AC

Civil Parish: **Kilturra**
Map Grid: 25
RC Parish: see Co. Mayo
Diocese: AC

Civil Parish: **Kilvarnet**
Map Grid: 18
RC Parish: see Ballysodare
Diocese: AC

Civil Parish: **Rossinver**
Map Grid: 2
RC Parish: see Rossinver (3), Co. Leitrim
Diocese: KM

Civil Parish: **St. John's**
Map Grid: 6
RC Parish: Sligo
Diocese: EL
Earliest Record: b. 10.1858; m. 10.1858
Parish Address: Rev. Charles Travers, Adm, St. Mary's, Sligo

Civil Parish: **Shancough**
Map Grid: 36
RC Parish: Geevagh, see Kilmactranny
Diocese: EL

Civil Parish: **Skreen**
Map Grid: 12
RC Parish: Skreen and Dromard
Diocese: KA
Earliest Record: b. 7.1848; m. 7.1848
Missing Dates: m. 8.1869-7.1878
Parish Address: Rev. Michael Cawley, Beltra, Ballysodare, Co. Sligo

Civil Parish: **Tawnagh**
Map Grid: 33
RC Parish: Riverstown, see Kilmacallan
Diocese: EL

Civil Parish: **Templeboy**
Map Grid: 11
RC Parish: Templeboy and Kilmacshalgan
Diocese: KA
Earliest Record: b. 9.1815; m. 10.1815; d. 11.1815
Missing Dates: b. 11.1816-5.1826, 11.1838-6.1868; m. 12.1837-1.1868; d. 11.1816-10.1824, 12.1833
Parish Address: Rev. Patrick Hegarty, PP, Templeboy, Co. Sligo

Civil Parish: **Toomour**
Map Grid: 24
RC Parish: part Drumrat; part Toomore, Co. Mayo
Diocese: AC

Commercial and Social Directories

1824
J. Pigot's *City of Dublin & Hibernian Provincial Directory* includes traders, nobility, gentry, and clergy lists of Ballisodare, Ballymote, Collooney, and Sligo.

1839
"Sligo Independent's" in *Sligo-Derry Directory* lists traders, gentry, etc.

1846

Slater's *National Commercial Directory of Ireland* lists nobility, clergy, traders, etc., in Ballymote, Collooney and Ballysodare, and Sligo.

1856

Slater's *Royal National Commercial Directory of Ireland* lists nobility, gentry, clergy, traders etc., in Ballymote, Collooney and Ballysodare, and Sligo.

1865

Sligo Independent Almanac.

1870

Slater's *Directory of Ireland* contains trade, nobility, and clergy lists for Ballymote, Collooney and Ballysodare, and Sligo.

1881

Slater's *Royal National Commercial Directory of Ireland* contains lists of traders, clergy, nobility, and farmers in adjoining parishes of the towns of Ballymote, Collooney and Ballysodare, Enniscrone and Easkey (see Ballina, Co. Mayo), and Sligo.

1889

Sligo Independent Directory of Ballymote, Cliffoney, Easkey, Coolaney, Drumcliff, Collooney, Carney, Dromore West, Riverstown and Bunnemadden, Rosses Point and Enniscrone, Sligo, and Tubercurry.

1894

Slater's *Royal National Directory of Ireland* lists traders, police, teachers, farmers, and private residents in each of the towns, villages, and parishes of the county.

Family History

Byrne, Celeste. "Hillas of Co. Sligo." *Ir. Anc.* 4 (1972): 26-29.

Downey, L. *A History of the Protestant Downeys of Cos. Sligo, Leitrim, Fermanagh and Donegal* (also of the Hawksby family of Leitrim and Sligo). New York, 1931.

"The Family of Wood, Co. Sligo." *Ir. Gen.* 3 (8) (1963): 300-09; 3 (9) (1964): 364-65.

Irwin – see Co. Roscommon.

The McDermots of Moylurg. Typescript in Sligo Co. Library.

The McDonagh Family of Co. Sligo. McDonagh Mss. No. 5, Sligo Co. Library.

O'Connor, Watson B. *The O'Connor Family: Families of Daniel and Matthias O'Connor of Corsallagh House, Achonry, Co. Sligo, Ireland, A.D. 1750.* Brooklyn, 1914.

Particulars Concerning Co. Sligo Families. McDonagh Mss. No. 2, Sligo Co. Library.

Pedigrees of the McDonagh Clan of Corann & Tirerill and Other Families of Co. Sligo. McDonagh Mss. No. 1, Sligo Co. Library.

Pedigrees of Co. Sligo Families. McDonagh Mss. No. 23, Sligo Co. Library.

Newspapers

Although there was a Sligo paper, *The Sligo Journal,* published as early as 1807, there are no copies of it before 1822. Mayo, Galway, and other county papers may also be consulted for early notices of relevance to this county.

Title: *The Champion* or *Sligo News* (continued as *Sligo Champion* from 1853)
Published in: Sligo, 1836-current
NLI Holdings: 10.1879-in progress (with gaps)
Sligo Co. Library Holdings: 1836-70; 1897-1925
BL Holdings: 6.1836-in progress

Title: *Sligo Chronicle*
Published in: Sligo, 1850-93
Sligo Co. Library Holdings: 4.1850-4.1893

Title: *Sligo Independent*
Published in: Sligo, 1855-1961
NLI Holdings: 1.1879-12.1961 (with gaps)
Sligo Co. Library Holdings: 9.1855-12.1859 (with gaps)
BL Holdings: 9.1855-7.1869; odd numbers 1870; 1.1875-7.1876; 2-9.1877; 3.1879-9.1921

Title: *Sligo Journal*
Published in: Sligo, ca. 1807-66
NLI Holdings: 3-12.1823

Sligo Co. Library Holdings: 3-7.1822; 1828-3.1866
BL Holdings: 1.1828-3.1866

Title: *Sligo Observer*
Published in: Sligo, 1828-31
NLI Holdings: 10.1828-2.1831
Sligo Co. Library Holdings: 10.1828-2.1831
BL Holdings: 10.1828-2.1831

Wills and Administrations

A discussion of the types of records, where they are held, their availability and value is given in the Wills section of the Introduction. The availability of prerogative wills, administrations, and marriage license records is also described in the relevant parts of the same section. Where available, published sources of these records are given in the Miscellaneous Sources.

Pre-1858 Wills and Administrations

Prerogative Wills. see p. xli.

Consistorial Wills. County Sligo is in the dioceses of Killala, Elphin, Achonry, and (one parish each) Ardagh and Kilmore. The guide to Catholic parish records in this chapter shows the diocese to which each civil parish belonged. The wills of residents of each diocese were usually proven within that diocese (see the Wills section for exceptions). The following records survive:

Wills. see p. xxxvii. County Sligo Wills (1705-32) NLI ms. 2164.

Abstracts. See p. xxxvii.

Indexes. Killala and Achonry (1698-1838). *Ir. Gen.* 3 (2): 506-19; *Ir. Anc.* 7: 55-61. Ardagh – see Co. Longford. Kilmore – see Co. Cavan.

Post-1858 Wills and Administrations

This county was served by the District Registry of Ballina. The surviving records are kept in the PRO.

Marriage Licenses

Indexes. Elphin, Killala, and Achonry (1740-1850). PRO; SLC film 100868. Kilmore and Ardagh (1691-1845). PRO; SLC film 100869.

Miscellaneous Sources

"Further Notes on the High Sheriffs of Co. Sligo." *Ir. Gen.* 2 (7) (1949): 197-203.

"Further Notes on the High Sheriffs of Co. Sligo." *Ir. Gen.* 2 (9) (1952): 269-75.

"The High Sheriffs of Co. Sligo." *Ir. Gen.* 1 (1) (1937): 16-18.

McDonagh, J. *History of Ballymote & the Parish of Emlaghfad.* 1936.

McPartlan, J. *Statistical Survey of Co. Sligo.* Dublin Society, 1801.

McTernan, J. *Historic Sligo: A Bibliographical Introduction to the Antiquities and History of Co. Sligo.* 1965.

O'Rourke, Rev. T. *History of the Parishes of Ballysadare & Killarnet.* 1878.

O'Rourke, Rev. T. *History of Sligo, Town & County.* 2 vols. 1889.

Wood-Martin, W.G. *History of Sligo.* 1882-1892.

Research Sources and Services

Libraries and Information Sources

Sligo County Library, The Courthouse, Sligo Ph: (071) 2212 (has extensive local collection and bibliography)

Research Services

Sligo Family History Society, c/o Columban Club, Castle Street, Sligo Ph: (071) 43728

See also research services in Dublin, p. xliv

Societies

Sligo Field Club, Mrs. Mary B. Murphy, Station Road, Ballysodare, Co. Sligo

Sligo Family History Society (see address above)

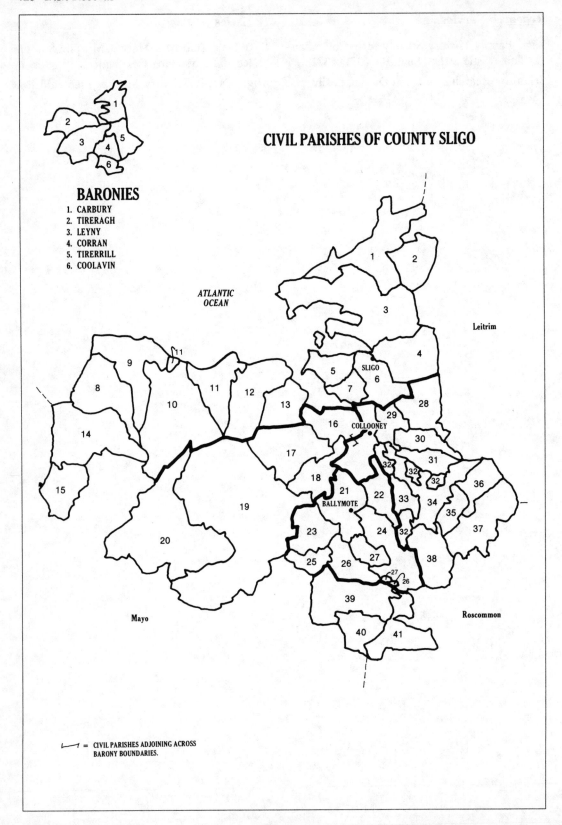

CIVIL PARISHES OF COUNTY SLIGO

BARONIES

1. CARBURY
2. TIRERAGH
3. LEYNY
4. CORRAN
5. TIRERRILL
6. COOLAVIN

ATLANTIC
OCEAN

Leitrim

Mayo

Roscommon

SLIGO

COLLOONEY

BALLYMOTE

⌐⌐ = CIVIL PARISHES ADJOINING ACROSS
        BARONY BOUNDARIES.

County Tipperary

A Brief History

Tipperary is an inland county with an area of just over 1 million acres, 80 percent of which is arable agricultural land. The county contains the towns of Clonmel, Nenagh, Thurles, Roscrea, Tipperary, Cashel, Cahir, Templemore, Carrick-on-Suir, and Fethard.

Historically the county was partly in the old Gaelic territory of Ormond and partly in Thomond. The major Irish families included the O'Fogartys, O'Briens, and O'Kennedys. Other names associated with the county are O'Moloney, O'Mulryan or Ryan, Meagher or Maher, Hourigan, Hayes, and Gleeson.

The county was invaded by the Normans in 1172. In 1185 it was granted by King John of England to Theobald Walter who was given the title Chief Butler of Ireland, from which the family took the surname "Butler." Among the Norman names now found in the county are Prendergast, Burke, Purcell, Fitzgerald, Everard, St. John, and Grace.

As elsewhere in the country, the Norman families assimilated into the local population and British cultural and administrative influence gradually waned. Among the vast majority of the people, English influence was negligible until the seventeenth century. Gaelic was the common language of the people, and even as late as 1841 around 8 percent of the population spoke Gaelic only.

In 1641 the Irish and Norman chieftains of Tipperary joined the rebellion of the Catholic Confederacy but were defeated by Oliver Cromwell in 1649. The lands of those who had rebelled were divided among English adventurers and among the soldiers of Cromwell's army. Most of these soldiers had no interest in the land and sold it to their officers and others who thereby managed to put together large estates in the county. There was little settlement by soldiers in the county.

Although not the worst affected area, Tipperary was relatively badly affected by the Great Famine of 1845-47. The population reached a peak of 436,000 in 1841. Following the large-scale failure of the potato crop, particularly in the years 1845-47, the population declined rapidly. Almost 70,000 people died in the county between 1845 and 1850, particularly in the years 1849 and 1850.

Huge numbers of people are known to have emigrated from the county during the nineteenth century. About 190,000 people are estimated to have emigrated from Tipperary between 1841 and 1891, particularly in the 1840s, '50s, and '60s. In the same period the rural population fell from 364,000 to 134,000 and the town population from 71,000 to 39,000.

County Tipperary is a largely agricultural

county with industries in the larger towns. It has a current population of 135,000.

Census and Census Substitutes

1551

Lists of Jurors in Various Towns in Co. Tipperary and of the County Generally, With a Writ to the Sheriff for Summoning Juries. NLI D 2553.

1595

Names of the Freeholders in Co. Tipperary, 1595. NLI P1700.

1641-63

"Proprietors of Fethard, Co. Tipperary." *Ir. Gen.* 6 (1) (1980): 5-8.

1653

"The Names of Soldiers and Adventurers who Received Land in Co. Tipperary Under the Cromwellian Settlement, 1653." In John Prendergast. *The Cromwellian Settlement of Ireland.* 386-400, Dublin, 1922.

1654-56

Civil Survey. Vol. 2. (eastern and southern parts).

1659

"Census" of Ireland. Edited by S. Pender. Dublin: Stationery Office, 1939; SLC film 924648.

1664

"The Dispossessed Landowners of Ireland: Co. Tipperary." *Ir. Gen.* 4 (5) (1972): 429-34.

1666-68

Three Hearth Money Rolls. Printed as *Tipperary's Families,* edited by Thomas Laffan, 9-193. Dublin, 1911.

1750

"Catholics in Parishes of Barnane, Bourney, Corbally, Killavanough, Killea, Rathnaveoge, Roscrea, Templeree, Templetouhy." *Ir. Gen.* 4 (6) (1973): 578-83; NLI ms. 8913.

1766

Religious Census of the Parishes of Athassel, Ballintemple, Ballycahill, Ballygriffin, Boytonrath, Brickendown, Bruis, Clerihan, Clonbeg, Cloneen, Clonoulty, Cloonbulloge, Clonpet, Colman, Cordangan, Corrogue, Cullen, Dangandargan, Drum, Dustrileague, Erry, Fethard, Gaile, Grean, Horeabbey, Killardry, Killbrugh, Killea, Kilconnell, Kilfeacle, Killevinogue, Knockgraffon, Killnerath, Kiltynan, Lattin, Magorban, Mealiffe, New Chapel (including number of children per household), Pepperstown, Railstown, Rathcoole, Relickmurry, Redcity, Shronell, St. John's Cashel, St. Patrick's Rock, Solloghodmore, Templebeg, Templemore, Templeneiry, Templenoe, Tipperary, and Toom. PRO 1A 46 49; Parishes of Ballingarry and Uskeane. GO 536.

1775

Catholic Qualification Roll Extracts (368 names, addresses, and occupations). 59th Report DKPRI: 50-84.

1776

Lists of Voters. PRO film 4912.

A Register of the Freeholders in Co. Tipperary. PRO film 1321-2; GO ms. 442.

1799

Census of Carrick-on-Suir (gives name, age, religion, and occupation of all inhabitants) NLI 28; BM ms. 11,722. A descriptive note on the census is in *Ir. Gen.* 5 (2) (1975): 271-72; *Decies* 21 (1982): 29-31.

1802

"Some Game Licenses of 1802." *Ir. Anc.* 8 (1): 38-47 (lists names and addresses of licensees in Clonmel, Cashel, and Tipperary).

1823-38

Tithe Applotment Survey (see p. xxvii).

1832-36

"Names of Excise License Holders and Applicants in Cashel and Clonmel (180 names and addresses). *Parl. Papers* 1837/38, 13 (2): Appendix 10, 13.

1832-37

"List of Voters Registered in the Boroughs of Clonmel and Cashel." *Parl. Papers* 1837, 11 (2): 217-33 (approximately 900 names, occupations, and residences in Clonmel; over 350 names and occupations in Cashel).

1834

"Census of Parish of Templebredin." *J. N. Munster Arch. & Hist. Soc.* (1976) (lists the heads of households in each townland with numbers of males and females).

1835

Census of Parishes of Birdhill and Newport (gives the name of the householder in each townland or street with numbers of males and females in each household). NLI P1561.

1837

"Lists of Freemen (since 1831) of Cashel and Clonmel" (120 names, occupations, and residences). *Parl. Papers* 1837/38, 13 (2): Appendix 3.

"Occupants of Clonmel, by Street, Giving Description of Premises and Valuation." *Parl. Papers* 1837, 11 (2): 247-64.

"Census of Protestant Parishioners in Clogheen Union, Co. Tipperary in 1837, '77, and '80." *Ir. Anc.* 17 (1) (1985): 25-29.

1840-44

"Names of All Persons Qualified to Serve as Jurors in the Northern Division of the County of Tipperary." *Parl. Papers* 1844, 43 (380): 1-29.

1845

List of Subscribers to Roscrea Chapel. In Catholic parish register of Roscrea and Kyle (see civil parish of Roscrea and Kyle in Roman Catholic records section).

1851

Griffith's Valuation (see p. xxvii).

1864-70

"Census of Protestants in the parishes of Shanrahan and Tullagherton Co. Tipperary in 1864-1870." *Ir. Anc.* 16 (2) (1984): 61-67.

1877-80

See 1837 (Clogheen).

1901

Census. PRO.

1911

Census. PRO.

Church Records

Church of Ireland
(shows starting date of record)

Parish: **Aghnameadle**
Existing Records: b. 1834; m. 1834; d. 1834
Status: LC

Parish: **Aghlishcloghane**
Status: Lost

Parish: **Ardcroney**
Status: Lost

Parish: **Ardfinnan**
Status: Lost

Parish: **Ardmayle**
Status: Lost

Parish: **Athassell** or **Relicmurray**
Status: Lost

Parish: **Ballingarry**
Existing Records: (earliest volume, 1785-1802 now extant, recovered in 1961) b. 1785; m. 1785; d. 1785
Missing Dates: b. 1803-15; m. 1803-15; d. 1803-1815
Status: PRO

Parish: **Ballingarry** and **Uskane**
Status: Lost

Parish: **Ballintemple**
Existing Records: b. 1805; m. 1805; d. 1805
Status: LC

Parish: **Ballymackey**
Status: Lost

Parish: **Ballysheehan**
Status: Lost

Parish: **Bansha** (see Templeneiry)

Parish: **Borrisokane**
Status: Lost

Parish: **Borrisoleigh**
Status: Lost

Parish: **Cahir**
Existing Records: b. 1801; m. 1802; d. 1804
Status: LC

Parish: **Carrick**
Existing Records: b. 1803; m. 1803; d. 1803
Status: LC

Parish: **Cashel Liberties**
Existing Records: m. 1654-57
Status: published by Parish Rec. Soc. I.

Parish: **Castletownarra**
Existing Records: b. 1802; m. 1802; d. 1802
Status: LC

Parish: **Clogheen** (see Shanrahan)

Parish: **Clonbeg**
Status: Lost

Parish: **Corbally**
Existing Records: b. 1834 (register of baptism
    1834-49 in local custody); d. 1849
Status: LC

Parish: **Cullen**
Existing Records: b. 1770; m. 1770; d. 1770
Status: LC

Parish: **Derrygrath**
Status: Lost

Parish: **Donohill** (see also Templeneiry)
Existing Records: b. 1856; d. 1859
Status: LC

Parish: **Dorrha**
Status: Lost

Parish: **Dunkerrin**
Existing Records: b. 1825; m. 1826; d. 1825
Status: LC

Parish: **Emly**
Status: Lost

Parish: **Fennor**
Status: Lost

Parish: **Finnoe** and **Cloughprior**
Status: Lost

Parish: **Galbally**
Status: Lost

Parish: **Glankeen**
Status: Lost

Parish: **Holy Cross**
Status: Lost

Parish: **Innislonnagh**
Status: Lost

Parish: **Kilbarron**
Status: Lost

Parish: **Kilcooly**
Status: Lost

Parish: **Kilfithnone**
Status: Lost

Parish: **Kilkeary**
Status: Lost

Parish: **Killaloan**
Status: Lost

Parish: **Killenaule**
Status: Lost

Parish: **Killodiernan**
Status: Lost

Parish: **Killoscully**
Status: Lost

Parish: **Kilmastulla** and **Templecalla**
Status: Lost

CASHEL. 41

William Scurlocke of Ballyngronty and Juane Kenedy of the same
in the Barrony of Clañwilliam married 13° January 1656°.

Teige Mulcroe of Boytonrath and Margarett Dooly of Woodins-
towne in the Barrony of Middlethird married 14° January
1656°.

Morgan Mackan of Darrymore and Catherin Ryane of the same
in the Barrony of Kilnemañagh married 16° January 1656°.

John Breanagh of Shanbally Duffe and Catherin Purcell of the
same in the Barrony of Middlethird married 20° Januarii
1656°.

Richard Ryane of Rathkenane and Margarett Dwyer of the same
in the Barrony of Kilnemannagh married 20° Januarij 1656°.

Edward Coñill of Kylltane and Margarett ny Danniell of Bansagh
in the Barrony of Clañwilliam married 20° Januarii 1656°.

Thomas Hiffernane of Ballynry and Gyles Meagher of the same
in the Barrony of Middlethird married 1° ffebr. 1656°.

Redmond Magrath of Ballymore and Ellis Butler of Culinure
in the Barrony of Kyllnemañagh married 17° Oct. 1656.

Donnogh Ryane of Cashell and Catherin Meehane of the same
married 4° Nov. 1656.

Teige mcConnor of Culinure and Uny Ryane of Clonisbeo in the
Barrony of Kylnemannagh married 4° Nov. 1656°.

Edmond Magrath of Cashell and Catherin Donoghie of Croghtina-
bluolie in the Barrony of Middlethird married 4° Nov. 1656°.

Teige Ryane of Dundrome and Margarett Ryane of Ballisidie
in the Barrony of Kylnemañagh married 12° Novbris 1656°.

Roger Higgin of Clounoultie in the Barrony of Kylnemañagh &
Honnora Devane of Ardmaile in the Barrony of Middlethird
married 13° Nov. 1656°.

Edmond Meagher of Cashell & Ellan Hacckett of the same married
13° Nov. 1656°.

Edmond Wailsh of Clounoultie and Sara Ryane of the same in
the Barrony of Middlethird married 15° Nov. 1656°.

Donnogh Arra of Ardmayle and Juane Dooly of the same in the
Barrony of Middlethird married 25° Nov. 1656°.

John fflood of Clonoultie in the Barrony of Kylnemañagh & Juane
Boorke of Collaghill in the Barrony of Eliogertie married
21 Dec. 1656°.

John Hickie of Boytonrath and Juane Hyffernane of the same
in the Barrony of Middlethird married 26° Decembr. 1656°.

Thomas Meagher of Cashell and Margarett ny Danniell of the
Barrony of Middlethird married 31° Dec. 1656°.

Willm Peñerton of Killteynane troop, and Añ Coogiñ of the Towne
of ffithard spinster married 5° Martij 1656.

Daniell ô Hallurane of Greistowne in the Barrony of Slyevardagh,
& Margarett Lemeasny of the same married March the 20th
1656.

John Henes of the parrish of Drañgane in the Barrony of Middlethird, & Catherin Bryen of the same married March the 16th
1656.

Derby Dalloghonty of Drañgane aforesd, & Juañ Carroll of the
same married die predicto

John Shea & Juañ Haly of Drañgane aforesd married the day
aforesd.

John Meagher of Priestowne in the sd Barrony, & Ellis Mahuny
of the same married March the 16th 56.

F

Page of 1656 marriage records from a published copy of the *Register of the Liberties of Cashel* (Co. Tipperary), Parish Register Society of Ireland, Volume 4, Dublin, 1907.

Parish: **Kilmore**
Status: Lost

Parish: **Kilruane**
Status: Lost

Parish: **Kilshane**
Status: Lost

Parish: **Kilvemnon**
Status: Lost

Parish: **Knockgraffon**
Status: Lost

Parish: **Lismalin**
Status: Lost

Parish: **Lisronagh**
Status: Lost

Parish: **Lockeene**
Status: Lost

Parish: **Lorrha**
Status: Lost

Parish: **Loughmoe**
Status: Lost

Parish: **Mealiffe**
Existing Records: b. 1791; m. 1795; d. 1792
Status: LC

Parish: **Modreeney**
Existing Records: b. 1811; m. 1811; d. 1811
Status: LC

Parish: **Magorban**
Status: Lost

Parish: **Monsea**
Status: Lost

Parish: **Moyne**
Status: Lost

Parish: **Nenagh**
Status: Lost

Parish: **Newchapel**
Status: Lost

Parish: **Rathronan**
Status: Lost

Parish: **Relickmurry** (see Arhassell)

Parish: **Roscrea**
Existing Records: b. 1784; m. 1784; d. 1784
Status: LC

Parish: **St. John Baptist**
Existing Records: b. 1668; m. 1668; d. 1668
Status: LC

Parish: **St. John Newport**
Existing Records: b. 1782; m. 1782; d. 1782
Status: LC

Parish: **St. Mary Clonmel**
Existing Records: b. 1766; m. 1766; d. 1766
Status: LC

Parish: **Shanrahan** and **Templetenny**
Status: Lost

Parish: **Shronell** and **Lattin**
Status: Lost

Parish: **Templederry**
Status: Lost

Parish: **Templemichael** (no church, no records)

Parish: **Templemore**
Existing Records: b. 1812; m. 1812; d. 1812
    (entries of baptisms, marriages, and burials
    1791 to 1809 from vestry book (1789-1872)
    ms.; Photostat M5364)
Status: LC

Parish: **Templeneiry** or **Bansha**
Status: Lost

Parish: **Templenor** (see Tipperary)

Parish: **Templetenny** (see also Shanrahan)
Status: Lost

Parish: **Templetuohy**
Status: Lost

Parish: **Terryglass**
Existing Records: b. 1809; m. 1809; d. 1809
Status: LC

Parish: **Thurles**
Status: Lost

Parish: **Tipperary**
Existing Records: b. 1779; m. 1779; d. 1779
Status: LC

Parish: **Toem** (includes entries from Holyford
   Mines)
Status: Lost

Parish: **Tubrid**
Status: Lost

Parish: **Tullamelan**
Existing Records: b. 1823; m. 1823; d. 1823
Status: LC

Parish: **Whitechurch** (see Tubrid)

Parish: **Youghalarra**
Status: Lost

Roman Catholic

Civil Parish: **Abington**
Map Grid: N28
RC Parish: Murroe, see Abington, Co.
   Limerick
Diocese: EM

Civil Parish: **Aghacrew**
Map Grid: S94
RC Parish: Annacarty, see Donohill
Diocese: CA

Civil Parish: **Aghnameadle**
Map Grid: N38
RC Parish: Aghnameadle and Toomavarra
Diocese: KL
Earliest Record: b. 3.1831; m. 8.1830

Missing Dates: b. 6.1856-5.1861; m. 9.1836-
   6.1861
Parish Address: Rev. John Mulqueen, PP,
   Toomevara, Co. Tipperary

Civil Parish: **Aglishcloghane**
Map Grid: N4
RC Parish: see Borrisokane
Diocese: KL

Civil Parish: **Ardcrony**
Map Grid: N13
RC Parish: Cloughjordan, see Modreeny
Diocese: KL

Civil Parish: **Ardfinnan**
Map Grid: S94
RC Parish: Ardfinnan
Diocese: LS
Earliest Record: b. 12.1809; m. 4.1814
Missing Dates: m. 2.1822-1.1827
Parish Address: Rev. J. McGrath, PP, Ardfin-
   nan, Clonmel, Co. Tipperary

Civil Parish: **Ardmayle**
Map Grid: S37
RC Parish: Boherlahan and Dualla
Diocese: CA
Earliest Record: b. 4.1810; m. 5.1810
Parish Address: Rev. J. Feehan, PP, Boher-
   lahan, Cashel, Co. Tipperary

Civil Parish: **Athnid**
Map Grid: N71
RC Parish: see Thurles
Diocese: CA

Civil Parish: **Ballingarry** (1) (Lower Ormond)
Map Grid: N10
RC Parish: see Borrisokane
Diocese: KL

Civil Parish: **Ballingarry** (2) (Slieveardagh)
Map Grid: S77
RC Parish: Ballingarry
Diocese: CA
Earliest Record: b. 6.1814; m. 4.1814
Missing Dates: b. 5.1827-8.1827; m. 2.1822-
   1.1826
Parish Address: Rev. P. Morris, PP, Ballingar-
   ry, Thurles, Co. Tipperary

Civil Parish: **Ballintemple**
Map Grid: S6
RC Parish: Knockavilla, see Oughterleague
Diocese: CA

Civil Parish: **Ballybacon**
Map Grid: S97
RC Parish: see Ardfinnan
Diocese: LS

Civil Parish: **Ballycahill**
Map Grid: N68
RC Parish: see Holycross
Diocese: CA

Civil Parish: **Ballyclerahan**
Map Grid: S101
RC Parish: Clerihan
Diocese: CA
Earliest Record: b. 4.1852; m. 8.1852
Parish Address: Rev. R. Fitzgerald, PP, Clerihan, Clonmel, Co. Tipperary

Civil Parish: **Ballygibbon**
Map Grid: N29
RC Parish: see Aghnameadle
Diocese: KL

Civil Parish: **Ballygriffin**
Map Grid: S14
RC Parish: Annacarty, see Donohill
Diocese: CA

Civil Parish: **Ballymackey**
Map Grid: N31
RC Parish: see Aghnameadle
Diocese: KL

Civil Parish: **Ballymurreen**
Map Grid: N79
RC Parish: see Moycarkey
Diocese: CA

Civil Parish: **Ballynaclogh**
Map Grid: N36
RC Parish: Silvermines, see Kilmore (2)
Diocese: KL

Civil Parish: **Ballysheehan**
Map Grid: S38

RC Parish: Boherlahan, etc., see Ardmayle
Diocese: CA

Civil Parish: **Baptistgrange**
Map Grid: S68
RC Parish: Powerstown, see Kilgrant
Diocese: LS

Civil Parish: **Barnane-Ely**
Map Grid: N51
RC Parish: see Drom and Inch
Diocese: CA

Civil Parish: **Barretsgrange**
Map Grid: S60
RC Parish: Fethard and Killusty, see Fethard
Diocese: CA

Civil Parish: **Borrisnafarney**
Map Grid: N47
RC Parish: Couraganeen, see Bourney
Diocese: KL

Civil Parish: **Borrisokane**
Map Grid: N8
RC Parish: Borrisokane
Diocese: KL
Earliest Record: b. 6.1821; m. 7.1821
Missing Dates: m. 1.1844-10.1844
Parish Address: Rev. J. Madden, PP, Borrisokane, Nenagh, Co. Tipperary

Civil Parish: **Bourney**
Map Grid: N45
RC Parish: Couraganeen, or Bourney and Corbally
Diocese: KL
Earliest Record: b. 7.1836; m. 6.1836
Missing Dates: b. 1873; m. 1873
Parish Address: Rev. P. Whelan, PP, Bournea, Roscrea, Co. Tipperary

Civil Parish: **Boytonrath**
Map Grid: S56
RC Parish: Golden, see Relickmurray
Diocese: CA

Civil Parish: **Brickendown**
Map Grid: S43

RC Parish: Boherlahan and Dualla, see Ardmayle
Diocese: CA

Civil Parish: **Bruis**
Map Grid: S27
RC Parish: see Lattin
Diocese: EM

Civil Parish: **Buolick**
Map Grid: S72
RC Parish: Gortnehoe
Diocese: CA
Earliest Record: b. 9.1805; m. 10.1805
Missing Dates: b. 12.1830-3.1831; m. 11.1830-10.1831
Parish Address: Rev. J. J. Lambe, PP, Gortnahoe, Thurles, Co. Tipperary

Civil Parish: **Burgesbeg**
Map Grid: N22
RC Parish: Burgess and Youghal
Diocese: KL
Earliest Record: b. 10.1828; m. 10.1820
Parish Address: Rev. John Minihan, PP, Newtown, Nenagh, Co. Tipperary

Civil Parish: **Caher**
Map Grid: S91
RC Parish: Caher
Diocese: LS
Earliest Record: b. 6.1776; m. 7.1776
Missing Dates: b. 3.1793-8.1809
Parish Address: Rev. J. P. Walsh, PP, Parochial House, Cahir, Co. Tipperary

Civil Parish: **Carrick**
Map Grid: S116
RC Parish: Carrick-on-Suir
Diocese: LS
Earliest Record: b. 9.1784; m. 1.1788
Missing Dates: b. 4.1803-5.1805, 7.1819-1.1823; m. 10.1803-1.1806, 2.1815-1.1823, 10.1825-1.1826
Parish Address: Rev. Laurence Walsh, PP, Parochial House, Carrick-on-Suir, Co. Tipperary

Civil Parish: **Castletownarra**
Map Grid: N19
RC Parish: Castletownarra

Diocese: KL
Earliest Record: b. 11.1849; m. 11.1849
Parish Address: Rev. Edmund Kennedy, PP, Portroe, Nenagh, Co. Tipperary

Civil Parish: **Clogher**
Map Grid: S1
RC Parish: see Clonoulty
Diocese: CA

Civil Parish: **Cloghprior**
Map Grid: N12
RC Parish: Cloghprior and Monsea
Diocese: KL
Earliest Record: b. 2.1834; m. 2.1834
Missing Dates: b. ends 12.1865
Parish Address: Rev. J. A. O'Brien, PP, Ballycommon, Nenagh, Co. Tipperary

Civil Parish: **Clonbeg**
Map Grid: S33
RC Parish: see Galbally, Co. Limerick
Diocese: CA

Civil Parish: **Clonbullogue**
Map Grid: S32
RC Parish: Bansha and Kilmoyler, see Templeneiry
Diocese: CA

Civil Parish: **Cloneen** or **Cloyne**
Map Grid: S54
RC Parish: see Drangan
Diocese: CA

Civil Parish: **Clonoulty**
Map Grid: S3
RC Parish: Clonoulty
Diocese: CA
Earliest Record: b. 10.1804; m. 10.1804
Missing Dates: m. 6.1809-10.1809
Parish Address: Rev. T. Kennedy, PP, Clonoulty, Gooldscross, Cashel, Co. Tipperary

Civil Parish: **Clonpet**
Map Grid: S28
RC Parish: see Lattin
Diocese: EM

Civil Parish: **Colman**
Map Grid: S66

RC Parish: Clerihan, see Ballyclerahan
Diocese: CA

Civil Parish: **Cooleagh**
Map Grid: S45
RC Parish: see Killenaule
Diocese: CA

Civil Parish: **Coolmundry**
Map Grid: S63
RC Parish: Fethard and Killusty, see Fethard

Civil Parish: **Corbally** (see also Co. Offaly)
Map Grid: N43
RC Parish: Couraganeen, see also Bourney and
   Roscrea
Diocese: KL

Civil Parish: **Cordangan**
Map Grid: S29
RC Parish: see Lattin and Cullen
Diocese: EM

Civil Parish: **Corroge**
Map Grid: S25
RC Parish: see Tipperary
Diocese: EM

Civil Parish: **Crohane**
Map Grid: S78
RC Parish: see Ballingarry (2)
Diocese: CA

Civil Parish: **Cullen**
Map Grid: S17
RC Parish: Lattin and Cullen, see Lattin
Diocese: EM

Civil Parish: **Cullenwaine**
Map Grid: N46
RC Parish: see Dunkerrin, Co. Offaly
Diocese: KL

Civil Parish: **Dangandargan**
Map Grid: S49
RC Parish: Golden, see Relickmurry
Diocese: CA

Civil Parish: **Derrygrath**
Map Grid: S92

RC Parish: see Ardfinnan
Diocese: LS

Civil Parish: **Dogstown**
Map Grid: S57
RC Parish: part New Inn, see Knockgraffon;
   part Golden, see Relickmurry
Diocese: CA

Civil Parish: **Dolla**
Map Grid: N35
RC Parish: part Silvermines, see Kilmore (2);
   part Killanave, etc., see Kilnaneave
Diocese: KL

Civil Parish: **Donaghmore**
Map Grid: S67
RC Parish: Powerstown, see Kilgrant
Diocese: LS

Civil Parish: **Donohill**
Map Grid: S2
RC Parish: Annacarty and Donohill
Diocese: CA
Earliest Record: b. 5.1821; m. 5.1821
Parish Address: Rev. Philip Kinane, PP, An-
   nacarty, Co. Tipperary

Civil Parish: **Doon**
Map Grid: N57
RC Parish: see Co. Limerick
Diocese: EM

Civil Parish: **Dorrha**
Map Grid: N2
RC Parish: Lorrha and Dorrha, see Lorrha
Diocese: KL

Civil Parish: **Drangan**
Map Grid: S48
RC Parish: Drangan (and Cloyne)
Diocese: CA
Earliest Record: b. 1.1811; m. 1.1812
Missing Dates: m. 10.1846-1.1847
Parish Address: Rev. James O'Rahilly, PP,
   Drangan, Thurles, Co. Tipperary

Civil Parish: **Drom**
Map Grid: N62
RC Parish: Drom and Inch

Diocese: CA
Earliest Record: b. 3.1827; m. 5.1827
Parish Address: Rev. James O'Connor, PP,
 Drom, Thurles, Co. Tipperary

Civil Parish: **Dromineer**
Map Grid: N15
RC Parish: Cloghprior and Monsea, see
 Cloghprior
Diocese: KL

Civil Parish: **Emly**
Map Grid: S22
RC Parish: Emly
Diocese: EM
Earliest Record: b. 7.1810; m. 4.1809
Missing Dates: m. 10.1838-1.1839
Parish Address: Rev. Michael English, PP,
 Emly, Co. Tipperary

Civil Parish: **Erry**
Map Grid: S39
RC Parish: Boherlahan, etc., see Ardmayle
Diocese: CA

Civil Parish: **Fennor**
Map Grid: S71
RC Parish: Gortnahoe, see Buolick
Diocese: CA

Civil Parish: **Fertiana**
Map Grid: N74
RC Parish: see Moycarky
Diocese: CA

Civil Parish: **Fethard**
Map Grid: S62
RC Parish: Fethard and Killusty
Diocese: CA
Earliest Record: b. 1.1806; m. 1.1806
Missing Dates: b. 1.1847-12.1847; m. 4.1820-
 1.1824
Parish Address: Rev. Philip Noonan, PP,
 Fethard, Co. Tipperary

Civil Parish: **Finnoe**
Map Grid: N7
RC Parish: see Kilbarron
Diocese: KL

Civil Parish: **Gaile** or **Geale**
Map Grid: S36
RC Parish: Boherlahan, etc, see Ardmayle
Diocese: CA

Civil Parish: **Galbooly** or **Boly**
Map Grid: N75
RC Parish: see Moycarky
Diocese: CA

Civil Parish: **Garrangibbon**
Map Grid: S106
RC Parish: Ballyneale, see Mothel, Co. Water-
 ford
Diocese: LS

Civil Parish: **Glenkeen**
Map Grid: N54
RC Parish: Borrisoleigh
Diocese: CA
Earliest Record: b. 11.1814; m. 11.1814
Parish Address: Rev. Thomas Kennedy, PP,
 Borrisoleigh, Thurles, Co. Tipperary

Civil Parish: **Glenbane**
Map Grid: S33
RC Parish: see Lattin
Diocese: EM

Civil Parish: **Grangemockler**
Map Grid: S84
RC Parish: Ballyneale, etc., see Mothel, Co.
 Waterford
Diocese: LS

Civil Parish: **Grange St. John**
Map Grid: S68
RC Parish: see Baptistgrange
Diocese: LS

Civil Parish: **Graystown**
Map Grid: S74
RC Parish: Bansha and Kilmoyler, see
 Templeneiry
Diocese: CA

Civil Parish: **Holycross**
Map Grid: N73
RC Parish: Holycross and Ballycahill
Diocese: CA
Earliest Record: b. 1.1835; m. 1.1835

Parish Address: Rev. Patrick Lynch, PP, Holycross, Thurles, Co. Tipperary

Civil Parish: **Horeabbey**
Map Grid: S41
RC Parish: Cashel, see St. John Baptist
Diocese: CA

Civil Parish: **Inch**
Map Grid: N66
RC Parish: Drom and Inch, see Drom
Diocese: CA

Civil Parish: **Inish-Lounaght**
Map Grid: S102
RC Parish: Clonmel, St. Mary's, see St. Mary's Clonmel
Diocese: LS

Civil Parish: **Isert-Kieran**
Map Grid: S82
RC Parish: Mullinahone, see Kilvemnon
Diocese: CA

Civil Parish: **Kilbarron**
Map Grid: N6
RC Parish: Kilbarron and Terryglass
Diocese: KL
Earliest Record: b. 7.1827; m. 9.1827
Parish Address: Rev. P. J. O'Connor, Terryglass, Nenagh, Co. Tipperary

Civil Parish: **Kilbragh**
Map Grid: S59
RC Parish: see Upperchurch
Diocese: CA

Civil Parish: **Kilcash**
Map Grid: S107
RC Parish: part Kilsheelan; part Powerstown, see Kilgrant
Diocese: LS

Civil Parish: **Kilclonagh**
Map Grid: N67
RC Parish: see Templetuohy
Diocese: CA

Civil Parish: **Kilcomenty**
Map Grid: N24
RC Parish: Ballinahinch

Diocese: CA
Earliest Record: b. 7.1839; m. 1.1853
Parish Address: Rev. Thomas Morris, PP, Ballinahinch, Birdhill, Limerick

Civil Parish: **Kilconnell**
Map Grid: S51
RC Parish: part Killenaule; part Boherlahan, etc., see Ardmayle
Diocese: CA

Civil Parish: **Kilcooly** (near Fennor)
Map Grid: N77
RC Parish: Gortnahoe, see Buolick
Diocese: CA

Civil Parish: **Kilcooly** (near Moyne, see also Co. Kilkenny)
Map Grid: S73
RC Parish: part Killenaule; part Gortnahoe, see Buolick
Diocese: CA

Civil Parish: **Kilcornan**
Map Grid: S16
RC Parish: Pallasgreen, see Grean, Co. Limerick
Diocese: EM

Civil Parish: **Kilfeakle**
Map Grid: S20
RC Parish: Golden, see Relickmurry
Diocese: CA

Civil Parish: **Kilfithmone**
Map Grid: N61
RC Parish: Drom and Inch, see Drom
Diocese: CA

Civil Parish: **Kilgrant**
Map Grid: S110
RC Parish: Powerstown
Diocese: LS
Earliest Record: b. 9.1808; m. 8.1808
Parish Address: Rev. Paul Beecher, PP, Rathronan, Clonmel, Co. Tipperary

Civil Parish: **Kilkeary**
Map Grid: N37
RC Parish: Toomeara, see Aghnameadle
Diocese: KL

Civil Parish: **Killaloan** (see Co. Waterford)
Map Grid: S114
RC Parish: part Powerstown, see Kilgrant; part
St. Mary's Clonmel

Civil Parish: **Killardry**
Map Grid: S31
RC Parish: Kilmoyler, see Templeneiry
Diocese: CA

Civil Parish: **Killavinoge**
Map Grid: N49
RC Parish: see Templemore
Diocese: CA

Civil Parish: **Killea**
Map Grid: N48
RC Parish: see Templemore
Diocese: CA

Civil Parish: **Killeenasteena**
Map Grid: S55
RC Parish: Golden, see Relickmurry
Diocese: CA

Civil Parish: **Killenaule**
Map Grid: S75
RC Parish: Killenaule
Diocese: CA
Earliest Record: b. 12.1742; m. 8.1812
Missing Dates: b. 1.1802-1.1814; m. 11.1851-
2.1852
Parish Address: Rev. T. O'Brien, Killenaule,
Thurles, Co. Tipperary

Civil Parish: **Killodiernan**
Map Grid: N11
RC Parish: Monsea, see Cloghprior
Diocese: KL

Civil Parish: **Killoscully**
Map Grid: N25
RC Parish: part Ballinahinch, see Kilcomenty;
part Newport, see Kilvellane
Diocese: CA

Civil Parish: **Killoskehan**
Map Grid: N56
RC Parish: part Upperchurch; part Cap-
pawhite, see Toem
Diocese: CA

Civil Parish: **Kilmastulla**
Map Grid: N23
RC Parish: Ballina, see Templeachally
Diocese: EM

Civil Parish: **Kilmore (1)** (Upper Ormond)
Map Grid: N34
RC Parish: Knockavilla, see Oughterleague
Diocese: CA

Civil Parish: **Kilmore (2)** (Kilnemanagh)
Map Grid: S7
RC Parish: Silvermines
Diocese: KL
Earliest Record: b. 11.1840; m. 1.1841
Parish Address: Rev. Timothy Mullaly, PP, Sil-
vermines, Nenagh, Co. Tipperary

Civil Parish: **Kilmucklin**
Map Grid: S12
RC Parish: Oola and Sohohead, see Oola,
Co. Limerick
Diocese: CA

Civil Parish: **Kilmurry**
Map Grid: S112
RC Parish: Ballyneale, see Mothel, Co. Water-
ford
Diocese: LS

Civil Parish: **Kilnaneave**
Map Grid: N39
RC Parish: see Templederry
Diocese: KL

Civil Parish: **Kilnarath**
Map Grid: N27
RC Parish: part Ballinahinch, see Kilcomenty;
part Newport, see Kilvellane
Diocese: CA

Civil Parish: **Kilpatrick**
Map Grid: S5
RC Parish: Knockvilla, see Oughterleague
Diocese: CA

Civil Parish: **Kilruane**
Map Grid: N30
RC Parish: Cloghjordan, see Modreeny
Diocese: KL

Civil Parish: **Kilshane**
Map Grid: S30
RC Parish: see Tipperary
Diocese: EM

Civil Parish: **Kilsheelan**
Map Grid: S111
RC Parish: Gambonsfield and Kilcash (Kilsheelan)
Diocese: LS

Civil Parish: **Kiltegan**
Map Grid: S109
RC Parish: Powerstown, see Kilgrant
Diocese: LS

Civil Parish: **Kiltinan**
Map Grid: S69
RC Parish: Fethard and Killusty, see Fethard
Diocese: EL

Civil Parish: **Kilvellane**
Map Grid: N26
RC Parish: Newport
Diocese: CA
Earliest Record: b. 2.1813; m. 2.1813; d. 2.1813
Missing Dates: b. 7.1859-11.1859; m. 2.1859-11.1859; d. ends 5.1839
Parish Address: Rev. Thomas O'Keeffe, Newport, Limerick

Civil Parish: **Kilvemnon**
Map Grid: S83
RC Parish: Mullinahone
Diocese: CA
Earliest Record: b. 7.1809; m. 2.1810
Parish Address: Rev. Henry Nash, PP, Mullinahone, Thurles, Co. Tipperary

Civil Parish: **Knigh**
Map Grid: N16
RC Parish: see Cloghprior
Diocese: KL

Civil Parish: **Knockgraffon**
Map Grid: S64
RC Parish: New Inn
Diocese: CA
Earliest Record: b. 3.1820; m. 6.1798
Parish Address: Rev. James Meehan, New Inn, Cashel, Co. Tipperary

Civil Parish: **Latteragh**
Map Grid: N40
RC Parish: see Aghnameadle
Diocese: KL

Civil Parish: **Lattin**
Map Grid: S26
RC Parish: Lattin and Cullen
Diocese: EM
Earliest Record: b. 12.1846; m. 9.1846
Parish Address: Rev. John Walsh, PP, Lattin, Tipperary, Co. Tipperary

Civil Parish: **Lickfinn**
Map Grid: S76
RC Parish: see Killenaule
Diocese: CA

Civil Parish: **Lisbunny**
Map Grid: N32
RC Parish: see Nenagh
Diocese: KL

Civil Parish: **Lismalin**
Map Grid: S80
RC Parish: Ballingarry, see Ballingarry (2)
Diocese: CA

Civil Parish: **Lisronagh**
Map Grid: S104
RC Parish: Powerstown, see Kilgrant
Diocese: LS

Civil Parish: **Lorrha**
Map Grid: N1
RC Parish: Lorrha and Dorrha
Diocese: KL
Earliest Record: b. 10.1829; m. 10.1829
Parish Address: Rev. Martin Ryan, PP, Lorrha, Nenagh, Co. Tipperary

Civil Parish: **Loughkeen**
Map Grid: N5
RC Parish: see Birr, Co. Offaly
Diocese: KL

Civil Parish: **Loughmoe East** (Callabeg)
Map Grid: N64
RC Parish: Loughmore, see Loughmoe West
Diocese: CA

Civil Parish: **Loughmoe West** (Loughmoe)
Map Grid: N64
RC Parish: Loughmore
Diocese: CA
Earliest Record: b. 3.1798; m. 4.1798
Missing Dates: m. 6.1840-9.1840
Parish Address: Rev. Patrick Cooney, PP, Loughmore, Templemore, Co. Tipperary

Civil Parish: **Magorban**
Map Grid: S44
RC Parish: see Killenaule
Diocese: CA

Civil Parish: **Magowry**
Map Grid: S45
RC Parish: see Killenaule
Diocese: CA

Civil Parish: **Modeshil**
Map Grid: S81
RC Parish: Mullinahone, see Kilvemnon
Diocese: CA

Civil Parish: **Modreeny**
Map Grid: N14
RC Parish: Cloughjordan
Diocese: KL
Earliest Record: b. 8.1833; m. 5.1833
Parish Address: Rev. Edward J. White, Cloughjordan, Co. Tipperary

Civil Parish: **Molough**
Map Grid: S99
RC Parish: see Newcastle, Co. Waterford
Diocese: LS

Civil Parish: **Monsea**
Map Grid: N17
RC Parish: see Cloghprior
Diocese: KL

Civil Parish: **Mora**
Map Grid: S65
RC Parish: Powerstown, see Kilgrant
Diocese: LS

Civil Parish: **Mortlestown**
Map Grid: S86
RC Parish: see Caher
Diocese: LS

Civil Parish: **Mowney**
Map Grid: S79
RC Parish: Ballingarry, see Ballingarry (2)
Diocese: CA

Civil Parish: **Moyaliff**
Map Grid: N59
RC Parish: see Upperchurch
Diocese: CA

Civil Parish: **Moycarky**
Map Grid: N78
RC Parish: Moycarky and Borris
Diocese: CA
Earliest Record: b. 10.1793; m. 10.1793
Missing Dates: b. 11.1796-1.1801, 10.1809-6.1810, 11.1810-1.1817, 4.1818-1.1830; m. 10.1796-1.1810, 11.1817-1.1830, 5.1854-9.1854
Parish Address: Rev. Daniel M. Ryan, PP, Moycarkey, Thurles, Co. Tipperary

Civil Parish: **Moyne**
Map Grid: N65
RC Parish: see Templetuohy
Diocese: CA

Civil Parish: **Neddans**
Map Grid: 398
RC Parish: see Ardfinnan
Diocese: LS

Civil Parish: **Nenagh**
Map Grid: N18
RC Parish: Nenagh
Diocese: KL
Earliest Record: b. 1.1792; m. 1.1792
Missing Dates: b. 11.1809-11.1830, 12.1842-1.1845, 4.1858-1.1859; m. 2.1794-9.1818
Parish Address: Rev. John Hogan, PP, Nenagh, Co. Tipperary

Civil Parish: **Newcastle**
Map Grid: S100
RC Parish: see Newcastle, Co. Waterford
Diocese: LS

Civil Parish: **Newchapel**
Map Grid: S103
RC Parish: Clerihan, see Ballyclerahan
Diocese: CA

Civil Parish: **Newtownlennan**
Map Grid: S113
RC Parish: Carrick-on-Suir, see Carrick
Diocese: LS

Civil Parish: **Oughterleague**
Map Grid: S8
RC Parish: Knockavilla
Diocese: CA
Earliest Record: b. 5.1834; m. 7.1834
Parish Address: Rev. John J. O'Mahony, PP,
    Knockavilla, Dundrum, Co. Tipperary

Civil Parish: **Outeragh**
Map Grid: S70
RC Parish: see Caher
Diocese: LS

Civil Parish: **Peppardstown**
Map Grid: S53
RC Parish: Drangan, see Drangan
Diocese: CA

Civil Parish: **Rahelty**
Map Grid: N72
RC Parish: see Thurles
Diocese: CA

Civil Parish: **Railstown**
Map Grid: S50
RC Parish: Fethard and Killusty, see Fethard
Diocese: CA

Civil Parish: **Rathcool**
Map Grid: S52
RC Parish: see Killenaule
Diocese: CA

Civil Parish: **Rathkennan**
Map Grid: S1a
RC Parish: see Clonoulty
Diocese: CA

Civil Parish: **Rathlynan** or **Rathliney**
Map Grid: S13
RC Parish: Knockavilla, see Oughterleague
Diocese: CA

Civil Parish: **Rathnaveoge**
Map Grid: N44

RC Parish: Dunkerrin, see Dunkerrin, Co. Of-
    faly
Diocese: KL

Civil Parish: **Rathronan**
Map Grid: S108
RC Parish: Powerstown, see Kilgrant
Diocese: LS

Civil Parish: **Redcity**
Map Grid: S61
RC Parish: Fethard and Killusty, see Fethard
Diocese: CA

Civil Parish: **Relickmurry** and **Athassel**
Map Grid: S21
RC Parish: Golden
Diocese: CA
Earliest Record: b. 5.1833; m. 5.1833
Parish Address: Rev. Michael A. O'Dwyer, PP,
    Golden, Cashel, Co. Tipperary

Civil Parish: **Rochestown**
Map Grid: S93
RC Parish: see Ardfinnan
Diocese: LS

Civil Parish: **Roscrea** (see also Co. Offaly)
Map Grid: N42
RC Parish: Roscrea and Kyle
Diocese: KL
Earliest Record: b. 1.1810; m. 2.1810
Missing Dates: m. 8.1822-4.1823
Parish Address: Rev. John Cuddy, PP, Roscrea,
    Co. Tipperary

Civil Parish: **St. John Baptist**
Map Grid: S42
RC Parish: Cashel
Diocese: CA
Earliest Record: b. 11.1793; m. 1.1793
Missing Dates: m. 6.1831
Parish Address: Rev. Christopher Lee, PP,
    Cashel, Co. Tipperary

Civil Parish: **St. Johnstown** or **Scaddanstown**
Map Grid: S46
RC Parish: Killenaule, see Killenaule
Diocese: CA

Civil Parish: **St. Mary's Clonmel** (see also Co. Waterford)
Map Grid: S114
RC Parish: Clonmel (St. Mary's); also SS. Peter and Paul, Clonmel, see St. Mary's below; also Powerstown, see Kilgrant
Diocese: LS
Earliest Record: b. 2.1790; m. 4.1797
Missing Dates: b. 12.1790-3.1793, 12.1793-1.1795, ends 1.1864; m. ends 1.1836
Parish Address: Rev. Gregory Power, PP, St. Mary's Clonmel, Co. Tipperary

Civil Parish: **St. Mary's**
Map Grid: S114
RC Parish: St. Peter's and St. Paul's, Clonmel
Diocese: LS
Earliest Record: b. 2.1836; m. 2.1836
Parish Address: Rev. R. Coady, PP, Parochiol House, SS Peter's and Paul's, Clonmel, Co, Tipperary.

Civil Parish: **St. Patricksrock**
Map Grid: S40
RC Parish: Cashel
Diocese: CA

Civil Parish: **Shanrahan**
Map Grid: S88
RC Parish: Clogheen
Diocese: LS
Earliest Record: b. 6.1815; m. 7.1814
Missing Dates: m. ends 4.1867
Parish Address: Rev. Thomas Morrissey, PP, Parochial House, Clogheen, Cahir, Co. Tipperary

Civil Parish: **Shronell**
Map Grid: S24
RC Parish: Lattin and Cullin, see Lattin
Diocese: EM

Civil Parish: **Shyane**
Map Grid: N70
RC Parish: see Thurles
Diocese: CA

Civil Parish: **Solloghodbeg**
Map Grid: S11

RC Parish: Oola and Solohead, see Oola, Co. Limerick
Diocese: EM

Civil Parish: **Solloghodmore**
Map Grid: S12
RC Parish: Oola and Solohead, see Oola, Co. Limerick
Diocese: EM

Civil Parish: **Templeachally**
Map Grid: N21
RC Parish: Ballina
Diocese: EM
Earliest Record: b. 3.1832; m. 5.1832
Parish Address: Rev. Martin Morrissey, PP, Ballina, Killaloe, Co. Clare

Civil Parish: **Templebeg**
Map Grid: N56
RC Parish: Kilcommon
Diocese: CA
Earliest Record: b. 3.1813; m. 6.1813
Missing Dates: m. 1.1840-5.1840
Parish Address: Rev. John Fogarty, PP, Kilcommon, Thurles, Co. Tipperary

Civil Parish: **Templebredon**
Map Grid: S15
RC Parish: Pallasgreen, see Grean, Co. Limerick
Diocese: EM

Civil Parish: **Templederry**
Map Grid: N41
RC Parish: Killanave and Templederry, see Kilnaneave
Diocese: KL
Earliest Record: b. 9.1840; m. 2.1839
Missing Dates: m. ends 2.1869
Parish Address: Rev. John Greed, PP, Templederry, Nenagh, Co. Tipperary

Civil Parish: **Templedowney**
Map Grid: N33
RC Parish: Tullamore, see Aghnameadle
Diocese: KL

Civil Parish: **Temple-etney**
Map Grid: S105
RC Parish: see Kilsheelan
Diocese: LS

Civil Parish: **Templemichael**
Map Grid: S85
RC Parish: Ballyneale, see Mothel, Co. Waterford
Diocese: LS

Civil Parish: **Templemore**
Map Grid: N60
RC Parish: Templemore
Diocese: CA
Earliest Record: b. 8.1807; m. 11.1807
Missing Dates: m. 1.1820-2.1834
Parish Address: Rev. William Noonan, PP, Templemore, Co. Tipperary

Civil Parish: **Templeneiry**
Map Grid: S34
RC Parish: Bansha and Kilmoyler
Diocese: CA
Earliest Record: b. 11.1820; m. 1.1822
Parish Address: Rev. Patrick Purcell, PP, Bansha, Co. Tipperary

Civil Parish: **Templenoe**
Map Grid: S19
RC Parish: see Tipperary
Diocese: CA

Civil Parish: **Templeree**
Map Grid: N52
RC Parish: Loughmore, see Loughmoe West
Diocese: CA

Civil Parish: **Templetenny**
Map Grid: S87
RC Parish: Ballyporeen
Diocese: LS
Earliest Record: b. 11.1817; m. 1.1818
Parish Address: Rev. John Murphy, PP, Ballyporeen, Cahir, Co. Tipperary

Civil Parish: **Templetuohy**
Map Grid: N53
RC Parish: Moyne and Templetuohy
Diocese: CA
Earliest Record: b. 1.1809; m. 2.1804

Parish Address: Rev. Joseph Bergin, PP, Templetuohy, Thurles, Co. Tipperary

Civil Parish: **Terryglass**
Map Grid: N3
RC Parish: see Kilbarron
Diocese: KL

Civil Parish: **Thurles**
Map Grid: N69
RC Parish: Thurles
Diocese: CA
Earliest Record: b. 3.1795; m. 4.1795
Missing Dates: b. 11.1821-8.1822; m. 2.1820-8.1822
Parish Address: Rev. J. J. O'Rourke, Adm, Cathedral Presbytery, Thurles, Co. Tipperary

Civil Parish: **Tipperary**
Map Grid: S18
RC Parish: Tipperary
Diocese: CA
Earliest Record: b. 1.1810; m. 2.1793
Missing Dates: m. 5.1809-1.1810
Parish Address: Rev. Dermot Clifford, PP, St. Michael's Street, Tipperary

Civil Parish: **Toem**
Map Grid: S9 and N58
RC Parish: Cappawhite
Diocese: CA
Earliest Record: b. 10.1815; m. 2.1804
Parish Address: Rev. Timothy English, PP, Cappawhite, Co. Tipperary

Civil Parish: **Tubbrid**
Map Grid: S89
RC Parish: Ballylooby
Diocese: LS
Earliest Record: b. 5.1828; m. 5.1828
Parish Address: Rev. Michael Power, PP, Ballylooby, Cahir, Co. Tipperary

Civil Parish: **Tullaghmelan**
Map Grid: S95
RC Parish: see Ardfinnan
Diocese: LS

Civil Parish: **Tullaghorton**
Map Grid: S96

RC Parish: Ballylooby, see Tubbrid
Diocese: LS

Civil Parish: **Tullamain**
Map Grid: S58
RC Parish: part Cashel, see St. John Baptist;
    part Fethard

Civil Parish: **Twomileborris**
Map Grid: N76
RC Parish: see Moycarkey
Diocese: CA

Civil Parish: **Upperchurch** or **Templeoutragh**
Map Grid: N55
RC Parish: Upperchurch
Diocese: CA
Earliest Record: b. 10.1829; m. 2.1829
Parish Address: Rev. James O'Meara, PP, Up-
    perchurch, Co. Tipperary

Civil Parish: **Uskane**
Map Grid: N9
RC Parish: see Borrisokane
Diocese: KL

Civil Parish: **Whitechurch**
Map Grid: S90
RC Parish: Ballylooby, see Tubbrid
Diocese: KL

Civil Parish: **Youghalarra**
Map Grid: N20
RC Parish: see Burgesbeg
Diocese: KL

Commercial and Social Directories

1788
Richard Lucas's *General Directory of the
Kingdom of Ireland* contains lists of traders
in Borrisoleigh, Carrick-on-Suir, Cashel,
Clonmel, Nenagh, Thurles, Tipperary.
Reprinted in *Ir. Gen.* 3 (11) (1966): 468-76.

1820
J. Pigot's *Commercial Directory of Ireland*
contains information on the gentry, nobility,

and traders in and around the town of Clonmel.

1824
J. Pigot's *City of Dublin & Hibernian Provin-
cial Directory* includes traders, nobility,
gentry, and clergy lists of Cahir, Carrick-on-
Suir, Cashel, Clogheen, Clonmel, Fethard,
Killenaule, Nenagh, Roscrea, Templemore,
Thurles, and Tipperary.

1839
T. Shearman's *New Commercial Directory for
the Cities of Waterford and Kilkenny, Towns
of Clonmel, Carrick-on-Suir, New Ross and
Carlow* lists traders, gentry, etc., in Carrick-
on-Suir and Clonmel.

1840
F. Kinder's *New Triennial & Commercial
Directory for 1840, '41 & '42* contains lists of
traders, nobility, and others for Clonmel and
Carrick-on-Suir (rare volume).

1846
Slater's *National Commercial Directory of
Ireland* lists nobility, clergy, traders, etc., in
Borrisoleigh, Cahir, Carrick-on-Suir,
Cashel, Clogheen, Clonmel, Fethard, Kil-
lenaule, Nenagh, Newport, Roscrea,
Templemore, Thurles, and Tipperary.

1856
Slater's *Royal National Commercial Directory of Ireland* lists nobility, gentry, clergy,
traders, etc., in Borrisoleigh, Cahir, Carrick-
on-Suir, Cashel and Golden, Clogheen,
Clonmel, Fethard, Killenaule, Nenagh, Newport, Roscrea, Templemore, Thurles, and
Tipperary.

1866
G.H. Bassett's *Directory of the City and
County of Limerick and of the Principal
Towns in the Cos. of Tipperary and Clare* has
traders lists for Clonmel, Cashel, Nenagh,
Newport, Thurles, and Tipperary and an al-
phabetical list of the gentry in the county.

1870
Slater's "Directory of Ireland" contains trade,
nobility, and clergy lists for Borrisoleigh,
Caher, Carrick-on-Suir, Cashel, Clogheen,
Clonmel, Fethard, Killenaule, Nenagh, New-

port, Roscrea, Templemore, Thurles, and Tipperary.

1881

Slater's *Royal National Commercial Directory of Ireland* contains lists of traders, clergy, nobility, and farmers in adjoining parishes of the towns of Borrisoleigh, Cahir, Carrick-on-Suir, Cashel, Clogheen, Clonmel, Fethard, Killenaule, Nenagh, Newport, Roscrea, Templemore, Thurles, and Tipperary.

1886

Slater's *Royal National Commercial Directory of Ireland* contains lists of traders, clergy, nobility, and farmers in adjoining parishes of the towns of Cahir and Ballylooby, Carrick-on-Suir, Cashel, Clogheen, Clonmel, Fethard, Killenaule, Nenagh, Newport, Roscrea, Templemore, Thurles, and Tipperary.

Francis Guy's *Postal Directory* of Munster lists gentry, clergy, traders, principal farmers, teachers, and police sergeants in each postal district of the county and has a listing of magistrates, clergy, and the professions for the whole county.

1889

Bassett's *Book of Co. Tipperary* lists traders, farmers, and prominent residents in even small villages in the county.

1893

Francis Guy's *Postal Directory of Munster* lists traders and farmers in each of the postal districts and has a general alphabetical index to prominent persons in the county.

1894

Slater's *Royal National Directory of Ireland* lists traders, police, teachers, farmers, and private residents in each of the towns, villages, and parishes of the county.

Family History

"Armstrong of Tipperary." *Swanzy Notebooks.* RCB Library, Dublin.

"Bell of Tipperary." *Swanzy Notebooks.* RCB Library, Dublin.

"The Bourkes of Illeagh." *N. Munster Antiq. J.* 1 (2) (1937): 67-77.

Callanan, M. *Records of Four Tipperary Septs: the O'Kennedys, O'Dwyers, O'Mulryans, O'Meaghers.* Galway, 1938.

Carden, J. *Some Particulars Relating to the Family and Descendants of John Carden of Templemore.* 1912.

Chapman, E. *Memoirs of My Family: Together with Some Researches into the Early History of the Morris Families of Tipperary, Galway, and Mayo.* Frome, 1928.

"The Family Register of the O'Briens of Newcastle, Ballyporeen." *Ir. Gen.* 2 (1953): 308-10.

"Family Register of the O'Briens of Newcastle, Co. Tipperary." *Ir. Gen.* 2 (1953): 308-10.

"Going of Munster." *Ir. Anc.* 9 (1) (1977): 21-43.

"The Grant Families of Co. Tipperary." *J. Cork Arch. & Hist. Soc.* 226 (1972): 65-75.

The Grubbs of Tipperary: Studies in Heredity and Character. Cork, 1972 (a good bibliography pages 229-31).

"Limerick and Gerald Griffin." *N. Munster Antiq. J.* 2 (1) (1940): 4-13.

Matthew, David. "Father Mathew's Family: the Mathews in Tipperary." *Capuchin Annual* (1957): 143-52.

"Pedigree of Smith Family of King's Co. & Co. Tipperary 1666–1881." *J. Ass. Pres. Mem. Dead* 8 (1910-12): 208.

"Power Papers (Kilsheelan, Co. Tipperary)." *Anal. Hib.* 25: 57-75.

Seymour, St. John D. "Family Papers Belonging to the Purcells of Loughmoe, Co. Tipperary." *N. Munster Antiq. J.* 3 (1914): 124-29, 191-203.

"Tobin of Kilnagranagh, Co. Tipperary." *Ir. Gen.* 5 (4) (1977): 491-95.

Wolfe – see Kildare.

Gravestone Inscriptions

The major series of published gravestone inscriptions for this county is that published by Ormond Historical Society (see Research Sources and Services section).

Ballygibbon: published by Ormond Historical Society.

Ballynaclogh: published by Ormond Historical Society.

Borrisokane: published by Ormond Historical Society.

Castletownarra: published by Ormond Historical Society.

Cloughprior: published by Ormond Historical Society.

Dolla: published by Ormond Historical Society.

Kilbarron: published by Ormond Historical Society.

Kilkeary: published by Ormond Historical Society.

Killaneave: published by Ormond Historical Society.

Kilmore: *Ir.Gen.* 2 (10) (1953): 317-21.

Kilruane: published by Ormond Historical Society.

Nenagh: published by Ormond Historical Society.

Uskane: *Ir.Gen.* 3 (2) (1957): 74-75.

Newspapers

Tipperary is a large county which published many newspapers. For the south of the county Clonmel is the major center of publication. The towns of Nenagh, Thurles, Roscrea, and Cashel also produced newspapers at various times.

Limerick and Waterford newspapers also contain notices regarding the parts of county Tipperary that are adjacent to them. The *Kings County Chronicle* (see Co. Offaly) also contains notices of relevance to the north of the county.

An index to the biographical notices up to 1821 in newspapers from Clonmel, Limerick, Ennis, and Waterford, which contains 50,000 items, is available on microfiche in the library of University College, Dublin. Microfiche copies are available from the compiler, Ms. R. ffolliott, Glebe House, Fethard, Co. Tipperary.

Title: *Cashel Gazette*
Published in: Cashel, 1864-93
BL Holdings: 5.1864-7.1866; 10.1868-9.1871; 10.1871-7.1893

Title: *Clonmel Advertiser*
Published in: Clonmel, ca. 1811-38
NLI Holdings: 7.1813-7.1819; 1.1828-4.1838
BL Holdings: 1.1828-4.1838

Title: *Clonmel Gazette, Powers*
Published in: Clonmel, ca. 1792
NLI Holdings: 6.1802-11.1804 (incomplete)

Title: *Clonmel Gazette* or *Hibernian Advertiser*
Published in: Clonmel, 1788-93
NLI Holdings: 4.1788-2.1795; one volume of old issues from 1788 to 1793
BL Holdings: odd numbers 9-12.1792

Title: *Clonmel Herald*
Published in: Clonmel 1813-41
NLI Holdings: 5.1813; 1.1828-3.1841
BL Holdings: 5.1813; 1.1828-3.1841

Title: *County Tipperary Independent and Tipperary Free Press*
Published in: Clonmel, 1882-91; Waterford, 1891-1907
BL Holdings: 11.1882-4.1905; 5.1907-11.1907

Title: *Midland Counties Advertiser*
Published in: Roscrea, 1854-1948
NLI Holdings: 8.1927-6.1947
BL Holdings: 1.1854-11.1881; 9.1882-1.1893; 3.1893-9.1948

Title: *Nationalist and Tipperary Advertiser* (continued as *Nationalist & Munster Advertiser* in 1908)
Published in: Thurles, 1881; Clonmel, 1886-present
NLI Holdings: 1.1892; 1.1905-2.1908
BL Holdings: 2.1890-2.1908

Title: *Nenagh Gazette*
Published in: Nenagh, 1841-42
NLI Holdings: 1.1841-6.1842
BL Holdings: 1.1841-6.1842

Title: *Nenagh Guardian* or *Tipperary (North Riding) & Ormond Advertiser* (continued as *The Nenagh Guardian*)
Published in: Nenagh, 1838-in progress
NLI Holdings: 4.1860; 6.1859-1861; 1.1862-12.1868; 1.1875-12.1876; 12.1899
BL Holdings: 7.1838-12.1925; 1.1927-in progress

Title: *Nenagh News & Tipperary Vindicator*
Published in: Nenagh, 1898-1924
NLI Holdings: several issues in 1921
BL Holdings: 7.1898-2.1923; 4.1923-12.1924

Title: *Tipperary Advocate*
Published in: Nenagh, 1858-89
NLI Holdings: 1.1860-10.1889
BL Holdings: 3.1858-9.1869; two numbers for 10.1889

Title: *Tipperary and Clare Independent*
Published in: Nenagh, 1867-69
BL Holdings: 4.1867-9.1869

Title: *Tipperary Champion*
Published in: Clonmel, ca. 1898-1910
BL Holdings: 8.1903; 1.1904-12.1910

Title: *Tipperary Constitution*
Published in: Clonmel, 1835-48
NLI Holdings: 12.1835-5.1848
BL Holdings: 12.1835-5.1848

Title: *Tipperary Examiner* (includes Limerick, Waterford, and Kilkenny)
Published in: Clonmel, 1858-59
BL Holdings: 4.1858-5.1859

Title: *Tipperary Free Press*
Published in: Clonmel, 1826-81
NLI Holdings: 12.1826-7.1881
BL Holdings: 12.1826-7.1881

Title: *Tipperary Leader*
Published in: Thurles (first series), 1855-85; (second series), 9.1822-4.1885

NLI Holdings: 9.1882-4.1885
BL Holdings: 1.1855-3.1856; 9.1882-4.1885

Title: *Tipperary Nationalist & Southern Irishman*
Published in: Clonmel, ? to 1890
BL Holdings: 5.1889-2.1890

Title: *Tipperary People*
Published in: Clonmel, 1865-66
NLI Holdings: 1920-21
BL Holdings: 7.1865-7.1866; 8.1876-12.1877; 1.1879-12.1891; 1.1893-12.1904; 1.1906-11.1918

Title: *Tipperary Vindicator* (continued as *Limerick Reporter & Tipperary Vindicator* in 1849)
Published in: Nenagh, 1844-49
NLI Holdings: 12.1844-12.1849; 4.1856-12.1895
BL Holdings: 1.1844-12.1849; 4.1859-10.1877

Title: *Tipperary Weekly News and Advertiser*
Published in: Tipperary, ca. 1857-58
BL Holdings: 1-2.1858

Wills and Administrations

A discussion of the types of records, where they are held, their availability and value is given in the Wills section of the Introduction. The availability of prerogative wills, administrations, and marriage license records is also described in the relevant parts of the same section. Where available, published sources of these records are given in the Miscellaneous Sources section.

Pre-1858 Wills and Administrations

Prerogative Wills. see p. xli.
Consistorial Wills. This county is in the dioceses of Cashel, Emly, Killaloe, and Lismore. The guide to Roman Catholic parish records in this chapter shows the diocese to which each civil parish belonged. The wills of residents of each diocese were usually proven within that diocese (see the Wills section for exceptions). The following records survive:

Wills. see p. xxxvii.

Abstracts. see p. xxxvii.

Indexes. Cashel and Emly (1618-58 and up to 1800) published by Phillimore. Killaloe (1704-1857). Lismore (1648-1858) published to 1800 by Phillimore.

Post-1858 Wills and Administrations

This county was served by the District Registries of Limerick (North County) and Waterford (South County). The surviving records are kept in the PRO.

Marriage Licenses

Indexes. Cashel and Emly (1664-1857). PRO; SLC film 100861. Killaloe (1691-1845). PRO; SLC 100869. Lismore (1661-1750). PRO; SLC film 100872.

Miscellaneous Sources

Bassett, G.H. *The Book of Co. Tipperary.* Dublin, 1889.

Burke, W.P. *History of Clonmel.* Dublin, 1907. Reprint. Kilkenny, 1983.

Cunningham, G. *Roscrea & District.* Roscrea, 1976.

"Emigration from the Workhouse of Nenagh Union, Co. Tipperary 1849-1860." *Ir. Anc.* 17 (1) (1985): 10-17.

"Extracts from the Minutes of the Corporation of Fethard, Co. Tipperary: Freemen of the Corporation." *Ir. Gen.* 5 (3) (1976): 370-82.

"Proprietors of Fethard, Co. Tipperary, 1641-1663." *Ir. Gen.* 6 (1) (1980): 5-8.

"The Seneschals of the Liberty of Tipperary." *Ir. Gen.* 52 (10): 294-302; 2 (11): 326-36; 2 (12): 368-76; 3 (2): 46-59; 3 (3): 109-15; 3 (4): 120-23.

Research Sources and Services

Journals

Cork Historical & Archaeological Society Journal (for south Tipperary, see Research Sources and services Section, Co. Cork)

Eile (published by Roscrea Heritage Society)

North Munster Antiquarian Journal

Libraries and Information Sources

Tipperary County Library, Castle Avenue, Thurles, Co. Tipperary Ph: (0504) 21102

Research Services

Brú Ború, Cashel, Co. Tipperary

Midwest Regional Archives (see Research Sources and Services section, Co. Limerick) (see also research services in Dublin, p. xliv)

Nenagh Heritage Centre, Nenagh, Co. Tipperary (local parish indexes)

Roscrea Heritage Centre – Castle Courtyard, Roscrea, Co. Tipperary (local parish indexes only)

Societies

Brú Ború Heritage Group, Una O'Murchin, Bohereenglas, Cashel Co. Tipperary Ph: (062) 61552

Nenagh District Heritage Society, Mrs. Geraldine McNulty, Mount Pleasant, Ballymackey, Nenagh, Co. Tipperary

Old Cashel Society, c/o Mr. J.P. Knightly, The Green, Cashel, Co. Tipperary

Ormond Historical Society, Dr. Denise Foulkes, Stoneyhigh, Gortlandroe, Nenagh, Co. Tipperary

Roscrea Heritage Society (publishers of *Eile*), Mrs. Carmel Cunningham, c/o Damer Annexe, Castle Courtyard, Roscrea, Co. Tipperary

Templemore Historical Society, Mr. Donal J. O'Regan, Manna, Templemore, Co. Tipperary

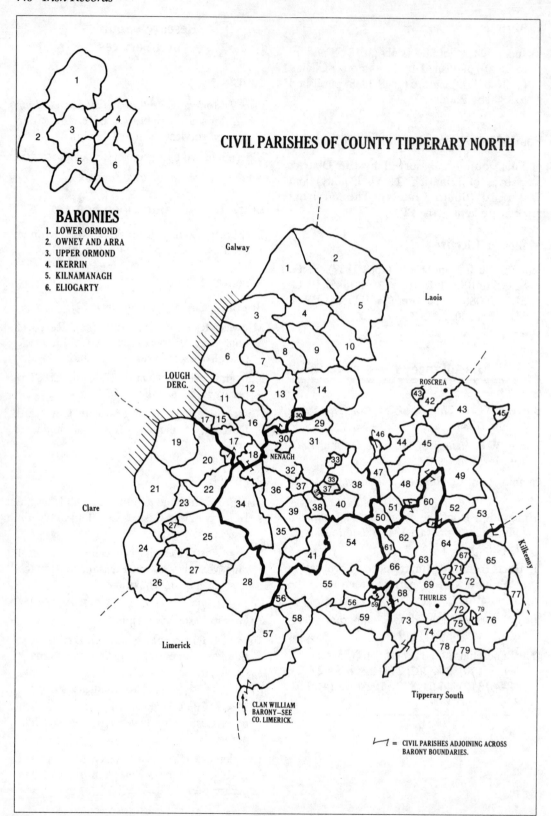

CIVIL PARISHES OF COUNTY TIPPERARY NORTH

BARONIES
1. LOWER ORMOND
2. OWNEY AND ARRA
3. UPPER ORMOND
4. IKERRIN
5. KILNAMANAGH
6. ELIOGARTY

Galway

Laois

LOUGH DERG.

ROSCREA

Clare

NENAGH

Kilkenny

THURLES

Limerick

CLAN WILLIAM
BARONY—SEE
CO. LIMERICK.

Tipperary South

⌐ = CIVIL PARISHES ADJOINING ACROSS
BARONY BOUNDARIES.

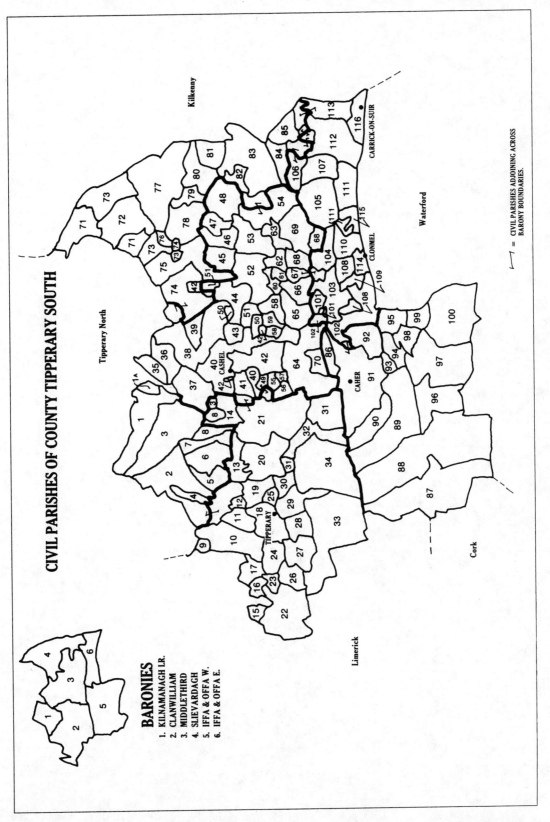

CIVIL PARISHES OF COUNTY TIPPERARY SOUTH

BARONIES
1. KILNAMANAGH LR.
2. CLANWILLIAM
3. MIDDLETHIRD
4. SLIEVARDAGH
5. IFFA & OFFA W.
6. IFFA & OFFA E.

= CIVIL PARISHES ADJOINING ACROSS BARONY BOUNDARIES.

COUNTY TYRONE

A Brief History

An inland Ulster county, Tyrone contains the towns of Strabane, Omagh, Clogher, Dungannon, and Ballygawley. Before the establishment of the present county, this area was part of the territory of Tirowen from which the county was named. The ruling family in the area was the O'Neills, and other important families were O'Quinn, O'Donnelly, O'Hamill, McGurk, MacMurphy, O'Hegarty, O'Devlin, O'Lunney, McGilmartin, MacGettigan, MacCloskey, MacColgan, O'Mulvenna, MacGilligan, O'Laverty, and MacNamee.

The Norman invasion had little effect on this area because of the power of the O'Neills and the other chieftains. The O'Neills' base was at Dungannon, but all trace of their castle has now disappeared. In 1594, as a result of various attempts by the English to obtain control of Ulster land, Hugh O'Neill, the leader of the Irish in Ulster began a rebellion. With Red Hugh O'Donnell of Donegal and the other major families of Ulster, he defeated successive armies sent to subdue the rebellion. In 1601 the Spanish sent an army to assist the Irish in this war. However, the Spanish army landed in Kinsale in County Cork, forcing O'Neill to march the length of the country to link up with them. This proved a serious tactical mistake. O'Neill's army was forced to abandon this attempt and was subsequently defeated in 1603.

Shortly afterwards, O'Neill and many of his ally chieftains and their families left the country. This so-called "Flight of the Earls" marked the final breakdown of the old Gaelic order in Ulster. Most of the O'Neill territories and those of his allies were confiscated and divided into six of the present Ulster counties. Tyrone was divided up between various English and Scottish adventurers who undertook to bring over settlers to their estates. The native Irish were also allotted some portions of these lands and others remained as laborers on the estates of the new settlers. The "armed men" of Ulster were forced to resettle in the province of Connaught.

The major undertakers and large tenants who arrived in Tyrone during this "Ulster Plantation" included Hamilton, Buchanan, Galbraith, Stewart, Newcomen, Drummond, Ridgwaie, Lowther, Burleigh, Leigh, Cope, Parsons, Sanderson, Lindsey, Caulfield, Ansley, Wingfield, and Chichester.

In the 1641 rebellion there was severe disturbance in this county. Sir Phelim O'Neill led the Catholic Irish in the county and successfully defeated several English armies. In 1649, however, the rebellion was finally defeated and the lands of those taking part were confiscated.

New proprietors took over the remaining lands of the Irish chieftains.

During the eighteenth century many Ulster Presbyterians, the so-called Scots-Irish, left Ireland as a result of the discrimination against them in the Penal Laws. These laws had been instituted in the 1690s primarily against Catholics. An indication of the origins of Tyrone inhabitants can be generally determined from the religious persuasions of its inhabitants. This is possible because the native Irish are predominantly Catholic, the Scottish, Presbyterian, and the English Protestant (Episcopalian). In 1861, when the census first determined the religion of respondents, the relative proportions were 57, 22, and 20 percent respectively.

The county was relatively badly affected by the Great Famine of 1845-47. The population, which was 313,000 in 1841, fell to 256,000 by 1851. Of this drop, some 28,000 died between 1845 and 1850, and the remainder emigrated to the cities or abroad. The population continued to fall throughout the century and by 1891 was 171,000.

In 1921 this county was one of the six which remained within the United Kingdom on the establishment of the Irish Free State.

Census and Census Substitutes

1612-13
"Survey of Undertakers Planted in Tyrone" (names, acreages allotted, and account of the progress of each). Hist. Mss. Comm. Rep. (Hastings Mss.) 4 (1947): 159-82.

1631
Muster Roll of Clogher and Strabane. PRONI T934; BL add. ms. 4770.

1654-56
Civil Survey. Vol. 3. SLC film 975121.

1662-63
Poll Tax Return for Aghaloo Parish. SLC film 258551.

1664-68
"Hearth Money and Subsidy Rolls for Barony of Dungannon." *Seanchas Ardmhacha* 6 (1) (1971): 24-45; SLC film 258551 .

1666
Hearth Money Roll. NLI mss. 9584-85. The part of Tyrone in Clogher diocese is covered in *The Clogher Record* 5 (3) (1965): 379-87; SLC film 258551.

1666-68
"Subsidy Rolls (for Clogher Diocese)." *The Clogher Record* 5 (3) (1965): 379-87.

1740
Protestants in the Parishes of Derryloran and Kildress. RCB Library; SLC film 258517; GO 539.

1766
Religious Census of Parishes of Aghalow, Artrea, Carnteel, Clonfeacle, Derryloran, Donaghendry, Errigalkerrouge, Kildress. PRO 1A 46 49, 1A 41 100; SLC film 258517.

Religious Census of Parishes of Aghalow, Carnteel, Derryloran, Drumglass, Dungannon, and Tullaniskan. *Seanchas Ardmhacha* 4 (1) (1960/61): 147-70.

1796
See Mayo 1796 (List of Catholics).

1823-38
Tithe Applotment Survey (see p. xxvii).

1834
"Occupants of Dungannon Arranged by Street, Giving Property Values." *Parl. Papers* 1837, 11 (1), Appendix G, 203-06.

1860
Griffith's Valuation (see p. xxvii).

1901
Census. PRO.

1911
Census. PRO.

Church Records

Church of Ireland
(shows starting date of record)

Parish: Aghalurcher
Existing Records: b. 1788; m. 1788; d. 1788
Status: LC

Parish: Altedesert, Pomeroy Church
Status: Lost (earlier entries in Termonmaguirk)

Parish: Arboe
Existing Records: b. 1773; m. 1773; d. 1773
Status: LC

Parish: Ardstraw
Status: Lost

Parish: Ardtrea
Existing Records: b. 1811; m. 1811; d. 1811
Status: LC

Parish: Badoney Lower
Existing Records: b. 1818; m. 1817; d. 1820
Status: LC

Parish: Badoney Upper
Status: Lost

Parish: Ballinderry
Existing Records: b. 1802; m. 1802; d. 1802
Status: LC

Parish: Ballyclog
Existing Records: b. 1828; m. 1828; d. 1828
Status: LC

Parish: Ballygawley (see also Errigal Keerogue)
Status: Lost

Parish: Bar
Status: Lost

Parish: Baronscourt
Status: Lost

Parish: Benburb (see Clonfeacle)

Parish: Caledon or **Aghaloo**
Existing Records: b. 1791; m. 1791; d. 1791
Status: LC

Parish: Camus (Mourne)
Existing Records: b. 1803; m. 1825; d. 1825
Status: LC

Parish: Cappagh
Existing Records: b. 1758; m. 1758; d. 1758
Status: LC

Parish: Carnteel (Aughnactsy)
Existing Records: b. 1805; m. 1805; d. 1805
Status: LC

Parish: Carrickmore (see Termonmaguirk)

Parish: Clanabogan
Existing Records: b. 1863; d. 1863
Status: LC

Parish: Clogher
Existing Records: b. 1763; m. 1763; d. 1763
Status: LC

Parish: Clogherny
Existing Records: b. 1824; m. 1825; d. 1825
Status: LC

Parish: Clonfeacle
Status: Lost

Parish: Clonoe
Existing Records: b. 1824; m. 1812; d. 1824
Status: LC

Parish: Cooley or **Sixmilecross**
Existing Records: b. 1836; m. 1836; d. 1836
Status: LC

Parish: Derg
Existing Records: b. 1807; m. 1807; d. 1839
Status: LC

Parish: Derrygortrevy
Status: Lost

Parish: Derryloran
Existing Records: b. 1796; m. 1796; d. 1796
Status: LC

Parish: **Desertcreat**
Existing Records: b. 1812; m. 1812; d. 1812
Status: LC

Parish: **Donagheady**
Existing Records: b. 1754; m. 1826; d. 1826
Missing Dates: b. 1766-1825
Status: LC

Parish: **Donaghenry**
Existing Records: b. 1734; m. 1811; d. 1811
Missing Dates: b. 1769-1809
Status: LC

Parish: **Donaghmore**
Existing Records: b. 1777; m. 1777; d. 1777
Status: LC

Parish: **Donaghmore, Upper**
Status: Lost

Parish: **Dromore**
Status: Lost

Parish: **Drumakelly**
Status: Lost

Parish: **Drumclamph**
Status: Lost

Parish: **Drumglass**
Existing Records: b. 1600; m. 1754; d. 1754
Missing Dates: b. 1767-1822; m. 1768-1813
Status: LC

Parish: **Drumrath**
Existing Records: b. 1800; m. 1800; d. 1800
Status: LC

Parish: **Dunnalong**
Status: Lost

Parish: **Edenderry**
Existing Records: b. 1841; d. 1849
Status: LC

Parish: **Errigal Keerogue**
Existing Records: b. 1812; m. 1812; d. 1812
Status: LC

Parish: **Errigle-Portclare**
Existing Records: b. 1835; m. 1835; d. 1835
Status: LC

Parish: **Errigle-Trough**
Existing Records: b. 1809; m. 1803; d. 1802
Status: LC

Parish: **Findonagh** or **Donacavey**
Existing Records: b. 1777; m. 1800; d. 1800
Status: LC

Parish: **Fivemiletown** (see also Clogher)
Existing Records: b. 1804; m. 1804; d. 1804
Status: LC

Parish: **Kildress**
Existing Records: b. 1794; m. 1799; d. 1864
Status: LC

Parish: **Killeeshill**
Status: Lost

Parish: **Killyman**
Existing Records: b. 1741; m. 1741; d. 1741
Status: LC

Parish: **Kilskeery**
Existing Records: b. 1772; m. 1772; d. 1772
Status: LC

Parish: **Longfield Lower**
Status: Lost

Parish: **Longfield Upper**
Status: Lost

Parish: **Leckpatrick**
Status: Lost

Parish: **Lislimnaghan**
Existing Records: b. 1862; d. 1864
Status: LC

Parish: **Mountfield**
Status: Lost

Parish: **Moy**
Status: Lost

Parish: **Newtownsaville**
Status: Lost

Parish: **Pomeroy** (see also Altedesert)
Status: Lost

Parish: **St. Mary, Portclare** (see Errigle-Portclare)
Status: Lost

Parish: **Sixmilecross** or **Cooley**
Existing Records: b. 1836; m. 1836; d. 1836
Status: LC

Parish: **Termonamongan**
Existing Records: b. 1825; m. 1825; d. 1825
Status: LC

Parish: **Termonmaguirk** (earlier entries in Termonmaguirk) (see also Drumakelly)

Parish: **Tullyniskin**
Existing Records: b. 1794; m. 1794; d. 1809
Status: LC

Parish: **Urney** (Strabane)
Existing Records: b. 1813; m. 1814; d. 1815
Status: LC

Presbyterian

Parish: **Albany** (Stewartstown)
Starting Date: 1838

Parish: **Ardstraw**
Starting Date: 1837

Parish: **Aughataire** (Fivemiletown)
Starting Date: 1836

Parish: **Aughnacloy**
Starting Date: 1843

Parish: **Ballygawley**
Starting Date: 1843

Parish: **Ballygorey** (Cookstown)
Starting Date: 1834

Parish: **Ballynahatty** (Omagh)
Starting Date: 1843

Parish: **Ballyreagh** (Ballygawley)
Starting Date: 1843

Parish: **Brigh** (Stewartstown)
Starting Date: 1836

Parish: **Carland** (Castlecaulfield)
Starting Date: 1759

Parish: **Castlederg**
Starting Date: 1823

Parish: **Cleggan** (Cookstown)
Starting Date: 1848

Parish: **Clenanees** (Castlecaulfield)
Starting Date: 1840

Parish: **Clogher**
Starting Date: 1819

Parish: **Coagh**
Starting Date: 1839

Parish: **Cookstown**
Starting Date: 1836

Parish: **Donagheady** (Strabane)
Starting Date: 1838

Parish: **Drumguin**
Starting Date: 1845

Parish: **Dungannon**
Starting Date: 1790

Parish: **Edenderry** (Omagh)
Starting Date: 1845

Parish: **Eglish** (Dungannon)
Starting Date: 1839

Parish: **Fintona**
Starting Date: 1836

Parish: **Gillygooly** (Omagh)
Starting Date: 1848

Parish: **Gortin**
Starting Date: 1843

Parish: **Leckpatrick** (Strabane)
Starting Date: 1838

Parish: **Minterburn** (Caledon)
Starting Date: 1829

Parish: **Moy**
Starting Date: 1851

Parish: **Newmills** (Dungannon)
Starting Date: 1850

Parish: **Omagh**
Starting Date: 1821

Parish: **Orritor** (Cookstown)
Starting Date: 1831

Parish: **Pomeroy**
Starting Date: 1841

Parish: **Sandholey** (Cookstown)
Starting Date: 1844

Parish: **Strabane**
Starting Date: 1828

Parish: **Urney** (Sion Mills)
Starting Date: 1837

Roman Catholic

Civil Parish: **Aghaloo**
Map Grid: 38
RC Parish: Aghaloo (Aughnacloy)
Diocese: AM
Earliest Record: b. 1.1846; m. 1.1832
Missing dates: m. 5.1834-10.1837
Parish Address: Rev. Brendan McHugh, PP, Parochial House, 19 Caledon Road, Aughnacloy, Co. Tyrone

Civil Parish: **Aghalurcher**
Map Grid: 43

RC Parish: see Co. Fermanagh
Diocese: CG

Civil Parish: **Arboe** (see also Co. Derry)
Map Grid: 27
RC Parish: Ardboe or Arboe
Diocese: AM
Earliest Record: b. 11.1827; m. 11.1827
Parish Address: Rev. Bernard Donnelly, PP, Parochial House, Mullanahoe, Ardboe, Dungannon BT71 5AU

Civil Parish: **Ardstraw (1)**
Map Grid: 6
RC Parish: Ardstraw East (Newtown Stewart); also Ardstraw West, see below
Diocese: DE
Earliest Record: b. 12.1861; m. 12.1860
Parish Address: Rev. Daniel McNicholl, PP, Parochial House, 41 Moyle Road, Newtownstewart, Co. Tyrone BT78 4AP

Civil Parish: **Ardstraw (2)**
Map Grid: 6
RC Parish: Ardstraw West and Castlederg
Diocese: DE
Earliest Record: b. 6.1846; m. 5.1843
Missing dates: b. 3.1850-1.1852
Parish Address: Rev. Patrick Grant, PP, 16 Castlefinn Road, Castlederg, Co. Tyrone BT81 7EB

Civil Parish: **Artrea**
Map Grid: 22
RC Parish: Moneymore, see Artrea, Co. Derry
Diocese: AM

Civil Parish: **Ballinderry**
Map Grid: 24
RC Parish: see Co. Derry
Diocese: AM

Civil Parish: **Ballyclog**
Map Grid: 26
RC Parish: see Ardboe
Diocese: AM

Civil Parish: **Bodoney Lower**
Map Grid: 8
RC Parish: see Bodoney Upper
Diocese: DE

Civil Parish: **Bodoney Upper**
Map Grid: 7
RC Parish: Bodoney Upper (Plumbridge or Cranagh)
Diocese: DE
Earliest Record: b. 10.1866
Parish Address: Rev. Joseph Doherty, PP, Parochial House, Plumbridge, Omagh, Co. Tyrone BT79 8EF

Civil Parish: **Camus**
Map Grid: 5
RC Parish: Clonleigh and Camus (Strabane)
Diocese: DE
Earliest Record: b. 4.1773; m. 8.1788
Missing dates: b. 2.1795-1.1836, 5.1837-3.1853; m. 9.1781-3.1843
Parish Address: Rev. John G. Farren, PP, Parochial House, Barrack St., Strabane, Co. Tyrone

Civil Parish: **Cappagh**
Map Grid: 9
RC Parish: Cappagh (Killyclogher)
Diocese: DE
Earliest Record: b. 7.1843; m. 7.1843; d. 7.1843
Parish Address: Rev. Francis Murray, PP, 14 Killyclogher Road, Omagh, Co. Tyrone BT79 OAX

Civil Parish: **Carnteel**
Map Grid: 37
RC Parish: part Aghaloo; part Errigal Kieran
Diocese: AM

Civil Parish: **Clogher**
Map Grid: 40
RC Parish: Clogher
Diocese: CG
Earliest Record: b. 4.1856; m. 9.1825
Missing dates: m. 11.1835-3.1840
Parish Address: Rev. Francis McKenna, PP, Clogher, Co. Tyrone

Civil Parish: **Clogherny**
Map Grid: 15
RC Parish: Beragh (Ballintacker)
Diocese: AM
Earliest Record: b. 9.1832; m. 7.1834

Parish Address: Rev. Francis Quigley, PP, Parochial House, Beragh, Omagh, Co. Tyrone

Civil Parish: **Clonfeacle** (see also Co. Armagh)
Map Grid: 35
RC Parish: Clonfeacle (Moy)
Diocese: AM
Earliest Record: b. 10.1814; m. 11.1814
Missing dates: b. 3.1840-8.1840
Parish Address: Rev. James J. Devlin, PP, Parochial House, 9 Benburb Road, Moy, Dungannon, Co. Tyrone

Civil Parish: **Clonoe**
Map Grid: 31
RC Parish: Clonoe
Diocese: AM
Earliest Record: b. 2.1810; m. 12.1806; d. 12.1806
Missing dates: b. 5.1816-10.1822; m. 5.1816-1.1823; d. ends 5.1816
Parish Address: Rev. Kieran MacKeone, PP, Parochial House, 18 Annaghmore Road, Coalisland, Dungannon BT71 4QZ

Civil Parish: **Derryloran** (see also Co. Derry)
Map Grid: 21
RC Parish: see Desertcreat
Diocese: AM

Civil Parish: **Desertcreat**
Map Grid: 25
RC Parish: Desertcreat and Derryloran (Cookstown)
Diocese: AM
Earliest Record: b. 10.1858; m. 1.1859
Parish Address: Rev. John Donaghy, PP, Parochial House, 1 Convent Road, Cookstown, Co. Tyrone BT80 8QA

Civil Parish: **Donacavey**
Map Grid: 39
RC Parish: Donaghcavey (Fintona)
Diocese: CG
Earliest Record: b. 11.1857; m. 10.1857
Parish Address: Rev. Joseph McDermott, PP, Fintona, Omagh, Co. Tyrone

Civil Parish: **Donaghedy**
Map Grid: 1
RC Parish: Donaghedy (Dunamanagh)
Diocese: DE
Earliest Record: b. 4.1854; m. 11.1858; d. 12.1857
Missing dates: m. 7.1859-12.1862, ends 5.1863; d. ends 7.1859
Parish Address: Rev. George Doherty, PP, 78 Lisnaragh Road, Dunmanagh, Co. Tyrone BT82 OQN

Civil Parish: **Donaghenry**
Map Grid: 28
RC Parish: Stewartstown (Coalisland)
Diocese: AM
Earliest Record: b. 2.1849; m. 5.1853; d. 1.1854
Parish Address: Rev. Patrick Coyle, CC, 55 West Street, Stewartstown, Dungannon, Co. Tyrone BT71 5HT

Civil Parish: **Donaghmore**
Map Grid: 32
RC Parish: Donaghmore (see also Killeeshil)
Diocese: AM
Earliest Record: b. 2.1837; m. 3.1837
Parish Address: Rev. Michael Ward, PP, 63 Castlecaulfield Road, Donaghmore, Dungannon, Co. Tyrone BT70 3HF

Civil Parish: **Dromore**
Map Grid: 16
RC Parish: Dromore
Diocese: CG
Earliest Record: b. 11.1835; m. 10.1835
Parish Address: Rev. T. Flood, PP, Dromore, Omagh, Co. Tyrone

Civil Parish: **Drumglass**
Map Grid: 33
RC Parish: Drumglass, Killyman, and Tullyniskin (Dungannon)
Diocese: AM
Earliest Record: b. 10.1821; m. 10.1821; d. 10.1821
Missing dates: m. 12.1829-5.1831, 5.1833-8.1833; d. 11.1829-4.1831
Parish Address: Rev. Francis Dean McLarnon, PP, The Deanery, Circular Road, Dungannon, Co. Tyrone

Civil Parish: **Drumragh**
Map Grid: 13
RC Parish: Drumragh (Omagh)
Diocese: DE
Earliest Record: b. 5.1846; m. 6.1846; d. 5.1846
Missing dates: b. 11.1846-11.1853; m. 8.1846-11.1853; d. 7.1846-11.1853
Parish Address: Rev. Martin Rooney, PP, Parochial House, Omagh, Co. Tyrone

Civil Parish: **Errigal Keerogue**
Map Grid: 41
RC Parish: Errigal Kieran (Ballygawley or Ballymacelroy)
Diocese: AM
Earliest Record: b. 1.1847; m. 1.1864
Parish Address: Rev. Patrick McPeake, PP, Parochial House, Glencull, Ballygawley, Co. Tyrone BT70 2AG

Civil Parish: **Errigal Trough** (see Co. Monaghan)
Map Grid: 42
RC Parish: see Co. Monaghan
Diocese: CG

Civil Parish: **Kildress**
Map Grid: 20
RC Parish: Kildress
Diocese: AM
Earliest Record: b. 1.1835; m. 3.1835; d. 3.1835
Missing dates: b. 12.1852-1.1857, 8.1859-1.1861, 2.1865-1.1878; d. ends 12.1842
Parish Address: Rev. Patrick Smyth, PP, 10 Cloughfin Road, Kildress, Cookstown, Co. Tyrone BT80 9JB

Civil Parish: **Killeeshil**
Map Grid: 36
RC Parish: Tullyallen, Killeeshil, and Donaghmore
Diocese: AM
Earliest Record: b. 1.1816; m. 1.1816; d. 1.1816
Missing dates: b. 1.1834-3.1837, 8.1844-8.1845; m. 1.1836-3.1837, 7.1844-9.1845; d. 5.1834-3.1837, 8.1844-8.1845
Parish Address: Rev. J. Crowley, PP, Parochial House, 65 Tullyallen Road, Dungannon, Co. Tyrone

Civil Parish: **Killyman**
Map Grid: 34
RC Parish: Dungannon, see Drumglass
Diocese: AM

Civil Parish: **Kilskeery**
Map Grid: 17
RC Parish: Kilskeery (Trillick)
Diocese: CG
Earliest Record: b. 10.1840; m. 8.1840
Parish Address: Rev. Thomas Gormley, PP,
    Trillick, Omagh, Co. Tyrone

Civil Parish: **Learmount**
Map Grid: 3
RC Parish: see Cumber Upper, Co. Derry
Diocese: DE

Civil Parish: **Leckpatrick**
Map Grid: 2
RC Parish: Leckpatrick; also part Donaghedy
Diocese: DE
Earliest Record: b. 9.1863; m. 9.1863
Parish Address: Rev. J. Harkin, PP, Parochial
    House, Ballymagorry, Strabane, Co. Tyrone

Civil Parish: **Lissan**
Map Grid: 19
RC Parish: Lissan
Diocese: AM
Earliest Record: b. 7.1839; d. 9.1839
Parish Address: Rev. Thomas Mallon, PP,
    Parochial House, 2 Tullynure Road,
    Cookstown, Co. Tyrone

Civil Parish: **Longfield East**
Map Grid: 12
RC Parish: see Longfield West
Diocese: DE

Civil Parish: **Longfield West**
Map Grid: 11
RC Parish: Drumquin (Longfield)
Diocese: DE
Earliest Record: b. 9.1846; m. 9.1846; d. 7.1853
Missing dates: d. ends 2.1856
Parish Address: Rev. Thomas O'Doherty, PP,
    Parochial House, 6 Willmount Road, Drum-
    quin, Co. Tyrone BT78 4PG

Civil Parish: **Magheracross**
Map Grid: 18
RC Parish: see Derryvullan, Co. Fermanagh
Diocese: CG

Civil Parish: **Pomeroy**
Map Grid: 29
RC Parish: Pomeroy
Diocese: AM
Earliest Record: b. 2.1837; m. 3.1837; d. 3.1837
Missing dates: b. 11.1840-12.1841, 5.1852-
    4.1857, 8.1865-2.1869; m. 12.1840-12.1841,
    6.1865-7.1869; d. 12.1840-4.1857, 4.1861-
    7.1871
Parish Address: Rev. Brendan O'Neill, PP, 9
    Cavanakeeran Road, Pomeroy, Dungannon,
    Co. Tyrone

Civil Parish: **Tamlaght** (see also Co. Derry)
Map Grid: 23
RC Parish: see Ardboe
Diocese: AM

Civil Parish: **Termonamongan**
Map Grid: 10
RC Parish: Termonamongan (Aghyaran)
Diocese: DE
Earliest Record: b. 3.1863; m. 9.1863
Parish Address: Rev. Brendan McGinn, PP, 11
    Church Road, Aghyaran, Castlederg, Co.
    Tyrone

Civil Parish: **Termonmaguirk**
Map Grid: 14
RC Parish: Termonmaguire (Carrickmore)
Diocese: AM
Earliest Record: b. 12.1834; m. 10.1834
Missing dates: b. ends 2.1857; m. ends 12.1857
Parish Address: Rev. Hugh McGrath, PP, Car-
    rickmore, Sixmilecross, Omagh, Co. Tyrone

Civil Parish: **Tullyniskan**
Map Grid: 30
RC Parish: see Drumglass
Diocese: AM

Civil Parish: **Urney**
Map Grid: 4
RC Parish: Urney, see Co. Donegal
Diocese: DE

Commercial and Social Directories

1819
Thomas Bradshaw's *General Directory of Newry* lists traders in Dungannon.

1820
J. Pigot's *Commercial Directory of Ireland* contains information on the gentry, nobility, and traders in and around the town of Strabane.

1824
J. Pigot's *City of Dublin & Hibernian Provincial Directory* includes traders, nobility, gentry, and clergy lists of Aughnacloy, Cookstown, Dungannon, Moy and Charlemont, Newtown-Stewart, Omagh, Stewartstown, and Strabane.

1842
Martin's *Belfast Directory* lists residents of principal streets, gentry, and traders in Cookstown, Dungannon, and Stewartstown.

1846
Slater's *National Commercial Directory of Ireland* lists nobility, clergy, traders, etc., in Aughnacloy, Cookstown and Desertcreat, Dungannon, Coal Island and Donaghmore, Moy and Charlemont, Newtownstewart, Omagh, Stewartstown, and Strabane.

1852
Henderson's *Belfast & Province of Ulster Directory* has lists of inhabitants, traders, etc., in and around the towns of Aughnacloy, Cookstown, Dungannon, Moy, and Charlemont.

1854
Further edition of the above covers Aughnacloy, Bellaghy, Clogher, Cookstown, Dungannon, Moy and Charlemont, Omagh, Stewartstown, and Strabane. Further editions issued in 1856, 1858, 1861, 1863, 1865, 1868, 1870, 1877, 1880, 1884, 1890, 1894, 1900.

1856
Slater's *Royal National Commercial Directory of Ireland* lists nobility, gentry, clergy, traders, etc., in Aughnacloy and Ballygawley, Clogher and Five-Mile-Town, Cookstown, Dungannon, Coal Island and Donaghmore, Moy and Charlemont, Newtown-Stewart, Omagh, Stewartstown, and Strabane.

1865
R. Wynne's *Business Directory of Belfast* covers Cookstown, Dungannon, Omagh, Strabane.

1870
Slater's *Directory of Ireland* contains trade, nobility, and clergy lists for Aughnacloy, Caledon, Castlederg, Clogher and Five-Mile-Town, Cookstown, Moy, Newtownstewart and Gortin, Omagh, Stewartstown, and Strabane.

1881
Slater's *Royal National Commercial Directory of Ireland* contains lists of traders, clergy, nobility, and farmers in adjoining parishes of the towns of Aughnacloy, Castlederg, Clogher and Five-Mile-Town, Cookstown and Stewartstown, Dungannon, Newtownstewart and Gortin, Omagh, and Strabane.

1882
The *Omagh Almanac* has lists of clergy, school staff, medical practitioners, and gentry for the county. It also lists traders in Cookstown, Dungannon, Fintona, Omagh, and Strabane.

1885
Further edition of above.

1887
Derry Almanac of Castlederg, Fintona, Gortin, Newtown-Stewart, Omagh, and Strabane (issued annually from 1891).

1888
Further edition of *Omagh Almanac* (see 1882).

1891
Further edition of *Omagh Almanac* covering traders and lists of residents (with *): Aughnacloy*, Augher*, Ballygawley, Beragh, Clogher, Cookstown, Dromore, Drumquin*,

Dungannon, Fintona, Gortin, New-townstewart, Omagh*, Sixmilecross, Strabane, and Trillick.

Family History

Campbell, F. *The Genealogy of Robert Campbell of Co. Tyrone.* New York, 1909.

Develin, J. *The O'Devlins of Tyrone: the Story of an Irish Sept.* Rutland, Vermont, 1938.

Godfrey, Earnest H. (comp.) *The Lindesays of Loughry, Co. Tyrone: a Genealogical History.* London, 1949.

Hamilton – see Fermanagh.

"Irwin family, Altmore, Pomeroy." *Family Links* 1 (7) (1983): 17-20.

"Notes on the Family of Cairnes, Co. Tyrone." *J. Ass. Pres. Mem. Dead* 12 (1926-31): 297.

Gravestone Inscriptions

Clogher: Johnston, John I.D. *Clogher Cathedral Graveyard.* 1972.

Donaghcavey: *Clogher Record* 7 (2) (1970): 299-320.

Drumglass: *Seanchas Ardmhacha* 9 (2) (1974): 316-19.

Kilskeery (Old): *Clogher Record* 8 (1) (1973): 51-57.

Newspapers

For biographical notices from 1772 onwards, the *Londonderry Journal* (see Co. Derry) should also be consulted as its circulation covered much of Tyrone.

Title: *Mid-Ulster Mail*
Published in: Cookstown, 1891-current
NLI Holdings: 1.1899-5.1915; 1.1950-in progress

BL Holdings: 2.1891-5.1915; 1.1923-12.1925; 1.1927-12.1940; 1.1942-in progress

Title: *Strabane Chronicle*
Published in: Strabane, 1896-current
NLI Holdings: 1.1950-in progress
BL Holdings: 1.1899-in progress

Title: *Strabane Morning Post*
Published in: Strabane, 1812-37
BL Holdings: 1.1823-4.1837

Title: *Tyrone Constitution*
Published in: Omagh, 1844-current
NLI Holdings: 1.1885-12.1941
BL Holdings: 11.1844-4.1853; 2.1854-3.1861; 3.1862-12.1927; 1.1929-in progress

Title: *Ulster Chronicle* (continued as *Tyrone Courier and Dungannon News* in 1921 and as *Dungannon News and Tyrone Courier* from 6.1968)
Published in: Dungannon, 1807-ca. 1824
NLI Holdings: 1.1885-12.1913; 6.1921-8.1947; 1.1954-5.1968
BL Holdings: 1.1880-12.1889; 1.1904-12.1916

Wills and Administrations

A discussion of the types of records, where they are held, their availability and value is given in the Wills section of the Introduction. The availability of prerogative wills, administrations, and marriage license records is also described in the relevant parts of the same section. Where available, published sources of these records are given in the Miscellaneous Sources section.

Pre-1858 Wills and Administrations

Prerogative Wills. see p. xli.

Consistorial Wills. County Tyrone is divided among the dioceses of Armagh, Derry, and Clogher. The guide to Catholic parish records in this chapter shows the diocese to which each civil parish belonged. The wills of residents of each diocese were usually proven within that diocese (see the Wills section for exceptions). The following records survive:

Wills. see p. xxxvii.

Abstracts. see p. xxxvii.

Indexes. Armagh–see Co. Armagh. Derry (1612-1858) published to 1858 by Phillimore. Clogher (1661-1858).

Post-1858 Wills and Administrations

This county was served by the District Registries of Londonderry and Armagh. The surviving records are kept in the PRO.

Marriage Licenses

Indexes. Armagh (1727-1845). PRO; SLC film 100859-860. Clogher (1709-1866). PRO; SLC film 100862.

Miscellaneous Sources

An Introduction to the Abercorn Letters (as Relating to Ireland, 1736-1816). Omagh, 1972 (correspondence of the Duke of Abercorn's family relating to their estates in Ireland).

Gebbie, Canon J.H. *Ardstraw (Newtownstewart): Historical Survey of a Parish (1600-1900).* Omagh: Strule Press, 1968.

MacEvoy, J. *Statistical Survey of County Tyrone.* 1802.

"The Survey of Armagh and Tyrone 1622." *Ulster J. Arch.* 23 (1960): 126-37; 27 (1964): 140-54.

"Volunteer Companies of Ulster 1778-1793." *Tyrone Irish Sword* 8 (1968): 210-17 (officer's names only).

Research Sources and Services

Journals

Seanchas Ardmhacha

Clogher Record

Libraries and Information Sources

Western Education & Library Board, Library Headquarters, Dublin Road, Omagh, Co. Tyrone Ph: (08 0662) 44821

Research Services

Irish World Citizen Organization, 26 Market Square, Dungannon, Co. Tyrone

See also research services in Belfast, p. xlvi

Societies

West Tyrone Historical Society, Mr. J. Gilmour, Ulster-American Folk Park, Camphill, Omagh, Co. Tyrone

Stewartstown Historical Society, Mrs. J.F. Laverty, The Castle Farm, Stewartstown, Co. Tyrone

Donaghmore Historical Society, P.H. Raffetty, St Patrick's Boys Secondary School, 41 Killymeal Road, Dungannon, Co. Tyrone

Muintirevlin (Ardboe) Historical Society, P. Coney, 27 Battery Road, Mullawhitra, Cookstown, Co. Tyrone

Clogher Historical Society, Cumann Seanchais Clochair, J.I.D. Johnston, Corick, Clogher, Co. Tyrone

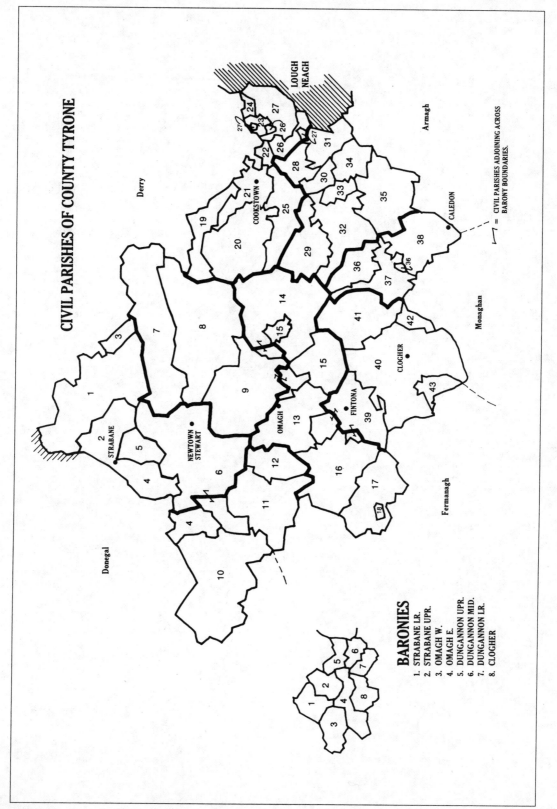

CIVIL PARISHES OF COUNTY TYRONE

LOUGH NEAGH

Armagh

Derry

Monaghan

COOKSTOWN

CALEDON

CLOGHER

STRABANE

NEWTOWN STEWART

OMAGH

FINTONA

Fermanagh

Donegal

BARONIES

1. STRABANE LR.
2. STRABANE UPR.
3. OMAGH W.
4. OMAGH E.
5. DUNGANNON UPR.
6. DUNGANNON MID.
7. DUNGANNON LR.
8. CLOGHER

= CIVIL PARISHES ADJOINING ACROSS BARONY BOUNDARIES.

County Waterford

A Brief History

Home of the manufacture of the famous Waterford crystal, this coastal Munster county contains the city of Waterford and the towns of Dungarvan, Tramore, Lismore, and Cappoquin.

Most of the present county was originally in the Kingdom of Decies. The major families were the O'Phelans, McGraths, O'Briens, and O'Keanes.

The town of Waterford itself was founded by the Danish Vikings in A.D. 853. The Danes successfully defended the town against the local inhabitants and remained a powerful force in the county until the eleventh century when the city was taken by the Normans. However, as the Danes did not use surnames, there is little evidence of the Viking heritage in the names now found in the county.

After the Norman invasion the county was granted to Robert de Poer, whose family is the ancestors of the Powers. Other Norman names now common in the county are Aylward, Wyse, and Wall. Wadding, an Anglo-Saxon name, has also been found in Waterford since Norman times. The city of Waterford became a stronghold of the Normans and was second only to Dublin in its importance.

Following the unsuccessful insurrection of the Earl of Desmond, (see Co. Kerry) part of

Waterford was confiscated from its owners and planted with English settlers in 1583. Many of these left again in 1598 during the war with Hugh O'Neill (see Co. Tyrone). In the 1641 rebellion of the Catholic Confederacy (see Co. Kilkenny) the city sided with the Irish Catholics and successfully withstood a siege by Oliver Cromwell's army. The city finally surrendered the following year following a second siege by Cromwell's army led by General Ireton. Neither the 1583 nor the 1650 settlements were very significant, however.

Waterford has been an important port since its establishment and has had extensive trading links with many countries. There is, for instance, a long established link with eastern Canada, particularly Newfoundland. Considerable emigration to Canada from Waterford took place, and there is much evidence of Waterford people travelling to and from eastern Canadian ports, even to the extent of families bringing children back to Waterford to be baptized.

The county suffered considerably in the Great Famine of 1845-47. The population in 1841 was 196,000 and by 1851 had fallen 20 percent to 164,000. Approximately 25,000 people died in the years 1845-50, and the remainder emigrated to the cities or, more usually, abroad. Between 1851 and 1855, for instance, over 28,000 people emigrated from the county. During the remainder of the century the popula-

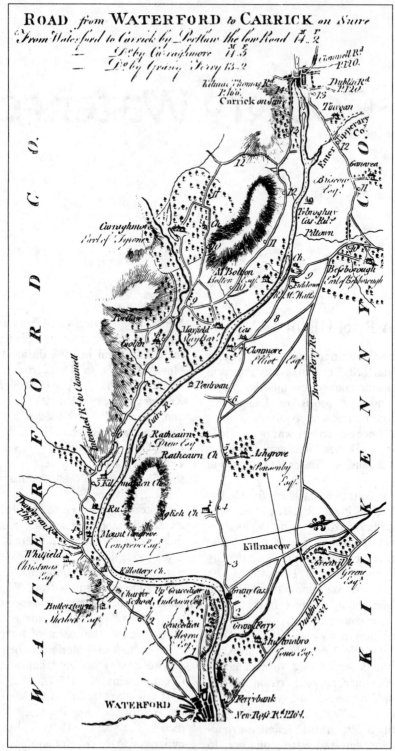

A 1783 map of the road from Waterford to Carrick-on-Suir.
From Taylor and Skinner's *Maps of the Roads of Ireland.*
Dublin, 1783.

tion continued to decline through emigration, so that by 1891 it was only 98,000. It is currently 89,000.

The town is still an important port, and also has several major industries: a dairy industry which processes the produce of the county's many dairy herds, engineering, and the previously mentioned Waterford crystal glass which was first manufactured here in 1783.

Census and Census Substitutes

1542-1650
"The Freemen of Waterford." *Ir. Gen.* 5 (5) (1978): 560-72.

1641
"Proprietors of Waterford" (name and street). *J. Cork Hist. & Arch. Soc.* 51 (173) (1946): 10-30.

1659
"Census" of Ireland. Edited by S. Pender. Dublin: Stationery Office, 1939; SLC film 924648.

1662
"Subsidy Roll." (tax payers of over £1 annual land value or £3 annual goods value). *Anal. Hib.* 30 (1982): 47-96.

1663
"Inhabitants of Waterford City, Showing Trade or Profession." *J. Cork Hist. & Arch. Soc.* 51.

1663-64
"Tenants or Possessors of Waterford" (name and street). *J. Cork Hist. & Arch. Soc.* 51 (173) (1946): 10-30.

1664-66
Civil Survey, Vol. 6. SLC film 973123.

1700
"Members of Some Waterford Guilds." *J. Waterford and S.E. Ire. Arch. Soc.* 7 (1901): 61-65.

1760
"Tenants of Bellew Properties in and Adjoin-

ing Dungarvan" (index to estate map). *J. Waterford and S.E. Ire. Arch. Soc.* 19 (4) (1911): 103-07 (some fifty-five names, addresses, and property and lease details).

1766
Religious Census of Parish of Killoteran, Waterford City. PRO 1A 46 49; SLC film 100158.

1775
Catholic Qualification Roll Extracts (174 names, addresses, and occupations). 59th Report DKPRI: 50-84.

"Principal Gentry of Co. Waterford." *J. Waterford and S.E. Ire. Arch. Soc.* 16 (2) (1913): 49-55.

1778
"Inhabitants of Waterford City." *Freeman's J.* 16 (30) (29 October 1778); 16 (32) (3 November 1778); 16 (33) (5 November 1778); SLC film 993913.

1792
"The Leading Catholics of Waterford in 1792." *Ir. Anc.* 8 (2) (1976): 80-81.

1793
Tenants of Lands, etc., belonging to City of Waterford and Other Accounts. NLI; GO 1917 (gives original lessees, current tenants of described premises, plus names of suppliers or employees paid by city, with description of the service provided; over 300 names).

1807
"How Waterford City Voted in 1807" (voters lists). *Ir. Anc.* 8 (11): 18-32.

1821
"Extracts from the Census of the City of Waterford." *Ir. Gen.* 4 (1) (1968): 17-26; 4 (2) (1969): 122-30; PRO; SLC film 100158.

"Transcript of 1821 Government Census Returns for Townland of Callaghane." *Decies* 17 (1981): 67-70.

1823-38
Tithe Applotment Survey (see p. xxvii).

1831 and 1841
Extracts from Government Census for the

Parish of Dungarvan Mainly for the Names Walsh and Kelly. QUB; SLC film 100158; PRO.

1841

Ratepayers, Contractors, and Suppliers to Waterford County. Statement of Accounts, Spring Assizes. NLI I 6551.

1846

Ratepayers, Contractors, and Suppliers to Waterford County. Statement of Accounts, Spring Assizes. NLI I 6551.

1847

"Names of Principal Fishermen in Ring, with Names of Boats, etc." Alcock, J. *Facts from the Fisheries 1848*. Waterford, 1848. NLI I6551.

1848-51

Griffith's Valuation (see p. xxvii).

1849

"Ballysaggart Estate." *Decies* 27 (1984): 4-12 (account of evictions and trial; gives some tenant's names).

1851

Extracts from the Government Census of Drumcannon (Tramore) Mainly for the Names Walsh and Kelly. QUB; SLC film 100158.

1857

"The Estate of George Lane Fox." *Decies* 26 (1984): 52-59 (mainly parish of Kilbarry; gives tenant's names and holdings).

1901

Census. PRO.

1911

Census. PRO.

Church Records

Church of Ireland
(shows starting date of record)

Parish: **Ardmore** and **Ballymacart**
Status: Lost

Parish: **Ballynakill**
Status: Lost

Parish: **Cappoquinn**
Existing Records: b. 1844
Status: LC

Parish: **Carrickbeg** (see Dysart)

Parish: **Clashmore**
Status: Lost

Parish: **Clonegam**
Existing Records: (1 register (1820-25) in custody of rector of Fethard-on-Sea) b. 1741; m. 1742; d. 1743
Status: LC and PRO

Parish: **Dungarvan**
Existing Records: b. 1741; m. 1741; d. 1741 (in PRO b. 1741-1802; m. 1808-27, 1827-75)
Status: PRO

Parish: **Dunhill**
Status: Lost

Parish: **Dysart**
Status: Lost

Parish: **Guilcagh**
Status: Lost

Parish: **Innislonagh**
Existing Records: b. 1801; m. 1800; d. 1805
Status: PRO

Parish: **Kill St. Nicholas**
Existing Records: b. 1730; m. 1730; d. 1730
Status: LC and PRO

Parish: **Killea** (see also Kill St. Nicholas)
Existing Records: b. 1816; m. 1816; d. 1816

Parish: **Killoteran**
Existing Records: b. 1770; m. 1768; d. 1758
Missing Dates: b. 1829-76; d. 1773-1838
Status: PRO

Parish: **Kilmeadon**
Existing Records: b. 1683; m. 1683; d. 1683
Status: LC and PRO

Parish: **Kilronan**
Status: Lost

Parish: **Kilrosanty**
Existing Records: b. 1806; d. 1858
Status: LC and PRO

Parish: **Kilwatermoy** (see also Tallow)
Existing Records: b. 1860; d. 1858
Status: LC and PRO

Parish: **Kinsalebeg** and **Grange**
Existing Records: b. 1817; m. 1827; d. 1841
Status: LC

Parish: **Lismore**
Existing Records: b. 1693; m. 1692; d. 1741
Status: LC and PRO

Parish: **Macollop**
Status: Lost

Parish: **Macully** or **Kilculliheen**
Status: Lost

Parish: **Monksland**
Existing Records: b. 1836; m. 1837; d. 1836
Status: LC

Parish: **Mothel**
Status: Lost

Parish: **Ringagonagh**
Status: Lost

Parish: **Rossmire**
Existing Records: b. 1834; m. 1803; d. 1836
Status: LC and PRO

Parish: **St. Olave** (see also Trinity)
Existing Records: b. 1741; m. 1741; d. 1785
Status: LC and PRO

Parish: **St. Patrick's, Waterford**
Existing Records: b. 1723; m. 1725; d. 1723
Status: LC and PRO

Parish: **Stradbally**
Existing Records: b. 1798; m. 1798; d. 1798
Status: LC and PRO

Parish: **Tallow** and **Kilwatermoy**
Existing Records: b. 1772; m. 1772; d. 1772
Missing Dates: b. 1810-28; m. 1810-28; d. 1810-28
Status: LC and PRO

Parish: **Templemichael**
Existing Records: b. 1821; m. 1804; d. 1823
Status: PRO

Parish: **Trinity** and **St. Olave's**
Existing Records: b. 1658; m. 1658; d. 1658
Status: LC and PRO

Parish: **Whitechurch**
Status: Lost

Presbyterian

Parish: **Waterford**
Starting Date: 1770

Roman Catholic

Civil Parish: **Affane**
Map Grid: 19
RC Parish: see Modeligo
Diocese: LS

Civil Parish: **Aglish**
Map Grid: 68
RC Parish: Aglish
Diocese: LS

Earliest Record: b. 5.1837; m. 1.1877
Parish Address: Rev. W. Callanan, PP, Aglish, Cappoquin, Co. Waterford

Civil Parish: **Ardmore**
Map Grid: 69
RC Parish: Ardmore; also part Aglish
Diocese: LS
Earliest Record: b. 1.1823; m. 1.1823
Parish Address: Rev. Thomas Flynn, CC, Ardmore, Youghal, Co. Cork

Civil Parish: **Ballygunner**
Map Grid: 58
RC Parish: see Waterford City, Trinity Within
Diocese: WA

Civil Parish: **Ballylaneen**
Map Grid: 34
RC Parish: see Stradbally
Diocese: LS

Civil Parish: **Ballymacart**
Map Grid: 74
RC Parish: see Ardmore
Diocese: LS

Civil Parish: **Ballynakill**
Map Grid: 51
RC Parish: see Waterford City, St. John's Within
Diocese: WA

Civil Parish: **Clashmore**
Map Grid: 71
RC Parish: Clashmore
Diocese: LS
Earliest Record: b. 1.1811; m. 1.1810
Parish Address: Rev. Joseph Murphy, PP, Kinsalebeg, Youghal, Co. Cork

Civil Parish: **Clonea**
Map Grid: 32
RC Parish: see Kilgobinet
Diocese: LS

Civil Parish: **Clonegam**
Map Grid: 11
RC Parish: Portlaw
Diocese: LS
Earliest Record: b. 1.1809 (3 registers for some periods); m. 1.1805
Parish Address: Rev. Joseph Murphy, PP, Kinsalebeg, Youghal, Co. Cork

Civil Parish: **Colligan**
Map Grid: 27
RC Parish: see Kilgobnet
Diocese: LS

Civil Parish: **Corbally**
Map Grid: 66
RC Parish: Tramore, see Drumcannon
Diocese: WA

Civil Parish: **Crooke**
Map Grid: 60
RC Parish: see Killea
Diocese: WA

Civil Parish: **Drumcannon**
Map Grid: 47
RC Parish: Tramore
Diocese: WA
Earliest Record: b. 1.1798; m. 1.1786
Parish Address: Rev. John Shine, PP, Parochial House, Tramore, Co. Waterford

Civil Parish: **Dungarvan (1)**
Map Grid: 30
RC Parish: Dungarvan; also Abbeyside, see below
Diocese: LS
Earliest Record: b. 2.1787; m. 5.1809
Missing Dates: b. 4.1798-9.1811; m. 5.1823-7.1823
Parish Address: Rev. T. Cassidy, PP, Parochial House, Dungarvan, Co. Waterford

Civil Parish: **Dungarvan (2)**
Map Grid: 30
RC Parish: Abbeyside
Diocese: LS
Earliest Record: b. 7.1828; m. 7.1828
Missing Dates: m. 2.1842-5.1842
Parish Address: Rev. M. Farrell, PP, Abbeyside, Dungarvan, Co. Waterford

Civil Parish: **Dunhill**
Map Grid: 44
RC Parish: Dunhill and Fenor
Diocese: LS

Earliest Record: b. 4.1829 (2 registers for period 1852-176); m. 11.1836; d. 1.1879
Missing Dates: d. ends 11.1881
Parish Address: Rev. G. Purcell, PP, Dunhill, Fenor P.O., Co. Waterford

Civil Parish: **Dysert**
Map Grid: 6
RC Parish: Carrickbeg, see Kilmoleran
Diocese: LS

Civil Parish: **Faithlegg**
Map Grid: 53
RC Parish: see Killea
Diocese: WA

Civil Parish: **Fenoagh**
Map Grid: 8
RC Parish: Carrickbeg, see Kilmoleran
Diocese: LS

Civil Parish: **Fews**
Map Grid: 25
RC Parish: see Kilrossanty
Diocese: LS

Civil Parish: **Grange** or **Lisgrennan**
Map Grid: 73
RC Parish: see Ardmore
Diocese: LS

Civil Parish: **Guilcagh** or **Guilco**
Map Grid: 12
RC Parish: Portlaw, see Clonegam

Civil Parish: **Inish-Lounaght**
Map Grid: 1
RC Parish: see Inish-Lounaght, Co. Tipperary

Civil Parish: **Islandikane**
Map Grid: 48
RC Parish: see Dunhill
Diocese: WA

Civil Parish: **Kilbarry**
Map Grid: 54
RC Parish: see Waterford City, Trinity Without
Diocese: WA

Civil Parish: **Kilbarrymeaden**
Map Grid: 36

RC Parish: Kill (Newtown)
Diocese: LS
Earliest Record: b. 3.1797; m. 4.1797
Missing Dates: b. 8.1830-2.1831
Parish Address: Rev. Jeremiah Condon, CC, Kill, Co. Waterford

Civil Parish: **Kilbride**
Map Grid: 46
RC Parish: see Dunhill
Diocese: WA

Civil Parish: **Kilburne**
Map Grid: 42
RC Parish: see Waterford City, Trinity Without
Diocese: WA

Civil Parish: **Kilcaragh**
Map Grid: 57
RC Parish: Kilcaragh
Diocese: WA

Civil Parish: **Kilcockan**
Map Grid: 17
RC Parish: Knockanore
Diocese: LS
Earliest Record: b. 5.1816; m. 2.1854
Missing Dates: b. 4.1833-9.1833
Parish Address: Rev. James Mulcahy, PP, Knockanore, Tallow, Co. Waterford

Civil Parish: **Kilcop**
Map Grid: 59
RC Parish: see Killea
Diocese: WA

Civil Parish: **Kilculliheen**
Map Grid: 13
RC Parish: Slieverue, see Rathpatrick, Co. Kilkenny
Diocese: LS

Civil Parish: **Kilgobnet**
Map Grid: 23
RC Parish: Kilgobinet
Diocese: LS
Earliest Record: b. 4.1848; m. 10.1848
Missing Dates: b. 10.1872-3.1873
Parish Address: Rev. Patrick Butler, CC, Kilgobinet, Dungarvan, Co. Waterford

Civil Parish: **Killaloan**
Map Grid: 4
RC Parish: see St. Mary's Clonmel, Co. Tipperary
Diocese: LS

Civil Parish: **Killea**
Map Grid: 65
RC Parish: Killea and Crooke (Dunmore East)
Diocese: WA
Earliest Record: b. 5.1815; m. 1.1780
Missing Dates: b. 7.1820-10.1845; m. 10.1791-1.1793, 2.1798-4.1815, 7.1820-8.1837, 7.1838-10.1845
Parish Address: Rev. James Aylward, PP, Killea, Dunmore East, Co. Waterford

Civil Parish: **Killoteran**
Map Grid: 38
RC Parish: see Waterford City, Trinity Without
Diocese: WA

Civil Parish: **Kill St. Lawrence**
Map Grid: 55
RC Parish: Kill St. Lawrence
Diocese: WA

Civil Parish: **Kill St. Nicholas**
Map Grid: 52
RC Parish: see Killea
Diocese: WA

Civil Parish: **Killure**
Map Grid: 56
RC Parish: Killure
Diocese: WA

Civil Parish: **Kilmacleague**
Map Grid: 62
RC Parish: see Killea
Diocese: WA

Civil Parish: **Kilmacomb**
Map Grid: 63
RC Parish: see Killea
Diocese: WA

Civil Parish: **Kilmeaden**
Map Grid: 37
RC Parish: Portlaw, see Clonegam
Diocese: LS

Civil Parish: **Kilmolash**
Map Grid: 28
RC Parish: part Cappoquin, see Lismore; part Aglish
Diocese: LS

Civil Parish: **Kilmoleran**
Map Grid: 7
RC Parish: Carrickbeg
Diocese: LS
Earliest Record: b. 1.1842; m. 1.1807
Missing Dates: b. 10.1846-2.1847
Parish Address: Rev. John Morrissey, PP, Carrickbeg, Carrick-on-Suir, Co. Tipperary

Civil Parish: **Kilronan (1)**
Map Grid: 2
RC Parish: see Newcastle
Diocese: LS

Civil Parish: **Kilronan (2)**
Map Grid: 43
RC Parish: Ballybricken, see Waterford City, Trinity Without
Diocese: WA

Civil Parish: **Kilrossanty**
Map Grid: 24
RC Parish: Kilrossanty
Diocese: LS
Earliest Record: b. 7.1822; m. 1.1859
Missing Dates: b. 8.1858-1.1859
Parish Address: Rev. Robert Arthure, PP, Kilrossanty, Kilmacthomas, Co. Waterford

Civil Parish: **Kilrush**
Map Grid: 31
RC Parish: see Dungarvan
Diocese: LS

Civil Parish: **Kilsheelan**
Map Grid: 5
RC Parish: see Kilsheelan, Co. Tipperary
Diocese: LS

Civil Parish: **Kilwatermoy**
Map Grid: 16
RC Parish: Knockanore, see Kilcockan
Diocese: LS

Civil Parish: **Kinsalebeg**
Map Grid: 72
RC Parish: see Clashmore
Diocese: LS

Civil Parish: **Leitrim**
Map Grid: 13a
RC Parish: see Kilworth, Co. Cork
Diocese: CY

Civil Parish: **Lickoran**
Map Grid: 21
RC Parish: see Modelligo
Diocese: LS

Civil Parish: **Lisgrenan**
Map Grid: 73
RC Parish: see Grange
Diocese: LS

Civil Parish: **Lismore** and **Mocollop (1)**
Map Grid: 14
RC Parish: Ballyduff; also Lismore, see below
2; also Cappoquin, see below 3.
Diocese: LS
Earliest Record: b. 6.1849; m. 11.1853
Missing Dates: m. 1.1861-6.1861
Parish Address: Rev. Patrick Quealy, PP, Bal-
lyduff, Co. Waterford

Civil Parish: **Lismore** and **Mocollop (2)**
Map Grid: 14
RC Parish: Lismore
Diocese: LS
Earliest Record: b. 3.1820; m. 11.1822
Missing Dates: b. 2.1831-7.1840, 7.1848-2.1849,
4.1858-8.1866; m. 10.1839-2.1840
Parish Address: Rev. John Power, PP,
Parochial House, Lismore, Co. Waterford

Civil Parish: **Lismore** and **Mocollop (3)**
Map Grid: 14
RC Parish: Cappoquin
Diocese: LS
Earliest Record: b. 4.1810; m. 1.1807
Parish Address: Rev. John Walsh, PP, Cappo-
quin, Co. Waterford

Civil Parish: **Lisnakill**
Map Grid: 41
RC Parish: see Waterford City, Trinity Without
Diocese: WA

Civil Parish: **Modelligo**
Map Grid: 20
RC Parish: Modelligo
Diocese: LS
Earliest Record: b. 7.1846
Parish Address: Rev. Michael Russell, PP,
Parochial House, Modeligo, Co. Waterford

Civil Parish: **Monamintra**
Map Grid: 61
RC Parish: see Waterford City, Trinity Within
Diocese: WA

Civil Parish: **Monksland**
Map Grid: 35
RC Parish: see Inish-Lounaght, Co. Tipperary
Diocese: LS

Civil Parish: **Mothel**
Map Grid: 10
RC Parish: see Rathgormuck
Diocese: LS

Civil Parish: **Newcastle**
Map Grid: 40
RC Parish: Newcastle
Diocese: LS
Earliest Record: b. 7.1814; m. 1.1822
Parish Address: Rev. Daniel O'Byrne, PP, Bal-
lymacarbery, Clonmel, Co. Tipperary

Civil Parish: **Rathgormuck**
Map Grid: 9
RC Parish: Mothel and Rathgormack
Diocese: LS
Earliest Record: b. 3.1831; m. 3.1845
Parish Address: Rev. Michael Wall, PP, Clonea,
Carrick-on-Suir, Co. Tipperary

Civil Parish: **Rathmoylan**
Map Grid: 67
RC Parish: see Killea
Diocese: WA

Civil Parish: **Reisk**
Map Grid: 45
RC Parish: Reisk
Diocese: WA

Civil Parish: **Rinagonagh**
Map Grid: 70
RC Parish: Ring and Old Parish
Diocese: LS
Earliest Record: b. 8.1840; m. 1.1841
Parish Address: Rev. Piaras Jackson, CC, Ring, Dungarvan, Co. Waterford

Civil Parish: **Rossduff**
Map Grid: 64
RC Parish: see Killea
Diocese: WA

Civil Parish: **Rossmire**
Map Grid: 26
RC Parish: see Stradbally
Diocese: LS

Civil Parish: **St. Mary's Clonmel** (see also Co. Tipperary)
Map Grid: 3
RC Parish: Clonmel, St. Mary's
Diocese: LS
Earliest Record: b. 2.1836; m. 2.1836
Parish Address: Arch. Richard Coady, PP, Parochial House, SS. Peter and Paul, Clonmel, Co. Tipperary

Civil Parish: **Seskinan**
Map Grid: 22
RC Parish: Touraneena
Diocese: LS
Earliest Record: b. 7.1852; m. 7.1852
Parish Address: Rev. John Keating, PP, Tournaeena, Ballinamult, Clonmel, Co. Tipperary

Civil Parish: **Stradbally**
Map Grid: 33
RC Parish: Stradbally
Diocese: LS
Earliest Record: b. 11.1806; m. 8.1805
Parish Address: Rev. William Phelan, PP, Stradbally, Kilmacthomas, Co. Waterford

Civil Parish: **Tallow**
Map Grid: 15
RC Parish: Tallow
Diocese: LS
Earliest Record: b. 4.1797; m. 4.1798
Missing Dates: b. 9.1842-1.1856; m. 4.1803-10.1808
Parish Address: Rev. Michael Walsh, PP, Tallow, Co. Waterford

Civil Parish: **Templemichael**
Map Grid: 18
RC Parish: Knockanore, see Kilcockan
Diocese: LS

Waterford City

Civil Parish: **St. John's Within**
Map Grid: 49
RC Parish: St. John's
Diocese: WA
Earliest Record: b. 4.1706; m. 4.1706
Missing Dates: b. 3.1730-3.1759, 3.1787-8.1807, 3.1816-6.1818 (microfilm ends in 1837); m. 3.1730-2.1760, 1.1817-9.1828
Parish Address: Rev. John Boyle, Adm, St. John's Presbytery, New Street, Waterford

Civil Parish: **St. John's Without**
Map Grid: 50
RC Parish: see St. John's Within
Diocese: WA

Civil Parish: **St. Michael's**
Map Grid: 49
RC Parish: part St. John's Within; part Trinity Within
Diocese: WA
Earliest Record: b. 12.1732; m. 6.1796
Missing Dates: m. ends 11.1796
Parish Address: see St. John's Within

Civil Parish: **St. Olave's**
Map Grid: 49
RC Parish: see Trinity Within
Diocese: WA

Civil Parish: **St. Patrick's**
Map Grid: 49

RC Parish: St. Patrick's, see Trinity Within
Diocese: WA
Earliest Record: b. 4.1731; m. 4.1731
Missing Dates: b. 9.1791-5.1795, 3.1801-4.1827;
    m. 5.1791-1.1799, 12.1800-9.1826
Parish Address: see Trinity Within

Civil Parish: **St. Peter's**
Map Grid: 49
RC Parish: see Trinity Within
Diocese: WA
Earliest Record: b. 11.1737; m. 11.1743
Missing Dates: b. ends 8.1746; m. ends 1.1787
Parish Address: see Trinity Within

Civil Parish: **St. Stephen's Within**
Map Grid: 49
RC Parish: part of St. John's
Diocese: WA
Earliest Record: b. 9.1731
Missing Dates: b. ends 3.1749
Parish Address: see St. John's Within

Civil Parish: **St. Stephen's Without**
Map Grid: 49
RC Parish: see St. John's
Diocese: WA

Civil Parish: **Trinity Within**
Map Grid: 49
RC Parish: Trinity Within
Diocese: WA
Earliest Record: b. 1.1729; m. 9.1747
Missing Dates: b. 7.1775-2.1793; m. 12.1756-
    2.1761, 8.1777-1.1791, 6.1795-1.1797
Parish Address: Rev. Nicholas O'Mahony,
    Adm, Cathedral Presbytery, Waterford

Civil Parish: **Trinity Without**
Map Grid: 39
RC Parish: Trinity Without
Diocese: WA
Earliest Record: b. 1.1797; m. 1.1797
Parish Address: Rev. Francis Hopkins, PP, St.
    Anne's Presbytery, Convent Hill, Waterford

Civil Parish: **Whitechurch**
Map Grid: 29
RC Parish: see Aglish
Diocese: LS

Commercial and Social Directories

1788
Richard Lucas's *General Directory of the Kingdom of Ireland* contains lists of traders in Dungarvan, Passage, and Waterford. Reprinted in *Ir. Gen.* 3 (10) (1965): 392-416.

1809
Holden's *Triennial Directory* has an alphabetical list of traders in the city of Waterford.

1820
J. Pigot's *Commercial Directory of Ireland* contains information on the gentry, nobility, and traders in and around the towns of Dungarvan and Waterford.

1824
J. Pigot's *City of Dublin & Hibernian Provincial Directory* includes traders, nobility, gentry, and clergy lists of Cappoquin, Dungarvan, Kilmacthomas, Lismore, Tallow, Tramore, and Waterford.

1839
T.S. Harvey's *Directory of Waterford* contains alphabetical lists of gentry, merchants, and traders; it also has a house-by-house street directory.

T. Shearman's *New Commercial Directory for the Cities of Waterford...* lists traders, gentry, clergy, etc., in Waterford.

1840
F. Kinder's *New Triennial & Commercial Directory for 1840, '41, & '42* contains traders and other lists for Waterford City (rare volume).

1846
Slater's *National Commercial Directory of Ireland* lists nobility, clergy, traders, etc., in Dungarvan, Dunmore, Kilmacthomas, Lismore, Portlaw, Tallow, Tramore, and Waterford.

1856
Slater's *Royal National Commercial Directory of Ireland* lists nobility, gentry, clergy, traders, etc., in Bonmahon, Dungarvan,

Dunmore, Kilmacthomas, Lismore and Cappoquin, Portlaw, Tallow, Tramore, and Waterford.

1866

T.S. Harvey's *Waterford Almanac and Directory* has an alphabetical list of residents and traders. It also has a useful period map of the city.

1869

Newenham Harvey's *Waterford Almanac and Directory* has a house-by-house directory, an alphabetical list of residents, and a list of traders.

1870

Slater's *Directory of Ireland* contains trade, nobility, and clergy lists for Bonmahon, Dungarvan, Dunmore, Kilmacthomas, Lismore and Cappoquin, Portlaw, Tallow, Tramore, and Waterford.

1881

Slater's *Royal National Commercial Directory of Ireland* contains lists of traders, clergy, nobility, and farmers in adjoining parishes of the towns of Dungarvan, Dunmore, Kilmacthomas, Lismore, Cappoquin and Tallow, Portlaw and Fiddown, Tramore, and Waterford.

1886

Francis Guy's *Postal Directory of Munster* lists gentry, clergy, traders, principal farmers, teachers, and police sergeants in each postal district of the county and has a listing of magistrates, clergy, and the professions for the whole county.

1893

Francis Guy's *Postal Directory of Munster* lists traders and farmers in each of the postal districts of the county and has a general alphabetical index to persons in the whole county.

1894

Slater's *Royal National Directory of Ireland* lists traders, police, teachers, farmers, and private residents in each of the towns, villages, and parishes of the county.

Family History

"Ancient and Illustrious Waterford Families: The Dobbyns and Waddings." *J. Waterford & S.E. Ire. Arch. Soc.* 4 (1955): 247-50.

"The Anthony Family of Carrigcastle and Seafield." *Decies* 16 (1981): 15-22.

"The Barkers of Waterford." *Decies* 17 (1981): 17-28.

"Distinguished Waterford Families: Baron." *J. Waterford & S.E. Ire. Arch. Soc.* 17 (1914): 47-65, 128-34, 137-52; 18 (1915): 69-87, 91-104.

"Distinguished Waterford Families, I. Sherlock." *J. Waterford and S.E. Ire. Arch. Soc.* 9 (1906): 120-28, 171-75; 10 (1907): 42-44, 171-73.

"The Fitzgeralds of Farnane, Co. Waterford. Redmond." *J. Waterford & S.E. Ire. Arch. Soc.* 14 (1911): 27-39, 72-81; 15 (1912): 168-76.

Genealogia Dell' Antica e Nobile Famiglia Smyth di Ballynatray Nella Contea di Waterford in Irlanda. Estratta dagli antichi dal fu Cavaliere William Betham'. Lucca, 1868.

Genealogical Account of the Bagge Family of Co. Waterford. Dublin, 1860.

Higgins, P. "Ancient and Illustrious Waterford Families. The Wyses of the Manor of St. John's, Waterford." *J. Waterford & S.E. Ire. Arch. Soc.* 5 (1899): 199-206.

"Kavanagh Papers" (Borris, Co. Carlow). *Anal. Hib.* 25: 15-30.

Lloyd, A.R. *Genealogical Notes on Lloyd Family in Co. Waterford.* N.p., n.d.

"Pedigree of Ryland of Dungarvan and Waterford." *R.S.A.I.* 15 (1881): 562-65.

O'Shee – see Power-O'Shee

"Power-O'Shee Papers" (Gardenmorris, Co. Waterford). *Anal. Hib.* 20: 216-58.

"The Powers of Clashmore, Co. Waterford." *J. Cork Hist. & Arch. Soc.* 47 (1924): 121-22.

"The Rivers Family of Co. Waterford." *Decies* 12 (1979): 32-61.

"The Roberts Family of Waterford." *J. Waterford and S.E. Ire. Arch. Soc.* 2 (1896): 98-103.

"Sherlock of Butlerstown, Co. Waterford." *Ir. Gen.* 4 (2) (1969): 131-41.

"Tandy of Sion Lodge." Pedigree in *Swanzy Notebooks.* RCB Library, Dublin.

"Ussher Papers" (Cappagh, Co. Waterford). *Anal. Hib.* 15: 63-78.

Wadding–see Dobbyn.

"The Waterford Merrys." *J. Waterford and S.E. Ire. Arch. Soc.* 16 (1913): 30-35.

Wright, W.B. *The Ussher Memoirs, or Genealogical Memoirs of the Ussher Families in Ireland.* London, 1899.

Gravestone Inscriptions

Affane: *Ir. Gen.* 2 (9) (1952): 285-89.

Churchtown (Dysert): *Decies* 25 (1984): 32-39.

Clashmore: *Ir. Gen.* 2 (8) (1950): 246-49.

Faha Chapel of Ease: *Decies* 17 (1981): 71-78.

French Church (Franciscan): *R.S.A.I.* (1973).

Stradbally: *Decies* 16 (1981): 61-68; 17 (1982).

Waterford, St. Patrick's: Power, Rev. P. *Catholic Record of Waterford and Lismore.* Vol. 4. 1916.

Whitechurch: *Ir. Anc.* 5 (1), 1973.

Newspapers

A card index to biographical notices in Waterford, Ennis, Clonmel, and Limerick newspapers up to 1821 (50,000 items) is available on microfiche from Ms. R. ffolliott, Glebe House, Fethard, Co. Tipperary. A copy of this is held by the Library of University College, Dublin. Note also that many of the biographical notices from Ramsay's *Waterford Chronicle* have been abstracted and published. See the Miscellanous Sources section for details.

Title: *The Citizen* (see *The Waterford Citizen*)

Title: *The Mail* (see *The Waterford Mail*)

Title: *Mail and Waterford Daily Express*
Published in: Waterford, 1855-60
NLI Holdings: 1-11.1856; 1-12.1857; 1-6.1859
BL Holdings: 7.1855-6.1860

Title: *Munster Express* (and *Co. Tipperary Independent and Celt*)
Published in: Waterford, 1860-current
NLI Holdings: 1863-68 (with gaps); 1908-23 (with gaps); 1926-40
BL Holdings: 7.1860-7.1869; 1.1870-3.1905; 9.1906-in progress

Title: (Ramsey's) *Waterford Chronicle* (called *The Chronicle* from 1884).
Published in: Waterford, 1771-1910
Note: Index for some years from 1776-96 published in *Irish Genealogist* (see Miscellaneous Sources section)
NLI Holdings: 1771; 1777; 1811-12; 1.1814-12.1814; 1816-17; 1.1818-12.1818; 1819-23; 7.1827-12.1827; 1.1829-5.1849; 1.1905-12.1910
BL Holdings: 1771; 1.1811-12.1812; 1.1816-12.1817; 1.1819-12.1822; odd numbers 1826, 1827; 1.1829-5.1849; 8.1859-12.1875; 1.1889-12.1910

Title: *The Waterford Citizen & Waterford Commercial Record* (also *New Ross News* from 1902)
Published in: Waterford, 1859-1906
BL Holdings: 9.1859-6.1876; 12.1876-2.1906

Title: *Waterford Freeman*
Published in: Waterford, 1845-47
NLI Holdings: 7.1845-4.1847
BL Holdings: 7.1845-4.1847

Title: *Waterford Herald*
Published in: Waterford, ca. 1789-96
NLI Holdings: 6-11.1791; 1-11.1792; 1-10.1793; 11.1793-9.1794
BL Holdings: odd numbers 1793-96

Title: *The Waterford Mail* (plus several additional titles from 1853-84)
Published in: Waterford, 1823-1908
BL Holdings: 8.1823-3.1905; 6.1907-9.1908

Title: *Waterford Mirror*
Published in: Waterford, ca. 1798-1843
NLI Holdings: 1804-40 (one volume, odd issues); 1-12.1807; 8.1808-7.1809; 2.1821-12.1824; 1.1827-9.1840
BL Holdings: 8.1808-7.1809; 1.1827-9.1843

Title: *Waterford Mirror and Tramore Visitor*
Published in: Waterford, 1860-1910
BL Holdings: 8.1860-7.1869; 4.1870-6.1873; 1-8.1875; 1.1884-12.1910

Title: *Waterford News*
Published in: Waterford, 1848-1958
NLI Holdings: 9.1848-3.1857; 1.1860-12.1883; 1.1885-12.1913; 5-12.1920; 8.1927-1.1959
BL Holdings: 9.1848-7.1869; 1.1870-12.1929; 1.1931-12.1958

Wills and Administrations

A discussion of the types of records, where they are held, their availability and value is given in the Wills section of the Introduction. The availability of prerogative wills, administrations, and marriage license records is also described in the relevant parts of the same section. Where available, published sources of these records are given in the Miscellaneous Sources section.

Pre-1858 Wills and Administrations

Prerogative Wills. see p. xli.
Consistorial Wills. County Waterford is mainly in the dioceses of Waterford and Lismore. One parish is in Cloyne diocese. The guide to Catholic parish records in this chapter shows the diocese to which each civil parish belonged. The wills of residents of each diocese were usually proven within that diocese (see the Wills section for exceptions). The following records survive:

Wills. see p. xxxvii. NLI holds 1660 Waterford Wills and Administrations. NLI D 9248-9413 .

Abstracts. see p. xxxvii and Miscellaneous Sources.

Indexes. Waterford and Lismore (1648-1858) up to 1800 published by Phillimore. Cloyne – see Co. Cork.

See also Miscellaneous Sources section.

Post-1858 Wills and Administrations

This county was served by the District Registry of Waterford. The surviving records are kept in the PRO.

Marriage Licenses

Indexes. Waterford and Lismore (1661-1750). PRO; SLC film 100872.
License Bonds. Jennings Mss., *Decies* 24 (1983): 20-24 (mainly for families Bray and Ronayne).

Miscellaneous Sources

"Business Records Relating to Co. Waterford in the PRO." *Decies* 21 (1982): 43-55.

"Extracts from the *Waterford Herald* 1792." *Ir. Gen.* 6 (2) (1981): 154-58.

"Extracts from the *Waterford Herald* 1793, 1794, 1796." *Ir. Gen.* 6 (3) (1982): 334-52.

"Genevese Exiles in County Waterford." *J. Cork. Hist. & Arch. Soc.* 75 (1970): 29-35.

"How Waterford City Voted in 1807." *Ir. Anc.* 8 (1) (1976): 18-32.

"Index to Waterford Wills 1583-1810." *J. Waterford and S.E. Ire. Arch. Soc.* 8 (31) (1902): 24-29 (over 400 names, dates, and occupations); 8 (32) (1903) (over 300 names, dates, and addresses).

"Marriage License Bonds, Chancery Bills, etc., in the Jennings Mss." *Decies* 24 (1983): 20-24 (mainly for families Bray, Ronayne).

"Old Wills." *J. Waterford and S.E. Ire. Arch. Soc.* 16 (4) (1913): 183-94 (extracts of biographical information etc.); 17 (1) (1914): 17-32; 17 (2) (1914): 71-91; 17 (3) (1914): 170-81; 18 (1) (1915): 32-39; 18 (4) (1915): 152-74; 19 (1) (1920): 34-47.

"Ramsay's *Waterford Chronicle* 1776. Births, Marriages and Deaths." *Ir. Gen.* 5 (3) (1976): 335-67.

"Ramsay's *Waterford Chronicle* 1777. Births, Marriages and Deaths." *Ir. Gen* 5 (4) (1977): 471-90; 5 (5) (1978): 625-42.

"Ramsay's *Waterford Chronicle* 1791. Births, Marriages and Deaths." *Ir. Gen.* 5 (6) (1979): 735-59.

"Ramsay's *Waterford Chronicle* 1778 and from the *Waterford Herald* 1650. Births, Marriages and Deaths." *Ir. Gen.* 6 (1) (1980): 22-37.

"Some 17th Century Funeral Entries." *J. Waterford and S.E. Ire. Arch. Soc.* 6 (1900): 165-70.

"Village of Kill (Part of Kilbarrymeadon)" (all census and other surveys listed). Supplement to *Decies* 8 (1978): 19-42.

"Wills Relating to Waterford" 3 (Index A-K). *Decies* 19 (1982): 39-52; 4 (Index L-Z). *Decies* 20 (1982): 51-60; *Decies* 22 (1983): 50-54; 6. *Decies* 23 (1983): 17-22.

Smith, Charles. *The Ancient and Present State of the County and City of Waterford.* 2 vols. 1746.

Research Sources and Services

Journals

Journal of the Waterford and South East Ireland Archaeological Society

Decies (Journal of the old Waterford Society)

Libraries and Information Sources

Waterford County Library, Lismore, Co. Waterford Ph: (058) 54128

Waterford Central Library, Lady Lane, Waterford Ph: (051) 73501.

Research Services

Irish Origins (see Research Sources and Services section, Co. Kilkenny)

Waterford Heritage Survey, St. John College, Waterford

See also research services in Dublin, p. xliv

Societies

Waterford Literary & Historical Society, 37 The Quay, Waterford

Old Waterford Society, Mrs. Nellie Croke, 208 Viewmount Park, Waterford

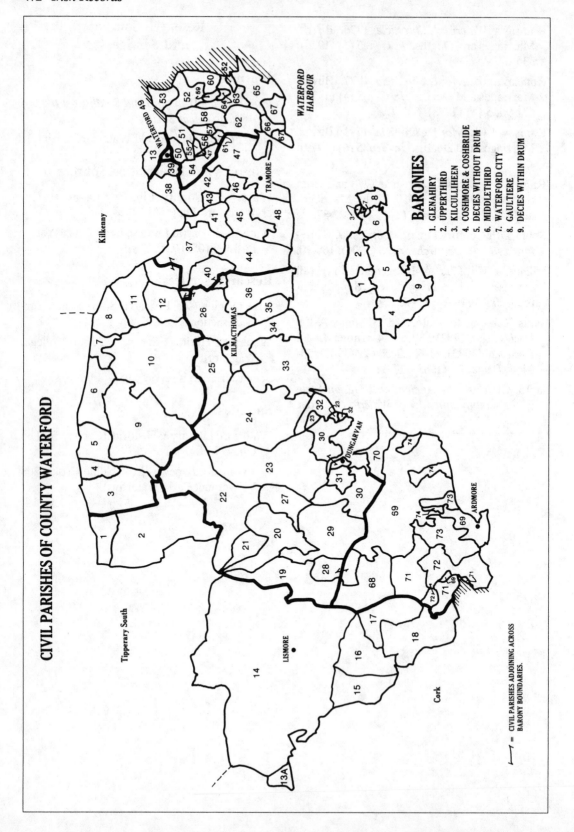

CIVIL PARISHES OF COUNTY WATERFORD

BARONIES

1. GLENAHIRY
2. UPPERTHIRD
3. KILCULLIHEEN
4. COSHMORE & COSHBRIDE
5. DECIES WITHOUT DRUM
6. MIDDLETHIRD
7. WATERFORD CITY
8. GAULTIERE
9. DECIES WITHIN DRUM

= CIVIL PARISHES ADJOINING ACROSS
   BARONY BOUNDARIES.

Kilkenny

Tipperary South

Cork

WATERFORD HARBOUR

TRAMORE

KILMACTHOMAS

DUNGARVAN

ARDMORE

LISMORE

County Westmeath

A Brief History

This Leinster county contains the towns of Mullingar, Athlone, Castlepollard, Moate, and Kilbeggan.

In the old Irish administrative divisions Westmeath was part of the Kingdom of Meath. This was the part of the country reserved as the territory of the High King. The major Irish families of the county were (Mc)Geoghegans, O'Growney, Brennan, O'Coffey, O'Mulleady, O'Malone, O'Curry, O'Daly, McAuley, O'Finlan, and McLoughlin.

After the arrival of the Normans in the late twelfth century this area was given to Hugh de Lacy. Other Norman families who obtained lands and settled in the county were Nugent, Tyrrell, Petit, Tuite, Delamar, Dalton, Dillon, Fitzsimon(ns), Hope, Ware, Ledwich, Dardis, and Gaynor.

The county was centrally involved in the rebellion of 1641 and was also active in the Williamite wars. Following these wars there was very extensive confiscation of land, and very few of the Irish or Norman families who held land before 1641 retained their properties. The major families who obtained grants of land were those of Packenham, Wood, Cooke, Swift, Handcock, Gay, Handy, Winter, Levinge, Wilson, Judge, Rochfort, Ogle, Middleton, Burtle, and St. George. The families of Fetherston, Chapman, Smith, O'Reilly, Purdon, Nagle, Blacquiere, and North later obtained property by purchase.

In the eighteenth and early nineteenth centuries the county was mainly composed of large farms under pasture. The Great Famine of 1845-47 did not affect the county as badly as others. In 1845 the population was 141,000. In 1851 it had fallen by 21 percent to 111,000. Between 1845 and 1850 almost 16,000 people died, and further thousands emigrated. The population continued to decline for the remainder of the century and beyond and is currently around 63,000.

Census and Census Substitutes

1640
"Irish Proprietors in Moate and District." In Cox's *Moate, Co. Westmeath: A History of the Town and District.* Athlone, 1981. Appendix 11.

1659
"Census" of Ireland. Edited by S. Pender. Dublin: Stationery Office, 1939; SLC film 924648.

1666

"Hearth Money Roll of Mullingar." *Franciscan College Journal* (1950); PRO.

1761-88

The Names of Owners of Freeholds in Co. Westmeath, Compiled for Electoral Purposes, 1761-1788. NLI mss. 787-788.

1761

Co. Westmeath Poll Book. GO ms. 443; SLC film 100181.

1766

Religious Census of the Parish of Russagh. SLC film 258517.

1802-03

"Census of Protestants in the Parishes of Ballyloughloe, Castletown Delvin, Clonarney, Drumraney, Enniscoffey, Kilbridepass, Killallon, Kilcleagh, Killough, Killua, Killucan, Leney, Moyliscar, and Rathconnell." *Ir. Anc.* 5 (2) (1973): 120-26.

1823-34

Tithe Applotment Survey (see p. xxvii).

1832

Westmeath Voters for Baronies of: Brawney-Clonlona, Kilkenny W., Moycashel and Rathconrath. *Ir. Gen.* 5 (2) (1975): 234-49.

Corkaree, Delvin, Demifore, and Farbill. *Ir. Gen.* 5 (6) 1979: 772-89.

Fartullagh, Moycashel and Magherdernan, and Moygoish. *Ir. Gen.* 6 (1) (1980): 77-98.

1832-36

"List of Holders of, or Applicants for, Licenses to Sell Liquor in Athlone" (over 100 names and addresses). *Parl. Papers* 1837, 13 (2): Appendix 10.

1835

Census of the Parish of Tubber (gives age, occupation, and religion of each person in each townland). NLI P 1994.

1837

"List of Those Made Freemen of Athlone Since 1831" (approximately 170 names, addresses, and occupations). *Parl. Papers* 1837, 11 (1): Appendix B1; 1837/38, 13 (2): Appendix 3.

1838

"Lists of Marksmen (illiterate voters) in Athlone" (forty-two names, occupations, and residences). *Parl. Papers* 1837, 11 (1): Appendix A3; and 1837/38, 13 (2): Appendix 4.

1854

Griffith's Valuation (see p. xxvii).

1901

Census. PRO.

1911

Census. PRO.

Church Records

Church of Ireland
(shows starting date of record)

Parish: **Abbyshrule**
Existing Records: b. 1821; m. 1821; d. 1821
Status: LC

Parish: **Almorita**
Status: Lost

Parish: **Ardnurcher** or **Horseleap**
Status: Lost

Parish: **Mount Temple Church**
Existing Records: b. 1793; m. 1776; d. 1803
Status: LC

Parish: **Ballymore** and **Killare**
Status: Lost

Parish: **Balnalack** (see Leney)
Status: Lost

Parish: **Benowen**
Status: Lost

Parish: **Carrick** (see Moylisker)

Parish: **Castlelost**
Status: Lost

Parish: **Castletown Kindalen** or **Vastina**
Status: Lost

Parish: **Churchtown**
Status: Lost

Parish: **Clonfadforan**
Status: Lost

Parish: **Clonmellon** (see Killallon)

Parish: **Collinstown**
Existing Records: b. 1838; m. 1838
Status: LC

Parish: **Delvin**
Existing Records: b. 1817; m. 1817; d. 1817
Status: LC

Parish: **Drumcree** (Kilcumne)
Existing Records: b. 1800; m. 1800; d. 1800
Status: LC and PRO

Parish: **Enniscoffey**
Status: Lost

Parish: **Foyran**
Status: Lost

Parish: **Kilbeggan**
Status: Lost

Parish: **Kilbixy**
Existing Records: b. 1815; m. 1814; d. 1816
Status: LC

Parish: **Kilbride** (Veston) (no church, see Moylisker and Castlelost)

Parish: **Kilcleagh** (Moate)
Status: Lost

Parish: **Kilkenny West**
Existing Records: b. 1809; m. 1809; d. 1809
Status: LC

Parish: **Killagh** (see Drumcree)
Status: Lost

Parish: **Killallon**
Status: Lost

Parish: **Killucan**
Existing Records: b. 1787; m. 1787; d. 1700
Missing Dates: d. 1779-87
Status: LC

Parish: **Kinnegad**
Status: Lost

Parish: **Leney**
Status: Lost

Parish: **Mayne** (Castelpollard)
Existing Records: b. 1808; m. 1809; d. 1808
Status: LC

Parish: **Moylisker**
Status: Lost

Parish: **Mullingar**
Status: Lost

Parish: **Newtown Fertullagh**
Status: Lost

Roman Catholic

Civil Parish: **Ardnurcher** or **Horseleap**
Map Grid: 50
RC Parish: Clara, see Kilbride (1), Co. Offaly
Diocese: ME

Civil Parish: **Ballyloughloe**
Map Grid: 46
RC Parish: Moate, see Kilcleagh (1)
Diocese: ME

Civil Parish: **Ballymore**
Map Grid: 36
RC Parish: Ballymore
Diocese: ME
Earliest Record: b. 9.1824; m. 4.1839
Missing Dates: m. 9.1870-2.1872
Parish Address: Rev. Joseph Conway, PP, Ballymore, Mullingar, Co. Westmeath

Civil Parish: **Ballymorin**
Map Grid: 38
RC Parish: Milltown, see Rathconrath
Diocese: ME

Civil Parish: **Bunown**
Map Grid: 30
RC Parish: see Drumraney
Diocese: ME

Civil Parish: **Carrick**
Map Grid: 59
RC Parish: part Rochefortbridge, see
   Castlelost; part Mullingar
Diocese: ME

Civil Parish: **Castlelost**
Map Grid: 63
RC Parish: Rochfortbridge
Diocese: ME
Earliest Record: b. 6.1823; m. 12.1816
Parish Address: Rev. Eamonn O'Brien, PP,
   Rochfortbridge, Co. Westmeath

Civil Parish: **Castletownkindalen**
Map Grid: 51
RC Parish: Castletown-Geoghegan
Diocese: ME
Earliest Record: b. 8.1829 (2 registers from
   1861-80); m. 2.1829 (2 registers from 1861-
   80); d. 4.1829
Missing Dates: d. ends 4.1835
Parish Address: Rev. M. J. Coleman, PP,
   Castletown-Geoghegan, Co. Westmeath

Civil Parish: **Churchtown**
Map Grid: 40
RC Parish: Churchtown
Diocese: ME
Earliest Record: b. 8.1836; m. 2.1825
Missing Dates: m. ends 2.1862
Parish Address: Rev. Francis X. O'Reilly,
   Dysart, Mullingar, Co. Westmeath

Civil Parish: **Clonarney**
Map Grid: 24
RC Parish: Clonmellon, see Killua
Diocese: ME

Civil Parish: **Clonfad**
Map Grid: 62

RC Parish: Rochfortbridge, see Castlelost
Diocese: ME

Civil Parish: **Conry**
Map Grid: 39
RC Parish: see Churchtown
Diocese: ME

Civil Parish: **Delvin**
Map Grid: 27
RC Parish: Castletowndelvin
Diocese: ME
Earliest Record: b. 1.1785; m. 2.1785; d. 2.1785
Missing Dates: b. 3.1789-7.1792, 7.1812-7.1830;
   m. 3.1789-7.1792, 7.1812-9.1830; d. 3.1789-
   7.1792, 7.1812-1.1849, ends 4.1855
Parish Address: Rev. Joseph Troy, PP,
   Parochial House, Delvin, Co. Westmeath

Civil Parish: **Drumraney**
Map Grid: 32
RC Parish: Drumraney (Noughaval)
Diocese: ME
Earliest Record: b. 4.1834; m. 5.1834
Parish Address: Rev. Andrew Rispin, PP,
   Drumraney, Athlone, Co. Westmeath

Civil Parish: **Durrow** (see also Co. Offaly)
Map Grid: 54
RC Parish: see Durrow, Co. Offaly
Diocese: ME

Civil Parish: **Dysart**
Map Grid: 43
RC Parish: see Churchtown
Diocese: ME

Civil Parish: **Enniscoffey**
Map Grid: 58
RC Parish: Rochfortbridge, see Castlelost
Diocese: ME

Civil Parish: **Faughalstown**
Map Grid: 7
RC Parish: Turbotstown, see Mayne
Diocese: ME

Civil Parish: **Foyran**
Map Grid: 1
RC Parish: Castlepollard
Diocese: ME

Civil Parish: **Kilbeggan**
Map Grid: 52
RC Parish: Kilbeggan
Diocese: ME
Earliest Record: b. 11.1818; m. 10.1818; d. 9.1818
Missing Dates: b. 8.1824-4.1825; d. ends 12.1843
Parish Address: Rev. Gerard Herbert, PP, Parochial House, Kilbeggan, Co. Westmeath

Civil Parish: **Kilbixy**
Map Grid: 13
RC Parish: Sonna and Ballinacargy
Diocese: ME
Earliest Record: b. 9.1837; m. 11.1838
Parish Address: Rev. Michael Deegan, PP, Parochial House, Ballincargy, Co. Westmeath

Civil Parish: **Kilbride**
Map Grid: 60
RC Parish: Mountnugent, see Kilbride (1), Co, Meath
Diocese: ME

Civil Parish: **Kilcleagh (1)**
Map Grid: 47
RC Parish: Kilcleagh (Moate and Mount Temple); also Ballynahowen, etc., see Kilcleagh (2).
Diocese: ME
Earliest Record: not on microfilm
Parish Address: Rev. James O'Beirne, PP, Moate, Co. Westmeath

Civil Parish: **Kilcleagh (2)**
Map Grid: 47
RC Parish: Ballynahowen, Boher, and Pollough
Diocese: ME
Earliest Record: b. 8.1821; m. 1.1830; d. 11.1829
Missing Dates: b. 12.1824-2.1826, 2.1839-2.1841; m. 8.1845-10.1854; d. 9.1845-9.1854
Parish Address: Rev. Patrick McKeown, PP, Ballinahowen, Athlone, Co. Westmeath

Civil Parish: **Kilcumny**
Map Grid: 23
RC Parish: see St. Feighin's
Diocese: ME

Civil Parish: **Kilcumreragh**
Map Grid: 49
RC Parish: see Kilmanaghan, Co. Offaly
Diocese: ME

Civil Parish: **Kilkenny West**
Map Grid: 31
RC Parish: Kilkenny West (Glasson)
Diocese: ME
Earliest Record: b. 8.1829
Parish Address: Rev. F. Gillooly, PP, Tubberclaire, Glasson, Athlone, Co. Westmeath

Civil Parish: **Killagh**
Map Grid: 28
RC Parish: Castletown-Delvin, see Delvin
Diocese: ME

Civil Parish: **Killare**
Map Grid: 37
RC Parish: see Ballymore
Diocese: ME

Civil Parish: **Killua**
Map Grid: 25
RC Parish: Clonmellon
Diocese: ME
Earliest Record: b. 1.1759; m. 1.1757; d. 12.1787
Missing Dates: b. 11.1809-6.1819; m. 9.1809-7.1819, 7.1845-1.1846; d. 10.1809-11.1819, ends 7.1850
Parish Address: Rev. Sean Garland, PP, Clonmellon, Navan, Co. Meath

Civil Parish: **Killucan (1)**
Map Grid: 44
RC Parish: Killucan (Raharney); also Kinnegad, see Killucan (2)
Diocese: ME
Earliest Record: b. 5.1821; m. 5.1821
Parish Address: Rev. Liam Murtagh, PP, Killucan, Co. Westmeath

Civil Parish: **Killucan (2)**
Map Grid: 44
RC Parish: Kinnegad
Diocese: ME
Earliest Record: b. 6.1827; m. 7.1844; d. 2.1869 (anointings from 1741-63; rents 1757)
Parish Address: Rev. Eamonn Marron, PP, Kinnegad, Co. Westmeath

Civil Parish: **Killulagh**
Map Grid: 26
RC Parish: see Delvin
Diocese: ME

Civil Parish: **Kilmacnevan**
Map Grid: 12
RC Parish: see Rathconrath
Diocese: ME

Civil Parish: **Kilmanaghan**
Map Grid: 48
RC Parish: see Co. Offaly
Diocese: ME

Civil Parish: **Kilpatrick**
Map Grid: 8
RC Parish: Collinstown, see St. Feighin's
Diocese: ME

Civil Parish: **Lackan**
Map Grid: 15
RC Parish: see Multyfarnham
Diocese: ME

Civil Parish: **Leny**
Map Grid: 17
RC Parish: see Multyfarnham
Diocese: ME

Civil Parish: **Lickbla**
Map Grid: 2
RC Parish: Castlepollard, see Rathgarve
Diocese: ME

Civil Parish: **Lynn**
Map Grid: 56
RC Parish: see Mullingar
Diocese: ME

Civil Parish: **Mayne**
Map Grid: 3
RC Parish: Turbotstown, Coole, or Mayne
Diocese: ME
Earliest Record: b. 8.1777; m. 11.1777; d. 8.1777
Missing Dates: b. 5.1796-1.1798, 11.1820-
    4.1824, 4.1835-2.1847; m. 4.1796-1.1798,
    12.1820-5.1824, 7.1843-8.1846, 7.1863-
    11.1864; d. 11.1796-2.1803, 9.1820-4.1824,
    8.1844-1.1846, ends 12.1850

Parish Address: Rev. Christopher King, PP,
    Coole, Co. Westmeath

Civil Parish: **Moylisker**
Map Grid: 57
RC Parish: see Mullingar
Diocese: ME

Civil Parish: **Mullingar**
Map Grid: 42
RC Parish: Mullingar
Diocese: ME
Earliest Record: b. 7.1742; m. 10.1737; d. 7.1741
    (anointings from 1741-63; rents 1757)
Missing Dates: b. 4.1816-1.1833, 11.1842-
    11.1843; m. 7.1754-1.1779, 4.1824-1.1833,
    4.1859-5.1860; d. 1797-1.1833, 5.1838-2.1843
Parish Address: Rev. Wiliam Cleary, Adm,
    Cathedral House, Mullingar, Co.
    Westmeath

Civil Parish: **Multyfarnham**
Map Grid: 16
RC Parish: Multyfarnham
Diocese: ME
Earliest Record: b. 2.1824; m. 2.1824; d. 1.1831
Missing Dates: d. ends 7.1844
Parish Address: Rev. Michael Murchan, PP,
    Multyfarnham, Co. Westmeath

Civil Parish: **Newtown**
Map Grid: 53
RC Parish: see Castletown
Diocese: ME

Civil Parish: **Noughaval**
Map Grid: 29
RC Parish: see Drumraney
Diocese: ME

Civil Parish: **Pass of Kilbride**
Map Grid: 61
RC Parish: Rochfortbridge, see Castlelost
Diocese: ME

Civil Parish: **Piercetown**
Map Grid: 33
RC Parish: see Forgney, Co. Longford
Diocese: ME

Civil Parish: **Portloman**
Map Grid: 22
RC Parish: see Mullingar
Diocese: ME

Civil Parish: **Portnashangan**
Map Grid: 19
RC Parish: see Multyfarnham
Diocese: ME

Civil Parish: **Rahugh**
Map Grid: 55
RC Parish: see Kilbeggan
Diocese: ME

Civil Parish: **Rathaspick**
Map Grid: 11
RC Parish: Rathaspick and Russagh
Diocese: AD
Earliest Record: b. 3.1822; m. 12.1819; d. 3.1822
Missing Dates: b. 9.1826-7.1832, 4.1833-5.1836,
    10.1846-3.1847; m. 2.1826-10.1832, 10.1833-
    1.1838; d. 2.1826-8.1832, 11.1833-8.1837
Parish Address: Rev. Owen Devaney, Adm,
    Rathowen, Mulligar, Co. Westmeath

Civil Parish: **Rathconnell**
Map Grid: 41
RC Parish: part Taghmon; part Mullingar
Diocese: ME

Civil Parish: **Rathconrath**
Map Grid: 34
RC Parish: Milltown
Diocese: ME
Earliest Record: b. 1.1781; m. 1.1781; d. 1.1781
Missing Dates: b. 9.1808-4.1809; m. 2.1805-
    4.1809; d. 11.1808-4.1809, ends 10.1869
Parish Address: Rev. John O'Reilly, PP,
    Milltown, Rathconrath, Co. Westmeath

Civil Parish: **Rathgarve**
Map Grid: 4
RC Parish: Castlepollard
Diocese: ME
Earliest Record: b. 1.1795; m. 3.1793; d. 1.1793
Missing Dates: b. 6.1825-11.1825; m. 8.1793-
    1.1795, 6.1825-11.1825; d. ends 6.1825
Parish Address: Rev. P. J. Regan, PP,
    Castlepollard, Co. Westmeath

Civil Parish: **Russagh**
Map Grid: 10
RC Parish: see Rathaspick
Diocese: AD

Civil Parish: **St. Feighin's**
Map Grid: 5
RC Parish: Collinstown
Diocese: ME
Earliest Record: b. 2.1807; m. 6.1784; d. 4.1784
Missing Dates: b. 4.1815-3.1821, 11.1843-
    3.1844, ends 10.1849
Parish Address: Rev. Christopher Gibney, PP,
    Colinstown, Co. Westmeath

Civil Parish: **St. Mary's**
Map Grid: 6
RC Parish: Collinstown, see St. Feighin's
Diocese: ME

Civil Parish: **St. Mary's Athlone**
Map Grid: 45
RC Parish: Athlone
Diocese: ME
Earliest Record: b. 1.1813; m. 1.1813; d. 1.1813
Missing Dates: b. 9.1826-5.1839, 4.1852-2.1853;
    m. 4.1827-1.1834, 12.1851-2.1854; d. ends
    12.1826
Parish Address: Rev. James Brennan, Adm, St.
    Mary's Presbytery, Athlone, Co. Westmeath

Civil Parish: **Stonehall**
Map Grid: 18
RC Parish: see Rathconnell
Diocese: ME

Civil Parish: **Street**
Map Grid: 9
RC Parish: see Street, Co. Longford
Diocese: AD

Civil Parish: **Taghmon**
Map Grid: 21
RC Parish: Taghmon
Diocese: ME
Earliest Record: b. 9.1781; m. 1.1782; d. 9.1809
Missing Dates: b. 3.1790-3.1809, 12.1850-
    1.1864; m. 6.1791-8.1809, 5.1848-9.1868; d.
    ends 2.1848

Parish Address: Rev. Fintan Cassidy, PP, Tagh-mon, Crookedwood, Mullingar, Co. Westmeath

Civil Parish: **Templeoran**
Map Grid: 14
RC Parish: Sonna House
Diocese: ME

Civil Parish: **Templepatrick**
Map Grid: 35
RC Parish: Moyvore
Diocese: ME
Earliest Record: b. 9.1831; m. 2.1832; d. 8.1831
Missing Dates: d. 4.1852-5.1863, ends 9.1865
Parish Address: Rev. John Kiernan, Adm, Parochial House, Moyvore, Co. Westmeath

Civil Parish: **Tyfarnham**
Map Grid: 20
RC Parish: see Rathconnell
Diocese: ME

linagore, Kinnegad, Moate, Mullingar, and Tyrrell's Pass.

1870
Slater's *Directory of Ireland* contains trade, nobility, and clergy lists for Athlone, Castlepollard, Castletowndelvin, Kilbeggan, Kinnegad, Moate, and Mullingar.

1881
Slater's *Royal National Commercial Directory of Ireland* contains lists of traders, clergy, nobility, and farmers in adjoining parishes, of the towns of Athlone, Castlepollard, Castletowndelvin, Kilbeggan and Tyrrell's Pass, Moate, and Mullingar.

1894
Slater's *Royal National Directory of Ireland* lists traders, police, teachers, farmers, and private residents in each of the towns, villages, and parishes of the county.

Commercial and Social Directories

1820
J. Pigot's *Commercial Directory of Ireland* contains information on the gentry, nobility, and traders in and around the town of Athlone.

1824
J. Pigot's *City of Dublin & Hibernian Provincial Directory* includes traders, nobility, gentry, and clergy lists of Athlone, Ballymore, Castletowndelvin, Kilbeggan, Kinnegad, and Mullingar.

1846
Slater's *National Commercial Directory of Ireland* lists nobility, clergy, traders, etc., in Athlone, Castlepollard, Kilbeggan and Ballinagore, Kinnegad, and Mullingar.

1856
Slater's *Royal National Commercial Directory of Ireland* lists nobility, gentry, clergy, traders, etc., in Athlone, Castlepollard, Castletowndelvin, Kilbeggan and Bal-

Family History

"McKeoghs of Moyfinn." *J. Old Athlone Soc.* 1 (4) (1974/75): 234-37; 2 (5) (1978): 56-70.

"Magawlys of Calry." *J. Old Athlone Soc.* 1 (2) (1970/71): 61-73; 1 (3) (1972/73): 147-60.

"Malones of Westmeath." *Gaelic Gleanings* 1 (1) (1981): 9-12; 1(2): 46-48; 1 (3): 81-84; 1 (4) 127-30; 2 (1) (1982): 9-10.

"Robinson of Killogeenaghan—a West Meath Quaker Family." *Ir. Anc.* 14 (1) (1982): 1-5.

"Smyth Papers" (Drumcree, Co. Westmeath). *Anal. Hib.* (20): 279-301.

Tyrrell—see Co. Dublin.

Gravestone Inscriptions

Ballyloughloe (Mount Temple): *Ir. Anc.* 4 (2): 1972.

Delvin (St. Mary's Churchyard): *Ir. Anc* 14 (1) (1982): 39-57.

Kilcleagh, CI: Cox, Liam. *Moate, Co. Westmeath: A History of the Town and District.* N.p., 1981.

Killomenaghan, CI: Cox, Liam. *Moate, Co. Westmeath: A History of the Town and District.* N.p.,1981.

Moate (St. Mary's, CI, and Quaker graveyards): Cox, Liam. *Moate, Co. Westmeath: A History of the Town and District.* N.p.,1981.

Street: *Riocht na Midhe* 4 (3) (1969): 28-29.

Newspapers

There were no newspapers published in this county before 1823. For earlier notices relevant to the county the newspapers from neighboring counties should be searched depending on the area of interest within the county.

Title: *Athlone Conservative Advocate & Ballinasloe Reporter*
Published in: Athlone, 1837
NLI Holdings: 6-9.1837
BL Holdings: 6-9.1837

Title: *Athlone Independent*
Published in: Athlone, 1833-36
NLI Holdings: 11.1833-11.1836
BL Holdings: 11.1833-11.1836

Title: *Athlone Mirror, Westmeath & Roscommon Reformer*
Published in: Athlone, 1841-42
NLI Holdings: 9.1841-7.1842
BL Holdings: 9.1841-7.1842

Title: *Athlone Sentinel*
Published in: Athlone, 1834-61
NLI Holdings: odd numbers 1846-47
BL Holdings: 11.1834-7.1861

Title: *Athlone Times*
Published in: Athlone, 1889-1902
NLI Holdings: 1899
BL Holdings: 5.1889-1.1902

Title: *Westmeath Examiner*
Published in: Mullingar, 1882-current
NLI Holdings: 1.1906-in progress
BL Holdings: 9.1882-in progress

Title: *Westmeath Guardian and Longford Newsletter*
Published in: Mullingar, 1835-1928
NLI Holdings: 6.1921-10.1928
BL Holdings: 1.1835-10.1928

Title: *Westmeath Herald*
Published in: Athlone, 1859-60
BL Holdings: 4.1859-4.1860

Title: *Westmeath Independent*
Published in: Athlone, 1846-1968
NLI Holdings: 1.1885-12.1913; 2.1923-7.1968
BL Holdings: 6.1846-8.1880; odd numbers 1881-84; 2.1884-10.1920; 2.1922-7.1968

Title: *Westmeath Journal*
Published in: Mullingar, 1823-34
BL Holdings: 1.1823-5.1834

Title: *Westmeath Nationalist & Midland Reporter* (*Midland Reporter* from 1897)
Published in: Mullingar, 1891-1939
BL Holdings: 4.1891-12.1928; 1-10.1930; 1.1931-9.1939

Wills and Administrations

A discussion of the types of records, where they are held, their availability and value is given in the Wills section of the Introduction. The availability of prerogative wills, administrations, and marriage license records is also described in the relevant parts of the same section. Where available, published sources of these records are given in the Miscellaneous Sources section.

Pre-1858 Wills and Administrations

Prerogative Wills. see p. xli.
Consistorial Wills. County Westmeath is mainly in the diocese of Meath with three parishes in Ardagh. The guide to Catholic parish records in this chapter shows the diocese to

which each civil parish belonged. The wills of residents of each diocese were usually proven within that diocese (see the Wills section for exceptions). The following records survive:

Wills. see p. xxxvii.

Abstracts. see p. xxxvii. The Upton papers also contain Westmeath abstracts. RIA Library.

Indexes. Meath – see Co. Meath; Ardagh (1695-1858) published in *Ir. Anc.* (1971).

Post-1858 Wills and Administrations

This county was served by the District Registry of Mullingar. The surviving records are in the PRO.

Marriage Licenses

Indexes. Meath and Ardagh (1691-1845). PRO; SLC film 100869.

Miscellaneous Sources

"Athlone in the Civil War 1641-1652." *Irish Sword* 10 (38) (1977): 38-55.

"Constabulary Employed in the District of Moate, Co. Westmeath." *Ir. Anc.* 7 (1) (1975): 35-38.

Cox, Liam. *Moate, Co. Westmeath, A History of the Town and District.* Athlone, 1981 (history of the area with extensive family references).

"Early 19th Century Lists of Protestant Parishioners in the Dioceses of Meath." *Ir. Anc.* 5 (2) (1973): 113-26.

Grand Juries of Westmeath 1727 to 1853 with Their Genealogies. NLI 34779.

Kieran, K. *Bibliography of the History of Co. Westmeath.* Mullingar, 1959.

"Westmeath in the 1798 Period." *Irish Sword* 9 (1969) 34: 1-15.

Research Sources and Services

Journals

Riocht na Midhe (published by Meath Archaeological and Historical Society, see Research Sources and Services section, Co. Meath)

Libraries and Information Sources

County Library, Dublin Road, Mullingar, Co. Westmeath Ph: (044) 40781/2/3

Research Services

See research services in Dublin, p. xliv

Offaly Heritage Centre (see Research Sources and Services section, Co. Offaly)

Societies

Old Athlone Society, Miss N. Egan, 'Lara', Court Devenish, Athlone, Co. Westmeath

Moate Historical Society, Mr. Jeremiah Sheehan, 'Avila', Moate, Co. Westmeath

CIVIL PARISHES OF COUNTY WESTMEATH

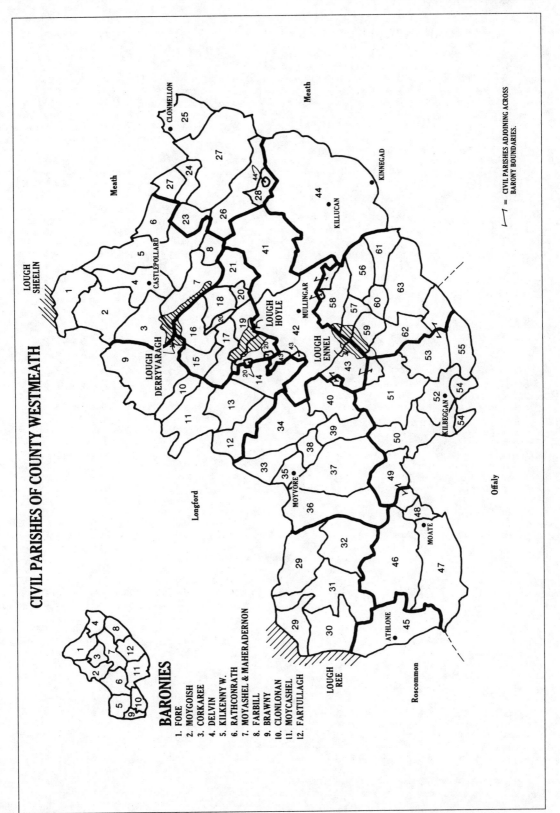

BARONIES

1. FORE
2. MOYGOISH
3. CORKAREE
4. DELVIN
5. KILKENNY W.
6. RATHCONRATH
7. MOYASHEL & MAHERADERNON
8. FARBILL
9. BRAWNY
10. CLONLONAN
11. MOYCASHEL
12. FARTULLAGH

⌐ = CIVIL PARISHES ADJOINING ACROSS BARONY BOUNDARIES.

LOUGH SHEELIN

Meath

Meath

CLONMELLON

KINNEGAD

KILLUCAN

CASTLEPOLLARD

MULLINGAR

LOUGH DERRYVARAGH

LOUGH HOYLE

LOUGH ENNEL

KILBEGGAN

Longford

MOYVORE

MOATE

Offaly

LOUGH REE

ATHLONE

Roscommon

County Wexford

A Brief History

Located in the southeastern corner of Ireland, County Wexford contains the towns of Wexford, Enniscorthy, New Ross, and Gorey. The county was traditionally the territory of the McMurroughs, Kavanaghs, and Kinsellas. Other Irish families in the county included O'Day, O'Leary, Murphy, O'Byrne, O'Dugan, and Bolger.

A settlement on the site of Wexford town was shown on the maps drawn by Ptolemy in the second century A.D. The modern town of Wexford was founded and named (Waesfjord) by the Norse Vikings as a trading settlement in the ninth or tenth century and became a large town and a major port. Following the Norman invasion the Norse were driven from Wexford town to the area around Rosslare where they gradually assimilated into the local population. However, because the Norse did not use surnames, there is little evidence of their heritage in the family names of the county.

It was in County Wexford that the first Normans, led by Robert Fitzstephen, landed in 1169. Evidence of their establishment in Wexford can be seen in the many Norman names now common in the county. These include Sinnott, Esmond, Stafford, Codd, Furlong, Wadding, Hore, and Devereux. The name Meyler, of Welsh origin, is also found in the county since Norman times. These Norman invaders gradually assimilated into the native population except in the baronies of Bargy and Forth where, cut off from the rest of the county, they developed a distinct culture and a dialect, called Yola, which is a mixture of old English and Irish. This survived until the nineteenth century.

In 1610 there was a small plantation of the county in which part of the land of the McMurroughs in the northern part of the county was confiscated and given to English settlers. The McMurroughs, in return, got full title to the remainder of their lands. As a result of local protests over this plantation, many local families were transported to Virginia. The records of contemporary Virginia settlements show many Murphy, Bolger, Kavanagh, and Byrne families. In 1641, Wexford joined the rebellion of the "Confederacy" of Irish Catholics (see Co. Kilkenny) and Wexford town became one of the major centers. In 1649 Oliver Cromwell besieged Wexford and, on its surrender, massacred the inhabitants. The lands of the rebel chieftains were confiscated and many were transported to the West Indies, or ordered to move west of the Shannon. Their lands were given either to those loyal to the English Parliament or as payment to Cromwell's soldiers and officers.

In 1661 many hundreds of English families were brought into Enniscorthy to man the ironworks which were growing rapidly in that town. The county was not extensively involved in the Williamite/Jacobite conflict of the 1690s.

The county was a major center of the 1798 rebellion of the United Irishmen. A huge army of Wexfordmen, incited by the burning of a church at Boolavogue, took Wexford and Enniscorthy and controlled the entire county. The insurgents were finally defeated at Vinegar Hill near Enniscorthy.

The county has always been noted for its prosperous farms and industrious farmers. Perhaps for this reason it was less affected than many others by the Great Famine of 1845-47. The rural population density in 1841 was one of the lowest in the country at 217 persons per square mile. The total population in 1841 was 202,000, and ten years later it had fallen to 180,000. There was considerable emigration, particularly from the north of the county. As elsewhere, emigration continued throughout the nineteenth century. The population by 1891 was 112,000 and is currently around 100,000.

Wexford is commonly regarded as an ethnically distinct part of the country because of the blend of Irish, Norse, and Norman blood.

Census and Census Substitutes

1654-56
Civil Survey. Vol. 9.

1659
"Census" of Ireland. Edited by S. Pender. Dublin: Stationery Office, 1939; SLC film 924648; some baronies in *The Past*, vols. 4 and 5.

1766
Religious Census of Parish of Ballynaslaney PRO 1A 41 100.

Protestants in Parish of Edermine (list householders, names of wives, and total number of children and servants). GO 537; SLC film 258517.

1775
Catholic Qualification Roll Extracts (twen-

ty-three names, addresses, and occupations). 59th Report DKPRI: 50-84.

1776
"The Freemen of Wexford." *Ir. Gen.* 5 (1) (1973): 103-21; 5 (3) (1973): 314-34; 5 (4) (1973): 448-63.

1789
"Protestant Householders in the Parish of Ferns." *Ir. Anc.* 13 (2) (1981): 93-94.

1792
Some Protestant Householders in the Parishes of Ballycanew and Killtrisk. *Ir. Anc.* 13 (2) (1981): 93-94.

1798
List of Persons Who Suffered Loss in '98 Rebellion. NLI JLB 94107 (over 2,000 names, addresses, and occupations).

1821
Extracts from Government Census for St. Mary's Parish (New Ross) mainly for surnames Walsh and Kelly. QUB; SLC film 100158.

1823-38
Tithe Applotment Survey (see p. xxvii).

1853
Griffith's valuation (see p. xxvii).

1861
Census of Inhabitants of the Catholic Parish of St. Mary's, Enniscorthy on April 17, 1861. (included in the parish register, see RC records section; possibly a copy of official census – now destroyed).

1867
Census of Catholics in the RC parish of Marshalstown and Kilmeashal (in parish register: see Monart, RC records section); *Ir. Gen.* 6 (5) (1984).

1901
Census. PRO.

1911
Census. PRO.

Church Records

Church of Ireland
(shows starting date of record)

Parish: **Ardamine**
Existing Records: b. 1807; m. 1807; d. 1807
Status: LC

Parish: **Ardcandrisk** (see Wexford)

Parish: **Ardcolm**
Status: Lost

Parish: **Ballycanew**
Existing Records: b. 1733; m. 1733; d. 1733
Status: LC

Parish: **Ballycarney**
Existing Records: b. 1835; m. 1836; d. 1836
Status: LC

Parish: **Ballyhuskard** (see also St. Mary's Enniscorthy)
Status: Lost

Parish: **Bannon**
Status: Lost

Parish: **Carne**
Status: Lost

Parish: **Carnew**
Existing Records: b. 1808; m. 1808; d. 1808
Status: LC

Parish: **Carrig** (see Wexford)

Parish: **Castlebridge** (see Ardcolm)

Parish: **Churchtown**
Status: Lost

Parish: **Clone** (see also Ferns and Kilbride)
Status: Lost

Parish: **Clonegal**
Existing Records: b. 1792; m. 1792; d. 1792
Status: LC

Parish: **Coolstuff**
Status: Lost

Parish: **Duncormick**
Existing Records: b. 1760; m. 1760; d. 1760
Status: LC

Parish: **Edermine**
Status: Lost

Parish: **Ferns** and **Kilbride**
Existing Records: b. 1775; m. 1775; d. 1775
Status: LC

Parish: **Fethard**
Status: Lost

Parish: **Glasscarrig**
Existing Records: b. 1835; m. 1835; d. 1807
Status: LC

Parish: **Gorey**
Existing Records: (volume acquired by purchase from papers of Dr. R. Caulfield.) b. 1801; m. 1801; d. 1867
Status: LC

Parish: **Hooke** and **Templetown**
Status: Lost

Parish: **Horetown**
Status: Lost

Parish: **Inch**
Existing Records: b. 1726; m. 1726; d. 1726
Status: LC

Parish: **Kilcormick**
Status: Lost

Parish: **Killann**
Existing Records: b. 1771; m. 1771; d. 1795
Status: LC

Parish: **Killegney**
Existing Records: b. 1800; m. 1800; d. 1800
Status: LC

Parish: **Killesk**
Existing Records: b. 1788; d. 1788
Status: LC

Parish: **Killinick and Ballybrennan**
Status: Lost

Parish: **Killurin**
Existing Records: b. 1816; m. 1798; d. 1816
Status: LC

Parish: **Kilmallog**
Existing Records: b. 1813; m. 1813; d. 1813
Status: LC

Parish: **Kilmuckridge** or **Ballyvalden**
Status: Lost

Parish: **Kilnehue** (see also Gorey)
Existing Records: b. 1817; m. 1817; d. 1817
Status: LC

Parish: **Kilnemanagh**
Existing Records: b. 1818; d. 1818
Missing Dates: b. ends 1836; d. ends 1836
Status: LC

Parish: **Kilpatrick**
Status: Lost

Parish: **Kilrane** (see Tacumshane)

Parish: **Kilrush**
Status: Lost

Parish: **Kilscorane** (see Tacumshane)

Parish: **Kiltennell**
Existing Records: b. 1806; m. 1806; d. 1806
Status: LC

Parish: **Leskinfere**
Existing Records: b. 1802; m. 1802; d. 1802
Status: LC

Parish: **Monamolin**
Status: Lost

Parish: **Monart**
Status: Lost

Parish: **Mulrankin**
Existing Records: b. 1786; m. 1786; d. 1786
Status: LC

Parish: **Newtownbarry**
Existing Records: b. 1779; m. 1779; d. 1779
Status: LC

Parish: **Old Ross** (see also St. Mary, New Ross)
Status: Lost

Parish: **Owenduff**
Existing Records: (with lists of baptisms, marriages, and burials 1806-29, and register of baptisms, marriages, and burials 1841-92) b. 1752; m. 1752; d. 1752
Status: LC

Parish: **Rathaspick**
Existing Records: b. 1844; m. 1844; d. 1844
Status: LC

Parish: **Rathmacknee**
Status: Lost

Parish: **Rossdroit**
Existing Records: b. 1828; m. 1832; d. 1828
Status: LC

Parish: **St. Iberius, Wexford** (see Wexford)

Parish: **St. Mary** (see Wexford)

Parish: **St. Mary, Enniscorthy**
Existing Records: b. 1798; m. 1798; d. 1798
Status: LC

Parish: **St. Mary, New Ross**
Existing Records: b. 1763; m. 1764; d. 1764
Status: LC

Parish: **St. Michael of Feagh** (see Wexford)

Parish: **St. Patrick** (see Wexford)

Parish: **St. Peter** (see Wexford)

Parish: **St. Selsker** (see Wexford)

Parish: **St. Tullogue** (see Wexford)

Parish: **Tacumshane (Union of Kilscoran)**
Existing Records: b. 1832; m. 1832; d. 1832
Status: LC

Parish: **Taghmon**
Status: Lost

Parish: **Templescobin**
Existing Records: b. 1802; m. 1819; d. 1835
Status: LC

Parish: **Templeshanbow**
Existing Records: b. 1815; m. 1815; d. 1815
Status: LC

Parish: **Templeshannon** (see St. Mary, Enniscorthy)

Parish: **Templetown** (see Hooke)

Parish: **Templeudigan** (see also St. Mary, New Ross)
Status: Lost

Parish: **Tomhaggard**
Existing Records: b. 1809; m. 1813; d. 1809
Status: LC

Parish: **Toombe**
Existing Records: b. 1770; m. 1770; d. 1770
Missing Dates: b. 1819-20, ends 1821; m. 1819-20, ends 1821; d. 1819-20, ends 1821
Status: LC

Parish: **Wexford**
Existing Records: b. 1674; m. 1674; d. 1674
Missing Dates: b. 1754-77; m. 1754-77; d. 1754-77
Status: LC

Parish: **Whitechurch** and **Kilmokea**
Status: Lost

Presbyterian

Parish: **Wexford**
Starting Date: 1844

Roman Catholic

Civil Parish: **Adamstown**
Map Grid: 50
RC Parish: Adamstown
Diocese: FE
Earliest Record: b. 1.1807 (2 registers at some periods); m. 12.1849; d. 9.1823
Missing Dates: b. 10.1848-4.1849; d. ends 1.1832
Parish Address: Rev. Noel Hartley, PP, Adamstown, Wexford

Civil Parish: **Allock**
Map Grid: 65
RC Parish: Crossabeg, see Kilpatrick
Diocese: FE

Civil Parish: **Ambrosetown**
Map Grid: 102
RC Parish: part Bannow; part Rathangan, see Duncormick
Diocese: FE

Civil Parish: **Ardamine**
Map Grid: 30
RC Parish: Ballygarrett, see Kiltennell
Diocese: FE

Civil Parish: **Ardcandrisk**
Map Grid: 71
RC Parish: Glynn, see Killurin
Diocese: FE

Civil Parish: **Ardcavan**
Map Grid: 85
RC Parish: Castlebridge, see Ardcolm
Diocese: FE

Civil Parish: **Ardcolm**
Map Grid: 86
RC Parish: Castlebridge
Diocese: FE

Earliest Record: b. 10.1832; m. 12.1832
Parish Address: Rev. Declan Cleary, PP,
    Castlebridge, Co. Wexford

Civil Parish: **Artramont**
Map Grid: 84
RC Parish: Crossabeg, see Kilpatrick
Diocese: FE

Civil Parish: **Ballingly**
Map Grid: 80
RC Parish: Ballymitty, see Bannow
Diocese: FE

Civil Parish: **Ballyanne**
Map Grid: 46
RC Parish: Cushinstown, see Carnagh
Diocese: FE

Civil Parish: **Ballybrazil**
Map Grid: 89
RC Parish: Sutton's, see Kilmokea
Diocese: FE

Civil Parish: **Ballybrennan**
Map Grid: 126
RC Parish: Tagoat
Diocese: FE

Civil Parish: **Ballycanew**
Map Grid: 24
RC Parish: Camolin, see Toome
Diocese: FE

Civil Parish: **Ballycarney**
Map Grid: 6
RC Parish: see Ferns
Diocese: FE

Civil Parish: **Ballyconnick**
Map Grid: 103
RC Parish: Rathangan, see Duncormick
Diocese: FE

Civil Parish: **Ballyhoge**
Map Grid: 53
RC Parish: Bree, see Clonmore
Diocese: FE

Civil Parish: **Ballyhuskard**
Map Grid: 58

RC Parish: part Oylegate, see Edermine; part
    Oulart
Diocese: FE

Civil Parish: **Ballylannon**
Map Grid: 79
RC Parish: see Clongeen
Diocese: FE

Civil Parish: **Ballymitty**
Map Grid: 81
RC Parish: see Bannow
Diocese: FE

Civil Parish: **Ballymore**
Map Grid: 129
RC Parish: Ballymore (and Mayglass)
Diocese: FE
Earliest Record: b. 5.1840; m. 2.1840
Parish Address: Rev. N. Doyle, PP, Ballymore,
    Killinick, Co. Wexford

Civil Parish: **Ballynaslaney**
Map Grid: 64
RC Parish: Oylegate, see Edermine
Diocese: FE

Civil Parish: **Ballyvaldon**
Map Grid: 62
RC Parish: Blackwater, see Killila
Diocese: FE

Civil Parish: **Ballyvaloo**
Map Grid: 68
RC Parish: Blackwater, see Killila
Diocese: FE

Civil Parish: **Bannow**
Map Grid: 105
RC Parish: Bannow or Carrick-on-Bannow
Diocese: FE
Earliest Record: b. 8.1832; m. 9.1830
Parish Address: Rev. Henry Sinnott, PP, Ban-
    now, Wexford, Co. Wexford

Civil Parish: **Carne**
Map Grid: 138
RC Parish: see Lady's Island
Diocese: FE

Civil Parish: **Carnagh**
Map Grid: 54
RC Parish: Carnagh (Cushinstown)
Diocese: FE
Earliest Record: b. 1.1759; m. 11.1752; d. 5.1794
Missing Dates: b. 8.1759-1.1778, 1.1830-7.1851;
   m. 2.1759-1.1778, 2.1824-8.1851, 9.1862-
   4.1863; d. 7.1808-5.1863
Parish Address: Rev. Vincent Buckley, PP,
   Cushinstown, Newbawn, Wexford, Co. Wex-
   ford

Civil Parish: **Carnew**
Map Grid: 3
RC Parish: see Carnew, Co. Wicklow
Diocese: FE

Civil Parish: **Carrick**
Map Grid: 78
RC Parish: Glynn, see Killurin
Diocese: FE

Civil Parish: **Castle-ellis**
Map Grid: 60
RC Parish: part Oulart; part Blackwater, see
   Killila
Diocese: FE

Civil Parish: **Chapel** (Charon)
Map Grid: 44
RC Parish: Glynn, see Killurin; see also Killeg-
   ney
Diocese: FE

Civil Parish: **Clone**
Map Grid: 11
RC Parish: Monageer (separate register for
   Boolavague, Monagear, for b. 1842 and m.
   1847)
Diocese: FE
Earliest Record: b. 11.1838; m. 11.1838; d.
   8.1838
Parish Address: Rev. James Greenan, PP,
   Monageer, Ferns, Co. Wexford

Civil Parish: **Clongeen**
Map Grid: 72
RC Parish: Clongeen
Diocese: FE
Earliest Record: b. 1.1847; m. 4.1847

Parish Address: Rev. Matthew L. Cleary, PP,
   Clongeen, Foulksmills, Co. Wexford

Civil Parish: **Clonleigh**
Map Grid: 42
RC Parish: see Killegney
Diocese: FE

Civil Parish: **Clonmines**
Map Grid: 97
RC Parish: see Tintern
Diocese: FE

Civil Parish: **Clonmore**
Map Grid: 45
RC Parish: Bree; also part Davidstown, see
   Templescoby
Diocese: FE
Earliest Record: b. 1.1837; m. 1.1837
Parish Address: Rev. Aidan Kavanagh, PP,
   Bree, Enniscorthy, Co. Wexford

Civil Parish: **Coolstuff**
Map Grid: 76
RC Parish: part Glynn, see Killurin; part Tagh-
   mon
Diocese: FE

Civil Parish: **Crosspatrick**
Map Grid: 13
RC Parish: Tomacork, see Carnew, Co. Wick-
   low
Diocese: FE

Civil Parish: **Donaghmore**
Map Grid: 31
RC Parish: Ballygarrett, see Kiltennell
Diocese: FE

Civil Parish: **Donowney**
Map Grid: 51
RC Parish: part Taghmon; part Newbawn, see
   Inch
Diocese: FE

Civil Parish: **Drinagh**
Map Grid: 120
RC Parish: Piercestown, see Rathmacknee
Diocese: FE

Civil Parish: **Duncormick**
Map Grid: 106
RC Parish: Rathangan
Diocese: FE
Earliest Record: b. 1.1803; m. 6.1803
Missing Dates: b. 8.1805-1.1813; m. 6.1806-
1.1813
Parish Address: Rev. Felix Byrne, PP, Rathan-
gan, Duncormick, Co. Wexford

Civil Parish: **Edermine**
Map Grid: 63
RC Parish: Oylegate
Diocese: FE
Earliest Record: b. 3.1804; m. 4.1803
Missing Dates: b. 12.1820-8.1832; m. 10.1820-
10.1832
Parish Address: Rev. Tobias Kinsella, PP,
Oylegate, Co. Wexford

Civil Parish: **Ferns**
Map Grid: 7
RC Parish: Ferns
Diocese: FE
Earliest Record: b. 5.1819; m. 5.1819
Missing Dates: b. 2.1840-9.1840; m. 1.1840-
11.1840
Parish Address: Rev. Patrick Doyle, PP, Ferns,
Co. Wexford

Civil Parish: **Fethard**
Map Grid: 99
RC Parish: see Templetown
Diocese: FE

Civil Parish: **Hook**
Map Grid: 100
RC Parish: see Templetown
Diocese: FE

Civil Parish: **Horetown**
Map Grid: 74
RC Parish: part Adamstown; part Taghmon
Diocese: FE

Civil Parish: **Inch** (near Clongeen)
Map Grid: 73
RC Parish: see Clongeen
Diocese: DU

Civil Parish: **Inch** (near Kilgorman)
Map Grid: 16
RC Parish: Arklow, see Co. Wicklow
Diocese: FE

Civil Parish: **Ishartmon**
Map Grid: 133
RC Parish: see Ballymore
Diocese: FE

Civil Parish: **Kerloge**
Map Grid: 117
RC Parish: see Wexford
Diocese: FE

Civil Parish: **Kilbride**
Map Grid: 8
RC Parish: see Ferns
Diocese: FE

Civil Parish: **Kilbrideglynn**
Map Grid: 77
RC Parish: Glynn, see Killurin
Diocese: FE

Civil Parish: **Kilcavan** (near Gorey)
Map Grid: 19
RC Parish: Kilanieran, see Kilnenor
Diocese: FE

Civil Parish: **Kilcavan** (near Bannow)
Map Grid: 101
RC Parish: see Bannow
Diocese: FE

Civil Parish: **Kilcomb**
Map Grid: 4
RC Parish: see Ferns
Diocese: FE

Civil Parish: **Kilcormick**
Map Grid: 25
RC Parish: part Monageer, see Clone; part
Oulart, see Meelnagh
Diocese: FE

Civil Parish: **Kilcowan**
Map Grid: 107
RC Parish: Rathangan, see Duncormick
Diocese: FE

Civil Parish: **Kilcowanmore**
Map Grid: 52
RC Parish: Bree, see Clonmore
Diocese: FE

Civil Parish: **Kildavin**
Map Grid: 118
RC Parish: Piercestown, see Rathmacknee
Diocese: FE

Civil Parish: **Kilgarvan**
Map Grid: 69
RC Parish: see Taghmon
Diocese: FE

Civil Parish: **Kilgorman**
Map Grid: 17
RC Parish: Arklow, see Co. Wicklow
Diocese: DU

Civil Parish: **Killag**
Map Grid: 109
RC Parish: Rathangan, see Duncormick
Diocese: FE

Civil Parish: **Killann**
Map Grid: 36
RC Parish: see Killegney
Diocese: FE

Civil Parish: **Killegney**
Map Grid: 43
RC Parish: Killegney (Cloughbawn)
Diocese: FE
Earliest Record: b. 3.1816; m. 3.1816; d. 3.1816
Missing Dates: b. 9.1850-1.1853; m. 9.1850-2.1853; d. 9.1850-2.1861
Parish Address: Rev. Brendan Kirby, PP, Clonroche, Enniscorthy, Co. Wexford

Civil Parish: **Killenagh**
Map Grid: 29
RC Parish: part Ballygarrett, see Kiltennell; part Monamolin
Diocese: FE

Civil Parish: **Killesk**
Map Grid: 93
RC Parish: Sutton's, see Kilmokea
Diocese: FE

Civil Parish: **Killiane**
Map Grid: 122
RC Parish: Piercestown, see Rathmackee
Diocese: FE

Civil Parish: **Killila**
Map Grid: 61
RC Parish: Blackwater
Diocese: FE
Earliest Record: b. 1.1815 (only few legible entries before 1818); m. 1.1815; d. 1.1843
Parish Address: Rev. Seamus Cummins, PP, Blackwater, Co. Wexford

Civil Parish: **Killincooly**
Map Grid: 33
RC Parish: see Kilmuckridge
Diocese: FE

Civil Parish: **Killinick**
Map Grid: 125
RC Parish: Moyglass, see Ballymore
Diocese: FE

Civil Parish: **Killisk**
Map Grid: 59
RC Parish: part Castlebridge, see Ardcolm; part Oulart, see Meelnagh
Diocese: FE

Civil Parish: **Killurin**
Map Grid: 70
RC Parish: Glynn
Diocese: FE
Earliest Record: b. 1.1817; m. 1.1817; d. 1.1823
Parish Address: Rev. James Finn, PP, Glynn, Co. Wexford

Civil Parish: **Kilmacree**
Map Grid: 123
RC Parish: Piercestown, see Rathmacknee
Diocese: FE

Civil Parish: **Kilmakilloge**
Map Grid: 21
RC Parish: Gorey
Diocese: FE
Earliest Record: b. 5.1845; m. 6.1845
Parish Address: Rev. John Gahan, PP, Gorey, Co. Wexford

Civil Parish: **Kilmannon**
Map Grid: 104
RC Parish: Rathangan, see Duncormick
Diocese: FE

Civil Parish: **Kilmokea**
Map Grid: 92
RC Parish: Suttons (Horsewood)
Diocese: FE
Earliest Record: (separate registers for Suttons, Ballykelly, from 1862) b. 11.1824; m. 2.1825; d. 5.1827
Missing Dates: d. 11.1836-1.1858
Parish Address: Rev. William Anglim, PP, Horeswood, Campile, Co. Wexford

Civil Parish: **Kilmore**
Map Grid: 110
RC Parish: Kilmore
Diocese: FE
Earliest Record: b. 4.1752; m. 4.1752; d. 4.1752
Missing Dates: b. 3.1785-6.1790, 11.1794-1.1798, 3.1826-7.1828; m. 3.1785-6.1790, 11.1794-1.1798, 3.1826-11.1827; d. 3.1785-6.1790, 11.1794-1.1798, ends 3.1826
Parish Address: Rev. Thomas O'Neill, PP, Kilmore, Wexford

Civil Parish: **Kilmuckridge**
Map Grid: 34
RC Parish: Kilmuckridge (Litter)
Diocese: FE
Earliest Record: b. 10.1789; m. 1.1788
Missing Dates: m. 4.1798-9.1806
Parish Address: Rev. Edmund Connolly, PP, Kilmuckridge, Co. Wexford

Civil Parish: **Kilnahue**
Map Grid: 18
RC Parish: Craanford, see Rossminoge
Diocese: FE

Civil Parish: **Kilnamanagh**
Map Grid: 32
RC Parish: Oulart, see Meelnagh
Diocese: FE

Civil Parish: **Kilnenor**
Map Grid: 15
RC Parish: Kilanieran
Diocese: FE

Earliest Record: b. 1.1852; m. 1.1852
Parish Address: Rev. Patrick O'Brien, PP, Kilanerin, Gorey, Co. Wexford

Civil Parish: **Kilpatrick**
Map Grid: 83
RC Parish: Crossabeg
Diocese: FE
Earliest Record: b. 1.1856
Parish Address: Rev. Michael McCarthy, PP, Crossabeg, Co. Wexford

Civil Parish: **Kilpipe**
Map Grid: 14
RC Parish: Killaveny, see Kilpipe, Co. Wicklow
Diocese: FE

Civil Parish: **Kilrane**
Map Grid: 131
RC Parish: Tagoat
Diocese: FE

Civil Parish: **Kilrush**
Map Grid: 2
RC Parish: Kilrush
Diocese: FE
Earliest Record: b. 5.1841
Missing Dates: b. 11.1846-3.1855
Parish Address: Ref. Patrick O'Keeffe, PP, Kilrush, Co. Wexford

Civil Parish: **Kilscanlan**
Map Grid: 55
RC Parish: Cushinstown, see Carnagh
Diocese: FE

Civil Parish: **Kilscoran**
Map Grid: 130
RC Parish: Tagoat
Diocese: FE

Civil Parish: **Kiltennell**
Map Grid: 28
RC Parish: Ballygarrett
Diocese: FE
Earliest Record: b. 11.1828; m. 8.1828; d. 8.1830
Missing Dates: b. ends 1863; m. ends 1865; d. 4.1857-10.1865, ends 4.1867
Parish Address: Rev. Patrick Doyle, PP, Ballygarrett, Gorey, Co. Wexford

Civil Parish: **Kiltrisk**
Map Grid: 27
RC Parish: Ballygarrett, see Kiltennell
Diocese: FE

Civil Parish: **Kilturk**
Map Grid: 111
RC Parish: see Kilmore
Diocese: FE

Civil Parish: **Lady's Island**
Map Grid: 136
RC Parish: Lady's Island
Diocese: FE
Earliest Record: b. 8.1737; m. 2.1753; d. 6.1868
Missing Dates: b. 5.1740-5.1752, 3.1763-1.1766,
    12.1802-1.1807, 1.1818-10.1827; m. 12.1759-
    2.1764, 5.1800-1.1807, 2.1818-10.1827; ends
    2.1838
Parish Address: Rev. Robert Staples, PP, Our
    Lady's Island, Broadway, Co. Wexford

Civil Parish: **Liskinfere**
Map Grid: 23
RC Parish: Camolin, see Toome
Diocese: FE

Civil Parish: **Maudlintown**
Map Grid: 116
RC Parish: see Wexford
Diocese: FE

Civil Parish: **Mayglass**
Map Grid: 124
RC Parish: see Ballymore
Diocese: FE

Civil Parish: **Meelnagh**
Map Grid: 35
RC Parish: Oulart
Diocese: FE
Earliest Record: b. 10.1837; m. 11.1837
Missing Dates: b. 1.1853-10.1863; m. 11.1852-
    11.1874
Parish Address: Rev. S. de Val, PP, Oulart,
    Gorey, Co. Wexford

Civil Parish: **Monamolin**
Map Grid: 26
RC Parish: Monamolin; also part Kilmuckridge
Diocese: FE

Earliest Record: b. 3.1858; m. 10.1859
Parish Address: see Kilmuckridge

Civil Parish: **Monart**
Map Grid: 10
RC Parish: Marshalstown; also part Ballindag-
    gin, see Templeshanbo
Diocese: FE
Earliest Record: b. 5.1854; m. 11.1854; d.
    10.1854
Parish Address: Rev. Brendan Kehoe, PP, Mar-
    shallstown, Enniscorthy, Co. Wexford

Civil Parish: **Moyacomb**
Map Grid: 1
RC Parish: see Co. Wicklow and Co. Carlow
Diocese: FE

Civil Parish: **Mulrankin**
Map Grid: 108
RC Parish: see Kilmore
Diocese: FE

Civil Parish: **Newbawn**
Map Grid: 49
RC Parish: see Adamstown
Diocese: FE

Civil Parish: **Oldross**
Map Grid: 48
RC Parish: Cushinstown, see Carnagh
Diocese: FE

Civil Parish: **Owenduff**
Map Grid: 91
RC Parish: see Tintern
Diocese: FE

Civil Parish: **Rathaspick**
Map Grid: 119
RC Parish: Piercestown (separate register for
    Murrintown, 1839-54), see Rathmacknee
Diocese: FE

Civil Parish: **Rathmacknee**
Map Grid: 121
RC Parish: Piercestown
Diocese: FE
Earliest Record: b. 12.1811; m. 1.1812
Parish Address: Rev. James B. Curtis, PP, Pier-
    cestown, Co. Wexford

Civil Parish: **Rathroe**
Map Grid: 95
RC Parish: Hook, see Templetown
Diocese: FE

Civil Parish: **Rossdroit**
Map Grid: 38
RC Parish: Rathnure
Diocese: FE
Earliest Record: b. m. and d. 10.1846
Parish Address: Rev. Patrick McDonald, PP, Rathnure, Co. Wexford

Civil Parish: **Rosslare**
Map Grid: 128
RC Parish: Tagoat and Kilrane
Diocese: FE
Earliest Record: b. 1.1853; m. 2.1853; d. 10.1875
Parish Address: Rev. Patrick Browne, PP, Tagoat, Co. Wexford

Civil Parish: **Rossminoge**
Map Grid: 20
RC Parish: Craanford
Diocese: FE
Earliest Record: b. 8.1871; m. 11.1871
Parish Address: Rev. Francis Staples, PP, Craanford, Gorey, Co. Wexford

Civil Parish: **St. Bridget**
Map Grid: 114
RC Parish: see Wexford
Diocese: FE

Civil Parish: **St. Doologe**
Map Grid: 116
RC Parish: see Wexford
Diocese: FE

Civil Parish: **St. Helen**
Map Grid: 132
RC Parish: Tagoat, see Rosslare
Diocese: FE

Civil Parish: **St. Iberius**
Map Grid: 135
RC Parish: see Lady's Island
Diocese: FE

Civil Parish: **St. Iberius**
Map Grid: 114

RC Parish: see Wexford
Diocese: FE

Civil Parish: **St. James and Dunbrody**
Map Grid: 94
RC Parish: see Templetown
Diocese: FE

Civil Parish: **St. John (1)** (near Wexford)
Map Grid: 113
RC Parish: Davidstown, see Templescoby
Diocese: FE

Civil Parish: **St. John (2)** (near Enniscorthy)
Map Grid: 40
RC Parish: part Davidstown, see Templescoby; part St. Mary's, Enniscorthy
Diocese: FE

Civil Parish: **St. Mary**
Map Grid: 114
RC Parish: see Wexford
Diocese: FE

Civil Parish: **St. Mary Enniscorthy**
Map Grid: 12
RC Parish: St. Mary Enniscorthy
Diocese: FE
Earliest Record: b. 5.1794; m. 5.1794; d. 10.1815
Missing Dates: m. ends 11.1861
Parish Address: Rev. T. Eustace, Adm, St. Aidan's, Enniscorthy, Co. Wexford

Civil Parish: **St. Mary, New Ross**
Map Grid: 47
RC Parish: New Ross
Diocese: FE
Earliest Record: b. 11.1789; m. 2.1859; d. 5.1794
Missing Dates: d. 4.1822-11.1851, ends 2.1849
Parish Address: Ven. Wiliam J. Shiggins, PP, New Ross, Co. Wexford

Civil Parish: **St. Mary, Newtownbarry**
Map Grid: 5
RC Parish: Newtownbarry
Diocese: FE
Earliest Record: b. 1834; m. 5.1834; d. 1834;
Missing Dates: d. 1857-1858, 1872-1873
Parish Address: Rev. Richard Breen, PP, Bunclody, Co. Wexford

Civil Parish: **St. Margaret (1)** (near Carne)
Map Grid: 137
RC Parish: see Lady's Island
Diocese: FE

Civil Parish: **St. Margaret (2)**
Map Grid: 87
RC Parish: Castlebridge, see Ardcolm

Civil Parish: **St. Michael** (near Rosslare)
Map Grid: 127
RC Parish: Tagoat, see Rosslare
Diocese: FE

Civil Parish: **St. Michael's of Feagh**
Map Grid: 114
RC Parish: see Wexford
Diocese: FE

Civil Parish: **St. Mullin**
Map Grid: 41
RC Parish: see St. Mullins, Co. Carlow and
 Whitechurch-Glynn
Diocese: FE

Civil Parish: **St. Nicholas**
Map Grid: 66
RC Parish: Castlebridge, see Ardcolm
Diocese: FE

Civil Parish: **St. Patrick**
Map Grid: 114
RC Parish: see Wexford
Diocese: FE

Civil Parish: **St. Peter**
Map Grid: 115
RC Parish: see Wexford
Diocese: FE

Civil Parish: **St. Selskar**
Map Grid: 114
RC Parish: see Wexford
Diocese: FE

Civil Parish: **Skreen**
Map Grid: 67
RC Parish: Castlebridge, see Ardcolm
Diocese: FE

Civil Parish: **Tacumshin**
Map Grid: 134
RC Parish: see Lady's Island
Diocese: FE

Civil Parish: **Taghmon**
Map Grid: 75
RC Parish: Taghmon
Diocese: FE
Earliest Record: b. 5.1801; m. 5.1801; d. 1.1828
Missing Dates: b. 12.1865-3.1866; m. 3.1835-
 4.1866; d. 12.1846-2.1866
Parish Address: Rev. Thomas McCormack, PP,
 Taghmon, Wexford

Civil Parish: **Tellarought**
Map Grid: 90
RC Parish: Cushinstown, see Carnagh
Diocese: FE

Civil Parish: **Templeudigan**
Map Grid: 37
RC Parish: see Killegney
Diocese: FE

Civil Parish: **Templescoby**
Map Grid: 39
RC Parish: Davidstown
Diocese: FE
Earliest Record: b. 1.1805; m. 6.1808
Parish Address: Rev. P. Kehoe, Davidstown,
 Enniscorthy, Co. Wexford

Civil Parish: **Templeshanbo**
Map Grid: 9
RC Parish: Ballindaggin; also part St. Mary's
 Newtownbarry
Diocese: FE
Earliest Record: b. 7.1871; m. 7.1871
Parish Address: Rev. Martin F. Clancy, PP, Bal-
 lindaggin, Enniscorthy, Co. Wexford

Civil Parish: **Templeshannon**
Map Grid: 57
RC Parish: part St. Mary, Enniscorthy; part
 Monageer
Diocese: FE

Civil Parish: **Templetown (1)**
Map Grid: 98
RC Parish: Hook; also Templetown (2)

Diocese: FE
Earliest Record: b. 11.1835; m. 11.1875; d. 10.1835
Missing Dates: b. 8.1840-3.1844; d. ends 1854
Parish Address: Rev. John Butler, PP, Ramsgrange, New Ross, Co. Wexford

Civil Parish: **Templetown (2)**
Map Grid: 98
RC Parish: Templetown and St. James
Diocese: FE
Earliest Record: b. 12.1792; m. 11.1792; d. 1.1816
Missing Dates: b. 10.1793-1.1795, 11.1798-4.1805
Parish Address: Rev. William Mernagh, PP, Templetown, New Ross, Co. Wexford

Civil Parish: **Tikillin**
Map Grid: 82
RC Parish: Crossabeg, see Kilpatrick
Diocese: FE

Civil Parish: **Tintern**
Map Grid: 96
RC Parish: Tintern (Ballycullane)
Diocese: FE
Earliest Record: b. 9.1827 (in bad condition); m. 10.1827; d. 10.1828
Missing Dates: d. ends 1.1832
Parish Address: Rev. Patrick Jordan, PP, Ballycullane, New Ross, Co. Wexford

Civil Parish: **Tomhaggard**
Map Grid: 112
RC Parish: see Kilmore
Diocese: FE

Civil Parish: **Toome**
Map Grid: 22
RC Parish: Camolin (Ballyoughter)
Diocese: FE
Earliest Record: b. 9.1810; m. 8.1815
Missing Dates: b. 12.1811-8.1815, 11.1832-8.1844; m. 2.1868-7.1871
Parish Address: Rev. Matthew Doyle, PP, Camolin, Co. Wexford

Civil Parish: **Wexford**
Map Grid: 114
RC Parish: Wexford

Diocese: FE
Earliest Record: b. 5.1671; d. 5.1671
Missing Dates: b. 1.1689-1.1694, 3.1710-2.1723, 8.1787-6.1815; m. 1.1685-4.1724
Parish Address: Rev. John McCabe, PP, The Presbytery, Wexford

Civil Parish: **Wexford, St. Bridget**
Map Grid: 114
RC Parish: see Wexford
Diocese: FE

Civil Parish: **Wexford, St. Doologe**
Map Grid: 114
RC Parish: see Wexford
Diocese: FE

Civil Parish: **Wexford, St. Iberius**
Map Grid: 114
RC Parish: see Wexford
Diocese: FE

Civil Parish: **Wexford, St. Mary**
Map Grid: 114
RC Parish: see Wexford
Diocese: FE

Civil Parish: **Wexford, St. Michael's of Feagh**
Map Grid: 114
RC Parish: see Wexford
Diocese: FE

Civil Parish: **Wexford, St. Patrick**
Map Grid: 114
RC Parish: see Wexford
Diocese: FE

Civil Parish: **Wexford, St. Selskar**
Map Grid: 114
RC Parish: see Wexford
Diocese: FE

Civil Parish: **Whitechurch**
Map Grid: 88
RC Parish: Horeswood, see Kilmokea
Diocese: FE

Civil Parish: **Whitechurch-Glynn**
Map Grid: 56
RC Parish: Glynn, see Killurin
Diocese: FE

Commercial and Social Directories

1788
Richard Lucas's *General Directory of the Kingdom of Ireland* contains lists of traders in Enniscorthy, Gorey, New Ross, Taghmon, and Wexford. Reprinted in *Ir. Gen.* 3 (10) (1965): 392-416.

1820
J. Pigot's *Commercial Directory of Ireland* contains information on the gentry, nobility, and traders in and around the towns of New Ross and Wexford.

1824
J. Pigot's *City of Dublin & Hibernian Provincial Directory* includes traders, nobility, gentry, and clergy lists of Enniscorthy, Gorey, New Ross, Taghmon, and Wexford.

1839
T. Shearman's *New Commercial Directory* lists traders, gentry, etc., in New Ross.

1840
F. Kinder's *New Triennial & Commerical Directory for 1840, '41 & '42* contains trader's and other lists for New Ross.

1846
Slater's *National Commercial Directory of Ireland* lists nobility, clergy, traders, etc., in Enniscorthy and Ferns, Gorey, New Ross and Rossbercon, Taghmon, and Wexford.

1856
Slater's *Royal National Commercial Directory of Ireland* lists nobility, gentry, clergy, traders, etc., in Enniscorthy and Ferns, Fethard, Gorey, New Ross and Rossbercon, Newtownbarry, Taghmon, and Wexford.

1870
Slater's *Directory of Ireland* contains trade, nobility, and clergy lists for Enniscorthy, Fethard, Gorey, New Ross, Newtownbarry, Taghmon, and Wexford.

1872
Griffith's *County Wexford Almanac* has lists of traders in Enniscorthy and Ferns and an alphabetical list of medical doctors in the county.

1881
Slater's *Royal National Commercial Directory of Ireland* contains lists of traders, clergy, nobility, and farmers in adjoining parishes of the towns of Enniscorthy and Ferns, Fethard, Gorey, New Ross, Newtownbarry, and Wexford.

1885
G.H. Bassett's *Wexford County Guide and Directory* has an alphabetical list of persons and traders for Wexford borough, and traders, farmers, and landholders in all postal districts in the county.

1894
Slater's *Royal National Directory of Ireland* lists traders, police, teachers, farmers, and private residents in each of the towns, villages and parishes of the county.

Family History

"Alcock Wilton of Wexford." *Irish Builder.* N.p., 1888.

Codd – see Esmond

"Devereux of the Leap." *Ir. Gen.* 4 (5) (1972): 450-60.

"The Dormer Family of New Ross." *R.S.A.I.* 19 (1889): 133-35.

"Doyle Wells of Gorey." *Irish Builder.* 1888.

"Dunne Papers (Brittas, Co. Wexford)." *Anal. Hib.* 30: 123-47.

"The Early Cullen Family." *Reportorium Novum* 2 (1) (1958): 185-202.

"Frayne of Co. Wexford." *Ir. Gen.* 4 (3) (1970): 213-20.

Genealogies of Esmond, Codd, Jacob, and Redmond. GO film 279.

"Goodall of Wexford." *Ir. Gen.* 3 (12) (1967): 487-500.

"The Harvey-Waddy Connection." *J. Old Wexford Soc.* 8 (1980-81).

"Harvey Family of Co. Wexford, 16 Births 1798-1801." *J. Ass. Pres. Mem. Dead* 9 (1912-16): 572.

"Hatchell of Co. Wexford." *Ir. Gen.* 4 (5) (1972): 461-76.

"Houghton of Kilmannock." *Irish Builder.* 1888.

"The Ivory Family of New Ross." *R.S.A.I.* 80 (1950): 242-61.

Jacob – see Esmond.

"Lambert of Wexford." *Past* 2 (1921): 129-38.

Loftus – see Co. Kilkenny.

Murphy, Hilary. *Families of Co. Wexford.* Dublin: Geography Publications, 1986.

"Notes on Brown of Mayglass (inc. pedigree)." *J. Ass. Pres. Mem. Dead* 9: 403.

"Notes on Cooke of Tomduff." *J. Ass. Pres. Mem. Dead* 1 (1888-91): 519.

"Notes on the Moore Family, Tinraheen, Co. Wexford." *J. Ass. Pres. Mem. Dead* 9: 189; and 10: 252.

Redmond – see Esmond.

Redmond, G.O. *Account of the Anglo-Norman Family of Devereux of Balmagir, Co. Wexford.* Dublin, 1891.

"Roches of Wexford." *J. Old Wex. Soc.* 2 (1969): 39-48.

"The Rossiters of Rathmacknee Castle (Co. Wexford), 1169-1881." *Past* 5 (1949): 103-16; 6 (1950): 13-44.

Waddy – see Harvey.

Wells – see Doyle.

West – see Co. Wicklow

Wilton – see Alcock.

Gravestone Inscriptions

This is one of the most comprehensively recorded counties. The inscriptions are available in the series *Memorials of the Dead*, vols. 5-7. These are compiled and published in a limited number of copies by Brian J. Cantwell. Copies are available in the NLI and PRO.

Memorials of the Dead, vol. 5 (North Wexford):
 Ardamine
 Askamore

Ballinclay (Quaker)
Ballindagen
Balloughter
Ballycanew
Ballycarney
Ballyduff
Ballyfad
Ballygarrett
Ballymore
Brideswell
Bunclody
Camolin
Castledockrill
Castletown
Clonatin
Clone
Craanford
Donoughmore
Ferns
Gorey
Holyfort
Inch
Kilanerin
Kilcashel
Kilcavan
Kilgorman
Killenagh
Kilmyshall
Kilnahue
Kilnenor
Kilrush
Kiltennel
Knockbrandon
Leskinfere
Limbrick
Monaseed
Prospect
Riverchapel
Rosminogue
Scarawalsh
Templeshanbo
Toberanierin
Toome

Memorials of the Dead, vol. 6 (Southeast Wexford):
 Ardcavan Old
 Ardcolm (CI; Castlebridge)
 Ardcolm Old
 Artramont Old
 Ballaghkeen (Ch. of St. John the Baptist) RC

Ballyfad
Ballyhuskard (CI)
Ballymurn (RC)
Ballynaslaney, St. David's Well
Ballyvaldon Old
Ballyvaloo Old
Beggerin Island Old
Blackwater, St. Brigid (RC)
Boolavogue, St. Cormac (RC)
Carrig (Wexford) Old
Castlebridge (RC)
Castle Ellis Old
Clone, St. Paul's (CI)
Cooladine Quaker
Crossabeg, SS Patrick and Brigid (RC)
Curracloe RC
Edermine Old
Enniscorthy, St. Aidan's Cathedral (RC)
Enniscorthy, St. Mary (CI)
Enniscorthy, St. Senan (RC)
Enniscorthy, Templeshannon Old
Glascarrig (CI)
Glenbrien, St. Peter (RC)
Kilcormack, St. Cormack (CI)
Killilla Old
Killincooly Old
Kilmallock Old
Kilmuckridge (CI)
Kilmuckridge (Litter) (RC)
Kilnamanagh, St. John's Ch., (CI)
Kilpatrick (Saunderscourt) Old
Meelnagh Old
Monagear (RC)
Monamolin (RC)
Monamolin (CI)
Oulart, St. Patrick (RC)
Oylegate (RC)
Screen (RC)
Solesborough Old (Quaker and CI)
Tykillen Old
Wexford, Church of the Assumption (RC)
Wexford, Church of the Immaculate Conception (RC)
Wexford, Paupers Graveyard
Wexford, Redmond Memorial
Wexford, Ch. of St. Francis (Merchants') (RC)
Wexford, St. Iberius Ch. (CI)
Wexford, St. John's Old
Wexford, St. Magdalen's Old
Wexford, St. Mary's Old
Wexford, St. Michael's Old
Wexford, St. Patrick's Old
Wexford, St. Selskar's Abbey

Memorials of the Dead, vol. 7 (Southwest Wexford):
Ambrosetown
Ballingly Old
Balloughton (CI)
Ballybrennan Old
Ballyconnick Old
Ballylannen
Ballymitty, St. Peter (RC)
Ballymore (RC)
Ballymore Old
Bannow, per Dr. and Mrs. Hetherington
Barntown, Church of Blessed Virgin and St. Alphonsus
Broadway, St. Iberius'
Carne, Churchtown (CI)
Carne, St. Margaret
Carne, St. Vogus
Caroreigh, St. Garvan
Carrick on Bannow, Church of Immaculate Conception and St. Joseph
Cleriestown, St. Mannan (RC)
Collstuff Old
Cullenstown (RC)
Cullenstown (near Cullenstown Strand)
Drinagh
Duncormick (CI)
Grange
Grantstown Priory, O.S.A. (RC)
Horetown, St. James (CI)
Isharton Old
Johnstown Castle Demesne
Kilcavan
Kilcowan
Kildavin
Kilgarvan
Killag
Killiane Old
Killinick (CI)
Kilmacree
Kilmannan
Kilmore, St. Mary (RC)

Newspapers

In the following listings, WCL denotes holdings in the Wexford County Library (see Research Sources and Services section).

Title: *County of Wexford Express* (*Wexford and Kilkenny Express* from 1878)
Published in: Wexford, 1875-1907
BL Holdings: 5.1878-4.1905; 6-11.1907

Title: *Enniscorthy News* (and *Co. Wexford Advertiser*)
Published in: Enniscorthy, 1860-1912
BL Holdings: 3.1861-3.1902; 1.1911-5.1912

Title: *Gorey Correspondent* (*Arklow Standard* from 1876)
Published in: Gorey, c.1856-92
BL Holdings: 2.1861-12.1892

Title: *Guardian*
Published in: Wexford, 1847-56 (incorporated with *The People*)
NLI Holdings: 11.1847-12.1848; odd numbers 1849-55
BL Holdings: 11.1847-12.1856

Title: *New Ross Standard*
Published in: New Ross, 1889-current
NLI Holdings: 12.1904-in progress
BL Holdings: 8.1889-in progress

Title: *New Ross Reporter & Wexford (Carlow & Kilkenny) Advertiser*
Published in: New Ross, 1871-95; Waterford, 1895-1910
BL Holdings: 8.1874-6.1875; 6-11.1875; 1.1850-8.1910

Title: *The Watchman*
Published in: Enniscorthy, 1869-86
BL Holdings: 7.1869-9.1886
WCL Holdings: 7.1869-1.1870; 3.1870-9.1886

Title: *Wexford Advertiser* (see *New Ross Reporter*)

Title: *Wexford Evening Post*
Published in: Wexford, 1826-30

NLI Holdings: 3.1826-3.1830
WXCL Holdings: 5 issues 9.1829-1.1830

Title: *Wexford Freeman*
Published in: Wexford, 1832-37
NLI Holdings: 5.1832-5.1837
BL Holdings: 5.1832-5.1837
WCL Holdings: 7 issues 11.1806-7.1807; 4.1808-3.1810; 1.1817-7.1817

Title: *Wexford Herald*
Published in: Wexford, 1788-1865
NLI Holdings: 7.1788-6.1789; 7.1792-6.1793; 4.1806-7.1810; 4.1812-2.1814; 1.1828-8.1832
BL Holdings: 5.1813; 1.1828-8.1832; 1.1861-4.1865

Title: *Wexford Independent* (continued as *The Independent,* 1843-70, and *The Wexford Independent,* 1870-1906)
Published in: Wexford, 1830-1906
NLI Holdings: 8.1837 (bound in "Miscellaneous Newspapers," Vol. 1); 1.1885-12.1905; 3.1906-8.1908
BL Holdings: 12.1830-7.1869; 7.1870-5.1873; 1.1874-8.1883; 1.1884-2.1906
WCL Holdings: 12.1830-12.1831

Title: *(Wexford) People*
Published in: Wexford, 1853-current
NLI Holdings: 1.1882-in progress
WCL Holdings: odd issues 10.1859; 1.1877; 3.1879; 7-11.1881; 6.1882; 9.1884-2.1887; 10.1888; 5.1891; 10.1892; 6.1893; 10.1898
Other Holdings: People Newspapers Ltd., Wexford holds all issues since 1861

Wills and Administrations

A discussion of the types of records, where they are held, their availability and value is given in the Wills section in the Introduction. The availability of prerogative wills, administrations, and marriage license records is also described in the relevant parts of the same section. Where available, published sources of these records are given in the Miscellaneous Sources section.

Pre-1858 Wills and Administrations

Prerogative Wills. see p. xli.

Consistorial Wills. County Wexford is mainly in the diocese of Ferns with two parishes in Dublin and one in Leighlin. The guide to Catholic parish records in this chapter shows the diocese to which each civil parish belonged. The wills of residents of each diocese were usually proven within that diocese (see the Wills section for exceptions). The following records survive:

Wills. see p. xxxvii.

Abstracts. see p. xxxvii.

Indexes. Ferns (1601-1858) (badly mutilated), up to 1800 published by Phillimore. The PRO has a copy (1603-1838) for F-V, with unproved wills 1616-1842 for W only. PRO 1A 4(16). A reconstructed copy of the index for 1800-57 (compiled by Ian Cantwell) is complete for F-T and 50 percent complete for the rest. This is also available in the PRO.

Post-1858 Wills and Administrations

This county was served by the District Registry of Waterford. The surviving records are in the PRO.

Marriage Licenses

See Miscellaneous Sources section.

Indexes. Ferns and Leighlin (1691-1845). PRO; SLC film 100870-71; GO ms. 612-617; SLC film 100169-72 (more complete copy).

Miscellaneous Sources

Bassett, George H. *Wexford County Guide and Directory.* Dublin, 1885.

Browne, Elizabeth, and Tom Wickham, eds. *Lewis's Wexford.* Enniscorthy, 1983.

Butler, Thomas. *History of the Parish of Carrick-on-Bannow.* N.p., 1985.

Cantwell, Brian J. *Memorials of the Dead for County Wexford.* vols. 5-10 (index).

County Wexford Almanac 1909. Wexford: John English & Co., 1909.

"Ferns Marriage Licenses 1662-1806 (except 1701-25 and 1693/94)." *J. Kildare Arch. Hist. Soc.* (A-B) 9 (1) (1918-21): 34-59; (C) 9: 178-90; (D-F) 9: 227-45; (G) 9: 292-300; (H) 9: 366-75, 9: 454-56, and 10: 29-31; (H contd. - P) 10: 61-99; (R-S) 10: 125-49; (T-Z) 10: 174-94.

Flood, W.H.G. *A History of Enniscorthy.* 1898.

Fraser, R. *Statistical Survey of the County of Wexford.* Royal Dublin Society, 1807.

Grattan-Flood, W. *History of the Diocese of Ferns.* Waterford, 1916.

Griffiths, George. *Chronicles of Co. Wexford to 1877.* Enniscorthy, 1877.

Hore, P.H. *The History of the Town and County of Wexford.* London, 1906.

Jeffrey, William H. *The Castles of Co. Wexford.* Old Wexford Society Presentation to Co. Library, Wexford, 1979.

Kinsella, A. *The Waveswept Shore – A History of the Courtown District.* Wexford, 1982.

Lacy, Thos. *Sights and Scenes in Our Fatherland.* London, 1863.

Leslie, J.B. *Ferns Clergy and Parishes.* Dublin, 1936.

"Passenger List of Ticonderoga 1850" (many from Killaveney parish, Wexford). *The Past* 12 (1978): 49-52 (including part of a group which founded New Wexford, Missouri).

"Population Trends in Co. Wexford." *The Past* 6 (1950): 118-37.

"Quakers in Wexford." *Old Wexford Soc. J.* 3 (1): (1970): 36-41.

Hennessy, Patrick. *Davidstown, Courtnacuddy – A Wexford Parish.* Enniscorthy, 1986.

"Some 18th Century Petitions." *The Past* 9 (1972): 8-38.

Whelan, K., ed. *A History of Newbawn.* Newbawn Macra na Feirme, 1986.

Research Sources and Services

Journals

The Past (Journal of the Ui Cinsealaigh Society)

Journal of the Wexford Historical Society

Journal of Waterford and SouthEast of Ireland Archaeological Society.

Libraries and Information Sources

Wexford County Library, Abbey Street, Wexford Ph: (053) 22211

Research Services

Irish Origins (see Research Sources and Services section, Co. Kilkenny)

St. Mullins Muintir Na Tire (see Research Sources and Services section, Co. Carlow)

See also research services in Dublin. p. xliv

Societies

Ui Cinsealaigh Historical Society, Rev. M. Glynn, St. Aidan's, Enniscorthy, Co. Wexford

New Ross Literary & Historical Society, Mr. James Doyle, Ard Ross, New Ross, Co. Wexford

Wexford Historical Society, 61 Talbot Green, Wexford

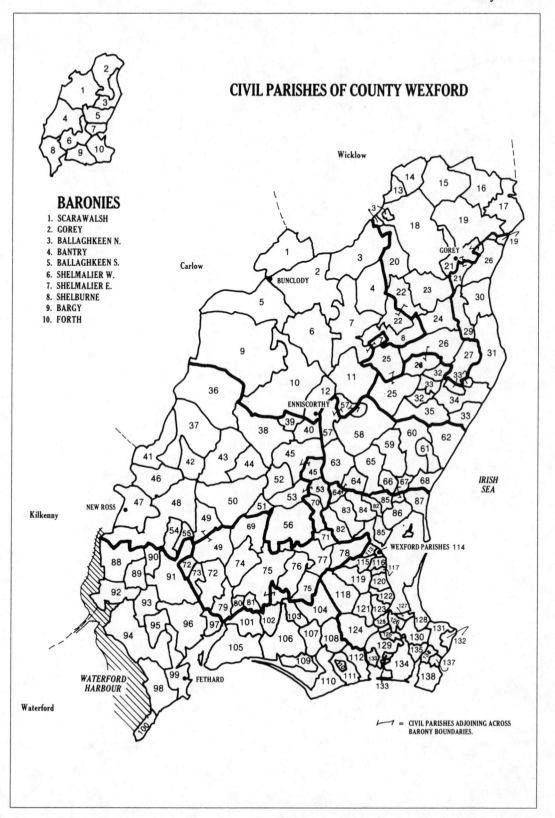

CIVIL PARISHES OF COUNTY WEXFORD

BARONIES

1. SCARAWALSH
2. GOREY
3. BALLAGHKEEN N.
4. BANTRY
5. BALLAGHKEEN S.
6. SHELMALIER W.
7. SHELMALIER E.
8. SHELBURNE
9. BARGY
10. FORTH

Wicklow

Carlow

BUNCLODY

GOREY

ENNISCORTHY

IRISH SEA

Kilkenny

NEW ROSS

WEXFORD PARISHES 114

Waterford

WATERFORD HARBOUR

FETHARD

⌐ = CIVIL PARISHES ADJOINING ACROSS BARONY BOUNDARIES.

County Wicklow

A Brief History

This scenic, wooded Leinster coastal county contains the towns of Wicklow, Bray, Rathnew, Arklow, Rathdrum, Enniskerry, Greystones, and Baltinglass. Because of its scenery and fine woodlands it is known as the "Garden of Ireland" and has been a popular resort area since the eighteenth century. The county has a wide coastal strip of fertile land, and the inland parts are mountainous.

In pre-Norman times this county was the territory of the O'Byrnes and O'Tooles. The families of O'Cullen, O'Kelly, O'Teige (Tighe), (O')Gahan, and McKeogh (or Kehoe) are also associated with the county. There were a number of Viking settlements on the Wicklow coast, including the towns of Arklow and Wicklow whose names are of Danish origin. The family name of Doyle, which is common in the county (and elsewhere in Leinster), is also of Scandinavian origin.

After the Norman invasion the coastal parts of the county came under the control of various Norman adventurers. These included the families of Archbold, Cosgrave, and Eustace. Wicklow town itself was granted to Maurice Fitzgerald who fortified it against the constant attacks from the O'Byrnes and O'Tooles who retained control of the more extensive mountaneous parts of the county.

These families continued to rule most of Wicklow for many centuries afterwards and made constant raids on the city of Dublin and on the Norman settlements in Wicklow. Their power was severely curtailed after the rebellion of the Irish Catholics in 1641 when Cromwell took every fort and stronghold in the county. However, the mountains of Wicklow continued to provide refuge for rebels until after the 1798 rebellion when the so-called Military Road was built through the heart of the mountains to provide military access.

During the Great Famine of 1845-47 the county was not as badly affected as others. Nevertheless, the population dropped by over 20 percent between 1841 (126,000) and 1851 (99,000). Almost 13,000 people died in the county between 1845 and 1850.

The north of Wicklow and particularly the towns of Bray, Greystones, and Enniskerry have become increasingly populated during the last century. These towns are now large commuter areas for the city of Dublin. The population of the county is currently over 90,000.

Census and Census Substitutes

1669
Hearth Money Roll. GO 667; PRO M4909;

SLC film 100248; abbreviated copy published in *R.S.A.I.* 61: 165-78.

1766

Protestants in Parishes of Ballymaslaney, Dunganstown (with the surnames of Catholics), Rathdrum (with the surnames of Catholics), and Wicklow. GO 537; SLC films 100173, 258517.

1798

List of Persons Who Suffered Losses in the '98 Rebellion. NLI JB 94017 (approximately 950 names, addresses, and occupations).

1823-38

Tithe Applotment Survey (see p. xxvii).

1852-53

Griffith's Valuation (see p. xxvii).

1901

Census. PRO.

1911

Census. PRO.

Church Records

Church of Ireland
(shows starting date of record)

Parish: **Arklow**
Status: Lost

Parish: **Ashford** (see Killiskey)

Parish: **Ballinaclash** (Rathdrum)
Existing Records: b. 1839; m. 1843; d. 1842
Status: LC

Parish: **Ballintemple** (Arklow)
Existing Records: b. 1823; m. 1823; d. 1848
Status: LC

Parish: **Ballynure**
Existing Records: b. 1815; m. 1818; d. 1818
Status: LC

Parish: **Baltinglass**
Status: Lost

Parish: **Blessinton**
Existing Records: b. 1695; m. 1683; d. 1683
Status: LC

Parish: **Bray**
Existing Records: b. 1666; m. 1666; d. 1666
Status: LC

Parish: **Calary**
Status: Lost

Parish: **Castlemacadam** (Avoca)
Existing Records: b. 1720; m. 1720; d. 1720
Status: LC

Parish: **Crosspatrick** and **Kilcommon**
Existing Records: b. 1830; m. 1830; d. 1830
Status: LC

Parish: **Delgany**
Existing Records: (entries for Newcastle, 1666-1777 in first volume of Delgany records) b. 1666; m. 1666; d. 1666
Status: LC

Parish: **Derralossory**
Status: Lost

Parish: **Donard** and **Crehelp**
Status: Lost

Parish: **Donoghmore**
Existing Records: b. 1720; m. 1720; d. 1720
Status: LC

Parish: **Drumkey** (see Wicklow)

Parish: **Dunlavin**
Existing Records: b. 1697; m. 1698; d. 1698
Status: LC

Parish: **Glanely** (see also Wicklow)
Existing Records: b. 1825; m. 1825; d. 1825
Status: LC

Parish: **Glenealy** (see Glanely)

Parish: **Greystones**
Status: Lost

Parish: **Hollywood**
Status: Lost

Parish: **Kilbride (1)** (Blessington)
Status: Lost

Parish: **Kilbride (2)** (Bray)
Status: Lost

Parish: **Kilbride (3)** (Enorily)
Status: Lost

Parish: **Kilcommon** (see Glanely and Wicklow)
Status: Lost

Parish: **Killiskey** (see also Wicklow)
Existing Records: b. 1818; m. 1818; d. 1824
Status: LC

Parish: **Killoughter** (see Wicklow)

Parish: **Kiltegan** and **Kilranelagh**
Status: Lost

Parish: **Moyne**
Existing Records: b. 1838; m. 1841; d. 1836
Status: LC

Parish: **Mullinacuff** (Tinahely)
Existing Records: b. 1698; m. 1698; d. 1797
Status: LC

Parish: **Newcastle**
Existing Records: (entries for Newcastle, 1666-
    1777 in first volume of Delgany records)
    b. 1677; m. 1662; d. 1663
Status: LC

Parish: **Powerscourt**
Existing Records: b. 1727; m. 1727; d. 1724
Status: LC

Parish: **Preban** (Tinahely)
Existing Records: b. 1739; m. 1739; d. 1739
Status: LC

Parish: **Rathdrum**
Existing Records: b. 1827; m. 1829; d. 1828
Status: LC

Parish: **Rathnew** (see Wicklow)

Parish: **Redcross**
Status: Lost (for some earlier entries see
    Castlemacadam)

Parish: **Shillelagh**
Existing Records: b. 1833; m. 1833; d. 1833
Status: LC

Parish: **Stratford-on-Slaney** (Ballinglass)
Existing Records: b. 1812; m. 1804; d. 1804
Status: LC

Parish: **Wicklow**
Existing Records: b. 1655; m. 1729; d. 1729
Status: LC

Presbyterian

Parish: **Bray**
Starting Date: 1836

Roman Catholic

Civil Parish: **Aghowle** (Agharle)
Map Grid: 55
RC Parish: Clonmore, see Co. Carlow
Diocese: FE

Civil Parish: **Ardoyne**
Map Grid: 54
RC Parish: Ardoyne
Diocese: FE

Civil Parish: **Arklow**
Map Grid: 50
RC Parish: Arklow
Diocese: FE
Earliest Record: b. 5.1809; m. 1.1818

Missing Dates: b. 6.1809-12.1817; m. 10.1856-1.1857

Parish Address: Rev. Liam Breen, PP, Maryville, St. Mary's Road, Arklow

Civil Parish: **Ballinacor**
Map Grid: 34
RC Parish: see Rathdrum
Diocese: FE

Civil Parish: **Ballintemple**
Map Grid: 47
RC Parish: see Arklow
Diocese: FE

Civil Parish: **Ballykine**
Map Grid: 37
RC Parish: see Rathdrum
Diocese: FE

Civil Parish: **Ballynure**
Map Grid: 15
RC Parish: see Baltinglass
Diocese: FE

Civil Parish: **Baltinglass** (see also Co. Carlow)
Map Grid: 20
RC Parish: Baltinglass
Diocese: FE
Earliest Record: b. 5.1807; m. 2.1810
Missing Dates: b. 2.1810-7.1810, 4.1811-10.1813; m. 4.1811-11.1813, 9.1815-4.1816, 2.1866-5.1866
Parish Address: Rev. Thomas F. Brophy, PP, Baltinglass, Co. Wicklow

Civil Parish: **Blessington**
Map Grid: 2
RC Parish: Blessington; also part Blackditches, and part Ballymore Eustace, see Co. Kildare
Diocese: DU
Earliest Record: b. 4.1852; m. 2.1852
Missing Dates: b. 8.1825-5.1830, 6.1830-2.1833; m. 8.1825-8.1826
Parish Address: Rev. Maurice O'Moore, PP, Crosschapel, Blessington, Co. Wicklow

Civil Parish: **Boystown**
Map Grid: 4
RC Parish: Valleymount or Blackditches
Diocese: DU

Earliest Record: b. 6.1810; m. 2.1810; d. 8.1824
Parish Address: Rev. M. Duffy, PP, Parochial House, Valleymount, Co. Wicklow

Civil Parish: **Bray**
Map Grid: 12
RC Parish: Bray
Diocese: DU
Earliest Record: not on microfilm
Parish Address: Rev. John O'Connell, PP, The Presbytery, Herbert Road, Bray, Co. Wicklow

Civil Parish: **Burgage**
Map Grid: 3
RC Parish: see Blessington
Diocese: DU

Civil Parish: **Calary**
Map Grid: 23
RC Parish: part Bray; part Glendalough; part Kilquade, see Kilcoole
Diocese: DU

Civil Parish: **Carnew** (see also Co. Wexford)
Map Grid: 59
RC Parish: Tomacork (Carnew)
Diocese: FE
Earliest Record: b. 1.1785; m. 6.1793; d. 5.1794
Missing Dates: b. 5.1786-2.1791, 11.1797-1.1807; m. 2.1797-1.1807, 3.1845-6.1847; d. 12.1797-5.1847, 11.1856-5.1864, 1.1871-4.1873
Parish Address: Rev. John McCarthy, PP, Carnew, Co. Wicklow

Civil Parish: **Castlemacadam**
Map Grid: 44
RC Parish: part Avoca, see Rathdrum; part Kilbride, see Dunganstown
Diocese: DU

Civil Parish: **Crecrin**
Map Grid: 53
RC Parish: Clonmore, see Co. Carlow
Diocese: DU

Civil Parish: **Crehelp**
Map Grid: 6
RC Parish: see Dunlavin
Diocese: DU

Civil Parish: **Crosspatrick** (see also Co. Wexford)
Map Grid: 57
RC Parish: Tomacork, see Carnew
Diocese: FE

Civil Parish: **Delgany**
Map Grid: 13
RC Parish: part Bray; part Kilquade, see Kilcoole
Diocese: DU

Civil Parish: **Derrylossary**
Map Grid: 24
RC Parish: Glendalough
Diocese: DU
Earliest Record: b. 6.1807; m. 1.1808
Missing Dates: b. 1.1838-8.1839; m. 6.1838-5.1840
Parish Address: Rev. John Doyle, PP, Glendalough, Co. Wicklow

Civil Parish: **Donaghmore**
Map Grid: 19
RC Parish: see Dunlavin
Diocese: DU

Civil Parish: **Donard**
Map Grid: 9
RC Parish: see Dunlavin
Diocese: DU

Civil Parish: **Drumkay**
Map Grid: 41
RC Parish: Wicklow, see Kilpoole
Diocese: DU

Civil Parish: **Dunganstown**
Map Grid: 43
RC Parish: Kilbride and Barndarrig
Diocese: DU
Earliest Record: b. 1.1858; m. 2.1858
Parish Address: Rev. James Murphy, PP, Barndarrig, Co. Wicklow

Civil Parish: **Dunlavin**
Map Grid: 8
RC Parish: Dunlavin
Diocese: DU

Earliest Record: b. 10.1815 (ink badly faded); m. 2.1831
Parish Address: Rev. Brian M. Byrne, PP, Parochial House, Dunlavin, Co. Wicklow

Civil Parish: **Ennereilly**
Map Grid: 46
RC Parish: Newbridge and Baronisky
Diocese: DU

Civil Parish: **Freynestown**
Map Grid: 16
RC Parish: see Dunlavin
Diocese: DU

Civil Parish: **Glenealy**
Map Grid: 33
RC Parish: Wicklow, see Kilpoole
Diocese: DU

Civil Parish: **Hacketstown**
Map Grid: 35
RC Parish: see Hacketstown, Co. Carlow
Diocese: DU

Civil Parish: **Hollywood**
Map Grid: 7
RC Parish: Ballymore-Eustace, see Co. Kildare
Diocese: DU

Civil Parish: **Inch**
Map Grid: 51
RC Parish: see Arklow
Diocese: DU

Civil Parish: **Kilbride (1)** (near Blessington)
Map Grid: 1
RC Parish: see Blessington
Diocese: DU

Civil Parish: **Kilbride (2)** (near Arklow)
Map Grid: 48
RC Parish: Newbridge and Baronisky
Diocese: DU

Civil Parish: **Kilcommon (1)** (near Rathdrum)
Map Grid: 32
RC Parish: Wicklow, see Kilpoole
Diocese: DU

Civil Parish: **Kilcommon (2)** (near Preban)
Map Grid: 38
RC Parish: Killaveny, see Kilpipe
Diocese: FE

Civil Parish: **Kilcoole**
Map Grid: 27
RC Parish: Kilquade and Kilmurray
Diocese: DU
Earliest Record: b. 8.1826; m. 8.1826
Missing Dates: b. 6.1855-12.1861
Parish Address: Rev. Henry Regan, PP, Parochial House, Kilquade, Co. Wicklow

Civil Parish: **Killahurler**
Map Grid: 49
RC Parish: see Arklow
Diocese: DU

Civil Parish: **Killiskey**
Map Grid: 30
RC Parish: Wicklow, see Kilpoole
Diocese: DU

Civil Parish: **Kilmacanoge**
Map Grid: 11
RC Parish: see Bray
Diocese: DU

Civil Parish: **Kilpipe** (see also Co. Wexford)
Map Grid: 40
RC Parish: Killaveny
Diocese: FE
Earliest Record: b. 11.1800; m. 11.1800
Missing Dates: m. 9.1836-1.1837
Parish Address: Rev. Thomas Curtis, PP, Killaveny, Tinahely, Co. Wicklow

Civil Parish: **Kilpoole**
Map Grid: 42
RC Parish: Wicklow
Diocese: DU
Earliest Record: b. 1.1748; m. 1.1748
Missing Dates: b. 6.1781-5.1796; m. 2.1778-2.1779, 10.1780-11.1795
Parish Address: Rev. Patrick Dowling, PP, Parochial House, Wicklow

Civil Parish: **Kilranelagh**
Map Grid: 21

RC Parish: Rathvilly, see Co. Carlow
Diocese: LE

Civil Parish: **Kiltegan**
Map Grid: 22
RC Parish: Hacketstown, see Co. Carlow
Diocese: LE

Civil Parish: **Knockrath**
Map Grid: 25
RC Parish: see Rathdrum
Diocese: DU

Civil Parish: **Liscolman**
Map Grid: 52
RC Parish: Clonmore, see Co. Carlow
Diocese: LE

Civil Parish: **Moyacomb**
Map Grid: 58
RC Parish: see Arklow, see also Co. Carlow and Co. Wexford
Diocese: DU

Civil Parish: **Moyne**
Map Grid: 36
RC Parish: see Hackettstown, Co. Carlow
Diocese: DU

Civil Parish: **Mullinacuff**
Map Grid: 56
RC Parish: Clonmore, see Co. Carlow
Diocese: LE

Civil Parish: **Newcastle Lower**
Map Grid: 29
RC Parish: Kilquade and Kilmurray, see Kilcoole
Diocese: DU

Civil Parish: **Newcastle Upper**
Map Grid: 28
RC Parish: Kilquade and Kilmurray, see Kilcoole
Diocese: DU

Civil Parish: **Powerscourt**
Map Grid: 10
RC Parish: Enniskerry
Diocese: DU

Earliest Record: b. 10.1825; m. 11.1825
Parish Address: Rev. Patrick McCabe, PP, Parochial House, Enniskerry, Co. Wicklow

Civil Parish: **Preban**
Map Grid: 39
RC Parish: Killaveny, see Kilpipe
Diocese: FE

Civil Parish: **Rathbran**
Map Grid: 18
RC Parish: see Baltinglass
Diocese: LE

Civil Parish: **Rathdrum (1)**
Map Grid: 26
RC Parish: Rathdrum; also Avoca, see below
Diocese: DU
Earliest Record: b. 1.1795; m. 11.1816
Missing Dates: b. 1.1799-10.1816
Parish Address: Rev. Timothy O'Brien, PP, Parochial House, Rathdrum, Co. Wicklow

Civil Parish: **Rathdrum (2)**
Map Grid: 26
RC Parish: Avoca
Diocese: DU
Earliest Record: b. 6.1791; m. 10.1778
Missing Dates: b. 2.1805-5.1809; m. 2.1805-11.1812, 2.1843-4.1844
Parish Address: Rev. J. K. O'Sullivan, PP, Parochial House, Avoca, Co. Wicklow

Civil Parish: **Rathnew**
Map Grid: 31
RC Parish: part Ashford; also part Wicklow, see Kilpoole
Diocese: DU
Earliest Record: b. 9.1864; m. 10.1864
Parish Address: Rev. G. A. Taylor, PP, Parochial House, Ashford, Co. Wicklow

Civil Parish: **Rathsallagh**
Map Grid: 14
RC Parish: see Dunlavin
Diocese: DU

Civil Parish: **Rathtoole**
Map Grid: 17
RC Parish: see Dunlavin
Diocese: DU

Civil Parish: **Redcross**
Map Grid: 45
RC Parish: Avoca, see Rathdrum
Diocese: DU

Civil Parish: **Tober**
Map Grid: 5
RC Parish: see Dunlavin
Diocese: DU

Commercial and Social Directories

1788
Richard Lucas's *General Directory of the Kingdom of Ireland* contains lists of traders in Arklow, Bray, and Wicklow. Reprinted in Ir. Gen. 3 (10) (1965): 392-416.

1824
J. Pigot's *City of Dublin & Hibernian Provincial Directory* includes traders, nobility, gentry, and clergy lists of Arklow, Baltinglass, Blessington, Bray, Newtown Mount Kennedy, Rathdrum, and Wicklow.

1846
Slater's *National Commercial Directory of Ireland* lists nobility, clergy, traders, etc., in Arklow, Baltinglass, Blessington, Bray, Newtown Mount Kennedy and Delgany, Rathdrum, and Wicklow.

1856
Slater's *Royal National Commercial Directory of Ireland* lists nobility, gentry, clergy, traders, etc., in Arklow, Baltinglass, Blessington, Bray and Enniskerry, Newtown Mount Kennedy, Delgany and Kilcoole, Rathdrum, Wicklow, and Ashford.

1870
Slater's *Directory of Ireland* contains trade, nobility, and clergy lists for Arklow, Baltinglass, Blessington, Bray, Newtown Mount Kennedy, Rathdrum, and Wicklow.

1881
Slater's *Royal National Commercial Directory of Ireland* contains lists of traders, clergy, nobility, and farmers in adjoining parishes, of the towns of Arklow, Baltinglass, Donard and Dunlavin, Blessington, Bray and

Enniskerry, Newtown Mount Kennedy, Greystones and Delgany, Rathdrum, and Wicklow.

1894

Slater's *Royal National Directory of Ireland* lists traders, police, teachers, farmers, and private residents in each of the towns, villages, and parishes of the county.

Family History

Collection Concerning the Family of Yarner of Wicklow. N.p., 1870.

"The Family of Saunders of Saunders' Grove, Co. Wicklow." *J. Kildare Hist. Arch. Soc.* 9 (1918-22): 125-33.

"Fitz-Eustace of Baltinglass." *J. Waterford & S.E. Ire. Arch. Soc.* 5 (1899): 190-95.

Fitzgerald, Lord Walter. "Hollywood, Co. Wicklow: With an Account of its Owners to the Commencement of the Seventeenth Century." *J. Kildare Arch. Hist. Soc.* 8 (1915-17): 185-96.

O'Toole, P.L. *History of the Clan O'Toole and Other Leinster Septs.* Dublin, 1890.

O'Toole, John. *The O'Tooles, Anciently Lords of Powerscourt . . .* Dublin, n.d.

"Percy of Co. Wicklow." Pedigree in *Swanzy Notebooks.* RCB Library.

"The Wests of Ballydugan, Co. Down; the Rock, Co. Wicklow; and Ashwood, Co. Wexford." *Ulster J. Arch.* 2nd series 12 (1906): 135-41, 159-65.

Gravestone Inscriptions

The following references may be found in Cantwell, Brian J., *Memorials of the Dead* (Vol. 1, Northeast Wicklow 1974; Vol. 2, Southeast Wicklow 1975; Vol. 3, Southwest Wicklow 1976; Vol. 4, Northwest Wicklow 1978):

Aghold: Vol. 3
Aghowle: Vol. 3
Annacurragh: Vol. 3

Ardoyne: Vol. 3
Arklow: Vol. 2
Ashford: Vol. 1
Askanagap: Vol. 3
Aughrim: Vol. 3
Avoca: Vol. 2
Ballinatone: Vol. 2
Ballintemple: Vol. 2
Ballycooge: Vol. 2
Ballycore: Vol. 4
Ballymaconnell: Vol. 3
Ballymaghroe: Vol. 3
Ballynure: Vol. 4
Baltinglas: Vol. 4
Baltyboys: Vol. 4
Barndarrig: Vol. 2
Barranisky: Vol. 2
Blacklion: Vol. 1
Blessington: Vol. 4
Bray: Vol. 1
Burgage: Vol. 4
Calary: Vol. 1
Carnew: Vol. 3
Castlemacadam: Vol. 2
Castletimon: Vol. 2
Cloghleagh: Vol. 4
Connary: Vol. 2
Coolafancy: Vol. 3
Coronation Plantation Obelisk: Vol. 4
Cranareen: Vol. 4
Crossbridge: Vol. 3
Crosschapel: Vol. 4
Crosspatrick: Vol. 3
Curraghlawn: Vol. 3
Curtlestown: Vol. 1
Davidstown: Vol. 4
Delgany: Vol. 1
Derralossary: Vol. 2
Donard: Vol. 4
Donoughmore: Vol. 4
Dunganstown: Vol. 2
Dunlavin: Vol. 4
Ennereilly: Vol. 2
Ennisboyne: Vol. 2
Enniskerry: Vol. 1
Glencree: Vol. 1
Glendalough: Vol. 4; "Monumental Inscription at Glendalough." *Ir. Gen.* 2(3): 88-93 (1945)
Glenealy: Vol. 2
Grangecon: Vol. 4

Greenan: Vol. 2
Greystones: Vol. 1
Hollywood: Vol. 4
Kilbride: Vol. 1, 2, and 4
Kilcarra: Vol. 2
Kilcommon: Vol. 2 and 3
Kilcoole: Vol. 1
Kilfea: Vol. 1
Killadreenan: Vol. 1
Killahurler: Vol. 2
Killamoat: Vol. 3
Killavany: Vol. 3
Killegar: Vol. 1
Killiskey: Vol. 1
Killoughter: Vol. 1
Kilmacanogue: Vol. 1
Kilmagig: Vol. 2
Kilmurry: Vol. 1
Kilpipe: Vol. 3
Kilquade: Vol. 1
Kilquiggan: Vol. 3
Kilranelagh: Vol. 4
Kiltegan: Vol. 3
Knockanana: Vol. 3
Knockanarrigan: Vol. 4
Knockarigg: Vol. 4
Knockloe: Vol. 3
Lackan: Vol. 4
Laragh: Vol. 4
Leitrim: Vol. 4
Liscolman: Vol. 3
Macreddin: Vol. 3
Moyne: Vol. 3
Mullinacuff: Vol. 3
Newcastle: Vol. 1
Newtown Mount Kennedy: Vol. 1
Nunscross: Vol. 1
Powerscourt: Vol. 1
Preban: Vol. 3
Rathbran: Vol. 4
Rathdrum: Vol. 2
Rathnew: Vol. 2
Redcross: Vol. 2
Redford: Vol. 1
Rossahane: Vol. 3
Scurlocks: Vol. 4
Shillelagh: Vol. 3
Stratford: Vol. 4
Templeboodin: Vol. 4
Templemichael: Vol. 2
Templerainy: Vol. 2

Tober: Vol. 4
Tomacrok: Vol. 3
Tornant: Vol. 4
Trinity: Vol. 1
Valleymount: Vol. 4
Whaley Abbey: Vol. 2
Wicklow: Vol. 2
Yewtree: Vol. 3

Newspapers

The earliest newspaper for this county is 1857. However, Dublin papers contain some relevant notices for the north of the county. For the other parts of the county the relevant adjoining county newspapers should be consulted.

Title: *Bray Gazette* (continued as *Kingstown and The Bray Gazette* in 1872)
Published in: Bray, 1861-73
BL Holdings: 6.1861-3.1873

Title: *Bray Herald* (continued as *South Dublin Herald* in 1922, and as *Bray Herald* again 1923-27)
Published in: Bray, 1876-1927
NLI Holdings: 1.1905-4.1927
BL Holdings: 10.1876-1927

Title: *Wicklow Newsletter and County Advertiser*
Published in: Wicklow, 1857-1927
NLI Holdings: 1.1885-4.1927
BL Holdings: 1.1858-5.1873; 6.1874-12.1919; 1.1922-12.1926

Title: *Wicklow People*
Published in: Wicklow, 1886-current
NLI Holdings: 12.1904-8.1908; 3.1909-in progress
BL Holdings: 6.1889-in progress

Title: *Wicklow Star*
Published in: Wicklow, 1895-1900
BL Holdings: 10.1895-2.1900

Wills and Administrations

A discussion of the types of records, where they are held, their availability and value is given in the Wills section in the Introduction. The availability of prerogative wills, administrations, and marriage license records is also described in the relevant parts of the same section. Where available, published sources of these records are given in the Miscellaneous Sources section.

Pre-1858 Wills and Administrations

Prerogative Wills. see p. xli.

Consistorial Wills. County Wicklow is in the dioceses of Dublin, Ferns, Leighlin, and (one parish) Kildare. The guide to Catholic parish records in this chapter shows the diocese to which each civil parish belonged. The will of residents of each diocese was usually proven within that diocese (see the Wills section for exceptions). The following records survive:

Wills. see p. xxxvii.

Abstracts. see p. xxxvii. The Lane-Poole Papers in NLI contain will abstracts from Co. Wicklow. NLI ms. 5359.

Indexes. Dublin–see Co. Dublin. Ferns–see Co. Wexford. Leighlin–see Co. Carlow. Kildare–see Co. Kildare.

Post-1858 Wills and Administrations

This county was served by the District Registry of Dublin. The surviving records are in the PRO.

Marriage Licenses

Indexes and Abstracts. Dublin–see Co. Dublin. Ferns–see Co. Wexford. Kildare–see Co. Kildare.

Original Records. Kildare–see Co. Kildare.

Miscellaneous Sources

A Hundred Years of Bray and Neighbourhood: 1770-1870 by "an old inhabitant." Blackrock, 1907, 1978.

Research Sources and Services

Journals

Journal of the West Wicklow Historical Society

Bray Historical Record

Journal of Cualann Historical Society

Arklow Historical Society Journal

Libraries and Information Sources

Wicklow County Library, Greystones, Co. Wicklow Ph: (01) 874387

Bray Urban District Council, Public Library, Florence Road, Bray, Co. Wicklow Ph: (01) 862600

Research Services

See research services in Dublin, p. xliv

Societies

Arklow Historical Society, Mrs. Mae Greene, 23 St. Peter's Place, Arklow, Co. Wicklow

Cualann Historical Society, Bray Town Hall, Bray, Co. Wicklow

Rathdangan Historical Society, Ms. Kathleen P. Cullen, Killamoat, Rathdangan, Co. Wicklow

West Wicklow Historical Society, Mr. Paul Baker, Ladystown, Rathvilly, Co. Carlow

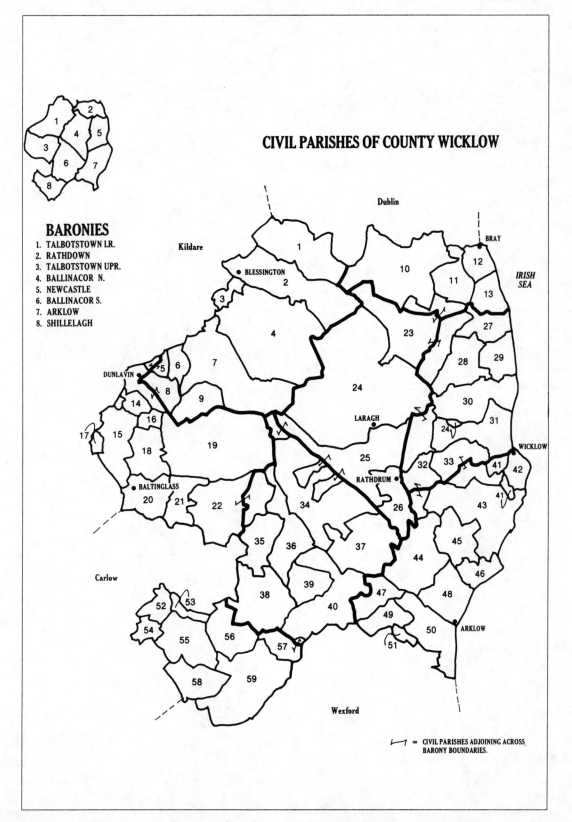

CIVIL PARISHES OF COUNTY WICKLOW

BARONIES
1. TALBOTSTOWN LR.
2. RATHDOWN
3. TALBOTSTOWN UPR.
4. BALLINACOR N.
5. NEWCASTLE
6. BALLINACOR S.
7. ARKLOW
8. SHILLELAGH

⌐ = CIVIL PARISHES ADJOINING ACROSS
    BARONY BOUNDARIES.

Appendix (Belfast)

Belfast Newspapers

The city of Belfast is in both County Down and Antrim. These newspapers, therefore, are relevant in particular to Antrim and Down but also to the other Ulster counties. The *Belfast Newsletter,* in particular, is of great value since it is both early in publication (1737) and also covered a large part of northeast Ulster. The Linen Hall Library in Belfast has a good set of this paper and also a partial index.

Title: *Banner of Belfast*
Published in: Belfast, 1842-69
BL Holdings: 6.1842-8.1869

Title: *Belfast Advertiser* (continued as *Belfast Weekly Advertiser* in 1880)
Published in: Belfast, 1879-86
BL Holdings: 10.1879-2.1886

Title: *Belfast Commercial Chronicle*
Published in: Belfast, 1805-55
NLI Holdings: 4-8.1807; 2-10.1809
BL Holdings: odd numbers 1809, 1813, 1820-22, 1.1823-12.1827; 1.1832-8.1855

Title: *Belfast Daily Post*
Published in: Belfast, 1882
BL Holdings: 3-4.1882

Title: *Belfast Evening Star*
Published in: Belfast, 1890
BL Holdings: 1-5.1890

Title: *Belfast Evening Telegraph* (continued as *Belfast Telegraph* in 1918)
Published in: Belfast, 1870-current
BL Holdings: 3.1871-4.1918; 4.1918-in progress

Title: *Belfast Mercantile Register*
Published in: Belfast, old series c.1838-52; new series 1852-93
BL Holdings: 1.1840-3.1852; 3.1852-4.1893

Title: *Belfast Mercury* (continued as *Belfast Daily Mercury* in 1854)
Published in: Belfast, 1851-61
NLI Holdings: 1.1853-12.1857
BL Holdings: 3.1851-11.1861

Title: *Belfast Mercury or Freeman's Chronicle* (continued as *Belfast Evening Post* in 1786)
Published in: Belfast, 1783-86
NLI Holdings: 8.1783-8.1787
BL Holdings: 4.1784-3.1786

Title: *Belfast Morning News* (incorporated with *Irish News* in 1892)
Published in: Belfast, 1857-92
NLI Holdings: 1.1860-12.1865; 7.1882-8.1892
BL Holdings: 11.1857-8.1892

Title: *Belfast Newsletter*
Published in: Belfast: 1737-current
NLI Holdings: 10.1738-12.1835; 1.1837-9.1962
BL Holdings: odd numbers 1747, 1792, 1799, 1813, 1.1825-9.1962

Title: *Belfast Times* (also called *Belfast Daily Times*)
Published in: Belfast, 1872
BL Holdings: 1.1872-8.1872

Title: *Belfast Weekly Mail*
Published in: Belfast, 1852-54
BL Holdings: 11.1852-9.1854

Title: *Belfast Weekly News* (merged with *Belfast Newsletter* in 1942)
Published in: Belfast, 1855-1942
NLI Holdings: 6.1921-12.1924
BL Holdings: 7.1855-6.1942

Title: *Belfast Weekly Telegraph* (continued as *Cityweek* in 1964)
Published in: Belfast, 1873-1964
NLI Holdings: 1.1913-2.1916; 6-10.1964
BL Holdings: 8.1874-10.1964

Title: *Evening Press*
Published in: Belfast, 1870-74
BL Holdings: 5.1873-5.1874

Title: *Irish News*
Published in: Belfast, 1891-current
NLI Holdings: 8.1892-in progress
BL Holdings: 8.1891-in progress

Title: *Irish Weekly*
Published in: Belfast, 1891-1981
NLI Holdings: 6.1921-12.1922
BL Holdings: 8.1891-1981

Title: *Morning Post*
Published in: Belfast, 1855-58
BL Holdings: 1-4.1858

Title: *Northern Herald*
Published in: Belfast, 1833-36
BL Holdings: 9.1833-1.1836

Title: *Northern Star*
Published in: Belfast, 1792-96
NLI Holdings: 1.1792-12.1796
BL Holdings: 1.1792-12.1796

Title: *The Northern Star*
Published in: Belfast, 1868-72
NLI Holdings: 1.1870-11.1872
BL Holdings: 2.1868-11.1872

Title: *Northern Whig*
Published in: Belfast, 1824-1963
NLI Holdings: 1.1824-4.1829 (not published 8.1826-5.1827); 1.1839-12.1850; 3.1856-9.1963
BL Holdings: 1.1832-9.1963

Title: *Ulster Echo* (incorporated with *The Witness*)
Published in: Belfast, 1874-1916
BL Holdings: 5.1874-6.1916

Title: *Ulster Examiner* (incorporated with *Morning News*)
Published in: Belfast, 1868-82
Note: called *Daily Examiner* (1870-82)
NLI Holdings: 1.1870-6.1882
BL Holdings: 3.1868-7.1882

Title: *Ulster Observer*
Published in: Belfast, 1862-68
BL Holdings: 7.1862-1.1868

Title: *Ulster Times*
Published in: Belfast, 1836-43
NLI Holdings: 3.1836-8.1843
BL Holdings: 3.1836-8.1843

Title: *Ulster Weekly News* (incorporated with *Weekly Examiner*)
Published in: Belfast, 1873-82
BL Holdings: 3.1873-10.1881

Title: *Vindicator*
Published in: Belfast, 1839-48
NLI Holdings: 5.1839-2.1848
BL Holdings: 5.1839-2.1848

Title: *Weekly Examiner* (incorporated with *Irish Weekly News*)
Published in: Belfast, 1870-92
BL Holdings: 11.1870-8.1892

Title: *Weekly Northern Whig*
Published in: Belfast, 1858-1940
BL Holdings: 2.1858-4.1840

Title: *Weekly Observer*
Published in: Belfast, 1868-72
NLI Holdings: 1.1868-11.1872
BL Holdings: 1.1868-11.1872

Title: *Weekly Press*
Published in: Belfast, 1858-75
BL Holdings: 5.1858-6.1875

Title: *Weekly Vindicator*
Published in: Belfast, 1847-52
BL Holdings: 2.1847-8.1852

Title: *Witness*
Published in: Belfast, 1874-1941
NLI Holdings: 10.1906-1.1941
BL Holdings: 7.1875-1.1941

Church Records

Church of Ireland
(shows starting date)

Parish: **All Saints** (University Street)
Existing Records: b. 1888; m. 1893; d. 1952
Status: LC

Parish: **Antrim Road** (see St. James and St. Peter)

Parish: **Ballymacarrett** (see St. Patrick)

Parish: **Ballynafeigh** (see St. Jude)

Parish: **Ballysillan** (see St. Mark)

Parish: **Beersbridge Road** (see St. Donard)

Parish: **Belfast Cathedral** (see St. Anne)

Parish: **Christ Church** (College Square North)
Existing Records: b. 1835; m. 1837; d. 1838
Missing Dates: b. 1859
Status: PRONI

Parish: **Cliftonville** (see St. Silas)

Parish: **Craven Street** (Shankill, see St. Michael)

Parish: **Cregagh** (see St. Finnian)

Parish: **Crumlin Road** (see St. Mary)

Parish: **Donegall Pass** (see St. Mary Magdalene)

Parish: **Drew Memorial** (see St. Philip)

Parish: **Duncairn Gardens** (see St. Barnabas)

Parish: **Dundela** (see St. Mark)

Parish: **Eglantine Avenue** (see St. Thomas)

Parish: **Falls** (see St. Luke and St. John the Baptist)

Parish: **Glencairn** (see St. Andrew)

Parish: **Grosvenor Road** (see St. Philip)

Parish: **Holy Trinity** (Trinity St.)
Existing Records: b. 1844; m. 1855
Status: PRONI and LC

Parish: **Knock** (see St. Columba)

Parish: **Knockbreda** (Co. Down)
Existing Records: b. 1785; m. 1784; d. 1787
Status: PRONI and LC

Parish: **Lisburn Road** (see St. Nicholas and St. Thomas)

Parish: **Lower Falls** (see St. Luke)

Parish: **Malone** (see St. John)

Parish: **Mariners Chapel** (see also St. Anne)
Existing Records: b. 1868; m. 1868; d. 1868
Status: PRONI

Parish: **Millfield** (see St. Stephen)

Parish: **Orangefield** (see St. John the Evangelist)

Parish: **St. Aidan** (Blythe Street)
Existing Records: b. 1893; m. 1895
Status: LC

Parish: **St. Andrew** (Glencairn)
Existing Records: b. 1881; m. 1870
Status: LC

Parish: **St. Anne** (Shankill)
Existing Records: b. 1745; m. 1745; d. 1745
Status: PRONI and LC

Parish: **St. Barnabas** (Duncairn Gardens)
Existing Records: b. 1892; m. 1893
Status: LC

Parish: **St. Clement** (Templemore)
Existing Records: b. 1897; m. 1902
Status: LC

Parish: **St. Columba** (Knock)
Existing Records: b. 1890; m. 1896
Status: LC

Parish: **St. Donard** (Beersbridge Road)
Existing Records: b. 1900; m. 1903
Status: LC

Parish: **St. Finnian** (Cregagh)
Existing Records: b. 1928; m. 1834
Status: LC

Parish: **St. George** (High Street)
Existing Records: b. 1817; m. 1817
Status: PRONI and LC

Parish: **St. James** (Antrim Road)
Existing Records: b. 1871; m. 1871
Missing Dates: b. ends 1934; m. ends 1950
Status: LC

Parish: **St. John** (Malone)
Existing Records: b. 1842; m. 1842
Missing Dates: b. ends 1847; m. ends1844
Status: PRONI

Parish: **St. John the Baptist** (Upper Falls)
Existing Records: b. 1855; m. 1863
Status: PRONI and LC

Parish: **St. John the Evangelist** (Orangefield)
Existing Records: b. 1853; m. 1853
Status: LC and PRONI (births only)

Parish: **St. Jude** (Ballynafeigh)
Existing Records: b. 1873; m. 1874; d. 1874
Status: LC

Parish: **St. Luke** (Northumberland Street, Lower Falls)
Status: Lost

Parish: **St. Mark (1)** (Ballysillan)
Existing Records: b. 1856: m. 1860
Status: LC and PRONI (baptisms only)

Parish: **St. Mark (2)** (Dundela)
Existing Records: b. 1869; m. 1879
Status: LC and PRONI (baptisms only)

Parish: **St. Mary** (Crumlin Road)
Existing Records: b. 1867; m. 1869; d. 1867
Status: LC and PRONI (baptisms and burials only)

Parish: **St. Mary Magdalene**
Existing Records: b. 1855; m. 1862
Status: LC and PRONI (baptisms only)

Parish: **St. Mathew** (Woodvale Road)
Existing Records: b. 1846; m. 1856; d. 1887
Status: LC and PRONI (baptisms only)

Parish: **St. Michael** (Craven Street)
Existing Records: b. 1893; m. 1900
Status: LC

Parish: **St. Nicholas** (Lisburn Road)
Existing Records: b. 1901; m. 1902
Status: LC

Parish: **St. Patrick** (Ballymacarrett)
Existing Records: b. 1827; m. 1827
Status: LC and PRONI

Parish: **St. Paul** (York Street)
Existing Records: b. 1851; m. 1921
Missing Dates: b. 1851-79
Status: LC

Parish: **St. Peter** (Antrim Road)
Existing Records: b. 1896; m. 1901
Status: LC

Parish: **St. Philip** (Drew Memorial)
Existing Records: b. 1871; m. 1872
Status: LC

Parish: **St. Silas** (Cliftonville)
Existing Records: b. 1899; m. 1902
Status: LC

Parish: **St. Stephen** (Millfield)
Existing Records: b. 1868; m. 1869
Status: LC

Parish: **St. Thomas** (Eglantine Avenue)
Existing Records: b. 1871; m. 1871
Status: LC

Parish: **Shankill** (see St. Anne and St. Mathew)

Parish: **Templemore Avenue** (see St. Clement)

Parish: **Upper Falls** (see St. John the Baptist)

Parish: **Willowfield** (Down)
Existing Records: b. 1872; m. 1872
Status: LC

Parish: **Woodvale Road** (see St. Mathew)

Parish: **York Street** (see St. Paul)

Presbyterian
(shows starting date)

Parish: **Albert Street**
Existing Records: b. 1852
Status: PRONI

Parish: **Argyle**
Existing Records: b. 1853
Status: LC

Parish: **Ballymacarret**
Existing Records: b. 1837
Status: PRONI

Parish: **Ballysillan**
Existing Records: b. 1839
Status: PRONI

Parish: **Belmont**
Existing Records: b. 1862
Status: PRONI

Parish: **Berry Street**
Existing Records: b. 1853
Status: PRONI

Parish: **Carnmoney**
Existing Records: b. 1708
Status: PRONI

Parish: **Castlereagh**
Existing Records: b. 1809
Status: LC

Parish: **College Square, North**
Existing Records: b. 1845
Status: PRONI

Parish: **Crescent**
Existing Records: b. 1831
Status: PRONI

Parish: **Donegall Street** (Cliftonville)
Existing Records: b. 1824
Status: PHSA

Parish: **Duncairn**
Existing Records: b. 1861
Status: PRONI

Parish: **Dundonald**
Existing Records: b. 1678
Status: PHSA

Parish: **Dunmurry**
Existing Records: b. 1860
Status: LC

Parish: **Ekenhead** (Academy Street)
Existing Records: b. 1864
Status: PRONI

Parish: **Eglinton**
Existing Records: b. 1840
Status: PRONI

Parish: **Fisherwick**
Existing Records: b. 1810
Status: PRONI

Parish: **Fitzroy**
Existing Records: b. 1820
Status: PRONI

Parish: **Gilnahirk**
Existing Records: b. 1797
Status: LC

Parish: **Great Victoria Street**
Existing Records: b. 1860
Status: PRONI

Parish: **Malone**
Existing Records: b. 1845
Status: PRONI

Parish: **May Street**
Existing Records: b. 1835
Status: PRONI

Parish: **Newtownbreda**
Existing Records: b. 1845
Status: PRONI

Parish: **Rosemary Street**
Existing Records: b. 1718
Status: PRONI

Parish: **St. Enoch**
Existing Records: b. 1853
Status: LC

Parish: **Sinclair Seamen's**
Existing Records: b. 1854
Status: PRONI

Parish: **Townsend Street**
Existing Records: b. 1835
Status: LC

Parish: **Westbourne**
Existing Records: b. 1880
Status: PRONI

Parish: **York Street**
Existing Records: b. 1840
Status: PRONI

Non-Subscribing Presbyterian Churches

Parish: **Dunmurry**
Existing Records: b. 1807
Status: PRONI

Parish: **Rosemary Street (1)**
Existing Records: b. 1757
Status: PRONI

Parish: **Rosemary Street (2)**
Existing Records: b. 1817
Status: PRONI

Methodist
(shows starting date)

Parish: **Agnes Street**
Existing records: b. 1864; m. 1868
Status: LC

Parish: **Carlisle Memorial**
Existing Records: b. 1877; m. 1877
Status: LC

Parish: **Crumlin Road**
Existing Records: b. 1878; m. 1878
Status: LC

Parish: **Donegal Square**
Existing Records: b. 1815-1928; m. 1863-1911
Status: PRONI

Parish: **Duncairn Gardens**
Existing Records: b. 1890; m. 1895
Status: LC

Parish: **Falls Road**
Existing Records: b. 1882; m. 1863
Status: LC

Parish: **Frederick Street**
Existing Records: b. 1841-1904
Status: LC

Parish: **Grosvenor Hall**
Existing Records: b. 1895; m. 1896
Status: LC

Parish: **Hydepark** (North Belfast Mission)
Existing Records: b. 1834; m. 1868
Status: LC

Parish: **Jennymount**
Existing Records: b. 1873; m. 1913
Status: LC

Parish: **Knock**
Existing Records: b. 1874; m. 1872
Status: LC

Parish: **Ligoniel**
Existing Records: b. 1870; m. 1893
Status: LC

Parish: **Mountpottinger** (called Ballymacarret
  until 1891)
Existing Records: b. 1885; m. 1888
Status: LC

Parish: **Ormeau Road**
Existing Records: b. 1870; m. 1884
Status: LC

Parish: **Osborne Park**
Existing Records: b. 1894; m. 1878
Status: LC

Parish: **Primitive Street**
Existing Records: b. 1885; m. 1878
Status: LC

Parish: **Salem New Connection**
Existing Records: b. 1829; m. 1904
Status: LC

Parish: **Sandy Row**
Existing Records: b. 1885; m. 1878
Status: LC

Parish: **Shankill Road**
Existing Records: b. 1874; m. 1815
Status: LC

Parish: **University Road**
Existing Records: b. 1865; m. 1815
Status: LC

Baptist and Congregationalist
(shows starting date)

Parish: **Albert Bridge**
Existing Records: b. 1867; m. 1868
Status: LC

Parish: **Antrim Road**
Existing Records: m. 1897
Missing Dates: m. ends 1924
Status: LC

Parish: **Clifton Park**
Existing Records: b. 1876; m. 1878
Status: LC

Parish: **Great Victoria Street** and **Finaghy**
Existing Records: b. 1869
Status: LC

Parish: **Regent Street**
Existing Records: m. 1878
Missing Dates: m. ends 1896
Status: LC

Parish: **Rugby Avenue**
Existing Records: b. 1904; m. 1863
Status: LC

Parish: **Whiteabbey**
Existing Records: b. 1884; m. 1888
Status: LC

Parish: **Spamount**
Existing Records: b. 1880; m. 1874; d. 1894
Missing Dates: d. ends 1898
Status: LC

INDEX

Researchers should note that in many instances there are spelling variations for Irish proper nouns. Entries in this index will refl.ect certain variations, but the reader is advised to pursue all possible spellings.

M